THE POEMS OF
EMILY DICKINSON

*an annotated guide to commentary published in
English, 1978–1989*

A
Reference
Publication
in
Literature

Jack Salzman
Editor

THE POEMS OF EMILY DICKINSON

an annotated guide to commentary published in English, 1978–1989

JOSEPH DUCHAC

G.K. HALL & CO.
An Imprint of Macmillan Publishing Company
New York

Maxwell Macmillan Canada
Toronto

Maxwell Macmillan International
New York   Oxford   Singapore   Sydney

G.K. Hall & Co.
An Imprint of Macmillan Publishing Company
866 Third Avenue
New York, NY 10022

Maxwell Macmillan Canada, Inc.
1200 Eglinton Avenue East
Suite 200
Don Mills, Ontario M3C 3N1

Macmillan Publishing Company is part of the Maxwell Communication Group or Companies.

Library of Congress Catalog Card Number: 92-32694

Printed in the United States of America

printing number
1 2 3 4 5 6 7 8 9 10

Library of Congress Cataloging-in-Publication Data

Duchac, Joseph.
   The poems of Emily Dickinson : an annotated guide to commentary published in English, 1978–1989 / Joseph Duchac.
      p.   cm. — (A Reference publication in literature)
   ISBN 0-8161-7352-4
   1. Dickinson, Emily, 1830–1886—Bibliography.   I. Title.   II. Series.
Z8230.5.D83   1993
[PS1541]
016.811′54—dc20   92-32694
                                                                              CIP

The paper used in this publication meets the minimum requirements of American National Standard for Information Sciences—Permanence of Paper for Printed Library Materials. ANSI Z39.48-1984. ∞™

Contents

The Author

Joseph Duchac holds an MA in English from New York University and an MLS from Columbia University. He is currently Head Reference Librarian at the Brooklyn Campus of Long Island University. Professor Duchac is also the author of *The Poems of Emily Dickinson: An Annotated Guide to Commentary Published in English, 1890–1977* (G.K. Hall, 1979).

Introduction

This volume is a continuation of and a supplement to the original work, *The Poems of Emily Dickinson: An Annotated Guide to Commentary Published in English, 1890–1977*. It covers the years 1978 through 1989, thus adding twelve years of coverage. Taken together, the two volumes include the first hundred years of Dickinson criticism. As in the original volume, only published material in English is included.

In the original volume I noted that over 25 percent of the numbered poems and fragments in Thomas H. Johnson's edition of Dickinson's works had escaped critical attention. This second volume adds a number of items to the "critically considered" list, but 15 percent of them remain unexamined. Many are fragments, or works that perhaps require no elucidation, but the number of poems that have not been discussed seems high for a poet of Dickinson's stature.

Two trends may be observed in the period covered here. First, the fact that Dickinson is a *woman* poet has emerged as a major concern. The focus has shifted from earlier criticism, which emphasized ways in which Dickinson was a peculiarly *American* poet, to significant ways in which she is a *woman* poet. Her role in her family and as a woman in the society of her time has come under close and repeated scrutiny. As George Monteiro remarked in a 1985 review, "Gendrification in Dickinson studies is well underway."* The second major trend has been consideration of the

**American Literary Realism, 1870–1910* 18. 1-2 (Spring/Autumn 1985): 250.

poems in relation to their place in the fascicles. A number of critics have attempted to discern the patterns (if any) that exist in the fascicles and have studied the importance of a poem's placement in the context of the poems preceding and following it. Much of this attention is undoubtedly due to the publication of *The Manuscript Books of Emily Dickinson* (edited by R. W. Franklin, Cambridge, MA: Belknap-Harvard University Press, 1981, 2 vols.), which has joined the short list of books indispensable to Dickinson scholarship.

This work is designed to enable students, teachers, scholars, or general readers to locate all published discussion of individual poems. Some of the books on Dickinson lack an index to explication, while others contain indexes that are incomplete or inaccurate. The present volume permits the reader to find explications in the former and provides supplementary indexing for the latter.

Not limited to discussion of any specified length, this volume includes all extensive discussions and many relatively short ones. I have been more likely to include brief items if they refer to poems not discussed previously or if the nature of the commentary is original or unusual. I have also considered the context of the discussion: frequently comments on an individual poem are brief, but the context may be highly illuminating.

Although thoroughness has been my goal, one group of items has proved particularly elusive. In the past twenty years or so a remarkably large amount of Dickinson criticism has been published in Japan, a country that now has its own Emily Dickinson Society. Existing bibliographic coverage of this material is unreliable, incomplete, and often inaccurate. Items in Japanese may be listed as being in English. Titles of journals and books are often "supplied" in English, and even when citations prove to be trustworthy, efforts to locate copies are often fruitless. I have included all English-language items published in Japan that I could obtain, but I make no pretense to complete coverage of a class of materials that demand a book of their own.

This work is arranged alphabetically by the poems' first lines; the citation form used is that employed by Johnson in the index of his 1960 edition of Dickinson's poems. After the first line is the number assigned by Johnson to the poem. (Critics frequently cite Dickinson's poems by this number, sometimes prefaced by a *J* for Johnson.) Citations of works containing commentary follow in chronological order from earlier to later works. The form used is author (last name only, except in cases where same surname requires use of first-name initial), brief title (significant words from the title), and pages on which references to the poem appear. (The full citation appears in the bibliography.) Each citation is followed by an annotation consisting of either a brief description of aspects of the poem that the commentary discusses or, when possible, a brief quotation that either summarizes or is considered representative of the critic's style, tone, and approach to the poem. Following the annotation is a list of the works in which the commentary in question has been either reprinted, reprinted in part, or revised and reprinted, and its location.

Following the Guide to Commentary is the Bibliography, which contains full information for the works cited. It is arranged alphabetically by author, and authors' names are given exactly as they appear in the work. Capitalization and punctuation in titles are those employed by the authors. (But titles that are printed in all capital letters have been standardized.)

There are no references to works published after 1989, but, although the scope is primarily 1978 through 1989, I have included several works from earlier years that either escaped my attention before or about which I have had second thoughts. For criticism published since 1989, the reader is referred to annual listings in the *MLA International Bibliography,* and to *American Literary Scholarship,* which is particularly useful for its critical evaluations and coverage of foreign-language materials. Also relevant are issues of *American Literature, Dickinson Studies,* and the *Higginson Journal.*

My thanks go to the Board of Trustees of Long Island University for granting me the time to complete the lion's share of the research required in this project. I am also grateful for the cooperation of countless libraries and the many librarians whose eagerness to help in any way possible and whose encouragement helped to lighten the inevitable drudgery. Special thanks to Jay Redfield and Milton Wenger of the Long Island University Library for facing the flood of interlibrary loan requests bravely and dispatching them with good humor and resourcefulness.

In the hundred years since the first critical observation on Dickinson was published, a remarkable outpouring of commentary has occurred. It shows no signs of abating.

*   *   *

Owners and users in general of the original volume may want to note the following inaccuracies:

The date for the AIKEN entries on pages 121 and 623 should be 1929, not 1919.

The date for the HAGENBÜCHLE entry on page 428 should be 1974, not 1968.

THE POEMS OF
EMILY DICKINSON

*an annotated guide to commentary published in
English, 1978–1989*

Guide to Commentary

"A bee his burnished carriage" (1339)

1980   GROSS and RASHID, "Dickinson and the Erotic," pp. 25–28
   "We freely acknowledge that the poem is in all probability not consciously a poem about sex. . . . But . . . [it] is so pervasively sexual in its
imagery, we believe that sexual passion is what the poem is really about."

1982   OLPIN, "Hyperbole: Part One," p. 14
   "The bee as comic character receives its sharpest and most distinctive portrayal" in this "well-known and overtly sexual" poem.

1983   SHURR, *Marriage*, pp. 158, 173–74
   "Dickinson surely knew the difference between *humility* and *humiliation*, and she chooses here a word that signifies the lover's devout
submission to the beloved, rather than any charge of exploitation of the
female by the male."

1984   MARTIN, W., *American Triptych*, p. 158
   Relates to other instances of flower imagery in Dickinson's poems
which illuminate "her evolution from passive, dependent femininity to
autonomous womanhood."

1987   DI GUISEPPE, "Maiden and the Muse," pp. 53–55
Discusses relationship of bee/poet with flower/muse; focuses on poet's use of the word "Cupidity."

"A bird came down the walk" (328)

1972   RAO, *Essential Emily Dickinson*, pp. 20–21, 134–35
General introduction to the poem aimed at "postgraduate students of literature in Indian Universities."

1978   HECHT, "Riddles," pp. 3–5
". . . might not this be a shy and modest allegory of human possibility?"
Reprinted: Hecht, *Obbligati*, pp. 93–95

1979   CAMERON, *Lyric Time*, pp. 6–7
The poem "exemplifies a typical pattern of development in a good number of Dickinson's utterances, as they linger on concrete, often trivial but entirely comprehensible phenomena, and then alter their focus in a tensile shift of the received lines into a shape that utterly perplexes them."
Reprinted: Mullane and Wilson, *Nineteenth-Century*, pp. 75–76

1981   PADDOCK, "Metaphor as Reason," pp. 71–72, 73, 75
". . . style and content become integral and inextricable; the hiatus in logical progression itself becomes an expression of the cleavage between man and nature which is the subject of the poem."

1982   MARCUS, *Emily Dickinson*, pp. 22, 23–24, 25
General consideration as one of the poet's nature poems.

1983   ALLEN, M., *Animals*, pp. 49–50
Relates to the birds, "unconventional in their immediacy," in other Dickinson poems.

BUDICK, "Dangers of the Living Word," pp. 217–20, 222
". . . the symbolic correspondences of the poem . . . signal to the reader the dangerous distortion of both natural and theological truths which can occur when biological happenstance is promulgated as divine gospel."
Revised and reprinted: Budick, *Emily Dickinson*, pp. 61–65, 67, 187, 191–93

WALKER, N., "Humor as Identity," pp. 59, 60
The poem illustrates the poet's "preferred relationship with the

natural world. . . . Instead of raising herself to the level of nature, she lifts it to her own superior level."

1984   ALLARD, "Regulation of Belief," pp. 28–30, 40 n. 5
"The poem is powerful because it charts a failed . . . attempt by the poet to approach a seemingly simple mystery of nature, to participate in 'otherness'. The poem's power and meaning have little to do with birds or works or beetles . . . ."

ANDERSON, D., "Presence and Place," pp. 221–22
"Presence is elusive and, in a small way, dangerous here . . . but it is also deeply captivating."

HATTENHAUER, "Feminism," pp. 54–55
The poem's "masculine" bird "has a freedom and ease denied to humans, especially nineteenth-century women of proper Massachusetts society."

KELLER, L., and MILLER, "Rewards of Indirection," pp. 546–47
"By the end of the poem, we are more interested in the observer than in what she sees. . . . the real drama of such a poem seems to lie in its speaker's idiosyncratic mental processes."

1986   LOVING, *Emily Dickinson,* pp. 55–56, 62
"If there is any suggestion of danger, it comes when the human narrator offers the bird a crumb. The truth is that nature is a nice place, a pastoral scene until man blunders on stage with the full weight of his past and future."

MOREY, "Dickinson-Kant: The First Critique," pp. 37–38, 42
Examines poem along with "Within my garden rides a bird" in order to explore a Dickinson-Kant relation.

ROBINSON, J., *Emily Dickinson,* pp. 71–72
"She is plainly standing up for a 'Pink and Pulpy multitude'—as one of them. Must we not be proud of ourselves if *even God* has us for breakfast?"

1987   MILLER, C., *Emily Dickinson,* pp. 38–39, 62
Comments on effect of syntactic doubling.

1988   WOLFF, *Emily Dickinson,* pp. 487–88, 523
"Oddly, although the speaker fails in her attempt to comprehend and describe the bird's nature, the poem itself does not fail to the same degree, for the use of these inadequate social categories to deal with the

activities of an essentially unknowable bird serves nicely to highlight nature's impenetrable enigma."

1989   GUERRA, "Dickinson's 'A Bird,'" pp. 29–30
"Initially, the speaker's choice of verbs seems to express a desire to anthropomorphize the bird; however, in the final stanzas, verbs that reflect the speaker's recognition of the bird's separateness from the human world create the poem's thematic climax."

KNAPP, *Emily Dickinson*, pp. 11, 106–11
It "depicts the voracity of nature as well as its beauty and cyclicality." Detailed examination of poem's images as they shift and expand in significance.

"A cap of lead across the sky" (1649)

1982   OLPIN, "Hyperbole: Part One," p. 16
"The comedy is in the contrast of surly thugs and pretty ladies. A punk has as many charms as winter and hell."

"A charm invests a face" (421)

1985   CARTON, *Rhetoric*, pp. 128–29
"Wish and denial, satisfaction and annulment, are delicately tensed at the poem's end. If a desire . . . has been met, a corresponding lack . . . has been acknowledged as its price."

1987   ST. ARMAND, "Veiled Ladies," pp. 36–37
"The poem is in many respects a self-portrait of the masked artist, expressing Dickinson's own delight in veiled mystery and anticipatory revery," but now she "sees the veil as a limit to the face that peers beyond it as well as a barrier to the face that seeks to penetrate through it."

"A clock stopped" (287)

1979   CAMERON, *Lyric Time*, pp. 103–04
"If part of Dickinson's intention in the poem is to make us 'guess what' or 'guess who' the subject is, it is largely a consequence of her insistence on our participation in the mystery of death's temporal transcendence."
Reprinted: Cameron, *"Et in Arcadia,"* pp. 51–53

1982   MARCUS, *Emily Dickinson*, p. 88
The poem "mixes the domestic and the elevated in order to communicate the pain of losing dear people and also to suggest the distance

of the dead from the living." Relates to other Dickinson poems on death and immortality.

1983 BENVENUTO, "Words within Words," pp. 51–52
Suggests instances where examining definitions and etymologies of key words in the poem, as they appear in the dictionary Dickinson used, may shed light on poem's meaning.

1984 MARDER, *Exiles at Home,* p. 136
The poet's vision of death is black and bitter in this poem, "where life itself is meaningless, a mere functioning of God's mechanism."

1986 ROBINSON, J., *Emily Dickinson,* pp. 121–23
". . . it is separation and inaccessibility which the poem ultimately dramatizes. What cannot be done and what will not be done is that the clock will not be made to go again. The actuality is now no different from the analogy."

1988 STOCKS, *Modern Consciousness,* pp. 46–47
"The poem can be read not only at its face value, but as a little parable of death and time; man ('the puppet bowing') with his little span, his built-in obsolescence, tied through the clock-world to the celestial mechanics."

WOLFF, *Emily Dickinson,* pp. 190–94, 197, 209, 233, 340, 359, 395
The poem is "a virtuoso demonstration of Dickinson's ability to manipulate mathematics and science and to insinuate them into her work, a deliberate appropriation of one essential element in God's great 'Design.'"

1989 GALPERIN, "Assignment," pp. 178–79
A sample assignment for study of this poem, including questions and suggestions.

KNAPP, *Emily Dickinson,* pp. 171–76
The poem explores the "poetics of various types of space/time relationships, and their impact upon thought."

"A coffin is a small domain" (943)

1978 CAMERON, "Naming as History," pp. 236–37, 238, 248
In this definitional poem the point of the definition is "to reveal the speaker's knowledge of its inadequacy."
Reprinted: Cameron, *Lyric Time,* pp. 38–39, 52; reprinted in part: Ferlazzo, *Critical Essays,* pp. 200, 201

1979 ESTES, "Search for Location," pp. 212–13
"... 'circumference' simultaneously suggests to the reader the tension between the two poles of Dickinson's thought—expansive inclusion and fearful exclusion, the hope for a universal order in which she finds her location and the knowledge of being lost."

"A day! Help! Help! Another day" (42)

1984 WALLACE, *God Be with the Clown*, pp. 98–99, 104
"In a way the poem is a kind of pep talk to her self to face experience head-on and not shirk responsibility for her own life. It is also a comic defense against real terrors."

WOLOSKY, *Emily Dickinson*, pp. 39–40
"Although this poem was written . . . before the Civil War had actually commenced, the rhetoric of war and the conflict of issues were already making themselves felt in the national consciousness. That rhetoric is suggested here."

"A death blow is a life blow to some" (816)

1982 MARCUS, *Emily Dickinson*, p. 76
Relates to other Dickinson poems on "Suffering and Growth." This poem contains a version of Emerson's doctrine of compensation.

1984 WALLACE, *God Be with the Clown*, pp. 96–97
"The playful repetition of opposites leads almost to nonsense, ridiculing the Christian notion of afterlife while asserting it at the same time."

"A deed knocks first at thought" (1216)

1981 KIMPEL, *Dickinson as Philosopher*, pp. 116–18
"No moral philosopher could make a basic moral distinction more clearly than is made in this poem."

"A dew sufficed itself" (1437)

1987 BARKER, *Lunacy of Light*, p. 69
The poem "treats the anguish Dickinson experienced because of her inability to pursue her creative life openly and consistently . . . ."

1988 TRIPP, *Mysterious Kingdom,* pp. 120–21
Comments on use of "by" in the poem.

"A doubt if it be us" (859)

1982 MOSSBERG, *Emily Dickinson,* p. 29
". . . while the voice of the poet is anguished, it is operative, and even seems to be fueled by the distress caused by its own fragmentation and ruptures in sensibility."

1986 NEW, "Difficult Writing," pp. 23–24
"The poet gains not an ideal or transcendental reality but an 'Unreality,' not vision of Paradise, but a 'Mirage' in the desert. Transcendental possibility is ceded to a precarious and existential 'living' that purges itself both of the certainty of center and of circumference."

ROBINSON, J., *Emily Dickinson,* p. 111
Contrasts with "Pain has an element of blank," both being "poems of analysis."

"A drop fell on the apple tree" (794)

1982 OLPIN, "Hyperbole: Part One," p. 16
"The wind gives a ready-made metaphor for shifting and varied perspective in language, image, and personification in [this poem]."

1989 DOWNEY, "Mathematical Concepts," pp. 25–26
Exemplifies Dickinson's use of mathematical concepts of "distributivity" and "transitivity."

"A dying tiger moaned for drink" (566)

1979 POLLAK, "Thirst and Starvation," pp. 45–46
The poem is "a brilliant vision of the frustration of generous nurturing impulses in a dream-like setting charged with anxious sexuality."

1988 PHILLIPS, *Emily Dickinson,* pp. 52, 53, 222 n. 34
Considers this poem and several others as the poet's response to the death of Frazar Stearns.

1989 OLIVER, *Apocalypse of Green,* pp. 81, 228
The poem illustrates "Dickinson's efforts to understand the unknown side of death through the moment of death."

"A face devoid of love or grace" (1711)

1984   WALLACE, *God Be with the Clown*, p. 36
"The venom in this satiric portrait is kept in check only by the surprising word *successful* and by the comic analogy of face and stone to old acquaintances."

"A field of stubble lying sere" (1407)

1988   WOLFF, *Emily Dickinson*, pp. 523–25
"Entirely intelligible standing alone, the poem is even more interesting when it is put into the context of its inception." It "addresses certain private preoccupations with ultimates and endings."

"A full fed rose on meals of tint" (1154)

1981   CUDDY, "Expression and Sublimation," p. 32
Relates to other Dickinson "bee poems." Here there is "no longer any question about whether or not a submitting flower . . . will lose the respect and love of the bee. The answer is YES since her belief now . . . is that the flower is only used by the bee for his own selfish, instinctual purpose."

1987   BARKER, *Lunacy of Light*, pp. 66–67
"No wonder Dickinson so often wrote . . . of preferring hunger and isolation. She feared that in feasting *she* would be the food—she would be the one exploited." Related to Dickinson's use of sun imagery in other poems.

"A fuzzy fellow without feet" (173)

1978   MILLER, R., "Transitional Object," pp. 459–60
"This is a simple, uncomplicated poem describing with precision the butterfly that emerges from a cocoon."

1983   ALLEN, M., *Animals*, p. 55
"Dickinson's immense compliment to her male animals is not only in granting them practically sole rights to the nobility of work and art but in replacing masculine strength with the delicacy usually considered feminine."

KHAN, "Dickinson's Phenomenology of Evolution," p. 62
The butterfly "is directed by an inward tendency (entelechy) in its course. The '*Damask* Residence' is the instinct of life for a stay-at-home

existence which conceals the potentiality of evolution or impetus responsible for the organization of matter."
Revised and reprinted: Khan, *Emily Dickinson's Poetry,* pp. 105–06

"A great hope fell" (1123)

1988   WOLFF, *Emily Dickinson,* pp. 458, 459
Notes poem's "attenuated religious language." The Son's "hold over the elements of this poem is so feeble that the verse seems more plausibly to refer to some entirely personal disillusionment, a particular 'Hope' that was not fulfilled."

"A happy lip breaks sudden" (353)

1979   DIGGORY, "Armored Women," p. 138
"Though the speaker is aware of each emotion beneath its plating, awareness of any sort is denied to the 'unqualified' others. Indeed, the gilding . . . provides not only a defense through concealment but a badge of superiority."

"A house upon the height" (399)

1978   PERRINE, "Dickinson's 'A House,'" pp. 14–15
Interpretation based on identifying the poem's "House" as a metaphor for heaven.

1984   WILT, "Playing House," pp. 156–57
Considered as one of the "scores of highly charged lyrics" in which "the poet confronts the house she is before, or within, or has become." Explores the poem's "knot of meanings."

1985   SALSKA, *Walt Whitman and Emily Dickinson,* pp. 155–56, 190
The poem "feels closer to compulsive talking from some powerful but hardly specified need than to a deliberate effort at clarifying meaning and designing an aesthetically ordered space in the expanse of the unknown."

"A lady red amid the hill" (74)

1977   AGRAWAL, *Emily Dickinson,* p. 109
The poem captures the "transitional period between autumn and winter."

"A light exists in spring" (812)

1979   CAMERON, *Lyric Time,* pp. 5, 178–80, 181, 183, 185, 199
". . . here light is metamorphosed into its magic hue by the way in which it rides above the year ('on' it), an essence or extract of luminosity. The representation . . . throws into relief the spatial depth of the world being perceived."

1984   MARTIN, W., *American Triptych,* pp. 127–28
The poem demonstrates that Dickinson "understood the extent to which everyday social circumstances would impoverish her receptivity to her surroundings."

1985   RENAUX, "Seasons of Light," pp. 28–29, 30–42, 50–51
Employs A. J. Zokovskij's "theory of amplification" to analyze the poem; "it is through amplification that we can trace how form and content interact to convey meaning."

1986   NEWMAN, "Dickinson's Influence," pp. 38–40
Examines parallels to suggest that Roethke used Dickinson's poem as "an unconscious blueprint for 'In Evening Air.'"

REGUEIRO ELAM, "Haunting of the Self," pp. 85–87, 88, 99 n. 3
"The poem's trade in the sense of a metaphysical exchange encroaches on a sacrament that can only be apprehended through that trade, so that the poem here witnesses its own absence, its 'internal difference' from itself. What it apprehends, finally, is its own otherness . . . ."

1988   RENAUX, "Dickinson's 'A Light,'" p. 21
Suggests that the poet's use of the word "Trade" may be illuminated by reference to Hermes, who not only "presides over commerce and is symbolic of creative intelligence, but he is also the god of perverted intellect and the protector of thieves."

WOLFF, *Emily Dickinson,* pp. 446–47
In this poem "the meaning must be extracted not merely from the verse's reference to some independent world of myth (here latter-day American Puritanism), but also from Dickinson's own system of encoded meaning."

"A little east of Jordan" (59)

1979   PATTERSON, *Dickinson's Imagery,* pp. 49–50, 159, 194
Explores implications of the poet's "identification of herself with Jacob."

1981 DIEHL, "Dickinson and Bloom," pp. 424–27, 428, 429, 438, 441 n. 18
In this poem Dickinson confronts "an anxiety that grows from the fear that she is at once dependent upon another for her source of inspiration and that this other may demand a commensurate repayment, a reimbursal of poetic afflatus of which the poet may find herself incapable."

DIEHL, *Romantic Imagination,* pp. 23, 38–39, 113 n. 98
"Both this poem and Wordsworth's 'Voluntary' delineate a process which characterizes each poet's predominant vision of the relationship between the self and the 'Dread Power.'"

1985 ANANTHARAMAN, *Sunset in a Cup,* pp. 103–05
Compares with "Two swimmers wrestled on the spar."

1988 WOLFF, *Emily Dickinson,* pp. xviii, 151–53, 532, 579 n. 7
"It is impossible to emphasize too strongly the importance of the transition that took place at Peniel: God concealed His face and gave us a *word* in its place—humankind's first tragic fall into language. And Dickinson's poem recalls the immediate effects of this transaction, too."

"A little madness in the spring" (1333)

1979 BARNES, "Telling It Slant," pp. 237–38
Notes allusion to King Lear; "here as elsewhere throughout her letters and poems Dickinson's Shakespeare is proverbialized."

1986 ANDERSON, CHARLES, "Modernism," pp. 37, 40
"The spring 'madness' of the artist, painter, or poet, in fancying that he can perceive the true reality of Nature is 'wholesome' for a moment. But if he thinks he possesses Nature and can express its truth, he is worse than mad—he is the king's fool, a clown."

1989 HAFLEY, "Green Experiment," pp. 18–20
Examines ways in which the poem exemplifies Dickinson's "achievement of amplitude in economy." The poem refuses "to admit of any absolute or definitive interpretations: it is cagey like *Hamlet.*"

"A little road not made of man" (647)

1988 TRIPP, *Mysterious Kingdom,* pp. 119–20
Comments on poet's use of "of" rather than "by" in first stanza.

"A long, long sleep, a famous sleep" (654)

1985 JOHNSON, *Emily Dickinson*, pp. 161–62
The poem "uses the rhetorical question (a familiar device in the death poetry) for ironic purposes, but here the execution is remarkably subtle and concise, focusing sharply upon the inert 'idleness' and 'independence' of the dead and contrasting this attitude with the symbolic noon of fulfillment."

"A loss of something ever felt I" (959)

1980 JOHNSON, " 'Pearl of Great Price,' " p. 204
Dickinson's "expressions of doubt," as in this and most of her mature works, "are more often statements of intellectual honesty than confessions of psychological vulnerability or depression."
Revised and reprinted: Johnson, *Emily Dickinson*, pp. 125–26

1981 PORTER, *Dickinson*, p. 173
"As explicit as the poem seems in its assertive language, there is simply no definition of the loss. . . . In place of meaning, as in her life, we have commotion, intuitive knowledge mixed with ignorance."

1982 MARCUS, *Emily Dickinson*, pp. 69–70
Related to other Dickinson poems about childhood deprivation.

1986 MCNEIL, *Emily Dickinson*, pp. 12, 21–22
"The goal of the poem is to know and depict what is in fact a classic human state of loss—even if this knowledge contradicts received Victorian truths about childhood."

POLLAK, "Second Act," pp. 164–65
"The poem's theme is the relationship between self-knowledge and lost access to experience."

1987 FINCH, "Patriarchal Meter," pp. 170–171
"The metrical ambivalence evident in this poem's pattern of alternating nine- and eight-syllable lines . . . parallels the ambivalent relationship with Christianity described in the poem."

GELPI, "Emily Dickinson's Word," pp. 42–43
"Having lost paradise, she is looking for it—futilely, this poem seems to be saying—in the bereft consciousness itself, as if consciousness could repair itself, could fill and heal and seal its own emptiness."

1989   OLIVER, *Apocalypse of Green,* pp. 198–99, 235
"She does not reveal to the reader, and perhaps she does not know, in what new direction she will look nor in what wrong direction she had been looking. It is safe to assume, however, that her gaze turned increasingly inward rather than outward for understanding the nature of immortality."

"A man may make a remark" (952)

1979   PATTERSON, *Dickinson's Imagery,* p. 108
Comments on poem's chemical metaphor.

"A mien to move a queen" (283)

1981   GUTHRIE, "Modest Poet's Tactics," pp. 231–32, 233, 237 n. 7
"Caught between a timidity greater than the wren's and an urge to enlarge upon those subjects addressed in her poems—subjects which are the badge and seal of her queenliness, her rank—she cannot find a suitable position for herself in society."

1985   EBERWEIN, *Dickinson,* pp. 12, 31
"The strength comes from chosen patterns of behavior, such as adopting a haughty mien or speaking in a commanding voice. The smallness prevents men from fearing this aristocratic mite, and distance, while cutting short opportunities for affection, precludes contempt."

1988   PHILLIPS, *Emily Dickinson,* pp. 171–72, 185
"Although there is no record that she read Robert Southey's *Joan of Arc* (1796), Dickinson seems to have adapted his dramatic narration of the history of the eighteen-year-old heroine for a twenty-five-line poem."

"A moth the hue of this" (841)

1982   OLPIN, "Hyperbole: Part One," p. 13
Comments on poem's irony. ". . . nature's 'trinkets' here take on an ironic black humor quality."

"A murmur in the trees to note" (416)

1988   OAKES, "Welcome and Beware," pp. 189–90, 192, 195
Examines relationship of poem's speaker to the masculine reader. "Telling and not telling, invoking metonymic proximity and metaphoric

distance, she underlines her ambivalence about relationships which involve secrets and intimacy."

"A narrow fellow in the grass" (986)

1972   RAO, *Essential Emily Dickinson,* pp. 152–54
General introduction to the poem aimed at "postgraduate students of literature in Indian Universities."

1979   KELLER, K., *Only Kangaroo,* pp. 190, 199, 268–69
"Sexual contact is here made comic; it makes no sense." In this poem and in "In winter in my room," she is "shocked and attracted by the male erection . . . and she is fascinated with the male sexual processes," but there is "no significance in the sex; it is fun and games."

1981   PADDOCK, "Metaphor as Reason," pp. 72–73
The poem demonstrates "a terror of the utterly alien, cold-blooded aspects of nature; but the concluding stanzas make it clear that she regards the snake—in part, no doubt, because of its archetypal role as the agent of man's alienation from God and nature—as an exception."

PORTER, *Dickinson,* pp. 16, 45, 57, 91
Here the poet "shows us less the way a snake looks than how ingenuity can reanimate language and put it up to saying new things, make us see afresh the life within language itself apart from an exterior reality."

SCIARRA, "Woman Looking Inward," pp. 36, 37–38, 39, 40
"It is not so much the snake itself which interests Dickinson, but rather its mystery, its quality of unseen presence. She has made a tangible object into an abstraction . . . ."

1982   MARCUS, *Emily Dickinson,* pp. 22–23, 25
General consideration as one of the poet's nature poems. "The poem is both descriptive and philosophical, and it runs counter to the tradition of poems that claim to see good intentions in nature."

1983   ALLEN, M., *Animals,* pp. 39–40
The snake's "only crime is to inspire . . . terror. But unlike the bone marrow fear of the more ambiguous poems of dread, this is a stimulating voyeuristic fright brought on by something exterior to man—something that does go away."

BENVENUTO, "Words within Words," pp. 47–48
Suggests instances where examining definitions and etymologies of

key words in the poem, as they appear in the dictionary Dickinson used, may shed light on the poem's meaning.

KNIGHTS, "Defining the Self," pp. 367–68
"The snake has not ceased to be a snake, but he is also a representative of the inhuman, the utterly alien, the 'earlier and other creation' invoked in Eliot's 'The Dry Salvages.'"
Reprinted: Ford, B., *New Pelican Guide*, pp. 160–161

1985   JOHNSON, *Emily Dickinson*, pp. 35–37, 42, 197 n. 35
This "apparently harmless 'Fellow' brings to the speaker's mind her sense of estrangement within nature, and in his mythic implications becomes a reminder of mortality as well."

1986   MOREY, "Dickinson-Kant: The First Critique," p. 42
"This is a good example of an object changing from simply pictorial to symbolic within the same poem."

ROBINSON, J., *Emily Dickinson*, pp. 25–26, 139, 147–48
The snake "is about its own business, not interacting. Its purposes are so deeply concealed that it moves through its poem as a set of images and not as an identity. . . . He, too, is outside a community of everyday expectation . . . ."

1988   MARHAFER, "Reading a Poem," pp. 59–63
Describes method by which a class of students "in advanced junior English used a Freudian model to explore the meanings inherent in [this poem]."

WOLFF, *Emily Dickinson*, pp. 245, 488–90, 582 n. 23
The poem "resolutely declines to identify the snake with Satan or with evil, the standard Christian 'meanings' of snake. Instead, the speaker voices his inclination to establish connections between humanity and nature."

1989   GUTHRIE, "Near Rhymes," pp. 73–74
The poem "demonstrates the way Dickinson used rhyme to achieve a crescendo."

KNAPP, *Emily Dickinson*, pp. 50, 105–06
Comments on poetic techniques and moral implications.

MORTON, "How Language Works," pp. 48–49
Suggestions for teaching the poem to college freshmen.

"A nearness to tremendousness" (963)

1979 CAMERON, *Lyric Time,* pp. 10, 160–61, 168, 170, 205
Here "we see the ways in which pain taxes language, creating nouns out of adjectives, words out of syllabic addition, sentences out of hyperbole."

ESTES, "Search for Location," p. 213
The poem "expresses the psychological pain of a person whose life lacks the order of limits and location. Significantly placed in the two lines at the center of the poem is the message that contentment exists in 'Vicinity to Laws.'"

1980 JUHASZ, "'To make a prairie,'" pp. 21–22, 25
"This companion poem to 'No Man can compass a Despair' is also concerned with situation and boundaries of emotional events, but it presents a different attitude towards the subject, admiring instead of fearing illocality."
Revised and reprinted: Juhasz, *Undiscovered Continent,* pp. 43–44, 51

1981 EDDINS, "Dickinson and Nietzsche," p. 99
"The most explicit demonstration of the *Angst* accompanying the revelation of ultimates, and of the anti-Apollinian [*sic*] nature of this revelation, is found in [this poem]."

JUHASZ, "'Peril as a Possession,'" pp. 35–36
"The poem distinguishes between kinds of mental space and maintains that the place toward which intensest pain draws one is not only enormous but without end. If we are tempted to equate that place with immortality, there is precedent for this perspective elsewhere in Dickinson's writing."

1984 BENFEY, *Problem of Others,* pp. 73–74
"The poem seems to be *about* nearness, how words and phrases assume meaning by their contiguity to other words."

1985 SMITH, B.J., "'Vicinity to Laws,'" p. 43
Examines poem's legal vocabulary. "Man is safe as long as he stays within the limits of the law, within the society of men, . . . but is in danger of life, sanity and peace if he ventures beyond these limits to the edge of knowing, to God, to the Sublime."

1987 MILLER, C., *Emily Dickinson,* pp. 41–42
"Polysyllabic circumlocution appropriately describes a place that is neither here nor there and has substance only as insubstantial qualities

might be imagined to have: 'nearness to Tremendousness' is neither local nor circumscribed."

"A pang is more conspicuous in spring" (1530)

1979 PATTERSON, *Dickinson's Imagery,* pp. 127, 177
Relates to bluebird references in other Dickinson poems.

1988 PHILLIPS, *Emily Dickinson,* p. 156
"The contrarieties of mood in the poem are inextricable from her need to believe beyond belief in the miracles of Christianity and the promise of redemption." The poem "locates the nineteenth century woman between a 'modern' and a traditional sensibility."

"A pit but heaven over it" (1712)

1978 ROBINSON, D., "Text and Meaning," pp. 45–52
As reconstructed by Franklin, this is one of Dickinson's "most straightforward portrayals of the mind's struggle to maintain itself, a portrayal whose force is increased dramatically when it is read with the benefit of the poet's intended conclusion."

1979 KELLER, K., *Only Kangaroo,* pp. 82–83
"She spits out her words in this poem because she is repulsed by the hell of the human condition, and her heartrending rhythms express the pathos she feels at this fact . . . ."

1980 FRANKLIN, "Houghton Library," pp. 245–57
Examination of manuscripts indicates that lines included in Johnson version of "I tie my hat, I crease my shawl" properly belong to this poem.

1983 SHURR, *Marriage,* pp. 32, 182–83, 214 n. 43
"The dangerous moral situation remains vague, until a metaphor for it is introduced in lines 20–21: 'we got a Bomb— / And held it in our Bosom.' The metaphor surely derives from conception . . . ., gestation, and nursing." Relates to other Dickinson "pregnancy musings."

1984 OLPIN, "Hyperbole: Part II," pp. 33–34
"The colloquial and the abstract, the familiar and the strange are brought together in a single poem."

WOLOSKY, *Emily Dickinson,* pp. 6–9
"The poem's form has its source in a sense of disorientation, as Dickinson's grasp on the orders of her universe and of her place within it

becomes tenuous. Such disorientation is expressed in a technique commensurate with it."
Reprinted: Wolosky, "Syntax of Contention," pp. 165–67

1988 PARKER, *Unbeliever,* pp. 34–36
Connects with Elizabeth Bishop's "The Unbeliever." "Though Dickinson relies more on resentment and anger than on unbelief, like Bishop she concentrates on the intensity of imagination in an indifferently hostile universe." Dickinson's "concern is not to find solutions but rather to seize the thrill of suffering without them."

STOCKS, *Modern Consciousness,* pp. 69–70
"Human life—or, rather, consciousness, the poet's consciousness—seems to dwell in it between two dimensions of felt reality— 'Heaven' and the 'Pit.' But towards the end of the poem a third dimension seems to be emerging—an implicit recognition of nature, with its stabilities and cyclical recurrences, as man's ground of being and ultimate security . . . ."

WOLFF, *Emily Dickinson,* pp. 322–23, 460, 587 n. 16
The poem suggests "that the intrinsic construction of the cosmos is itself so radically destabilizing that we are in constant menace of a disintegration that would pitch self into plumbless 'fathoms' of oblivion."

1989 OLIVER, *Apocalypse of Green,* pp. 153–54
Discusses along with other Dickinson poems on "judgment."

"A plated life diversified" (806)

1984 WOLOSKY, *Emily Dickinson,* pp. 64–65
"Life is 'diversified' by its gold and silver mixture of experiences; and, in contributing to this diversity, pain enriches. Value emerges through struggle. The poet sees this as affirming man's capacity to face annihilation . . . ."

1986 BAKKER, "Emily Dickinson's Secret," pp. 342–43
Here "she actually seems to view theodicy as the only way of endowing suffering and pain with significance."
Reprinted: Bunt et al., *One Hundred Years,* pp. 240–41

1988 STOCKS, *Modern Consciousness,* pp. 55–56
Here is "the essence of the basic existentialist situation and response. . . . It is basically a despairing attitude; yet, within its conceptual framework, a noble one, giving to the authentically human a sort of tragic grandeur."

"A poor torn heart, a tattered heart" (78)

1985 JOHNSON, *Emily Dickinson,* pp. 16, 17–18, 191 n. 10
Contrasts with "Adrift! A little boat adrift." Both are "songs of innocence recreated by the experienced poet; their speakers remain serene in their assurance that the bark will be saved through the intervention of an established spiritual world."

"A precious mouldering pleasure 'tis" (371)

1984 TSELENTIS-APOSTOLIDIS, "I will be Socrates," pp. 7, 8
"ED has not really discussed anything with the ancients; no issue has troubled her mind, no inspection like the scrutiny with which she meets the Bible has taken place. . . . The quest for the ancients has been a superficial quest and her conclusion the result of no great labor."

"A prison gets to be a friend" (652)

1979 ESTES, "Search for Location," pp. 215–16
Here the poet "imagines the contentment of living in a world the size of a cell. . . . Because contentment can come only when she is assured of regularity, she is willing to trade her liberty."

1984 CHERRY, "Sexuality and Tension," p. 21
"Memory and skepticism are the active ingredients of this poem. . . . In fact, the limitations of the prison are what keep her writing. She needs the boundaries so she can attempt to overcome them."

POLLAK, *Dickinson,* pp. 129–31, 134
". . . by the end of the poem, which is structured around a single extended analogy between external and internal inhibition, she is avoiding any pleasurable recall of the past, because she has transferred her allegiance from joy to despair."

1988 STOCKS, *Modern Consciousness,* pp. 95–96, 97
Considers with other Dickinson poems that present "the imprisonment of real human value in the socio-economic necessities of the system."

1989 GARBOWSKY, *House without the Door,* pp. 85–87
". . . although the whole poem implies an acceptance of the imprisoned life, the last stanza recalls the terrors of agoraphobia . . . ."

19

"A rat surrendered here"

"A rat surrendered here" (1340)

1984 WILT, "Playi___ _se," p. 166
Considered as ___ f the "scores of highly charged lyrics" in which "the poet confronts tl ___ se she is before, or within, or has become."

"A route of evanescence" (1463)

1980 DUNCAN, "Joining Together," p. 117
". . . instead of handing over the unadorned thing itself—a simple unassuming hummingbird—she sounds out the idea of the thing with all the adornment of rococo."

1981 THOMAS, J., "Emerson's Influence," pp. 38, 40–42
This poem and "Within my garden rides a bird" illustrate "growth in the poet's attitude toward nature and herself, as well as the influence of Emerson's theories of nature."

1982 MARCUS, *Emily Dickinson,* pp. 25–26
General line-by-line consideration as one of the poet's nature poems.

SALSKA, *Poetry of the Central Consciousness,* pp. 158–59
Compares with Whitman's "Cavalry Crossing a Ford." Whitman's poem "is a realistic scene executed with loving care for the detail while Dickinson's—an impressionistic view in which the object becomes decomposed into elements of color and movement. It is replaced on the canvas by the analysis of the effect produced on the artist's mind."
Revised and reprinted: Salska, *Walt Whitman and Emily Dickinson,* pp. 147–48, 160 nn. 35, 37

1983 ALLEN, M., *Animals,* pp. 52–54
"As purely aesthetic as this hummingbird is, he is also given the role of common laborer—a mailman following his route, and completing that appointed task with breathtaking efficiency. . . . Dickinson could not have found a more exquisite model in nature for so much that she values."

1985 ANANTHARAMAN, *Sunset in a Cup,* pp. 67–72, 105, 151
". . . the mind or more truly the consciousness of the poet becomes the garden, and the humming bird is an image therein." Compares with D. H. Lawrence's poem on the hummingbird.

BUDICK, *Emily Dickinson,* p. 10
". . . there is a hint of frenzy that is intended not simply to replicate the motion of a bird but to warn us that both the bird and the poem are teetering at the edge of confusion and disarray."

1986 BUELL, *New England Literary Culture,* pp. 112–13
"A poem about a hummingbird becomes a poem about disoriented perceptions occasioned by a hummingbird." Compares with "Within my garden rides a bird."

MOREY, "Dickinson-Kant: The First Critique," pp. 36, 43
The poem's second half "adjusts to daily speech of Anglo-Saxon and Norman extraction. It is almost as if the bird were a Latin magician, hypnotizing the audience."

ROBINSON, J., *Emily Dickinson,* pp. 148–49
"The poem is not looking for anything: it is confronted. The senses are assaulted—that is, they do not identify and anticipate, and they cannot name. This leaves us . . . with a performance."

1987 MILLER, C., *Emily Dickinson,* p. 152
"Even in poems about action or change in nature, the poet emphasizes process, causality, and relationship more than temporal acts. . . . The poem is full of action, but there is only one verb . . . ."

"A saucer holds a cup" (1374)

1981 KIMPEL, *Dickinson As Philosopher,* pp. 168–69
"In entertaining the idea that human beings are not the undisputed superiors of every other living creature, she is not far from the point of view affirmed in *Ecclesiastes* that 'man has no advantage over the beasts'."

"A science so the savants say" (100)

1977 KELLER, K., "Alephs, Zahirs," pp. 310–11
"The 'representative' flower (perhaps herself) stands, after the Emersonian manner of each and all, as typal synecdoche of the whole of nature. The plebeian method thus justifies/rationalizes/enlivens one's own small world."

1988 WOLFF, *Emily Dickinson,* pp. 296–97
". . . the speaker of this poem has surely learned her lessons in geology and fossil findings from [Edward Hitchcock]."

"A secret told" (381)

1989 GARBOWSKY, *House without the Door,* p. 83
In the poem "Dickinson might well be addressing her own secret shame of agoraphobia and her need for silence."

"A sepal, petal, and a thorn" (19)

1987 HUGHES, J., "'I bring my rose,'" p. 37
"The poem makes identification with the rose a poetic process that outlasts any real rose that ED could have known and given."

"A shade upon the mind there passes" (882)

1984 WOLOSKY, *Emily Dickinson*, pp. 101–02
"The sincerity of the question posed at the end establishes this poem as a true attempt to address divinity. But the religious posture is undercut by the nature of the poet's question."

"A sickness of this world it most occasions" (1044)

1988 TRIPP, *Mysterious Kingdom*, pp. 127–29
Comments on poem's syntax; reference to other Dickinson poems is useful.

"A single clover plank" (1343)

1979 ESTES, "Search for Location," p. 214
This poem "joins the plank image with the fearfulness of circumference. . . . Note the specifically harmful power of circumference which sweeps the bee away so that even the plank offers no permanence."

1981 MONTEIRO and ST. ARMAND, "Experienced Emblem," pp. 259–60, 266
Relates to the emblem of "Walking by Faith" in Holmes and Barber's *Emblems and Allegories.*

1984 OLPIN, "Hyperbole: Part II," pp. 32–33
". . . the carefully constructed metaphor of safety versus threat and the colloquial versus the grandiose language collapse in the ironic repetition of 'nought' and 'not.' The whole poem puns elaborately on nothing as this beautiful bee, 'Alas,' is gone."

1985 BUDICK, *Emily Dickinson*, pp. 180–81
The poet "alone, it seems, can put the natural drama in its full context of meaning. But it is the 'single Clover Plank' that saves the bee, not the poet. Without the clover (and the bee) there can be no drama . . . ."

EBERWEIN, *Dickinson,* pp. 164, 165, 170

The poem demonstrates "the distorted perspective of the circuit world when confronted with the prospect of escape beyond its immediate margin. . . . Like other flying creatures, the bee symbolized for Dickinson the possibility of soaring *to* circumference without passing *through* it."

"A single screw of flesh" (263)

1983   HOMANS, " 'Oh, Vision,' " pp. 128–30

"As the notion of 'standing for,' or metaphor, becomes metonymy (in the figure of the name as keepsake), a dualistic heaven is revised into a perpetual breaking of boundary."

SHURR, *Marriage,* pp. 176–77

This "troubled and difficult" poem is clarified by knowledge that "screw" in Dickinson's time referred to a small package. The poem "memorializes a small human being, intimately connecting her and the 'thee' of the fascicles, taken out of this world before its time."

1984   WOLOSKY, *Emily Dickinson,* pp. 170–71

"Here are aligned the various terms of Dickinson's contention with her inherited metaphysic. . . . Spirit and flesh comprise the self, but only the former can partake in the immutable realm."

1985   BUDICK, *Emily Dickinson,* pp. 204–05

"The 'single Screw of Flesh,' . . . suggests that the eternality of consciousness . . . cannot be made synonymous with immortality. It is instead a power that may actually usurp or subvert immortality, or at least our understanding of it."

1987   ST. ARMAND, "Veiled Ladies," pp. 26–27

"For the initiated soul, a totally new kind of seeing as well as a new name and a new order of being are in force, while those who remain 'this side of the veil,' . . . can only await their own swift summons to the realm of unimpeded vision."

1988   WEISSMAN, " 'Transport's Working Classes,' " pp. 408–09

Dickinson "speaks more blasphemy than many whole volumes by other nineteenth-century writers. Souls are not supposed to be pinned to each other by screws of flesh—and we can suspect that Dickinson knows what 'screw' means in obscene slang. Furthermore, one human soul is not supposed to stand for deity to another."

"A slash of blue" (204)

1987 LEDER and ABBOTT, *Language of Exclusion*, pp. 114–15
Considers the poem's "interesting and suggestive color imagery."

"A soft sea washed around the house" (1198)

1988 WOLFF, *Emily Dickinson*, p. 484
Poems such as this "may begin strongly and conclude weakly because a striking trope can neither be sustained nor brought to succinct and effective conclusion."

"A solemn thing it was I said" (271)

1979 KELLER, K., *Only Kangaroo*, pp. 22–23
"The religious terms are joined with sexual terms to argue her productivity. She has by nature a world within that can be used to prove that a woman is not small but full of life. . . . This pattern was one she developed often: a religious definition of herself as a woman leading to her creativity."

1980 PORTERFIELD, *Feminine Spirituality*, pp. 131–32
"Like many of Dickinson's poems, this one is about herself. And also, like many of her poems, this one suggests that the poet is God."

1983 GILBERT, "Wayward Nun," pp. 31–32, 33, 40
"Though it is in some ways obscure . . . this poem is particularly clear about one point: Dickinson's white dress is the emblem of a 'blameless *mystery*,' a kind of miraculous transformation that rejoices and empowers her."

1985 EBERWEIN, *Dickinson*, pp. 34–35
The poet's white costume is here linked to "the themes of smallness and renunciation that characterized her personal mythology of growth."

1986 BENNETT, *Loaded Gun*, pp. 75–76
The final stanza may be read "as a paen [*sic*] of praise to the potential lying within her as she makes the transition from girl to woman or as a rejection of all that has gone before and an assertion of the validity of the 'small' life to which she clings."

ROBINSON, F., "Strategies of Smallness," pp. 31–32

Dickinson "maintains the role of a woman who speaks softly despite her power because it is at once useful as irony . . . and necessary to her sense of self: she never ceases to be a 'woman,' she wishes to experience her womanhood as large without thereby becoming a Sage."

STONUM, "Calculated Sublime," pp. 109, 114

Notes way in which mathematics is "enlisted in the sublime combat between freedom and power. . . . Aside from her life, mathematical skill is the only resource in the poem that is the speaker's own."

1987   COOK, C., "Psychic Development," pp. 130–31

"She appears to equate wearing white with the mystery of her ability. There was nothing wrong with her secret . . . but it would not be understood by the 'Sages' of her time who considered women's lives too inconsequential to be worth anything."

SMITH, M., " 'To Fill a Gap,' " pp. 12–13, 24 n. 19

Reviews first publication. "Loomis Todd's changes are gender-determined in that she edits out the erotic poet who blasphemes the social order. In Dickinson's poem . . . the spinster is made huge and powerful by her unorthodox contentment."

1988   MOREY, "Dickinson-Kant III," p. 50

Considered as "a religious poem with an erotic vehicle."

1989   FALK, "Poem 271," pp. 23–27

The poem is "*not* about choosing to be a bride or a nun, but about the process by which the speaker comes to reject such a choice. . . . it is about the overthrowing of roles and idealizations in favor of embracing an autonomous, self-created life."

FALK, MOSSBERG, and SIMON, "Workshop Discussion," pp. 39–52

Transcript of a workshop discussion of the poem.

MOSSBERG, "Dressing for Success," pp. 29–34

In this poem "we see themes which will emerge as pivotal: self-reliance, creation and control, the giving of the self over to art, the concept of stature . . . and finally, the focus on the process of writing itself."

SIMON, "Poem 271," pp. 36–37

This is "a poet's poem: that is, one that focuses upon the poet's relationship to her own power and that ultimately exposes her willingness to submit to that power."

"A solemn thing within the soul" (483)

1986   ROBINSON, J., *Emily Dickinson*, pp. 41–42
"The attraction of the poem is in the boldness which risks comparing the ripening of fruit in an orchard with the approach of death and possible immortal life and the delicacy which sustains both the image and the reality as occurring under the same universal 'Sun'."

1988   WOLFF, *Emily Dickinson*, pp. 305–07
" 'The Maker's Ladders' are an explicit invocation of Jacob—not yet having wrestled with the Lord, and privileged to see into Heaven itself. . . . Her glimpse into Heaven . . . is not glorious but terrifying."

"A spider sewed at night" (1138)

1979   CAMERON, *Lyric Time*, pp. 5–6, 7
"Here the relationship between what is visible and what is not strains toward formulation in the last stanza, but the polysyllabic abstractions that link appearance, calculated effort, and an intimated other world cohere more as a consequence of verbal patterning . . . than of any demonstrated semantic connection."
Reprinted: Mullane and Wilson, *Nineteenth-Century*, pp. 75, 76

GILBERT and GUBAR, *Madwoman*, pp. 635–38, 640, 641
Examines implications of poem's images. The poet was "profoundly confident that the spider-artist spinning his yarn of pearl in the dark chasm of her life would triumph in mysterious ways."

1981   DIEHL, *Romantic Imagination*, pp. 92–93
"The spider at once gives the web both its function and its importance; completely dependent upon its maker for its physical shape, the web becomes a mirror of the artist's features."

1982   MARCUS, *Emily Dickinson*, pp. 44, 45–46
General consideration as one of Dickinson's poems on "Poetry, Art, and Imagination."

SALSKA, *Poetry of the Central Consciousness*, pp. 89–91, 92, 141
"This poem emphasizes the absolute self-sufficiency of the creator be it spider, God, or, by implication, the maker of the poem. It is his inscrutable autonomy that makes him divine." Contrasts with Whitman's "A Noiseless Patient Spider."

Revised and reprinted: Salska, *Walt Whitman and Emily Dickinson,* pp. 78–79, 129

1983   ALLEN, M., *Animals,* pp. 42–43

"The super artist of the nocturnals is the spider. . . . This artist's sense of form is intrinsic, though no mere animal instinct drives him. It is a creator's plan, charmingly turned to logic, a strategy."

1984   ST. ARMAND, *Dickinson and Her Culture,* pp. 36, 37, 76, 159

"Her poem tantalizes by promising the time-tested, applied wisdom of the proverb (folk), or the epigrammatic, bourgeois, obvious truth of the moral apologue (popular). At its core, however, is an exclusive, transcendent, antididactic theory of art for art's sake (elite)."

1985   BUDICK, *Emily Dickinson,* pp. 87, 89, 91

"In an idealist view of the universe, it may be that only a 'Spider'-like deity can know whether the phenomenal web of creation is a harmless decorative 'Ruff' or a suffocating 'Shroud.' . . . As he is portrayed in the poem, he is concerned solely with his own egomaniacal goals: to 'Himself himself inform.' "

JOHNSON, *Emily Dickinson,* pp. 42–44

Considers several of Dickinson's "spider" poems. Here she "symbolizes the value of artistic endeavor within her larger, always preeminent concerns of death and immortality."

1986   BUELL, *New England Literary Culture,* pp. 128–29

"The spider's action, as usual for a Protestant meditation on the insect kingdom, is an exemplum that teaches something about immortality. . . . What is not so usual is that the poem refuses to demystify [the mysteriousness of God's ways] by rendering the proposition explicitly or by allowing it to stand as the only possible inference."

1987   GELPI, "Emily Dickinson's Word," p. 50

"In the weaving of the web . . . the spider-artist 'informs' herself in a double sense: reporting or articulating her inner being, and thereby giving form to that inner being, her otherwise inchoate and unrealized consciousness, in its aesthetic creation. The text is the embodiment of consciousness."

MOREY, "Dickinson–Kant II," pp. 5–6

"The dark night of the soul and the ars moriendi are certainly hinted at." The poem is "built on abstractions, both nouns and pictorial expressionism."

"A stagnant pleasure like a pool" (1281)

1981 PORTER, *Dickinson,* pp. 71, 73–74
"This, one can say, is a modern poem because it gives enough to engage but withholds all the rest, leaving the reader resignedly in a quandary of urgent words and incomplete disclosure."

"A still volcano life" (601)

1979 PATTERSON, *Dickinson's Imagery,* pp. 37, 48, 81, 136, 174, 192–193, 223 n. 78
Relates to volcano images in other Dickinson poems.

1981 DIEHL, *Romantic Imagination,* p. 177
"What distinguishes this from Emerson's volcano is Dickinson's insistence on secrecy, on individuality, and on destruction."
Reprinted: Bloom, H., *American Poetry,* p. 459; Bloom, H., *Emily Dickinson,* p. 155

1985 COOK, A., *Figural Choice,* pp. 35–36
"As often with Dickinson, the word yields and totters before alternative possibilities. . . . The word itself suffers something akin to the approximations of her imaginal thinking."

PHILIP, "Valley News," p. 70
". . . one cannot help noticing the similarity between the forces embodied here, and those inner dynamics as mapped by Freud and his inheritors."

1986 ROBINSON, J., *Emily Dickinson,* p. 152
Relates to "On my volcano grows the grass."

1987 BARKER, *Lunacy of Light,* pp. 117–19, 202 n. 25
"Whether genital or linguistic, these 'lips' hold a power she recognizes and acknowledges as strength derived from darkness, in the same way a volcano is fire emerging from the dark compression of the 'female' earth."

MONTEFIORE, *Feminism and Poetry,* pp. 149–51
The final stanza "reads almost like a prophetic allegory of female language, especially if one accepts . . . that anger as well as alienation characterize female identity . . . ."

1988   REYNOLDS, *Beneath the American Renaissance*, p. 415
Dickinson "brought a full self-consciousness to the use of volcano imagery, recognizing that it applied both to women's lives and to women's literary style."

1989   DOBSON, *Strategies of Reticence*, pp. 107–08
"The destructive power here is as sexual as it is verbal. In a nineteenth-century America still marked by the vestiges of its Puritan origins, the possessor of such power is under divine obligation to Christian civilization to maintain reticence."

"A thought went up my mind today" (701)

1972   RAO, *Essential Emily Dickinson*, pp. 147–48
General introduction to the poem aimed at "postgraduate students of literature in Indian Universities."

"A toad can die of light" (583)

1985   JOHNSON, *Emily Dickinson*, pp. 168–69, 215 n. 13
"Death is inevitable, absolute, but life represents continuous potential, an unmeasured wine; the poem's final question implies that the wine of life must be refined, contained, and individuated to form the personal 'Ruby' of identity and status."

"A tooth upon our peace" (459)

1980   MURPHY, "Definition by Antithesis," pp. 22–23
Poem illustrates development in Dickinson's use of "definition by antithesis." "Suffering is no longer a merely contrastive device for heightening the experience of joy, but a force which acts on that experience, literally giving it life."

1984   WOLOSKY, *Emily Dickinson*, p. 67
Dickinson here "suggests that the journey through sorrow to redemption may be an unnecessary peripety. Its value eludes her, and its reward does not outweigh the rigors demanded for it—rigors that seem superfluous."
Revised and reprinted: Wolosky, "Dickinson's War Poetry," pp. 28–29

"A train went through a burial gate" (1761)

1981 KIMPEL, *Dickinson As Philosopher,* pp. 195–96
The poem has "the stamp of spiritual greatness, and enters into the tradition of the loftiest of Buddhist tributes to the sensitivities of nonhuman beings."

"A transport one cannot contain" (184)

1984 CARTON, " 'True Romance,' " pp. 97–98
The poem represents "the mind's power of transcendence as inadequate and finally illusory. . . . The understanding or imagination can render only an obviously inadequate diagram of rapture, can approach divine mysteries only by turning them into cheap circus acts."
Revised and reprinted: Carton, *Rhetoric,* pp. 10, 56

"A visitor in marl" (391)

1985 BUDICK, *Emily Dickinson,* p. 124
"The analogy between poetry and frost is as much a reflection on art as it is on nature."

JOHNSON, *Emily Dickinson,* p. 112
This poem describes "the frost's evanescent beauty" whereas "The frost was never seen" uses frost as "an analogue for deeper mysteries."

1988 WOLFF, *Emily Dickinson,* pp. 313–14
"Here at last is the promised face-to-face 'Interview' with the force of divinity, but instead of fulfilling existence, it erases it. There is an indecent familiarity . . . and there is . . . an eradication so thorough that both being and all recollection of it are utterly nullified."

"A weight with needles on the pounds" (264)

1979 JUHASZ, "But most, like Chaos," pp. 226, 234–35
Relates to other poems that are also "about *during* and *after* 'great pain' that reveal insights into the nature of pain and also Dickinson's methods for measuring it."
Revised and reprinted: Juhasz, *Undiscovered Continent,* pp. 77–78

"A wife at daybreak I shall be" (461)

1981 STEINER, "Image Patterns," p. 66

The poem "can be read in a secular way, with the 'Bride' leaving behind her 'maiden' state . . . or as a poem in which the female *persona* awaits Death, an unearthly lover, who is by no means a rare object of the Dickinson-*persona*'s wooing . . . ."

1982 MARCUS, *Emily Dickinson*, pp. 60–61

Relates to other Dickinson "marriage" poems. "The poem may represent a suicidal impulse, or a blending of the idea of spiritual marriage with the idea of a union in heaven."

1983 JUHASZ, *Undiscovered Continent*, pp. 110, 116–19, 120

Pairs with "Good morning, midnight." Both poems are "about love, and together they represent the movement from before to during to after, or from not having to having to not having again. . . . The paired poems form a chart of anticipation and loss."

1984 ST. ARMAND, *Dickinson and Her Culture*, p. 141

"Love and Death are one, for the 'Childhood's prayer' fumbled at by the speaker is obviously *The New England Primer*'s 'Now I Lay Me Down to Sleep,' with its Puritanical stress on the 'Lord' both keeping and taking the trusting soul of those young Elect who are 'willing to die.'"

SALSKA, "Emily Dickinson's Lover," p. 138

"In the last analysis the lover in this poem is a presence typifying all the major mysteries of existence, while the framing first night situation serves to concretize the psychic content of the encounter with the unknown."

Revised and reprinted: Salska, *Walt Whitman and Emily Dickinson*, pp. 139–40

1985 BRASHEAR, "Dramatic Monologues," p. 68

"This monologue is of particular interest, for its setting is a metaphoric house of life."

EBERWEIN, *Dickinson*, pp. 174–75

"The natural analogies here serve to reinforce the bridal theme by summoning routine if spectacular natural initiations to clarify this emotionally complex human transition."

1986 DOBSON, "'Invisible Lady,'" pp. 51, 54 n. 14

"Christ, Death, and the husband are indistinguishable one from the

other here, and the marriage experience is thoroughly overlaid with implications of death—the final invisibility."
Reprinted: Dobson, *Strategies of Reticence,* pp. 74, 146 n. 11

JONES, R., "'Royal Seal,'" pp. 43, 49–50 n. 18
"A hushed anticipation prevails as the poem mounts to its climax: reunion in 'Eternity' with a 'Savior' whom she has known before." Reviews critical arguments as to whether the poet "intended to exalt a human or a divine lover."

1988 MOREY, "Dickinson-Kant III," p. 51
"It is a mutability poem, on the borderline between two major phases of life: from child to wife overnight. Such rapid conversion suggests a death-in-life spiritual stage, rather than a human husband."

1989 WALKER, N., "Voice, Tone," pp. 109–10
Suggests contrasting with "She rose to his requirement" for teaching purposes. "From a cultural standpoint, these poems reveal Dickinson's understanding of the myth and the reality of marriage for women in the nineteenth century . . . ."

"A wind that rose" (1259)

1981 MURPHY, "Wind Like a Bugle," p. 33
"The combination of the 'North' imagery, the infinity of Circumference that is implied, the ability of the wind to 'rise' of its own accord, and its ineffable invisibility provides an unmistakable parallel to the imagery that Dickinson uses in her most serious attempts to penetrate the mystery of God."

1986 CARRUTH, "Emily Dickinson's Unexpectedness," p. 57
An appreciation, noting attitude similar to that of Camus.

ROBINSON, J., *Emily Dickinson,* p. 105
The "nature of the wind is established by exclusions. . . . It stirs no leaves and it is 'Beyond the Realm of Bird'. . . . It has its presence in the not-world of the mind, the same place where witchcraft in Salem and Empires of Evil exist, but also where love between people is sustained, as also fear of them."

"A winged spark doth soar about" (1468)

1983 ALLEN, M., *Animals,* p. 41
". . . the lightning bug. The joke that he is taken for lightning, posing minute against cosmic, in Dickinson's scheme reverses the usual

priorities. Violent power is not the greater marvel; more extraordinary is that a living being, especially one so small, can make his own light."

"A word dropped careless on a page" (1261)

1979   GILBERT and GUBAR, *Madwoman*, pp. 45, 51–53, 92
The poet's "observations about 'infection in the sentence,' . . . resonate in a number of different ways . . . for women writers, given the literary woman's special concept of her place in literary psychohistory."

1985   COTTLE, *Language of Literature*, pp. 101–02
A note on use of subjunctive.

1988   TRIPP, *Mysterious Kingdom*, pp. 118–19
Comments on key words and their possible implications.

"A word made flesh is seldom" (1651)

1980   DUNCAN, "Joining Together," pp. 120–21
"Rather than asserting that the structure of language proves the truth of the doctrine [of the Incarnation], she modestly indicates that the doctrine is borrowed from the structure of language. More subversively, she suggests that the Incarnation of doctrine may be inferior to its prototype . . . ."

HOMANS, *Women Writers*, pp. 212–14
The poem "aligns the poet's linguistic powers with the incarnation of the Word that represents a masculine God's specifically masculine powers of creation. . . . she is entertaining a long tradition of the inheritance of divine language by human language."
Reprinted: Homans, "Emily Dickinson," pp. 446–48

REISS, "Dickinson's Self-Reliance," pp. 32–33
"In this poem, Emily Dickinson is primarily concerned with poetry. . . . The poet is saying that while words can live and redeem in poetry, she is not aware of any communion on the part of 'the Word made Flesh.'"

1981   DIEHL, "Dickinson and Bloom," pp. 432–33, 434, 441 n. 27
"In these lines the communion of self and word, its sovereignty, supplants the descendental and essentially unequal relationship between divine authority and its recipient. As the poet's Word usurps the Christian Logos, so the lover of the Word becomes the preferred, superior vision of the imagination."

DIEHL, *Romantic Imagination,* pp. 124–25
"The competition between Christ's love and Philology ends in her choosing the consent of language. Appropriating theological language to her alternative poetics, Dickinson signals her antinomian intent."

MCGREGOR, "Standing with the Prophets," p. 20
"The association of poetry with the scriptural Incarnate Word . . . implies . . . that both she and the Evangelist–poet are responding to similar things, to instances of divinity making its presence felt among men."

1982 BARNSTONE, "Women and the Garden," pp. 158–59
"By writing poetry, she steps outside of not only God's authority but outside of the breed of fathers whose reign is sanctified by the Bible."

MARCUS, *Emily Dickinson,* pp. 40, 42, 43, 92
General consideration as one of Dickinson's poems on "Poetry, Art, and Imagination."

MILLER, C., "Terms and Golden Words," pp. 54–55, 59
"Somewhat paradoxically, the condescension of Christ, or our possession of the absolute Word, would strengthen our language instead of replacing it by releasing the human word from its necessity to be immortal; language would no longer be obligated to prove human and divine stability."

1983 BUELL, "Literature and Scripture," pp. 20, 28 n. 67
"The living word, though immortal in itself, depends for its 'expiration' on the truth of the Incarnation in the Christian as well as in the linguistic sense."

DIEHL, " 'Ransom,' " pp. 157–58
"In a stunning inversion of orthodoxy, Dickinson takes the Word of God and makes it her own, which then serves as the criterion for measuring all power outside the self. Transubstantiation thus becames [*sic*] a trope for poetic inspiration."
Reprinted: Bloom, *American Women Poets,* pp. 24–25

HOMANS, " 'Oh, Vision,' " pp. 127–28
Here Dickinson "uses the image of the Incarnation as God's 'condescension' to criticize patriarchal religion and patriarchal language use; the poem proposes the revision of that condescension into the relationship of 'consent' implied by the definition of language as 'This loved Philology.' "

1984 BENFEY, *Problem of Others*, pp. 95–96
Like "My life had stood a loaded gun," this is an allegory of the body, "centrally concerned with expression, and the relation between expression and finitude."

MARTIN, W., *American Triptych*, p. 117
"The clue to Dickinson's cosmology can be found in the contrast between condescension and consent; the former is a descent from a superior position and implies disdain while the latter indicates a harmony and accord that springs from union."

RUDDICK, " 'Synaesthesia,' " pp. 67–68
Examines poem's initial image for synaesthetic qualities.

WOLOSKY, *Emily Dickinson*, pp. 145–49
"The final verse makes clear . . . that Dickinson is indeed addressing the theological Logos in this poem, and not only immanent words, if only in order that the former be contrasted with the latter. Language consents to be among us in a way that the Logos does not."

1985 EBERWEIN, *Dickinson*, pp. 150, 191
"Language here plays Christ's role, consenting to share its strength with those who love it and condescending as a compound of humanity and divinity to fulfill man's needs."

1986 BUELL, *New England Literary Culture*, pp. 186–87, 447 nn. 67–68
The poem "shields itself from recognizing, yet acknowledges all the same, that secular philology remains on the merely emotive level unless authorized by sacred philology."

NORRIS, "Let Emily Sing," pp. 227–28
"The poem is her assertion that she prefers poetry to religion. She will not unravel any of the contradictions and puzzles here. The poem is a mystery, she says: dwell in it."

1987 GELPI, "Emily Dickinson's Word," pp. 49–50
"Here, Dickinson the Calvinist and Dickinson the Transcendentalist come as close as they ever do to speaking as one."

MILLER, C., *Emily Dickinson*, pp. 1, 147, 153, 171–72, 173
"Contrasting God's 'condescension' with philology's 'consent,' the poet appears to say that the ability to expire—breathe as well as die— is crucial in language and perhaps inseparable from its relation to human need and use."

1988   WEISSMAN, " 'Transport's Working Classes,' " pp. 421–22
"Philology . . . is beloved because the true knowledge of words 'consents' to Dickinson's secret meaning, the sanctified love of the body which is the same as the word. The authority of the words of the Bible and the experience of the body confirm each other."

1989   DIEHL, "Loving Language," pp. 177–80
The poem "may be read as Dickinson's assertion of her alternative power in the face of a potentially crippling external authority, the sovereignty of a male-identified God."

DIEHL, MILLER, and SIMON, "Workshop Discussion," pp. 189–206
Transcript of a workshop discussion of the poem.

GIBBONS, "Poetry and Self-Making," pp. 111–12
Here the poet "began with the Biblical creation of the Word made Flesh in order to suggest that all language that is 'breathed distinctly,' such as a poem, can defeat death in some way, and would only be *unnec-essary* if indeed God were to return."

LARSEN, "Text and Matrix," pp. 245, 255–58
Considers the following questions: "How does this poem incarnate its defiance of patriarchal logocentric language; how does it literally 'deconstruct' and 'reconstruct' . . . its very words?"

MILLER, C., "Poem 1651," pp. 181–84
The poem is "above all about choice or choosing language, but it is also about a nearly Puritan sense of being chosen."

RICHWELL, "Poetic Immortality," pp. 20–21
"That poetry, as well as the poet, serves a religious function in the Dickinsonian scheme of things is most obvious in those poems, like [this one], where she equates the poetic word with the biblical word."

SIMON, "Poem 1651," pp. 185–87
Examines the poem's "controlling metaphor: language is a sacrament; thus the poet's diction is linked with Christ's incarnation. The poem employs eucharistic imagery to dramatize the magical and transcendent forces of language."

"A world made penniless by that departure" (1623)

1986   ROBINSON, J., *Emily Dickinson,* p. 103
"If we read the syntax 'that departure/Of minor fabrics,' or even if we read 'that departure' on its own, I take it that what is being referred

to is the collapse of religious doctrines. They do not matter. "Sustenance' is an inward thing. It survives without dogmas . . . ."

"A wounded deer leaps highest" (165)

1977 KELLER, K., "Alephs, Zahirs," p. 308
In this poem, which exhibits her "most conventional use of typological icons from the Bible," Dickinson "refreshes Augustus Toplady's popular 'Rock of ages, cleft for me' by personalizing and parodying the conventional images of Christ that had come down from the Middle Ages."

LANDOW, "Moses Striking the Rock," pp. 338–39
Examines the "commonplace typological significance" of the line "The *Smitten* Rock that gushes!" ". . . only by recognizing the original importance of the image as a type of Christ do we allow it full impact."

1982 SALSKA, *Poetry of the Central Consciousness*, pp. 146–47
"The poet's most extensive comment on the way conditions of extreme stress stimulate to performance comes in this early poem."
Revised and reprinted: Salska, *Walt Whitman and Emily Dickinson*, pp. 133–34, 158 n. 12

1983 WILLIAMS, D., " 'This Consciousness,' " p. 369
The poem's "Smitten Rock" refers to "the typological symbol of Christ that followed the Children of Israel through the wilderness."
Reprinted: Williams, D., *Wilderness Lost*, p. 203

1984 WALLACE, *God Be with the Clown*, pp. 99–100
"In this poem Dickinson defines 'Mirth' as a kind of armor, a defense against further vulnerability. Laughter confines a hurt to the individual involved, preventing others from compounding it by remarking upon it."

1988 WOLFF, *Emily Dickinson*, pp. 205–06, 218
"Dickinson's acquaintance with Shakespeare may first have introduced her to that Elizabethan commonplace, the trope of Hunter and Deer for courtship . . . ."

1989 KNAPP, *Emily Dickinson*, pp. 142–45
"Dickinson's use of the image of the deer to convey the pain and the volcanic resentment felt by the narrator reveals the depth and religious nature of her hurt."

"Above oblivion's tide there is a pier" (1531)

1989 OLIVER, *Apocalypse of Green,* pp. 109–10
Relates to other Dickinson poems dealing with the doctrine of election. She emphasizes "the paucity of the number of the elect when placed side by side at the end of time."

"Abraham to kill him" (1317)

1983 BUELL, "Literature and Scripture," pp. 7–8, 24 n. 32
Contrasts Dickinson's use of the biblical story with that of Nathaniel Parker Willis.
Revised and reprinted: Buell, *New England Literary Culture,* pp. 173–74, 443 n. 31

1987 MONTEIRO, G., "Dickinson's 'Abraham,'" pp. 32–33
Examines ways in which "Dickinson's redaction of Genesis 22 deviates sharply and boldly from Scripture."

"Absence disembodies, so does death" (860)

1985 DICKENSON, *Emily Dickinson,* pp. 63–64
Suggests that "the first pair of lines is about love: absence and death heighten our feeling for the loved one—taken for granted when alive, perhaps. Memory hides the beloved from fleshly mortality."

"Absent place an April day" (927)

1981 PORTER, *Dickinson,* pp. 85, 90
This poem illustrates the importance to the poet of first lines. While the poem "as a whole is disarranged and unclear, the opening is undistorted and an effective lead-in."

"Adrift! A little boat adrift" (30)

1985 JOHNSON, *Emily Dickinson,* pp. 16–17, 146, 191 n. 9
The poem's "childish manner is appropriate to its underlying theme: the delusive nature of unquestioning faith."

1988 STOUT, "Breaking Out," p. 41
"Foundering indeed in our human dimension, and witnessed in its foundering by 'sailors,' people of ordinary perception, the 'little boat' of the self departs triumphantly into another dimension recognized only by very special beings, 'angels.'"

"Advance is life's condition" (1652)

1989 OLIVER, *Apocalypse of Green*, pp. 86, 233
"Two possible interpretations of this poem can be made: the 'wall' can be considered as the end of life, as terminus, or it can be considered as a shield to protect man from certain knowledge of his annihilation."

"Afraid! Of whom am I afraid" (608)

1989 GARBOWSKY, *House without the Door*, p. 109
"In each stanza, the speaker asks the question—first of death, then of life, and finally of resurrection—and in each instance she denies her fears." The poem "asks a question the poet may have asked herself as she became more phobic and housebound."

"After a hundred years" (1147)

1988 TSURI, "The Wind," pp. 7–12
"Dickinson is contemplating her own enactment of agony and coming death, while mourning for a dead soldier."

"After all birds have been investigated and laid aside" (1395)

1988 WOLFF, *Emily Dickinson*, p. 527
". . . the activities of this 'Blue-Bird' are reminiscent of the course of Emily Dickinson's own 'conscientious' creative life." Contrasts with "The most triumphant bird I ever knew or met" and "Before you thought of spring."

"After great pain a formal feeling comes" (341)

1977 AGRAWAL, *Emily Dickinson*, pp. 90–91, 133, 137, 140
"Such moments of painful experience of existential agony lie too heavily, like load [*sic*], on human psyche. They crush man's total consciousness . . . ."

1979 CAMERON, *Lyric Time*, pp. 15, 167–69, 170, 202, 260
" 'Great pain' is the predicate on which the sentence of fixity lies, the prior experience against which feeling hardens in intransigent difference." Here the poet "probes a feeling by describing its progressions."

HELMS, "Sense of Punctuation," pp. 178, 187–90
Examines techniques and effects of poem's punctuation.

"After great pain a formal feeling comes"

JUHASZ, " 'But most, like Chaos,' " pp. 226, 235–38, 239
"Lack of feeling, or various forms of 'death,' occasions the metaphoric transfers which interweave in [this poem] to measure the effect of pain on the mind and body and, in consequence, to tell us something about the nature of pain itself."
Revised and reprinted: Juhasz, *Undiscovered Continent*, pp. 45, 78–81, 82

KAMMER, "Art of Silence," pp. 154–56, 158, 160
"The connections the reader must discover or create in 'After Great Pain' are connotative, imaginative ones, independent of the expected resolutions of syntax."

1980 TAYLOR, M., "Shaman Motifs," pp. 6–7
Relates poem to elements of the "shaman experience." The poet uses a group of metaphors "all relevant to the process of trance as well as of death."

1982 MARCUS, *Emily Dickinson*, pp. 71–72, 73, 75
Relates to other Dickinson poems about "Suffering and Growth." This poem is pervaded by "a sense of terrible alienation from the human world."

1983 GALINSKY, "Northern and Southern," p. 137
Comments on sound and symbolic qualities of "quartz."

KHAN, "Agony of the Final Inch," p. 22–23
"The covert suggestion is that the death-like apoplectic effect of pain on the perceptive level, tho a psycho-physiological experience, transforms itself into a purely psychical experience like paranoia."
Revised and reprinted: Khan, *Emily Dickinson's Poetry*, pp. 21–23

1984 BARNSTONE, "Houses within Houses," pp. 130, 139, 142–43
"The death imagery, the contentment, the 'letting go,' coalesce into the Nirvana principle of abandonment to nothingness, which is a release and a liberation, the necessary state for revelation."

POLLAK, *Dickinson*, pp. 199, 206–11
". . . perhaps Dickinson's major psychological insight into the symptomatology of suffering is that rebirth necessitates the death of a rigid set of impulses grown comfortable and familiar; that pain signifies a loyalty to frustrated aspirations which is both heroic and dysfunctional; and that the unconscious is the unwitting conservator of personal history."

1986   MARSTON, "Metaphorical Language," pp. 112–13, 114
"The event that has caused pain is not named; thus, pain may be understood as either loss or physical pain, the one prefiguring grief, the other, death. . . . The speaker cares about effect, not cause—about what it is like to live out the aftermath of pain."

ROBINSON, J., *Emily Dickinson,* pp. 114–16, 126, 180, chap. 5 n. 1
"Its message which is orderly and analytic is dramatically enacted in terms which challenge that control and even threaten the message."

1987   FINCH, "Patriarchal Meter," pp. 173, 175 n. 10
". . . as the meter of the past poets overtakes the poem, the poet uses iambic pentameter to present an image of helpless, frozen stupor."

MARCUS, "Dickinson and Frost," pp. 16–29
Contrasted and compared with Frost's "Acquainted with the Night" in order to "deepen one's understanding of both poems. . . . Further light is shed on the poems by comparison of their imagery, figuration, symbolism, diction, and prosody."

TAYLOR, L. J., "Form, Process," pp. 91–101
Compares poem's characteristics with those of poems by Eliot, Yeats, and Stevens. These comparisons "show a greater kinship between Dickinson and the great seminal poets of modernity than we have yet documented, and help to establish a place for her in the mainstream of the tradition of post-romantic poetry in English."

1988   REYNOLDS, *Beneath the American Renaissance,* pp. 416–17
"Though she may be treating a gender-specific theme for gender-specific reasons, she succeeds in escaping to the gender-free realm of imaginative artistry."

WOLFF, *Emily Dickinson,* pp. 154, 468–70, 589 Part 5:1 n. 2
The poem derives "its haunting power from the radical compression of several subjects." Among them are "themes of violation and disorder" and "poetry that has been fatally wounded by the pain of its creator."

1989   GARBOWSKY, *House without the Door,* pp. 134–35
"The poem suggests the panic attack where the individual is numbed with anxiety and fear, feeling as if death has come."

MORTON, "How Language Works," p. 50
Suggestions for teaching the poem to college freshmen.

"Again his voice is at the door" (663)

1980   CUNNINGHAM, *Dickinson,* pp. 37–38
"The poem depicts . . . a recurrent fantasy of visitation by a spectral lover."

1983   SHURR, *Marriage,* pp. 149–50
Relates to a meeting with Wadsworth. ". . . this recorded visit . . . becomes the first one they enjoyed after the marriage event had taken place."

1988   PHILLIPS, *Emily Dickinson,* pp. 189–90, 235 n. 22
"Dickinson never wrote a more personal-impersonal poem. It is both subtle and obvious: subtle in the language that carries two states of being concurrently, and obvious in its knowledge of the mind in the act of recollecting a significant hour in one's life."

1989   MILLER, C., "Dickinson's Language," p. 83
Comments on the poem's "toss" and "plummet." "The reader must unravel the relation between the words . . . ."

"Ah! Necromancy sweet" (177)

1982   MOSSBERG, *Emily Dickinson,* pp. 191–92
"Dickinson's 'necromancy' . . . is related to her strategy to 'haunt' her 'house of art' with her 'maturer childhood.' She may ordain her future as a poet with her haunting use of words, but she identifies with evil in the process."

"Ah, Teneriffe" (666)

1988   WOLFF, *Emily Dickinson,* p. 434
In this poem the "image of nature as distant from human concerns and utterly independent both of God's force and of mankind's needs is . . . invoked as an example of strength and endurance."

"Air has no residence, no neighbor" (1060)

1978   HORIUCHI, *Possible Zen Traits,* pp. 353–54
"The Light of the soul, the lightened soul is a required acquisition of the spiritual awakening and without the protecting air it cannot breathe, metaphysically."

1985   PHILIP, "Valley News," p. 71
"There is no pantheistic absorption of the person into the element; nor . . . is there a celebration of the mind's power to absorb all material fact into higher law. What happens rather is a process of 'accosting' and 'persuasion'—the intuited freedom and pervasiveness of the air provoking the recognition of undeniable longings within the self."

"All but death can be adjusted" (749)

1988   WOLFF, *Emily Dickinson*, p. 219
"In the midst of these metaphors of creation and destruction, of accounts come due and final payments, there is the delicate undertone of a last, futile wish to mend and make anew. . . . But death is an ultimate barrier to solace."

"All I may if small" (819)

1988   WOLFF, *Emily Dickinson*, p. 194
". . . the student-become-poet knew that 'small' . . . could be transformed into a declaration of power. . . . Just as 'noon' contains both zero and infinity and 'snow' contains 'no,' so 'small' contains 'all.'"

"All that I do" (1496)

1982   THOTA, *Emily Dickinson*, p. 113
In the poem's final lines the poet is "referring to her lover whose bride she hopes to become after her death. But the words also echo the theological concept of the 'bride of Christ.' The poem deals with three phases of temporal experiences—past, present, and future . . . ."

"All the letters I can write" (334)

1985   HOMANS, "Syllables of Velvet," pp. 583–86, 587, 591
". . . the sexuality of the poem is its diffuse intersubjectivity and mutuality, the circularity of its reference, and its freedom from any desiring fetishization of referential objects."

"All these my banners be" (22)

1987   LEDER and ABBOTT, *Language of Exclusion*, pp. 141, 142, 145
This poem, "concerned with the contrast between earthly spring and eternal life," is part of "a sequence of poems concerning risk, loss, death . . . ."

43

"Alone and in a circumstance" (1167)

1979 GILBERT and GUBAR, *Madwoman,* pp. 619, 631–33
Relates to "the longstanding mythic tradition which associates virgin women—women who spin, or spin/sters—with spinning spiders."

"Alone I cannot be" (298)

1981 STEINER, "Image Patterns," p. 61
"The visitant evidently represents a Power which is experienced as haunting and inescapable; whether it comes as a blessing or as a curse is not easy to decide. . . . since the Muse is conceived in terms of Power, it has a masculine connotation and its effect is one of over-powering."

1989 MUNK, "Musicians Wrestle," pp. 4–5, 6, 7
"Like a dream this poem is abbreviated and tightly condensed, the intimation of psychological facts that we may grasp, in part, by association." Relates to Jung's insistence on "the autonomy of the creative complex."

"Although I put away his life" (366)

1983 JUHASZ, *Undiscovered Continent,* pp. 121, 125–127
"Surely, what Dickinson is portraying here, emphasizing by exaggeration, is the traditional female role, by which she is both attracted and repelled. . . . This poem shows her first rejecting it; then experiencing it imaginatively, in the subjunctive mood."

1985 EBERWEIN, *Dickinson,* pp. 29, 115
The poem is "spoken from the perspective of a woman who has already renounced the lover but fantasizes the comforts she might have brought him. . . . Inspected closely, this love-in-a-cottage picture seems to scream slavery!"

"Always mine" (839)

1985 COOK, A., *Thresholds,* p. 184
"Here the slightly submerged metaphor of eternity as a school makes itself recognized by no property other than the lack of intermittence . . . ."

"Ample make this bed" (829)

1985 EBERWEIN, *Dickinson,* p. 201
Relates to other poems employing "human contrivances like gates and doors" to represent death.

1988 WOLFF, *Emily Dickinson,* pp. 497–98, 503, 504
"Here there is paradox, but not bitterness. No grave's bed is ample in the usual sense; however, every grave is large enough: it is the equal portion to which all are ultimately brought."

"An altered look about the hills" (140)

1984 BADDELEY and BISHOP, "Perpetual Noon," p. 11
"The images of the springtime land, intensified and seen as a living affirmation of the promise of the Resurrection, make the poem seem an orison, a deeply-felt prayer of the heart."

"An awful tempest mashed the air" (198)

1980 LAIR, "Fracture of Grammar," p. 162
Comments on poet's interchange of adjective and noun functions in the poem.

"An everywhere of silver" (884)

1981 PORTER, *Dickinson,* pp. 131–32
"The poem is sheer style, without observation, composed of metaphor, an abstract image or two . . . , an oxymoronic twist, and a bit of irony."

1982 MADIGAN, "Mermaids," p. 40
The poem's "memorable quality . . . is achieved by the hints of the threatening power of the sea."

"An honest tear" (1192)

1981 DIEHL, *Romantic Imagination,* pp. 62–63
Here Dickinson echoes Horace, "to revise his meaning." "Dickinson shifts the Horation [*sic*] comparison from ode and artifact to unmediated emotion and physical memorial. Without the spontaneous, honest tear, the cenotaph is devoid of meaning."

"An hour is a sea" (825)

1982 MADIGAN, "Mermaids," p. 43
"The poem attempts a definition of time in terms of space: although a relatively short time could bring her to friends, that hour seems an eternity and an infinite distance, either because of the excitement of anticipation or the knowledge that the 'Sea' cannot be crossed."

1983 SIMPSON, "Dependent Self," p. 36
Discussion of Dickinson's "friendship poems"; here "friends represent safety."

"An ignorance a sunset" (552)

1985 LAWSON, "Slant on Immortality," pp. 26, 32
The poet uses "Circumference" here as "part of a set of 'earthly' terms against which 'Amber Revelation' and the Immortality it figures and prefigures is vividly contrasted."

"And this of all my hopes" (913)

1979 PATTERSON, *Dickinson's Imagery*, pp. 41, 107, 197
Notes that the poem "uses what appears to be castration symbolism."

"Angels in the early morning" (94)

1985 BUDICK, *Emily Dickinson*, p. 70
"Precisely because it is so easy for the narrator and the angels to manage their depredations upon nature, faith is put into jeopardy."

1987 BARKER, *Lunacy of Light*, pp. 68–69
The poet "connects youthful hopes with the moisture of early morning and mature disappointment with the dry heat of noon. . . . this poem offers a grim picture of reality for many women of Dickinson's era."

"Apparently with no surprise" (1624)

1972 RAO, *Essential Emily Dickinson*, pp. 161–62
General introduction to the poem aimed at "postgraduate students of literature in Indian Universities."

1978 FLEISSNER, "Dickinson's 'Moor,'" pp. 8, 9
Suggests possible allusions to *Othello*.

FLEISSNER, " 'Frost . . . at . . . Play,' " pp. 28–39
Compares and contrasts Dickinson's poem with Frost's "Fire and Ice" regarding content and technique, including "the irony, the deliberate use of paradox, and the religious or Puritan elements either explicitly or covertly implied."

1982 FAULKNER, "Emily Dickinson," pp. 809–10
The poem unites Dickinson's "attitudes toward nature and God. . . . In common with many American writers, she reverses the conventional association of white and purity . . . ."

MARCUS, *Emily Dickinson,* pp. 91–92
"The subtleties and implications of this poem illustrate the difficulties that the skeptical mind encounters in dealing with a universe in which God's presence is not easily demonstrated."

1985 ERKKILA, "Emily Dickinson," pp. 103–04
This is one of several Dickinson poems whose subject is the "struggle between female fecundity and a potentially destructive male force."

1987 BARKER, *Lunacy of Light,* p. 72
"The 'blonde Assassin' . . . may refer not only to the frost but also to the sun, which after this act of floral cerebral castration, continues calmly measuring out the day, carrying out the orders of god, which clearly do not include stooping to protect such tiny entities as frost bitten flowers."

BLASING, *American Poetry,* pp. 183–85
In this poem "Dickinson descends below even syllables to the level of letters and graphemes and walks the line between the rational and the irrational, the 'circumference' of what makes discourse discourse . . . .

" 'Arcturus' is his other name" (70)

1979 BUDICK, "Assignable Portion," pp. 1, 7–8
"In desiring to see nature as a comprehensible symbol of something beyond nature, both poet and scientist succeed only in particularizing, reducing, fragmenting, and even destroying it."
Revised and reprinted: Budick, *Emily Dickinson,* pp. 126–27, 193

GILBERT and GUBAR, *Madwoman,* pp. 592–93
The poem is "an exceptionally lighthearted example of what Dickinson could do with an ironically childlike perspective. . . ." In the last

stanza she "is deliberately parodying both the sentimental pieties of Victorian households and her own carefully created childishness."

PATTERSON, *Dickinson's Imagery,* pp. 87, 95–96, 107–08
Consideration of "pearl" imagery in Dickinson poems; "here the barrier appears to be no more than a rather arch version of the pearly gates of the heavenly city and is religious, if anything."

1984   WALLACE, *God Be with the Clown,* pp. 85–86
"Like Walt Whitman's 'When I Heard the Learn'd Astronomer,' this poem contrasts the individual's superior sensual appreciation of the skies with the experts' inferior intellectualism."

1985   COOK, A., *Thresholds,* pp. 181–82
"The reassurance that the difficult transition will survive the bepuzzlement of naming, indicated by the three terms placed between quotes in [the penultimate stanza], is affirmed by the quotes around the intensity and loveliness of the analogic last term, 'Pearl.'"

1986   MOREY, "Dickinson–Kant: The First Critique," pp. 40–41, 59
"This is a transitional poem from objectivity to subjectivity. The academic Newtonian-Linnean world is poked fun at. . . . The superstitions and myths of childhood and noble savagery are preferred to the scientific reserve and impersonal point of view."

1987   COOPER, M. F., "Androgynous Temper," p. 142
"In regard to nature . . . she feels like a child—small and impotent, though not in any oppressive sense. We learn that she treasures this childlikeness with a grin, since it provides a stage for her devilish resistance to adult concepts of order."

1988   WOLFF, *Emily Dickinson,* p. 451
"Such a meditation is entirely different from poems that act as a verbal assault upon God. Here it is not the speaker who raises doubts, but 'Science'; and these doubts deal not with the *nature* of Divinity or of Heaven, but with their very *existence*."

1989   OLIVER, *Apocalypse of Green,* pp. 192–93
"The tone of this poem is playful and anything but serious, but it illustrates the way she often thought of Heaven—in terms probably made habitual through church hymns and sermons."

"Are friends delight or pain" (1199)

1983   JUHASZ, *Undiscovered Continent,* pp. 99–100
". . . again we see the close relationship that must exist between

delight and pain. But here the cause, 'Friends,' provides a basis that makes ratio a concern more than mathematical."

"Art thou the thing I wanted" (1282)

1979   PATTERSON, *Dickinson's Imagery,* pp. 24, 34
The poem is "aimed, it would seem, at Abby Wood Bliss, fiercely repudiating the old school friend who had given her a scanty, disappointing affection."

1980   HOPES, "Uses of Metaphor," pp. 13–16
Here Dickinson's "imagery has the tang of divisement [*sic*] rather than discovery." The poem "takes on something of the appearance of a riddle . . . by giving a reader more options than necessities."

1981   ALEXANDER, "Reading Emily Dickinson," pp. 10–11
Comparison of two versions of this poem illustrates "how subtle changes in language can result in important changes in perspective."

1982   MOSSBERG, *Emily Dickinson,* pp. 135, 144–45
". . . starving has made her spiritually more consequential. Indeed, 'dining without' makes her now 'Like God' for she needs nothing: creator, not created: mother, not child."

"As by the dead we love to sit" (88)

1978   PERRINE, "Dickinson's 'As by the dead,' " pp. 32–33
Examines the phrase "fading ratio" and suggests that it is "a ratio of the *emotional value* of the *one recently lost friend* to the *collective emotional value* of the *friends who remain* (in which the emotional value of any friend as compared to another is inconstant and unequal)."

1980   JOHNSON, " 'Broken Mathematics,' " pp. 21–23, 202 n. 4
Reviews critical misreadings of the poem, resulting largely from "a failure to recognize its rhetorical structure." The poem "states a kind of formula which indicates the heightened value of any perception as the perception's object fades from our sight or possession."
Revised and reprinted: Johnson, *Emily Dickinson,* pp. 82–83

1986   BURBICK, "Economics of Desire," p. 373
"In the language of exchange and measure, the other increases in price as it recedes into death. In a simple economy of desire, death ironically enhances the value of the desired, the corpse is most precious."

STONUM, "Calculated Sublime," p. 110

Ratio is a "crucial" mathematical idea in Dickinson's poetry. "She uses the word here . . . to set an experience she possesses in relation to one that is absent. . . . The mathematics here is broken, both imperfectly executed and victimized by the incommensurability between the finite and the infinite."

"As far from pity as complaint" (496)

1988   STOCKS, *Modern Consciousness,* p. 49

Examines connection between time and history conveyed by this poem.

"As from the earth the light balloon" (1630)

1983   UNO, "Expression by Negation," pp. 9–10

The concept of "release" is important in this poem, and Dickinson emphasizes it by her use of negation.

1989   OLIVER, *Apocalypse of Green,* p. 207

"The poem captures the ambiguity of the soul's desire for earthly release from captivity; yet at the same time it recognizes the incomplete nature of the soul separated from the body."

"As frost is best conceived" (951)

1979   PATTERSON, *Dickinson's Imagery,* pp. 41, 48, 187

The poem describes "the action of the frost in terms of a symbolic castration."

1987   BARKER, *Lunacy of Light,* pp. 72–73

Considers sun and frost imagery here and in other poems. In this poem, "the effects of the frost are seen as damaging only in the sun's light."

1988   WOLFF, *Emily Dickinson,* pp. 312–13

Although the poem "begins and ends with the language of birthing, the ability to breed has been nullified. God has imposed His will upon the world, and He leaves only wilt and putrefaction to signify His passing."

"As if I asked a common alms" (323)

1989   DOBSON, *Strategies of Reticence,* pp. 100–01

The poem, whose subject "is replaced by two metaphors, . . . could be an expression of religious awe or a response to a declaration of love, as easily as what it seems to be, an expression of profound gratitude for some unstated favor or compliment."

"As if some little arctic flower" (180)

1978 HECHT, "Riddles," pp. 20–21
Suggests poem may be read as being "in fact about the evolutionary process of survival with regard to the flower."
Reprinted: Hecht, *Obbligati*, pp. 111–13

1979 PATTERSON, *Dickinson's Imagery*, pp. 106–07, 188
The poem may illustrate Dickinson's "practice of analogizing from important developments of her time [here, botanical findings of Asa Gray] and thus conferring upon a personal and limited event the grandeur of great intellectual discoveries and stirring historic occasions."

"As if the sea should part" (695)

1983 JUHASZ, *Undiscovered Continent,* pp. 136–37, 138, 150–51, 153, 166, 167
". . . the key words in this poem are as much *as if, presumption, to be,* as they are *sea* and *shore*. These phrases . . . indicate that the very existence of eternity is dependent upon them, upon the mind."

1986 MOREY, "Dickinson-Kant: The First Critique," pp. 65–66
". . . as each spiritual insight is activated, there is an accumulation of them. One's understanding of the unconscious expands on the Great Chain of Being and one is metamorphized gradually to a new level. The sea is symbolic of these stages and changes."

"As imperceptibly as grief" (1540)

1981 DIEHL, *Romantic Imagination,* pp. 98–99
"The pain of summer's passing provokes Dickinson to assume a determining power over the past as well as the future, so she extends the province of her artistic control by shaping memory according to desire."

1982 MARCUS, *Emily Dickinson,* pp. 33, 35
General consideration as one of Dickinson's "philosophical poems of nature."

1983 HOOK, *American Literature,* pp. 56–61, 64
"Seasonal change becomes a metaphor for the transformation of grief into its own kind of beauty. Change, the poem says, does not always

"As plan for noon and plan for night"

mean change for the worse." Examines poem's rhymes, images, structure.

1985   JOHNSON, *Emily Dickinson,* pp. 104, 106–08, 203 nn. 7–9
Relates to other Dickinson poems "describing the movement of summer into fall" and discusses stanzas from an earlier draft.

RENAUX, "Seasons of Light," pp. 28–29, 42–48, 50–51
Employs A. J. Zokovskij's "theory of amplification" to analyze the poem; "it is through amplification that we can trace how form and content interact to convey meaning."

"As plan for noon and plan for night" (960)

1989   OLIVER, *Apocalypse of Green,* pp. 84–85
"In this poem life and death are described not as complementary but as polar processes; life is not a process leading to or through death, but in the opposite direction."

"As summer into autumn slips" (1346)

1982   MOSSBERG, *Emily Dickinson,* pp. 81–82
"Dickinson's choice of 'Autumn' instead of winter to symbolize the inevitability of our 'Declivity' is important, for she is emphasizing that maturity is a gradual downward slope into death: old age is emblematic of maturity as well as death."

"As the starved maelstrom laps the navies" (872)

1977   BENNETT, "Language of Love," p. 16
The poem's sexual images are clearly homoerotic in nature.

1979   CAMERON, *Lyric Time,* pp. 16–17
In this poem "verbal designation seems to guard the meaning it ostensibly specifies."

1981   PORTER, *Dickinson,* pp. 91, 174
The poem illustrates Dickinson's "outrageous appetite for the sensations of language and the power with which she fed it. . . . It is a poem of craving and appetite, of instinctive need, but without understanding."

1988   LOUIS, "Sacrament of Starvation," pp. 358–59
The poem's speaker, "like the tiger, has only learned to prefer a new diet to a more innocent and more readily procurable nutriment. The

persnickety wrongheadedness of these impractical epicures creates their suffering, while at the same time it constitutes their quixotic triumph of identity within a world too easily satisfied."

1989 MILLER, C., "Approaches," pp. 224–25
"Dickinson's three analogies tell what the speaker's hunger is like but also unlike—leaving interpretation of the speaker's 'finer Famine' in a middle ground that the reader must locate and describe."

"As watchers hang upon the east" (121)

1985 BUDICK, *Emily Dickinson*, p. 54
". . . by ending the poem with an ominous 'if true' Dickinson is more than subtly suggesting that the very process of seeking sacramental unities may leave us with a painfully conditional and tentative faith."

JOHNSON, *Emily Dickinson*, pp. 97–98, 200 n. 19
Reviews "critical confusion" resulting from "the attempt to reconcile this poem with Dickinson's characteristic skepticism."

1988 WOLFF, *Emily Dickinson*, pp. 289–90
"Perhaps nothing displays the Deity's cunning so well as His ability to wound us with the force of our own desire for His presence, for even this glorious expectation is transformed into pain when it must remain uncertain so long as we live."

"As we pass houses musing slow" (1653)

1984 WILT, "Playing House," p. 156
"The meanings knotted typically into Dickinson's grammar here are several."

"At half past three a single bird" (1084)

1979 ATTEBERY, "Dickinson, Emerson," pp. 17, 21
Examines abstractions in final stanza. "Dickinson is inserting her abstractions . . . into a syntactical framework which would ordinarily hold concrete nouns."

CAMERON, *Lyric Time*, pp. 176–77, 185
The poem "implies that in the fight for the finite space of being, something must be sacrificed. . . . Much of what serves to isolate mo-

ments of a single event and to sever them from each other is that their departure is not a gradual giving way but an abrupt disappearance."

1980   HARTMAN, *Criticism in the Wilderness,* pp. 122, 126–30
Considered along with "The birds begun at four o'clock." "Read in sequence, their quest for purity appears in a revealing and frightening way. We glimpse . . . the link between nature poetry and language purification; between questions of representation and purity of diction; and we understand that nature enters . . . as a privative and admonitory force."

1981   PADDOCK, "Metaphor as Reason," pp. 75–76
All the birds "fall silent as the sun rises. This occurrence can be seen as a metaphor for Dickinson's poetic method: the action of a given poem begins with a single perception that provokes a deluge of images that ceases abruptly at the moment of conceptualization."

1984   ANDERSON, D., "Presence and Place," pp. 209–11, 212, 213, 218–19, 222
"The music of the bird provides one sort of luminous 'presence' for the speaker, but the sheer joy of listening . . . is the poem's genuine subject."

HATTENHAUER, "Feminism," p. 55
An example of Dickinson's feminization of the bird when it "stands directly for the poet." Comments on poem's use of numbers three, four, and seven.

1985   COOK, A., *Thresholds,* pp. 194–95
"The metaphor here of a logical progression through experiment, proof, and something like a totally assimilated law exhibits its figurativeness, and it does so progressively."

1986   MOREY, "Dickinson–Kant: The First Critique," p. 44
"Along with the admirable example of the Doppler effect, this poem is an outstanding example of presence absent, with the silent Place reminding the writer of the divine music heard there previously."

STONUM, "Calculated Sublime," pp. 120–22
Examines changes from "The birds begun at four o'clock," of which this "seems to be a direct revision."

1988   WOLFF, *Emily Dickinson,* pp. 364–65
". . . the abstract nouns throughout this poem compel the reader

to infer that Dickinson is dealing here not with the material world, but with mythic time and archetypal events."

"At last to be identified" (174)

1978   MILLER, R., "Transitional Object," pp. 455–56
"The poem shows a perhaps inordinate belief in the significance of identity through publication, but, so it was. To Emily Dickinson it meant she would have place in her time and immortality for all time."

1982   MOSSBERG, *Emily Dickinson,* pp. 18, 19, 67
"Dickinson essentially lived as an unknown, as regards her 'true' identity as a poet, and in this poem, she presents a consciousness that has waited a lifetime for such identification."

"At least to pray is left, is left" (502)

1980   REISS, "Dickinson's Self-Reliance," pp. 31–32
"The poet presents a person who knocks everywhere and yet no door is opened. The earth is shaken and the sea is whirled, all by God's might, but there is no forcing of the person praying in this poem."

1984   WOLOSKY, *Emily Dickinson,* pp. 59–61
The poem is "strangely situated between its own universality and the unavoidable but barely hinted fact of the war raging in the background of its composition." The poet asserts divine power "only in its aspect of unleashing catastrophe."

1986   OBERHAUS, "'Engine against th' Almightie,'" pp. 161–63, 171 n. 25
Relates to "Jesus! thy crucifix" and other "prayer" poems of Dickinson.

"At leisure is the soul" (618)

1981   STEINER, "Image Patterns," p. 65
Relates to other Dickinson poems dealing with "the woman in her dealings with Power."

"Aurora is the effort" (1002)

1978   MANN, "Poet as Namer," p. 481
The poem shows how the poet was able to develop a "name-generated definition" poem "with terse speed and complex metaphor."

"Awake ye muses nine, sing me a strain divine" (1)

1980 BRASHEAR, " 'Awake ye muses nine,' " pp. 90–99
Examines as a prototypical Dickinson poem, "a key to her metrical development and the earliest record of the imagery and themes which inform her later work."

1981 DIEHL, Romantic Imagination, p. 17
". . . Dickinson's version of erotic bliss is shadowed by her awareness of the other side of life. Within this highly conventional romantic frame, death and the swift punishment of God's law reside."

1982 MOSSBERG, Emily Dickinson, pp. 9, 83, 103–06, 108, 109, 123, 158, 206 n. 4
"What emerges from the poem is not a conventional valentine message so much as a criticism of the romantic rituals prescribed by church and state, accomplished through the use of poetic as well as thematic convention."

"Away from home are some and I" (821)

1982 MOSSBERG, Emily Dickinson, p. 122
"According to the daughter construct, Dickinson has internalized her family structure so that she carries her sensibility as a daughter—and her corresponding alienation and homelessness—with her. This accounts for poems such as [this one]. . . . In these poems heaven is a paradigm of alienation for the little girl."

"Banish air from air" (854)

1979 PATTERSON, Dickinson's Imagery, p. 103
The poem is "so clotted with scientific metaphors as to be almost unreadable."

1981 PORTER, Dickinson, pp. 67–78
The poet's "allegory of fate" is "compressed, seemingly confident in its procedure, employing single words of unarguable meaning but joined in a chain that curves in and out of the intelligible and loops, finally, out of the real world into the autonomous system of language."

1982 RUDDICK, "Dickinson's 'Banish Air,' " pp. 31–33
"The poem is an astonishingly succinct and allusive variation on the theme of the essential unity of creation, a unity which the poet feels is entirely misunderstood by the kind of mind that seeks to analyze and compartmentalize phenomena."

1985   BUDICK, *Emily Dickinson,* pp. 84–85
"No matter how hard he or she tries, the individual cannot carve out a safe space between the crowding, suffocating densities of 'Air' and 'Light' that define phenomenal reality in each of the succeeding emanations of the cosmic plan."

EBERWEIN, *Dickinson,* pp. 155–56
In this poem describing her "fragmented, condensed art," Dickinson applies "a chemical analogy of water's distillation into steam to exemplify her distinctive aesthetic process in both its stylistic and thematic dimensions."

"Beauty be not caused—it is" (516)

1979   WINTHER, "Editing Emily Dickinson," p. 32
Notes effect of capitalization in bringing into focus "the thematically most important phrase in the whole poem": "It Is."

"Because I could not stop for death" (712)

1972   RAO, *Essential Emily Dickinson,* pp. 34–36, 51, 85, 148–51
General introduction to the poem aimed at "postgraduate students of literature in Indian Universities."

1978   ABAD, *Formal Approach,* pp. 59n, 139–40, 141–43, 181–82, 292, 293, 391
The poem "is rather a *lyric meditation* than a lyric of reaction."

COOPER, P., "Central Image," pp. 295–96
Examines second line of fourth quatrain ("At Recess—in the Ring—") and its superiority to version previously used ("Their lessons scarcely done"), which "lost the image of physical contact so relevant to the lady's peril . . . ."

PRIVRATSKY, "Irony," pp. 25–29
This is "a thoroughly ironic poem, and recognition of Dickinson's use of irony is essential to one's understanding of the poem's meaning." The poem "concerns separation from life . . . [and] it may stand as her testimonial of the value of that life left behind."

1979   CAMERON, *Lyric Time,* pp. 51, 112, 121–23, 124–26, 127–28, 129–32, 133, 137, 204, 208
"The poem presumes to rid death of its otherness, to familiarize it, literally to adopt its perspective and in so doing to effect a synthesis

between self and other, internal time and the faster, more relentless beat of the world."

Reprinted: Cameron, *"Et in Arcadia,"* pp. 58–59, 65–68, 69–71, 72–73, 74

KAPLAN, "Indefinite Disclosed," p. 76

Here "the dream is a secondary frame for a poem in which the primary convention is a classical or medieval reference to death as driver, boatman or charioteer . . . ."

Reprinted: Kaplan, *Sea Changes,* p. 113

O'HARA, "'Designated Light,'" pp. 180–83, 185–86, 196 n. 1, 197 n. 12

Kierkegaard's "understanding of 'unmastered irony' . . . seems to illuminate much of Tate's New Critical or 'modernist' interpretation" of Dickinson's poetry.

1980   TAYLOR, M., "Shaman Motifs," p. 10

The poem "speaks eloquently of a soul who has endured the shamanic crisis and is able to pass on the treasures of rare vision to those who like her are ready to move beyond the discrete objects of the earthly plane of consciousness."

1981   CROSTHWAITE, "Ride with Death," pp. 18–27

"The poet is not talking of her own death at all but of her encounter with death in the death of another. The poem is immediately clarified by this simple, but pivotal, understanding. . . . She is a mourner, not a corpse."

McGANN, "Historical Method," pp. 278–84, 287 nn. 12, 15, 17, 19, 20

Examines Allen Tate's 1936 study of this poem to illustrate problems inherent in specific critical approaches. The poem's power "rests in its ability to show us not merely the thoughts and feelings of Dickinson and her fictive speaker, but the attitudes of her implied readers as well."

1982   DOWNEY, *Child's Emily Dickinson,* pp. 88, 92

"This poem that she writes about death is like the Cinderella story. Death is the kind Prince who comes for Cinderella, and Emily herself plays the part of Cinderella."

FAULKNER, "Emily Dickinson," p. 812

"Death, Dickinson's essential metaphor and subject, is seen in terms of a moment of confrontation. Absence thus becomes the major presence, confusion the major ordering principle."

LEWIS, "Theologian," pp. 13–17, 21
"Here she is affirming her destiny, consolidating her manifest resources of character, and making poetic capital out of the poetic self she has purchased at the price of renouncing the receding possibility of a genuine love relationship."

MARCUS, *Emily Dickinson*, pp. 86–87, 96
Related to other Dickinson poems on death and immortality. "The presence of immortality in the carriage may be part of a mocking game or it may indicate some kind of real promise."

1983 BUDICK, "Temporal Consciousness," pp. 235–37, 238 nn. 6, 7, 239 n. 8
Immortality, "as it is presented in the poem, is not just something toward which human beings journey in death. . . . Rather it is apparently also a component of consciousness itself, somehow coextensive not only with death, but with life as well . . . ."
Revised and reprinted: Budick, *Emily Dickinson*, pp. 211–12, 223–28

DAICHES, *God and the Poets*, pp. 159–60
The imagination displayed in this poem is one "that could only have developed in post-Puritan New England with its neatly materialist daily life coexisting with its mutated Calvinist heritage, with Romanticism and Transcendentalism blowing round."

HARRIS, N., "Naked and Veiled," pp. 23, 29–30, 33
Contrasted with Plath's "Death & Co." Each involves "a woman who is courted by death."

ROGERS, W. E., *Three Genres*, pp. 94, 97–102
". . . the poem attempts to bring about a shocking encounter of the mind of the work with itself while it is in the very process of constructing its protective sentimental fictions." The poem should be read as lyric rather than as drama.

1984 ALLARD, "Regulation of Belief," pp. 32–33
"Rather than an allegory of her own death the stopping of Death in the poem surely represents her first intimation of mortality and her entrance into History."

BZOWSKI, "Continuation of the Tradition," pp. 33–42
"Altho some of these allusions may be subconscious, there are suggestions not only of Christian's pilgrimage, but also of the medieval Dance of Death and of seventeenth century emblems permeating the poem."

"Because I could not stop for death"

GALPERIN, "Marriage Hearse," pp. 62–73
Reviews various critical approaches to the poem. "Feminist writing succeeds [in this poem] not only as an oppositive rhetoric but as a prelude to its deconstruction which, like the passage to 'Eternity,' is necessarily uncompleted."

KAZIN, "Wrecked, Solitary, Here," pp. 174, 179–80
"The effect of the poem is 'dying'—stanza by stanza we see less and less of what we are passing through, what is soon behind us."

MARDER, *Exiles at Home*, p. 135
"Although the dead one has gone to eternity, the focus is totally on the life that has been lost. . . . Eternity is apparently an empty place where the soul longs endlessly for life. Death is the loss of consciousness, with its drunken, exhilarating moments of heaven."

OLPIN, "Hyperbole: Part II," pp. 16–18, 20
Examines comic techniques employed by Dickinson in this poem, including "the genteel and comic personification of death."

POLLAK, *Dickinson*, pp. 190–93, 196, 197
"Dickinson shapes the crucial event of dying from within in order to suggest that life contains many such deaths. The self is a function of its relationships, and once these relationships have been extinguished, there emerges a concept of being without essence."

ST. ARMAND, *Dickinson and Her Culture*, pp. 34, 71–73, 135, 137, 258
"In this poem all the clichés of the sentimental gospel are emptied of their well-intended meanings and become props by which Dickinson constructs a surreal 'tribute' to her own special brand of spiritual materialism."

STAUB, "Dickinson Diagnosis," pp. 44–46
"A stanza-by-stanza analysis of J712 reveals the motif of forces held in opposition. This tension lends the poem a swaying cadence—between life and death, between temporal and eternal, between hope and despair. Repeatedly in J712 the symbolic fabric of sentimentality is sliced thru with doubt."

WALLACE, *God Be with the Clown*, pp. 98, 214
"Seen from the proper comic perspective, the perspective of compensation, death could be a friend rather than an enemy, paradoxically giving life while taking it away. At best you might end up in heaven."

1985 ANANTHARAMAN, *Sunset in a Cup,* pp. 25–35, 42, 47, 48, 54, 147, 162
"The setting of the poem is deeply religious. The narrator's consciousness assimilates past, present and future into a consciousness which is made of the imagination." Considers poem's descriptive, symbolic, and poetic meanings.

COOK, A., "Figural Choice, pp. 35, 180
"In Emily Dickinson's eschatology the strange elisions of visual registering when her speaker travels through the afterlife forbid our univocal assignment of metaphor to *gazing* or to *grain.*"

COOK, A., *Thresholds,* pp. 185–86, 188, 191, 288 n. 8
"Here the process of recognizing one's location in the afterlife is rendered as a gradual census of dissimilarities-in-similarity."

DOWNEY, "ED's Appeal," p. 26
Children may read this as "a sequel to the Cinderella story" and the "happy ending of this poem will help give the child a positive attitude toward death."

EBERWEIN, *Dickinson,* pp. 123, 183, 216–19
"Rather than attending to mysteries, this speaker focuses only on the familiar until a novel perspective on the sunset jolts her into awareness of her own transitional state." The poem confronts the problem of "the assertiveness of the circuit world against the claims of complementary vision."

ESTES, "Granny Weatherall," pp. 438–39, 440, 441, 442
Examines allusions to this poem in Katherine Anne Porter's "The Jilting of Granny Weatherall."

LOVING, "'Hansom Man,'" pp. 93, 94, 96–97, 98, 99
"The poem describes her assignation with the lover she had always remembered—which is to say that it is not about life's so-called happy ending but about the union of Love and Death." Compares with "There came a day at summer's full."

RAINA, "Dickinson's 'Because I could not stop,'" pp. 11–12
Suggests a reading of the first two lines translates "the persona's not stopping for death into an imaginative perception of the nonreality of death. Death is death only to those who live within the time-bound finite world outside of the imaginative infinity of consciousness."

"Because I could not stop for death"

1986   BENNETT, *Loaded Gun*, pp. 46–47
This is not a "personal poem" but rather "it uses the speaker's situation as the basis for a generalized rumination on the affective quality of eternity. . . ." Compares and contrasts with "I often passed the village."

LOVING, *Emily Dickinson*, pp. 11–12, 32, 33, 37, 40–41, 45, 47–48, 94, 109
"This poem is about the day in every life when we realize that the desire for love is the desire for death. All we have finally, Dickinson knew, is the desire to love."

MCNEIL, *Emily Dickinson*, pp. 129, 131
"Dickinson doesn't depict her soul flying from her house to a home above. The ambiguous status of the house actually serves a surprising function as a hedge against dualism."

ROBINSON, J., *Emily Dickinson*, pp. 51–53, 54–55, 171
"We are unsettled by the discrepancy between the matter and the manner. . . . As we proceed we are given a heightened sense of social conventions being firmly applied and yet drastically inappropriate."

1988   MONTEIRO, G., "Dickinson's 'Because I could not stop,'" pp. 20–21
Speculates on possible significance of the poem's schoolyard game, which might well be "Ring-a-ring-a-roses."

PHILLIPS, *Emily Dickinson*, pp. 85–87, 91, 92, 225 n. 12, 234 n. 38
"The idea for the poem must . . . have originated in an event about which the poet knew: the death of a distant cousin, Olivia Coleman, at the age of twenty . . . ."

WOLFF, *Emily Dickinson*, pp. xviii, 235, 274–277, 294, 464
The poem "might best be read against a purely literary model, the novel of seduction. . . . Still, the novel of seduction is external to the essential import of [this poem], the speaker's refusal to submit to God's demands. It is a pattern to a manipulated, nothing more."

1989   GALPERIN, "Posthumanist Approach," pp. 113, 114, 116, 117
Describes a "nexus . . . of humanism and feminism" as the basis of an approach to teaching Dickinson. ". . . by redefining death so that it meant a woman's co-optation by culture, the poem similarly redefined immortality as a woman's self-possession, or the result, in turn, of a refusal to allow 'society' the prerogative of selecting her."

HOCKERSMITH, "'Into Degreeless Noon,'" pp. 279, 280–81, 282–83, 286, 294 n. 7
The poem "portrays a dead speaker who wishes to be freed from the awareness of time, who wishes to be freed from consciousness."

KNAPP, *Emily Dickinson,* pp. 91–95
The poem "may be looked upon as a religious adventure in the largest sense of the world: an Orphic descent into the world of death." Detailed examination of development of poem's images.

LAKOFF and TURNER, *More Than Cool Reason,* pp. 2–10, 15, 68–69, 107, 174
Examines the nature of poem's metaphors, specifically to illustrate "the range of common, unconscious, automatic basic metaphors which are part of our cultural knowledge and which allow us to communicate with each other . . . ."

OLIVER, *Apocalypse of Green,* pp. 88–91, 231
This poem "as an imaginative metaphor for death and dying encompasses most of Dickinson's attitudes about death."

"Because that you are going" (1260)

1978 KHAN, "Romantic Tradition," pp. 61–63
"Dickinson's vision of love . . . is symbolic of both the worlds— the world of Platonic Ideas and the world of neo-Platonic emanations from its plenitude, the world of supersensuous love (Eros) and the world of human love. The identity of love in both the worlds remains human in its centrality and focus."
Revised and reprinted: Khan, *Emily Dickinson's Poetry,* pp. 74–77

1983 SHURR, *Marriage,* pp. 158–59
". . . the last meeting of lovers until eternity is a moment lifted 'Above Mortality.' Eternity is then the subject."

"Because 'twas riches I could own" (1093)

1985 JOHNSON, *Emily Dickinson,* p. 89
Relates to Dickinson's use of economic metaphors in other writings.

"Bee! I'm expecting you" (1035)

1984 WALLACE, *God Be with the Clown,* pp. 2–3, 77
"Although the hint of loneliness and longing in the poem adds a slightly deeper emotional resonance, there is not much serious import here—just the shadow of a cloud."

"Bees are black with gilt surcingles" (1405)

1981 CUDDY, "Expression and Sublimation," pp. 32–33
". . . taken in the context of all her bee poems, there is a great deal of mockery, sarcasm, and disdain for this self-important, self-satisfied insect that would not even exist without the help of the (female) flower. There is an obvious assumption of authority and control over the male figures who had once humbled the poet."

PADDOCK, "Metaphor as Reason," pp. 74–75
The poem attempts "to reconcile a concrete instance of apprehension with a conceptual verbal tag through the projection of a series of metaphors. The drama of discovery thus engendered is, essentially, the action of the poem and itself a metaphor for the reasoning process."

1982 OLPIN, "Hyperbole: Part One," pp. 13–14
"The surface of the poem focuses on the Bucaneers [*sic*], but the ministerial bees with their 'Fuzz ordained' and their jugs are at the heart of the comedy."

1986 ROBINSON, J., *Emily Dickinson,* p. 92
"If belief were simply a matter of accepting a satisfactory blueprint for life, it would be like declaring, as she wittily does (#1405), that bees do not live in a haphazard world but in a universe that is purposefully planned and whose plan therefore makes it invulnerable to accident . . . ."

"Before I got my eye put out" (327)

1978 CARTON, "Dickinson and the Divine," pp. 243–45
"The danger of the sun . . . is that its light will satisfy the quester and thus disengage her from the pursuit of a light beyond, detach her from God."
Revised and reprinted: Carton, *Rhetoric,* pp. 48–50

MANN, "Poet as Namer," pp. 478–79
"She records her joy at the thought of seeing once again by listing the names of things she most yearns for. . . . Dickinson's insistent use of 'mine' reflects her excitement at possessing what she has just named."

1979   BUDICK, "When the Soul Selects," pp. 352, 360–63

The poem "is a veritable symbolograph which demonstrates the consequences of that kind of Neoplatonic refining of human perception in which the attempt to isolate ideal essences from the living whole ironically results in a contrary explosion outward into material grossness and multiplicity."

Revised and reprinted: Budick, *Emily Dickinson*, pp. 117–21, 187, 191

GILBERT and GUBAR, *Madwoman*, pp. 58, 595–96

"In the context of the elaborate drama she was enacting . . . her metaphorical (and perhaps occasionally literal) blindness seems to have functioned in part as a castration metaphor . . . ."

O'HARA, " 'Designated Light,' " pp. 176–78, 197 n. 5

"Dickinson's poem is as much a critical commentary on 'the sublime' as an instance of it." She "redirects attention from the transcendental posing of Emerson to what are perhaps the more authentic sublimities of the household seer."

PATTERSON, *Dickinson's Imagery*, pp. 43, 44, 127–28

"Her blindness . . . is the consequence of the cruel treatment she has received—but, in some curious way, has deserved. Other items in the poem . . . represent aspects of the faithless beloved."

1980   TAYLOR, M., "Shaman Motifs," p. 10

Relates poem to elements of the "shaman experience." The poet "accepts interior vision rather than attempt participation in a transcendent one for which she is not ready."

1982   GUTHRIE, "Dickinson's Illness," pp. 19, 21

Relates to the poet's eye problems. "The poem becomes her own warning to those individuals who might scrutinize the world too closely, as she had, that there is something there which God does not want them to see."

JOHNSON, "Emily Dickinson," pp. 4–7, 8–9

The poem "contrasts two kinds of perception, visual and intuitive, and contains ambiguities deliberately left unresolved. . . ." It is also "a potent satire, an attack upon complacency . . . and perhaps against empty assertions of spiritual vision made by other poets."

Revised and reprinted: Johnson, *Emily Dickinson*, pp. 9, 48–51, 52, 53, 198 n. 5, 198–99 n. 8

1983   ROSENTHAL and GALL, *Modern Poetic Sequence*, pp. 48, 50–53, 54, 68–69, 71–72

Dickinson's poem "presents the aftermath of a heart's voyage into lovely, unexpectedly deadly places, and it offers something like a resolution—all in the elusive context of envisioned moments of choice and crisis, each with its own storm center of language." Relates to other poems in fascicles 15 and 16.

1984   ANDERSON, D., "Presence and Place," pp. 220–21, 222
"The condition of perception that Dickinson describes here is both something less and something more than ordinary human power. . . . To maintain its poise between the remembered fact and the present miracle of memory is the poem's chief objective."

1986   BUELL, *New England Literary Culture*, pp. 124–25
"This and a number of other poems of the absent center could be seen as arising from a specifically feminist consciousness."

McNEILL, *Emily Dickinson*, pp. 104–05, 189 n. 3
This is a poem "about both literal blindness and feminine constraint."

ROBINSON, J., *Emily Dickinson*, pp. 65–66
". . . the superiority of insight over visual sight is given in the claim that she now sees more when blinded than she did sighted. This is joined with another idea, that total knowledge would be unendurable because it would amount to being immortal (having the all-knowing mind of God), hence being dead."

1988   PHILLIPS, *Emily Dickinson*, pp. 72, 73–74, 75, 100–01, 104, 115, 123, 208, 227–28 n. 4
The poem's burden "is not just that it began in the anxieties of the poet, or that she knew there was more than one way to see. It is also that she used the resources of language to transcend the limits and terrors of finite eyes." Notes literary source in *Jane Eyre*.

1989   GARBOWSKY, *House without the Door*, pp. 103–04, 110–11
"Eye problems are common complications of the agoraphobic syndrome." Suggests that this poem might "reflect the phobia that kept her hidden within her house, 'safe' from the outside world."

"Before you thought of spring" (1465)

1988   WOLFF, *Emily Dickinson*, pp. 527–28
Contrasts with "The most triumphant bird I ever knew or met" and "After all birds have been investigated and laid aside."

"Behind me dips eternity" (721)

1977 AGRAWAL, *Emily Dickinson,* pp. 99–101
Here Dickinson "blasts the foundations of the Biblical doctrine of eternity and immortality by exploiting its own tenets."

1978 CAMERON, " 'Loaded Gun,' " pp. 430–31, 434
"As she presses against the poles of eternity and immortality with the force of life's disorder, we know that the price of her collapse—the disappearance of the middle term—is not only personal extinction but the omission of life itself . . . ."
Reprinted: Cameron, *Lyric Time,* pp. 74–76, 84, 111, 244, 259–260; Bloom, H., *Emily Dickinson,* pp. 115–17, 124

CARTON, "Dickinson and the Divine," pp. 245–46, 252 n. 6
". . . in the structure of Dickinson's poem, the state of ultimate selfhood that [the kingdom] represents is 'the Term between' two depictions of a present self's inundation. The third stanza is an ominous mirror image of the first."
Revised and reprinted: Carton, *Rhetoric,* pp. 51–52, 270 n. 6

MILLER, R., "Transitional Object," pp. 463–64
"Thus she satisfied herself; thus she quieted her longings; thus she understood her isolation: she was the mortal simulacrum of Christ."

1981 DIEHL, *Romantic Imagination,* pp. 151–53
"The form of these lines and the vision of the self surrounded by time, the waiting, open sea, and the prospect of a possible, future kingdom closely resemble" lines in Shelley's "The Triumph of Life."

ORSINI, "Romantic Use of Science," pp. 65–66
This is "the poem that best exemplifies her scientific approach to revelation . . ., perhaps *the* central poem in the Dickinson canon inasmuch as it both dramatizes and analyzes her objective and empirical methods."

1982 ANDERSON, P., "Dickinson's 'Son of None,' " pp. 32–33
Examines the phrase "Son of None." "To anyone familiar with the Bible, the phrase suggests 'Son of Nun,' which very often follows any mention of Joshua . . . ."

MARCUS, *Emily Dickinson,* p. 90
Related to other Dickinson poems on death and immortality. "The poem is primarily an indirect prayer that her hopes may be fulfilled."

1987 BLASING, *American Poetry,* pp. 173–74
Comments on effect of poem's alliteration.

LEDER and ABBOTT, *Language of Exclusion,* p. 115
The poem "may be interpreted as an illustration of Dickinson's personal response to the crisis of her country."

1988 PHILLIPS, *Emily Dickinson,* pp. 201–02
"The imagery of the natural world in awesome disorder is the imagery of a dark night of the soul."

WOLF, *Emily Dickinson,* pp. 292–94, 322, 323, 356, 479
"Fated to disintegrate into some other state, the speaker attempts to define the place that is the fabled prize awaiting those who possess faith. Yet her effort . . . leads only to a wasteland."

1989 HOCKERSMITH, "'Into Degreeless Noon,'" pp. 290–93, 294–95 n. 21
"Several critics suggest that this poem reflects Dickinson's metaphysical and ontological stance. In fact, it reflects her epistemological problem. . . . [It] offers neither a definite metaphysic nor a fixed ontology; instead, it seeks the limits of human knowledge."

McCLURE, "Expanding the Canon," pp. 78–79
"Dickinson's use of frontier imagery illustrates how she adapted cultural mythology to express a personal vision."

WALKER, C., "Feminist Critical Practice," pp. 9, 15, 18–19
Considers the poem in a "gendered historical context." "This poem can be read as the poet's self-insertion of the female into history . . . ."

"Behold this little bane" (1438)

1985 ANANTHARAMAN, *Sunset in a Cup,* p. 83
"The speaker is a person of wildly separated halves, who is being shuttled between duo-consciousness and mono-consciousness. The duo-consciousness gives her a startled recognition that love is a boon, huge and multi-dimensional. But mono-consciousness conceals this fact from her, and love becomes a 'small bane.'"

"Belshazzar had a letter" (1459)

1987 MOREY, "Dickinson-Kant II," pp. 10–11
Notes a "possible undercurrent . . . that God should be more generous with his letters and presence."

"Bereaved of all, I went abroad" (784)

1981   KNOX, "Metaphor and Metonymy," pp. 50–55
"The poem, by providing a means for the actual bipolarity of figurative thinking to find expression, provides the poet the means for imaginative transformation, if not elimination, of her anxiety about death."

1982   BURBICK, "Irony of Self-Reference," pp. 89–90
" 'It,' the pronoun that signifies the unknown, the inanimate object
or the impersonal subject, rides in awesome pursuit of the speaker in this
poem."

"Best things dwell out of sight" (998)

1980   JOHNSON, " 'Pearl of Great Price,' " pp. 210–11
"The pearl, symbol of concentrated artistic value (a symbol en-
compassing both Dickinson's work and the poet herself), dwells out of
sight . . . : it is being nurtured within a protective shell. The pearl, like
the poet's 'Thought,' is a rarefied essence."
Revised and reprinted: Johnson, *Emily Dickinson,* pp. 72–73, 135–36

1981   PORTER, *Dickinson,* p. 123
"The poem demonstrates Dickinson's language moving into the
realm of referentless, quasi-mathematical expression."

1983   WALKER, J., "ED's Poetic," pp. 21–22
The poem suggests that "this poet CHOSE privacy in her poetry,
and chose it as the means by which to attain a personal and poetic sense
of liberation."

1984   BENFEY, *Problem of Others,* pp. 37–40
Discussion of Porter's 1981 interpretation.

"Best witchcraft is geometry" (1158)

1987   OATES, "Soul at the White Heat," pp. 809–10
"The 'witchcraft' of art is (mere) geometry to the practitioner: by
which is meant that it is orderly, natural, obedient to its own rules of logic;
an ordinary event. What constitutes the 'feat' is the relative ignorance of
others—nonmagicians."
Reprinted: Oates, *(Woman) Writer,* p. 168

"Better than music! For I who heard it" (503)

1982 MOSSBERG, *Emily Dickinson*, pp. 153–54
In this poem "Dickinson continues a child's interest in the loss of Paradise and her identification with Eve's hunger and rebellion as a daughter and poet."

1983 SHURR, *Marriage*, p. 173
"The poem is a nature poem, but Eve's sexual life intrudes."

1985 CARTON, *Rhetoric*, pp. 42–43
"For the persona of [this poem] the harmony of her receptive and expressive selves remains a 'promise.' The hearer stands momentarily in the presence of the sublime; the speaker stands in its absence."

"Bind me, I still can sing" (1005)

1989 HOCKERSMITH, "'Into Degreeless Noon,'" p. 290
Here the poet's "use of the objective pronoun suggests that what is subject to death is the *object* of the speaker's consciousness— her awareness of *being*. On the other hand, the poem clearly equates the speaker's 'soul' with her 'mandolin' . . . which represents her poetry."

"Blazing in gold and quenching in purple" (228)

1981 KNOX, "Metaphor and Metonymy," p. 50
Examines the "three-level metaphor" in the poem's first two lines.

1983 BUDICK, "Dangers of the Living Word," pp. 208–10, 213, 215, 216, 217, 218, 223, nn. 4, 6
Here the poet "wants to convey the implicit connection between language and reality in which language, attempting to convey cosmic beauty, cannot but recapitulate and deepen its immanent discreteness, its apparent disorder."
Revised and reprinted: Budick, *Emily Dickinson*, pp. 1–6, 7, 8, 13, 14, 20, 26, 27, 29, 44

1988 MOREY, "Dickinson–Kant III," pp. 25–26, 32, 45
"Despite all the gaiety and artistry there is the underlying sadness of permanent departure. . . ." Comments on prosody.

"Bloom is result to meet a flower" (1058)

1981   PORTER, *Dickinson*, p. 196
   "Her figure is a flower but the concern of the poem . . . is in view. With a primitivist wisdom, it has to do with result, coming into fulfillment, wholeness, all the things she had not attained herself in a way she could name."

1984   MARTIN, W., *American Triptych*, pp. 157–58
   Linked with other instances of flower imagery in Dickinson's poems that illuminate "her evolution from passive, dependent femininity to autonomous womanhood."

"Bloom upon the mountain stated" (667)

1983   MILLER, C., "How 'Low Feet' Stagger," pp. 149–151
   This poem "repeats the concerns of Dickinson's other poems about women poets, this time in implicit contrast to a male creator and male audience."

1984   HAGENBÜCHLE, "Concept of Ambiguity," pp. 217–21
   A discussion of the poem dealing with "the following linguistic features: lexical ambiguity/indeterminancy, referential ambiguity/indeterminacy, and syntactic ambiguity/indeterminacy."

1986   ROBINSON, J., *Emily Dickinson*, pp. 165, 167–68
   In this poem "the sun is, as in a metaphysical conceit, the seed, and the glowing light which it casts upon the mountain is the 'Bloom' or flower of the opening line and the 'Solemn Petals' of the last but one stanza."

"Bound a trouble" (269)

1979   PATTERSON, *Dickinson's Imagery*, pp. 102, 135
   The poem "suggests that if one could only foresee the end of pain, if the depth of the bleeding and the 'drops of vital scarlet' were limited, then it would be bearable."

1986   STONUM, "Calculated Sublime," pp. 108–09, 112
   The second stanza "advises that calibrated accounts can make life bearable, as any laborer knows when he counts the hours until quitting time and as any poet knows when she sings the fall of what had seemed a just and kindly natural world."

"Bring me the sunset in a cup" (128)

1981 HERNDON, "Dickinson and Job," pp. 47–50, 51
Finds "compelling" parallels with the Book of Job in this poem.

1984 WALLACE, *God Be with the Clown,* pp. 93–94
"The poem is structured as a series of comic questions about who is responsible for the world's wonders. . . . The humorous attempt to know the unknowable, to explain the inexplicable, leads to an ominous moment of existential doubt."

"By homely gift and hindered words" (1563)

1988 IWATA, "Something from Nothing," pp. 133–37
". . . for Dickinson 'nothing' represented a very positive and fundamental principle of some sort."

"By my window have I for scenery" (797)

1982 MADIGAN, "Mermaids," pp. 40–42, 44
"God has allowed the poet an insight . . . , a mental grasp, of the fact that the pine tree is a kind of microcosm of Infinity, the limitless space associated in this poem and elsewhere with the sea image and with the divine."

MILLER, C., "Terms and Golden Words," pp. 56–57
Although this poem is not about language, "structurally and dramatically [it] illustrates the process by which the use of metaphor may carry us beyond both conventional naming and the control of our initial linguistic intent and perception . . . ."

1985 BUDICK, *Emily Dickinson,* pp. 164, 182–86
The poem "expresses the poet's highly skeptical attitude toward conventional symbolic machinery."

1986 MCNEIL, *Emily Dickinson,* pp. 119–20, 137
"Transcendent presence would seem to silence the kind of non-metaphysical metaphor of knowledge that plays with proportion and takes pleasure in nature."

"Circumference thou bride of awe" (1620)

1981 DIEHL, *Romantic Imagination,* pp. 138–40, 143, 144
"She writes a distinct and original poem which banishes the hope

at the heart of *Epipsychidion* and, in the process, appropriates several images from Shelley's poem to inform her own ambivalent response."

1984 MARTIN, W., *American Triptych,* p. 124
"Here Dickinson celebrates joyous fusion of self and other—seeking and finding are no longer eternal opposites. Circumference, from the Latin 'to carry around,' then, is the perception of the universe as an eternal and cyclic whole."

1985 ANANTHARAMAN, *Sunset in a Cup,* pp. 88–89, 117
"This brief contextual poem is Emily's nearest approach to imaginative perception of love within the structure of her religious consciousness."

EBERWEIN, *Dickinson,* pp. 194–95, 218
Dickinson asserts here "that the artist must seek out the limits of human possibility, knowing that the limiting point is death. He must, in fact, desire death actively and pursue it as a goal, confident that its intimacy with 'Awe' . . . would lead him to glory."

"Civilization spurns the leopard" (492)

1979 PATTERSON, *Dickinson's Imagery,* pp. 151, 152–53, 161, 170
The poem's "Ethiopian" symbols "are somehow involved in the central idea of love as tropical heat, vitality itself . . . ."

1986 MCNEIL, *Emily Dickinson,* pp. 42–43, 171
The poem illustrates Dickinson's sensitivity "to her difference, not only from a masculine model, but also from the received model for feminine writing."

"Cocoon above! Cocoon below" (129)

1982 MOSSBERG, *Emily Dickinson,* p. 172
"*She* is the cocoon, bursting with words, yet confined and 'shut up;' she has a 'secret' creation no one can see; her dutiful daughter image contains, protects, and hides her present and future greatness as a poet."

"Come slowly, Eden" (211)

1983 JUHASZ, *Undiscovered Continent,* pp. 103–04, 105, 106
"Even as sexuality dominated events in the original garden, so the erotic implications of this poem's drama are emphasized. Love is the subject: the delight, the Eden in question."

KHAN, *Emily Dickinson's Poetry,* pp. 12–13
"The experience of love through the senses is akin to the primal experience in the garden of Eden, mainly in its brevity and abrupt termination."

1984 POLLAK, *Dickinson,* p. 113
"Building on her anxiety of gender, Dickinson achieves an insight into the relationship between the quality of an experience and the duration of it."

SALSKA, "Emily Dickinson's Lover," p. 137
". . . in what seems at first glance a very conventional though also a very sensuous allegory of the sexual act, there occurs a confusion of roles which effectively subverts the orthodox ecstasy of the intensely erotic."
Revised and reprinted: Salska, *Walt Whitman and Emily Dickinson,* pp. 138, 159 n. 21

1987 DI GIUSEPPE, "Maiden and the Muse," pp. 52–53, 54
Examines poem's "bee" metaphor and relates it to other "bee" poems by Dickinson.

1988 WOLFF, *Emily Dickinson,* pp. 382–83, 416
The poem "defines the lovers' relationship in language that explicitly reverses the usual Christian implications of nature."

"Conferring with myself" (1655)

1980 DIEHL, "American Self," p. 4
"Within its naturalistic frame, this poem describes an interior dialogue, an examination of a consciousness which exorcises the Self's Stranger; for the dialogue between Stranger and Self achieves its effect to the extent that it diminishes the recognized Self's private concerns."

"Conjecturing a climate" (562)

1986 DORESKI, "'Exchange of Territory,'" pp. 63–64
"This poem adds to Dickinson's grammar of poetic knowledge by creating a metaphorical structure in which the overt allegory is strong enough to recognize (and is emphasized by the poem's position in the sequence), yet is finally inextricable."

"Conscious am I in my chamber" (679)

1982   VAN DYNE, "Double Monologues," pp. 465, 467–68
The poem shows us "Dickinson's speaker standing watchfully by her subjective self in order to examine the dimensions and co-habitants of her chamber of consciousness."

1983   JUHASZ, *Undiscovered Continent,* pp. 155–57
"The poem has consistently employed comparisons with social rituals to define the nature of the speaker's relationship with eternity." Relates to other Dickinson poems about the experience of eternity.

1984   ANDERSON, D., "Presence and Place," pp. 213–14, 216
"Dickinson's point" in this poem appears to be: "the instinct of immortality is peace without knowledge." Considers significance of the poem's "Presence."

1985   JOHNSON, *Emily Dickinson,* pp. 71–72
"Especially intriguing here is the speaker's unwillingness to 'Forfeit Probity'; . . . here perception is sober, cautious, making no claims to knowledge outside the central 'instinct' that she is not alone."

"Contained in this short life" (1165)

1981   PORTER, *Dickinson,* pp. 32–33
Examination of the worksheet shows Dickinson laboring "to speak the idea of apogean experiences the senses are unequipped to handle. . . . The variants for the lines explicitly define for us as they did for the poet the limits of sense-linked images."

1982   MADIGAN, "Mermaids," pp. 40–41, 42–43, 44
"It is only in dreams that adults approach the great unknown depths with the security and lack of self-consciousness of the child." This poem "treats the human curiosity to learn about infinity."

1986   ROBINSON, J., *Emily Dickinson,* p. 142
The poem's most significant feature is not its "thrilled sense of the travelling soul . . . but rather the oscillation between the secure and the precarious . . . ."

"Could I do more for thee" (447)

1987   MILLER, C., *Emily Dickinson,* p. 55
"The poem's question calls attention to the comparison (Queen,

Bumble Bee) and to the speaker's role, leaving the analogy itself flexible in its implications."

"Crisis is a hair" (889)

1978 TAYLOR, C., "Kierkegaard," p. 579
The absurdity of the poem's premise "reveals a truth: the perilous nature of a crisis is just such a 'hair's breadth,' and God's relation to the balance of life and death is as powerful and arbitrary as the touch of a hand adjusting a hair."

1981 JUHASZ, "'Peril as a Possession,'" pp. 37–38
The "ultimate risk of crisis" is that "it occurs precisely at the interface between vision and conclusion. . . . Concentrating upon the nature of the balance itself, the poem is . . . purposefully ambiguous about what happens afterwards."
Revised and reprinted: Juhasz, *Undiscovered Continent*, pp. 60–62

1985 EBERWEIN, *Dickinson*, pp. 177, 196
"By representing the crisis as a hair, the poet emphasizes the fragility of the barriers protecting the circuit world, which can defend itself only by preternatural stillness . . . ."

"Crisis is sweet and yet the heart" (1416)

1983 SHURR, *Marriage*, pp. 187–88
Relates poem to others dealing with pregnancy and childbirth.

"Crumbling is not an instant's act" (997)

1988 WOLFF, *Emily Dickinson*, pp. 233–34
"The definition comprised by this verse states that time is linear and undifferentiated." The device "that mimics this linear process is . . . the slow, incremental accumulation of examples that follows the definition in the first stanza."

1989 OLIVER, *Apocalypse of Green*, pp. 172–73, 234
The poem reveals how well Dickinson recognized "the diabolical influences at work in the world." "The Devil's work is insidious and slow, yet persistent, but to be effective must have some cooperation from the object of this slow destruction."

"Dare you see a soul at the white heat" (365)

1979 CAMERON, *Lyric Time,* pp. 198–200
"Desire must suffer a conversion, whether to language or to the exigencies of other loss. . . ." But conversion "is process rather than end—until death (that designation for the final conversion) puts out the mortal light in the brilliance of its own inextinguishable shine."

GILBERT and GUBAR, *Madwoman,* pp. 611–13, 621, 696 n. 57
Although the poem concedes that the "fiery process of self-creation is painful," the poet's "real emphasis here is not upon her pain but upon her triumph."

O'HARA, " 'Designated Light,' " pp. 194–95
The poem "seems to achieve a balanced resolution of possibly conflicting responses to the transcendental revision of that Christian paradigm which sanctions the belief in the beatific compensations of suffering." Examines poem's irony.

1982 MARCUS, *Emily Dickinson,* p. 79
Relates to other Dickinson poems on "Suffering and Growth." This is "an unconstrained celebration of growth through suffering."

SALSKA, *Poetry of the Central Consciousness,* pp. 100–02, 103, 108 n. 49
"The poem makes it clear that in the final count, art, for Dickinson, consists in conscious craft. It is through technique that experience can be shaped and put at a distance so that, eventually, it 'repudiates the forge'. It is also technique that makes vision possible."
Revised and reprinted: *Walt Whitman and Emily Dickinson,* pp. 88–90, 91, 100 n. 49

1984 WILT, "Playing House," pp. 162–63, 169 n. 10
Considered as one of the "scores of highly charged lyrics" in which "the poet confronts the house she is before, or within, or has become."

1986 MILLER, C., " 'A letter is a joy,' " p. 35
"This poem's metaphor may apply to the cryptic compression and distortions of Dickinson's language. Ordinary language exists as unrefined ore, the unexamined life. It must undergo painful and unnatural or artful manipulation to become pure."

1987 DI GIUSEPPE, "Maiden and the Muse," pp. 43–44
Examines poem's images regarding the refining of the creative will and metamorphosis.

1988 MOREY, "Dickinson-Kant III," pp. 14–15
The poem "deals almost exclusively with the purposeful pain and craft of the sublime."

1989 LOEFFELHOLZ, "Dickinson Identified," pp. 170–71, 172, 173–74, 175
Describes a classroom approach; views this as "a poem that makes problematic both readerly identification and ideas of 'experience,' two mainstays of humanist (and much feminist) literary criticism."

"Death is a dialogue between" (976)

1984 BENFEY, *Problem of Others*, p. 101
"What is startling, here, is the second stanza, and the skeptical perspective it gives voice to. Indeed, it is the allowance *for* different perspectives, one canceling the other, that is of interest here."

"Death is like the insect" (1716)

1984 MARTIN, W., *American Triptych*, pp. 146–47
"Dickinson was concerned with the full range of positive and negative aspects in her experience, and she remained especially fascinated by death, in the natural as well as the human world."

OLPIN, "Hyperbole: Part II," p. 28
". . . the central paradox is that this poem which so painfully attempts to describe a plan for defeating death makes a strong case for the fact that nothing can be done about it."

"Death is the supple suitor" (1445)

1978 CAMERON, "Naming as History," p. 239
In this definitional poem "the definition takes the form of a progression. Isolating the steps in the process is a strategy for asserting knowledge over something, half of whose threat lies in its insistence that we cannot know it."
Reprinted: Cameron, *Lyric Time*, pp. 41–42, 137; Ferlazzo, *Critical Essays*, pp. 202–03

1982 LEE, " 'This World is not Conclusion,' " pp. 230–31
Related to other Dickinson poems on death. "The stages of Death's 'wooing' resemble a lover's progress. . . . The imagery is at once domestic and ritual, in part the conventional courtship but also the robber princeling cheating life of breath."

1984   OLPIN, "Hyperbole: Part II," pp. 18–19, 20
"A central irony of the poem is that despite the concrete personification of death and the explicit statement of his purpose, the poem finally drops the concrete for the nebulous ambiguity of the final lines in
which the carriage and its occupants seem to drop into a world beyond
the poet's descriptive powers."

"Death leaves us homesick, who behind" (935)

1981   KIMPEL, *Dickinson as Philosopher*, p. 269
"The poem takes account of the fact that even though the one who
died can no longer remember those who love him, still they who live continue to love as though death had not occurred."

"Death warrants are supposed to be" (1375)

1989   OLIVER, *Apocalypse of Green*, pp. 141–42, 153
"A mistake which would grant a reprieve to someone undeserving
might seem to be merciful, but not if the mistake consigned one deserving
to an opposite fate; therefore, it can be assumed that the word *merciful* is
intended to be ironic."

"Delight becomes pictorial" (572)

1983   JUHASZ, *Undiscovered Continent*, pp. 90–91, 92
"It is delight's relationship to pain that makes it 'pictorial': its distance gives it outline and separateness. As a picture, it is art (which makes
pain life)."

1985   JOHNSON, *Emily Dickinson*, p. 86
Examines the poem's "analogical structure."

1986   McNEIL, *Emily Dickinson*, pp. 120–21
"The fixed 'pictorial' perspective is one of suffering. Any 'view'
is framed; the window of pain makes pleasure such a framed view."

"Delight is as the flight" (257)

1980   JOHNSON, "'Broken Mathematics,'" pp. 24–25, 26 n. 8
The poem "focuses upon perception as the source of experiential
value." Examines way in which "Dickinson's rhetorical structure clarifies her meaning."

"Delight's despair at setting"

Revised and reprinted: Johnson, *Emily Dickinson*, pp. 83, 84–85, 86, 203 n. 7

1983 JUHASZ, *Undiscovered Continent*, pp. 87–90, 98, 99, 100, 102, 115, 116, 121, 131
"The ratio that must be measured and understood is the proportion between having and losing, presence and absence. Obviously, if rainbows are the eccentricity, empty skies the common way, this proportion is weighted in favor of pain."

1985 MORRIS, T., "Free-rhyming Poetry," pp. 233–34
"Two formal features—inexact rhyme and verse syntax—mark this poem as uniquely Dickinson's rather than Emerson's in style."

"Delight's despair at setting" (1299)

1979 NATHAN, "Slanted Truth," p. 39
Compares with "Sunset that screens reveals" concerning Dickinson's views on the elusiveness of truth.

NATHAN, "Soul at White Heat," p. 45
"In the distinction it makes between the genuine and the false, the poem suggests the Augustinian preoccupation with penetrating to the source of spiritual life."

1983 JUHASZ, *Undiscovered Continent*, pp. 30, 94–95, 183 n. 1
"The spatial configurations of the poem are those of circular trajectories: orbits upon which the location of bodies are charted." Relates to other Dickinson poems that show "how delight and despair, albeit emotional opposites, inform one another."

"Denial is the only fact" (965)

1989 OLIVER, *Apocalypse of Green*, pp. 178, 179–80
"Though there may be an experiential referent [*sic*] in the poet's life for this poem, the tone of dejection and loss of hope suggest that Dickinson found the idea of life without belief in some form of immortality a greater loss than mere earthly loss would bring."

"Departed to the judgment" (524)

1980 DUNCAN, "Joining Together," pp. 125–26
The last two lines "make us wonder if the soul is finally dead or alive, and denying the very distinction we insist upon, they make us keep wondering."

1984 ANDERSON, D., "Presence and Place," p. 217
This poem, "explicitly addressing the subject of mutable and immutable worlds, portrays one individual's surrender of the flesh and assumption of spirit in the company of two vast audiences that represent all
mutable creation and the immutable heavens."

1986 ROBINSON, J., *Emily Dickinson*, pp. 49–50
"We are left uncertain about whether we have had the judgement
or whether the judgement is now about to begin, but the isolation is dis-
concerting indeed when the imagined drama of religious tradition simply
dissolves as if it were quite inadequate to represent the real truth."

1988 WOLFF, *Emily Dickinson*, pp. 329–31
In this poem "desolation derives not from punishment, but from
solitude. . . . This is clearly God's realm, but Dickinson employs poetic
devices that the great Christian poets had conventionally used to depict
Hell."

1989 OLIVER, *Apocalypse of Green*, pp. 148, 150
"Although the belief in the immortality of the soul was common
enough and also an official doctrine, the solitude and loneliness of the
soul after death and judgment . . . was not preached from New England
pulpits in the nineteenth century. This is Dickinson structuring her own
forlorn view of such solitude . . . ."

"Deprived of other banquet" (773)

1988 PHILLIPS, *Emily Dickinson*, pp. 103–04
Dickinson "derives metaphors" for this poem from *Jane Eyre*.

"Despair's advantage is achieved" (799)

1980 MURPHY, "Definition by Antithesis," p. 24
The poem illustrates development in Dickinson's method of defining by use of opposites.

1984 WOLOSKY, *Emily Dickinson*, pp. 85–86
"Dickinson refuses to name suffering by any euphemism. In this
poem, where 'Advantage' should be, there is only despair, the very term
with which the poem began. There is no redemption, only redundance."

1986 BAKKER, "Emily Dickinson's Secret," p. 344
The poem's conclusion states that "we can only feel affliction, if
we are afflicted ourselves, and what we feel is just affliction, nothing else,
not some higher truth which might have redemptive value."
Reprinted: Bunt et al., *One Hundred Years*, p. 242

"Dew is the freshet in the grass" (1097)

1982 THOTA, *Emily Dickinson*, pp. 83–84
"The 'imitation to the state of self-identification' lies at the root of all romantic poetry. In her role as a 'spy' poet, Dickinson only considers how lilies grow and blossom. . . . She scrutinises them to find a human relevance to their biological process."

"Did life's penurious length" (1717)

1984 MARTIN, W., *American Triptych*, p. 162
"Here Dickinson asserts that if there were an accurate understanding of life's parsimonious brevity, 'the men' who focus on utilitarian concerns would alter their lives so radically that the extreme multiplicity of life could no longer be reduced to pragmatic goals."

1986 ROBINSON, J., *Emily Dickinson*, p. 164
"It is not permitted to see God and live. But she has begun the approach, for she is not identified with 'The men that daily live'—she lives on a different scale than one of day-to-day perspectives and it is notable that such an emphasis on sweetness . . . threatens movement and sequence . . . ."

1987 MILLER, C., *Emily Dickinson*, p. 94
"Here, although the syntax is complex, the difficulty of the poem lies in the density of its metaphorical predications."

"Did our best moment last" (393)

1983 JUHASZ, *Undiscovered Continent*, pp. 82–83, 86
"Delight, 'Our Best Moment,' is temporary. It has to be, or else it becomes the ultimate danger."

1985 JOHNSON, *Emily Dickinson*, pp. 69–70
The poem is "an example of Dickinson's didacticism, her assertion of spiritual realities through the creation of a comprehensible poetic 'definition.'"

1986 DORESKI, "'Exchange of Territory,'" pp. 64–65, 66, 67 n. 12
In the context of the poem's fascicle "it becomes clear that the actual subject is poetic insight, the elation that through Emerson and Wordsworth we have learned to associate with epiphany and transcendence."

1989   OLIVER, *Apocalypse of Green,* pp. 196, 205
"In this poem, Dickinson's view of man's soul conforms more nearly to the Biblical view, especially that of the Old Testament, rather than to the Greek, which considered the soul . . . an immortal part of man which separated from the body at death."

"Did the harebell loose her girdle" (213)

1981   CUDDY, "Expression and Sublimation," p. 31
"It is an interesting problem she has posed, a problem involving essence, for if a man loves a woman in her completeness, just as she is at that moment in all her innocence, would he still love her in a different form." Relates to other Dickinson "bee poems."

DIEHL, *Romantic Imagination,* pp. 86–87
"The coy intrusion of society's conventions upon the natural union of bee and flower develops into an abiding mode in Dickinson's nature poems . . . ."

1983   SHURR, *Marriage,* pp. 17, 21, 171
". . . resists intercourse on the traditional grounds that the lover would lose his respect for her afterward, and for himself as well. The poem is dated by handwriting at about 1860, the year of Wadsworth's first visit."

WALKER, N., "Humor as Identity," pp. 65–66
Here the poet "acknowledges the conventional transformation of 'good' woman into 'bad' woman, and her extension of this convention to the 'innocent' world of bees and flowers testifies to its absurdity."

1984   POLLAK, *Dickinson,* pp. 24–25
"The poem's reason for being is to free Emily Dickinson from the specific circumstances within which her sexual frustration is meaningless. The poem's achievement is that it both endorses and disparages the terms of its own self-debate."

1985   JOHNSON, *Emily Dickinson,* p. 209 n. 16
This poem "clarifies Dickinson's identification of her consecrated poetic identity with her sexual identity."

1986   MOREY, "Dickinson-Kant: The First Critique," pp. 40, 50, 54–55, 56
The poem's two stanzas pose the same question, "the first on a sexual level, the second on a Transcendental level." Suggests "non-duality" as a "possible subject" of this "ambiguous poem about success."

"Did you ever stand in a cavern's mouth"

1989 WALKER, N., "Voice, Tone," pp. 107–08
Suggestions for teaching the poem, which is a clear example of Dickinson's "flirtatious voice and method."

"Did you ever stand in a cavern's mouth" (590)

1989 GARBOWSKY, *House without the Door*, pp. 138–39
Suggests that Dickinson was "a victim of the agoraphobic syndrome" and that this poem reflects her "fear of loneliness."

OLIVER, *Apocalypse of Green*, p. 150
". . . expresses vividly the utter loneliness and terror of anticipation of judgment."

"Do people moulder equally" (432)

1988 WOLFF, *Emily Dickinson*, pp. 182–83, 423
Considers the poem's poetic "Voice." "The very *vitality* of this Voice is proof of the argument the Voice intends to make . . . ."

"Dominion lasts until obtained" (1257)

1981 DIEHL, *Romantic Imagination*, pp. 94–95
"The lesson is clear: anticipation surpasses fulfillment and so should be preserved. Desire alone assures permanence."

1985 CARTON, *Rhetoric*, pp. 126–27
". . . dominion and possession exist prospectively; they may be imagined but they are lost in the moment of their realization. It would be a mistake, however, to infer that they do not really exist, for they are products not merely of their final achievement but also of their pursuit."

"Don't put up my thread and needle" (617)

1986 HUGHES, G., "Subverting the Cult," pp. 18–19
"By equating domestic activities with those of a poet, she implies that she values sewing and gardening as highly as poetry."

McNEIL, *Emily Dickinson*, pp. 158–60
This poem "located the Dickinson speaker firmly in the world of woman's work. She neither wishes to transcend or ignore her sex; her

'work' is different but the way all women's labour is degraded trivializes her own work too."

1988   PHILLIPS, *Emily Dickinson*, pp. 72–73, 75, 223 n. 68, 224 n. 69
Considers in regard to Dickinson's "visual disorder" along with "Before I got my eye put out."

WOLFF, *Emily Dickinson*, pp. 207–09, 238
"The explicitly poetic element here is the line that is repeatedly appealed to, though never named, as the measure of straight seams; these are an accomplishment of eye as well as of hand and have a royal stamp in this poem."

1989   GUTHRIE, "Near Rhymes," pp. 72–73
"Ironically, her near rhymes and her irregular rhyme scheme permit her to achieve effects here that might have been impossible using regular exact rhyme."

"Doom is the house without the door" (475)

1978   CAMERON, "Naming as History," pp. 234–35, 236
In this poem "a disjunction between the initial naming in line one and the lines which follow it lead the reader to interpretive despair . . . ."
Reprinted: Cameron, *Lyric Time*, pp. 36–37, 38; Ferlazzo, *Critical Essays*, pp. 198, 199

MANN, "Dream," p. 20
"For the dead, in an inversion of the usual opposition, reality outside the tomb is only a dream and cannot be grasped as a living, concrete force."

1984   WILT, "Playing House," pp. 158–59, 164
Examines the "knot of meanings" in this, one of many poems in which "the poet confronts the house she is before, or within, or has become."

1988   WOLFF, *Emily Dickinson*, pp. 331–32
"If it were not for the words 'Doom' and 'Escape,' the first stanza might offer a relatively conventional depiction of Paradise. . . . The second stanza reveals wherein the 'Doom' of Heaven lies; it is static, a prison of ennui. Too late, earth is recognized as preferable to heaven."

1989   GARBOWSKY, *House without the Door*, p. 88
Relates to other images of claustrophobia in Dickinson poems. Here "not even a dream of liberty is possible."

"Doubt me! My dim companion" (275)

1979 KELLER, K., *Only Kangaroo*, pp. 31–32
Here she "complains against the oppressive relationship between God and woman (read *man* and woman): she taunts God for thinking her less than she is, for assigning her a secondary role, for keeping her low."

1983 BENVENUTO, "Words within Words," pp. 52–53
Suggests instances where examining definitions and etymologies of key words in the poem, as they appear in the dictionary Dickinson used, may shed light on poem's meaning.

SHURR, *Marriage*, pp. 72–73, 172
"*En route* through the poem we are faced with a much more aggressive lover than conjectures about Wadsworth have allowed." Connected to other poems in the fascicles that deny her "a fall from virginity."

1988 WOLFF, *Emily Dickinson*, pp. 380–82, 414
The poem's "most striking characteristic is the speaker's command over a supple series of verbal attitudes in her wooing of the 'Caviler' who has raised suspicions about her sincerity. . . . Like many of the other love poems, this one merges Old and New Testament language."

"Down time's quaint stream" (1656)

1979 BARNES, "Telling It Slant," pp. 227–28
Dickinson was "seriously hampered by her choice of this proverb as the proposition for a poem. The speaker may be oarless; the poem is rudder-bound."

"Drama's vitallest expression is the common day" (741)

1986 ROBINSON, J., *Emily Dickinson*, pp. 99–100
"Emerson would have liked the Platonism of this but her sense of 'the best' and the hint of disdain in the idea of a Hamlet who does not need the publicity given to him points as much to Calvin."

"Dreams are the subtle dower" (1376)

1978 MANN, "Dream," p. 21
"Dreams, the poet says, are, metaphorically, a kind of personal

property. Bestowed like a dowry, a gift of nature, they . . . mock those who attempt to possess their transitory power, leaving them only with a sense of what they have lost."

"Dreams are well, but waking's better" (450)

1978   MANN, "Dream," pp. 21–22
   "Dreaming becomes the real waking, since it is the activity of the imagination which makes the outside world come to the mind's terms."

1981   PORTER, *Dickinson*, p. 103
   Examines syntax that is "garbled because of syllabic count" in this "allegory of passage into immortality."

"Dropped into the ether acre" (665)

1986   McNEIL, *Emily Dickinson*, pp. 135, 136
   Comments on the nature of the image "Whip of Diamond."

"Drowning is not so pitiful" (1718)

1981   ROSENTHAL, "Volatile Matter," pp. 814–15
   "This prototype of the modern lyric poem using humor as part of a deadly serious strategy is both sardonic and compassionate. The humor of its closing is oddly compatible with the pathos of its opening . . . ."

1982   MADIGAN, "Mermaids," p. 50
   "All the mixed feelings of the poet toward Eternity, Infinity and the unknown are summarized in this powerful poem. . . . The poet makes clear that it is not death itself that is the horror, but the hopeless situation in a mind that rejects the very thing it seeks."

   MARCUS, *Emily Dickinson*, p. 91
   Although this is "a poem about death, it has a kind of naked and sarcastic skepticism which emphasizes the general problem of faith."

1989   OLIVER, *Apocalypse of Green*, pp. 169–70, 233
   "Paradoxically, it is the attempt to rise to heaven and the hoping that are more devastating than would be the drowning if there had been no hope."

"Dust is the only secret" (153)

1982 LEE, "'This World is not Conclusion,'" pp. 222–23
Relates to other Dickinson poems on death. Here the poet is playful, "the usual image of Death as menace undercut by her willingness to speak of him as an object of gossip . . . ."

SOULE, "Robin," pp. 77–78
". . . the irony of the poem with its image of cosmic bird-snatching and the possible pun on 'Robin' and 'robbing' hints that Christ is closely related to Death, 'the only One.'"

1984 WALLACE, God Be with the Clown, pp. 39–40
"In effect, Dickinson is gossiping behind death's back, getting away with it by means of a series of gentle ironies that result in death's ultimate comeuppance. While the poet talks, Christ and comedy . . . smuggle death's treasures away from him and gaily escape."

1988 WOLFF, Emily Dickinson, pp. 298–99
"Traditionally the risen Christ was figured as a bird whose soaring flight promised His followers a miraculous rebirth into life eternal. Here, however, it is death who 'Builds, like a Bird . . . .'"

"Dying! Dying in the night" (158)

1984 POLLAK, Dickinson, pp. 140–41, 142
"The sequence Jesus-Dollie suggests that the speaker is more likely to be rescued by her friend than by the proverbial 'Savior' who 'doesn't know the House.' The cause of her desperation may be her friend's absence."

ST. ARMAND, Dickinson and Her Culture, pp. 54–55
Notes "Calvinist elements" in this "relatively early dress rehearsal for death": "the dying soul has only two 'ways' to trudge into the blankness of eternity, and the longed-for vision is that of Jesus, who will escort Dickinson along the dark road of death to a homelike heaven . . . ."

"Dying! To be afraid of thee" (831)

1984 WOLOSKY, Emily Dickinson, p. 72
"Battle signifies not glory but the confrontation between a certainty of love's conquest of death and a radical doubt as to its victory."

"Each life converges to some centre" (680)

1979   ESTES, "Search for Location," pp. 209–10, 211, 215, 216
"The poem expresses the poet's adjustment to the disappointment of not reaching her heaven. . . . the relative location of the poet within her world rather than the possession of particular objects is the source of meaning which controls chaos."

1984   WOLOSKY, *Emily Dickinson*, pp. 21–23
The poem's "prosody underscores the goal as that which governs process. It also underscores how tenuous relations between goal and process can be."
Reprinted: Wolosky, "Syntax of Contention," pp. 177–78

1985   CARTON, *Rhetoric*, pp. 127–28
"So long as the goal remains a goal, it remains both pursuable and supreme. . . . although one may claim to persevere toward it *despite* 'the Distance,' the distance is precisely what protects it and makes the perseverance possible."

1989   KNAPP, *Emily Dickinson*, pp. 138–39
"The 'Centre' in the first stanza, considered as Principle or absolute Reality, refers to God. . . . That each 'Life Converges' . . . or moves toward a single point, approaching a limit as the number of terms increases without limit, signifies a universal and infinite presence."

OLIVER, *Apocalypse of Green*, pp. 178–79
"There must be a central focus for each person in life. Though heaven seems inaccessible, the poet urges all to eschew timidity of approach and advocates boldness and perseverance. . . . Some critics do not see this as a religious poem."

"Each scar I'll keep for him" (877)

1981   PORTER, *Dickinson*, p. 110
"With its syntax inversions and ellipsis, the syllable count is the only fulfilled element in this contorted poem."

"Elysium is as far as to" (1760)

1972   RAO, *Essential Emily Dickinson*, pp. 163–64
General introduction to the poem aimed at "postgraduate students of literature in Indian Universities."

"Empty my heart, of thee"

1982   MARCUS, *Emily Dickinson,* pp. 48, 49
Relates to other Dickinson poems about lost friends.

"Empty my heart, of thee" (587)

1984   WALLACE, *God Be with the Clown,* pp. 100, 101
"The intrusion of humor into this intensely painful, personal poem
is an incongruity that twists the true sentiment grotesquely out of shape,
focusing the suffering as much as deflecting it."

"Endanger it, and the demand" (1658)

1984   BENFEY, *Problem of Others,* pp. 42, 44
"It seems to be a poem . . . about the attractions of danger. It is a
poem in praise of the sublime." Examines significance of "tickets" in
Dickinson's poetry.

"Ended, ere it begun" (1088)

1981   BEAUCHAMP, "Riffaterre's *Semiotics,*" pp. 36–47
Textual analysis of the poem is used to illustrate Riffaterre's theory
of literary semiotics, exploring "how readers generate meaning when
cued by the structures encoded in a poetic text."

1982   MOSSBERG, *Emily Dickinson,* pp. 169–70, 173
In this poem "she appears resigned to God's will that 'The Story'
remain unrevealed: she is sure that when she dies . . . she will be rewarded for her obedience. Her poetry will be discovered, and people will
recognize her real identity as God's poet."

1984   WOLOSKY, *Emily Dickinson,* pp. xix-xx
"The poem is an assault. It does not declare the independence of
immanent language from divine decrees, but rather asserts divine decree
only to attack, defame, and denounce it."
Reprinted: Wolosky, "Voice of War," pp. 21–22

"Escape is such a thankful word" (1347)

1981   KIMPEL, *Dickinson as Philosopher,* pp. 75–76
In this poem Dickinson "characterizes a mode of thinking which
commonly occurs in hours in which one has become too tired or too dis-

couraged to think clearly about the advantage of the discipline of character."

1982   MOSSBERG, *Emily Dickinson*, p. 195
"Dickinson is grateful for the word because she can use it to get away from her posed conventional life. In this way, she saves herself from a traditional eclipsed identity as a woman."

1987   MILLER, C., *Emily Dickinson*, pp. 92, 151
The poem's second stanza is "altogether typical of Dickinson's poetry. Even with the repeated subject (Escape—it), the hypotaxis, and the inversion in the last two lines of this stanza, the syntax does not confuse. The poem's complexity is conceptual."

1989   OLIVER, *Apocalypse of Green*, p. 132
"The desired escape is not from life but from the fate awaiting the person at death. In extremity, salvation is a longed-for condition. The motive displayed in the poem is not the expected Christian one—to see the savior—but to save self-identity."

"Escaping backward to perceive" (867)

1978   CARTON, "Dickinson and the Divine," pp. 246–47
"Dickinson's mingled desire and fear to be consumed is consistent with the overtones of sexual seduction in this poem and others like it."
Reprinted: Carton, *Rhetoric*, p. 53

1982   MADIGAN, "Mermaids," pp. 48–49
"The poem is notable not for any great profundity, but for its suggestion of a life of unceasing activity where at every turn the individual faces the great unknown."

1986   NEW, "Difficult Writing," p. 13
"The poet is no longer centering her circumference. . . . No longer confined by, or borrowing the privileges of, the Romantic self, she has in Kierkegaard's terms 'let go.'"

"Essential oils are wrung" (675)

1978   MILLER, R., "Transitional Object," p. 455
The poem's "metaphor derives from the activity of the perfumer, pressing the rose petals bit by bit in order to extract the oil. What is lingering in the lady's drawer is not sachet but packets and packets of poems."

1979   CAMERON, *Lyric Time,* pp. 195–96, 205
"Whether the oils are perfume from the rose or speech from the lyric, to arrive at either essence, life must be pressed to the thinness of its own immemorial finish, must be condensed and, in the condensation, lost to the extract that will symbolize it."

1982   MARCUS, *Emily Dickinson,* pp. 37–38, 96
General consideration of this "allegorical comment on poems as a personal challenge to death" as one of Dickinson's poems on "Poetry, Art, and Imagination."

1983   MILLER, C., "How 'Low Feet' Stagger," pp. 138–39, 144, 146–47, 148, 149, 151
Examines Dickinson's use of uninflected verbs; here they "demonstrate how one enables meaning—whether as scent or as poetry—to remain vital."

   SHURR, *Marriage,* p. 102
"Pointing to her poems with 'this' in the sixth line, Dickinson indicates the exact place where her sister Lavinia would find those poems after Dickinson's funeral."

1984   CHERRY, "Sexuality and Tension," pp. 17–18
"It is the condensed perfume of suffering which has a lasting fragrance, not the rose which expires naturally." Considers poem's tension and passivity.

1986   ARNDT, "Limits of Language," pp. 23, 24–27
As in many of Dickinson's poems, this poem achieves "ambiguity of meanings and manages to force these meanings into refining, suggestive, and qualifying relationships by denying language its limiting logic."

1987   BAWER, "Audacity," p. 10
This poem "succinctly summarizes Dickinson's poetic theory." The "art of writing poetry is superior not only to that of the distiller of attar, but to that of the God Himself who created the rose."

   MILLER, C., *Emily Dickinson,* pp. 2–5, 21, 25, 27, 34, 39–40, 43, 44, 45, 47–49, 56, 58, 59, 61, 64–65, 68, 87–88, 97, 98, 103, 119–20, 121, 129, 153, 185, 189 n. 2, 192–193 n. 19
"By presenting poetic creation metaphorically as the expressing of essence and suggesting a connection between this process and a woman's life or death, Dickinson strikingly anticipates twentieth-century feminist metaphors for female creativity."

1988   MOREY, "Dickinson–Kant III," pp. 28–29, 31, 32
This poem on composition "goes to the heart of the Kantian esthetics: how does the beautiful become sublime?"

1989   RICHWELL, "Poetic Immortality," pp. 23–24
Shakespeare's sonnet 54 "provides a helpful gloss" on this poem.

"Estranged from beauty none can be" (1474)

1986   ROBINSON, J., *Emily Dickinson*, pp. 95–96
Links with "Witchcraft has not a pedigree." "Beneath the images of the two poems we have a recurrence—two separate maps of the same place: of what precedes our birth and exceeds our death."

"Except the heaven had come so near" (472)

1985   ANANTHARAMAN, *Sunset in a Cup,* pp. 13–15
Paraphrase. The poem "verges on the border of riddle, as the speaker does on the border of heaven."

"Except to heaven, she is nought" (154)

1981   CUDDY, "Expression and Sublimation," p. 30
Relates to other Dickinson "bee poems." Here "the masculine bee's recognition of the value of a flower (herself)" is notable.

1983   UNO, "Expression by Negation," p. 8
"The flower is described by the repetition of negations, but negation is used, paradoxically, to emphasize the positive importance of the inconspicuous flower to 'somebody.'"

"Exhilaration is within" (383)

1977   AGRAWAL, *Emily Dickinson*, pp. 62–63, 119
"The self-awareness of soul is an exhilarating and intoxicating experience which has no parallel in the realm of the outer world seen through sense-perception."

1981   DIEHL, *Romantic Imagination*, pp. 112–13
"She chooses to provide her own sacrament, rather than accept the stimulation of an inferior, external brand. To her mythic 'visitor,' she will offer only the wine of the self as a match for his own ample store."

KIMPEL, *Dickinson as Philosopher*, pp. 72–74
"If the poem were somewhat pared of its jubilant imagery, it would soberly affirm that there is no equivalent in life's good fortune to the culture of character, to which the Greeks referred as 'paideia'. . . ."

PORTER, *Dickinson*, pp. 56, 102, 117
The poem's closing lines "are so disarranged to fit the syllabic necessities that a reader is hard put to find a meaning."

1983 GALINSKY, "Northern and Southern," pp. 136–137
Comments on functions of Rhine scenery.

1989 OLIVER, *Apocalypse of Green*, pp. 204–05
"This poem clearly reveals Dickinson's belief that within man there is a consciousness of the divine which can provide guidance."

"Expanse cannot be lost" (1584)

1985 EBERWEIN, *Dickinson*, pp. 230, 231
"Rather than speculating on the child's newly ethereal condition, his aunt pushes her speculation now against God's nature—particularly his infinity, which contrasts so sharply with human limitation and loss."

1988 STOCKS, *Modern Consciousness*, pp. 22, 78–79
"It is the shutting down of the traditional order in the new emergent consciousness of our age. The 'Tent' of the traditional order is still there, but emptied of its content."

"Expectation is contentment" (807)

1983 JUHASZ, *Undiscovered Continent*, pp. 92–94, 95, 102, 121
Here Dickinson "demonstrates how pleasure must be defined with pain within its boundaries." The poem, "essentially abstract in vocabulary, relies on linguistic position—apposition and opposition—to establish psychological value."

"Experience is the angled road" (910)

1978 CAMERON, "Naming as History," pp. 235–36
"The lack of explicit connection between the statements" in this definitional poem "results in speech that is almost unintelligible."
Reprinted: Cameron, *Lyric Time*, pp. 37–38; Ferlazzo, *Critical Essays*, pp. 198–99

1984 LEONARD, D. N., "Dickinson's Religion," p. 341
". . . the 'angled road' of experience can never be traveled through pure activity. Even action requires contemplation because it must first be chosen."

1985 DICKENSON, *Emily Dickinson*, pp. 60–61
"This is an entirely typical poem: the half-rhymes, the abstraction, the Latinate words balanced against the Lutheran hymn rhythms, the envoy of the word 'pain'. But perhaps the paradoxical juxtaposition of seeming opposites, practical experience and abstract thought is particularly typical."

"Experiment escorts us last" (1770)

1986 ROBINSON, J., *Emily Dickinson*, p. 89
"We do not know what the final experience, death, will bring—she is saying—so we cannot establish doctrines because they may not take account of this experience. This view, however, has its origins as much in a feeling about life as in her eschatology."

"Extol thee, could I? Then I will" (1643)

1981 KIMPEL, *Dickinson as Philosopher*, pp. 260–61
"In the last two lines of this poem, the Poet affirms a version of love possibly influenced by her knowledge of the Pauline doctrine that a human being who enters with Christ in His death, partakes of His nature in coming to life again, and thereby acquires immortality."

1983 SHURR, *Marriage*, pp. 167–68
"While the poem is not complete, it obviously falls into the class of love poems which 'extol' the qualities of the beloved."

"Exultation is the going" (76)

1972 RAO, *Essential Emily Dickinson*, pp. 109–10
General introduction to the poem aimed at "postgraduate students of literature in Indian Universities."

1982 MADIGAN, "Mermaids," pp. 44–45
"The exultation of the poem . . . is the feeling caused by a new experience or fresh insight, a kind of ecstasy that frees the individual temporarily from mundane reality and allows him a glimpse into 'Eternity.'"

1983   JUHASZ, *Undiscovered Continent*, pp. 132, 133, 136, 137, 166
Relates to other Dickinson poems about eternity. "This poem is primarily concerned with using the journey metaphor to make the equation between delight and the suspension of time."

1985   BUDICK, *Emily Dickinson*, pp. 52–53
The "sacramental identities established" in this poem "create more problems than they solve. The departures of natural phenomena . . . put us in mind of death, but they do not finally prove to us whether or not God exists."

1986   HAGENBÜCHLE, "Aesthetics of Process," pp. 138–39
"It is characteristic of Dickinson's strategy to focus on the turning point as such . . . which alone can be grasped in language, while 'deep Eternity' must forever remain inexpressible."

ROBINSON, J., *Emily Dickinson*, pp. 162–63
The poem "is not so far gone that it does not keep both sea *and* land in sight. . . . It still has its reference-points and this explains not only its coherence as an art-work but also its 'exultation'."

1988   MOREY, "Dickinson-Kant III," pp. 18–19
This is "a definition poem of a subjective, ineffable feeling. The sea represents truth or theodicy . . . ."

"Facts by our side are never sudden" (1497)

1984   BENFEY, *Problem of Others*, p. 72
"The Gothic mode in this poem—the specter and the fear, and the fairly obvious phallic attributes of the 'neighbor'—clothes a meditation on nearness and knowledge."

"Fairer through fading, as the day" (938)

1978   TILMA-DEKKERS, "Immortality," p. 165
"Although the poem is about exaltation and ensuing disillusion, the end position of the word 'look' and the lack of the full stop seem to suggest a meaning extended beyond the poem, a view beyond the 'expiring,' with the noun 'look' taking on its verbal meaning."

1985   JOHNSON, *Emily Dickinson*, pp. 87, 89
The poem describes "the 'perfect' perception one may achieve at the moment when deprivation is imminent."

" 'Faith' is a fine invention" (185)

1980 FRY, "Writing New Englandy," pp. 25–26
The poem "asserts that *faith* is an *invention* in an age remarkable for inventions. It is man-made and hardly the gift of God her church and her believing family and friends certainly held that it was."

1981 MONTEIRO and ST. ARMAND, "Experienced Emblem" pp. 212–14
Examines implications of "a visual referent for the poem: Holmes and Barber's emblem for 'Prudence and Foresight.'. . . As the emblem argues, sight and prudence are both necessary . . . ."

1984 SIEGFRIED, "Bridge Poem," pp. 22–23
This is "a bridge poem" between Dickinson's "statements about poetry, conversion, and spiritual experience and the following series of longer poems in the fascicle that focus on affliction and the person of Jesus."

1988 UNO, "Optical Instruments," pp. 228–29, 230, 237
Suggests various interpretations. "Dickinson must have wanted to say scientific devices are useful . . . in our daily life, while religion is important for our inner life in the long run."

"Faith is the pierless bridge" (915)

1981 MONTEIRO and ST. ARMAND, "Experienced Emblem," pp. 256–258, 266
Relates to the emblem of "Walking by Faith" in Holmes and Barber's *Emblems and Allegories*.

1985 JOHNSON, *Emily Dickinson*, p. 73
"Though 'faith' has a relatively subordinate role in the drama of Dickinson's evolving soul, she sometimes does assert that 'I better see—/Through Faith,' an idea which [this poem] places specifically in the context of perceptual quest."

1986 LOVING, *Emily Dickinson*, pp. 78–79
Dickinson may have intentionally spelled the word "necessity" in the manuscript "as an attempt to conflate 'necessity' and 'nescience,' for the absence of knowledge makes faith our necessity."

1988 WOLOSKY, "Rhetoric or Not," pp. 218–21
Contrasts with Watts's "Faith is the brightest evidence." Dickinson "fissures the unity of figuration and assertion by erecting an explicitly

theological framework and then refusing to allow the figures supporting it properly to do so.''

"'Faithful to the end' amended" (1357)

1981   KIMPEL, *Dickinson as Philosopher,* pp. 98–102
"The provision that fidelity is pledged to another only so long as one lives is, according to her, a contradiction of the moral meaning of fidelity.''

"Far from love the Heavenly Father" (1021)

1979   NATHAN, "Soul at White Heat," pp. 47–48
Poem's elements are related to those of Augustinian meditation.

1989   OLIVER, *Apocalypse of Green,* pp. 102–04, 163 n. 86
"There is no element of fatalism here displayed; although the child has been elected, . . . he cannot remain passive but rather must make efforts to prepare himself for sanctification by facing the trials of this life under the guidance of the 'heavenly Father.' ''

"Fate slew him, but he did not drop" (1031)

1988   PHILLIPS, *Emily Dickinson,* pp. 182–83, 185
The "strong, sure verbs and the relentless rhythms expressing the repeated attacks upon him are matched by rhythms that snap back in the account of the man's continued opposition to Fate.''

"Finding is the first act" (870)

1979   CAMERON, *Lyric Time,* pp. 43–44
"In this case the step past the final one is really the step upon which all other deceptions are predicated.''

1983   WILLIAMS, D., " 'This Consciousness,' '' p. 378
Relates to Calvinist teaching. "To go in search of identity and to find oneself a sham was a prerequisite for proceeding beyond to totality. One had to accept one's own annihilation and learn to live not for self but for Being.''
Revised and reprinted: Williams, D., *Wilderness Lost,* pp. 211–12

1984   TSELENTIS-APOSTOLIDIS, "I Will Be Socrates," p. 15
Dickinson's "perception of a different tragic structure in life crushes Jason's myth. ED sees myth primarily as a force in life.''

1985   CARTON, *Rhetoric,* pp. 130–31
". . . the quest, whatever the obscure truth of its origin, casts discovery as a prospect, and any prospect is necessarily a fiction that heralds
a possible fact. To embrace one's fiction, then, need not be to abandon
fact . . . ."

JOHNSON, *Emily Dickinson,* pp. 178–79
This poem "represents a spiritual nadir, the moment when she is
prepared to abandon all her efforts in despair."

1986   McNEIL, *Emily Dickinson,* pp. 19–20
In this poem "Dickinson unravels the myth of quest, using the tale
of Jason and the Golden Fleece as a narrative basis for her own negative
parable."

1987   GELPI, "Emily Dickinson's Word," p. 48
"Two terse quatrains condense and invert the heroic and epic pretensions of western culture, and the drama of disillusionment strips away
the final illusion of the hero—that of his own existential truth and integrity."

MILLER, C., *Emily Dickinson,* p. 33
"Because the first lines have no context, Jason's expedition and
'sham' seem to represent all 'finding' and quest. Every hopeful venture
may end thus."

"Fitter to see him, I may be" (968)

1978   KHAN, "Romantic Tradition," pp. 64–65
"The human drama of love of which the terms of reference and
drawn from both the temporal and the non-temporal worlds, is the centre
of [Dickinson's] imaginative vision."
Revised and reprinted: Khan, *Emily Dickinson's Poetry,* pp. 78–79

1984   WOLOSKY, *Emily Dickinson,* pp. 80–82
". . . if, at the end, the poet's lack, grief, and loss are declared
means to attainment and gain, the redemption thus obtained remains a
strange one. . . . The greatest reward in redemption is that the scrutiny,
severity, and demands of the Redeemer will at last cease."

1985   EBERWEIN, *Dickinson,* p. 182
The poem may be read as "a report on the speaker's experience of
sanctifying changes in herself since Christ's grace first assured her of
election, so that her only remaining fear is that the Savior may not rec-

ognize the gradually developed beauty of his bride when he comes to claim her."

"Floss won't save you from an abyss" (1322)

1981 MONTEIRO and ST. ARMAND, "Experienced Emblem," pp. 246–47
Relates to emblem tradition of the poet's time. "Dickinson's grim transaction takes on an added resonance when we realize that a 'souvenir rope' was, in the late eighteenth and early nineteenth centuries, the memento of one's having attended a public hanging."

"Flowers—Well if anybody" (137)

1987 COOPER, M. F., "Androgynous Temper," pp. 138–39
The poem's "second stanza portrays the poet as witness, not creator and not even participant in nature's drama. She creates a persona in this poem who is a simple soul who feels the butterflies, representing Nature, have a greater sense of artistry than she does."

"Follow wise Orion" (1538)

1971 LEVIN, "Some Uses of the Grammar," pp. 21, 23–24, 25, 26
Examines poem's "nonrecoverable deletions" and the way in which they evoke "a response of compression."

"For death or rather" (382)

1982 SALSKA, *Poetry of the Central Consciousness,* pp. 60–61
"It is interesting to notice that what Dickinson singles out as life's essential quality is 'opportunity,' that is, possibility and expectation. In this she is rather like Whitman, though without Whitman's insistence on the fertile abundance."
Revised and reprinted: Salska, *Walt Whitman and Emily Dickinson,* pp. 50–51

1984 WOLOSKY, *Emily Dickinson,* pp. 110–11
Immortality is "the antithesis of the least pleasing aspects of the mortal condition and represents a refuge from them. At the same time, it entails the loss of this world. . . . The whole sacrifice is based on an unknown, against whose worth the poet asserts the worth of what she has . . . ."

"For each ecstatic instant" (125)

1980   JOHNSON, "'Broken Mathematics,'" pp. 23, 26 n. 17
The poem's focus is "the poet's attempt to state accurately the relationship between value and loss."
Revised and reprinted: Johnson, *Emily Dickinson*, pp. 83, 84, 203 n. 6

1986   BURBICK, "Economics of Desire," p. 375
"Desire is restrained merely through an inflated assignment of cost. The reason the cost of joy is so high is not disclosed; only the harsh ratio that rigidly extracts 'years' of payment for 'hours' of bliss is articulated. The punishment of joy by pain is measured in time and emotional strain."

1989   DOWNEY, "Mathematical Concepts," pp. 20–21
Poem exemplifies Dickinson's use of "direct variation."

"For every bird a nest" (143)

1978   MONTEIRO, G., "Dickinson's 'For every Bird,'" pp. 28–29
An examination of the wren in folklore suggests that this poem "says as much about sexual love as it does about poetic ambition."

1981   GUTHRIE, "Modest Poet's Tactics," pp. 232, 233–34, 237 n. 8
In this poem Dickinson "uses bird symbolism and rhyme adroitly to explain both her system of aesthetics and her conception of the modest artist's proper demeanor in society."

1985   EBERWEIN, *Dickinson*, pp. 12, 13
Examines wren and lark images in Dickinson's poetry. "Looking from the ground like a foolish little flutterer, the wren proves herself an aristocrat who refuses to settle for the 'households' available on every tree but attempts to select the most rarefied lodging . . . ."

1989   GUTHRIE, "Near Rhymes," pp. 76–77
Consideration of poem's rhyme scheme. The poem's subject may be the "relation between ambition and vanity."

"For largest woman's heart I knew" (309)

1982   TOEGEL, *Emily Dickinson*, p. 84
"Seen in the context of this poem, Emily Dickinson displays an attitude far more modern than the conventions of her time would have allowed."

"For this accepted breath" (195)

1983 SHURR, *Marriage,* pp. 23, 78, 137
Here "Dickinson presents as a riddle some human experience that is most like glory in heaven. The answer is marriage, and one of the features of the heavenly bestowal of glory is Gabriel's announcement of it." Considers poet's use of "Gabriel" in her poetry.

1984 WOLOSKY, *Emily Dickinson,* pp. 158–59
"This is human language invested with a power whose source remains divine. It is equally a divine language that has descended into the human word, opening to man a world above which is also figured as linguistic."

"Forbidden fruit a flavor has" (1377)

1977 BENNETT, "Language of Love," p. 16
"Joining images from *Genesis* and the *Song of Songs* to basic vegetation metaphors for the female anatomy, she gives precise expression to the physical nature of her love as well as to the fact that it is a tabooed attachment."

"Forever at his side to walk" (246)

1983 SHURR, *Marriage,* pp. 17, 63
"The first stanza is filled with references to the Christian marriage ceremony. The rest of the poem recounts the idea of mutual sharing and sacrifice, and the life of joy which is transformed into still finer joy for the Christian couple in Heaven."

1988 WOLFF, *Emily Dickinson,* pp. 369–71, 414
"This New Testament of passion and devotion replaces the Bible as a model for human behavior and mortal hope, and it is lovers who truly merit the language that has traditionally been reserved for the Divinity."

1989 WILSON, *Figures of Speech,* pp. 269–70
That Dickinson could write this poem as well as "I cannot live with you" illustrates her "capacity to write poems from disparate and even contradictory points of view . . . ."

"Forever is composed of nows" (624)

1983 JUHASZ, *Undiscovered Continent,* pp. 150–51, 152, 157
Relates to other Dickinson poems about eternity. Here "eternity is

presented as a place where social rituals and social systems do not literally apply, but the idea of society still organizes definition."

1985   BUDICK, *Emily Dickinson,* pp. 200, 205
"Eternity, this poem insists, can be 'experienced Here.' 'Forever' can be inferred from the 'Nows' of mortal existence. Time, in other words, would seem to be what makes eternity manageable and comprehensible in human terms."

1986   ROBINSON, J., *Emily Dickinson,* pp. 38, 94
Here the poet "seems to reassure herself by saying . . . that God's time is like our time only unrestricted . . . ."

1988   WOLFF, *Emily Dickinson,* pp. 234, 237
". . . because God has not imparted privileged moments of truthful narrative to the passage of time, the poet must repair God's deficiency by recounting the privileged insights from her moments of heightened perception."

"Four trees upon a solitary acre" (742)

1978   MILLER, R., "Transitional Object," pp. 450–51
"Just as the acre gives location to the trees, so do the trees give place, geographic identity to the acre; . . . they may be participating in a larger general plan; but what the plan is, whether the four trees advance or slow down the plan, is not known to the poet."

TAYLOR, C., "Kierkegaard," p. 571
"The speaker is impressed by a self-contained system without any evident purpose outside itself, and yet the design so compels her attention that the possibility of revelation necessarily arises."

1981   ALEXANDER, "Reading Emily Dickinson," pp. 3–5, 13, 14, 15
"The reading of the poem hinges on the reading of the pronoun. . . . The gender of the pronoun is not the sole determinant, and if God can be an it, a patch of land can be a him."

LEONARD, J., "Poems of Definition," pp. 23–24
"The poem evokes an image of randomness and disorder by both its content and its form."

1983   BUDICK, "Dangers of the Living Word," pp. 212–13, 217
In this poem "confusion and fragmentation . . . are products not just of external nature, but equally of the internal human thought process which attempts to comprehend nature."
Revised and reprinted: Budick, *Emily Dickinson,* pp. 16–18, 104

DIEHL, "'Ransom,'" pp. 164–66
The poem "resists any orthodox assertion of Divine omnipresence, proceeding instead to define other earthly relationships that are determined by chance and dependent upon the presence of an observer."
Reprinted: Bloom, *American Women Poets,* pp. 30–32

KNIGHTS, "Defining the Self," pp. 372–74
"The fact that the trees *are* there, in their simple undemanding relationships with other not especially remarkable things or persons, is a mystery worth contemplating: and in making it a matter for contemplation . . . she has affirmed, toughly, her own place in the world."
Revised and reprinted: Ford, B., *New Pelican Guide,* pp. 162–64

1984 BENFEY, *Problem of Others,* pp. 113–17
"Dickinson, in this poem, does not so much assert a skeptical view of the world as *accept* such a view, and build on it. The limits of human knowing do not controvert the view of the world that the poem exhibits."

WOLOSKY, *Emily Dickinson,* pp. 2–4, 7
"If God is present, he does not unite the scene. This remains a collection of isolated objects that do not cohere. The poem's grammatical construction is as discontinuous as the scene it presents."
Reprinted: Wolosky, "Syntax of Contention," pp. 162–64, 166

1985 JOHNSON, *Emily Dickinson,* pp. 37–38
"The poem itself may be said barely to exist: it speaks in a soft monotone at the very edge of silence, able only to sketch the lack of order in nature, to suggest the speaker's lack of knowledge, and to haunt the reader with its own ghostly yet profound uneasiness."

1987 MILLER, C., *Emily Dickinson,* pp. 70–71, 196 n. 46
Here "the nonrecoverable deletion that results from using the transitive verb 'Maintain' intransitively or without an obviously apparent direct object takes the form of syntactic doubling."

1988 TRIPP, *Mysterious Kingdom,* pp. 46–48, 49–51, 55, 121–22
"Significantly, her concern is not what the trees do after and by virtue of the fact that they have come into existence, but rather this very act itself: their *being* there."

WOLFF, *Emily Dickinson,* pp. 459–62, 470
". . . the 'Acre' and all the elements upon it stand in a perpetual state of existential isolation. . . . the task of pulling the visible world into some meaningful configuration, once God's right, now falls entirely to human beings."

WORTMAN, "The Place Translation Makes," pp. 130–42

Detailed examination of the poem and its translation into German by Paul Celan. "As in many of her poems, 'Four Trees' becomes both an opening to the uncanny possibility of *not* knowing and the brutal record of the chilling closure or absence at the heart of observation and knowledge."

1989   KNAPP, *Emily Dickinson*, pp. 113–16

"What at first seems to be a simple and forthright narration" in this poem "is in reality a search on the poet's part for meaning, determined by her need to relate objects to each other, and thus to *order disorder.*"

"Frigid and sweet her parting face" (1318)

1978   FADERMAN, "Homoerotic Poetry," pp. 21, 25, 27 n. 19

". . . the speaker, who has been deserted by the other woman, runs away herself and is everywhere a stranger and without hope. . . . Good fortune will be as sour to the speaker now as bad fortune."

"From blank to blank" (761)

1984   LEONARD, D. N., "Dickinson's Religion," pp. 337–38

"The absurdity of life, the unknowableness of its purpose, and sheer fatigue overwhelm the seeker and leave her in a state of spiritual apathy. Yet the very blankness becomes a kind of vision, its own reward for the heroic seeker after light."

WOLOSKY, *Emily Dickinson*, pp. 23–24

"When space has no definition, to see or not become functional equivalents—except that blindness raises no doomed expectations. Blindness is therefore chosen, but as a darkness which remains itself: an incomplete dialectic unsynthesized into any all-inclusive divine light."

Reprinted: Wolosky, "Syntax of Contention," p. 179

1986   NEW, "Difficult Writing," pp. 21–22, 24

Compares "this poem's self-referentiality—its double reference both to a religious and a poetic exodus—with the similarly reflexive 'I dwell in possibility,'. . . ."

1987   BARKER, *Lunacy of Light*, pp. 85–86

"In this poem life consists of sewing with blank thread upon blank cloth—an endeavor as impossible as one of the labors required of Hercules. But we have no hope that gods will soon be on the way to help the poet accomplish the impossible task."

1988 STOCKS, *Modern Consciousness,* p. 97
The poem's significance "extends beyond the purely personal and subjective into the consciousness of the age."

WOLFF, *Emily Dickinson,* pp. 473, 479
" 'Blank' is almost a totemic word in Dickinson's work to identify a course of human affairs that has been stripped of larger significance. Now . . . there are no defined beginnings or endings to be acknowledged or rejected. Even the structure that the drive toward death had imposed has been lost . . . ."

1989 GARBOWSKY, *House without the Door,* pp. 122–23
The poem's speaker "resembles the agoraphobic victim who during episodes of depersonalization admits to 'an oppressive sense of loss of spontaneity in movement, thought and feeling' and to 'automaton-like behavior.' "

KNAPP, *Emily Dickinson,* pp. 166–68
Examines implications and development of poem's images.

"From cocoon forth a butterfly" (354)

1978 CUDDY, "Latin Imprint," p. 77
The "complexity of construction" in the poem's first three lines "enforces an ambiguity that might seem to be poetic awkwardness . . . but is actually a sophisticated use of the Latin rule."

DOWNEY, "Antithesis," pp. 10–11
The poem "sets up a series of antitheses between struggling and relaxing. . . . Her faith must be at a very low ebb in this poem, because she does not even imply immortality."

1988 MONTEIRO, G., *Robert Frost,* pp. 14–15, 16, 18
Cites as an antecedent for Frost's "My Butterfly." Notes "thematic correspondences" and differences.

TRIPP, *Mysterious Kingdom,* pp. 54–56
"If the Lady Butterfly has any other 'Design,' except to be herself, it is difficult to trace, although the 'Clovers,' who share her mysterious wisdom, 'understood.' The burden of insight is upon the observer of this marvelous creature . . . ."

"Further in summer than the birds" (1068)

1978 FRANKLIN, "Manuscripts and Transcripts," pp. 552–60
Detailed examination of all existing versions of the poem, including an "explanation of the 'Norcross transcript.' "

1979 CAMERON, *Lyric Time,* pp. 182–84, 185
". . . taxed with representing a difference it can barely comprehend, speech is flung out into the farthest reaches of its permissible space. . . . The poem is very much concerned with the problem of inferring depth from a world whose visible dimensions deny it."

1980 DUNCAN, "Joining Together," pp. 111–12, 115–16, 117, 119, 122–23, 125, 127, 128
Dickinson's poem examines "not only the particular metaphor it uses, but, by implication, the nature of metaphor as such." It is, paradoxically, "perfectly agnostic" and "perfectly religious."

1981 DIEHL, *Romantic Imagination,* pp. 97–98
"Keats had stressed the continuity of bird and cricket; Dickinson emphasizes the fall from the free, singing birds to the lowly inhabitants of the grass. . . . Keats's cricket sang with increasing intensity of a reassuring companionship; Dickinson's expresses loss."

PORTER, *Dickinson,* pp. 21–23, 28–29, 91, 107–08, 260
In this "masterpiece in the art of the aftermath" the poet is "not celebrating the change but calibrating it, dissecting it, placing it in no system. In the starkest modernist way, the poem is an analysis without an explanation." Examines poem's syntax, diction, and images.

1982 MARCUS, *Emily Dickinson,* pp. 33–35
Line-by-line analysis; related to other "philosophical poems of nature" by Dickinson.

1984 HATTENHAUER, "Feminism," p. 56
"This poem's religious ceremony is a mass for the repose of the soul. Because the insects cannot be further into summer, literally, than any other creature, this time-as-space treatment of summer is a metaphor for the life cycle."

1985 EBERWEIN, *Dickinson,* pp. 63, 190–91
"A sense of holiness dominates this poem, a depth of reverence and faith." The poem "communicates invisible processes of change all of which testify to the salvific effects of sacred action."

"Further in summer than the birds"

JOHNSON, *Emily Dickinson,* pp. 104–06, 206 nn. 4–6
Relates to other Dickinson poems "describing the movement of summer into fall" and discusses stanzas from an earlier draft to clarify the poet's intent.

RASHID, "Voice of Endings," pp. 23, 24, 25–26, 28, 29, 30–33, 34 nn. 3–4, 8, 35 n. 13, 36 nn. 23–24
Examines poem's "conceptual frame." It is "a poem of endings" as well as "a poem of its time which attempts to apply the artistic solutions and methods of the past and, finding them no longer viable, anticipates those of the future."

1986 MUNK, "Recycling Language," pp. 236–37, 249 nn. 21, 23
"That Dickinson transforms the language of orthodoxy is clear. That she does so without irony, however, is remarkable—her crickets in no way parody a requiem mass."

ROBINSON, J., *Emily Dickinson,* pp. 32, 173–77
Examination of poem's religious imagery, effect of verb forms. "The poem's great reach is into the human character of time with its contrary sensed terminus and unknown infinite extension."

1987 BARKER, *Lunacy of Light,* pp. 129–32, 134
Explores the nature of the poem's "minor Nation" and implications of use of "Antiquest." ". . . that the ritual described in this poem is a *mass* seems in itself to be anti-Calvinist, although not quite anti-Christ."

EBERWEIN, "Sacramental Tradition," pp. 67, 68, 75–77, 80 n. 29
Examines the poem "within the specific context of Calvinist sacramental theology as understood by the nineteenth-century Congregational community within which Dickinson received her Christian formation."

HESFORD, "Creative Fall," pp. 84–85, 87
"It is not merely about coming to rest; rather, it is a type, a symbolic representation of that event. Dickinson's assessment of nature here draws on the Judeo-Christian tradition of reading and interpreting nature as a book, a second scripture, replete with meaning."

MILLER, C., *Emily Dickinson,* pp. 88–89, 101–02, 103
". . . the unusual use of the opening conjunction, omitted words and phrases, and syntactic inversions help create a sense of the delicate momentary Grace the speaker finds it so difficult to describe."

1988 WOLFF, *Emily Dickinson,* pp. 307, 309–11

This is "a poem of ineluctable loss, and one way of defining the focus of the verse is to construe it as concerned with the problem of naming." The poet invokes "a succession of religious vocabularies."

1989 KNAPP, *Emily Dickinson,* pp. 119–21

". . . what is arresting in this poem is the poet's allusion to Druidism as opposed to the Christian Passion in the first stanza." The poem's poignancy comes from "its association with the Last Supper/Holy Communion."

MILLER, C., "Dickinson's Language," p. 80

Comments on effect of poem's uninflected verbs. "The verbs prevent place and time from being easily categorized."

PARSONS, "Refined Ingenuities," pp. 16–17

"With 'Druidic Difference' she condenses the theme and protects this personal, private intuition of divinity against association with conventional theology by giving it a primordial, pre-Christian cast."

"Given in marriage unto thee" (817)

1983 SHURR, *Marriage,* p. 134

This is the only "unequivocally mystical poem in the whole canon of Dickinson's poetry." It "reveals a solid conviction of salvation, of the presence of grace in her soul, not of the more special mystical relationship to God."

WILLIAMS, D., " 'This Consciousness,' " p. 374

Suggests that a familiarity with "the use New Englanders made of their rich tradition of typological symbolism" is essential for a proper understanding of this poem.

1985 EBERWEIN, *Dickinson,* p. 182

"The imagery by which Dickinson expressed her shifting relationships with God deviated often from traditional Calvinist language." This poem "sounds more Catholic than Congregational."

1989 OBERHAUS, "Dickinson as Comic Poet," p. 122

The poem's speaker "uses the language of sacred parody, marital or sexual love as metaphor for divine love, a recurring trope in biblical and Christian poetry."

RICHWELL, "Poetic Immortality," p. 7

"This cryptic poem becomes less opaque when we recognize the 'marriage' she portrays therein as a symbol for poetic immortality."

"Glass was the street in tinsel peril" (1498)

1981   PORTER, *Dickinson*, pp. 71, 72–73
In this poem "the crossing from image to figural significance is so abrupt that a reader is hard put to make the connection." Analyzes poem's use of the word "italic."

1986   ROBINSON, J., *Emily Dickinson*, p. 88
"Her sense of the present has been built up out of experience. However, she was transmitting her sense of life and not lecturing in epistemology and it is important not to have too limited a conception of what experience might mean."

1987   BLASING, *American Poetry*, p. 237 n. 10
"The contract of meaning by absenting the literal present, by making the 'Present' 'Past,' diminishes the present even as it endows it with significance. . . . Dickinson's poetic truth . . . is a diacritical truth that draws the line between presence and loss in representation."

"Glee—The great storm is over" (619)

1985   EBERWEIN, *Dickinson*, pp. 111, 139
Compares with Longfellow's "The Wreck of the Hesperus." Dickinson's poem "is not actually a poem about a wreck but about the problem of telling about one adequately afterward . . . ."

1988   TRIPP, *Mysterious Kingdom*, pp. 124–27
Examines poem's diction. Dickinson's "use of words tends to transform them into *roots,* so that they again command their larger undifferentiated meanings."

1989   KNAPP, *Emily Dickinson*, pp. 74–77
"The antithesis in the opening word *Glee* (joy-death) . . . sums up Dickinson's need to know truth and the realization that the infinite is beyond her understanding." Considers significance of poem's "Four" and "Forty."

"Glowing is her bonnet" (72)

1985   BUDICK, *Emily Dickinson*, pp. 124–25
It is "a light poem that aims at a simple celebration of nature. But it is useful to consider that what stands opposed to nature in this poem is not science or philosophy but art itself."

1988   MORRIS, T., "Development," pp. 34–36
The way in which Dickinson "elaborated the detail and the rhetorical structure" of this poem into "It bloomed and dropt, a single noon" illustrates her stylistic development.

"Go not too near a house of rose" (1434)

1977   AGRAWAL, *Emily Dickinson,* pp. 85–86
Here the poet "makes the momentary glimpse of ecstasy both a measure and the cause of despair which is the essence of the human condition."

1978   HORIUCHI, *Possible Zen Traits,* pp. 359–60
"The quality that insures the continuance of joy is the insecurity about its perpetuity, thus hinting that so frail a charm is to be preciously handled so that it will be safe. Zen would approve of the thought."

1979   KELLER, K., *Only Kangaroo,* pp. 147, 155–56, 157, 159, 326
The subject of "remoteness from nature" is a warning in Emerson, but in Dickinson"an apocalyptic fear which, with Edwardsian logic, she turns into a more positively arguable position; his terms are soft and sweet, hers determined and tough."

1988   FONTANA, "Dickinson's 'Go not,' " pp. 26–29
Contends that Dickinson's poem "evokes Keats' ODE ON MELANCHOLY as a precursor text not merely to restate it, but instead to interrogate and subvert it."

"Go slow, my soul, to feed thyself" (1297)

1984   WOLOSKY, *Emily Dickinson,* p. xiv
In this poem "Dickinson presents her patience and timidity—and unmasks them. In appearance a litany of instruction to her modest soul, the poem ends as an attack upon her subject. The final stroke denounces God as a traitor who demands a Judas kiss for his mercy."
Reprinted: Wolosky, "Voice of War," pp. 17–18

" 'Go tell it'—What a message" (1554)

1980   CLEARY, "Classical Education," pp. 126–28
"The literalness with which parts of the Simonides epitaph are incorporated" into this poem suggests that Dickinson "understood the Greek poem in the original."

"God gave a loaf to every bird"

1983   SHURR, *Marriage,* p. 164
   "Her 'death,' the changeless mode her life took after the marriage, was like the death of the Spartans at Thermopylae: it was in strict conformity to 'law' as she and her times understood it."

1984   TSELENTIS-APOSTOLIDIS, "I Will Be Socrates," pp. 12–13
   Dickinson refers to Thermopylae in three poems and "to a different purpose each time." Only this poem "is able to appreciate the event without attempting to internalize it and without projecting anything to it."

"God gave a loaf to every bird" (791)

1981   KIMPEL, *Dickinson as Philosopher,* pp. 10–12
   "The modesty with which Emily Dickinson refers to the lean gifts bestowed upon her . . . may well be another expression of the stoical element in her independent nature which relates her more sympathetically to the Cynic Diogenes . . . than it does to the manner of life of many of her acquaintances."

1982   MOSSBERG, *Emily Dickinson,* pp. 135, 138–39, 141
   "Within the curious pathology of this poem, which purports to celebrate, even worship, a crumb, we recognize the daughter who is simply carrying obedience and gladness too far . . . in order to reveal the absurdity and irresponsibility of her authority figures."

1983   MOSSBERG, "Nursery Rhymes," p. 57
   ". . . in her 'Cinderella complex' she defines herself as superior *because* of the neglect and injustice she experiences; in fact, being singled out for special attention reassures her."

"God is a distant, stately lover" (357)

1978   MANN, "Poet as Namer," pp. 480–81
   "This poem illustrates one of Dickinson's most important structural devices: the use of a name both to begin a poem and to generate its own definition."

   TAYLOR, C., "Kierkegaard," pp. 578–79
   "The wit of the paradox lies in the fact that it is logically resolved, but in such a way that its resolution leaves a more absolute paradox: if God and Christ are one, then why make the distinction?"

1979   PATTERSON, *Dickinson's Imagery,* pp. 20, 214 n. 7
   The poem "pays a curious, backhanded compliment to Jesus as

the more appealing member of the Trinity. He is a kind of divine confidence man, a John Alden who might win for himself the love he has come to woo for Miles Standish-God, if the latter did not affirm with 'hyperbolic archness' that they two were one."

1981   ANDERSON, V., "Disappearance of God," pp. 8–9
It appears that "Dickinson did not truly believe that contact with or acceptance of Christ brought God as a presence into her life; rather, she was (in this one particular poem) simply playing detachedly . . . with the Church's doctrine of mediation."

1982   MOSSBERG, *Emily Dickinson*, pp. 124–25, 130
"The clergy and Bible are 'Miles Standishes' wooing her in the name of God. Craftily, she reveals the one loophole in the doctrine: she rejects the substitute suitor (society, parents, Church). Since they all purport to be 'synonymous' with God, she rejects—and outsmarts—God."

SALSKA, *Poetry of the Central Consciousness*, p. 61
Dickinson's "special regard for Christ is largely due to the fact that she sees Christ as co-victim of His Father's arbitrary plans."
Revised and reprinted: Salska, *Walt Whitman and Emily Dickinson*, p. 51

1984   OLPIN, "Hyperbole: Part II," p. 8
"In this poem an elaborate borrowing from two common 19th century sources—the Bible and Longfellow—culminates in a grandly absurd parody of the Trinity."

1985   BUDICK, *Emily Dickinson*, pp. 75–76
"The problem for Dickinson is not simply . . . that trinitarianism goes against human reason, but that the fixed image of a three-personed God threatens to confine the expansiveness and incomprehensibility of divinity within a symbol that is limited, reductive, and uncomfortingly numerical."

1986   ANDERSON, P., "Bride of the White Election," p. 6
". . . it is not the Trinity being described but the first and second persons of the Godhead, the Father and Son. . . . What Dickinson has done is offer a clever analogical gloss of St. John, chapter 17, where Jesus prays to his Father acknowledging their oneness."

1987   MOREY, "Dickinson-Kant II," pp. 14–16
"This is a powerful poem, succinctly stated with alliteration, a master metaphor, and a complete development in a short space." There is "no real blasphemy here, only a loving archness . . . ."

OBERHAUS, "Herbert and Emily Dickinson," pp. 353–54, 359
"While her tone here is comically irreverent, as is Herbert's when he asks God if He has nothing else to do but pursue his heart, in this poem . . . Dickinson makes clear her acceptance of the mystery of the Trinity."

1989   OBERHAUS, "Dickinson as Comic Poet," p. 122
"Students are delighted with the unconventionality of this poem, but because it *is* so unconventional they assume at first that it is blasphemous." The poem shows "that the comic can be a pose assumed to express a serious idea."

"God made a little gentian" (442)

1979   PATTERSON, *Dickinson's Imagery*, pp. 131–32, 184
"The gentian of this poem is a personal symbol, referring either to her belated love affair or to the dramatic efflorescence of her talent under the sharp stimulus of personal tragedy."

1984   KELLER, L., and MILLER, "Rewards of Indirection," pp. 543–44
". . . the poem's lesson is clear: loss or isolation can be useful; defeat may be the first step toward a new power instead of toward death; indirection may permit daring self-expression."

1987   BARKER, *Lunacy of Light*, pp. 81–82
Explores the nature of the gentian and its implications for Dickinson's view of herself.

"God permits industrious angels" (231)

1979   PATTERSON, *Dickinson's Imagery*, pp. 8, 194
"This schoolboy has been summoned from a game of 'Marbles' to play the game of love with an enchanting angel and stranger, two names Emily Dickinson repeatedly gave the lost beloved, with an obvious reference to the Bible . . . ."

1985   EBERWEIN, *Dickinson*, pp. 63, 254
Considers angels in Dickinson's poetry. ". . . her angels possessed no liberating power. . . . they provided no real assistance in man's efforts to look or penetrate beyond circumference."

1987   BARKER, *Lunacy of Light*, pp. 60–61
The poet is here "grappling still unsuccessfully with a sense of abandonment." The poem's subject may be the failure of her literary friendships.

"Going to Him! Happy letter" (494)

1981 SELLEY, "Kinky Kangaroo," pp. 5–6
Examines poem's virtuosity in making the form suit the content. "The poem is metrically irregular because its subject is an inexperienced writer."

1986 MILLER, C., "A letter is a joy," pp. 34, 38 n. 9
"For the poet, the poem exists beyond any personal use she may put it to. It is more general in address and broader in theme than a single mailing or context would signify."
Reprinted: Miller, C., *Emily Dickinson,* pp. 14, 190 n. 14

"Good morning, midnight" (425)

1983 JUHASZ, *Undiscovered Continent,* pp. 116–17, 119–20
Reading along with "A wife at daybreak I shall be" suggests that "both poems are about love, and together they represent the movement from before to during to after, or from not having to having to not having again."

"Good night! Which put the candle out" (259)

1989 GREENWALD, "Dickinson among the Realists," pp. 166–67
"In this poem, the physical world of nature and humanity is translated into symbolic form, reflecting the capacity of the soul to transcend the physical realm." Suggests classroom approaches.

"Good to hide and hear 'em hunt" (842)

1983 JUHASZ, *Undiscovered Continent,* pp. 35–36, 163
"The central message here is that the fox and the poet hide not only out of a desire for privacy but out of an interest in the game itself; out of a desire to test the hound and the audience, a wish to be found only by the appropriate seeker."

MATTHEWS, "Importance of Silence," p. 18
"It really is 'better to be found' than to hide, however much fun the hiding may be. The problem, tho, is that the perceptive reader is uncommon, and Dickinson knows it all too well."

1988 WOLFF, *Emily Dickinson,* pp. 128–29, 576 n. 64
Dickinson's "trope of fox and hound for poet and reader anticipates by a century the insights of twentieth-century psychologists and psychiatrists."

1989   DOBSON, *Strategies of Reticence,* pp. 104–05
   "While the tone of the poem in some ways is light . . . the implications of its imagery . . . are mystifying and horrific, creating a stylistic disjuncture not dissimilar to what was happening in other women's texts at the time."

"Great Caesar! Condescend" (102)

1980   CLEARY, "Classical Education," pp. 125–26
   The poem shows that Dickinson's "knowledge of Roman history was not superficial."

1983   SHURR, *Marriage,* p. 58
   "Dickinson's plea to her correspondent to 'Condescend' to accept the gift of 'Daisy' is . . . one of acid hostility, the fury of a woman who feels scorned. . . ." Considers the nature of the poem's speaker.

"Great streets of silence led away" (1159)

1977   AGRAWAL, *Emily Dickinson,* p. 99
   "God's despotism is the only principle of ordination here—there are no laws, none can dare to oppose His moves; He acts arbitrarily without giving any inkling of His intention."

1979   CAMERON, *Lyric Time,* pp. 45, 162–64, 170, 205–06, 241
   The poem "insists that while time no longer passes, it also fails to pass from the speaker, does not leave her be, but rather goads her with the shell of its own disembodied workings."

1983   JUHASZ, *Undiscovered Continent,* pp. 153–55, 157
   "Each stanza centers upon a phrase that effects a collision between spatial and temporal as well as between concrete and abstract." Relates to other poems by Dickinson about eternity.

1985   BUDICK, *Emily Dickinson,* p. 166
   " 'Silence' of the senses accompanies the ultimate 'Pause' of time, so that when the 'Period' at the end of time and of the poem exhales, i.e., when both time and the structure of linguistic meaning have died, there is simply nothing left—nor anything left to say."

"Grief is a mouse" (793)

1979   DIGGORY, "Armored Women," p. 139
   "She is expressing the insight of a woman who, confined to her

'proper place,' discovers not a prison but a valuable defense, as the house in the poem functions for its inhabitant."

1982 THOTA, *Emily Dickinson,* pp. 140–41
Compares with George Herbert's poem on grief, "Confession." "The difference between the two poems is the totally secular approach of Dickinson, as opposed to the theological approach of Herbert, who views, [*sic*] 'grief' as 'God's afflictions.'"

1988 PHILLIPS, *Emily Dickinson,* pp. 192, 194
Even though the poem is "written from the point of view of an author observant . . . the language persuades us that the author observant is observing herself."

"Growth of man like growth of nature" (750)

1982 MARCUS, *Emily Dickinson,* pp. 77, 78
The poem "declares that personal growth is entirely dependent on inner forces. External circumstances may reveal its genuineness but they do not create it. The poem praises determination, personal faith, and courage in the face of opposition."

MOSSBERG, *Emily Dickinson,* pp. 161–62
The poem "insists that indeed one can grow, in the way one wants to grow. The only thing we need is self-reliance, determination, and a will to succeed. Identity and potential proceed out of the daughter construct."

1985 BUDICK, *Emily Dickinson,* pp. 160–61
"The mind must accept the 'opposing forces' of the external world and of its own opposition to that world. For belief to remain intact these forces cannot be reconciled and thus abated. They must remain in eternal opposition."

JOHNSON, *Emily Dickinson,* pp. 61–62
In the poem's second half "Dickinson emphasizes the work and the loneliness of quest in a way that suggests for us a pertinent definition of 'the soul.'"

"Guest am I to have" (1661)

1979 PATTERSON, *Dickinson's Imagery,* p. 187
In this poem "anticipating some guest, she or perhaps Death gives command to light 'my northern room,' and the remainder of this grim little poem suggests that the 'northern room' is the actual grave." Discussion of "north" in Dickinson's poetry.

"Had I known that the first was the last" (1720)

1989   OLIVER, *Apocalypse of Green,* pp. 60–61, 93 n. 11
"By adding irony to the poem, the Biblical reference to the eschatological passage from Matthew 20:16 enriches and makes ambiguous the meaning of the poem."

"Had I not seen the sun" (1233)

1981   KIMPEL, *Dickinson as Philosopher,* pp. 148–49
The poem "affirms a contrast between two modes of herself which seem as if they are separated from each other, and are not merely distinguishable aspects of her one complex nature."

1988   WOLFF, *Emily Dickinson,* pp. 458, 459
Comments on the poem's "attenuated religious language." To Dickinson, "Sun," "Light," and "Wilderness" formerly had religious significance; here "the explicitly Biblical connotation has been virtually eliminated."

1989   KNAPP, *Emily Dickinson,* pp. 112–13
"Prior to the insights shed by light, the narrator could have lived in her bleak and darkened realm. . . . Once the search to know has begun, the agony experienced is untenable."

"Had I not this or this, I said" (904)

1982   MOSSBERG, *Emily Dickinson,* pp. 30, 144, 209 n. 9
"In the face of the self's jeers, the narrator is humbled into obsequious acknowledgment of vulnerability. . . ." One of several poems discussed in which "Dickinson discusses her need for pain, danger, etc."

"Had I presumed to hope" (522)

1982   JOHNSON, "Emily Dickinson," pp. 14–15
"Confidence in the reality of grace, despair at its incalculable distance—here the central paradox of Dickinson's poetic insight, that perception of an object requires its loss, is stated poignantly in terms of her religious quest as a whole."
Revised and reprinted: Johnson, *Emily Dickinson,* pp. 59–60

"Had this one day not been" (1253)

1983   SHURR, *Marriage,* pp. 157–58
"Her anomalous marriage is the only situation which contextualizes the poem satisfactorily."

"He ate and drank the precious words" (1587)

1972   RAO, *Essential Emily Dickinson,* pp. 159–60
General introduction to the poem aimed at "postgraduate students of literature in Indian Universities."

1981   KIMPEL, *Dickinson as Philosopher,* p. 243
". . . one cannot help thinking that this poem was written with a determination to convince herself that she had within herself and in her books all that she wanted, and therefore had a type of security which others do not likewise have."

1984   WOLOSKY, *Emily Dickinson,* p. 152
Words "strengthen and release man from his poverty and dust. . . . But in this poem, it is no longer necessary that it is indeed the Logos that bestows these gifts."

1985   EBERWEIN, *Dickinson,* pp. 73, 76–77, 93
"Appropriately, given the miraculous power here ascribed to literature, Dickinson writes the poem in sacramental language with an opening line that presents reading as a eucharistic action and associates literary diction with the incarnate Word."

1986   MCNEIL, *Emily Dickinson,* p. 98
"Dickinson seems to have chosen a male protagonist to permit her to examine untrammeled freedom without falsifying the case."

"He forgot and I remembered" (203)

1983   SHURR, *Marriage,* pp. 61–62
The poem seems "meant for the eyes only of the insider who participated in the event with her and who is addressed in the poem as 'Thee.'"

1987   MILLER, C., *Emily Dickinson,* pp. 175–76
". . . the speaker compares herself to Jesus as a way of marking both her perfect humility at receiving a slight and her potential power." Relates to other "poems of disdain."

"He fumbles at your soul"

OBERHAUS, "'Tender Pioneer,'" pp. 350–51
This "dramatization of Peter's denial of Christ" concerns the poet's "mental process in a disappointing situation" rather than a personal event or experience.

"He fumbles at your soul" (315)

1982 SALSKA, *Poetry of the Central Consciousness,* pp. 63, 179–80
"How nature produces her effect cannot be known. How the master performer achieves his is analysed in detail so that the full range of his calculating craftsmanship may be admired."
Reprinted: Salska, *Walt Whitman and Emily Dickinson,* pp. 53, 139, 180

THOTA, *Emily Dickinson,* p. 112
Dickinson "brings out intricate intellectual and emotional convulsions that a beloved feels about her lover, and she does so through organised metaphors."

1983 DOBSON, "'Oh, Susie,'" pp. 81–82, 88
"The somatic nature of this imagery denotes a concrete and vulnerable involvement in the situation. It also serves to accentuate the contrast with the 'He' of the poem, who is impersonal, who has no physical or psychic presence."

LINDENBERGER, "Walt Whitman and Emily Dickinson," pp. 221–23, 224, 225
The poet "is intent on portraying not so much either the deity or the self as she is the interaction between them." Her "deviation from earlier poets is thematic and stylistic at once."

1986 ROBINSON, J., *Emily Dickinson,* pp. 40–41, 171
"It is as though Emily Dickinson had found in the awesome forces of nature an indication of the scale and power she associated with the thrilling dramas of the pulpit."

1987 LEONARD, D., "'Chastisement of Beauty,'" pp. 251–52, 255 n. 4
Here "Dickinson's use of the sublime serves to indicate the persona's profound ambivalence in response to the experience of intimacy between the self and God."
Reprinted: *University of Dayton Review,* pp. 42–44, 46 n. 4

MILLER, C., *Emily Dickinson,* pp. 29–30, 37–38, 40, 46, 47, 48, 51–52, 58, 61, 72–73, 83, 113–118, 126, 127, 128–129, 136, 199 n. 4, 200 n. 5, 9

Examines poetic techniques and reviews history of critical response. The poem "dramatizes a moment of anticipation and ambiguous fulfillment. Its contrasting metaphors and adjectives make the experience it relates seem both ecstatic and terrible . . . ."

1988 MOREY, "Dickinson-Kant III," pp. 26–27
 "This is a rare instance of Dickinson employing two analogies side by side to illustrate a third one." Comments on prosody.

 OAKES, "Welcome and Beware," pp. 198–99
 This poem "reveals the intensity and potential pain of the demands which a dialogical relationship between reader and speaker imposes."

 PHILLIPS, *Emily Dickinson*, pp. 179–81
 Considers along with other poetic portraits of real or imagined people in Dickinson's poems.

 WOLFF, *Emily Dickinson*, pp. 279–81, 306, 341, 361–62, 433
 "In the third stanza, this progress toward extinction is brought to an inclusive finale: God rapes us one by one; however, He has violated us collectively, too, for His violence has vitiated the very culture in which we have been reared."

1989 FAST, "Poem 315," pp. 55–59
 Line-by-line analysis, examining structural devices, connections to other poems, and "suggestive or perplexing words and phrases."

 FAST, JUHASZ, and RINGLER-HENDERSON, "Workshop Discussion," pp. 73–84
 Transcript of a workshop discussion of the poem.

 JUHASZ, "Poem 315," pp. 61–66
 The poem is "a multi-faceted analysis of the nature and uses of power itself. Even as it reveals the abuses of aggression, so it also shows why and under what circumstances it might be attractive."
 Revised and reprinted: Juhasz, "Reading Doubly," pp. 88–94

 MILLER, C., "Approaches," pp. 225, 226
 The poem is used to illustrate Dickinson's use of recoverable and nonrecoverable deletion.

 MILLER, C., "Dickinson's Language," pp. 79–80, 83
 Suggests some of the questions the poem's nonrecoverable deletion raises.

RINGLER-HENDERSON, "Poem 315," pp. 67–71

Reads the poem as "a description of the way in which grief plays itself out in the human psyche." The poem "fits centrally . . . into the large group of Emily Dickinson poems about grief, many of which were written in . . . 1862."

"He gave away his life" (567)

1981 ANDERSON, V., "Disappearance of God," pp. 10–11

The poem "may be about the public reaction either to Christ or to poets. . . . Dickinson is possibly reacting here to the problems she had in the publishing of her poems."

1987 OBERHAUS, "'Tender Pioneer,'" pp. 354–58

Stanza-by-stanza examination in context of other Dickinson poems on Christ's life.

1988 PHILLIPS, *Emily Dickinson,* pp. 53–54, 222 n. 34

This poem and three others may be considered as the poet's response to the death of Frazar Stearns.

"He outstripped time with but a bout" (865)

1986 ROBINSON, J., *Emily Dickinson,* p. 84

Here the poet "describes someone (herself disguised as 'He'? her lover?) as defeating Time, the Stars and Sun, and finally as challenging God in combat."

"He preached upon 'breadth' till it argued him narrow" (1207)

1972 RAO, *Essential Emily Dickinson,* pp. 157–58

General introduction to the poem aimed at "postgraduate students of literature in Indian Universities."

1979 NATHAN, "Slanted Truth," p. 38

"A lifelong truth-seeker, Dickinson was repelled by the glibness of the practiced orator. The 'plain' style of her Puritan ancestors prompted her to reject oleaginous rhetoric."

1981 ANDERSON, V., "Disappearance of God," p. 7

"Jesus would only react in confusion to this view of the gospel. It is not touched by simplicity, innocence, humanity; in fact, it is completely out of touch with man in its narrowness and smugness."

1982   MILLER, C., "Terms and Golden Words," pp. 51–52
Dickinson here distinguishes "the pure or truthful word and its impure uses. . . . In this optimistic poem, the true meaning of a word—that is Truth itself, the golden word—finally dominates any glib misrepresentation of its meaning."

1986   HURLEY, "Waiting for the Other Shoe," pp. 133–34
Discussion of the nature and effect of poem's rhymes.

1988   REYNOLDS, *Beneath the American Renaissance,* p. 37
"Here Dickinson uses the tools of antebellum imaginative preaching—paradox, humor, startling metaphor, stress upon the human Jesus—to undermine preaching itself. Even the broadest preacher, she suggests, is trapped . . . by the belief that truth flaunts 'a Sign.' "

1989   OBERHAUS, "Dickinson as Comic Poet," pp. 121, 122
Notes some of the comic techniques used to "cut down to size" the poem's "nineteenth-century preacher, a personification of the church of Dickinson's day."

"He put the belt around my life" (273)

1981   HYMEL, "Singing Off Charnal Steps," pp. 3, 5–7
The speaker's "marked response to the situation in which she finds herself is largely one of passivity."

1983   SHURR, *Marriage,* p. 63
"Marriage as the 'Belt,' Dickinson seems to be saying, puts limitations on one's life, but it also gives form and adornment to that life."

TACKES, "Dickinson's 'He put the Belt,' " pp. 26–27
Suggests that line 8, "A Member of the Cloud," is a reference to Swift's *Gulliver's Travels.*

1986   MUNK, "Recycling Language," pp. 241–42, 251 n. 40
The poem "is about poetic election . . . and the Crowd/Cloud substitution, a dual model of transformation and sublimation . . . , is crucial to a reading of the poem."

1988   WOLFF, *Emily Dickinson,* pp. 333–34
"Ironically, although the speaker contributes to God's grandeur, she is able to gain no eminence for herself: on her side, everything about this transaction spells loss."

1989 FADERMAN, "Ambivalent Heterosexuality," pp. 124–25
Like "My life had stood a loaded gun," this poem is about "Dickinson's ambivalence toward heterosexual relationships."

MUNK, "Musicians Wrestle," pp. 9–11
This poem "is a correlative for the poetic process—indeed, for a type of poetic possession—in which the creative complex, in Jung's words, takes the ego into its service."

"He strained my faith" (497)

1979 PATTERSON, *Dickinson's Imagery*, pp. 21, 41
"Here she drew upon the curious and widespread nineteenth-century conception of a humanly intimate, well-nigh erotic relationship between the beloved disciple and the Master in whose bosom he lay."

1982 MOSSBERG, *Emily Dickinson*, pp. 130–31
"In the poem, she depicts the neglect of both her father and brother: neither recognizes her loyalty or her true status as a poet or daughter."

1987 BISHOP, "Queen of Calvary," p. 54
"Dickinson here places in the character of John, the beloved disciple, those attributes which she might wish could be found reciprocally in the godhead: thoroughgoing faithfulness, strong trust, willingness to forgive."

"He touched me, so I live to know" (506)

1978 SADOWY, "Dickinson's 'He touched me,'" pp. 4–5
Explores possible significance of "Rebecca" and "Persian" references in final stanza.

1979 PATTERSON, *Dickinson's Imagery*, pp. 158–59, 161
Notes echoes from Thomas Moore's *Lalla Rookh*. In the poem "Dickinson appears to be both the Persian burning in the sacred fire and the appalled onlooker at her own immolation."

1980 PORTERFIELD, *Feminine Spirituality*, pp. 134–35
"In this poem, religious and sexual imagery are intertwined and both involve submission. . . . The experience described in this poem finds its prototype in the Old Testament story of Rebecca . . . ."

1985   ANANTHARAMAN, *Sunset in a Cup,* pp. 91–92
   "As the stream submerges its identity into the sea and gets its final repose, so the persona has lost its identity in the person of lover, and this experience has changed her profoundly."

"He was my host, he was my guest" (1721)

1981   DIEHL, "Dickinson and Bloom," pp. 422–23, 440 n. 13
   "In Dickinson's poem the host is at once parasite, eucharistic offering, and stranger—source of power and its destroyer."

1987   OBERHAUS, "Herbert and Emily Dickinson," pp. 362, 363–64
   Here Dickinson "describes the union of soul with Deity in the language of sacred parody."

"He was weak, and I was strong, then" (190)

1983   SHURR, *Marriage,* pp. 30–31, 60–61, 93–94, 171
   The poem "describes a nighttime meeting with the beloved . . . , the strength of the sexual forces which attracted them both, and their alternating weaknesses to resist."

1985   SALSKA, *Walt Whitman and Emily Dickinson,* p. 139
   The poem "does not dwell on the human price of this exercise in balance. The final simultaneous striving of both partners and their resulting poise are unmistakably presented as achievement."

1988   WOLFF, *Emily Dickinson,* pp. 366–67, 384, 579 n. 7
   "Not as uniformly strong as Dickinson's best love poetry, this verse nonetheless exhibits a number of themes and strategies that are repeated elsewhere in more effective form."

"Heart! We will forget him" (47)

1982   SALSKA, *Poetry of the Central Consciousness,* p. 66
   ". . . even as she calls the intellectual faculty 'I' and singles it out for the identifying feature, she makes it absolutely clear that the life of the heart and the life of the mind are as inseparable as warmth and light."
   Revised and reprinted: Salska, *Walt Whitman and Emily Dickinson,* p. 56

" 'Heaven' has different signs to me" (575)

1978 TILMA-DEKKERS, "Immortality," pp. 164–65
"We see an interplay of two movements: one from external world to the internal world of mind (the way the different phases of the sun act upon her imagination), and an inward-outward movement: the projection of the poet's yearning to be assured of heaven on to the world of nature."

1985 COOK, A., *Figural Choice,* pp. 33–35
Observes the poem's "attempt at definition-through-images."

"Heaven is so far of the mind" (370)

1981 KIMPEL, *Dickinson as Philosopher,* pp. 283–84
"This poem does not merely affirm the view that thought is conditioned by the human capacity to think. It rather affirms that apart from the thought itself about a heaven, there is no reality of heaven."

1987 COOK, C., "Psychic Development," p. 129
"The vast capacity and the fair idea of the mind control a person's acquaintance with heaven."

" 'Heaven' is what I cannot reach" (239)

1978 DOWNEY, "Antithesis," p. 16
"She antithetically defines Heaven by the unreachable relation of this tree to her."

1980 HOMANS, *Women Writers,* pp. 177–78
"It is not Canaan itself as an image of desirability that she satirizes, but God's method of consecration, inflating the value of Canaan for others by depriving Moses, making unattainability a pure and empty status symbol."
Reprinted: Homans, "Dickinson and Poetic Identity," pp. 140–41; Homans, "Emily Dickinson," p. 422

1986 MUNK, "Recycling Language," pp. 238–39, 250 n. 28
Examines poet's use of "naive irony." "In three quatrains, she effectively revises *Paradise Lost.* . . . The Miltonic Heaven is not Dickinson's."

1988   WOLFF, *Emily Dickinson*, pp. 350–51, 352
   "The poem is a compendium of the Judaeo-Christian experience. Its consummate woe is that of all the alluring delights it mentions, only the Edenic apple actually hung near enough for man and woman to grasp it and be lost: with this ancient irony the poem is begun."

"'Heavenly Father' take to thee" (1461)

1978   DAVIS, "'Heavenly Father,'" pp. 40–44
   The poem's theme is "the duplicity of God's actions. Clearly, there is also much duplicity in the words of the poem and therefore in the feelings of ED herself."

   TAYLOR, C., "Kierkegaard," p. 574
   This is one of a group of Dickinson poems that "utilize a stunningly rational analysis of religious language in order to demonstrate both the inconsistency of religious ideas and the logical absurdity of their application."

1980   ARMITAGE, "Crackerbox Humor," pp. 13, 14
   "The implication is that the narrator—the moral child—recognizes God's 'own duplicity': that if 'We are Dust' we are, after all, made in His image. Thus Dickinson jousts with conventionally awesome and common items by mixing or exchanging their characteristics."

1983   TEICHERT, "Divine Adversary," pp. 22, 24–25
   Examines poem's image of God. Because people are "just what He made them—weak and sinful creatures . . . He is implicated in their guilt."

1986   McNEIL, *Emily Dickinson*, pp. 107, 108
   As in many of her later poems, here the poet "is in no doubt that the negative, denying, tyrannical face of the Bible accurately represents the nature of its divine author."

   OBERHAUS, "'Engine against th' Almightie,'" pp. 164–65
   ". . . both the tone and the thought of the poem resemble the comic impertinence of Herbert's 'Judgement.'"

   ROBINSON, J., *Emily Dickinson*, p. 77
   ". . . she seems to genuflect into the Lord's Prayer, asking forgiveness for being, sinfully, herself, but actually spurning this charade

because it is God who set the whole thing up and is responsible for the 'supreme iniquity,' us, in the first place."

1988   WEISSMAN, " 'Transport's Working Classes,' " pp. 420–21
"Every word deflates the idea of sin. Iniquity becomes candid, the creation of mere duplicity; and it is only contraband, forbidden by the arbitrary laws of trade, not by eternal laws of right and wrong."

"Her breast is fit for pearls" (84)

1977   BENNETT, "Language of Love," p. 16
The poem's "erotic images traditionally associated with women" are used "with great precision in the description of a woman-to-woman relationship."

1984   POLLAK, *Dickinson*, pp. 135, 155 n. 17
"Symbolically castrating herself, Dickinson inhibits the boldness she associates with male identity and is drawn back into a nest which is also, uncomfortably, a womb."

"Her 'last Poems' " (312)

1982   SOULE, "Robin," pp. 69–70
This elegy to Elizabeth Barrett Browning "illustrates Dickinson's appreciation of the aristocracy of international poets, those who surpass even the robins of New England."

1983   MILLER, C., "How 'Low Feet' Stagger," pp. 142, 154 n. 15
Relates poem's "Ourself" to Dickinson's pattern of using "a singular ending with a reflexive plural."

SHURR, *Marriage*, pp. 44–45
"The poem is distinctly *about* Elizabeth Barrett Browning, but spoken from the ground of Dickinson's developing diction and personal concerns."

1984   POLLAK, *Dickinson*, pp. 240 n. 23, 241–44
"This transformation of jealousy into grief is among the most fundamental gestures of Dickinson's psyche. Consequently, hers is grief with a vengeance . . . ."

1987   MILLER, C., *Emily Dickinson*, pp. 53–54, 63, 163–64
"Significantly, the poem's poet remains a woman: rather than

change Barrett Browning's sex and make herself bride to the older poet, Dickinson alters the sex of her speaker."

"Her spirit rose to such a height" (1486)

1985   COOK, A., *Thresholds*, p. 196
   "The feelings engendered here enact their apocalyptic correlatives confusedly."

"Her sweet turn to leave the homestead" (649)

1981   PORTER, *Dickinson*, pp. 68–69
   Death "is presented alongside the terms of marriage until in a startling interpenetration of ritual imagery there is an ebb and flow of clarity."

1983   SHURR, *Marriage*, p. 112
   In this poem "a Bride dies on her wedding day. She is carried to the graveyard from her house, which is named 'the Homestead'—the name of the house in which Dickinson lived for most of her life."

1989   GARBOWSKY, *House without the Door*, p. 151
   "She is finally out of the house, out of the control of a father who overshadowed her life. . . . Dickinson finally achieves an adult selfhood, one unclaimed in her own life."

"Her sweet weight on my heart a night" (518)

1983   SHURR, *Marriage*, pp. 88–89, 135
   In this poem "Dickinson enters the mind of her clergyman lover and dreams the sentiments she would hope to find there."

1984   POLLAK, *Dickinson*, pp. 148–50
   "With its dreamlike nocturnal setting, this poem admits an image of physical intimacy rarely found in Dickinson's poetry of womanly love."

1987   MONTEFIORE, *Feminism and Poetry*, pp. 174–75
   "The bride's disappearance ought, rationally speaking, to prove her non-existent, but Dickinson makes the speaker insist that she is 'real,' whether because the speaker's own dream came true, or because the vanished bride actually dreamt herself into the poet's bed."

"Herein a blossom lies" (899)

1981 CUDDY, "Expression and Sublimation," p. 29
The poem "may be read several ways, esthetically, sexually, or theologically. But regardless of one's interpretation, what the bee represents must be 'overcome'. . . ."

"His bill is clasped, his eye forsook" (1102)

1988 WOLFF, *Emily Dickinson*, pp. 156, 196
These lines "function to refute the informing poetics of Milton, of Keats, and of the Psalmist . . . ."

"His heart was darker than the starless night" (1378)

1981 KIMPEL, *Dickinson as Philosopher*, pp. 151–52
Dickinson "reaffirms the Pauline anthropology that the human self can be so darkened that it is incapable of its own initiative to change its nature. . . . She affirms . . . a Calvinistic belief that some men are destined never to be saved from their evil natures."

"His little hearse like figure" (1522)

1986 ROBINSON, J., *Emily Dickinson*, pp. 79, 81
Here the poet scoffs at "the moral earnestness" produced by religious belief. The lilac "does absolutely nothing but idle around in 'the divine Perdition' of spring. If that (happiness on earth) is what damnation is, we must surely prefer it . . . ."

1988 WEISSMAN, "'Transport's Working Classes,'" p. 418
"The word Perdition has lost its meaning now that it has become divine; only people still obsessed with the false categories of law could see any danger in idleness and spring."

"His mansion in the pool" (1379)

1981 KIMPEL, *Dickinson as Philosopher*, pp. 153–54
"Under the gloss of charm of this little poem is . . . one of the heartbreaking commentaries on the plight of millions of human beings who come into life to 'blush unseen', and to waste what might have been their sweetness to enrich the desert air."

"His mind of man a secret makes" (1663)

1984   BENFEY, *Problem of Others*, pp. 28, 84–86, 111
The poem's intention appears to be "to make skepticism about other minds as important a question . . . as skepticism about the existence of God. In the other, God or man, if anywhere, lies our salvation."

"His oriental heresies" (1526)

1985   RASHID, "Voice of Endings," pp. 27–28, 35 n. 18
". . . perhaps no poem more clearly displays Dickinson's final regard for her own 'transcendental' moments than this one."

1988   MILLER, M. C., "Dickinson's Oriental Heresies," pp. 145–46
"It would seem that adequate scholarly attention has not been given to the significant juxtaposition of "heresies'—'apostasy'—satiation (the 'jaded eye')—death—the subject matter in this poem from the last five years of Dickinson's life . . . ."

"His voice decrepit was with joy" (1476)

1983   SHURR, *Marriage*, p. 162
One of several poems that appear to describe a meeting with Wadsworth.

"Hope is a subtle glutton" (1547)

1979   CAMERON, *Lyric Time*, pp. 34, 38
The poem's conclusion is "redundant and hence gratuitous. . . . The second stanza glosses the first."

1988   WOLFF, *Emily Dickinson*, p. 476
Although "the thrust of the poem is centripetal, pulling 'Glutton' inward to clarify the import of 'Hope,' a faint connection is made between the inner and the outer worlds through this defining process."

" 'Hope' is the thing with feathers" (254)

1972   RAO, *Essential Emily Dickinson*, pp. 15, 119–21
General introduction to the poem aimed at "postgraduate students of literature in Indian Universities."

1977   AGRAWAL, *Emily Dickinson,* pp. 80–81, 117, 119
Hope is "the eternal music of soul, it is sweetest in the moments of grief and sorrow, yet it never makes any demand on soul. . . . Man's hope becomes strongest when his heart is lashed by the gale of unhappy situations . . . ."

1978   DITSKY, "Two Emilies," pp. 28–31
Contrasts with Emily Brontë's "Hope."

1982   THOTA, *Emily Dickinson,* pp. 141–42
Compares with George Herbert's "Hope."

1984   HATTENHAUER, "Feminism," p. 55
"Here the bird is a source of psychic power—a dynamo that keeps producing without asking for fuel, a superlatively masculine perpetual motion machine. No matter how trying the situation, the male muse keeps the soul moving without asking for sustenance . . . ."

1988   WOLFF, *Emily Dickinson,* p. 478
"'The thing with feathers—' is the source of unseen song, perhaps choristers in treetops whistling against the gale. Perhaps it is even every human's potential for music and poetry, brave stays against the brooding dark."

1989   ROGERS, K., "Introducing Dickinson," p. 54
Suggestions for teaching the poem to college students.

ST. ARMAND and MONTEIRO, "Dickinson's 'Hope,'" pp. 34–37
A pictorial emblem "available to her at the time" that shows a drowning man clinging to an albatross "stands behind Dickinson's famous poem."

"'Houses'—so the wise men tell me" (127)

1981   STEINER, "Image Patterns," p. 64
Relates to other Dickinson poems concerned with "the woman in her dealings with Power."

"How brittle are the piers" (1433)

1981   KIMPEL, *Dickinson as Philosopher,* pp. 226–27, 231
Consideration of whether poem's predominant trait is its "satirical character" or its "religious earnestness."

MONTEIRO and ST. ARMAND, "Experienced Emblem," pp. 264, 266
Dickinson here combines "the idea of the narrow plank of Faith, exemplified in Holmes and Barber's emblem of 'Walking by Faith,' with the idea of the various groups that take the different roads of Life and Death to produce a truly original and . . . unorthodox rendering."

1987   OBERHAUS, " 'Tender Pioneer,' " pp. 345–46, 349, 350
Relates to other Dickinson poems about Christ. "That God the Father is the craftsman who built the bridge and Jesus the 'Son' sent to test it manifests Dickinson's acceptance of the Christian Trinity . . . ."

"How dare the robins sing" (1724)

1989   OLIVER, *Apocalypse of Green,* pp. 55, 137, 152
"She feels that nature should suffer as she has and as those facing judgment do and join with her in a period of mourning."

"How firm eternity must look" (1499)

1984   LEONARD, D. N., "Dickinson's Religion," p. 348
This poem "states explicitly what is implicit in Dickinson's poetry as a whole: religion is fundamentally a search to realize the fulness [*sic*] of one's identity. . . . The creature can find his or her self only by submersion into the identity of the creator."

"How fits his umber coat" (1371)

1981   KIMPEL, *Dickinson as Philosopher,* p. 170–71
The poem is "not only a commentary on the 'Umber Coat' and its 'Tailor,' but also on peoples' [*sic*] restricted capacities to notice such wonders, and to do so with an awareness of what is involved in such creations, with such effectiveness that they equal or surpass the inventions of the most able of the minds of men."

"How fleet, how indiscreet an one" (1771)

1979   WELLS, A., "ED Forgeries," pp. 12–13
Suggests the poem is spurious and may be by Mabel Loomis Todd.

"How happy is the little stone" (1510)

1972   RAO, *Essential Emily Dickinson,* p. 159
   General introduction to the poem aimed at "postgraduate students of literature in Indian Universities."

1979   WILSON, "Problem of Career," pp. 455–56
   Examines how poem lays out "the logic of Emily Dickinson's concept of the poetic career."

1981   KIMPEL, *Dickinson as Philosopher,* pp. 197–98
   ". . . by virtue of attributing to 'the little Stone' an indifference for the sort of goals for which human beings destroy their lives, she credits it with a type of happiness which Stoics promise mankind, provided men learn the wisdom of relinquishing the many follies which ruin their well-being."

   PADDOCK, "Metaphor as Reason," pp. 77–78
   "The poem's ambivalence . . . signifies both Dickinson's uncertainty about man's place in the scheme of things and her triumphant mastery of her art."

1982   OLPIN, "Hyperbole: Part One," p. 15
   Examines poem's ironies. ". . . in the framework of the poem, whatever freedom there is belongs to the human being, not the stone."

   SALSKA, *Poetry of the Central Consciousness,* p. 57
   Relates to passage in Emerson's "Workship": "the two utterances show well the divergence in philosophical position between Emerson and Whitman on the one hand, and Dickinson on the other."
   Revised and reprinted: Salska, *Walt Whitman and Emily Dickinson,* pp. 47–48

1983   DURNELL, *Japanese Cultural Influences,* pp. 19–20
   "The little stone's life of silence, casual simplicity and quiet independence exemplifies Oriental religion, as well as the secluded, independent, soul-searching life of Emily Dickinson herself."

1986   ROBINSON, J., *Emily Dickinson,* p. 76
   ". . . the trouble with the so-wholly satisfactory and adaptable object is that it is, after all, a soulless lump: it is as if it parodies its maker: a stone is his satisfactory expression."

1987   CULJAK, "Dickinson and Kierkegaard," pp. 152–53
   In this poem "Dickinson describes Kierkegaard's despair about the

eternal. She contemplates the absence of the process of selfhood in nature and demonstrates a desire for concreteness and finitude which are at odds with the eternal and infinite aspect of the process."

1988   TRIPP, *Mysterious Kingdom,* pp. 51–52, 55
   "Here we encounter another . . . 'knot of ideas': the paradox of abundant loneliness, but actual happiness and contentment in the society of creation itself, a lack of outward activity in the inner business of the universe, and survival through a divine indifference to survival."

"How know it from a summer's day" (1364)

1988   MORRIS, T., "Development," pp. 39–40
   Examines as part of a cluster of Dickinson poems on Indian summer to illustrate her stylistic development.

"How many times these low feet staggered" (187)

1981   STEINER, "Image Patterns," pp. 67–68
   "Domestic weakness is set off against masculine strength . . . on the one hand and nature imagery . . . on the other, as symbolizing the freedom and range of activity which is denied the woman."

1982   MARCUS, *Emily Dickinson,* pp. 83–84
   Relates to other Dickinson poems on death and immortality. This poem "skirts the problem of immortality."

1983   BENVENUTO, "Words within Words," pp. 48–49, 55 n. 6
   Suggests instances where examining definitions and etymologies of key words in the poem, as they appear in the dictionary Dickinson used, may shed light on poem's meaning.

   MILLER, C., "How 'Low Feet' Stagger," pp. 135, 137, 146, 149, 151
   The poem illustrates how Dickinson "restructures hierarchies of power or role associations through a parallel disruption of some word's normal use or meaning."

1986   SMITH, S. B., " 'Radical Dualism,' " p. 37
   Discussed along with other Dickinson poems in which "a housewife is used as a metaphor for a secondary, even menial, comparison for some larger concern."

"How much the present moment means"

1988   WOLFF, *Emily Dickinson,* pp. 206–07, 218, 225
Dickinson "chooses to focus not on extinction, but on the ever-shifting tension between the forces of death and the minute triumphs of everyday vitality."

1989   WOLFF, "Usable Past," pp. 642–43
"Intimately aware of society's increasing inclination to devalue 'mere' domestic work—even as it ever more rigidly defined a woman's world in terms of home and family—Emily Dickinson wrote anthems of simple eulogy that deplored this devaluation without ever resorting to argumentation."

"How much the present moment means" (1380)

1981   DIEHL, *Romantic Imagination* pp. 95–96
"To say the moment is enough in itself would border on heresy, because it is not the solace of forgetfulness but just its opposite that Dickinson hopes to win."

KIMPEL, *Dickinson as Philosopher,* pp. 150–51
"A fact of which this poem takes account is that the poverty of inner resources sets such unyielding restrictions upon an individual that he is condemned by his own impoverishment to clutch at a trivial content offered during a moment."

"How ruthless are the gentle" (1439)

1979   BARNES, "Telling It Slant," p. 229
In this poem Dickinson invites the reader "to see a causal relation which is at odds with that of the traditional proverb."

"How sick to wait in any place but thine" (368)

1983   SHURR, *Marriage,* pp. 19, 86, 87
"This is a love poem, springing from a specific occasion, addressed at several points to 'thee,' and recalling to him at the end the imagery of her earlier love poem 'Wild Nights—Wild Nights!' . . . He remains now, to her, as the only person who has ever gained the right to console her."

"How soft this prison is" (1334)

1980   HOPES, "Uses of Metaphor," pp. 16, 18
"Softness and incarceration are the twin principles of the poem,

but which is she employing as a metaphor for the other? Eventually we perceive that the blurring of the direction of her metaphor is the point of the matter."

1984   OLPIN, "Hyperbole: Part II," p. 21
This poem "can be read as an indictment of Dickinson's home environment, but this does not change the basic ironies of the poem . . . ."

"How the old mountains drip with sunset" (291)

1981   PORTER, *Dickinson,* pp. 29–32, 33, 35, 91
"The raw material . . . of the 'Dome of Abyss' image is not only a preverbal but a preconscious sensation: the feel of woods unseen that one yet knows are there . . . . It is . . . *an absence felt as a presence.*"

1985   HOMANS, "Syllables of Velvet," pp. 581–83, 591
"Eschewing representation, Dickinson offers a sunset that substitutes for representational the pure presence of self-referential words. . . . The sense that how the poem speaks is what it speaks comes closest to indicating the kind of sexuality that suffuses the poem."

1986   ROBINSON, J., *Emily Dickinson,* pp. 165–67, 168, 171
In this poem Dickinson "uses two main lines of imagery. One is fluid . . . and one is fiery . . . . Water blazes and fire flows, keeping both spectacular light and the sense of movement."

1988   WOLFF, *Emily Dickinson,* pp. 290–91, 302, 367, 437
". . . the transcendent truth inherent in sunset—that the visible world's most salient feature is its slow disintegration into nothingness— is perhaps not accessible to an artist of gloriously resplendent oil paints. How is it possible to *draw* extinction?"

1989   LEONARD, D. N., "Certain Slants," pp. 128, 131–33
In this poem "fascicle 13 culminates its running meditation on the relation between nature and the artist. Here nature's two great talents— art and murder—are fused; in the end the human artist is slain by beauty."

"I am afraid to own a body" (1090)

1978   DIEHL, "Come Slowly," p. 581
"The body and soul Dickinson is afraid to own would be the masculine sides of a self whose identity she assumes frequently in both her poems and letters."
Reprinted: Diehl, *Romantic Imagination,* p. 25

"I am alive I guess" (470)

1985   ANANTHARAMAN, *Sunset in a Cup,* pp. 92, 95–97, 154
"On the whole, this poem is a fine example of a centering in Dickinson's imagery of the various qualities of an object . . . into a single apperception. In this particular poem, life emerges as a totality, with all its glory, warmth and freshness."

1987   LEDER and ABBOTT, *Language of Exclusion,* p. 135
The poem sets forth "the terms on which a woman in America before the Civil War could own a house, or her own 'Girlhood' name, or even the 'Key' to her own identity." Discusses in relation to other "marriage poems" by Dickinson.

1989   GARBOWSKY, *House without the Door,* p. 122
"Alienation is present in [this poem] . . . . where the speaker can only be sure of life by the absence of death, the quality of life is questionable."

"I am ashamed, I hide" (473)

1983   SHURR, *Marriage,* pp. 12, 15, 109, 133
The poem is "a description of the new spiritual estate gained by a bride through marriage." Relates to other "Wife" and "Bride" poems by Dickinson.

1985   ANANTHARAMAN, *Sunset in a Cup,* pp. 88, 92, 93–95
". . . a dazzling imaginative experience of a bride-inebriate, charged with mental agility, idyllic beauty, and jaunty-consciousness moving amongst the babel of bright, presto images. The emotion, if there is any in the poem, is in the images."

EBERWEIN, *Dickinson,* pp. 103, 174, 188
Here "Dickinson presents us with a timorous bride persona, apprehensive of coping adequately with her new privileges. . . . she has no idea how to behave in her new station . . . ." Discusses bridal poems.

MORRIS, T., "Free-rhyming Poetry," pp. 232–33, 234
"Here we can see Dickinson deliberately following Emerson in trying to enact the meaning of the poem in its form." This poem is "a good example of her use of free-rhyming techniques in a nominally regular metrical pattern."

1986 JONES, R., "'Royal Seal,'" pp. 37, 38–40, 46
"Status conferred through baptism is the subject" of this poem.
The ritual of baptism "seals the speaker's confirmation as an adult in an
inner covenant of grace."

1989 OLIVER, *Apocalypse of Green,* pp. 114, 115–16
"She at first has no hope of God's grace until some sign is revealed
that she has been chosen. Then, when she realizes that for some reason
grace is withdrawn, her loss is a twofold one: the loss itself before hope
and the loss exacerbated by hope withdrawn . . . ."

"I asked no other thing" (621)

1981 DIEHL, *Romantic Imagination,* p. 167
The poem "asserts Dickinson's frustration in divine, mercantile
terms which combine the bitterness of defeat with an attack on the doc-
trine of compensation itself."
Reprinted: Bloom, H., *American Poetry,* p. 453; Bloom, H., *Emily
Dickinson,* p. 149

1982 WESTBROOK, *New England Town,* p. 197
"Dickinson was always slightly touchy about the fact that she had
never undergone conversion, and she expressed her feelings in terms descriptive of a village woman's frustration on a shopping errand to the local
dry-goods store."

1983 UNO, "Expression by Negation," p. 9
". . . the use of negatives effectively produces the ironic mood of
this poem."

1987 MOREY, "Dickinson-Kant II," pp. 12, 13
"The Mighty Merchant is trying to educate the speaker to ask for
something more worthwhile, one of the Transcendental postulates possibly."

"I breathed enough to take the trick" (272)

1989 GARBOWSKY, *House without the Door,* pp. 89, 119
". . . if we place the agoraphobic syndrome at the center of these
poems, we gain a deeper insight into the physical discomforts the poet
documents, as well as into the nature of the psychic disturbance that
fueled them."

"I bring an unaccustomed wine" (132)

1979 POLLAK, "Thirst and Starvation," pp. 45, 46–48
Relates to the poet's use of "food and drink imagery," which typically "describes a cycle of deprivation, self-deprivation, and attempted self-sustenance."

1988 WOLFF, *Emily Dickinson*, pp. 213–14
"Not blessed by the 'custom' of the church or tradition, this 'wine' ministers not by promising eternal reunion and transcendent glory, but by the eloquent offer of simple charity and the shared hope—not the guarantee—of eternity."

"I can wade grief" (252)

1978 CODY, "Dickinson's 'I can wade,'" pp. 15–16
"Pain strengthens and provides a stimulus to extraordinary action, but prosperity debilitates and renders ordinary." Paraphrase. Reviews critical interpretation.

DOWNEY, "Antithesis," pp. 9, 12
The poem expresses "the antithesis between grief and joy."

1983 JUHASZ, *Undiscovered Continent*, pp. 55, 58, 97–98, 103, 105
"Here she identifies power with pain, because, by means of one's own discipline, one can possess it. . . . Control is power. And, in this poem . . . delight cannot be controlled."

1988 WOLFF, *Emily Dickinson*, pp. 214–16
"Here Dickinson explicitly argues against accepting any surrogate: permit no one to suffer in your behalf, the poem entreats, for when you seek to evade sorrow, you only relinquish the means to strength. Even God's *mercy* can be castrating."

"I cannot buy it, 'tis not sold" (840)

1989 MILLER, C., "Dickinson's Language," pp. 81–82
"The conclusion reveals that 'it' is a person . . . but the impersonal pronoun metaphorically identifies him with the entire effect he has had on her . . . ."

"I cannot dance upon my toes" (326)

1982 MOSSBERG, *Emily Dickinson*, pp. 156–58, 170
"The poem champions self-reliance for a poet, giving the stratagem of defiance an intellectual and artistic rationale. . . . Dickinson shows that she is not ignorant of 'Customs.' If she dispenses with them, it is by choice."

1983 WALKER, J., "ED's Poetic," p. 20
"She has confidence that her art springs from a talent which is of equal quality with that which is popular, but she possesses no desire to acquire the skills of others."

1984 POLLAK, *Dickinson*, pp. 239–40
Dickinson's "uncompromising repression of the exhibitionism this poem so beautifully expresses heightened her sense of competitiveness with other women artists."

1985 OLPIN, "In Defense of the Colonel," pp. 11–12
This poem about "the art of the mind" also shows that the poet "really did not need or want too much criticism from Higginson however much she seems to ask for it."

1986 LOVING, *Emily Dickinson*, pp. 61–62
"The poem observes the paradox of experience—the gap between knowing and doing *anything*. . . . [It] expresses the anxiety of knowing."

1987 LEDER and ABBOTT, *Language of Exclusion*, pp. 185–86
Links to other Dickinson poems about women artists. "The ballet metaphor provides the key to this poem's unusual form. . . . The lines evoke the dancer's leaps because they alternate between three and four beats to each line . . . ."

1988 MOREY, "Dickinson-Kant III," pp. 24, 25
"Today the public can see this as a satire on her contemporaries . . . ."

1989 DOBSON, *Strategies of Reticence*, pp. 121–22
". . . the thought of such self-display might well have caused anxiety to a woman acculturated to see herself as essentially private. However, through a grammatical manipulation . . . the story can be distanced and thus safely told."

MOSSBERG, "Double Exposures," p. 249
The poem's "reference to the fact that the poem before our eyes is

a secret, its practice is a secret, her sense of its success is a secret, makes the true subject of the poem the process of deception itself."

"I cannot live with you" (640)

1978   CAMERON, "Loaded Gun," pp. 431–33, 434
"Although its catechism is one of renunciation, we must scrutinize the poem carefully to see how renunciation can be so resonant with the presence of what has been given up."
Revised and reprinted: Cameron, *Lyric Time,* pp. 78–82, 83, 84; Bloom, H., *Emily Dickinson,* pp. 118–21, 124

1981   KHAN, "Poetry of Ecstasy," pp. 21–24
"The emotionally central paradox of the poem—separation sustained by despair—runs through the whole poem, its shock value being enhanced by a boldly unconventional style . . . ."
Revised and reprinted: Khan, *Emily Dickinson's Poetry,* pp. 47–50

1982   MARCUS, *Emily Dickinson,* pp. 52–53, 54, 66, 67
Relates to other Dickinson poems about "the renunciation of a profferred love."

SALSKA, *Poetry of the Central Consciousness,* pp. 148, 154–55
"The incredibly condensed feeling disciplined with excruciating effort endows the poem with the quality of psychic violence on the one hand, and, of intellectual toughness, on the other."

1983   DONOHUE, "Lyric Voice," pp. 3–8
The poem contains three voices, and its "tension derives from the separateness of the voices, as well as from secondary disparities within each voice."

SHURR, *Marriage,* pp. 7, 38, 89–93, 95, 97, 98–99, 143
"The poem embodies one of the most complete scenarios to be found among Dickinson's poems. . . . The two figures are Dickinson's constant first person 'I' and the lover whose identity is hinted at in several places in the poem." It presents considerable evidence that her beloved is a clergyman, most likely Wadsworth.

1984   POLLAK, *Dickinson,* pp. 181–184
"Throughout, she excoriates the social and religious authorities that impede her union, but she remains emotionally unconvinced that she has correctly identified her antagonists."

SALSKA, "Emily Dickinson's Lover," p. 139

"Distance alone permits a safe connection with the superior powers whom the lover typifies, while the void felt within keeps the link vital. Despair of ever being united is this union's one immaculate sustenance."

Revised and reprinted: Salska, *Walt Whitman and Emily Dickinson,* pp. 135, 142–43, 145, 146

1986   BUELL, *New England Literary Culture,* pp. 121–22

Compares method with that of poem by Ellen Hooper. "Like Hooper, Dickinson uses the Transcendentalist method of taking as the coordinates of one's argument the Platonized terms of received orthodoxy . . . but inverts this method more thoroughly."

1987   CULJAK, "Dickinson and Kierkegaard," p. 152

In this poem "she expresses both the desire to merge with another self and the realization that this act would constitute a violation of selfhood."

DI GIUSEPPE, "Maiden and the Muse," pp. 45, 48–51

Examination of the poem's paradoxes, which are central to Dickinson's "poetic statement."

MONTEFIORE, *Feminism and Poetry,* pp. 170–73

"The drama is entirely subjective, comprising both the agonizing separation . . . and her own incapacity to conform like her lover to Heaven's demands, so that 'I cannot live with You' means both 'I am incapable' and 'I am prevented.' "

MOREY, "Dickinson-Kant II," pp. 9–10, 24–25

Examines last stanza of this "savage" poem as an expression of "the anguish of an atheist or an agnostic."

1988   WOLFF, *Emily Dickinson,* pp. 417–23, 472

"The poem is about love, of course. Yet taken in the larger context of Dickinson's mission, it spells the fate of the poet as well." Examines key structuring patterns at work in the poem.

1989   WALKER, N., "Voice, Tone," p. 112

In spite of "the quiet anguish of the speaker, the poem is organized as though it were an argumentative essay, which serves to intellectualize and objectify the emotional burden."

WILSON, *Figures of Speech,* pp. 267–69

The poem is "a fine working of a delicate conundrum on the impossibility of life together on earth for any two devout lovers, laying out all the options and rejecting each in turn."

"I cannot want it more" (1301)

1978   MANN, "Poet as Namer," p. 479
"Here the desire to own and the problems attending that desire are held in balance, and the poet cannot decide whether she prefers possession or deprivation."

"I can't tell you but you feel it" (65)

1988   WOLFF, *Emily Dickinson*, pp. 299–302
"Repeatedly . . . the poem returns explicitly to the problem of communication, especially communication through art."

"I cautious scanned my little life" (178)

1981   STEINER, "Image Patterns," p. 64
Relates to other Dickinson poems concerning "the woman in her dealings with Power."

1985   BUDICK, *Emily Dickinson*, p. 147
"Like so many other inadequate modes of synecdochic perception, this Puritan-like self-analysis proceeds along lines of all-consuming analogical hypotheses that not only reduce the soul to hay but then subject it to the hay's ultimate perishability."

EBERWEIN, *Dickinson*, p. 66
The poem shows that the poet's "strategies based on habitual loss offer no protection against anything but exaggerated hopes."

"I could die to know" (570)

1986   McNEIL, *Emily Dickinson*, p. 116
The poem is "unusual for her work in having a personal speaker writing throughout from a perspective fixed in a specific time and place."

"I could suffice for him, I knew" (643)

1983   SHURR, *Marriage*, pp. 7, 34, 106, 172–73
"The poem dramatizes his proposal and her acceptance, expressed through Dickinson's now conventional imagery of the feminine sea's response to the masculine moon."

"I cross till I am weary" (550)

1985 JOHNSON, *Emily Dickinson,* pp. 180–83, 185
". . . this complex vision of quest fulfillment, though presented as a narrative, actually describes a pattern of fulfillment in consciousness, charting the attainment of 'compound vision' in a viable (yet 'experimental') assessment of death."

1986 BURBICK, "Economics of Desire," p. 369
"Value increases in direct ratio to the threat of competition." Examines poem's use of the language of the marketplace.

"I did not reach thee" (1664)

1979 PATTERSON, *Dickinson's Imagery,* pp. 39, 149, 201
"In the end she has apparently crossed three rivers, a hill, two deserts, and the sea, only to learn that death has taken her lover."

"I died for beauty, but was scarce" (449)

1972 RAO, *Essential Emily Dickinson,* pp. 137–38
General introduction to the poem aimed at "postgraduate students of literature in Indian Universities." It "epitomizes Emily Dickinson's sensuous approach to life."

1978 ABAD, *Formal Approach,* pp. 139, 140–41, 292, 293
"The speaker is *responding to her own life's situation*: that is the primary ground of our own response to the poem. It is a poetic lyric of reaction."

1979 CAMERON, *Lyric Time,* pp. 209–10, 221
Although the poem's "voice tells us what silences voice, it is still talking, is *after* its end relating its end."

1981 DIEHL, *Romantic Imagination,* pp. 120–21
"This is . . . a double failure, for not only have they died, but their names will not live after them as the obliterating moss destroys the possibility that they will be remembered for their sacrifice."

PORTER, *Dickinson,* pp. 10, 21, 19, 221–22
"The offbeat diction . . . and the off-rhymes play against the syllabic and metrical regularity of the lines so that the nihilism at the end is already sanctioned as it stands in wicked independence from the conventional sentiment with which the little poem began."

1982 MARCUS, *Emily Dickinson,* pp. 38–39
General consideration as one of Dickinson's poems on "Poetry, Art, and Imagination."

1983 SHURR, *Marriage,* pp. 36, 101, 143
The "professional obligations" of Dickinson, the poet, and Wadsworth, the clergyman, are stated here: "if one should die for Truth, the other would die for Beauty."

1984 FLEISSNER, "Beauty-Truth RE-Echoed," pp. 19–21
Suggests that Dickinson had Shakespeare's "The Phoenix and the Turtle" "on the back of her mind when she composed her own monody linking beauty with death . . . ."

1985 BUDICK, *Emily Dickinson,* pp. 112–15, 118, 121, 179, 186, 187, 188–91, 192, 212
The poem's "principal subject . . . is language itself, in particular the word's symbolizing function." It describes "a process in which a series of meticulously delineated steps issues in a suggestion of the poet's hoped-for result."

1986 ROBINSON, J., *Emily Dickinson,* pp. 50–51
"It is not the substance of the poem which carries its charge but its change in modes. It begins in a highly symbolic Gothic fantasy which is then intersected by the naturalism of weathering tombstones."

"I dreaded that first robin so" (348)

1972 RAO, *Essential Emily Dickinson,* pp. 136–37
General introduction to the poem aimed at "postgraduate students of literature in Indian Universities."

1976 SHANDS, "Malinowski's Mirror," p. 322
"What Miss Dickinson does, time after time, is to *translate,* in a personal sense, a status as *victim* into a status as *monarch,* thus demonstrating, in her own life, the enormous power of the central theme of Christian theology."

1978 MANN, "Poet as Namer," pp. 486–88
The poem "finds its subject in the clash between the exposed nerve of the poet's sensibility and the rebirth, the metamorphosis of nature in spring."

1982 MARCUS, *Emily Dickinson,* pp. 66–68
Relates to other Dickinson poems on "Suffering and Growth."

"The poem expresses anger against nature's indifference to her suffering, but it may also implicitly criticize her self-pity."

SOULE, "Robin," pp. 71–74, 82 n. 15
"The paradox which underlies the poem is that creation of any sort exposes the creator to criticism and possibly to spiritual suffering and death."

1983 SHURR, *Marriage,* pp. 46–48, 80
In this poem "Nature is secondary, used to clarify the interior emotions which are her primary focus." Here nature "provides an analogue for fuller exploration of Dickinson's marriage situation . . . ."

1984 ALLARD, "Regulation of Belief," pp. 31–32
The poem is Dickinson's comment on our "total alienation from beautiful but foreign and inaccessible nature. . . . She is but one more creature of nature, but with the tragic difference of an awareness of self and of passing."

1986 ROBINSON, J., *Emily Dickinson,* pp. 130, 131–33
"The great irony of the closing ritual is that she, deferred to as a Queen, is being persecuted by this attention. The salute is a crucifixion . . . ."

1987 MOREY, "Dickinson-Kant II," pp. 25, 27
Considers poem's images as "a pioneering effort to evince emotion by synethesia [*sic*], a mixing of the senses . . . foreshadowing Rimbaud's 'Le Batteau Ivre.' "

"I dwell in possibility" (657)

1978 MILLER, R., "Transitional Object," pp. 449–50
"Emily Dickinson's Paradise is that of poetic accomplishment; her occupation is the concrete task of creating poems; her visitors are the Muses, and her place of dwelling, personified as a house, is nature."

1982 MARCUS, *Emily Dickinson,* pp. 42–43, 44, 69, 96
General consideration as one of Dickinson's poems on "Poetry, Art, and Imagination."

1983 JUHASZ, *Undiscovered Continent,* pp. 15, 19–20, 25, 138–39
"Paradise is the farthest space conceivable, and the mind can expand to include it. When this happens, because of the power of the imagination, the 'housewife' can be a poet."

WALKER, J., "ED's Poetic," p. 21
"The process of writing the poem generates the pleasure which stimulates the process of writing the poem. It is a totally self-contained experience."

1984 BENFEY, *Problem of Others,* pp. 28, 33–34, 49
There is a "defensive posture in the poem, and an implicit claim that poetry and privacy are closely related. . . . The doors and windows of the first stanza seem . . . to be there less in the service of openness than for the possibility of closing them when necessary . . . ."

1986 NEW, "Difficult Writing," pp. 6–7, 10, 21–22
The poem "does double duty as both religious and poetic manifesto. . . . [The poem] promises all in one leap the simultaneous ventilation of both poetry and religion."

1988 MOREY, "Dickinson-Kant III," p. 33
"Using the imagination as well as the understanding, one can work up a transcendental feeling with the barest of materials. . . . This poem is approaching teleology . . . ."

1989 ROBINSON, DOUGLAS, "Two Dickinson Readings," pp. 25, 29, 34
In this poem "Dickinson's apocalyptic imagination is as it were deadlocked, split in an agon between an Emersonian expansion and a Poeian constriction that seems irresolvable."

"I envy seas whereon he rides" (498)

1983 SHURR, *Marriage,* pp. 31, 77–78
This is "a love poem in which the speaker envies the seas and hills on which the beloved travels, . . . the light that awakens him, and the bells which tell him it is noon. . . . The poem ends with the religious sanction opposing their union . . . ."

1987 MOREY, "Dickinson-Kant II," pp. 23–24
"The meaning seems to be that sumptuous destitution and fantasy are better than an actual attempt to make contact with the lover. Noon stands for imagination or vision, Night for the Despair which is really at the bottom of this poem."

"I fear a man of frugal speech" (543)

1984 WALLACE, *God Be with the Clown,* pp. 19–20
"Dickinson's pose of silence and frugality is as much a means of

self-aggrandizement as is Whitman's more straightforward boast and blab."

1988   PHILLIPS, *Emily Dickinson,* pp. 181–82
  "As a poet, knowing the lure of words, she was also wary of them; and, knowing that words serve a profound need, she respected the dignity of silence but dreaded absolute silence."

"I felt a cleaving in my mind" (937)

1979   CAMERON, *Lyric Time,* pp. 28, 45, 164, 170, 205
  ". . . the very sequence the speaker claims she is at a loss to reconstruct is that structure which elements the poem."

  GILBERT and GUBAR, *Madwoman,* pp. 627–28, 639
  Considers as "a kind of revisionary companion piece" to "I felt a funeral in my brain." This latter poem is "far more frank in its admission that madness is its true subject, and that psychic fragmentation . . . is the cause of this madness."

1981   ALEXANDER, "Reading Emily Dickinson," pp. 6–7, 15
  "The cleaving of the brain opens to perusal, however brief, the moment behind speech where experience assumes sequence (syntax) and sound (language). This is the dangerous, empty landscape that Emily Dickinson tried to describe, delineate, or embody so often in her poems."

1982   MOSSBERG, *Emily Dickinson,* pp. 29, 201 Part I n. 3
  "The important aspect of the poem to stress is not whether what it describes is true for Dickinson, but that the persona is engaged in the process of describing this disintegration with full possession of her poetic faculties and sense."

1984   OLPIN, "Hyperbole: Part II," p. 35
  "The poem gives two surprises, the surprise of the initial incongruity and finally the surprise of an incongruity turned to a hard-won congruity in the recognition of the harmony of the metaphor in its total effect."

  WOLOSKY, *Emily Dickinson,* pp. 162–63
  In this poem "silence represents a failure to articulate, derived in the failure of order and coherence."

1988   WOLFF, *Emily Dickinson,* pp. 471–72
  "There is a linguistic countermovement to this descent into gibberish, a thread of tangible, domestic terms that suggest a speaker straining toward the Voice of the 'Wife.' "

"I felt a funeral in my brain" (280)

1972 RAO, *Essential Emily Dickinson,* pp. 34, 55–56, 81, 123–26
General introduction to the poem aimed at "postgraduate students of literature in Indian Universities." Notes similarity of theme or attitude between this poem and Eliot's "Gerontion."

1977 AGRAWAL, *Emily Dickinson,* pp. 45, 46, 92–93, 151–55
"The poet develops the imagery of funeral in [this poem] for enacting the drama of despair on the stage of the inner self. There are four scenes in this drama, each taking place in 'Brain,' 'Mind,' 'Soul,' and 'Being' respectively."

1979 CAMERON, *Lyric Time,* pp. 51, 96–98, 100, 110, 159
It is "in the tension between the two modes of knowing and of representation, between an allegorical structure and an ironic one, that the poem's interest lies."
Reprinted: Cameron, *"Et in Arcadia,"* pp. 45–47, 57

GILBERT and GUBAR, *Madwoman,* pp. 620, 626–28, 639
"Death, here as in much of Dickinson's other poetry, is ultimately a metaphor for madness, specifically for the madness attendant upon psychic alienation and fragmentation." Authors compare with "I felt a cleaving in my mind."

1980 PORTERFIELD, *Feminine Spirituality,* pp. 141–43
The poem is "not a literary conjecture about what madness or death might feel like nor is it a metaphorical meditation on funerals. It is simply—and powerfully—a record of an event. The event occurred . . . within the poet's brain."

TAYLOR, M., "Shaman Motifs," pp. 7–8
Relates poem to elements of the "shaman experience." "There is a mythic antithesis set up in the poem as the speaker splits and reconciles two human faculties: Sense and Mind."

1981 PORTER, *Dickinson,* pp. 10, 20, 91, 120–21, 172, 174, 227–28, 284–85
This poem "is the first coolly targeted modern interior in American poetry, and it is handled adroitly with modernist attention not to moral judgment but to judgment-free description."

SCIARRA, "Women Looking Inward," pp. 36, 37, 38–39, 40
Dickinson here is "interested in the reality of death only insofar as it sparks off contemplation of the abstract, the emotion." The poem is "a powerfully visual expression of Dickinson's fear of loss of self."

1982 FAULKNER, "Emily Dickinson," pp. 810–11
Suggests final line may be read that the speaker is "finished with 'knowing' not as a gerund object, but as the participial modifier, so that even at the moment of her death, she dies knowing."

LEE, "'This World is not Conclusion,'" pp. 226–28, 230
"This 'funeral' . . . signifies the internalized comprehension of what it is to envisage the end of one's earthly being, the Brain as it were witness to its own obsequies." Relates to other Dickinson poems on death.

MARCUS, *Emily Dickinson,* pp. 72–73, 74, 75
The poem is "a dramatization of mental anguish leading to psychic disintegration and a final sinking into a protective numbness like that portrayed in 'After great pain.'" Relates to other Dickinson poems about "Suffering and Growth."

MOSSBERG, *Emily Dickinson,* pp. 29, 30
"The persona is so detached that she is able to describe the burial of her consciousness and senses. It is important to note that the deceased is plural. . . . In other words, the persona describes the death of a multiple self."

NIGRO, "Imp of the Perverse," p. 8
"Rational knowing gives way to intuitive unknowing, and thus is death once more the mother of beauty."

1983 BUDICK, "Temporal Consciousness," pp. 230–33, 234–35
Here Dickinson deals with "the dilemma of a temporal consciousness that must persist into eternity and yet that must simultaneously step aside to admire the supervention of immortality."
Revised and reprinted: Budick, *Emily Dickinson,* pp. 144, 205–11, 212, 220–21, 224, 227–28

GIBSON, "Poetry of Hypothesis," pp. 232, 233–34
"The poem is usually read as an account of spiritual catastrophe, but . . . [Dickinson] also hints, with a characteristic adventurousness, that catastrophe may be next to revelation."

KHAN, "Agony of the Final Inch," pp. 23–25, 26
"The allegory of funeral which is psychogenic in nature, compares to a psychic trauma. The psychodrama is structured on the pagan-Christian funeral ritual."
Revised and reprinted: Khan, *Emily Dickinson's Poetry,* pp. 23–26, 28

PESCHEL and PESCHEL, "'Am I in Heaven,'" pp. 475–76

"What this poem dramatizes . . . is that even if the experience of dying may be terrifying initially, it is, ultimately, easeful. For the dying person loses consciousness and, therefore, fear."

WILLIAMS, D., "'This Consciousness,'" pp. 366–67

"Here in a nondoctrinaire, nondogmatic form, are the classic Calvinist images of the crisis of conversion as they apply to the sinner first awakened to the terrors of the wrath of God."

Revised and reprinted: Williams, D., *Wilderness Lost,* p. 200

1984 OLPIN, "Hyperbole: Part II," p. 36

"The poem is comic only in the furthest reaches of the term, in its heroic confrontations with terms of the grotesque and the absurd. The comic grotesquery lies in the boldness of the metaphor."

POLLAK, *Dickinson,* pp. 211–14

". . . the text's most ambiguous element is less the hazardous action with which it concludes than Dickinson's moral evaluation of it."

ST. ARMAND, *Dickinson and Her Culture,* pp. 107–08, 109, 135

"Whether an ultimate knowledge of an individual's destiny is gained or lost, what swallows up all exegesis is the very terror of the question itself."

1985 ANATHARAMAN, *Sunset in a Cup,* pp. 35–43, 44, 47–48, 50, 154

The poem is "a psychic projection, in metaphorical language, of the loss of the poet's vision of Circumference, having its poetic parallel in the image of death, represented here purely as an adventure of consciousness."

PHILIP, "Valley News," pp. 67–68, 69

"Poems of this kind have such a vertiginous speed that we imagine their unstated conclusions can only be in breakdown and madness. But we should remember that the very writing of them implies a certain degree of control and manipulation."

1986 MARSTON, "Metaphorical Language," pp. 115–16

"In the most complex of all her poems involving the projection of self into and beyond the grave, Dickinson's treatment of death incorporates both existential and biological notions of nonbeing." The poem's "allegorical structure . . . mirrors the dualities of mind and body, self and negation."

REGUEIRO ELAM, "Haunting of the Self," pp. 89–91, 93, 95, 98

The funeral "reveals itself to be a funeral of the imagination, and the poem an account of the process by which poetic vision breaks down."

ROBINSON, J., *Emily Dickinson,* pp. 112–16, 126, 171, 175
Although "some of the poem's force comes from Gothic sensation-alism . . . a weird inversion takes place and the congregation seem more insensible than the poet. . . . Utterly a receiver, the poet uses a ceremony for the dead to define herself as a helpless victim, not of persons but of orders."

1987 COOK, C., *Psychic Development,"* pp. 126–27
"All Dickinson finds in an attempt to reach her collective uncon-scious are the trappings of death . . . . She has no success in communi-cation; it is as though she does not exist."

1988 PHILLIPS, *Emily Dickinson,* pp. 46–58 passim, 72, 208, 220 nn. 15–17, 221 nn. 22, 25, 31, 225 n. 69
This poem's origins are most likely "not in the poet's personal col-lapse but in her sympathetic and imaginative participation with those she loved in the rites for [Frazar Stearns]."

REYNOLDS, *Beneath the American Renaissance,* pp. 436–37
"This poem may be called a condensed, interiorized reconstruc-tion of the American Subversive imagination, with its dour themes and its bizarre imagistic transpositions. . . . [It] departs notably from popular sensational texts in several ways . . . ."

WOLFF, *Emily Dickinson,* pp. xviii, 227–35, 237, 261, 266, 271, 275, 471, 479, 584 n. 40
Examines the poem's three major forces: the funeral ritual, the "disruptive capacity of death," and time.

1989 GARBOWSKY, *House without the Door,* pp. 90, 105–07, 108, 109, 110, 111, 129, 140
The poem "depicts a figurative funeral . . . setting up a metaphor for a vivid exploration of agoraphobia with panic attack."

HAGENBÜCHLE, "Visualization and Vision," p. 67
"It is simply impossible to separate the spheres of material reality and inner experience. The delineating element (here, the 'floor') belongs at once to two realms—it is used as a *biform.*"

HOCKERSMITH, "'Into Degreeless Noon,'" pp. 283–84, 285, 286, 294 nn. 11, 12, 14
"The poem's structure is clearly the sequence of perceptions in a dying mind." Compares with "I heard a fly buzz when I died."

KNAPP, *Emily Dickinson,* pp. 86–90, 166
"Once the deceased (narrator) has divested herself of categories, once she has put a stop to systematizing and attempting to find coherence

in life's processes . . . she has stepped into a new order of her own manufacture, that of poetry."

> RICHMOND, "Teaching ED," pp. 36–37
> "The transformation of an observation—here a funeral ceremony—into a state of feeling is given a literalness which is less defined as a poetic figure, as traditional metaphor could be defined, than immediately felt."

"I felt my life with both my hands" (351)

1981 FAST, "'The One Thing Needful,'" pp. 162–63
"The orthodox heaven threatens individual identity, just as accepting others' definitions of 'paradise' and 'home' would undermine the integrity of one's own mind and experience. . . . she recognizes the price of the conventional."

1982 MOSSBERG, *Emily Dickinson*, p. 24
The poem "describes her alienation from her very being." The persona is "possessed by an unknown Owner, dispossessed of herself: the result is her sensation of being dead, in 'Heaven.'"

1989 GARBOWSKY, *House without the Door*, pp. 121–22
"There is a dramatic divorce between the person of the speaker and the self, as if the speaker were two separate people, one who does the weighing and the other who is weighed."

> OLIVER, *Apocalypse of Green*, pp. 193–94
> Discusses along with other Dickinson poems presenting a view of heaven.

"I fit for them" (1109)

1935 ALLEN, G. W., *American Prosody*, pp. 312, 317
Comments on poem's rhymes and meter.

1982 MOSSBERG, *Emily Dickinson*, pp. 143–44
"Dickinson's hunger strategy is built on a foundation of commitment and confidence in her poetic career. Her 'abstinence' provides a 'purer food' (the immortal word) than the kind made in the kitchen . . . ."

1985 MOSSBERG, "Rose in Context," p. 212
Relates to other Dickinson "hunger poems" that describe "an anorexic's strategy: by not allowing herself to be nurtured, she can avoid her mother's fate, become something different, herself . . . ."

"I found the words to every thought" (581)

1979   CAMERON, *Lyric Time,* pp. 193–94
   In this poem "we see the pain of a space that will not let itself be worded."

1988   MOREY, "Dickinson-Kant III," p. 28
   ". . . the allusion would seem to be a firmly theistic base, not necessarily Christian, but agnostic like Kant."

"I gained it so" (359)

1979   BUDICK, "Assignable Portion," p. 7
   This is one of Dickinson's "anti-symbolic poems" in which "the poet is concerned with demonstrating more how symbolic perception corrupts nature than with how it disturbs faith."
   Revised and reprinted: Budick, *Emily Dickinson,* p. 160

1985   JOHNSON, *Emily Dickinson,* pp. 114, 186
   This is one of many poems "in which Dickinson warns herself of the treacherous conditions of her quest, its cyclical rather than linear progress, and of her subjection to the friable and essentially patternless dimension of time."

"I gave myself to him" (580)

1980   CUNNINGHAM, *Dickinson,* pp. 39–41
   "It is a poem of earthly marriage . . . not of symbolic or spiritual marriage, and hence not autobiographical."

1983   ROSENTHAL and GALL, *Modern Poetic Sequence,* pp. 60, 61–62, 67
   Considers aspects of the poem that relate to the poems preceding and following it in the poetic sequence of fascicle 15.

   SHURR, *Marriage,* pp. 14, 82–83, 133, 173
   Rejects a mystical interpretation. ". . . the giving of lovers to each other is 'Mutual Risk'; one of the lovers might not realize the inferiority of the other until the commitment is made. Neither would be true in the case of the mystical marriage."

1984   WOLOSKY, *Emily Dickinson,* pp. 107–08
   Dickinson "denies the validity of the contract posed in rhetoric reminiscent of that between man and God. She suspects its terms, its promises, and its Transactor."

1985   EBERWEIN, *Dickinson,* p. 103
"Relatively late among her bridal poems, this one expresses doubt about the bride-speaker's own value. . . . she also suggests doubts about the bridegroom's value."

1987   MILLER, C., *Emily Dickinson,* pp. 60–61
Examines nature of experimental use of grammar in the line "The Daily Own—of Love."

MONTEFIORE, *Feminism and Poetry,* pp. 173–74
The final stanza is "beautiful as well as erotic. Yet its metaphor of circular exchange, with the payment passing endlessly between the cosy couple, suggests a certain scepticism about actual as opposed to anticipated pleasure . . . ."

"I got so I could take his name" (293)

1977   AGRAWAL, *Emily Dickinson,* pp. 83–85
"Faith begets hope, but because she has no faith in all these scriptural principles, she has no hope of salvaging herself from anguish. Thus a personal emotion teaches a universal truth that man devoid of faith loses all hopes in life."

1979   CAMERON, *Lyric Time,* pp. 58–61, 62, 146, 205
The poem, perhaps unintentionally, "is about what it is like to trivialize feeling because, as is, feeling has become unendurable. Better to make it nothing than to die from it."

1980   REISS, "Dickinson's Self-Reliance," pp. 29–31
"Shaping her hands in petition, she prays an unCalvinistic and unEmersonian prayer. . . . The woman in this poem prays for an end to her misery, altho she has little faith in her act." Stanza-by-stanza examination of the poem.

1983   KHAN, "Agony of the Final Inch," pp. 28–39
"The poem has two emotional referents: the present neurasthenic state of recovery in which separation becomes emotional reality; and the agony of separation as recollected by the newly recovered sensibility, thru a type of psychosomatic device."
Revised and reprinted: Khan, *Emily Dickinson's Poetry,* pp. 31–33

1984   POLLAK, *Dickinson,* pp. 177–80
Dickinson "spells out the difficulty of transferring her loyalty from a godlike man to an inhumane deity and concludes that this transference

cannot be effected. . . . As a principle of cosmic justice, 'God' exists in this poem only to reveal the futility of the speaker's quest for order."

WOLOSKY, *Emily Dickinson,* pp. 118–21
"Her prayer has, through successive syntactic disguises, been defeated and become blasphemous. From petition it becomes a description of utterance turned back upon itself."

1985 EBERWEIN, *Dickinson,* pp. 25–26, 119, 129, 257
"The total breakdown—possibly of the speaker, surely of the poem—comes in the final stanza with its unresolved pileup of phrases that fail to constitute a sentence or articulate an idea."

1987 MOREY, "Dickinson–Kant II," pp. 25–27
Examines the "theme of control." Considers poem's poetic techniques.

1989 WALKER, N., "Voice, Tone," pp. 111, 112
Suggestions for teaching the poem; its "skepticism about religion" saves it from sentimentality.

"I groped for him before I knew" (1555)

1983 SHURR, *Marriage,* p. 164
"The 'him' of the first line must be the husband of the marriage poems. . . . The crushing restriction sensed throughout the fascicles is reiterated near the end of the poem: such love must be 'consecrated' to be enjoyed."

"I had a daily bliss" (1057)

1980 JOHNSON, " 'Broken Mathematics,' " p. 25
This poem "embodies the familiar Dickinson theme of value heightened through its remoteness, and finally suggests her method of coping with this anguished insight."
Revised and reprinted: Johnson, *Emily Dickinson,* pp. 90, 125, 203 n. 13

"I had been hungry all the years" (579)

1979 PATTERSON, *Dickinson's Imagery,* pp. 34, 107, 191
The poem "appears to reflect on a moment of near consummation . . . ." However, "her 'Noon' to dine comes after years of hunger,

and she turns in discomfort and revulsion from the proffered food of love."

POLLAK, "Thirst and Starvation," pp. 42–44

The poem contains "Dickinson's fullest poetic statement of the relationship between external deprivation and internal inhibition."

Revised and reprinted: Pollak, *Dickinson,* pp. 127–29

1981 DIEHL, *Romantic Imagination,* pp. 104–05

"Hunger is Dickinson's strategy for overcoming her earlier exclusion from the communion table. . . . Thus, Dickinson cannot relinquish her acknowledged hunger because it has become a way of satisfying the starvation such exclusion implies."

1982 MARCUS, *Emily Dickinson,* pp. 68–69

Relates to other Dickinson poems about childhood deprivation.

MOSSBERG, *Emily Dickinson,* pp. 38, 135, 137, 139–40, 154, 207 n. 15

". . . to swallow that 'Bread,' is to become a part of a social or religious structure, and Dickinson, whose identity has been based on her hunger, refuses to give up that which distinguishes her from society."

Revised and reprinted: Mossberg, "Nursery Rhymes," pp. 59, 60, 61

1983 ROSENTHAL and GALL, *Modern Poetic Sequence,* pp. 54, 57, 67–68

Considers in relation to the poems that precede it in fascicle 15. "Essentially, [the poem] narrates a moment of triumph that has come too late and is fraught with sick and weary disillusion."

1988 REED, "Masculine Identity," pp. 280–81

"Without deprivation, there is no wanting; hence, deprivation is a necessity which defends against the oral fear of deprivation."

"I had no time to hate" (478)

1983 GIBSON, "Poetry of Hypothesis," pp. 226–27

"In the original version, the verb in the last line is subjunctive ('Be' and not 'Was')." The use of the subjunctive "throws the argument of the poem into question, and thus alerts us to its complexity of tone."

"I had not minded walls" (398)

1976 BUDICK, "'I had not minded,'" pp. 5–12

"The poem proposes two antithetical metaphors for primordial cosmic unity and its postlapsarian dispersion into multiplicity."

Revised and reprinted: Budick, *Emily Dickinson,* pp. 80–82, 88–89, 97–99, 101–11, 118, 168, 179, 187, 191, 192

1982 SALSKA, *Poetry of the Central Consciousness,* pp. 96–97, 155
"The poem is organized by syllogism. All the images in the major premise point to monolithic structures . . . , corresponding desires . . . , and definite directions in which to act . . . ."
Revised and reprinted: Salska, *Walt Whitman and Emily Dickinson,* pp. 84–85, 145

WALKER, C., *Nightingale's Burden,* pp. 112–15
"This is a poem about the forbidden lover, and as such it reminds us of what Dickinson could do with conventional female subjects." Examines poem's language, compression, and structure.

1983 SHURR, *Marriage,* pp. 31, 87–88
The final stanzas "provide five analogues for the 'law' which keeps [the poet and her beloved] apart, and then expands a sixth with the sense of danger in their precarious moral situation."

1985 SMITH, B. J., "'Vicinity to Laws,'" pp. 39–40
Examines poem's "legal word-echoes."

"I had some things that I called mine" (116)

1982 THOTA, *Emily Dickinson,* p. 116
"Dickinson always feels that there is constant rivalry between herself and God, who was snatching away from her all the dearly 'loved' persons. Her success as a poet lies in the fact that she turns this idea into a legal battle between herself and God."

1984 EBERWEIN, "Dickinson's 'I had some things,'" pp. 31–33
Suggests that variants in the manuscript might affect interpretation, particularly regarding the poem's "Action" and "Shaw."

1985 DICKENSON, *Emily Dickinson,* pp. 89–90
"Whimsy, business metaphor and the family hauteur combine in this broadside against the 'rival claims' of the revivalists" in this poem that "epitomizes Dickinson's concern for privacy in religious matters."

SMITH, B. J., "'Vicinity to Laws,'" pp. 40, 41–42
Here "the law is accepted as an arena of recourse in disputes with God. The poem is boisterous and uses an extended legal metaphor of civil action."

"I had the glory—that will do" (349)

1983 JUHASZ, *Undiscovered Continent,* pp. 123, 127–28
"Although this poem takes a generalized, proclamatory stance towards the mind's control of the relationship between past and future, bliss and loss, its opening line establishes the personal, experiential basis for its subsequent remarks."

"I have a bird in spring" (5)

1978 FADERMAN, "Homoerotic Poetry," pp. 20, 21, 22–23, 26 n. 12
The poem's bird is "not just the one woman she loves and is now losing to another, but all those that she loved and lost to heterosexual marriages . . . in the past."

"I have a king who does not speak" (103)

1976 KHAN, "'King' Symbolism," pp. 14–15
The poem "deals with 'King' as a lover; a preceptor who can guide the poet's genius; the Muse who can inspire but on her own terms; even God who can send poetic revelations."
Revised and reprinted: Khan, *Emily Dickinson's Poetry,* pp. 3–5

1983 DOBSON, "'Oh, Susie,'" pp. 86–87
In this poem "Dickinson gives unmistakable evidence of her awareness of a masculine presence in her psychic makeup."

GILBERT, "Wayward Nun," pp. 27–28, 29
Notes the act of "poetic prestidigitation" by which Dickinson converts "the mysterious figure she romanticizes from a lover into a male muse. Significantly . . . he is strangely passive and silent . . . ."

SHURR, *Marriage,* pp. 57–58
In this "plea to her silent correspondent," the poet characterizes her beloved as "the ruler of her moods: she is ecstatic if she dreams of him, utterly unhappy if she does not."

1985 SMITH, B. J., "'Vicinity to Laws,'" pp. 40–41
Examines as early example of Dickinson's "use of things legal." "It is essential to recognize that this early poem presumes a contract between the poet-child and the Father."

1988 HARRIS, S., "'Cloth of Dreams,'" pp. 9, 10
"The ambiguity of the perjury, which reflects her rejection of the social system and yet reveals a guilt for that rejection, is representative

of her manner in dealing with the anger and frustration she feels toward the limitations imposed . . . upon her by society."

"I have never seen 'Volcanoes'" (175)

1979 PATTERSON, *Dickinson's Imagery,* pp. 136, 152, 171, 172–73
Although she describes "as volcanic the passionate suffering that threatens to destroy her," the poem "may be less desperate than it looks. . . . the last puzzling stanza may be more playful than self-pitying."

1986 ROBINSON, J., *Emily Dickinson,* pp. 153–55, 157
"It is a restatement of the powerful Christian paradox that losing life is finding it, but so structured as to suggest that pain might be rewarded and thus justified. . . . But the poem is a might-be, its grammar never completed."

"I have no life but this" (1398)

1981 CAMPBELL, "Poetry as Epitaph," pp. 667, 668
The poem "asserts her desire to persist *actively* in the world. It clarifies precisely the kind of immortality Dickinson hoped for."

"I heard a fly buzz when I died" (465)

1972 RAO, *Essential Emily Dickinson,* pp. 34, 139–41
General introduction to the poem aimed at "postgraduate students of literature in Indian Universities."

1977 AGRAWAL, *Emily Dickinson,* pp. 93–94, 152
Paraphrase. "The word 'uncertain' is the keynote of the whole poem; what appeared to be a factual truth in the first line of the poem has now become doubtful. Is it really a fly that is buzzing? No, perhaps, or, is it a meaningless sound, carrying no message of immortality."

1978 GOHDES, "Emily Dickinson's Blue Fly," pp. 425–31
Reviews critical commentary on the nature and meaning of the poem's bluebottle fly.

SHARMA, "'I Heard a Fly Buzz,'" pp. 50–54
Overemphasis by critics on the poem's "fly" is responsible for "a misinterpretation of the other metaphors and symbols" and a falsification of "the pattern of meaning available in the poem."

161

1979   BUDICK, "Assignable Portion," pp. 1, 8–13, 15 n. 7
     The poem is Dickinson's "defense of symbolic perception, her def-
inition of the 'Assignable,' i.e., symbolizable, 'portion' of cosmic experience." One of its major purposes is "to describe this process whereby
symbolic perception destroys Christian faith."
     Revised and reprinted: Budick, *Emily Dickinson*, pp. 168–74, 176–77,
186, 187–88, 192, 198–99, 205, 207, 212, 216, 224

     CAMERON, *Lyric Time*, pp. 51, 112–15, 118, 119, 120–21, 125, 130,
     132, 133, 134, 137, 204, 208
     ". . . two notions logically exclusive—that death is the end of life,
specifically conceived of as a loss of consciousness, and that perception
is the end of life (consciousness continued, even heightened)—are in the
poem stalwartly presented as if they were the same thing."
     Reprinted: Cameron, *"Et in Arcadia,"* pp. 58–61, 63, 64, 65, 68, 72,
74

     KELLER, K., *Only Kangaroo*, pp. 322–23
     "The point of view is deliberately funny: a woman sitting some-
where hereafter telling other dead how *she* died. There was, she remembers with her flip tale, really nothing to it."

1981   HYMEL, "Singing Off Charnal Steps," pp. 3, 5, 7, 11, nn. 8, 11
     The poem's speaker is "restored from the Grave in order to . . .
facilitate the relating of the passive, and decidedly ambivalent, nature of
the speaker's experience of Death."

     RACHAL, "Probing the Final Mystery," pp. 44–46
     This poem and "I've seen a dying eye" "complement each other
by offering two closely connected perspectives on death."

1982   LEE, "'This World is not Conclusion,'" pp. 226, 228–29, 230
     Relates to other Dickinson poems on death. The concluding stanza
"manages nothing less than to force us to imagine our own parting moment, the point at which the random, alien energies of life other than our
own . . . mark the difference between conscious existence and the enduring total stasis of death."

     MARCUS, *Emily Dickinson*, pp. 80–81, 86
     Relates to other Dickinson poems on death. "The fly may be loath-
some, but it can also signify vitality."

1983   ALLEN, M., *Animals*, pp. 46–47, 53
     "Displayed against this backdrop of death, [the fly] is unmistak-
ably potent, first in holding the poem together as a reflector of weaker

forms of life and then in his independent journey outward, leaving death behind."

HARRIS, N., "Naked and Veiled," pp. 23, 27–29, 30, 33
Contrasts with Plath's "Paralytic." Both poems "depict speakers who experience feelings of alienation at the onset of death."

1984 ALLARD, "Regulation of Belief," pp. 33–34
"The force of the poem is not to do with futurity or immortality so much as with the final moments of life." Relates to other Dickinson poems on the moment of death.

BOGUS, "Not So Disparate," p. 42
Suggests source in Elizabeth Barrett Browning's *Aurora Leigh.*

MONTEIRO, G., "Dickinson's 'I heard a fly buzz,'" pp. 43–45
The conjunction of "Fly" and "King" in the poem may be rooted in "the religious legend surrounding the death of Jesus Christ and the flies which gathered on His body at the time of the crucifixion."

OLPIN, "Hyperbole: Part II," pp. 31–32
The poem exemplifies Dickinson's insertion of "the clown or the lowly" into her speculations on the "nature of God, time, and death."

POLLAK, *Dickinson,* pp. 193–98
The poem's theme is fraud, and "Dickinson tells us that fraud is not merely the essence of life, it is the essence of death as well. . . . Only an artist who had staked her all on resolving the incomprehensible hiatus between her past and her future could have written such a poem."

RAFFEL, *How To Read a Poem,* pp. 17–18
Dickinson permits us to see "not a thing that is personal in the imaginatively dying poetic persona she has 'interposed' between her reader and herself."

RUDDICK, "'Synaesthesia,'" p. 77
Comments on intersensory elements in poem's final stanza.

ST. ARMAND, *Dickinson and Her Culture,* pp. 55, 56, 60–61, 71, 73, 108, 135, 159
This poem "is similar to hundreds of mortuary effusions that dwell on the details of deathbed scenes . . . . The telling difference is that Dickinson makes a shorthand of conventional imagery while also questioning the whole meaning of the spiritual significance of material things."

WALLACE, *God Be with the Clown*, pp. 94–96

The poem "is more than just a dark satire of conventional death watches or conventional religious belief. It is also a disturbing comic inquiry into human limitation . . . ."

1985   ANANTHARAMAN, *Sunset in a Cup*, pp. 43–48, 139

The narrator's "obsession with the fly is neither mental nor outwardly [*sic*], but has religious overtones. . . . Though she longs for salvation, damnation is her predestination—as she was not a devout Christian."

BACHINGER, "Dickinson's 'I heard a fly buzz,'" pp. 12–15

Suggests that Dickinson's symbolism in this poem is indebted to works of John Donne.

EBERWEIN, *Dickinson*, p. 219

"The fly . . . obscures the dying person's total consciousness to the point that even when narrating her ironic story from beyond circumference, she still concentrates on the circuit world and its final bitter deprivation."

ESTES, "Granny Weatherall," pp. 439–40, 441

Examines allusions to this poem in Katherine Anne Porter's "The Jilting of Granny Weatherall."

JOHNSON, *Emily Dickinson*, pp. 158, 165–66

The implications of the "relationship between the two types of seeing" in the final line "make the poem one of total hopelessness."

KAJINO, "Moment of Death," pp. 41–43, 44

". . . the final dash seems to imply her hesitation to declare herself a witness to the spiritual light. It seems that the poet notices her expanding consciousness reach its limit and decides to remain within the boundary of human cognition . . . ."

1986   BORUCH, "Dickinson Descending," pp. 870–72

"The poem focuses closely, almost myopically, on unnerving natural things. . . . Her detachment seems almost scientific in the twentieth-century sense . . . ."

BYERS, "Possible Background," pp. 35, 36–37

Considers Hawthorne's *The House of the Seven Gables* as a possible source for this poem.

LOVING, *Emily Dickinson,* pp. 62–64

This poem "is about the high cost of knowledge. . . . Of course [it] . . . is about literal death as well, but that is not its most important theme. . . . For Dickinson, death is always a metaphor for experience, because life is always measured by its loss."

MARSTON, "Metaphorical Language," p. 114

"Trying to comprehend what a self can *be* without a body, the speaker contemplates her final moments and sees herself as having been reduced to two sense-impressions: the buzzing of a fly, and the failing of light at the windows."

ROBINSON, J., *Emily Dickinson,* pp. 107, 116–18, 120, 126

"The fly interposes between the controlling effort of deathbed ritual and the state of feeling which is other than that which that ritual allows for." Relates this poem to the "literature of the *ars moriendi.*"

TURCO, *Visions and Revisions,* pp. 48–49

Considers nature and identity of poem's narrator.

1987 JEROME, "Type of the Modern," pp. 72–75

"No effort is being made to explain, to extract meaning, to moralize, to decorate: the concentration of the poet was upon providing us with the raw ingredients of an imagined experience—raw, but carefully selected, carefully arranged."

WILLIAMS, S., "'. . . omitted centers,'" pp. 30–33

"The cohesion in this poem evolves through its context rather than through a concurrence with a single, understood object, or the universality of an idea: through metonymy rather than through metaphor."

1988 WOLFF, *Emily Dickinson,* pp. xviii, 207, 225–27, 228, 276

The poem "maintains a tension between the capacity of vision and the meaning of its extinguishment, between that which is willed and that which must be accepted passively."

1989 GALPERIN, "Posthumanist Approach," pp. 113, 116

Examines the "feminist trajectory in Dickinson" through teaching a specific sequence of poems, including this one.

HOCKERSMITH, "'Into Degreeless Noon,'" pp. 284–85, 286

Compares with "I felt a funeral in my brain." In both poems Dickinson "ironically twists Christian imagery to emphasize the impotence she sees in the Christian promise of eternal perfection."

"I heard as if I had no ear" (1039)

1980 DUNCAN, "Joining Together," pp. 127–28

"Having acquired life, she inherits death, the awareness of time and her own mortality; but having inherited death, she acquires Life, the consciousness of eternity."

1981 DIEHL, "Dickinson and Bloom," pp. 428–29, 438

Considers "implications of invoking the Scene of Annunciation as a paradigm for poetic influence" that "in part determine the woman poet's perception of her precarious position as it creates its own distinct anxieties."

1984 WOLOSKY, *Emily Dickinson*, pp. 149–50

"In this poem, a distinction between heaven and earth, spirit and flesh, is assumed. But the two do not conflict. The Logos provides a bridge for crossing from the former to the latter."

1986 DIEHL, "Twilight of the Gods," pp. 184–85

Dickinson "shares a perception of the sublime with several other women poets . . . who experience the workings of the sublime as an essential process, but one that carries within it, ironically, the shattering capacity for splitting apart that self."

1987 MARTIN, J. E., "Religious Spirit," pp. 501–02

"The difference between illusion and reality has not even by Plato been captured more accurately."

"I held a jewel in my fingers" (245)

1982 DITTA, "Jewel and Amethyst," p. 36

"One can see clearly how Dickinson evaluates the two aspects of the creative mind . . . by comparing the symbolic values of the Jewel and Amethyst in [this poem]."

MOSSBERG, *Emily Dickinson*, pp. 171–72

Loss in this poem refers to "Dickinson's fear of losing her ability to create. . . . That the valued jewel is poetry, and the poem a metaphoric statement about art is suggested by the emphasis on 'fingers'. . . ."

1983 SIMPSON, "Dependent Self," p. 38

The poet employs the "gem metaphor to heighten the sense of the preciousness of her friends" in this poem, which is "a kind of miniature of the medieval poem PEARL without the redeeming vision."

1987   BARKER, *Lunacy of Light,* pp. 69–70, 198 n. 25
Notes that "jewels appear often in Dickinson's imagery as emblems for the poet's Self, or more specifically, for her artistic genius."

GELPI, "Emily Dickinson's Word," p. 44
"The awakening of consciousness to 'an Amethyst remembrance' is expressly here the transition from prose to poetry. Poetry is the owning of loss, the owning *up* of loss, the reclamation or repossession of absence."

"I hide myself within my flower" (903)

1988   O'KEEFE, "I Hide Myself," pp. 57–66
The poem appears with alterations in both fascicles 3 and 40. Examines variants to see how they relate to each fascicle as a whole.

"I keep my pledge" (46)

1989   OLIVER, *Apocalypse of Green,* pp. 72–73
The poem "combines Christian ideas of election and personification of Death within the metaphor of nature. . . . Her pledge of faith is based not on God's revealed word, the Bible, but on the supportive evidence of nature . . . ."

"I know a place where summer strives" (337)

1988   WOLFF, *Emily Dickinson,* p. 285
". . . nature *can* sometimes be a 'mirror' of mankind, but when she assumes that relationship to human beings, it is principally their wrestle with God that she reflects."

"I know some lonely houses off the road" (289)

1979   KELLER, K., *Only Kangaroo,* pp. 323–24
This poem illustrates Dickinson's use of "metaphor as a form of play. . . . The form surprises by being near to conventions and yet having a character—a voice—of its own. The poem, a tease, is therefore *about* teasing."

1984   WILT, "Playing House," p. 158
Considers as one of the "scores of highly charged lyrics" in which "the poet confronts the house she is before, or within, or has become."

"I know that he exists"

1985 BUDICK, *Emily Dickinson,* pp. 156–58
". . . the price that the solipsistic, idealist mind may pay for its reentry into the world is high. In this poem it is plundered of its wealth because it can find no way to reconcile its internal gifts with its external commitments."

1987 BARKER, *Lunacy of Light,* pp. 97–98
"Primarily playful, the poem nevertheless contains several images that again suggest Dickinson's sympathies with darkness and all it connotes."

"I know that he exists" (338)

1978 CARTON, "Dickinson and the Divine," pp. 249–50
"The maker of images and arguments to answer her own need to believe, she cannot but suspect at times that she is the only conjuror and that her entire enterprise amounts to a magnificent decoy."
Revised and reprinted: Carton, *Rhetoric,* pp. 57–58

PERRINE, "Emily Dickinson's 'I know,' " pp. 11–12
Stanza-by-stanza explication of this poem "in which an initial assertion of faith is gradually undermined until the poem ends up as an expression of profound skepticism."

1979 KELLER, K., *Only Kangaroo,* pp. 62–64
"There is tension between the trite language of the poem . . . and the ambiguously personal language . . . , just as there is between the phony ideology . . . and the cruel reality of life . . . ."

NATHAN, "Soul at White Heat," pp. 49–50
In this poem Dickinson "wrote a literal paraphrase of Augustine's declaration of knowing."

1980 DIEHL, "American Self," pp. 1–2, 9 n. 8
"Here God is a Stranger whose acts alone reveal His intent; His motives remain a mystery. To defend herself against this silence, Dickinson takes the available signs of His power and converts them into weapons that serve her alternative rebellious purposes."

MACHOR, "Feminine Rhetoric," p. 137
The poet's use of "equivocating syntax" achieves "a piercing irony."

1982 FAULKNER, "Emily Dickinson," pp. 807–08
This poem is typical of Dickinson's "explicitly religious poetry" in its movement "from apparent affirmation to resounding doubt."

MARCUS, *Emily Dickinson,* pp. 82–83, 96

Examines poem's irony. "It is as close to blasphemy as Emily Dickinson ever comes in her poems on death, but it does not express an absolute doubt. Rather, it raises the possibility that God may not grant the immortality that we long for."

1983 DOBSON, "'Oh, Susie,'" pp. 82–83

". . . in Dickinson's poetic universe possibility is commensurate with psychic reality, and the destructive potential inherent in interaction with the masculine leaps to the foreground of her mind and usurps the poem."

1984 LEONARD, D. N., "Dickinson's Religion," pp. 346–47

In this poem "Dickinson confronts the limits of the consciousness in its quest for knowledge of God. . . . In its final effect, the poem serves as an arsenal of contempt—for God, for faith, and for the self—ready to be detonated if the faith prove mistaken."

OLPIN, "Hyperbole: Part II," pp. 9–10

The poem's irony "is directed at the poet herself—or perhaps her religious background which has supplied pious assurances of God—who plays the dual role of ironist and victim."

1985 BUDICK, *Emily Dickinson,* pp. 92–93

". . . instead of rejoicing in this happy coincidence of scriptural authority and neoplatonic patterns, the poem concludes with an awful shudder that effectively denies all of the comfortable assumptions of Christian idealism on which the poem is built."

JOHNSON, *Emily Dickinson,* pp. 152–53, 213 n. 15

The poet here "views the relationship between her quest object (the unnamed 'He,' referring in this poem to God) and the possibly permanent obstacle of death, focusing upon visual perception as the means toward 'Bliss.'"

1989 KNAPP, *Emily Dickinson,* pp. 83–86, 132

"If God 'exists' as a transcendental, impersonal, silent, undefined power, He does not mitigate the narrator's fears." Considers development of poem's images.

"I learned at least what home could be" (944)

1981 PORTER, *Dickinson,* p. 202

"The view of a wife's day, surely, is naive in its homely idealism. Yet the lines create the feeling that the husband in this case has a real counterpart in the world."

1983 SHURR, *Marriage,* pp. 146–47, 152, 198
The poem is "a magnificent scenario imagining married life with her clergyman lover."

"I like a look of agony" (241)

1972 RAO, *Essential Emily Dickinson,* pp. 118–19
General introduction to the poem aimed at "postgraduate students of literature in Indian Universities."

1982 LEE, " 'This World is not Conclusion,' " pp. 223–24
Relates to other Dickinson poems on death.

MARCUS, *Emily Dickinson,* p. 76
"The second stanza rushes impetuously from the idea of terrible suffering to the absolute of death, as if the speaker were demanding that we face the worst consequences of suffering—death, in order to achieve authenticity."

1983 BENVENUTO, "Words within Words," pp. 53–54
Suggests instances where examining definitions and etymologies of key words in the poem, as they appear in the dictionary Dickinson used, may shed light on poem's meaning.

ROSENTHAL and GALL, *Modern Poetic Sequences,* pp. 69–70
Considers as it relates to the other poems in fascicle 16. This poem is "a remarkable foreshadowing of major affective modes in twentieth-century poets as far apart as Mayakovsky and Plath."

1984 BENFEY, *Problem of Others,* pp. 88, 91–92
"What the poem seems to be saying is: If you want certainty, if you demand to know whether a look corresponds to something inside, then you will be satisfied only with the dead, where the gaze or 'glaze' of the eyes means ('is') 'death.' All else *can* be . . . feigned."

"I like to see it lap the miles" (585)

1972 RAO, *Essential Emily Dickinson,* pp. 144–46
General introduction to the poem aimed at "postgraduate students of literature in Indian Universities."

1978 ABAD, *Formal Approach,* pp. 276–77, 342–44, 359
Considers why some of the poem's terms "are, *in relation to the subject* of the poetic description, metaphors" while "others are not."

1980 O'CONNELL, "Iron Horse," pp. 469–74
Detailed analysis of poem's tone and details shows that it "may be read as a pointed commentary on the perennial human capacity to create idols, and an ironic warning of impending technological catastrophe."

1982 FREEDMAN, "Dickinson's 'I Like to See,'" pp. 30–32
Shows that this may be read as "a poem about poetry and about itself."

MARCUS, *Emily Dickinson*, pp. 65–66
Although this is "Dickinson's most popular poem on a social theme," it is "devoid of both people and an explicit social scene."

1984 MARTIN, W., *American Triptych*, pp. 134–35
"Whitman's locomotive . . . dominates the landscape subject to no external restraints—while Dickinson's prodigious train follows definite tracks . . . ." The contrast reflects "the differences in traditional masculine and feminine consciousness in the nineteenth century."

1985 DOWNEY, "ED's Appeal," pp. 28, 30
A small child might enjoy the poem "as the journey of a train without perceiving that the journey symbolized is the journey of death."

PHILIP, "Valley News," pp. 74–75
"If the train is 'male', then the elements that surround and support it are 'female'. In social terms there is the provision of sustenance and comfort; in physical terms the pleasurable yielding to sexual advance."

1987 LEDER and ABBOTT, *Language of Exclusion*, pp. 145–46
"This juggernaut doesn't need human aid as it devours the landscape, so that now both time and space are altered. . . . In a teaming of opposites that perfectly describes machine servants, it is docile *and* omnipotent."

1989 MORTON, "How Language Works," pp. 48, 49
Suggestions for teaching the poem to college freshmen.

OBERHAUS, "Dickinson as Comic Poet," pp. 119–20, 121, 122, 123
Describes teaching the poem, which is "both a cartoon of the train and social criticism."

"I live with him, I see his face" (463)

1979 CAMERON, *Lyric Time*, pp. 82–83, 84
Here "reconstruction is tantamount to memory—the invention of presence where not to have it would leave the world absent even of pain."

1984   POLLAK, *Dickinson,* pp. 179–81
"... her ability to distinguish effectively between physical absence and emotional presence is undercut by her inability to distinguish between unreciprocated love and death."

1985   EBERWEIN, *Dickinson,* p. 176
"The poem strongly implies this woman's status as bride of Christ, and the compact between the lovers suggests election."

1989   HOCKERSMITH, "'Into Degreeless Noon,'" pp. 278–80, 286, 294 n. 6
The poem "represents death as a state of monotonous isolation of consciousness in time."

OLIVER, *Apocalypse of Green,* pp. 157–58, 215–16
The poem is "a positive, triumphant declaration of God's presence after death." It also "demonstrates the constructive role time plays in the achievement of immortality."

"I lived on dread" (770)

1981   JUHASZ, "'Peril as a Possession,'" pp. 31–32, 33, 34
"The poem's focus ... is neither on the awe nor on the suffering involved in the experience of dread; its concern is less with discipline and more with the excitement engendered."
Revised and reprinted: Juhasz, *Undiscovered Continent,* pp. 55–57, 83

1984   LEONARD, D. N., "Dickinson's Religion," pp. 338–39
"Dickinson shares with Kierkegaard the basic supposition that transcendence is achieved through recognition of limitations, renunciation of the self, and the taking of risks on the chance that one may truly find oneself in the end."

"I lost a world the other day" (181)

1983   SHURR, *Marriage,* pp. 11, 39, 72
In the context of the fascicle, the poem is seen as "a love poem, addressed to the same 'Sir' as the others are, recalling the Day of her marriage, and lamenting her loneliness without him."

"I make his crescent fill or lack" (909)

1978   CARTON, "Dickinson and the Divine," pp. 248, 252 n. 7
"That any relation between the self and the divine presupposes the

vanquishment of one by the other is the bitter implication of [this poem]."
Reprinted: Carton, *Rhetoric*, pp. 55–56, 270–71 n. 7

1983 SHURR, *Marriage*, pp. 121–22
"The poem is near the end of all of the fascicles, and rewards close investigation, especially since it is a later working of her early moon-sea imagery for the lovers."

"I many times thought peace had come" (739)

1972 RAO, *Essential Emily Dickinson*, pp. 151–52
General introduction to the poem aimed at "postgraduate students of literature in Indian Universities."

1979 ESTES, "Search for Location," p. 215
"The poet's hopelessness suggests the futility of any action since the many mirages she sees make a true sense of location impossible."

"I meant to find her when I came" (718)

1984 POLLAK, *Dickinson*, pp. 135–37
"Her personification of death suppresses key elements of her experience as a daughter, a sister, and a friend. The poem reenacts a partially repressed drama, reproducing the original triangle (a female figure, an 'I' of undefined gender, and a deathly male) in a less threatening form."

"I meant to have but modest needs" (476)

1978 BURKE, "Religion of Poetry," p. 20
This poem goes beyond "Papa above" for "it makes explicit the futility implied in the earlier poem."

1982 MOSSBERG, *Emily Dickinson*, pp. 126–27
"In poem after poem she tells us that obedience results in humiliation—as in [this one]. . . . God, in addition to being merely indifferent, mocks her."

1984 WALLACE, *God Be with the Clown*, pp. 87–88
"The humor in the poem is directed partly against human misinterpretation of divine will; it is also directed against a God so detached that he could allow such misunderstandings and callously laugh at the victims."

1985   EBERWEIN, *Dickinson,* pp. 254–56
"This is less a poem about loss of faith than about replacement of manipulativeness by a less hopeful kind of cynicism."

1986   OBERHAUS, " 'Engine against th' Almightie,' " pp. 159–60
"To the end, this protagonist remains oblivious to her arrogant self-centeredness." Relates to other "prayer" poems of Dickinson.

ROBINSON, J., *Emily Dickinson,* pp. 73–74
"Although it is a fairly robust piece of satire, it is dealing with essentially the same core of experience which far more delicate and difficult poems treat: the ways in which the profoundest matters of life do not match the received, or perhaps any, description of them."

1987   MOREY, "Dickinson–Kant II," pp. 12–13
The situation is similar to that in "I asked no other thing." Contrasts the two poems.

"I measure every grief I meet" (561)

1984   BENFEY, *Problem of Others,* pp. 64, 86, 88–91
"My grief is just as much a mystery to me as their grief. This is one argument against 'analogy,' that my relation to my grief is not necessarily privileged."

1986   DORESKI, " 'Exchange of Territory,' " pp. 58–59, 62, 63
"Wonder, measure, and classification join perception as an approach to knowledge" in this poem, which "assumes almost an anthropological tone. It proposes not to share but to measure and compare emotions, to compile not a record of a grief but a generic language of grief."

MUNK, "Recycling Language," pp. 242–45, 251 n. 43
In this poem Dickinson "may be subverting and parodying through wordplay *all* fashionable cults, especially those that are constantly being re-formed."

1988   PHILLIPS, *Emily Dickinson,* pp. 190–91
"The persona is fascinated by the question of why, when we are not alone, we are forever alone."

1989   DOBSON, *Strategies of Reticence,* pp. 96–97
Contrasts with Helen Hunt Jackson's "My Legacy" in order to reveal the "profound motivational gap between the two writers." For Dickinson, the purpose of language is "to provide personal insight and satisfaction and an apt embodiment of alienated anguish."

"I met a king this afternoon" (166)

1976 KHAN, "'King' Symbolism," pp. 16–17
"'King' in the poem may stand for some preceptor in real life, Muse, God, and even death, but they must correlate to the terms of the outer analogue."
Revised and reprinted: Khan, *Emily Dickinson's Poetry,* pp. 5–8

1983 DOBSON, "'Oh, Susie,'" pp. 87–88
"The masculine figure . . . is not singular in power as he is seen in other poems, but capable of multiplicity and associated with innovation and origins rather than with paralysis and destruction."

"I never felt at home below" (413)

1981 KIMPEL, *Dickinson as Philosopher,* pp. 59–60
Examines the "mode of loneliness" exhibited by this poem.

1982 MOSSBERG, *Emily Dickinson,* pp. 120–21
". . . the voice of the child in this poem is not only an emblem of hopelessness. It is also a means of rebellion in itself, for as a child Dickinson can criticize and complain with impunity."

1983 MOSSBERG, "Nursery Rhymes," pp. 48–49
Considers implications of the child's viewpoint, which is "cheekily humorous, serving to deflect any reprisals for such unorthodox but 'perfectly natural' thoughts."

1984 LLOYD, "Adult Voice," pp. 25–27, 28, 29
"In fashioning a child's voice which can express complex adult preoccupations, Dickinson performs a difficult balancing act."

· OLPIN, "Hyperbole: Part II," p. 6
"The description of God as ever-ready telescope is a description that both gives him inflated power and at the same time reduces him."

"I never hear that one is dead" (1323)

1978 TILMA-DEKKERS, "Immortality," pp. 176–77
"By this word ['Consciousness'] Emily Dickinson makes clear her special view of the nature of the human soul: it is not to gain immortality after death, but only consciousness of its immortality."

1980 DIEHL, "American Self," pp. 3–4
The poem "describes the Self's reaction to an awareness of its own mortality. Too much delving into consciousness . . . has driven her to the

brink of madness; annihilating the belief in life's continuation renders existence a nightmare."

1986   ROBINSON, J., *Emily Dickinson*, pp. 92–93
The poem shows how Dickinson "uses a disruption (death) of the smooth continuum of existence to make her mind confront once more the possibilities latent in life."

"I never hear the word 'escape' " (77)

1980   LAIR, "Fracture of Grammar," pp. 159–60
Comments on poem's syntactic ambiguity. "Two syntactic functions are . . . compressed into the single word 'childish'; it is both adjective and adverb, doubling the semantic force of the word."

1989   ROGERS, K., "Introducing Dickinson," p. 54
Suggestions for teaching the poem to college students.

"I never lost as much but twice" (49)

1972   RAO, *Essential Emily Dickinson*, pp. 107–08
General introduction to the poem aimed at "postgraduate students of literature in Indian Universities."

1980   FRY, "Writing New Englandy," p. 28
In the poem's penultimate line, "the poet has achieved such technical mastery of her language that she is able to say more about the irrationality of death than many theologians have been able to say in complete books."

MACHOR, "Feminine Rhetoric," pp. 139–40
". . . the series of epithets culminating in the sardonic implications of 'Father' denotes a frustration with and reaction against conventional attitudes of feminine resignation."

1982   MARCUS, *Emily Dickinson*, pp. 48–49
This poem is "a fine example of Dickinson's jocular blasphemy combined with a quite serious theme. We could place this poem under the headings of death and religion as easily as under friendship."

MOSSBERG, *Emily Dickinson*, pp. 113–15, 207 n. 7, 208 n. 5
The poem reveals "the correlation in Dickinson's mind between her own and her heavenly 'father.' . . . And like her own father, God is seen to be creating her dependence upon him at the same time that he sadistically refuses to satisfy her needs."

1987   LEDER and ABBOTT, *Language of Exclusion,* pp. 141, 142–43, 145
    Discusses as part of a sequence of poems from 1858 concerning "risk, loss, death." "All of them link aspects of modern male power positions—brokers, bankers, factory owners—with God-like qualities . . . in order to present her concerns in these dramas of the masculine sphere."

    MOREY, "Dickinson-Kant II," pp. 12, 14, 20
    This poem is "pivotal" in a consideration of Dickinson's prayer poems.

1988   KJAER, "Job's Sister," pp. 20–21
    Considers significance of poem's reference to Job.

    PHILLIPS, *Emily Dickinson,* pp. 82–83, 84, 87, 234 n. 38
    Considers as a combination of dramatic monologue and personal experience.

"I never saw a moor" (1052)

1978   FLEISSNER, "Dickinson's 'Moor,'" pp. 8, 9
    Notes possible allusions to *Othello.*

    MONTEIRO, G., *"Love & Fame,"* pp. 108–10
    Considers as one of the poet's "fame" poems. In it "cashing her 'Checks' characterizes the way in which the poet will participate in the ultimate transaction involving her death and immortality."

1979   KELLER, K., *Only Kangaroo,* pp. 291–92
    "God is friend and heaven a spot and salvation a quick ride. The metaphors bring the hoped-for down to earth, and the present known becomes itself a measure of that hoped for."

1981   CODY, "Hazards, Billowbees," pp. 202–17
    A playful, word-by-word exploration of possible readings of the poem, with speculations on Dickinson's intent and methods as well as on the hazards of interpretation.

1982   JOHNSON, "Emily Dickinson," pp. 12–13
    The poem's intent is clearly ironic.
    Revised and reprinted: Johnson, *Emily Dickinson,* pp. 47, 57–58, 59, 61, 146, 200 n. 19

1984   BENFEY, *Problem of Others,* p. 25
    The poem considers the "precise relation of knowing to sense experience, to the evidence (or testimony) of the eyes."

1985   Cottle, *Language of Literature,* p. 102
A note on poem's grammar.

1986   Hughes and Cortinez, "Where Do You Stand," pp. 233, 234–35
Examines possible interpretations of poem's "Checks."

1987   Perkins, "History of Explication," pp. 30–31
Suggests that reading "checks" as "cross points of furrows gives the geographical orientation to the stanza that the word spot requires" and "brings unity to the poem."

1988   St. Armand, "Heavenly Rewards," pp. 219–38
Relates poem's "checks" to "Rewards of Merit" handed out in schools and Sunday schools. "This recontextualization of 'Checks' also emphasizes the child-like caprice of the poem . . . and parodies the very physicality of the nineteenth-century arranged marriage of commodity with religious commitment."

"I never told the buried gold" (11)

1986   Bennett, *Loaded Gun,* pp. 50–52, 53
"The poet, the persona, and the poem are all left divided between conflicted and conflicting possibilities. . . ." The poem expresses Dickinson's feeling that her brother, Austin, "had stolen Susan from her."

"I often passed the village" (51)

1986   Bennett, *Loaded Gun,* pp. 45–46, 47–48
Compares and contrasts with "Because I could not stop for death."

"I play at riches to appease" (801)

1982   Mossberg, *Emily Dickinson,* pp. 141–42, 149, 150, 166, 172
In this poem Dickinson "introduces a rationale for cultivating *hunger* rather than another form of deprivation: she suggests that her identity as a poet is linked to her 'hunger' and to her refusal to *satisfy this hunger.*"
Revised and reprinted: Mossberg, "Nursery Rhymes," pp. 61–62

1983   Gibson, "Poetry of Hypothesis," p. 231
"The poem is a series of intricate but disjointed ruminations, and the disjointedness is an important part of its effect." Comments on effect of poem's "syntactical ambiguity."

"I prayed at first a little girl" (576)

1982 MOSSBERG, *Emily Dickinson,* pp. 122–24, 126, 207 n. 10
Perhaps "it is not God who suffers from her refusal to pray, but the God of doctrine and convention promoted and supported by the culture in which she lives."

1986 OBERHAUS, "'Engine against th' Almightie,'" p. 161
Relates to other "prayer" poems of Dickinson. This poem's "speaker regards as childish her earlier expectation that God responds to all prayers."

ROBINSON, J., *Emily Dickinson,* p. 127
Here the poet "describes praying as a little girl because she had been told to pray and later stopping when she had sufficient imagination to think what it must be like to be on the receiving end of one of her ensuing shopping lists to God."

"I read my sentence steadily" (412)

1978 HECHT, "Riddles," pp. 21–22
The poem "clearly speaks of a mind frighteningly divided, without an external orthodoxy to appeal to or to judge by, the nightmarish solipsism of the lonely who must work out their salvation without help or tradition."
Reprinted: Hecht, *Obbligati,* pp. 113–14

1979 CAMERON, *Lyric Time,* pp. 108–09, 112
In this poem "the wit of the intellectual construction hastens to announce its nonchalance at the 'sentence' of death, but the poem's cavalier railery [*sic*] and its matter-of-fact evenness of tone are belied by the profusion of pronouns and the schism within the self that they imply."
Reprinted: Cameron, *"Et in Arcadia,"* pp 55–56, 58

1982 DONOHOE, "Undeveloped Freight," pp. 43–48
The poet "here confronts the biblical doctrine of Adam's sin and the curse of death thereby laid on man. . . . Assuming that the 'I' is the persona, it is possible to say that 'Him' refers to Adam and 'she' to the soul of the persona."

MARCUS, *Emily Dickinson,* p. 75
Suggests possible interpretations of the poem's "sentence." The poem "provides a bridge between Emily Dickinson's poems about suffering and those about the fear of death . . . ."

1983 ROSENTHAL and GALL, *Modern Poetic Sequence,* pp. 48, 65, 66
The poem "presents an excruciating experience of rejection, couched in courtroom terminology." Considers in relation to the poems that precede and follow it in the poetic sequence of fascicle 15.

1984 KELLER, L., and MILLER, "Rewards of Indirection," p. 549
Here "Dickinson's diction and her manipulation of form draw attention away from the speaker's fear of dying."

WALLACE, *God Be with the Clown,* p. 100
"Both the legal matter . . . and the physical matter . . . end in the tranquil and amiable pun. The little joke comes as a surprise, undercutting the ominous tone with which the poem began."

1985 EBERWEIN, *Dickinson,* pp. 124–25
"Death triumphs here, with the unconscious mind that is its partner in a conspiracy against rational control."

1988 SHIMAZAKI, "'Dare you see,'" pp. 93–94
"In spite of the fact that the speaker is conscious of the duality of existence here, the poet is prudent enough . . . not to speak of the salvation of the soul directly, though it seems the sins committed by the body can be atoned in the soul with the help of God's mercy."

1989 GIBBONS, "Poetry and Self-Making," pp. 108–10
While the poem's "apparent" subject is "that all mortals are condemned to death," its "hidden" subject is the poet's "sense of why she writes."

"I reason earth is short" (301)

1978 TAYLOR, C., "Kierkegaard," pp. 575–76
"Like Ivan [in *The Brothers Karamazov*] Dickinson commingles the extremes of defiance and despair in a voice that exalts the reasoning ego. Its attack is not particularized, but directed against the totality of existence."

1980 MONTEIRO, G., "Dickinson's 'I reason,'" pp. 23–26
Notes "strong similarities—in idea, language, and phrasing" between this poem and an 1873 essay by W. R. Greg. Suggests "there may be profit in reading the texts . . . as if . . . each were a comment on, or an answer to, the other."

1981   EDDINS "Dickinson and Nietzsche," p. 100

The poem's " 'new Equation' represents the mathematics of eternity, a divine algebra by which the apparent chaos and lack of proportion that have rendered earthly existence a panorama of despair are suddenly revealed as part of a cosmic Apollinian [*sic*] structure that our finite vision has not been able to apprehend."

FAST, " 'The One Thing Needful,' " pp. 163–64

This poem "attacks the New England Calvinists' insistence on logical explanations and reassurances by using Calvinist reason to undermine Calvinist faith."

1985   EBERWEIN, *Dickinson*, p. 237

Dickinson's "most logically structured poem . . . demonstrated the failure of reason to buttress dreams of heavenly replenishment. Promised bliss failed to atone for absolute earthly anguish and the inevitability of loss."

1986   MOREY, "Dickinson–Kant: The First Critique," p. 42

Relates to other "poems about symbolism in nature." "The whole cast of the poem is negative, even blasphemous."

1988   MONTEIRO, G., *Robert Frost*, pp. 11-12

Frost's poem "The Birds Do Thus" was "influenced by this poem, and particularly by Dickinson's handling of the theme of death and its aftermath . . . ."

"I reckon when I count at all" (569)

1981   DIEHL, *Romantic Imagination*, pp. 90–91

"She asserts that Grace, freely given, is hardly worth waiting for, but denies the assurance that deeds will be justly rewarded." In this poem "Dickinson assesses her priorities and firmly establishes her own poetic primacy."

KIMPEL, *Dickinson as Philosopher*, pp. 35–37

"That she is using the ideal of poetry, or poetry in a normative sense, in making this list of comparative values can be understood if one thinks of the hierarchy of valued goods which Plato affirms in the *Phaedrus*."

1982   MARCUS, *Emily Dickinson*, pp. 40, 41, 42, 43

General consideration as one of Dickinson's poems on "Poetry, Art, and Imagination."

1984 WOLOSKY, *Emily Dickinson,* pp. 153–54
"This poem is not aestheticist, it is critique. The interest in language for its own sake is a function of lost proximity to the divine. Language is thus not finally defined in relation to itself as a closed, self-contained system."

1987 BARKER, *Lunacy of Light,* pp. 105–06
In this poem Dickinson "made clear her own priorities. . . . Poets are even more important than the sun itself, she asserts, in this list that reads like a ranking of cakes at the state fair."

DI GIUSEPPE, "Maiden and the Muse," pp. 44–45
"Dickinson attributes all power to the poet and all reality to the poem, and there seems to be little room left for God or the father."

SEWALL, "Emily Dickinson," pp. 75–76
The poem is "not so much a rejection of an old theology as it is a song of praise of the good things of this world—the sun, the summer—so good, indeed, that she chooses them over the promises of the preacher."

1988 HARRIS, S., " 'Cloth of Dreams,' " pp. 11–12
"That SHE is writing these words here in the poem emphasizes her power to act and to be 'All' unto herself as Poet."

1989 RICHWELL, "Poetic Immortality," pp. 15–17, 19
"Frankly religious in tone and vocabulary, the poem is a settlement of the rewards and penalties of being a poet." Considers Dickinson's uses of "the image of heaven as a trope for literary recognition."

WILSON, *Figures of Speech,* pp. 232–33, 236
The poem "may be just as much about salvation and eternity as about poets. The key words . . . could, in the end, be the theological terms of the final verse: 'prepare,' 'worship,' 'Grace,' and 'Justify.' "

"I rose because he sank" (616)

1984 GILBERT and GUBAR, "Tradition," pp. 23–24
"Taken as a narrative, Dickinson's poem implies that the deconstruction of male primacy is not necessarily matched by a construction of female potency. Rather, male dis-ease is often balanced by female unease . . . ."
Reprinted: Miller, N. K., *Poetics of Gender,* pp. 204–05; revised and reprinted: Gilbert and Gubar, *No Man's Land,* vol. 1: pp. 67, 172

1987 Di Giuseppe, "Maiden and the Muse," pp. 55–56
The poem illustrates development of the poet's relationship to her Muse.

Finch, "Patriarchal Meter," pp. 171–72
The poem's "metrical development parallels the story told in the poem, of gaining power through the weakness of an anonymous male and then using that power to help him—a story with possible Christian undercurrents."

1988 Martin, W., "Emily Dickinson," p. 621
"In addition to being a direct response to [*Jane Eyre*], this poem describing Jane's increasing strength and control is a paradigm for Emily Dickinson's emotional growth in general."

Phillips, *Emily Dickinson,* pp. 104–07, 228 n. 10
The poem is based on Jane Eyre's love for Rochester.

Wolff, *Emily Dickinson,* pp. 454–56
"Here, the speaker discovers 'Sinew from within,' a power of the verse to resurrect the God-made-man." The poet's "response to God's decline is a remarkable effort to revive Him."

"I saw no way—the heavens were stitched" (378)

1979 Cameron, *Lyric Time,* pp. 8–9, 157
In this poem, "which envisions a leavetaking of the known temporal world, abstraction invests utterance with the foreignness of the venture."
Reprinted in part: Mullane and Wilson, *Nineteenth-Century,* pp. 76, 77

Estes, "Search for Location," p. 211
In this poem "the poet moves 'out upon Circumference' not because of an ecstatic vision which reveals the coherence of all things, but because she has failed and has nowhere else to go." Relates to other "circumference" poems.

Juhasz, "'Undiscovered Continent,'" pp. 94–95
"The outer-spatial vocabulary here . . . with its dramatic exaggerations, grants to the mind an enormous width, depth, height . . . ."
Revised and reprinted: Juhasz, *Undiscovered Continent,* pp. 25–26

"I saw no way—the heavens were stitched"

1980   HOMANS, *Women Writers,* pp. 187–88, 204
"The departure from a dualistic universe takes her 'Beyond the Dip of Bell,' or beyond signification, especially beyond a system of signs with ties to conventional religion, if the bell here is a church bell."
Reprinted: Homans, "Emily Dickinson," pp. 429, 441

1982   SALSKA, *Poetry of the Central Consciousness,* pp. 63, 141–42
"The haunting image offered in [this poem] visualizes the appalling predicament of the mind rent between the alternatives of claustrophobic enclosure within the center and absolute alienation upon circumference."
Revised and reprinted: *Walt Whitman and Emily Dickinson,* pp. 53, 129–30

1983   BUDICK, "Temporal Consciousness," pp. 233–34, 235
". . . immortality exists at the fulcrum moment where the imaginary heaves and bells achieve temporary stasis not before they resume their analogy-making activity, but before they abandon such efforts at symbolic duplication altogether."
Revised and reprinted: Budick, *Emily Dickinson,* pp. 209–10, 224

JUHASZ, *Undiscovered Continent,* pp. 151–53, 166
"Although eternity is not named here, the location to which the speaker comes could be no other place. And yet . . . the 'movement' is entirely mental and happens within what is really only one place, the mind."

1985   EBERWEIN, *Emily Dickinson,* pp. 195–97, 198
The poem "cries out for a chalkboard and a geometry lesson from the poet. To make sense of it, we must visualize the speaker's position along the margin of an exploding circle . . . ."

1986   NEW, "Difficult Writing," pp. 13–15, 18, 21
The poem is "oddly modern, a poem whose images we would like to call surreal, whose isolation we would like to call existential, a poem of a provisional space alien to the nineteenth-century Calvinist universe in which Providence assigns to each his place."

REGUEIRO ELAM, "Haunting of the Self," pp. 91–93, 98, 99 n. 5
"The poem seems to stem from an impasse of interpretation, and repeatedly converges upon that impasse, reopening the space of impossibility."

1989   FRANK, "Dickinson's 'I saw no way,'" pp. 28–29
Suggests interpretations of several of the poem's elements; for example, "Dip of Bell" may refer to the diving bell.

GARBOWSKY, *House without the Door,* pp. 120–21
The poem's speaker "experiences both derealization and depersonalization."

"I see thee better in the dark" (611)

1986 LOVING, *Emily Dickinson,* pp. 50–51
"Though this poem can be read as an apostrophe to a lost lover, its meaning deepens when we see that apostrophe as an expression of self-love."

1988 WOLFF, *Emily Dickinson,* p. 378
The opening lines "are laden with erotic potential," but the poem is "more macabre than ardent."

"I send two sunsets" (308)

1983 WALKER, N., "Humor as Identity," pp. 61–62
The poem expresses Dickinson's "ideal relationship with nature," that of a "comfortable equality."

1986 DORESKI, "'Exchange of Territory,'" pp. 60–61
Relates to poetic sequence of fascicle 27. "Balancing natural and metaphorical sunsets, Dickinson determines not only the restrictiveness of artificial sunsets, but how far she can reasonably extend the metaphor . . . ."

1987 BARKER, *Lunacy of Light,* p. 113
The poem shows that Dickinson "felt a rivalrous superiority to the sun's public world of letters."

"I shall keep singing" (250)

1981 GUTHRIE, "Modest Poet's Tactics," p. 234
In this poem "Dickinson vows that she will be recognized as a poet despite her tardy arrival in 'summer,' long after the other robins will have arrived."

1982 SOULE, "Robin," pp. 70–71
Relates to other "robin" poems.

THOTA, *Emily Dickinson,* p. 83
"Here one can see how Dickinson was walking on the razor's edge by keeping both the English romantics and American neo-classicists at

bay, taken her own line of creative action, which circumstantially happens to coincide with that of the metaphysicals."

"I shall know why, when time is over" (193)

1981 ANDERSON, V., "Disappearance of God," p. 9
"The important point Dickinson is making is that suffering and 'anguish' are at the heart of her own and Christ's experience, and the two are thus bound together; in looking at his experience, she understands her own."

DIEHL, *Romantic Imagination,* pp. 102–03
"The final cry, a Keatsian repetition, signals her despair. Explanations lie beyond the province of the possible; they come too late to assuage her pain."

1984 WALLACE, *God Be with the Clown,* pp. 89–90
"Ostensibly about celestial reconciliation, this poem is structured on the terrible discrepancy between the pain of the moment and the explanation to come."

1985 JOHNSON, *Emily Dickinson,* p. 204 n. 16
Contrasts with " 'Tis one by one the Father counts."

1987 MILLER, C., *Emily Dickinson,* pp. 57, 168
"The speaker proves herself more generous than Christ both in her willingness to accept His refusal to care for her and in her anticipated empathy at His 'woe,' despite His apparent indifference to hers."

"I should have been too glad, I see" (313)

1978 CAMERON, "Loaded Gun," pp. 424–25, 434
"Underlying the dialectic . . . is the generative force of rage, an alternative voice that concludes the poem by disrupting or redefining its established meaning."
Reprinted: Cameron, *Lyric Time,* pp. 63–65, 84; Bloom, H., *Emily Dickinson,* pp. 105–07, 124

1979 BAYM, "God, Father, and Lover," p. 197
"God makes Heaven attractive by making earthly life painful; loss may school the human being into a desire for heaven, but it cannot possibly create love or trust for the schoolmaster."

BENNETT, "Value of Isolation," pp. 46, 47
"This lamb of God is far from satisfied with her good shepherd. If

denying us earthly happiness is God's way of endearing us to the 'Shore beyond,' something is terribly wrong."

HAGENBÜCHLE and SWANN, "Dialectic of Rage," p. 145

Takes issue with Cameron's 1978 interpretation. The poet "expresses in a finely balanced . . . dialectic the truth of an experience made meaningful in terms of that which is beyond experience and a 'beyond' that is, and can only be, realized in language."

1984 WOLOSKY, *Emily Dickinson*, pp. 95–97

"As in other theodicean poems, the poet contrasts the negative terms of penury and fear with the positive terms of gladness, salvation, and joy. And she refuses to integrate the negative terms into the positive ones."

1985 JOHNSON, *Emily Dickinson*, pp. 96–97, 204 n. 18

The poem's voice "seems largely overwhelmed by the suffering itself, and can only faintly assert the heightened insight her loss has produced."

1986 BAKKER, "Emily Dickinson's Secret," p. 347

The poem shows that Dickinson lacked the faith to "understand and accept" the gains of "unbearable loss," and it holds "the secret of her almost total seclusion."

Reprinted: Bunt et al., *One Hundred Years*, p. 245

BENNETT, *Loaded Gun*, pp. 88–89

". . . no poem Dickinson wrote captures more perfectly the heresy that lay at the heart of her vision of love and, therefore, her concept of self as queen of Calvary than this one."

MOREY, "Dickinson-Kant: The First Critique," pp. 51–52, 56

"The religious vocabulary . . . dominates the poem and shifts the poem from any possible lover directly over to God. It is not a blasphemous poem, altho the suffering is immense."

1987 MILLER, C., *Emily Dickinson*, pp. 57–58

Here "the exclamation mark works ironically. . . . Its repeated use contributes to the impression that the voice of the poem is spontaneous and intimate; there is no pretense of decorum or artificial formality here."

1989 DOBSON, *Strategies of Reticence*, pp. 115–18, 124

"The poem read in both extant versions indicates that only a hairline difference exists in the language between the expression of passive acceptance and the articulation of explosive fury."

"I should not dare to leave my friend"

OLIVER, *Apocalypse of Green,* pp. 129–30, 161 n. 52
". . . if the analogy of Christ's suffering on the cross is seen as central to the poem, with the poet's stress on the lesser human reenactment, . . . the two—the earthly circuit and the heavenly circumference—can be seen as necessarily complementary."

"I should not dare to leave my friend" (205)

1981 KIMPEL, *Dickinson as Philosopher,* pp. 102–05
"Her interpretation of such a normative version of loyalty parallels the interpretation which Josiah Royce affirms in *The Philosophy of Loyalty . . . .*"

1984 ALLARD, "Regulation of Belief," pp. 36–38
This poem "is a prime example of the mechanism Dickinson employs to capture the intensity of feeling in death's presence."

"I showed her heights she never saw" (446)

1978 FRANKLIN, "Three Additional," pp. 111–13
Description of manuscript found after variorum edition was published that completes the already known packet version beginning "He showed me Hights I never saw."

"I sometimes drop it, for a quick" (708)

1986 ROBINSON, J., *Emily Dickinson,* pp. 133–35
"It is wholly characteristic of Emily Dickinson in declaring the superiority of knowledge . . . over experience . . . but it is also characteristic of her to make this knowledge part of the experience."

"I started early, took my dog" (520)

1972 RAO, *Essential Emily Dickinson,* p. 66
The poem illustrates Dickinson's "romantic sensibility and her fundamental romantic attitudes to Nature and childhood."

1978 CARTON, "Dickinson and the Divine," p. 247
"In her successful flight . . . she not only has escaped violation but also has retreated from the sea's imperial realm and from its offer of precious metals and gems, symbols of eternity's splendor."
Reprinted: Carton, *Rhetoric,* pp. 53–54

EITNER, "Another Daphne?" pp. 35–39
Suggests the myth of Dapne offers "a rewarding parallel" to this poem.

1979   KAPLAN, "Indefinite Disclosed," pp. 76–77
"Because both sex and death are incorporated in the sea as symbol, . . . and because the dreamer's desire in relation to this lover-destroyer is also unstable, the mermaids and the frigate act as displacing images to decoy the reader away from the more erotic and unnerving implications of the poem . . . ."
Reprinted: Kaplan, *Sea Changes,* pp. 113–14

WINTHER, "Editing Emily Dickinson," pp. 32–33, 36
Notes effect of capital letters and dashes.

1981   STEINER, "Image Patterns," p. 68
"The pattern of [this poem] is based on the dichotomy of the mighty 'Tide' . . . which follows and threatens to rape the humble and frightened 'Mouse'. . . . The girl's identity is eventually restored and asserted when the gentleman withdraws voluntarily."

1982   FAULKNER, "Emily Dickinson," p. 809
The poem is characteristic of Dickinson "in its treatment of nature, although uncharacteristic in the romantic venturing forth of the persona."

MADIGAN, "Mermaids," pp. 52–56
"Love and death seem to swallow up the individual, reduce him to a 'drop,' yet the same individual will be constantly tempted to risk all in the search for greater knowledge, knowledge that might only be gained through ultimate loss of identity."

MARCUS, *Emily Dickinson,* pp. 51–52, 54, 55, 57
"The coy tone of the poet suggests that she may be taking refuge from a symbolic experience involving combined sexual attraction and threat by adopting a childlike attitude."

SALSKA, *Poetry of the Central Consciousness,* pp. 92–94
"The speaker's triumph in this poem is by no means final as the 'mighty look' sent by the sea at parting indicates. It is an achievement in a single confrontation (i.e., a single poem) and more encounters must be expected."
Revised and reprinted: Salska, *Walt Whitman and Emily Dickinson,* pp. 81–82, 140–41; Salska, "Emily Dickinson's Lover," pp. 138–39

1983   SHURR, Marriage, pp. 19–20
The poem "becomes a fairly clear allegory if the passionate male

"I started early, took my dog"

'sea' pursues the not entirely unwilling damsel all the way up to 'the Solid Town'—and then withdraws his pursuit when ethical bounds and social *mores* impede."

1984 CHERRY, "Sexuality and Tension," pp. 13–14
"The unboundedness of nature and sexuality are enticements which civilization, based on limitations, must deny for its stable continuance. Fantasy must be rejected for the sake of solidity."

WALLACE, *God Be with the Clown,* pp. 79–81
Compares with Whitman's "You sea! I resign myself to you also." Both poets "have had a sexual experience with the sea, they have gone beyond the narrow confines of the town with its conventional morality and security, and they have confronted elemental forces . . . ."

WILT, "Playing House," pp. 154–55
Considers as one of the "scores of highly charged lyrics" in which "the poet confronts the house she is before, or within, or has become." Here the poet's visit "is as to a house."

1985 ANANTHARAMAN, *Sunset in a Cup,* pp. 74, 77–79
"The poem's strength lies in the fact that it can accommodate all contradictory interpretations regarding its theme, and at the same time remain superbly dramatic and highly symbolic."

SWENSON, "Big My Secret," pp. 19–20
"The poem has the aura of a vivid dream. . . . It may also be a disguised love poem."

1986 FLETCHER, "Poetry, Gender," pp. 109, 134–38, 139
This poem and poems by Elizabeth Barrett Browning and Blake are examined "in order to disclose the way they work and rework fantasies that bear on sexual difference and desire."

POLLAK, "Second Act," pp. 165–67
"At the heart of the poem's insight into the complex relationship between risk and maturation lies a thanatized vision of love and an eroticized vision of death . . . ."
Revised and reprinted: Pollak, *Dickinson,* pp. 114–18

1987 BARKER, *Lunacy of Light,* pp. 115, 202 n. 22
This is "another poem about the 'Flood Subject,' immortality, and the workings of the imagination. . . . In many ways [it] seems to be about the comings and goings of the muse, the 'floods' and tides of writing fever."

MILLER, C., *Emily Dickinson,* pp. 58, 73–77
The poet's "combination of differing verb tense and mood in this narrative remove it from any simple, temporal context."

MOREY, "Dickinson–Kant II," pp. 21–22
"The abruptness and foreign novelty are too much for the speaker: psychologically she cannot cope with the new stage of life, puberty."

1988 STOCKS, *Modern Consciousness,* pp. 85–87
"If the relics of childhood are still present though transcended in the poem, that only adds to the poem's profound insight, expressing an abiding reality of the human consciousness."

1989 KNAPP, *Emily Dickinson,* pp. 70–74
"To be wary of the Tide, in any form, suggests the shifting nature of what excites and entices, the continuous dangers awaiting those whose vision is either undeveloped or veiled." Line-by-line commentary on poem's images.

"I stepped from plank to plank" (875)

1979 ESTES, "Search for Location," p. 214
"Related to the inability to discern a trustworthy order in life is Dickinson's apprehension about what the future holds." This poem expresses her fear of "where the next step on the journey leads."

JUHASZ, " 'Undiscovered Continent,' " p. 94
"Internal space is the setting for this adventure, and the poem specifically identifies the exploration that has brought her there as the quest for experience."
Reprinted: Juhasz, *Undiscovered Continent,* p. 25

1984 MARTIN, W., *American Triptych,* pp. 119–20
"Unlike Shelley, Wordsworth, and Keats, she does not use images of flight and escape from earthly restraints but as this poem reveals she proceeds cautiously and is connected to her actual experience, however perilous it seems to be."

1985 JOHNSON, *Emily Dickinson,* pp. 22, 192 n. 17
The poem "speaks explicitly of experience in terms of her quest and its progress. . . . Yet it is experience of a specially refined, purposeful kind, almost entirely inward."

1988   WOLFF, *Emily Dickinson*, pp. 478–79
The poem's "linguistic patterns . . . so clearly echo Dickinson's earlier works that they reveal her keen awareness of the poetic transformation that is taking place."

1989   GARBOWSKY, *House without the Door*, p. 121
The poem exhibits "*macropsia,* another facet of derealization, in which the individual perceives his or her surroundings as enlarged and near."

"I suppose the time will come" (1381)

1981   KIMPEL, *Dickinson as Philosopher*, pp. 119–20
Considers "the aspect of moral obligation" that the poem affirms.

"I taste a liquor never brewed" (214)

1972   RAO, *Essential Emily Dickinson*, pp. 115–17
General introduction to the poem aimed at "postgraduate students of literature in Indian Universities."

1978   CODY, "Dickinson's 'I taste,' " pp. 7–8
Reviews other interpretations of the poem's "tankards" and suggests that here the word refers to lungs.

PEARCE, "Bards and the Bees," pp. 293–94
Third stanza's image of the bee in the foxglove flower has its source in Keats.

1979   KELLER, K., *Only Kangaroo*, pp. 31, 150 n. 3, 155, 157, 159, 198
"Her drunk poet . . . is not at all an Emerson intellectual speaking wildly but, oxymoronically and humorously, a drunk Congregationalist, a *religious* drunk; the pure transcendental mind and chaste transcendental body have become by worldly standards debauched and by heavenly ones heretical."

1982   MARCUS, *Emily Dickinson*, pp. 26–27, 28
Stanza-by-stanza discussion. Here "Dickinson describes an intoxicated unity of self and nature without the alienation that haunts some of her other nature poems."

OLPIN, "Hyperbole: Part One," pp. 20–21
"The final line that places the 'Tippler' in the cosmos and leans him against the sun is a specific type of hyperbole that occurs again and again in frontier humor."

SALSKA, *Poetry of the Central Consciousness,* p. 58

The poem "establishes the self as essentially alien to nature, though subject to moods of longing for the mystic communion."

Revised and reprinted: Salska, *Walt Whitman and Emily Dickinson,* p. 48

1983   JUHASZ, *Undiscovered Continent,* pp. 106–08, 109, 115, 183 n. 7

". . . her intoxication is more than fun; it is also a sign of power. In this poem, lack of control, diminutive stature, are coyly representative of their opposites, as the final audacious image . . . indicates."

1985   BUDICK, *Emily Dickinson,* pp. 9–10

"For all the ecstasy of [this poem], there is a disruption of rhythm and a slightly slurring excess that, though not refuting the poet's giddy love of nature, do suggest how easily innocent intoxication with the physical world can turn into genuine chaos-producing bloat."

DALKE, " 'Devil's Wine,' " pp. 78–80

"The union with nature which Dickinson embraces throughout the poem leads, not to a union with an orthodox God, but to a division from Him." It is clear "that her idea of heaven is decidedly this-worldly."

MONTEIRO, G., "Manzanilla," pp. 16–17

Suggests that "Manzanilla" here refers to "chamomile the plant and especially to the tea brewed from that plant."

RASHID, "Voice of Endings," pp. 26–27

"Dickinson's willingness to entertain the possibility of unlimited joy is undercut by the reality of her experience. Nature, to which she turned for metaphors of permanent ecstasy, constantly proved the opposite . . . ."

1986   HURLEY, "Waiting for the Other Shoe," pp. 131–32, 134–35

Discussion of the nature and effect of poem's rhymes.

ROBINSON, J., *Emily Dickinson,* p. 163

"It is not a poem whose gaiety will be patient of the gravity of Calvinist divines, nor of the textual attentions of literary critics . . . but it is worth observing that . . . *she* is the centre of interest."

1987   COOPER, M. F., "Androgynous Temper," p. 142

"It seems to me the inns are a directional indicator pointing to her inner self—but are also used in the more denotative definition of a hotel. . . . She has become debauched, it appears, in the inns of nature's court."

1988 MOREY, "Dickinson-Kant III," pp. 13–14, 15, 34
"After the first half of the poem has depicted the present feeling, Dickinson lets the last half predict the future, how she intends to devote her life to the ingestion of beauty, even pass the prescribed limits . . . ."

1989 CADMAN, "Dickinson's 'I taste,'" pp. 30–32
If the poem's "speaker is the daisy, then the link between the language of the meadow and that of the tavern becomes clear, and the poem itself becomes a record of the flower through the seasons."

OBERHAUS, "Dickinson as Comic Poet," pp. 118, 119, 122
The poem "demonstrates Dickinson's comic spirit while illustrating comic themes, strategies, and figures."

"I tend my flowers for thee" (339)

1979 BUDICK, "Assignable Portion," pp. 1, 6–7, 9, 13
The poem is "a symbolic, allegorical drama in which the material flora of the natural world represents the poet's immaterial, heavenly soul. The consequences of the poet-gardener's idealist inclinations are anything but encouraging."
Revised and reprinted: Budick, *Emily Dickinson*, pp. 67–69, 70, 117, 118, 126, 168, 173

PATTERSON, *Dickinson's Imagery*, pp. 47, 81, 107, 134, 212 n. 13
Considers poem's use of botanical figures and notes that it borrows from Robert Browning and possibly Elizabeth Barrett Browning.

1983 SHURR, *Marriage*, pp. 21–22, 76
"It seems excessively naive to read these lines as a simple report on how her flowers are growing . . . ." Notes the "surprising frankness" with which the "erotic details of the bee-flower convention are explored."

1984 MARTIN, W., *American Triptych*, pp. 156–57
Links with other instances of flower imagery in Dickinson's poems that illuminate "her evolution from passive, dependent femininity to autonomous womanhood."

1986 HUGHES, G., "Subverting the Cult," pp. 19–20, 21, 22
". . . from the poem's dutiful opening stanza, through its erotic progression, to its final disclaimer, Dickinson is specifically satirizing a humiliation that she knew well but did not necessarily applaud—the humiliation of control-by-deprivation."

1988 HARRIS, S., "'Cloth of Dreams,'" p. 11
"What is particularly confusing in this poem, which suggests both

allurement and rape, is that 'Her Lord' is away; he is endowed with an almost omniscient ability to violate her dream state thru a silence of removal."

"I think I was enchanted" (593)

1980   PORTERFIELD, *Feminine Spirituality,* pp. 145–46
"In this poem, the art of black magic initiates a somber girl to the powers of womanhood."

1981   EDDINS, "Dickinson and Nietzsche," pp. 104–05
"This poem is an apotheosis of the Dionysian mode in her poetry."

1983   GILBERT, "Wayward Nun," pp. 27, 35–36, 37
In this poem, which lists "a series of witty transformations through which the common becomes the uncommon, the daily the divine," Dickinson tells us that "this transformation of the ordinary into the extraordinary is a bewitching female art she actually learned from Elizabeth Barrett Browning."

1986   DIEHL, "Twilight of the Gods," pp. 185–87
When "the external transformative power is perceived as feminine, the relationship between Dickinson and the Other momentarily frees itself from the corporeal anxieties that customarily mark such confrontations."

1987   BARKER, *Lunacy of Light,* pp. 99–101
Here Dickinson reveals how "such successful literary women as Elizabeth Barrett Browning and Charlotte Brontë . . . enabled her to find a literary tradition of her own and a deity of her own in the only room of her own she could imagine: the 'feminine' darkness."

MILLER, C., *Emily Dickinson,* pp. 164–65
"Dickinson's description of the 'Magic' that saves her as 'Witchcraft' underlines the gender identification in the poem."

1989   GILMORE, "Gaze of the Other Woman," pp. 83–84, 91–94, 97, 98, 99, 100, 101
Examination of what the poem reveals about "poetic engendering, inspiration, and the limits of narrative."

"I think just how my shape will rise" (237)

1979   PATTERSON, *Dickinson's Imagery,* p. 22
The poem "uses religious language so boldly as to suggest that she may be addressing God himself. A closer look shows that she is praying

to be *'forgiven'* by a godlike lover, to 'rise' into a human heaven, and to be considered the 'Sparrow' of this god's care."

1983   SHURR, *Marriage,* pp. 32, 71, 145–46, 192
The poem responds to words from Wadsworth's sermonizing. In the context of the fascicles, the "you" of lines 7 and 8 "is surely the beloved and the poem as a whole is a love poem addressed to him."

1985   BUDICK, *Emily Dickinson,* p. 73
"Divine forgiveness is not God's attempt to remake the individual, but His effort to unmake him. The poet, therefore, must come to understand that she will ascend to heaven only when she allows her heart to plummet to earth 'unshriven,' unforgiven and therefore untransformed."

EBERWEIN, *Dickinson,* pp. 235–36
"No sin is mentioned here, nor is there evidence even of unfocused guilt. The notion of forgiveness has been transmitted to her without its moral context. So has the spatial concept of heaven been imposed on her."

1988   WOLFF, *Emily Dickinson,* pp. 281–82
"Our only recourse is to turn God's methods back upon Himself, matching rage to primitive rage."

1989   OLIVER, *Apocalypse of Green,* pp. 137–39, 232
"She is frustrated, surely, by her inability to image an afterlife in terms of the experiences of this life, but this frustration must yield, not to rage, but to her 'long bright—and longer—trusting./'"

"I think the longest hour of all" (635)

1981   PORTER, *Dickinson,* p. 66
"We are not sure of the setting or the occasion or why the speaker is there or what her removal 'further North' portends. The lines are tense with pseudo-significance, the consequences crucial and yet we can't say what they are or why they have come about."

1983   SIMPSON, "Dependent Self," p. 40
The poem "gives a markedly Poesque treatment of this paradox of oppressive joy in greeting friends."

"I think to live may be a bliss" (646)

1986   JUHASZ, "Renunciation Transformed," pp. 258–61
"By placing the speaker initially in a state of renunciation and end-

ing there again, this poem not only reveals the nature of the transformation required but something, as well, about the process by which renunciation is transformed."

McNEIL, *Emily Dickinson*, pp. 12, 17–19
The poem ends "without clarifying whether 'Thee' is God, or a person, or both, or another fiction. 'Thee' is whatever would give the mind whatever the mind desires."

ROBINSON, J., *Emily Dickinson*, pp. 94–95
In this love poem the poet says "she can envisage a life . . . which 'may be a Bliss' and it becomes the more persuasive the more she thinks about it until it actually takes the place of what she has previously known."

1988   HARRIS, S., " 'Cloth of Dreams,' " pp. 5, 7, 16 n. 8
"The poet-dreamer who can no longer 'conceive' . . . loses not only the key to her creative imagination but perhaps even to a definition of her own existence." Reviews critical interpretation of the poem's "dream."

WOLOSKY, "Rhetoric or Not," pp. 229–32
In this poem "Dickinson restructures hymnal modes and tropes she borrows from Watts, clearly intending to subvert his doctrinal assertions. She then . . . proceeds to subvert her own subversions. . . ."

1989   FULTON, "Moment of Brocade," pp. 25–26
The poem's voice "uses negative definition to imagine a fuller life than the one currently known. In this poem . . . the speaker and her work are stymied, lacking the power to live and the power to die."

"I thought that nature was enough" (1286)

1979   PATTERSON, *Dickinson's Imagery*, pp. 99, 216–17 n. 8
Considers use of astronomical terms. "If the order of the sense is that flame absorbs parallax (firmament), then she may be saying that the great flame of these human suns annihilates the vast distances between them."

1984   BENFEY, *Problem of Others*, pp. 17–18, 51–52
"Dickinson wants to suggest . . . . a relation of reciprocity between container and contained: the contents, the 'other,' answer to (are responsive to) the capacity of the container."

"I thought the train would never come" (1449)

1983 SHURR, *Marriage,* pp. 159–60
The poem refers to Wadsworth's arrival by train.

1985 BRASHEAR, "Dramatic Monologues," p. 71
Discussion of "Dickinson's virtuoso development of her own kind of dramatic monologue."

"I tie my hat, I crease my shawl" (443)

1978 CAMERON, " 'Loaded Gun,' " pp. 431, 434
Here "life is represented as fury coming to terms with sexuality, and both are subject to the efforts of repression."
Reprinted: Cameron, *Lyric Time,* pp. 45, 46, 76–78, 83, 84; Bloom, H., *Emily Dickinson,* pp. 117–18, 124

1979 PATTERSON, *Dickinson's Imagery,* pp. 98, 111–12, 147, 216 n. 7
In the poem "she speaks of the trivial duties that must be done even though 'Existence' has effectually ended. . . . She remains in firm control of her poem, choosing figures that, far from exaggerating, seem to understate her dilemma.

1980 FRANKLIN, "Houghton Library," pp. 245–57
Examination of manuscripts indicates that lines included in Johnson version of this poem properly belong to "A pit but heaven over it."

1981 STEINER, "Image Patterns," p. 68
This poem ridicules "the woman's daily activities in the house." "The rebel woman mocks the seriousness with which the housewife performs her 'little duties,'. . ."

1982 MOSSBERG, *Emily Dickinson,* pp. 196–98, 209 n. 13
The poem "encapsulates her attitudes as a poet and her consciousness of her needs as a woman and poet."

1984 POLLAK, *Dickinson,* pp. 202–06
"Her subjective morbidity cannot be arrested by her objective perception that she is still capable of performing trivial tasks. Subjectively, time is meaningless to her; objectively, it continues to organize her behavior."

1985 PHILIP, "Valley News," pp. 63–65
"What is really being challenged is that whole network of theolog-

ical assumptions which had underpinned New England life from its Puritan origins . . . : the assertion of God as an unknowable but infinite power; the subjugations of women to men; etc."

1986 ROBINSON, J., *Emily Dickinson,* pp. 96–99, 171
"What is unusual . . . about this poem is that it allows us a sight of Emily Dickinson presenting herself to the eyes of other people and sustaining herself by the fact of that observation."

1988 DICKIE, "Discontinuous Lyric Self," pp. 545–57, 550–51, 552
This is "a poem about a life in which control is the only meaning and meaning the only control." It is "not about loss but about the refusal to give up loss."

TRIPP, *Mysterious Kingdom,* pp. 60–63
The poem focuses on "the trials of living one's dharma out."

UNO, "Optical Instruments," pp. 238–40
"In this poem we can see that Dickinson's fear that the inner world would be looked into is surely connected with the development of science, particularly the telescope."

1989 GARBOWSKY, *House without the Door,* pp. 125–26, 127–28
"The speaker's admission that the bomb is calm now reveals that the panic attacks are in remission, and although the bomb is still intact, she is in a state of relative ease, trying to appear normal."

"I took my power in my hand" (540)

1982 SALSKA, *Poetry of the Central Consciousness,* pp. 67, 98, 148
The poem "is an explanation of the core of her poetry: poems are battles between the poet and those larger powers against which creativity measures itself in order to make an experience meaningful."
Revised and reprinted: Salska, *Walt Whitman and Emily Dickinson,* pp. 57, 86–87, 135

1985 FITZGERALD, "Dickinson's 'I took my power,'" pp. 20–21
Suggests the poem's "power" may refer to her poetic talent; "it was her pen she let fly."

1986 POLLAK, "Second Act," p. 163
"Out of this self-critical dialogue between arrogance and humility, a third voice emerges: the voice of the poet mediating this conflict through language which calls attention to the instability of its ironic mode."

"I took one draught of life" (1725)

1989 OLIVER, *Apocalypse of Green,* pp. 145–46
The poem's theme seems to be "the costliness of Heaven. Here the use of the images from business makes the attainment of heaven seem perhaps a too business-like transaction, ignoring completely the element of love."

"I tried to think a lonelier thing" (532)

1983 SHURR, *Marriage,* p. 89
"Her sense of alienation and abandonment begets, it seems, the presence of 'Horror's Twin'—another person equally guilt-ridden and abandoned. . . . They are linked by their spiritual guilt—but it is precisely that guilt that forbids communication."

1985 BUDICK, *Emily Dickinson,* pp. 158–59
The poem's narrator discovers "that mental solipsism is no anti-dote for the dangers and tensions of mortality. When the mind, in its own self-circumscribing seclusion, looks out on death . . . it sees only an end-less repetition of the very same cycle of living and dying that the mind had hoped it could evade."

EBERWEIN, *Dickinson,* pp. 55, 57
This revealing poem demonstrates "how intensively Dickinson meditated on the isolation she regarded both as her troubling distinction from the rest of humanity and as an artistic resource."

1986 ROBINSON, J., *Emily Dickinson,* pp. 57, 107–08
"The pleasurable, if desperate, vigour of the lines has more to do with breaking a taboo and crossing into the extraordinary than it has with the protracted enduring of misery."

1987 COOPER, M. F., "Androgynous Temper," pp. 144–45
In this poem "she looks for her own duplicate and also comes up with something distinctly male. . . . the poem rests on a potential empa-thy between the poet's persona and the male figure who is her twin."

" 'I want'—it pleaded all its life" (731)

1986 GILBERT, "American Sexual Poetics," pp. 148–49
"Her slight, two-stanza-long encounter with 'its' assimilation into 'Eternity' occurs in a setting of absence, blankness: the little that the poet

speaks about death as an event is spoken nowhere and for nobody, in an atmosphere of bleak skepticism . . . ."

"I was a phoebe, nothing more" (1009)

1983   MOSSBERG, "Nursery Rhymes," pp. 55, 56, 57
"Her dwelling on her small size does not reflect her physical or psychological reality, so much as her conscious *choice* to be 'little,' to play along with society's view of her insignificance and turn it to her own advantage."

1984   POLLAK, *Dickinson*, pp. 231–32
"The singing bird is a conventional romantic emblem of the artist's harmonious relationship to nature's text, but the punishment motif, together with the emphasis on abstinent marginality . . . is specifically Dickinsonian."

"I was the slightest in the house" (486)

1981   KIMPEL, *Dickinson as Philosopher*, pp. 27–28
"This poem is a condensed description of a way of living which may be universalized, as the description may also be of the meaning of the Cross. . . . [It] confronts one with the fact that spiritual achievements have come about only upon the most demanding conditions of personal sacrifice."

MILLER, MARTHA, "Parallels," pp. 4–5
Notes similarity to poem by Rosalia de Castro. "Here the speaker's childlike posture and everyday tone contrast sharply with the seriousness of the thought contained in the last line . . . ."

1986   SINGLEY, "Reaching Lonely Heights," pp. 77–78
Notes "uncanny parallels" to Sarah Orne Jewett's story "A White Heron."

1987   LEDER and ABBOTT, *Language of Exclusion*, p. 152
Here "Dickinson exalts her poverty of person, both in her pride at small stature and her identification with small, unnoticed, weak objects."

1989   FULTON, "Moment of Brocade," p. 24
"Although the poem equates obscurity with integrity, in the last stanza the speaker realizes that because of her awkward ethics she might have no posthumous literary existence."

"I watched the moon around the house"

MUNK, "Musicians Wrestle," pp. 13–14
"Dickinson's poem is . . . a partial reconstruction of the biblical and of the classical myths of immaculate conception."

"I watched the moon around the house" (629)

1982   MOSSBERG, *Emily Dickinson,* pp. 145–46, 150
". . . the self-absorbed poet is defining the moon in terms of herself, projecting upon that orb all that she, by sharp contrast, is not . . . ."

1983   KNIGHTS, "Defining the Self," pp. 369, 370–71
In this poem "not only does the mind find objective forms for deep-seated attitudes, but the contemplation of those forms has played a necessary part in the discovery of what is in the mind: subject and object form an indissoluble whole."

1989   DIEHL, "Murderous Poetics," pp. 329–30
". . . Dickinson observes the female moon, who has gained her freedom at a price too high for the living woman to pay."

"I went to heaven" (374)

1979   PATTERSON, *Dickinson's Imagery,* pp. 52, 53, 82–83
Notes possible source known to her referring to "a Talmudic story that Noah's ark was lit . . . by a single great ruby; . . . her intimate little heaven may well share the symbolism of the protective ark."

1984   OLPIN, "Hyperbole: Part II," pp. 11–12
". . . the central irony of the poem is not found in the clash between the homely image of the town in juxtaposition to the 'Ruby' heaven, but rather in the irony directed at what in the final analysis is a very insubstantial heaven."

1988   WEISSMAN, " 'Transport's Working Classes,' " pp. 409–10
"The combination of the glowing ruby and the forms of downy softness produces a very strange picture of Heaven—but a startlingly graphic description of the female genitals. . . . The rereading suggests that Dickinson has found an alternative and available 'Heaven' in her own body."

"I worked for chaff and earning wheat" (1269)

1978   DOWNEY, "Antithesis," pp. 14–15
Examines poem's use of the chiasmus, here formed by "juxtaposition of meaning."

"I would not paint a picture" (505)

1978 DIEHL, " 'Come Slowly,' " p. 577
"Here language reflects the pull of attraction and terror that informs Dickinson's view of independence as a poet and the dangers attendant on creative self-sufficiency."
Revised and reprinted: Diehl, *Romantic Imagination,* pp. 19–20, 127–28

1984 CHERRY, "Sexuality and Tension," pp. 15–16
Focuses on final stanza. "She knows the power of language and of being a poet and will not give it up to be merely the passive reader or the passive housewife."

1985 CARTON, *Rhetoric,* pp. 43–44
"Artistic success and self-annihilation are bound, here, in an unhappy and unconsummated marriage."

EBERWEIN, *Dickinson,* pp. 192–93
"When the speaker of this poem disavows her aspiration to be a poet, it is because she has come to regard poetry in superhuman terms exciting awe and reverence."

1986 JUHASZ, "Writing Doubly," pp. 7, 8, 11–13, 14
In this poem "about the power of the poet, we encounter consummate ambiguity, occasioned by a tension between conflicting definitions of the poet and even the role of poetry."

McNEIL, *Emily Dickinson,* pp. 102–03
"This terminology of audience is unmitigatedly feminine; adoring another, but 'impotent' oneself, content to 'revere' the (poetic) license given to others without a hint of any desire of one's own."

MERMIN, "Damsel, Knight," pp. 78–79
"Being both poet and audience, both subject and object, would mean turning eroticism and aggression inward: both to marry ('dower') and to 'stun' oneself, to be 'impotent' and yet to wield the tools ('bolts') of violence—and to wield them against oneself."

1987 MILLER, C., *Emily Dickinson,* pp. 97–98, 128–29, 178
The poem's subject: the "special joy of being ravished by one's own creativity." "In its balance of giving and receiving . . . poetry feels indistinguishable from love: both demand full engagement and offer ultimate expression or release."

1988 DICKIE, "Discontinuous Lyric Self," pp. 548–50, 551, 552
"The supposed person that Dickinson might have called the rep-

resentative of this verse is less a person than the power of supposition."

MOREY, "Dickinson–Kant III," pp. 31, 32

The poem "concerns composition, or more exactly, not composing but imagining how someone else would translate the object into art. Imagining the nerve endings in the artist, the composer, or the poet would be better than creating the masterpiece."

WOLFF, *Emily Dickinson,* pp. 170, 171–74, 184, 313

This is "a superbly controlled, subtly complex examination of the plight of woman-as-poet." Here Dickinson postulates "a correlative female power of physical fecundity to match the man's literal potency . . . ."

1989 RICHWELL, "Poetic Immortality," pp. 6–7, 13

Links to other poems in which Dickinson relates her "affirmations of womanhood and her statements about poetic immortality."

"I years had been from home" (609)

1982 MOSSBERG, *Emily Dickinson,* pp. 154, 207 n. 16

The poem "does not describe an attitude towards a specific house; rather it outlines a renunciation strategy in which a long-denied fulfillment is renounced."

NIGRO, "Imp of the Perverse," pp. 7–8

"The poem is a distinctive variation of a recurrent theme in Dickinson's canon: the retreat from a figurative, and in this case a literal, threshhold [*sic*] that leaves the person estranged."

1984 WILT, "Playing House," pp. 157–58

Considers as one of the "scores of highly charged lyrics" in which "the poet confronts the house she is before, or within, or has become."

1985 ANANTHARAMAN, *Sunset in a Cup,* pp. 111, 112–16

"Even in a mood of despair and terrorised by the dictates of the scriptural notations, Emily does not demand that God, the owner of the house here, should give her grace and confidence that she needs for her salvation."

"I'd rather recollect a setting" (1349)

1981 KIMPEL, *Dickinson as Philosopher,* pp. 272–73

Considers poem as evidence that Dickinson's "complex nature included a 'Stoical' element."

1986 ROBINSON, J., *Emily Dickinson,* pp. 21–22

The poem is "a useful shorthand guide to her work." The poet "challenges the idea of having objectives and seeking to reach them, of judging life by targets which are or are not attained."

"If any sink, assure that this, now standing" (358)

1984 WOLOSKY, *Emily Dickinson,* pp. 87–88, 95

"The only justification for death in war is that it precludes more murder. This ironic theodicy is the very best that can be said of war."

Revised and reprinted: Wolosky, "Dickinson's War Poetry," pp. 39–40

1989 OLIVER, *Apocalypse of Green,* p. 66

Here Dickinson "compares the fear of death and death itself to the approach and penetration of a shot from a firearm. The fear lies in the anticipation; death itself is self-defeating . . . ."

"If he dissolve, then there is nothing more" (236)

1979 PATTERSON, *Dickinson's Imagery,* pp. 22, 41, 43, 98, 127, 135, 161, 186–87, 197

The poem's "'*Faint* Star of Bethlehem' . . . may be her hope or the defaulting lover or both."

1986 BENNETT, *Loaded Gun,* pp. 49, 77

In this "truly awful" poem, "Dickinson writes from the position of a woman whose womanhood and womanly power can only be confirmed through the presence and love of a man."

1989 OLIVER, *Apocalypse of Green,* pp. 82–83, 95 n. 45

"Whether the poem indeed expresses religious concerns or more secular thoughts, the words and images . . . pose the question of the possibility that death can be equated with nothingness."

"If I can stop one heart from breaking" (919)

1986 GILBERT, "American Sexual Politics," pp. 141–42

Relates to Whitman's "O Captain! My Captain!" ". . . in their flirtations with convention the two poems are telling, for they suggest relationships between genre and gender that are, paradoxically enough, deeply embedded in the 'not poetry' for which their authors became famous."

1987 SEWALL, "Emily Dickinson," p. 82
This poem "shows the Orphic in her—the impulse to alert people to sights, sounds, feelings—blended with a liberal amount of Puritan didacticism and outreach, too much, perhaps, for our sensibilities . . . ."

1989 DOBSON, *Strategies of Reticence,* pp. 91–92
"Although it is one of the very few in all her canon of 1,775 poems that express any overall concern for the needy, it is so non-specific as to be unconvincing."

"If I could tell how glad I was" (1668)

1986 STONUM, "Calculated Sublime," pp. 115–16
"The dilemma here is the familiar choice between eternity, apparently the source or destination of gladness, and selfhood, here identified with force, mathematics, and language."

"If I may have it when it's dead" (577)

1983 HOMANS, "'Oh, Vision,'" pp. 126–27, 128
"The signs made here have no identifiable content separate from the fact of sign-making itself, nor need they have. Language here signifies only its own process, without difference. Simply to communicate with the dead, to make signs and be noticed . . . is what is desired."

ROSENTHAL and GALL, *Modern Poetic Sequence,* pp. 57, 60, 63–65, 66, 69
Considers in relation to the poems that precede and follow it in the poetic sequence of fascicle 15.

1986 BURBICK, "Economics of Desire," pp. 373–74
"For the fulfillment of desire, death is required. A middle space between earth and Paradise, the grave becomes a sanctioned meeting place for love. Celestial love in this bizarre poem is undone by the materiality of the body."

1987 MILLER, C., *Emily Dickinson,* pp. 81–82
Examines poem's "it," which is "both personal and impersonal, and . . . collapses the distinction of 'this' and 'that.'"

1988 OAKES, "Welcome and Beware," pp. 190–92, 205 n. 20
Examines relationship of the poem's speaker to the masculine reader. "We learn from this speaker that reading as a masculine, desiring other can result in death."

WOLFF, *Emily Dickinson,* pp. 378–79, 588 n. 1
"Neither Dickinson nor her speaker, we must suppose, actually wanted the lover's dead body; what *is* at stake is the ability to present a vision of the afterworld to him—some preparation for the ordeal he is destined to encounter."

1989   DIEHL, "Murderous Poetics," pp. 328–29
"Religious terms vie with the secular as the poet apologizes for not embracing an orthodox 'paradise' rather than the corpse; but that other, be he 'it,' male lover, father, Christ, or Master, finally becomes the object of desire who must be subsumed."

"If I should cease to bring a rose" (56)

1989   OLIVER, *Apocalypse of Green,* p. 78
The poem "reveals the imperfection of the analogy between death in nature and human death, a difference which makes nature sometimes seem a doubtful analogue for life after death."

"If I should die" (54)

1984   WALLACE, *God Be with the Clown,* p. 22
In this "serious poem about mortality and loss, an unexpected word keeps solemnity and pain off-balance. . . . 'Gurgle' plays the role of clown here, disrupting any pretensions of undue solemnity."

1987   BARKER, *Lunacy of Light,* pp. 64–65
Discusses poem's "underlying sarcasm" and the difference between the poem's "apparent and intended" meanings.

LEDER and ABBOT, *Language of Exclusion,* pp. 141, 143–44, 145, 146
Considers this as one poem in "a sequence of poems concerning risk, loss, death. . . . All of them link aspects of modern male power positions—brokers, bankers, factory owners—with God-like qualities, excluding the feminine narrator who then has refuge only in sarcasm . . . or supplication . . . ."

"If I shouldn't be alive" (182)

1972   RAO, *Essential Emily Dickinson,* p. 115
General introduction to the poem aimed at "postgraduate students of literature in Indian Universities."

"If my bark sink"

1981 DIEHL, *Romantic Imagination*, p. 47
"The struggle of the granite lip to speak after death acknowledges the effort of the vital being as it confronts the pressures that urge her into silence; hence the need of another voice, the voice of the reader . . . ."

1982 MARCUS, *Emily Dickinson*, pp. 37, 38
General consideration as one of Dickinson's poems on "Poetry, Art, and Imagination."

1986 MARSTON, "Metaphorical Language," pp. 114–15
"The grotesquery of the metaphor implies the unnaturalness of a union between self and death, between the utterances of a conscious but disembodied mind and the immobility and silence of stone."

"If my bark sink" (1234)

1982 MADIGAN, "Mermaids," p. 43
"Life ('Mortality') is the surface of the sea that can be perceived readily by the senses. Beneath this surface is the afterlife, actually no more than the continuation of existence (time), or moving from one floor to another (space)."

1987 BLASING, *American Poetry*, p. 182
"The juxtaposition of 'Mortality' and 'Immortality' calls into question what the poem ostensibly asserts, for the very concept of immortality must be built upon the 'Ground Floor' of mortality by adding the negative prefix *im–* to the root word, and not the other way around."

1989 OLIVER, *Apocalypse of Green*, p. 91
"The interesting use of directions, with the condition after death appearing not as a heaven 'above' but as subsuming in solid fashion mortal life indicates the strength of its importance to Emily Dickinson."

"If nature smiles, the mother must" (1085)

1980 HOMANS, *Women Writers*, pp. 199, 200
"Knowing that nature is not to be possessed by means of any human construct, Dickinson is not taking Mother Nature to be a personification of nature, but a figure imported from tradition and extrinsic to nature."
Reprinted: Homans, "Emily Dickinson," pp. 437–38

"If pain for peace prepares" (63)

1978 TILMA-DEKKERS, "Immortality," pp. 169–70
"The idea of preparation and compensation, stated in three different ways, is in advance pervaded by doubt by the opening word 'If.' Yet doubt is suppressed in each of the three statements by the emphasis the poet puts on the thought that follows . . . ."

1982 JOHNSON, "Emily Dickinson," p. 11
"Despite the skeptical 'ifs,' the tone of the poem is joyous; it is remarkable for an early poem in its synthesis of so many symbols and ideas Dickinson continues to develop in her later poetry."
Revised and reprinted: Johnson, *Emily Dickinson,* pp. 55–56

THOTA, *Emily Dickinson,* pp. 81–82, 83
"What apparently looks like a nature poem . . . becomes a poem on death and resurrection." Notes "apparent Shelleyan connections."

"If recollecting were forgetting" (33)

1984 WALLACE, *God Be with the Clown,* pp. 27, 103
This is an example of "Dickinson's use of comic paradox to intensify seriousness."

"If the foolish call them 'flowers'" (168)

1979 PATTERSON, *Dickinson's Imagery,* pp. 49, 98–99
"The poem sentimentalizes religion in a way not native to her and romantically attacks the scientific discipline that in reality she found quite congenial . . . ."

"If this is 'fading'" (120)

1988 FURUKAWA, "'Finite Infinity,'" p. 16
"The italicized *Peacock* effectively functions as an 'objective correlative,' which unites the eternal radiant sun with the dying poet, for the dying *Peacock* is an image of the dying poet, which the peacock provides another image of the radiant sinking sun."

"If what we could were what we would" (407)

1986   ROBINSON, J., *Emily Dickinson,* p. 100
"If desire and attainment were identical what would be our means of measurement? Surely we calibrate and talk about inadequacy?"

"If you were coming in the fall" (511)

1972   RAO, *Essential Emily Dickinson,* pp. 141–42
General introduction to the poem aimed at "postgraduate students of literature in Indian Universities."

1981   KHAN, "Poetry of Ecstasy," pp. 24–26
"The theme is appropriately the ecstasy of despair and pain arising from the tantalizing prospect of union with the lover, which makes the troth itself a situation of Tantalus . . . ."
Revised and reprinted: Khan, *Emily Dickinson's Poetry,* pp. 50–52

1982   MARCUS, *Emily Dickinson,* pp. 55–56
Relates to other Dickinson poems dealing with "renunciation of a proffered love" and "love-separation and hope for earthly or heavenly reunion."

SALSKA, *Poetry of the Central Consciousness,* pp. 156, 157
". . . the succession of provisional situations presented in the first part of the poem seems invented to 'design' a void, a tauntingly indefinite reality. The multiplied conditions form stages in the mind's effort to cope with cosmic doubt."
Revised and reprinted: Salska, *Walt Whitman and Emily Dickinson,* pp. 143–44, 145; Salska, "Emily Dickinson's Lover," p. 140

1983   BUDICK, "Temporal Consciousness," pp. 227–28
The poem articulates "the belief that the concept or experience of time becomes treacherous and ultimately damning only when it begins to lose its manageable particularity. Only when human beings cease to be conscious of time is time dangerous."
Revised and reprinted: Budick, *Emily Dickinson,* pp. 201–02

SHURR, *Marriage,* pp. 29, 75–76
The poem "takes on a sudden new richness in the context of the fascicles, as a poem that precisely expresses the anguish of separation that followed their marriage, and the doubt that becomes crucial now regarding life after death."

1984 CHERRY, "Sexuality and Tension," p. 19
"Loss and desire are bound together. Tension in this poem and others is the visible result of their interaction. Here the desire for the absent lover is the issue . . . ."

1986 SHANDS, "Goblin Bee," pp. 24–25
"She puts the prosaic description of the objectless state of anxiety, into arresting metaphor in the notion of a *Goblin Bee* in a poem in which she emphasizes throughout the relation of unpredictability."

1988 WOLFF, *Emily Dickinson*, pp. 376–78, 383
". . . the beloved here is closely identified with a husband figure, and the ideal, away from which the poem moves with increasingly distressed strokes of imagery, is conjugal love. Given her choice, the speaker would elect a life in which marriage gives passion a permanent home."

"If your nerve deny you" (292)

1979 CAMERON, *Lyric Time*, p. 155
"If feeling at all is the equivalent of feeling negation . . . , the best way to repudiate negation is to transcend it, . . . is to appeal to a numbness imitative of death . . . ."

1989 LEONARD, D. N., "Certain Slants," p. 133
In this, the final poem in fascicle 13, "the speaker adopts the comic mode to exhort herself to live fearlessly, wittily suggesting that nothing is more of a spur to life than the fact of death."

"I'll clutch and clutch" (427)

1984 RUDDICK, " 'Synaesthesia,' " pp. 65–66
Examines poet's use of the phrase "golden touch" for connotations and intent.

"I'll tell you how the sun rose" (318)

1972 RAO, *Essential Emily Dickinson*, pp. 75, 129–31
General introduction to the poem aimed at "postgraduate students of literature in Indian Universities."

1982 MARCUS, *Emily Dickinson*, pp. 21–22
General consideration as one of the poet's nature poems.

1983   DURNELL, *Japanese Cultural Influences,* pp. 15–16
        The poem expresses "the Oriental concept of an endless continuity
of life—or of life as continual metamorphoses. It indicates symbolically
life and death as a unity in renewable but changing form."

1985   BUDICK, *Emily Dickinson,* pp. 7–8, 26, 194
        ". . . the silence that ends this poem represents not reassurance
but the loss of cheerful confidence that, at the end of time at least, human
beings will share in the restoration of cosmic oneness."

1986   ROBINSON, J., *Emily Dickinson,* pp. 165, 168–72
        One of several poems "which represent what might be regarded as
the passing away or dissolution of the material world in its familiarity,
security and quotidian insularity."

1988   MOREY, "Dickinson-Kant III," pp. 19–20
        "The entire poem covers the ground of Blake's *Songs of Innocence*
and *Experience.* . . . This poem is almost 100% objective, not directly
subjective but hinting about individuation and the taboo in general . . . ."

"I'm ceded, I've stopped being theirs" (508)

1980   REISS, "Dickinson's Self-Reliance," pp. 26–27
        "She is raised up, with free will to choose or reject, and she
chooses her crown—she gives recognition to her power as a poet."

1981   KHAN, "Poetry of Ecstasy," pp. 28–29
        "The theme is the opposition between two moods of dependent
incompleteness and freedom and fullness earned by a surrender to experience."
        Revised and reprinted: Khan, *Emily Dickinson's Poetry,* pp. 55–56

1982   MARCUS, *Emily Dickinson,* pp. 61–62
        Considers as a connection between Dickinson's "marriage poems
and the poems about growth and personal identity. . . . Probably the condition of a crowned queen here represents that being a poet gives her the
feeling that she is a whole person."

        MOSSBERG, *Emily Dickinson,* pp. 158–60
        "Rejecting external concepts, such as fame, prayer, faith, and even
parents, does not eliminate them; because her identity is given by society
and therefore tainted with society's restrictions for a daughter, she must
renounce herself as well."

1983   SHURR, *Marriage,* pp. 23–24, 83
    "A marriage involves the taking of a new name for the bride. Dickinson's version of this, with a larger celebration of the many changes caused by marriage, is [this poem]."

1984   LEONARD, D. N., "Dickinson's Religion," pp. 343–45
    "The poem's metaphysical conceit primarily addresses the subject of spiritual status, which for Dickinson is achieved by personal consent, grace, and a solemn covenant with God."

    MARTIN, W., *American Triptych,* p. 103
    ". . . 'ceded' refers to Dickinson herself—she is the territory that others must relinquish; self-centered, she now claims the right to devote her energy to her own work."

    POLLAK, *Dickinson,* pp. 118–23
    "The essential difference Dickinson posits between childhood and maturity is an awareness of competing systems of value and an ability to choose decisively between them." Examines "crown" symbolism.

1985   EBERWEIN, *Dickinson,* pp. 45, 188–89
    Examines significance of sacrament of baptism in New England Puritan churches and in Dickinson's poetry.

1986   ANDERSON, P., "Bride of the White Election," pp. 5–6
    The poem "shows Dickinson's expanding vision of the Christian life in her awareness of the believer's co-rulership with King Jesus as promised by the glorified Christ himself in Revelation 3:21 . . . ."

    BLOOM, C., " 'Occult' Experience," pp. 6–11
    "By the last stanza Dickinson is ready to choose her sexuality. Yet, she does *not* choose and thus the poem stands upon the brink of a revelatory fulfilment which is encapsulated in the poem but does not potentiate itself within the poem."

    JONES, " 'Royal Seal,' " pp. 37–38, 40
    "Whatever its particular application, the adult baptism marks an inner transformation . . . analogous to that signified and sealed by the traditional Puritan rite."

    STONUM, "Calculated Sublime," pp. 106–07
    This poem "articulates the central dilemma in Dickinson's poetry: the conflict between internal freedom and external power."

1987   COOK, C., "Psychic Development," pp. 125–26
    "This poem works with the image of Christian baptism to show

that Dickinson considered herself baptised into a new life by claiming her right to her creative soul."

DI GIUSEPPE, "Maiden and the Muse," pp. 46–48
The poem illustrates "how the poet bends dogma to her own use" and how she "employs religious doctrine to define her ordeal of self-definition."

EBERWEIN, "Sacramental Tradition," pp. 67, 71–72
Examines the poem "within the specific context of Calvinist sacramental theology as understood by the nineteenth-century Congregational community within which Dickinson received her Christian formation."

HUGHES, D., "Queen of Sheba," pp. 25–26
"The self-baptizing of this poem celebrates a history of the developed soul."

LEDER and ABBOTT, *Language of Exclusion,* p. 154
"In answer to the poems of physical renunciation, [this poem] exalts the passion and power which follow death and, in its coy ending, gives us a glimpse of a place in which women may choose freely to be themselves first."

1989   DIEHL, "Murderous Poetics," pp. 338–39
"The sense of insufficiency, of hunger for authority, the failure of orthodoxy to bestow identity, may indeed suggest submerged thoughts of murder, death of the father, the Church, and the representatives of patriarchal orthodox culture."

RICHWELL, "Poetic Immortality," pp. 18–19
"The theme of poetic immortality accounts for the image of royalty in the poem. . . . She is not claiming to be the queen of heaven, but the ruler of her own life and literary destiny."

"I'm nobody! Who are you" (288)

1972   RAO, *Essential Emily Dickinson,* pp. 58, 126
The poem "seems to be an illustration of Emily Dickinson's self-exile into a private world of her own." Paraphrase.

1982   MARCUS, *Emily Dickinson,* pp. 62, 65
Relates to other Dickinson poems on society. This poem "perhaps reflects Dickinson's resentment of shallow writers who gain undeserved

attention. Or she may be satirizing the character and situation of people who loom large in the eyes of society . . . ."

Salska, *Poetry of the Central Consciousness,* pp. 42–43, 44, 67, 71
Contrasts with poem by Whitman: "both poems are founded on the assumption that the self is central and, therefore, whatever comes in experience can only be viewed subjectively."
Revised and reprinted: Salska, *Walt Whitman and Emily Dickinson,* pp. 35–36, 37, 57, 61

1983 Eberwein, "Dickinson's Nobody," pp. 9–14
A possible source in Homer's *Odyssey* "provides an organizational structure for Dickinson's poem and a rationale for its tone of hushed triumphalism."

Loving, "Emily Dickinson's Workshop," pp. 195–201
Argues that the poet's manuscript version, with variant material, best represents her intentions.

1984 Wallace, *God Be with the Clown,* p. 19
Dickinson "uses the shy self-deprecation of the Yankee to ridicule and elevate herself. . . . The typical pose of diminution and ignorance both undermines and asserts a sense of power and prestige."

1985 Eberwein, *Dickinson,* pp. 61–62, 277 n. 8
The poem "seems to savor the 'Nobody' role, a tendency likely to make more sense to us when we recall Western mythology's most memorable exploiter of submerged identity: Ulysses proclaiming himself Noman to evade Polyphemus."

Ostriker, "Being Nobody Together," pp. 201–03, 207
"A poem like this is duplicitous in that it means both what it says and its opposite. . . . contrary meanings co-exist with equal force."
Revised and reprinted: Ostriker, *Stealing the Language,* pp. 39–41, 63, 149

1988 Oakes, "Welcome and Beware," pp. 195–96
"The poet's feminine discourse insists that the reader-other in the poem must choose between two roles, that of 'public' masculine frog or 'private' feminine playmate."

Reed, "Masculine Identity," pp. 281, 282–283
"Once more . . . we see the fear in Dickinson's poetry that into her comfortable situation, here the exclusiveness of two nobodies, someone will intrude and disrupt the relationship."

1989 OBERHAUS, "Dickinson as Comic Poet," pp. 118–19, 122
Considers poem's comic techniques and comic tone, which is "reinforced by its uneven metrics, its frequent pyrrhics, and Dickinson's typical condensation and brevity."

WOLFF, "Usable Past," p. 640
". . . perhaps this particular piece of verse (with all its mocking resonance) could only have been conceived by a poet who was 'nobody' *under the law.*"

"I'm the little 'Heart's Ease'" (176)

1981 KIMPEL, *Dickinson as Philosopher,* pp. 128–33
The poet "regards herself as different from objects in nature by virtue of her ability to be aware of herself as a thinking being."

"I'm 'Wife'—I've finished that" (199)

1979 GILBERT and GUBAR, *Madwoman,* p. 589
"The stops and steps of the mind that give this dramatic monologue its strength clearly indicate Dickinson's ironic view of her speaker's anxious rationalizations."

1981 KIMPEL, *Dickinson as Philosopher,* pp. 157, 158–60
"Notwithstanding the poetry which came into being in the quiet of her room, she still was aware that she was in a house in which others lived to whom she had responsibilities, and so this poem ends with the realization that she is still a housewife . . . ."

1982 MARCUS, *Emily Dickinson,* pp. 59–60, 62
Relates to other Dickinson "marriage" poems. "The poet's attitude toward her triumph is ambiguous; she seems uncertain about its nature, and yet she is reluctant to explore her state further, as if through further questioning she might lose everything."

MOSSBERG, *Emily Dickinson,* pp. 46–47, 48, 126, 129, 195, 207 n. 13
"Whether the persona is dead or merely married is not made clear, but the poem's humorous ambiguity on this point signifies that marriage or maturity is a kind of death for a woman. Ironically, the woman is betrayed by her own body . . . ."

THOTA, *Emily Dickinson,* p. 113
"That in an early poem . . . Dickinson could play with such complex ideas, is a testimony to her inherent metaphysical sensibility. The

216

point to be noted here is that she uses a theological concept, with which she never comes to terms for her aesthetic purpose."

1983 HOMANS, "'Oh, Vision,'" p. 119
"Being wife means stopping, both in the sense that the woman's life stops growing and in the sense that the poem comes to an end. . . . heterosexuality is imaged as leading to an end to communication."

SHURR, *Marriage*, pp. 14, 23, 60, 133
"The burden of the poem is to assert that a qualitative change has been made in her life, by marriage."

1984 POLLAK, *Dickinson*, pp. 172–73
". . . her loyalty to the odd, unclosed girl's life undercuts the marriage fiction she creates for herself and a fuller comparison of the old self and the new might reveal that they have more in common than she cares to admit here."

1985 EBERWEIN, *Dickinson*, pp. 103, 174
"A sense of satisfaction dominates, impressing the reader with the apparent sufficiency of marital bliss to correct earlier limitation; but the terminal line . . . abruptly cuts off speculation about later happiness."

1986 BENNETT, *Loaded Gun*, pp. 74–75, 76
However ambivalent the poem may be, it is "hard to escape" the "obvious implication—that marriage equals death."

DOBSON, "'Invisible Lady,'" pp. 50–51, 54 n. 14
Marriage "as Dickinson sees it here means not only transformation, but also an obscuration—whether of life or of the self is not specified. This eclipse may be painless, . . . perhaps even ecstatic, with suggestions of sexual transport, but it is nonetheless real."
Reprinted: Dobson, *Strategies of Reticence*, pp. 72–74, 146 n. 11

SMITH, S. B., "'Radical Dualism,'" pp. 38, 39
In this poem "being a wife may mean being static and unchanging, being concerned perhaps with the housewifely duties described in other poems."

1988 PHILLIPS, *Emily Dickinson*, pp. 124–26
Notes literary sources in poems of Elizabeth Barrett Browning.

REYNOLDS, *Beneath the American Renaissance*, pp. 421–23
"Dickinson's poem stands out not for any new statement about marriage it might contain but for its playful fusion of opposing views about the marriage relation that was circulating in American culture."

WOLFF, *Emily Dickinson,* pp. xviii, 203–05, 206, 217
The poem is "so spare with language that both problem and resolution must be inferred from method as much as from verbal content."

"Immortal is an ample word" (1205)

1982 MILLER, C., "Terms and Golden Words," pp. 55–56, 59, 61 n. 12
"Language becomes necessary, or we most clearly perceive its importance, when there is a gap between our needs and their fulfillment. . . . Understanding the word 'Immortal' becomes a psychological guarantee that the condition exists."

1984 WOLOSKY, *Emily Dickinson,* pp. 116–17
"This profession of satiric theism presents a God whom the poet cannot praise, but she cannot banish him either."

"In ebon box, when years have flown" (169)

1986 MILLER, C., "A letter is a joy," pp. 30–31
". . . letters provide a kind of communication somewhere between that of holy prayer and secular seduction."
Reprinted: Miller, C., *Emily Dickinson,* p. 8

"In falling timbers buried" (614)

1984 WILT, "Playing House," p. 160
Considers as one of the "scores of highly charged lyrics" in which "the poet confronts the house she is before, or within, or has become."

"In lands I never saw, they say" (124)

1980 HOMANS, *Women Writers,* pp. 202–03, 206
"The poem is about the invidiousness of ascribing conventional characteristics to the sexes."
Reprinted: Homans, "Emily Dickinson," pp. 439–40, 442–43

1983 GALINSKY, "Northern and Southern," pp. 135–36
Comments on function of Alpine scenery.

1985 BRASHEAR, "Dramatic Monologues," pp. 71–72, 75 n. 5
The poem's closing question "lays bare a tenuous imprecision in the relationship between the speaker and listener, who has apparently been oblivious to the price the speaker has paid in loss of self-esteem."

"In many and reportless places" (1382)

1985 CARTON, *Rhetoric,* pp. 83–85, 123–24
"Here, Dickinson's language does not un-name so much as it somewhat stealthily identifies that which it purports to be unidentifiable; . . . most importantly, it intricately involves itself with its object while ostensibly opposing itself to it."

"In snow thou comest" (1669)

1983 HESFORD, " 'In snow,' " pp. 15–19
The poem "is a riddle whose solution is at once simple and difficult. The 'thou' of the poem is Jesus. . . . The difficulty comes in trying to discern the relationship between the poet and the 'thou,' between the poem's speaker and the faith she bespeaks."

"In this short life" (1287)

1981 KIMPEL, *Dickinson as Philosopher,* pp. 80–83
"The thought in this poem both about the limits of what human effort can accomplish, and also about the extent to which it can be accomplished, is a fine example of the mean, the moral significance of which Aristotle makes so much."

"In winter in my room" (1670)

1978 MANN, "Dream," pp. 24–25
"The images suggest that the poem can be read as a dream-fable for the dark underside of poetic power, the dangers which attend the influx of inspiration."

1979 KELLER, K., *Only Kangaroo,* pp. 268–69
In this poem and "A narrow fellow in the grass" "she is shocked and attracted by the male erection . . . and she is fascinated with the sexual processes," but there is "no significance in the sex; it is fun and games."

PETRY, "Two Views of Nature," pp. 16–22
The poem can be read as "a symbolic rendering of the two aspects of nature as it is perceived by the human mind: it may seem friendly, like the pink worm over which man has easy dominion, or it may seem hostile, like the aggressive snake with its possibly diabolic dimension."

1982 MARCUS, *Emily Dickinson*, pp. 22, 50–51, 52, 54
". . . viewing the snake as a symbol of evil, in addition to seeing it as a sexual symbol, helps us to see how ambivalent is the speaker's attitude toward the snake—to see how she relates to it with a mixture of feelings . . . ."

PETRY, "Ophidian Image," pp. 598–601
Suggests possible literary antecedents in works of Oliver Wendell Holmes. Dickinson's poetry should be "perceived to belong within the contexts of the contemporaneous nineteenth-century literature which clearly she studied with care and profit."

1983 ALLEN, M., *Animals*, pp. 44–45
"Either this is a translation from a more phallic representation to a form from nature the poet was comfortable with, or she saw a worm."

1985 MORRIS, T., "Free-rhyming Poetry," pp. 225, 234–36
"The poem's crucial moment is described in the abstract in order to show that the terror of the snake is not merely physical; the aesthetic terror of the experience is what troubles the speaker most."

1986 ROBINSON, J., *Emily Dickinson*, p. 148
"If she had not done so, *he* would have had to leave . . . for if they had become well acquainted she would not have been able to record the thrill of fear as (unconvincing to her and us) a dream. The poem lives on the frisson."

1987 BARKER, *Lunacy of Light*, pp. 93–95
The snake "represents herself, her poems, her imagination, her energy, but it also, to the mind of a young woman raised with Calvinist notions of good and evil, represents evil."

1988 REED, "Masculine Identity," pp. 278, 279, 283, 285–86
Behind the theme of "sexual violation" in this poem is "the deeper infantile fantasy and the central fear of oral deprivation because of the father's desire for the mother."

1989 OLIVER, *Apocalypse of Green*, pp. 154–57, 234
Reviews critical interpretations. ". . . the poem's imagery can also be interpreted as religiously allegorical . . . ."

WALKER, N., "Voice, Tone," pp. 108–09
Suggestions for teaching the poem. "Students need only a light acquaintance with Freudian psychology to comprehend the phallic imagery of the poem, but they may not as readily understand the complexity of the speaker's stance . . . ."

"Inconceivably solemn" (582)

1983 MATTHEWS, "Importance of Silence," pp. 16–17
The poem "asserts that the truth, even if pleasant, is too poignant to know directly."

1987 LEONARD, D., " 'Chastisement of Beauty,' " p. 249
Argues that the poem "demonstrates especially well Dickinson's use of Burkean elements of the sublime."
Reprinted: *University of Dayton Review,* pp. 40–41

1988 PHILLIPS, *Emily Dickinson,* pp. 58–59
Along with several other poems, considers as the poet's response to the Civil War.

"Is bliss then such abyss" (340)

1981 MONTEIRO, G., and ST. ARMAND, "Experienced Emblem," pp. 243–44, 266
"It was the precarious, manic-depressive nature of her religious experience that prompted a poem such as [this one]."

1983 SHURR, *Marriage,* p. 172
One of several poems "denying herself a fall from virginity."

1984 OLPIN, "Hyperbole: Part II," pp. 34–35
The poem "presents a summary in microcosm of the elements of the comic that Dickinson brings to the abyss in her attempt to describe and control it."

1985 CARTON, *Rhetoric,* pp. 124–25
"Here, Dickinson's characteristic drama is enacted in low style: the questing spiritual self is represented by a foot, the threatened formal self is a boot, and the abyss into which the seeker of bliss must plunge is no more than a pothole."

EBERWEIN, *Dickinson,* pp. 109–10
". . . when brain and foot collide, the foot determines the issue: "Verdict for Boot!' As a venturer after pleasure and self-satisfaction, then, Dickinson presents herself as a failure."

"Is heaven a physician" (1270)

1984 WOLOSKY, *Emily Dickinson,* pp. 105–06
Here Dickinson "questions the value of heavenly promises and the whole framework in which they are offered."

1986 ROBINSON, J., *Emily Dickinson,* p. 80
Here she questions how she could "be held to be in debt to heaven when she was not party to the original contract?"

"It always felt to me a wrong" (597)

1983 TEICHERT, "Divine Adversary," pp. 22, 24
Examines poet's image of God in several poems; here God appears unjust and malicious.

1984 WOLOSKY, *Emily Dickinson,* pp. 139–40
"Scripture is questioned as a reliable text, and the only lesson the poet draws from it is her own indignation."

1986 NEW, "Difficult Writing," pp. 15–16, 21, 23
"What Dickinson guards against in this poem is the temptation to fill the void felt by the loss of self with a hagiography—a totemization of Christ cult—that would at once columnize the hero and pardon the assembly for whose foibles he suffers."

ROBINSON, J., *Emily Dickinson,* pp. 82–83
"She closes the poem with further observations on the justice of the case, but the core of the grievance has been given: to tantalize, to let him see but not take possession, to hold out a possibility but deny fulfilment."

1988 WOLFF, *Emily Dickinson,* pp. 348–49
The Lord "needed to create us so that He would have some means for affirming His sense of His own importance: over and over He must 'prove ability' by taunting humanity with its helplessness before His power."

"It bloomed and dropt, a single noon" (978)

1988 MORRIS, T., "Development," pp. 34–36
Examination of the ways in which Dickinson "elaborated the detail and the rhetorical structure" of "Glowing is her bonnet" into this poem illustrates her stylistic development. This poem "contains all the features of Dickinson's later style."

"It came at last but prompter death" (1230)

1983 SHURR, *Marriage,* pp. 184–85
The poem states that "a death would not have occurred if Love

had been prompt enough to step in and prevent it." Suggests this refers to the poet's child.

"It came his turn to beg" (1500)

1983   SHURR, *Marriage,* p. 161
     May refer to a meeting with Wadsworth. "The reversal of roles seems to indicate Dickinson's sense that she was the beggar originally, perhaps in her demands for more of his time and attention, if not for actual marriage. Now he is the beggar . . . ."

"It can't be 'summer'" (221)

1979   PATTERSON, *Dickinson's Imagery,* pp. 18, 135–36, 185
     The line "The *Dead* shall go in white" is "a complex reminiscence of the white robes of the martyred dead in Revelation and an allusion to these same passages by . . . Elizabeth Browning's Aurora Leigh."

"It ceased to hurt me, though so slow" (584)

1979   JUHASZ, "'But most, like Chaos,'" pp. 226, 232–34, 235, 237, 239, 241 n. 8
     Relates to other poems that are also "about *during* and *after* 'great pain' that reveal insights into the nature of pain and also Dickinson's methods for measuring it."
     Revised and reprinted: Juhasz, *Undiscovered Continent,* pp. 75–77, 78, 82

1989   FULTON, "Moment of Brocade," p. 27
     "In this reversal of synecdoche, 'It,' 'the Anguish,' is an immense whole standing for whatever part the reader cares to inscribe. The specifics of 'It' could include a failed love affair, the death of a loved one, or the knowledge of creative abnegation."

"It did not surprise me" (39)

1979   PATTERSON, *Dickinson's Imagery,* pp. 53, 54, 176
     The poem "appears to be related to 'Misconceptions,' a poem from Robert Browning's *Men and Women.*"

1986   BENNETT, *Loaded Gun,* pp. 44–45, 46
     "The poet's failure to state clearly either her anger or her loss give the poem an arch quality that is distasteful. . . . Nevertheless, the poem

"It dropped so low in my regard"

does help establish how closely Dickinson's feelings for Susan were tied into the initial stages of her poetic development."

"It dropped so low in my regard" (747)

1977 AGRAWAL, *Emily Dickinson*, p. 72
"We realize afterwards that fate has nothing to do with our love for illusions and mirages and consequently we denounce ourselves for it."

1979 NATHAN, "Slanted Truth," p. 37
The poem deals with a paradox "of the metaphysical mind: the co-existence of profound humility and an exalted sense of one's worth."

1983 SHURR, *Marriage*, p. 113
The poem "expresses a complexity of insights and emotions" regarding the end of a love affair.

1989 ROGERS, K., "Introducing Dickinson," p. 53
Suggestions for teaching the poem to college students.

"It feels a shame to be alive" (444)

1984 TSELENTIS-APOSTOLIDIS, "I will be Socrates," pp. 13, 14
The poem's "reference to Thermopylae merges the two histories to the glorification of the present event [the Civil War] thru its connection with the symbol of ultimate heroism."

1987 LEDER and ABBOTT, *Language of Exclusion*, pp. 109–11, 114
This elegy, which "links money and war," may be read as "a meditation by the excluded on institutions in which she has no part."

"It is a lonesome glee" (774)

1977 AGRAWAL, *Emily Dickinson*, pp. 117–18
"'A Bird' in [this poem] suggests mental faculty operating unhindered."

1988 WOLFF, *Emily Dickinson*, p. 481
"Validation comes only through the poet's own awareness of 'association,' human and bird each making music."

"It knew no lapse nor diminution" (560)

1981 PORTER, *Dickinson*, p. 55
The poem "sits on the page without a subject. It may be about love

or friendship, or, indeed, about the sun burning until it is extinguished, an image in the poet's mind, but never mentioned, associated with human relationships severed by time.''

1985   BUDICK, *Emily Dickinson,* pp. 83–84, 88
"The cosmic finale . . . portrayed here . . . is a total 'Dissolution' that is tantamount, in the language of the poem, to cosmic failure. . . . The sun's failing and the universe's dissolving are simply functions of mechanistic realities.''

1986   DORESKI, "Exchange of Territory," pp. 65–66
Examines poem in relation to its place in the poetic sequence of fascicle 27. "By omitting the initiating image . . . Dickinson focuses on her concern with the 'Exchange of Territory,' the 'expansion and con- traction' of language possibilities that constitute poetic knowledge.''

1989   OLIVER, *Apocalypse of Green,* p. 84
"Using the analogy of the apparent disappearance of a star or planet from human sight, Dickinson seems to suggest that the physical laws of matter deny the possibility of complete annihilation, permitting only change of form . . . .''

"It knew no medicine" (559)

1985   JOHNSON, *Emily Dickinson,* pp. 163–64
"The poem is a critique of faith because it blames the idea of 'Par- adise' for being simple-minded and for ignoring the tragic possibilities of death.''

1988   WOLFF, *Emily Dickinson,* pp. 328–29
This poem "attempts to infer what has been glimpsed on the other side, when the portal to 'Paradise' has been left 'momently ajar.' The unthinkable possibility offered . . . is that there is some essential part of God's afterlife that, could we but see it, would leave us 'sickened—ever afterward.' ''

"It might be lonelier" (405)

1981   KIMPEL, *Dickinson as Philosopher,* pp. 57–58
The poem "considers the mode of loneliness itself as the only al- ternative to a completely unrelieved loneliness.''

1985   EBERWEIN, *Dickinson,* pp. 187–88
The poem "suggests the speaker's sense of the penetration of in-

finity into the finite and her recognition of time as a human fallacy in trying to regulate eternity."

1986   ROBINSON, F., "Strategies of Smallness," p. 30
Here Dickinson "finds the loneliness of her house more comfortable than the intrusion of the holy."

ROBINSON, J., *Emily Dickinson*, pp. 107–08
"Using words admits the existence of other people's thought—even if, seemingly, you are using those words only to talk to yourself. By this means, paradoxically, the most private moment becomes public if it is recorded."

"It sifts from leaden sieves" (311)

1979   CAMERON, *Lyric Time*, pp. 174–75, 185, 202–03
"Having neither determinable origin nor explicable end, the existence of the unnamed substance in [this poem] is sheer middle, the spaces on either side of the pheomenon [*sic*] that would explain it blocked from human scrutiny."

1982   MARCUS, *Emily Dickinson*, pp. 20–21, 22
General consideration as one of the poet's nature poems.

1983   BICKMAN, "'Snow that never drifts,'" p. 140
". . . it is clear from other manuscripts of this poem and from her general practice that the initial 'it' is not supposed to have a clear noun referent, that 'it' is more a process, an event."

1987   BARKER, *Lunacy of Light*, pp. 83–84, 86, 89, 99, 113
". . . in this poem nature's 'Artisans' of snow become silent, allowing Dickinson's own mind and voice free range. The snow provides an ideal working climate, since it has no voice of its own to silence her."

1988   WOLFF, *Emily Dickinson*, pp. 434–39, 482–83
"Read once through, the poem might seem no more than a watercolor in words; read again, it might seem a bitter narrative of God's annihilation." Contrasts original with revised version.

"It sounded as if the streets were running" (1397)

1986   MOREY, "Dickinson-Kant: The First Critique," p. 47
"The abstractions, Eclipse and Awe, together with the words Streets and Window, are expected to do all the work of recreating the storm and its effects."

"It struck me every day" (362)

1983 SHURR, *Marriage,* p. 112
"The poem seems to combine equally her experiences with madness and with marriage, and to describe a moral revulsion that continues to the present."

1989 GARBOWSKY, *House without the Door,* pp. 116–17
"It is no coincidence that the image of lightning is used. It is one chosen by agoraphobic victims . . . ."

"It was a quiet seeming day" (1419)

1986 ROBINSON, J., *Emily Dickinson,* pp. 152–53
"There is the same sense of an impressive demonstration of the real before which human beings should be properly submissive, as if might manifests the superiority of the sublime over the mundane."

1983 DOBSON, "'Oh, Susie,'" pp. 90–91
"The 'He' of this poem is indeed a strange companion to exert such a compelling influence upon the speaker, yet elicit such an autistic response." Relates to "the motif of the masculine in its archetypal manifestation as the ghostly lover."

SHURR, *Marriage,* pp. 7, 105, 133
The poem insists on "the active role that the beloved took in their marriage. . . . [It] then develops her lyric response—affirmative—to his question." Relates to other "Wife" and "Bride" poems in the fascicles.

1985 EBERWEIN, *Dickinson,* p. 183
The poem "provides a happy report on the soul's journey with Christ to heaven."

"It was given to me by the gods" (454)

1982 MOSSBERG, *Emily Dickinson,* pp. 139, 182, 184, 205 n. 1
Here the persona is "proud of her 'difference'. . . . While Dickinson does not specify what 'it' is, 'it' distinguishes her from the crowd, and takes the visible shape of deprivation . . . ."
Revised and reprinted: Mossberg, "Nursery Rhymes," pp. 60–61

1987 BLASING, *American Poetry,* pp. 176–77
"The gift she keeps in her hand and guards so jealously is the gift of writing, the gods' present of the absent."

"It was not death, for I stood up" (510)

1977 AGRAWAL, *Emily Dickinson*, pp. 91–92
"Because despair kills, it is akin to death, but because it does not devour life absolutely, it is different from death. Emily Dickinson shows this gruesome human condition in [this poem]."

1978 CAMERON, "Naming as History," pp. 245–49, 250
The poem evades "metaphor and explicit naming" and this "evasion is the point, for insofar as names involve distance from and interpretation of what has been apprehended, they are precisely what certain experiences—perceived in complexity and multifaceted—will not yield."
Reprinted: Cameron, *Lyric Time*, pp. 48–50, 51, 52–53, 54, 83, 202

CRABBE, "Thing without Feathers," pp. 3–6
"The self identified here is a despairing one, isolated in an unpleasant and contradictory world, holding on to a life which has ceased to be dear, ready indeed for the letting go but uncertain where it would take her."

1979 JUHASZ, "'But most, like Chaos,'" pp. 226–31, 232–33, 234, 241 n. 5
". . . the closer she comes through the act of the poem to defining her condition, the less it is in fact one of complete isolation. The creation of an adequate language is what saves her."
Revised and reprinted: Juhasz, *Undiscovered Continent*, pp. 65–70, 73, 74, 75, 77, 182 nn. 9, 11

1980 PERRINE, "Structure and Pronominal Reference," pp. 34–36
Discussion that "corrects and complements" Crabbe's 1978 article. The poet "does not identify the experience because her primary interest . . . is not in the event itself but in defining as precisely as possible the state of mind and feeling that it brought about."

1981 DIEHL, *Romantic Imagination*, pp. 117–18
"The ceremonies of the altar . . . indicate that the moment is sacramental; however, it is not a time of redemption but of all-consuming unredeemed despair."

HYMEL, "Singing Off Charnal Steps," pp. 3, 5, 8–9
The speaker's "marked response to the situation in which she finds herself is largely one of passivity."

1982 FAULKNER, "Emily Dickinson," pp. 806–07
Here are "many of Dickinson's typical devices at work: the tightly

patterned form, based on an undefined subject, . . . the shifting of mood from apparent observation to horror, the grotesque images couched in emotionally distant language."

MARCUS, *Emily Dickinson,* pp. 73–74
"The ritualization of how the world persecutes her, the symbolizing of her suffering by landscape and seascape, and the analytical ordering of the material suggest some control over a suffering which she describes as irremediable."

1983   KHAN, "Agony of the Final Inch," pp. 26–27
"Consciousness survives near absolute insensation of the body to register painfulness of despair. The disembodied consciousness enables the protagonist to taste death as a living experience."
Revised and reprinted: Khan, *Emily Dickinson's Poetry,* pp. 28–30

1984   POLLAK, *Dickinson,* pp. 214–17
"The speaker is both exterior to and part of a landscape of death, an 'It' and an observer of 'It.' . . . the speaker's fragmentation is reflected in her mode of telling."

1986   ROBINSON, J., *Emily Dickinson,* pp. 118–21, 171
"In other poems she let go, could not see, finished knowing. In this she is trying to start knowing as the means of control which is, to that extent, a means of liberation—through language, by finding the right words."

1987   MILLER, C., *Emily Dickinson,* pp. 65, 78–80, 83, 97, 100–01, 102, 103, 136–37, 201 n. 9
Examines nature and implications of poem's "it."

1988   WOLFF, *Emily Dickinson,* pp. 338–42, 379, 446, 588 n. 1
"Nowhere else does Dickinson's arrogant, revisionary image of Heaven come so close to Milton's depiction of Hell. . . . There is no temporal or spatial structure whatsoever, merely an unmeasurable, unending state of flux and confusion."

1989   GARBOWSKY, *House without the Door,* pp. 112–13, 117, 119, 126, 136
"This experience parallels the panic attack in its physiological symptoms and its episodes of depersonalization where the victim is numb from extreme fear."

MORTON, "How Language Works," pp. 49–50
Suggestions for teaching the poem to college freshmen.

"It was too late for man" (623)

1984 BENFEY, *Problem of Others,* p. 69
"This poem describes a boundary situation, perhaps that of a dying person, beyond human aid, but not yet ready for relinquishment to God . . . ."

1985 ANANTHARAMAN, *Sunset in a Cup,* p. 140
"This poem, if understood in the light of its tone and speaker's attitude toward the situation, sums up . . . Emily's religious attitude."

1986 OBERHAUS, " 'Engine against th' Almightie,' " pp. 155, 157–58, 162
Relates to other "prayer" poems of Dickinson.

"It will be summer eventually" (342)

1980 MACHOR, "Feminine Rhetoric," pp. 143–44
Dickinson here demonstrates her ability to "manipulate the epiphoric process to create startling significance."

1987 EBERWEIN, "Sacramental Tradition," pp. 68–69, 77
". . . Dickinson grounds her hopefulness about nature's renewal in the concept of divine promise that is central to Calvin's definition of sacrament."

"It would have starved a gnat" (612)

1978 MILLER, R., "Transitional Object," pp. 460–61
"She compares herself to a gnat and finds herself lesser, less in her need for sustenance and less powerful in her control over her destiny."

1979 BAYM, "God, Father, and Lover," pp. 196–97
The poem "presents an almost Dickensian picture of adult sadism and childish suffering. The adult is God."

POLLAK, "Thirst and Starvation," pp. 44–45
The poem scrutinizes the "paralyzing consequences of prolonged emotional starvation. . . . Here, the attempt to renounce natural hunger is thwarted, as is the ability to gratify instinctual urges."
Revised and reprinted: Pollak, *Dickinson,* p. 131

1982 MARCUS, *Emily Dickinson,* pp. 68–69
Relates to other Dickinson poems on "Suffering and Growth." Here "Dickinson seems to be charging that when she was a child her family denied her spiritual nourishment and recognition."

MOSSBERG, *Emily Dickinson,* pp. 39, 135, 136–37, 138, 139, 143

Relates to other "deprivation" and "hunger" poems. "Her 'hunger' here seems to be the consequence of powerlessness. She cannot command food, nor can she 'coax' or merit reprieve from those responsible for her needs."

Revised and reprinted: Mossberg, "Nursery Rhymes," pp. 56–57, 58–59, 61

1984   BENFEY, *Problem of Others,* pp. 103–04

"The gnat on the pane is a kind of artist. He has 'the power to die,' while the speaker's only art is the art of hunger."

1985   EBERWEIN, *Dickinson,* p. 58

Relates to other poems in fascicle 21 that explore the nightmares of the abandoned child. "The poem builds upon Dickinson's characteristic themes of hunger, privation, confinement, and death."

1988   LOUIS, "Sacrament of Starvation," p. 356

"By reducing her aspirations to that of physical hunger, she disclaims all moral responsibility for her grief, and implicitly arraigns the cruelty of a society, or of a god, unwilling to feed its young."

PHILLIPS, *Emily Dickinson,* pp. 101–02, 104, 115

This poem is "allusively and substantively related to *Jane Eyre.*"

REED, "Masculine Identity," pp. 279–80

"What we see in this poem . . . is an oral fantasy that contains the fear of oral deprivation, a deprivation which is beyond the narrator's control."

1989   FULTON, "Moment of Brocade," pp. 24–25

Dickinson here "defines subtle states by saying what they are *not.* . . . The female self is seen as the negative space that allows the positive pattern to emerge."

"It would never be common more, I said" (430)

1979   PATTERSON, *Dickinson's Imagery,* pp. 32, 91, 130, 134, 160

Considers significance of poem's "drop—of India." It seems to "be related to all the nectars and dews and assorted liquors that represent ecstasy in her poetry, but it also incorporates all the vague riches of the India symbol . . . ."

1981   KIMPEL, *Dickinson as Philosopher,* pp. 245, 246–47

"It would be difficult to find any expression to surpass this poem

for describing occasions in her life out of which her religious response
occurred. . . . This poem . . . is a masterpiece for making so graphic this
type of crisis which is brought about by misdirecting trust."

1982 MILLER, C., "Terms and Golden Words," pp. 51, 55, 58–60, 62 nn.
14–16
"The speaker apparently cannot control the accessibility of epi-
phanic words of gold, but she can limit the extent to which she accepts
the broken words of 'Wilderness.' She prefers chaos to the 'old sort' of
ordinary life or meaning."

1983 DIEHL, "Ransom," pp. 170–72
"With its clearly delineated connection between linguistic power
and continuous war waged between the competing forces of self and
world, this poem serves as a paradigmatic expression of the conflict that
marks Dickinson's understanding of her relationship to everything outside
herself."
Reprinted: Bloom, H., *American Women Poets,* pp. 35–37

MILLER, C., "How 'Low Feet' Stagger," pp. 147–49, 151, 155 n.
22
"The poem tells a Cinderella story in which the speaker is her own
fairy godmother. She turns herself from a 'Common' woman into a poet,
and her magic gifts and husband Prince are all words."

1984 WOLOSKY, *Emily Dickinson,* pp. 155–57
"This poem perhaps merely describes the passing of poetic inspiration. But in recognizing that such inspiration passes, the poem recognizes the distinction between linguistic power and a power that does not
pass away."

1985 BUDICK, *Emily Dickinson,* pp. 71–73
"The attempt to characterize heaven in ordinary symbolic language, Dickinson argues, can only result in a disappointment and loss that
are both proximate and ultimate."

EBERWEIN, *Dickinson,* pp. 63–64
In this poem "Dickinson confronted the loss of dreams—deprivation of those imagined compensations that serve fanciful people as substitutes for the status, jewels, and property discovered to be elusive."

1988 WOLFF, *Emily Dickinson,* pp. 217–19, 383, 529
". . . even India ink cannot permanently dispel the forces of disintegration. . . . The ever-shifting balance of power between the creative
forces and the forces of destruction swings against the poet, and the effort
to impose order must begin once again."

1989 FULTON, "Moment of Brocade," pp. 27–42, 43

Detailed examination of poem's "syntactical deletion, compression, and blurred pronouns." It is possible to read the poem as one "in which a woman confronts literary effacement."

GARBOWSKY, *House without the Door,* pp. 128–29, 138

Relates to other Dickinson poems "of aftermath" that "deal with the concepts of wilderness and peace. [This poem] is dramatic in its description of 'Difference,' the state of life the speaker must endure."

"It's easy to invent a life" (724)

1980 NOWER, "Soul, Take Thy Risk, Part 2," p. 7

Here "God's perversity is seen as a part of the inscrutability against which we mortals forever bang our heads in vain. . . . Without enthusiasm, grudgingly, Emily Dickinson acknowledges that God can indeed casually and spontaneously alter what to us are eternal patterns."

1983 WALKER, N., "Humor as Identity," p. 67

"If creation is an enormous 'gambol' or frivolous activity, Dickinson suggests that human beings—themselves creations of a playful imagination—may likewise invent their own lives."

1984 OLPIN, "Hyperbole: Part II," pp. 10–11

"A desperate attempt to find God's 'plan' reveals that there is no plan in the real sense of the word, but rather a playful and 'Perturbless' pattern that has no logic at all."

WOLOSKY, *Emily Dickinson,* pp. 44–45, 106

Dickinson "had been taught that God's design appoints both life and death. Both are instances of his will. But to her eyes, he effaces as willingly as he creates. There then may be some flaw in the pattern itself or in the will directing it."

1986 ROBINSON, J., *Emily Dickinson,* pp. 75–76

The poem "contrasts the capricious indifference of a self-absorbed deity, casually, bureaucratically, carrying out his pet schemes, with the appalled consciousness which has to live out life in the schemes so arbitrarily bestowed."

1988 STOCKS, *Modern Consciousness,* pp. 80–82

"There is little left of the traditional Christian God in the God of this poem. But there is something in Him that is slightly reminiscent of Gloucester's gods in *King Lear.*"

WOLFF, *Emily Dickinson*, pp. 344–47, 349
In this poem Dickinson "returns to the Augustan master [Pope], not to imitate him but to explode the plausibility of his vision of an ordered world supervised by a God who is wise and kind."

"It's such a little thing to weep" (189)

1971 LEVIN, "Some Uses of the Grammar," pp. 21, 22, 23, 24, 26,
Considers how recoverable deletion operates in the poem.

"I've dropped my brain—my soul is numb" (1046)

1981 DIEHL, *Romantic Imagination*, pp. 45–46
"Dickinson has adopted the extreme language of the grave to characterize her unnamed crisis. And in the transfer of the action of carving on marble from the stone to the self, Dickinson lends the gesture sexual connotations."

1989 FULTON, "Moment of Brocade," pp. 22–23
"The poem implies that the ability to smite and stir, the narrator's poem, is linked to her disinheritance. For a woman to speak her mind is danger."

GARBOWSKY, *House without the Door*, pp. 135–36
Suggests that the poem's immobilizing and paralyzing experience may be related to "agoraphobia with panic attack."

"I've heard an organ talk sometimes" (183)

1981 KIER, "Only Another Suspension," pp. 40–48
Juxtaposes with Sir Arthur Sullivan's "The Lost Chord." "Whereas Sullivan's organist-speaker becomes a divine instrument, Dickinson's narrator is a mere receiver, struck dumb and impotent." The poem is "the utterance of the sober and skeptical Dickinson reflecting on religious sublimity *ex post facto*."

"I've known a heaven like a tent" (243)

1979 PATTERSON, *Dickinson's Imagery*, pp. 54, 150
"Consciously she may be using the tent and circus feats to recall a glorious experience that has now ended, but at a deeper level the tent,

like the bird, appears to represent the person who created the experience."

1984   WILT, "Playing House," pp. 164–65
Considers as one of the "scores of highly charged lyrics" in which "the poet confronts the house she is before, or within, or has become."

1986   ROBINSON, J., *Emily Dickinson,* p. 67
"I take 'heaven' to be a sky and the scene to be nightfall, the onset of blackness being like the decamping of a circus. The world is temporary."

1988   WOLFF, *Emily Dickinson,* pp. 302–04
"One of Dickinson's finest poems, it achieves its effect by maintaining a superb balance between summoning the immanent world and invoking transcendence. Without apparent effort, the poem compresses several images together . . . ."

"I've none to tell me to but thee" (881)

1981   PORTER, *Dickinson,* pp. 132–33, 191
The purpose of this "poem of separation and loss . . . is its *style* of rendering loss—in language violations, paradox, the displacement of viewpoints, and an unexpected metaphor."

1983   HOMANS, " 'Oh, Vision,' " pp. 126–27, 128
". . . at the end of the search for the source of speech there is a kiss. What it signifies is that and how it signifies: the act of communication is itself the love."

1984   WOLOSKY, *Emily Dickinson,* pp. 122–23
"Dickinson addresses herself to God in an act that defines both her conceived relation to him and her conception of language in that relation."

"I've nothing else to bring, you know" (224)

1983   SHURR, *Marriage,* pp. 9, 67, 137
"In a poem that concludes a bound fascicle of twenty-two poems, 'These' can hardly refer to anything but the poems themselves."

UNO, "Expression by Negation," p. 9
Notes poet's use of negation. Here one can "interpret this *nothing* not only as meaning 'not anything' but also as a substance 'nothing' in the positive sense."

"I've seen a dying eye" (547)

1981   RACHAL, "Probing the Final Mystery," pp. 44–46
"I heard a fly buzz when I died" and this poem "complement each other by offering two closely connected perspectives on death."

1985   COTTLE, *Language of Literature*, p. 101
A note on grammatical peculiarities.

EBERWEIN, *Dickinson*, p. 212
"A kind of anger smolders in this poem about the cruel insensitivity of the dead to the questions of the living whom they are luring toward circumference without giving adequate insight into the journey's goal."

ESTES, "Granny Weatherall," pp. 439, 440–41, 442
Examines allusions to this poem in Katherine Anne Porter's "The Jilting of Granny Weatherall."

1989   KNAPP, *Emily Dickinson*, pp. 12, 122–26
"The power and limitations of the Dickinsonian Eye or I is never better nor more terrifyingly depicted than in [this poem]. . . . Dickinson conveys the necessity of continuous probing even if it means increasing the excoriating anguish corroding every fiber of her being."

"Jesus! thy crucifix" (225)

1983   SHURR, *Marriage*, pp. 175–76
Relates to other Dickinson poems containing "pregnancy and childbearing metaphors."

1986   OBERHAUS, "'Engine against th' Almightie,'" pp. 161–62, 163
"The prayer's brevity, extreme condensation, and four exclamation points disclose the speaker's haste and urgency, a tone of immediate suffering suggesting that the two sentences are pleas rather than declarations . . . ."

"Joy to have merited the pain" (788)

1989   ROBINSON, DOUGLAS, "Two Dickinson Readings," pp. 30–34
". . . at once inside and outside the reader, the poem contains the writer as a house its inhabitant, and thereby both maintains the writer's isolation from the community and *in* that isolation integrates her into it."

"Just as he spoke it from his hands" (848)

1984 WOLOSKY, *Emily Dickinson,* pp. 137–38
"The world is a system of signs, issuing from the Godhead. But the poet cannot perceive heavenly love in it. This word declares God's distance rather than his proximity."

"Just lost, when I was saved" (160)

1972 RAO, *Essential Emily Dickinson,* pp. 80, 113–15
General introduction to the poem aimed at "postgraduate students of literature in Indian Universities." "The poem abounds in paradoxes. But they are eminently suited to express the paradoxical, rather the dual experience of the speaker."

1978 DOWNEY, "Antithesis," p. 13
Comments on poem's "use of opposing motions."

1982 MADIGAN, "Mermaids," pp. 49–50
The sea is associated with "both Eternity and the experience of the unknown." The narrator's attitude is ambiguous.

MARCUS, *Emily Dickinson,* p. 89
Relates to other Dickinson poems on death and immortality. Here Dickinson "expresses joyful assurance of immortality by dramatizing her regret about a return to life after she—or an imagined speaker—almost died and received many vivid and thrilling hints about a world beyond death."

1983 HARRIS, N., "Naked and Veiled," pp. 23, 31–32
Contrasts with Plath's "Lady Lazarus." Both poems are about "regretful returns to life from near-death."

1985 EBERWEIN, *Dickinson,* pp. 203–04
The poem "throbs with the frustrated expectancy of one making a purposeful assault on death for the sake of gaining a perspective denied within earth's horizon."

JOHNSON, *Emily Dickinson,* pp. 18, 19–21, 191 n. 12
Contrasts with " 'Twas such a little, little boat." Both poems deal "not with salvation but with being lost."

MORRIS, T., "Free-rhyming Poetry," pp. 231–32, 234
Techniques employed in this early free-rhyming poem, "a hybrid of several of Dickinson's typical verse-forms," are related to those used by Emerson.

1986 LOVING, *Emily Dickinson*, pp. 15–17
The poem "describes the vigilant moments of one who is forever trying to remember by contemplating his dis-memberment—one who dwells on the edge of insight into the ratio between life and death."

1988 WOLFF, *Emily Dickinson*, pp. 236–38
". . . the poet's willingness to confront even death can qualify her to understand both life and eternity, and to explicate the very process of annihilation. It is this ability that is asserted in [this poem]."

1989 GALPERIN, "Posthumanist Approach," pp. 114–15
Examines the "feminist trajectory in Dickinson" through teaching a specific sequence of poems, including this poem.

"Just once! Oh least request" (1076)

1989 OLIVER, *Apocalypse of Green*, p. 119
"It is not clear whether the petitioner wants a general assurance of the possibility of Heaven or a specific assurance of the petitioner's immortality. . . . again she considers the possibility of denial of grace."

"Just so—Jesus raps" (317)

1979 PATTERSON, *Dickinson's Imagery*, pp. 21, 53
"Kneeling on Sue's doorstep, she raps as patiently and unweariedly as Jesus."

1983 BUELL, "Literature and Scripture," pp. 8–9, 24–25 n. 33
Examines Dickinson's use of the biblical scenario, which exemplifies one "literary approach toward biblical narrative" in which the "scriptural antecedent . . . is made subservient to some other thematic principle."
Revised and reprinted: Buell, *New England Literary Culture*, pp. 174–75, 443 n. 34

1987 OBERHAUS, "Herbert and Emily Dickinson," pp. 346, 361–62
Notes similarities to poetry of George Herbert.

"Knock with tremor" (1325)

1988 WOLFF, *Emily Dickinson*, pp. 502–03
"Death seems to have very little to do with God at all here; it has become an entirely human affair, the final exploration of our birthright as men and women." This elegy "celebrates the dignity and heroism of every mortal who has passed into the unknown beyond."

"Knows how to forget" (433)

1979   PATTERSON, *Dickinson's Imagery*, p. 95
The poem is "remarkable largely for the determined and persistent use of school terms, especially those drawn from the sciences."

1983   SHURR, *Marriage*, pp. 8, 143, 152
The poem is "addressed to 'You' and begs for the knowledge and strength to forget him—not a sentiment the mystic would feel in reference to God."

"Lad of Athens, faithful be" (1768)

1981   KIMPEL, *Dickinson as Philosopher*, pp. 71–72, 95
"The Poet has selected two preeminently influential features of Athenian culture when she refers to the 'self' and to 'Mystery'."

1984   TSELENTIS-APOSTOLIDIS, "I will be Socrates," pp. 8–9
The poem's final line is Dickinson's "pagan declaration of faith in the self and the unknown. 'All the rest' strongly implies Christian dogma."

"Lain in nature, so suffice us" (1288)

1989   OLIVER, *Apocalypse of Green*, pp. 76–78
"In this poem Dickinson affirms the belief of the living in the future existence of the dead, . . . yet she finds no evidence in nature of anything but death; . . . Faith in an afterlife must come from another source."

"Lay this laurel on the one" (1393)

1979   PATTERSON, *Dickinson's Imagery*, pp. 164–65
"The poem has been interpreted as a tribute to her father, . . . but it is more plausibly read as Emily's tribute to herself."

1980   SUDOL, "Elegy and Immortality," pp. 10–15
Explores the poem's sources in Higginson's elegy "Decoration" and possibly in *King Lear*. Considers Dickinson's development of the elegy; those from her last years are celebrations of mortal existence rather than affirmations of "immortal existence."

1989   ELFENBEIN, "Unsexing Language," pp. 208–14, 216–22
"The poem's treatment of fame and poetic immortality lends resonance to its violation of patriarchal linguistic forms and literary formulas."

"Least rivers docile to some sea" (212)

1983   SHURR, *Marriage,* pp. 17, 19, 66
One of three love poems in its fascicle that "describe the awakening of an erotic sensibility." This poem is "remarkable . . . for its compact statement of entering and merging."

"Lest this be heaven indeed" (1043)

1989   OLIVER, *Apocalypse of Green,* p. 180
"Lest man become too . . . satisfied with this life, it is necessary both to have a belief in a larger existence and to have obstacles to overcome in its attainment. Otherwise, the poem suggests, earth might itself be Heaven."

"Let down the bars, oh death" (1065)

1988   FELSTINER, "Translating Celan," pp. 113–18
Examines German translation of the poem by Paul Celan.

"Let me not mar that perfect dream" (1335)

1978   MANN, "Dream," p. 22
"Here, as elsewhere, the poet's inner life constitutes her most valued reality, and the 'dream' becomes a perfect metaphor for her special communion with that mental realm."

JOHNSON, *Emily Dickinson,* pp. 123–24
This is an example of "what becomes a virtual genre for Dickinson after 1862: the reminiscence poem, in which she looks back upon the earlier self, takes stock of her progress, and usually draws some philosophical conclusion about her new freedom and access of power."

1986   MUNK, "Recycling Language," pp. 246–47
Examines "etymological wordplay" in second stanza. "Dickinson's 'Wine'—a synecdoche for the Lord's Supper—may be 'dry' . . . in a number of senses."

1988   STOCKS, *Modern Consciousness,* pp. 39–42, 43–44, 52, 53, 80
Compares and contrasts with Wordsworth's "Immortality Ode." "The poem presents and explores a view of the human situation and a response to it which . . . we can recognise as essentially existentialist."

1989   RICHWELL, "Poetic Immortality," pp. 7–10
"The characters in this spirited narrative poem detailing her

growth as a poet are the poet herself and an unidentified man who variously fills the roles of God, lover, teacher, and muse. At any rate his appearance in Dickinson's life heralds the birth of her writerly self."

"Let us play yesterday" (728)

1979 PATTERSON, *Dickinson's Imagery*, pp. 31, 44, 65, 94–95, 103, 197
Notes reference to Isaiah 35:5–6 and possible source in *Atlantic Monthly* article that "exalts the ellipse as the most beautiful of geometric forms."

1982 MOSSBERG, *Emily Dickinson*, pp. 136, 147–52, 154–55, 156, 190, 196, 205 n. 1, 208 n. 6
"It is an evocation of childhood which features the tormenting savior and daunted daughter and all the accompanying motifs of the daughter construct: famine, imprisonment, dependence, ambivalence, repression, accusation, and craftiness."

1983 SHURR, *Marriage*, pp. 113–14
In this poem Dickinson"reviews the three periods of her life": her life as a child, a stage when the poem's "you" opened a freer and larger life, and the third period when Dickinson anticipates "a return to the 'doomed' loneliness of her childhood."

1985 EBERWEIN, *Dickinson*, pp. 58, 172, 173
The poem's speaker "urges her friend to return imaginatively to childhood, to a point before adult freedom, and she uses an egg analogy to indicate how the friend had precipitated birth into a new identity . . . ."

" 'Lethe' in my flower" (1730)

1984 TSELENTIS-APOSTOLIDIS, "I will be Socrates," p. 20
Examines classical reference and suggests the poet may have confused "the action of 'lethe' which is in myth a drink given to the dead to forget their past lives so that they may return to the earth again."

"Life is what we make it" (698)

1981 KIMPEL, *Dickinson as Philosopher*, pp. 66–69, 70, 221–22, 224, 232, 241
"The way Jesus interprets the will of God for human life is, according to her, the one supremely trustworthy directive upon which she can unqualifiedly depend."

1987 OBERHAUS, "'Tender Pioneer,'" pp. 342–45, 350, 358
"This meditation's meaning centers on its astonishingly varied verb forms." Relates to other poems on Christ by Dickinson.
Revised and reprinted: Oberhaus, "Dickinson's Poem 698," pp. 21–25

1989 OLIVER, *Apocalypse of Green*, p. 87
The poem "proclaims the poet's willingness to accept responsibility for her life and relinquish fears about the unknown in death and the afterlife through faith in Christ . . . ."

"Lift it with the feathers" (1348)

1982 MADIGAN, "Mermaids," pp. 39–40
Discussion of sea imagery in Dickinson's poetry. The sea here "is perceived on two levels: the literal 'aquatic' sea experienced by the lower powers or senses, and the higher symbolic sea unperceived except by the imagination."

"Light is sufficient to itself" (862)

1978 WIENOLD, "Some Aspects," pp. 128, 132–35
Semantic analysis of linguistic structure, specifically "the verb-noun phrase-nexus with the noun phrase in the object position."

1979 KELLER, K., *Only Kangaroo*, pp. 156–57, 159
Compares with passage from Emerson's "Fable." In her poem "she catches her mentor looking too narrowly—at only the synecdoches—while she opens her eyes wider than he does his and calls his attention to a light (a grace?) larger than these vulgar considerations . . . ."

1988 WOLFF, *Emily Dickinson*, p. 480
Notes poem's "self-consciously Emersonian terms." "No universal sign, 'Light' exists entirely in its own right. It came into being for no purpose. It *is*. Nothing more."

"Lightly stepped a yellow star" (1672)

1983 WALKER, N., "Humor as Identity," p. 62
Dickinson "parodies the language of conventional nature poetry." In this poem she "assumes the same equality with God that she assumes with nature."

1984   OLPIN, "Hyperbole: Part II," p. 8
"God's powers are clearly understated in the emphasis on punctuality in the face of his immense power."

"Like brooms of steel" (1252)

1989   MONTEIRO, G., "Dickinson's 'Like Brooms,'" pp. 19–23
". . . when set against the more famous snowstorm poems of her New England elders, [this poem] reads like a reduced and fragmentary reduction of their 'completed' poems. For all its promise her poem remains unfinished . . . ."

"Like eyes that looked on wastes" (458)

1977   BENNETT, "Language of Love," pp. 15, 17 n. 11
The poem is "a tissue of code words" and describes a "homoerotic relationship."

1978   MILLER, R., "Transitional Object," pp. 461–62
". . . her image, her self, are locked in a compact of misery not merely endless but innately a part of the choice she has made—a divine compact to become a poet."

1979   CAMERON, *Lyric Time,* pp. 141–42, 171
In this poem "loss is the feature in which the speaker recognizes herself, the mirror where it all becomes clear. . . . In the self-reflexive parody of completion, pain is identity."

1980   PORTERFIELD, *Feminine Spirituality,* pp. 133, 135
"Although the vision of the Eyes and the vision of the poet are antagonistic, they are dependent on each other. Each antagonist requires the other to exist . . . ."

1981   PORTER, *Dickinson,* pp. 11, 169
"Here, with a mirror image anticipating Prufrock, is the particular Christology of Dickinson at the midpoint of the nineteenth century when the mediations of an habitual faith had, for her it seems, broken down."

1982   BURBICK, "Irony of Self-Reference," pp. 88–89
Examines pronominal language. "The reader is left attempting to distinguish between an objectification of the self and an encounter between the self and other."

MOSSBERG, *Emily Dickinson,* pp. 24, 178–81, 197
"This is a key poem in understanding Dickinson's life as a daughter

as it relates to her aesthetic strategy. . . . it serves as an important example of the process of objectification of the creating self for the purpose of art . . . ."

1983   HOMANS, " 'Oh,Vision,' " pp. 121–23, 124
    "Among the love poems that are gender-marked in such a way as to define both speaker and addressee as female, [this poem] presents both the advantages and the disadvantages of such a strategy both for life and for language and verse."

        MORRIS, A., " 'The Love of Thee,' " pp. 110–11
    This poem explores "the idea of a royal marriage between queens. . . . It is clear that unlike the union of king and queen this marriage would be mutually empowering . . . but it is also clear that the union cannot be achieved."

1984   POLLAK, *Dickinson*, pp. 144–45
    ". . . in a rare poem in which Dickinson implicates both women equally in this proud homosexual terror, freedom and impotence meet."

1989   FULTON, "Moment of Brocade," p. 43
    Suggests that the poem "can be read as a female writer's awaking to disenfranchisement."

"Like rain it sounded till it curved" (1235)

1981   PORTER, *Dickinson*, p. 60
    Here we see the poet "accelerating images into metaphors and then beyond that into a private phrase seemingly packed with meaning but in fact unintelligible."

1989   MUNK, "Musicians Wrestle," pp. 7–9
    Dickinson is here "describing poetic inspiration in terms of the divine *SPIRITUS* or *kneuma*."

"Like some old fashioned miracle" (302)

1978   MANN, "Dream," pp. 20–21
    Relates poem's use of "Dream" to that in other Dickinson poems. Here the word "signifies an analogy for the poet's recollection of those real objects of the summer, now disappearing in the seasonal cycle."

1985   BUDICK, *Emily Dickinson*, pp. 60–61
    "In some of her poems the poet wishes that the parallels between nature and Christian theology were indeed true, as in [this poem] in which she weeps for a plausibility that is painfully absent."

"Longing is like the seed" (1255)

1978 CAMERON, "Naming as History," pp. 233, 236
Exemplifies "Dickinson's definitional poems where the poem's conclusion follows poorly from its beginning."
Reprinted: Cameron, *Lyric Time,* pp. 34–35, 38; Ferlazzo, *Critical Essays,* pp. 196–97, 199

1987 BARKER, *Lunacy of Light,* p. 122
Dickinson "could be suggesting that the poet, like the seedling, reconciles the differences between dark and light, earth and sky. . . . In archetypal terms, of course, she is suggesting that by gaining strength from the feminine she will be able to confront—and enjoy—the masculine."

1988 WOLFF, *Emily Dickinson,* pp. 477–78, 579 n. 7
The "pale shades of Jacob at Peniel and revivals in mid-nineteenth-century Amherst can be discovered" in this "generally secular verse" that is permeated by "the spent terminology of the Christian myth."

"Look back on time with kindly eyes" (1478)

1981 KIMPEL, *Dickinson as Philosopher,* pp. 77, 79
"By persisting in thinking of what one morally ought to do, one actually can increase the oppressive weight of his life, adding to its already discouraging occurrences."

"Love is anterior to life" (917)

1982 THOTA, *Emily Dickinson,* p. 106
"Dickinson's definition of love . . . states love as a continuum through life and death. The sequence that emerges is: love-life-death-love, a cyclic process resembling that of the seasons in nature."

1983 JUHASZ, *Undiscovered Continent,* pp. 49, 50, 51, 184 n. 9
"A poem about idea, this epigram makes it clear that idea does not exist in a vacuum, as it maps with precision love's situation."

1984 BOGUS, "Not So Disparate," p. 40
Suggests poem was influenced by Elizabeth Barrett Browning's "Catarina to Comoens."

"Love is that later thing than death" (924)

1983 SHURR, *Marriage,* pp. 179, 198
The poem is "a definition of love, contextualized by the process

of procreation. . . . its elements . . . bring together love, pregnancy, birthing, and the early death of a child."

"Love thou art high" (453)

1988 BEPPU, " 'O, rare for Emily,' " pp. 185–86
". . . the subjunctive mood in the final stanza . . . indicates the supremacy of love and some hope beyond death in 'Eternity.' 'Just think of Antony and Cleopatra,' the poem seems to say."

"Make me a picture of the sun" (188)

1982 SOULE, "Robin," pp. 71, 73
In this poem "Dickinson resolves the disparity between artifice and nature by acknowledging the pretensions of art and by gently lampooning the species of cloistered art that can result from a failure to recognize artifice as artifice."

1988 OAKES, "Welcome and Beware," pp. 196–98
Examines relation of poem's speaker to "her auditor-reader."

"Many a phrase has the English language" (276)

1983 SHURR, *Marriage,* pp. 65–66
This love poem is a riddle; the answer is "I love you," which "had been spoken to Dickinson . . . presumably by the beloved whose presence is pervasive in the fascicles."

1985 PHILIP, "Valley News," pp. 72–73
This poem "fully demonstrates Dickinson's point that something powerful happens prior to any formulated response—that the poem is always in that sense 'Prospective', that it is always 'saying itself'."

1988 WOLFF, *Emily Dickinson,* pp. 368–69, 416
The poem "raises a fundamental query. Which is better, the 'bright Orthography' of love poetry or the 'Hush' of love enacted? Might not the presence of the beloved and the possibility of intimacy's sweet delight displace the value even of verse?"

"March is the month of expectation" (1404)

1979 PATTERSON, *Dickinson's Imagery,* pp. 176–77
Discussion of the significance of March to Dickinson. Considers evolution of ideas shown in work-sheet drafts.

"Me, come! My dazzled face" (431)

1983   SHURR, *Marriage*, p. 28
The poem contains one of the poet's "strongest assertions of faith."

1988   WOLFF, *Emily Dickinson*, p. 198
"This may seem at first to be a poem about the entrance into Heaven; however, the allusion to 'feet' . . . signals that the subject is in reality the kind of 'Election' conferred upon poets."

1989   RICHWELL, "Poetic Immortality," p. 15
This poem "provides an excellent introduction to the name/fame theme in Dickinson's poetry and its relationship to her religious vocabulary."

"Me from myself to banish" (642)

1979   JUHASZ, "Undiscovered Continent," pp. 89–91
Consideration of Dickinson poems in which "the enclosure and confinement experienced in the place of the mind is established with an architectural vocabulary."
Revised and reprinted: Juhasz, *Undiscovered Continent*, pp. 17–18, 24, 172

1980   BURBICK, "Revenge of the Nerves," pp. 101–02
"This poem takes the form of a residual *psycho-machia* or conflict of the soul."

1981   PORTER, *Dickinson*, pp. 54, 274
"This is the language of the psychic life of the modern: isolated, problematic, the mental event cut loose from any context that would make it intelligible. The poem is the drama without the plot, the pain without the cause, the existential phenomenon simply of self-destructive psychic energy."

1982   BURBICK, "Irony of Self-Reference," pp. 84–88, 90, 91, 94 nn. 13–14
Examines implications of poem's pronominal language. "In the battle of the Me and the Myself, Dickinson reconceptualizes the dynamics of the self and creates through the use of self-reflexive pronouns a disturbing language of the self."

MOSSBERG, *Emily Dickinson*, pp. 4, 30–31, 48, 101, 174–75, 206 n. 3
"Describing the persona's mind as engaged in civil war may be a

metaphor for the creation process that depends upon identity conflict. As long as the war manifests itself in madness and dissociation of sensibility, the general-poet exists."

SALSKA, *Poetry of the Central Consciousness,* pp. 65–66, 148
". . . unlike in Whitman where ideally the different aspects of self fuse into identity, in Dickinson they are contending forces, forever locked in an unresolvable conflict. Her self is a compound of . . . irrational impulses including subconscious and instinctive urges as well as affections . . . ."
Revised and reprinted: Salska, *Walt Whitman and Emily Dickinson,* pp. 55–56, 135

1986 MOREY, "Dickinson-Kant: The First Critique," pp. 60, 61, 62
"Here the ego-self axis of Jung is suggested strongly, or in a Kantian point of view, the two egos: the phenomenal and the transcendental. . . . This is an example of the Transcendental ego observing the phenomenal ego at work."

1987 LEONARD, G. M., "Necessary Strategy," p. 86
"Being impregnable to the outside world is brought about only by fragmenting oneself and thus subjugating consciousness: a sort of numbness reigns. But even this numb feeling is a precarious monarchy, since the banished self may attack at any time."

1989 GARBOWSKY, *House without the Door,* pp. 130, 132
The poem exhibits a "conflict between the soul or spirit and the self."

HOCKERSMITH, " 'Into Degreeless Noon,' " p. 281
The poem's speaker "has no 'peace' because of a perpetual 'assault.' . . . She is being tormented by her continual awareness of her own existence in time."

"Me prove it now, whoever doubt" (537)

1978 CARTON, "Dickinson and the Divine," pp. 247–48
"The self's completed quest for contact, its integration with God, not only is a self-annihilation but may be a self-deception as well."
Revised and reprinted: Carton, *Rhetoric,* pp. 54–55

1988 PHILLIPS, *Emily Dickinson,* pp. 110–11, 115
Suggests poem's debt to Eliot's *The Mill on the Floss.*

"Meeting by accident" (1548)

1983   SHURR, *Marriage,* p. 164
"She seems here to return to the idea of their marriage made in heaven, ratified by heaven even though it cannot be enjoyed on earth."

"Midsummer was it when they died" (962)

1983   SHURR, *Marriage,* p. 114
"The beloved had performed a function in her life . . . and now can disappear as a physical presence. The marriage now becomes a timeless, spaceless perfection. This is serenely expressed in [this poem]."

1989   OLIVER, *Apocalypse of Green,* pp. 73–74
"There is no equivocation here but rather a clear statement of the role of death in the process of perfecting a human life."

"Mine by the right of the white election" (528)

1979   KELLER, K., *Only Kangaroo,* pp. 25, 231, 289–90
"Self-sufficiency, self-reliance, and individual conscience were the promise of covenant theology, as she asserts in one of her most exclamatory, explicitly theological poems."

WESTBROOK, *Free Will and Determinism,* pp. 55–56
"The choice of words echoes not only the speech of Emily's lawyer father but also the old Puritan legalistic view of the Covenant of Grace whereby God enters into a contract with His elect."

1982   MARCUS, *Emily Dickinson,* pp. 56, 59
"The poet's frenetic attitude may influence even our perception of the poem's central purpose, which is to celebrate the possession of a beloved person, by leading us to suspect that considerable doubt may lie behind its overly emphatic affirmation."

1983   JUHASZ, *Undiscovered Continent,* pp. 101–03, 106, 108, 111, 183 n. 3
The poem's "focus is not external but internal; its concern is with what the speaker feels because she has what she wants. . . . our primary impression of the poem is of its tone, its delirious delight; form and vocabulary reveal something about how the speaker got that way."

SHURR, *Marriage,* pp. 36, 86–87
"In the fascicle . . . the poem follows an equally intense poem of possessiveness, obviously addressed to the husband. Thus contextual-

ized, [it] leaps suddenly into focus as another hymn to Dickinson's anomalous marriage . . . ."

1984   POLLAK, *Dickinson*, pp. 174–75
"This imbalance between a referential language of experience and a nonreferential language of language camouflages the delirious egoism the poem cannot conceal. God expands as nature recedes; the persona becomes godlike in an empty universe."

1986   ANDERSON, P., "Bride of the White Election," pp. 7–8
Relates to text of hymn, "Holy Bible, Book Divine." "Tracing the poem to a particular hymn bolsters theological interpretation."

JONES, "'Royal Seal,'" pp. 44–45, 46, 50 n. 19
The poem's "traditional terminology" seems to refer to "present experience, rendering what is human, 'divine.' The 'Charter' and the baptismal 'Seal' that signs it both allude to a fulfillment of human happiness won through earthly suffering."

1987   COOK, C., "Psychic Development," p. 131
"She has accomplished her goal of finding eternity, of joining with her inner self, and of capturing those moments of immortality in her writings. Nothing can ever take away what she has done . . . ."

EBERWEIN, "Sacramental Tradition," pp. 69–70
"Whether it celebrates an actual experience of assurance or is simply an imaginative rendering of what conversion would feel like to the saved, it shows the poet working brilliantly within an enduring Puritan system of language."

HUGHES, D., "Queen of Sheba," p. 22
"The Scarlet Prison is the body itself, necessary for the making of the poem, and the Vision and Veto are the rewriting of her poems that has left them so open."

1988   PHILLIPS, *Emily Dickinson*, pp. 113–15, 229 n. 26
The Scarlet Letter is a source for this poem. "Dickinson's Hester Prynne, in the language of Puritan theology and politics, passionately affirms her independence, her rightful beatitude . . . ."

REYNOLDS, *Beneath the American Renaissance*, pp. 433–34
"The lack of a clear referent for 'Mine' points up the radical openendedness of meaning that results from the creative fusion of opposing cultural elements."

WOLFF, *Emily Dickinson*, pp. 196–98, 200, 217, 396, 409, 531
"A traditional Christian lyric would celebrate God's supremacy;

this heretical hymn glorifies the individual's ability to remain intact despite cosmic threats and bribes."

1989   OLIVER, *Apocalypse of Green,* pp. 110–11
Considers biblical references and echoes. "The persona clearly has no doubts in this poem as she unhesitatingly proclaims her assurance of election, the vision of which is hers as is also the veto . . . ."

"Mine enemy is growing old" (1509)

1982   MOSSBERG, *Emily Dickinson,* pp. 193, 194–95
"The implication is that we 'grow' through recognizing and acting upon anger, dissatisfaction, and need. Dickinson wants to 'grow' to be a great poet; her aesthetic which cultivates hunger and pain would seem to imply that hunger-anger is necessary to grow 'fat.' "

"More life went out when he went" (422)

1979   CAMERON, *Lyric Time,* pp. 149–51, 269 n. 13
". . . we might say that the poem chills its readers with the dry ice of its words, verbally shaping the plenitude of thanatotic possibility, urging that we note the degree of terminal cold as one registered by individual difference."

1983   KHAN, "Agony of the Final Inch," pp. 25–26
"The poem employs life and death as sustained metaphors to describe love and separation in love respectively, thru the device of antithesis."
Revised and reprinted: Khan, *Emily Dickinson's Poetry,* pp. 26–28

1986   CARRUTH, "Emily Dickinson's Unexpectedness," pp. 52–55
An appreciation of poem's techniques and diction. Suggests reducing the poem to more conventional punctuation and word arrangement as an aid to understanding.

ROBINSON, J., *Emily Dickinson,* pp. 155–57, 180, chap. 6 n. 2
"There seems to me no doubt that the poet's preference is for the distinguished and the exceptional against the commonplace life, and we are encouraged to follow her."

1988   STOCKS, *Modern Consciousness,* pp. 56–57
"The existentialist death-theme, the 'authentic' and the 'inauthentic' dying, is presented in this poem, in vivid imagery, more than sixty years before Heidegger."

"More than the grave is closed to me" (1503)

1984 WOLOSKY, *Emily Dickinson,* pp. 27–28
"The grave, with all its secrets, is closed to her. Her faith cannot quite negotiate the distance between life and death. And she has glimpsed the crash that would follow a complete loss of faith."
Reprinted: Wolosky, "Syntax of Contention," pp. 182–83

1987 BLASING, *American Poetry,* p. 182
Comments on technique exhibited by poem, which "focuses on the syllable as a building block in order to show how it adds meanings . . . ."

"Morning is due to all" (1577)

1981 KIMPEL, *Dickinson as Philosopher,* p. 152
This poem "affirms a basic teaching in versions of Mahayana Buddhism. It is that, whereas all living beings are capable of some understanding of the Way or Dharma . . . the full light of enlightened living is a blessedness for only a relatively few."

" 'Morning' means 'milking' to the farmer" (300)

1988 WOLFF, *Emily Dickinson,* pp. 352–54
". . . 'Morning' is no more than a medium of communication between those on earth and the transcendent force that lies behind the material world. God communicates with us through such 'signs' as this, and it is the *meaning* of God's message that the poem tracks."

"Much madness is divinest sense" (435)

1978 ABAD, *Formal Approach,* pp. 132–34, 152, 369, 418
Discussion of whether poem is properly classifiable as "lyric of definition" or "lyric of reaction."

WOLFF, "Dickinson's 'Much Madness,' " pp. 3–4
In a sense this poem "is about itself. . . . structure itself has meaning here." The poem is "a gnomic riddle. It asks a question: 'What is Truth?' And in its form it gives the answer: 'To discover Truth, you must read between the lines.' "

1979 NATHAN, "Slanted Truth," p. 36
"The key to the riddle is obviously the 'discerning eye.' Since few are gifted with it, the majority is obviously incapable of *seeing* the truth."

1982   MARCUS, *Emily Dickinson*, p. 64
Relates to other Dickinson poems on society. This poem "leaves the picture and nature of the cruel behavior which it attacks so generalized that one may not immediately notice its social satire."

1983   WILLIAMS, D., "'This Consciousness,'" p. 369
In the poem's opening line Dickinson "was trying to get beyond the metaphor and symbol and to say directly that what people call madness is in fact the only way to heaven."
Revised and reprinted: Williams, D., *Wilderness Lost*, p. 203

1984   WALLACE, *God Be with the Clown*, pp. 102–03
"The incongruity between the tone of the first and last lines produces a comedy that refines to agony."

1986   ROBINSON, J., *Emily Dickinson*, p. 66
Most people "do not understand the vast forces with which they are playing. Emily Dickinson is aware of those forces . . . and the claim to superior understanding and proximity to divinity and death—or madness—which such divine knowledge entailed is explored in this poem."

"Musicians wrestle everywhere" (157)

1981   KIMPEL, *Dickinson as Philosopher*, pp. 173–75
". . . for her empathic identification with everything of which she took account in nature, she could easily believe that they 'wrestled' for her delight, the opposite of which occurred in her relations with people."

1984   RUDDICK, "'Synaesthesia,'" pp. 75–76
Rather than being a synaesthetic image, the poem's "silver strife" illustrates instead the poet's technique of transferring "color adjectives from real objects . . . to abstract nouns in some way connected with those objects."

"Must be a woe" (571)

1980   REISS, "Dickinson's Self-Reliance," p. 27
"There must be suffering and loss before one can gain . . . the poetic vision. This idea almost suggests a Calvinistic dying to things of the world, but in this poetic reparation it is the things of the world which die and depart."

1981   ANDERSON, V., "Disappearance of God," p. 14
"The beauty the poet perceives is of course embodied in her verse. The poetry itself, then, is the new life, the resurrection, that has emerged

as a result of rejection, suffering, defeat. It is a 'Grace' that, like Christ's, comes at great cost."

DIEHL, *Romantic Imagination,* pp. 57, 58, 59
"Crucifixion precedes the bliss of revelation in poetry as well as religion. . . . In this theory of aesthetic compensation, suffering yields an ability to witness beauty which depends directly upon the force of the pain."

KIMPEL, *Dickinson as Philosopher,* pp. 26–27
This is "a philosophical poem or is a philosophy affirmed in poetic form."

1989 RICHWELL, "Poetic Immortality," pp. 19, 29
"Often, as in [this poem], she likens the exquisite suffering of the crucifixion to the pain she endures in creating a life from which she can make poetry."

"Mute thy coronation" (151)

1983 HOMANS, "'Oh, Vision,'" pp. 117, 118, 130
"In poems of this kind, Dickinson imagines a possibility for placing herself as a woman that is at once seductive (because traditional and comfortable) and dangerous (because it defines her as silent)."

SHURR, *Marriage,* p. 191
This is one of two early poems that "connect the broken heart with Dickinson's husband of the marriage poems."

"My cocoon tightens, colors tease" (1099)

1982 MARCUS, *Emily Dickinson,* pp. 78–79
"Its metaphor of the self as a butterfly, desiring both power and freedom, makes us think that it is about the struggle for personal growth." Relates to other Dickinson poems on "Suffering and Growth."

MOSSBERG, *Emily Dickinson,* pp. 190, 208 n. 6
"We see Dickinson . . . straining to be released from the unesteemed identity of a little girl which society has imposed on her."

1983 BENVENUTO, "Words within Words," p. 51
Suggests instances where examining definitions of key words in the

poem, as they appear in the dictionary Dickinson used, may shed light on poem's meaning.

1984   CARTON, "True Romance," pp. 97, 115 n. 12
The poem "affirms, however equivocally, that a capacity for knowledge of the divine may be attained at the boundary of human experience."
Reprinted: Carton, *Rhetoric*, pp. 9–10, 266 n. 12

1985   EBERWEIN, *Dickinson*, p. 170
"The speaker hesitates, even fears, to push through the protective margin of her outgrown circuit to assume her 'Power of Butterfly' but has no choice about pressing outward into new identity and a freedom inconceivable within the homelike prison."

1986   MOREY, "Dickinson-Kant: The First Critique," pp. 40, 65
"The overall conceit of the cocoon stands for a generally better awareness of life, for personal intimations of growth, not just vague yearnings or hopes."

1988   MONTEIRO, G., *Robert Frost*, pp. 17, 27
Cites as antecedent for Frost's "In White."

"My faith is larger than the hills" (766)

1979   GONNAUD, "Nature, Apocalypse," p. 136
The poem "offers a playful treatment of the very unequal collaboration between Nature and the poet. Continuation and staying-power are on her side . . . ."

1984   LEONARD, D. N., "Dickinson's Religion," p. 338
"The poem avoids sentimental and credulous piety not so much by allowing for doubt, but by actually affirming the paradoxical action of a faith which grows stronger through feeding on its own unbelief."

WOLOSKY, *Emily Dickinson*, pp. 15–17
The poem's "subject, diction, and metric is decisively hymnal, but [its] purport is a denial of doubt which argues its presence."
Reprinted: Wolosky, "Syntax of Contention," pp. 172–73

1989   KNAPP, *Emily Dickinson*, pp. 135–37
"Strangely enough, the more Dickinson seems compelled to prove the depth of her faith, the greater is her recourse to antithetical imagery, coloration, dissonant nouns, and adverbs."

"My first well day since many ill" (574)

1982 GUTHRIE, "Dickinson's Illness," p. 18
Relates to the poet's eye problems. "Images suggesting obstructed or impaired vision are present in the poem . . . ."

JOHNSON, "Emily Dickinson," pp. 9–10
"She needs to 'measure' and establish ratios, to measure everything against the grave, but the poem also makes a statement about her perceptual stance. To see the sun through a 'Haze,' an awareness of imperfect human perception and of death, is to 'earn' a spiritual insight . . . ."
Reprinted: Johnson, *Emily Dickinson*, pp. 54–55

1983 SHURR, *Marriage*, pp. 137, 180–181
Suggests the poem, which "describes a whole summer of 'sickness' . . . unexplained in any biography," may allude to "a painful abortion which left her sick and bedridden."

"My life closed twice before its close (1732)

1972 RAO, *Essential Emily Dickinson*, p. 163
General introduction to the poem aimed at "postgraduate students of literature in Indian Universities."

1982 LUCKETT, "Dickinson's 'My Life Closed Twice,'" pp. 32–34
"Dickinson carefully subordinates elements of meaning, rhetoric, punctuation, metrical stress, syllabication, and stanzaic form to the thematic relationship between mortal and immortal closings developed within the lyric."

MARCUS, *Emily Dickinson*, pp. 48, 49
Relates to other Dickinson poems about lost friends.

1985 COTTLE, *Language of Literature*, pp. 102–03
A note on poem's grammatical peculiarities, alliteration, rhythm; notes "a polished perfection unusual in her work."

1986 MCNEIL, *Emily Dickinson*, p. 23
"Heaven and hell manifest themselves through the same effect: in practical terms—and these are the only terms the poem is considering—they are both hellish."

1988 FLATTO, "Archetypal Import," pp. 225–27
"This paper presents speculations on the imagistic role the number

two plays in contributing to the feeling of anguish characterizing [this poem]."

"My life had stood a loaded gun" (754)

1977   AGRAWAL, *Emily Dickinson,* pp. 146–47
"There is a perfect conceit of a loaded gun carried by its possessor as the harmonious operation of heart and mind in [this poem]. . . . The heart knows that it will live longer than the mind because if the mind is hurt, it affects the heart and almost kills it, though it itself does not die."

1978   CAMERON, "Loaded Gun," pp. 425–27, 428–29, 430, 434, 436–37 nn. 4–5
The poem "plays with the idea of death as explanation and concludes by despairing of both death and explanation. Its power is a direct consequence of the explosion that hovers over the individual incident each stanza narrates and provides a counterstrain to it."
Reprinted: Cameron, *Lyric Time,* pp. 65–69, 71–72, 73–74, 76, 84, 90, 121, 141, 181, 203, 205, 250, 266 nn. 8–9; Bloom, H., *Emily Dickinson,* pp. 107–09, 110, 112–14, 115, 124, 128

1979   GILBERT and GUBAR, *Madwoman,* pp. 607, 608–10, 611, 612
"The irony of the riddling final quatrain . . . hints that it is the Gun and not the Master, the poet and not her muse, who will have the last word." Relates to a possible source, Sir Thomas Wyatt's "The Lover Compareth His Heart to the Overcharged Gun."

HAGENBÜCHLE and SWANN, "Dialectic of Rage," p. 145
"Violence here is surely the poet's violation of the world, itself a twofold act, for to name things is to kill them in their 'thingness' and at the same time to violate the dimension of total meaning proper to the 'Owner,' the God-Thanatos figure in the poem."

KAPLAN, "Indefinite Disclosed," p. 77
"It is unclear throughout the poem who is in command, and the bullet-gun-master are welded into an androgynous fantasy—violent, fetishistic and atavistic. The poem toys with omnipotence, banishes femininity."
Reprinted: Kaplan, *Sea Changes,* p. 114

KELLER, K., *Only Kangaroo,* pp. 26–27, 267–68
In this poem "full of sexual puns . . . she watches the object of her attraction and her attraction itself and also her reaction to the attraction. As a poet, she can have her passion and observe it too."

"My life had stood a loaded gun"

PATTERSON, *Dickinson's Imagery,* pp. 14, 17, 37, 48, 128, 174, 211–12 n. 7
Notes echoes from Tennyson and Hawthorne.

1981 PORTER, *Dickinson,* pp. 1, 209–18, 256, 301 n. 6
"Three related functions create the signification of the poem: the poem's voice is language itself, the language gun has the power to kill, and language to be purposeful and not randomly destructive must be under some mature authority."
Revised and reprinted: Porter, "First Modern," p. 19

PORTER, "First Modern," p. 19
"The poem's semiotic message, then, lies in its very *indefiniteness. . . .* It is perhaps the most blindly forceful of all the works that reflect Dickinson's troubled freedom from experience, from meaning, and from identity."

1982 D'AVANZO, "Source in Wyatt," pp. 40–43
Dickinson may have borrowed the figure of the gun from a poem by Sir Thomas Wyatt and "used it as a conceit" that the poet invested with "psychological, sexual, and artistic dimensions."

MARCUS, *Emily Dickinson,* pp. 53–54, 55
The poem "presents an allegory about the pursuit of personal identity and fulfillment through love, and yet it is quite possible that the joy of the poem conceals a satire directed back against the speaker . . . ."

MOSSBERG, *Emily Dickinson,* pp. 19–23, 24, 26, 27, 65–66, 169, 194, 197, 201 Part I n. 2
"What this poem most significantly represents . . . is an array of conflicting attitudes toward art and the self, which result in severe identity conflict. According to this poem, speaking is a powerful and destructive activity for women. Poetry is not creation so much as it is annihilation . . . ."

STOCKER, "We Roam," pp. 43–50
"The Gun's narrative presents in allegory certain aspects of ED's career as a poet, prior to the date . . . when the poem was composed."
Line-by-line analysis.

1983 GILBERT, "Wayward Nun," pp. 27, 28, 29
". . . the central mystery-as-miracle the poem records is the woman writer's appropriation of her Master/owner's power. Though he has identified her, seized her, carried her away, it is finally she who, in a kind of prototypical role reversal, guards him with her deadly energy."

SHURR, *Marriage,* pp. 46, 110–11
Examines the sixth stanza. "The imagery of the gun . . . serves to focus much in Dickinson's mind regarding her marriage and its aftermath . . . ."

1984   CHERRY, "Sexuality and Tension," pp. 12–13, 20
"Activity and passivity constantly jar against one another in the poem. . . . Because of the power gained by the capacity for death, the master's life can have a completeness, while the speaker must face loss and incompletion."

POLLAK, *Dickinson,* pp. 150–55
"No other Dickinson poem testifies more urgently to the rage engendered by her suspicion of the feminine principle in her universe, seeks more urgently to expel it, or fails more absolutely in the attempt."

WOLOSKY, *Emily Dickinson,* pp. 92–95
". . . whether the poem is read finally in terms of psychic or divine forces, the problem of destructive power in the order of the world and, therefore, of the contradictions involved in a benevolent and omnipotent God remains preeminent for Dickinson."

1985   HOWE, *My Emily Dickinson,* pp. 24–138 passim
Extended exploration of poem's images, language, and significance. Relates to Shakespeare, Elizabeth Barrett Browning, Emily Brontë, Cooper. "This austere poem is the aggressive exploration by a single Yankee woman, of the unsaid words—slavery, emancipation, and eroticism."

LOVING, "'Hansom Man,'" pp. 98–99
"The phrase 'the power to die' appears oxymoronic until we recall that death is the power of change. . . . Death is a power because it makes life meaningful. With only the 'power to kill' there is no life."

1986   BAKKER, "Emily Dickinson's Secret," pp. 345–46
In this poem "Dickinson seems to give expression" to the view that "instead of a benevolent God the universe is ruled by a malignant, essentially destructive power." Discusses and expands on Wolosky's 1984 interpretation.
Reprinted: Bunt et al., *One Hundred Years,* pp. 243–44

BENNETT, *Loaded Gun,* pp. 5–8, 92–93, 267, 269 nn. 8–9, 11
"Whatever else [this poem] may be about, it is about the woman as artist, the woman who must deny her femininity, even perhaps her humanity, if she is to achieve the fullness of her self and the fullness of her power in her verse."

BORUCH, "Dickinson Descending," pp. 872–73
"By the poem's end, the gun is thoroughly sentient and strange, its power funneled through such violent calm . . . that we forget—then remember, startled—it is some dark inner substance in human experience she speaks of, something unfounded and unstoppable, inexplicable as the riddle that ends the soliloquy."

LOVING, *Emily Dickinson,* pp. xii, 18, 45–47, 61, 69, 73, 112
". . . the *truth* in [this poem] is that man may 'outlive' God in the sense that God's creation or will is eternal. . . . Hence, a man will go on infinitely in the mind of God, but—and this is Dickinson's tragic concern in the poem—not in the particular."

McNEIL, *Emily Dickinson,* pp. 104, 175–78
"Dickinson's relation to the post-Romantic model of sublimated artistic self may best be seen in [this poem] in which she most nearly approximates it . . . ." Examines characteristics of the poem's speaker.

ROBINSON, J., *Emily Dickinson,* pp. 158–62, 180 chap. 6 n. 3
". . . the situation celebrated is one of privilege and power expressed in exclusion and killing. . . . the poem is not a history in allegorical form, but a daydream which, knowingly, thrills at the power of its own imaginings."

1987 HOLLAND, "Emily Dickinson," pp. 137–45
The poem reveals "less her appropriation of or by a male Muse than her awareness of the problematic interactions between female poet and male precursor, and finally between language and reader."

MILLER, C., *Emily Dickinson,* pp. 28, 31, 32, 34–37, 49, 59, 61, 71–72, 90, 111, 122–26, 127, 136, 137, 174, 195 n. 36, 196 n. 47, 200 n. 14
Considers it as "an adolescent fantasy about coming of age that breaks down before what should be its happy conclusion—powerful adulthood. . . ." It may also be "a terrible fantasy of adult womanhood—that condition which allows none of the privileges of childhood but few of the privileges of male adulthood in their place."

1988 BONHEIM, "Narrative Technique," pp. 258–68
Structuralist analysis. The poem is "a narrative puzzle in lyric form, and under the kind of analysis appropriate to narrative it yields up some of its more hidden meanings . . . ."

PHILLIPS, *Emily Dickinson,* pp. 209–10, 236 n. 6
"Illustrating again Dickinson's capacity to develop the meanings

inherent in common language, [this poem] is the most uncommon of all of them because in it the *Word* itself is personified and speaks."

REED, "Masculine Identity," pp. 278, 279, 284–85

"In this poem, the narrator assumes the phallic role; she is the gun, and the . . . patterns of separation from others, the freedom from intrusion, security and happiness dominate the poem."

REYNOLDS, *Beneath the American Renaissance*, pp. 425–26, 427, 431

The poem "makes it clear that Dickinson is conjuring up an adventure-feminist fantasy and, simultaneously, suggesting the suspicion that this imagined power is an illusion."

WEISSMAN, " 'Transport's Working Classes,' " pp. 408, 410

"The speaker feels that her body is out of her control, unable to 'die' through orgasm without its owner, the man. To be unable to die is also a traditional form of damnation in Christian myth, the fate of the wandering Jew."

WOLFF, *Emily Dickinson*, pp. 441–46, 447

"Who am 'I,' and who is 'He'? To an Amherst audience . . . the answers would probably have been patent: death and Christ."

1989 DIEHL, "Murderous Poetics," pp. 334–35, 341, 343 n. 9

"The crucial power—what counts—is the ability to end, and this capacity the poem identifies with the Master, whether internalized or not, who has what the speaker most covets: the power to control life through closure."

DOBSON, *Strategies of Reticence*, pp. 123–26, 127

The poem's significance lies "in its embodiment of the expressive dilemma faced by any woman writer of Dickinson's time and place. . . . it embodies a superb ability and a pressing need to speak, filtered through a profound culturally conditioned anxiety about telling personal experience."

DOBSON, "Unreadable Poem," pp. 117–20

Although the poem "defies understanding," it is "in some sense a poem about utterance, an expression of the explosive or incendiary potential of speech."

DOBSON, FADERMAN, and RINGLER-HENDERSON, "Workshop Discussion," pp. 133–48

Transcript of a workshop discussion of the poem.

261

FADERMAN, "Ambivalent Heterosexuality," pp. 121–25
This poem, "like a number of other poems and letters by Emily Dickinson, is about her ambivalence toward heterosexuality, and particularly the role of a woman in a heterosexual relationship."

GILBERT, " 'Now in a moment,' " pp. 46–48, 53–54
Relates to Whitman's "Out of the Cradle Endlessly Rocking." Each work, "in some sense, records—even enacts—a ritual of aesthetic initiation."

RINGLER-HENDERSON, "Poem 754," pp. 127–31
"With imaginative insight the poet characterizes different facets of male companionship: its hierarchical dimensions, as well as its shifts of power and the way in which speaker and Master become hunting partners, bed-fellows, guard and guarded, protector and defended."

SHULLENBERGER, "My Class had stood," pp. 102–04
Suggestions for teaching the poem. "The poem's lucid and self-contained simplicity of story and the cleverness of the euphemistic metaphors . . . suggesting the cordiality of gunfire from the gun's point of view give students the pleasure of reading a fable and solving its riddles."

TRIPP, "Spiritual Action," pp. 282–303
"Close reading, comparison, and tradition . . . show that the spiritual 'form' of 'My Life' does not support currently popular sexual, aesthetic, or political 'profiles' of the poem. The poet's language, the body of her poems, and the larger cultural tradition behind them, all point to Emily Dickinson's spiritual awakening."

WALKER, C., "Feminist Critical Practice," pp. 15–18
"The poem is hysterical in certain ways and that hysteria must be understood in the historical context of a continent and a century in which women were invited to assume certain sorts of power while at the same time subtly tortured for their desires to do so."

"My period had come for prayer" (564)

1978 BURKE, "Religion of Poetry," pp. 18, 20, 22
"She sees divinity not as receptive to personal petitions, but as so impersonal and indifferent in an overwhelming way as to call for 'worship' rather than prayer."

1979 GUNN, *Interpretation of Otherness*, pp. 192–95, 202
The poem "is concerned to describe a fundamental change in at-

titude, really a basic alteration of belief. The significance of that change, however, lies less in its specific nature and character than in the reasons for it, and their consequent impact upon the shaken speaker."

O'HARA, " 'Designated Light,' " pp. 190, 192–94
"In this poem Dickinson presents the idea of the visionary quest in order to put it into question by critically repeating and reflecting on the traditional paradigm." The poem exhibits "Dickinson's ironic relationship to the idea of a god-image."

1982   MOSSBERG, *Emily Dickinson,* pp. 127, 205 n. 1
"She describes a metaphoric narrative about being driven, her previous 'Tactics' having failed, to confront God where He lives to know if He exists or not."

THOTA, *Emily Dickinson,* pp. 122–23
In this poem "she dramatises her visit to the Creator and perhaps reveals herself as having mystical experience like Henry Vaughan. . . . In no other poem she comes to terms with the Creator as clearly as in this poem."

1986   OBERHAUS, " 'Engine against th' Almightie,' " pp. 156, 159, 166–69
Relates to George Herbert's "Artillerie." Both poems are "colloquies with God as well as retrospective narratives" and "recount similar religious experiences."

1987   LEONARD, D., " 'Chastisement of Beauty,' " pp. 253–54
The poem "shows the primacy of awe in Dickinson's consciousness." It "treats the sublime experience of the soul encountering God, but this time the metaphor is a cosmic quest, in which the persona now becomes the aggressive partner in the relationship."
Reprinted: *University of Dayton Review,* pp. 44–45

MARTIN, J. E., "Religious Spirit," pp. 505–06
Dickinson here moves "the speaker from the mechanical exercise of routine prayer . . . to the radical confrontation with the Other. This experience takes her out of herself, transports her into a world indefinite, beyond and, above all, demanding a response of awe and worship."

1989   OLIVER, *Apocalypse of Green,* pp. 197–98
"The essential difference between man and God, and between earth and Heaven is that between finitude and infinity."

"My portion is defeat today" (639)

1982   MOSSBERG, *Emily Dickinson*, p. 128
   In this poem "Dickinson describes a pathetic scene that illustrates the tragic futility of believing in a powerful, merciful God—and hence, prayer."

1984   WOLOSKY, *Emily Dickinson*, pp. 56–59
   In this and "every other war poem, she scrupulously refrained from taking sides. She sympathized with the defeated without partisanship. She could not celebrate victory, regardless of the victors."
   Revised and reprinted: Wolosky, "Dickinson's War Poetry," pp. 34–35

1987   LEDER and ABBOTT, *Language of Exclusion*, pp. 26–27, 108, 112–13
   This Civil War poem, which stresses "the waste of defeat, the loss, and the preference for heroic victory, even at the risk of death," is in some ways a sequel to "Success is counted sweetest." It "explores a recurrent theme and clearly shows her consciousness of the physical price of war."

"My reward for being was this" (343)

1989   OLIVER, *Apocalypse of Green*, pp. 107–08
   "The Biblical references are clearly of an eschatological nature." Notes combination of political images with biblical ones.

   WOLFF, "Usable Past," p. 641
   The poem's "language is deliberately and deftly over-determined—toying simultaneously with Biblical and religious connotations, meanings that have to do with American politics and business, and diction that alludes rather specifically to the narrowness of a woman's particular choices."

"My river runs to thee" (162)

1981   KIMPEL, *Dickinson as Philosopher*, pp. 274–75
   This poem "expresses only a peaceful resignation toward death as a passage into a boundless, open expanse, and in this association of death with an unrestricted future, she expresses an acceptance of death without protest."

1982   MADIGAN, "Mermaids," pp. 45, 46
   "The tone of the poem, verging on desperation, indicates a passionate desire, not for Emersonian self-reliance, but for subordination to

some all-consuming beloved, whether an actual person . . . or Eternity itself."

1983   WILLIAMS, D., " 'This Consciousness,' " p. 374
"The Blue Sea was Eternity, the infinite depth of God personified by Christ. Hers was the classic position of the Christian mystic, betrothed to Christ."
Reprinted: Williams, D., *Wilderness Lost,* p. 207

My soul accused me and I quailed" (753)

1986   ROBINSON, J., *Emily Dickinson,* pp. 56–57, 58–59
". . . the position she takes up is the classic one of the Protestant conscience and . . . we can see that the underlying model is not a personal but a cultural one. The Protestant conscience fears no rebuke like its own . . . ."

"My triumph lasted till the drums" (1227)

1984   WOLOSKY, *Emily Dickinson,* p. 51
"The contrition of guns is, the poet concludes, 'Nothing to the Dead.' The future is not accessible to the present, and the pattern as a whole may finally be irrelevant."
Revised and reprinted: Wolosky, "Dickinson's War Poetry," pp. 31–32

"My wars are laid away in books" (1549)

1983   SHURR, *Marriage,* p. 163
"The 'Books' are surely the fascicles she has put together recording her mental life during the experience that stimulated the greatest of her poetry. The remaining 'Battle,' as is clear from the rest of the poem, is her own death."

"My wheel is in the dark" (10)

1935   ALLEN, G. W., *American Prosody,* pp. 316–17
Comments on poem's rhymes and grammar.

1977   AGRAWAL, *Emily Dickinson,* pp. 69–70
Dickinson"implies that how life moves remains a dark mystery, yet we know that it moves. Further, life's contrarities [*sic*] and heterogeneities disappear when one looks at it as an eternal cycle of recurrence."

1987   LEDER and ABBOTT, *Language of Exclusion,* pp. 141, 142, 145
   The poem "employs imagery from the textile mills to reflect metaphorically on one's narrow choices in life." This is part of "a sequence
of poems concerning risk, loss, death . . . ."

"My worthiness is all my doubt" (751)

1987   OBERHAUS, "Herbert and Emily Dickinson," pp. 356, 362–63
   "Much of this meditation's language and imagery is that of [George
Herbert's] *The Temple* and [Thomas à Kempis's] *The Imitation of Christ*
and thus may be responses to them. Or it may be simply that the discourse
of all three is that of Christian devotion."

1989   OLIVER, *Apocalypse of Green,* p. 105
   "The persona reasons that since God stoops to humanity in
Christ's incarnation, she must look to humanity to make her worth. . . .
the poet does not doubt that she has been 'elected,' simply that she does
not merit such consideration."

"Myself was formed a carpenter" (488)

1983   MILLER, C., "How 'Low Feet' Stagger," pp. 144, 146, 154–55 nn.
   17–18
   "The suggestion that 'We' may be female in this poem is particularly disruptive because traditionally one associates a Carpenter/poet
with Christ."

1984   WILT, "Playing House," pp. 160–61
   Examines the "knot of meanings" in this, one of many poems in
which "the poet confronts the house she is before, or within, or has become."

1988   WOLFF, *Emily Dickinson,* pp. 431–32
   "Although the poem claims to describe a process in which power
is transferred, the poem itself is finally without power. And if the image
of 'Scaffolds drop' indicates liberation, it also carries the shadow image
of an execution."

"Nature affects to be sedate" (1170)

1984   OLPIN, "Hyperbole: Part II," pp. 4–5
   There is "an element of parody in the portrayal of nature against a
Romantic tradition that sees it as all-important, even divine."

"Nature and God—I neither knew" (835)

1979 PATTERSON, *Dickinson's Imagery,* pp. 69–70, 96–97
The poem "almost certainly alludes to Leverrier's calculations respecting Mercury." Considers nature of the poem's "Secret."

1983 DIEHL, " 'Ransom,' " pp. 160–63
Examines the poem's "curiously inverted linguistic structures." Considers implications of "Herschel's private interest" and "Mercury's affair."
Reprinted: Bloom, H., *American Women Poets,* pp. 27–29

1984 BENFEY, *Problem of Others,* pp. 60–61
". . . Nature and God are 'like Executors,' for executors appear on the scene after a death to account for and dole out the property of the deceased. . . . The property in this case is the speaker's identity."

1986 McNEIL, *Emily Dickinson,* p. 37
In this poem "Dickinson is remarking that her knowledge is about as secret and unimportant as the most important astronomical discoveries about the universe."

1989 DIEHL, "Murderous Poetics," p. 337
"The alliance between nature and God becomes collusion in the face of the child, the parents withholding knowledge or a secret about her that they alone possess. They both execute (or kill) her identity and act it out by executing her will after her death . . . ."

"Nature assigns the sun" (1336)

1983 SIMPSON, "Dependent Self," pp. 40–41
The poem "underscores the intimate connection between friendship and mystery."

" 'Nature' is what we see" (668)

1979 GONNAUD, "Nature, Apocalypse," p. 134
Comments on implication of quotation marks around "Nature." "While it calls into question the commonsense notion of nature as an aggregate of objects individually perceived by the senses, it points to the abstracting faculty of the mind . . . ."

1980 HOMANS, *Women Writers,* pp. 190–91
The poem "exposes the futility of efforts to master nature by finding linguistic equivalencies for it."
Reprinted: Homans, "Emily Dickinson," pp. 431–32

JUHASZ, "'To make a prairie,'" pp. 17–19, 22, 25
"The poem is a dialogue, or perhaps a trio, in which concrete and abstract, object and interpretation, are contrasted."
Revised and reprinted: Juhasz, *Undiscovered Continent,* pp. 38–40, 47, 50, 51, 181 n. 11

1982   THOTA, *Emily Dickinson,* p. 78
"The strength of the poem lies in three factors: definition, 'miracle' of metaphors, and contrast. . . . Through the poem we can view the universe as an astronomer who views the skies through a telescope."

1985   ANANTHARAMAN, *Sunset in a Cup,* p. 66
"In the end, we have Dickinson trying to arrive at a conclusion by a negative process, and immediately repudiating it and leaving the problem with a few revealing insights but without resolving the doubts."

1987   COOK, C., "Psychic Development," p. 127
The poet states that "nature is more than what people see or hear; nature is eternal, like heaven; it is harmonious because all parts of nature work together to create the universe; it is indefinable, yet it is instinctively known."

"Nature sometimes sears a sapling" (314)

1984   MARTIN, W., *American Triptych,* p. 146
"By attending to the full range of her emotions, she avoided the excesses of the cult of scenery. Nature could be wantonly destructive as well as awesome or sublime."

1988   WOLFF, *Emily Dickinson,* pp. 149, 305
"Trees can tell us only about other trees. . . . The time to live is very short, and nothing endures but dissolution."

"Nature the gentlest mother is" (790)

1980   HOMANS, *Women Writers,* pp. 198–200
"Knowing that nature is not to be possessed by means of any human construct, Dickinson is not taking Mother Nature to be a personification of nature, but a figure imported from tradition and extrinsic to nature."
Reprinted: Homans, "Emily Dickinson," pp. 437, 438

1988   PHILLIPS, *Emily Dickinson,* pp. 203–04
"Is the conceit a description of Nature at 'her' best, the 'nature' of an ideal mother, or the poet's 'real' mother?"

"New feet within my garden go" (99)

1988   WOLFF, *Emily Dickinson,* pp. 297–98, 302
  Here Dickinson fuses "her insights with the direct, immediate experience of New England life." The poem "rests upon an assumption that nature's continuity is provided not by renewal, but by loss."

"No bobolink reverse his singing" (755)

1977   AGRAWAL, *Emily Dickinson,* p. 118
  Here Dickinson "uses 'Bobolink' as a symbol of the relentless inner self . . . which is deprived of its faith."

"No crowd that has occurred" (515)

1983   MILLER, C., "How 'Low Feet' Stagger," pp. 139, 153 n. 12
  Examines effect of uninflected verbs. "As befits a poem describing resurrection, there is no clear sense of time or of number here. Singular 'Dust' and plural 'Multitudes' refer to the same crowd of dead . . . ."
  Revised and reprinted: Miller, C., *Emily Dickinson,* pp. 68–70, 71

1986   ROBINSON, J., *Emily Dickinson,* pp. 47–49, 171
  The poem deals "with a location of Calvinism, but without its plan. It presents a moment, but without action. It has no outcome."

1987   OBERHAUS, "Herbert and Emily Dickinson," pp. 365–67
  "Whether or not it is a response to Herbert's 'Dooms-day,' Dickinson's dramatization of Judgment Day provides . . . evidence of the devotional nature of her mind and art . . . ."

"No man can compass a despair" (477)

1980   JUHASZ, " 'To make a prairie,' " pp. 19–21
  The poem "plays the inaccuracy of the concrete against the accuracy of the abstract in order to make a case for ignorance and lack of a fully realized consciousness."
  Revised and reprinted: Juhasz, *Undiscovered Continent,* pp. 41–43, 51, 73

1983   SHURR, *Marriage,* pp. 97–98
  "Despair is so vast that only our ignorance of its vastness keeps us going on through it."

1984   WOLOSKY, *Emily Dickinson,* pp. 24–25
  Dickinson "stops short of a declared unbelief in ends or in the

"No man saw awe, nor to his house"

structure that provided her with a teleology. Outright rejection of her faith would thrust such dislocation upon her. She therefore tries to retain her hold upon belief."
Reprinted: Wolosky, "Syntax of Contention," p. 180

"No man saw awe, nor to his house" (1733)

1982   SALSKA, *Poetry of the Central Consciousness,* pp. 67, 94
"It is a narrow escape and mere survival must count as success. . . . Her reverence for 'awe' only increases her loyalty to the mind coping as best it can with forces vastly surpassing its compass."
Revised and reprinted: Salska, *Walt Whitman and Emily Dickinson,* pp. 57, 63 n. 26, 82–83, 141

1984   WILT, "Playing House," pp. 163–64
Examines the "knot of meanings" in this poem, one of many in which "the poet confronts the house she is before, or within, or has become."

1985   SMITH, B. J., "'Vicinity to Laws,'" pp. 47–49
"The legal word-echoes of the poem prepare and re-inforce the importance of judgment and interpretation and action. They create a backbone in the poem for the abstraction of evidence and interpretation and judgment that resonates thruout. The legal words drive the poem to its law-giving end."

1986   ROBINSON, J., *Emily Dickinson,* p. 92
"It is of the very essence of human awe . . . that it skirts the edges of the familiar—as if we knew the house of awe but never went inside it. It stops our understanding and threatens life: 'A grasp on comprehension laid / Detained vitality.'"

1987   SMITH, L., "Some See God," pp. 302–09
This is "a key poem for understanding the curious mixture of orthodoxy and iconoclasm which characterizes Dickinson's later spirituality. . . . Dickinson blends Old Testament iconography with her own brand of lyrical syllogism to describe her personal apprehension of Christ's incarnation and redemption."

"No notice gave she, but a change" (804)

1980   LAIR, "Fracture of Grammar," pp. 160–61
Examines instances where poem "gains in semantic dimension through syntactic ambiguity."

"No other can reduce" (982)

1981 PORTER, *Dickinson,* pp. 27–28, 42
"It is in fact a bitterly wrought commentary on the Calvinist view of man as unworthy. But that sense is got only with great difficulty by sorting out syntax and finding the *no other . . . but* construction."

1984 WOLOSKY, *Emily Dickinson,* pp. 109–10
" 'Jehovah's Estimate' is not compatible with the estimate of mortality. . . . It represents a viewpoint that denies the stature and value of earthly existence."

1986 LEONARD, D., "Pictureless Trope," pp. 28–34
This is "a poem without image, a poem in which idea itself becomes trope and argument itself makes meter. . . . It is, among other things, Romantic in subjectivity, Victorian in doubt, metaphysical in paradox, Augustan in wit, and modern in existential irony." Examines alternative versions and other critical discussions of the poem.

"No rack can torture me" (384)

1982 SALSKA, *Poetry of the Central Consciousness,* pp. 68, 70, 71, 141
Juxtaposed with fragment of Whitman's "Song of Myself" to illustrate the "respective vision of self" in the two poets. Dickinson's "persona achieves not so much freedom 'from' as, rather, freedom 'in spite of' necessity."
Revised and reprinted: Salska, *Walt Whitman and Emily Dickinson,* pp. 58, 59, 60–61, 129

1987 COOPER, M. T., "Androgynous Temper," p. 141
"In the final two lines of this poem Dickinson is explaining how one can not only be aware of two members in a pair of opposites—in this case imprisonment and freedom; she also defines them both as consciousness. The opposites are within the same mind, the two in the one."

LEONARD, G. M., "Necessary Strategy," p. 81
"Dickinson fears attack only from within; self-betrayal is her sole enemy. . . . A free consciousness cannot be put on the rack."

1988 TRIPP, *Mysterious Kingdom,* pp. 123–24
Comments on syntax and verb forms.

1989 HOCKERSMITH, " 'Into Degreeless Noon,' " pp. 281, 290
"The final stanza implies that the soul, even if released from the body by death, can never be freed from consciousness. Consequently, the

soul's 'liberty' is still held 'captive' and imperfect by immortal consciousness."

"No romance sold unto" (669)

1981 KIMPEL, *Dickinson as Philosopher,* pp. 123–24
The poet maintains that "any analysis of the nature of self that was regarded as exhausting its nature . . . would not be a 'true' or informed interpretation . . . ."

1983 SHURR, *Marriage,* pp. 102, 131
This poem, which "argues that fiction 'dilutes' reality, that the real 'Romance' is the individual's own life," seems to sanction "a search for the 'biographical springs' of her art."

1984 CARTON, "True Romance," pp. 93–94
"Dickinson opposes the escapist literary commodity of the first line to another 'Romance,' the intimate imaginative formulation or representation of the self. . . . This latter romance is aligned . . . with precisely those things from which romance is usually differentiated: the novel and the truth."
Revised and reprinted: Carton, *Rhetoric,* p. 5

1988 REYNOLDS, *Beneath the American Renaissance,* pp. 435–36
The poem shows Dickinson "redirecting horrific themes away from the neutral realm of exterior sensationalism toward the deeper abysses of the human mind." The poem's message: "that the interior drama of the mind is far more exciting than any popular romance."

"Nobody knows this little rose" (35)

1985 BUDICK, *Emily Dickinson,* pp. 69–71
"Nobody, Dickinson admits, really 'knows' or pretends to know what nature is or what it 'might' mean in the cosmic scheme of things. . . . the question that the poem is asking is what if the implications of existence for the creatures are also the implications of existence for humankind?"

"None can experience stint" (771)

1980 MURPHY, "Definition by Antithesis," pp. 23–24
The poem illustrates development in Dickinson's use of "definition

by antithesis." Here the "process is reversed. . . . This is the antithesis of antithesis, to define the lack of a thing by the thing itself."

1984   WOLOSKY, *Emily Dickinson,* pp. 82–83
"Recompense is posited here: an art is 'Acquired by Reverse.' But it is the art of want, of stint, of famine. Attainment then becomes but another element in the economy of indigence."

"Not in this world to see his face" (418)

1981   FAST, " 'The One Thing Needful,' " p. 165
". . . the speaker prefers not to anticipate the future; in fact she prefers the 'Primer' of this world to 'the Skies,' implying her belief that heaven is perceptible within mortal experience, that she can 'see his face' now."

KIMPEL, *Dickinson as Philosopher,* pp. 137–38
"The aspect of herself which consists of hoping for a good which cannot be enjoyed in this life is spoken of, as it were, by another aspect of herself which chooses to be satisfied with what she already has, willing, as it were, to leave to the other part of her nature, 'the Skies.' "

1983   SHURR, *Marriage,* p. 75
"Those who would see Dickinson's lover as God or Christ . . . must run aground on such poems as this"; it records the "lonesome conditions of her marriage."

1984   WOLOSKY, *Emily Dickinson,* pp. 150–52
"The poet asserts that the life she has suffices her, not as a preface, but as complete in itself. . . . God's Word, as an otherworldly text, is dismissed."

1986   LOVING, *Emily Dickinson,* p. 87
The "final stanza makes it clear that the rewards of the next world—even the possession of a distant lover—simply will not satisfy the demands and needs of the self in the finite or selfless present."

"Not knowing when the dawn will come" (1619)

1981   KIMPEL, *Dickinson as Philosopher,* pp. 111–12
"The 'dawn' is predictable, as the occasion for a moral opportunity to fulfill an obligation is not. Hence, by virtue of the unpredictability of an occasion when she will be needed by another, she accepts a constant preparation as her obligation."

"Not probable—the barest chance" (346)

1984 WOLOSKY, *Emily Dickinson*, pp. 76–77
The poem "questions more than her own election. It suggests, in the trivial nature of damning offenses, doubt of the scheme itself. . . . The world seems created for the special purpose of tempting mortals to their damnation."

1986 ROBINSON, J., *Emily Dickinson*, p. 74
". . . even while she hurtled towards Judgement, she wondered what kind of world it was that could make something so awesome as one's eternal destiny depend on keeping in with God."

"Not seeing, still we know" (1518)

1978 TILMA-DEKKERS, "Immortality," p. 171
"All our attempts to gain knowledge turn out to be futile, and the poet takes refuge in the despairing attitude of presuming not to notice her incapacity."

1982 BARNSTONE, "Women and the Garden," p. 158
"Here Eden is personified as a gangster guarding the authority of the chief. Because Dickinson takes the 'dare' and does not heed 'Eden's innuendo,' she has lost the assurance of immortality on God's terms."

1989 OLIVER, *Apocalypse of Green*, pp. 86–87
In this poem, based "loosely on the New Testament passage, I Peter 1:8, . . . Dickinson is now able to accept belief in an afterlife without proof; it is to this faith that her hope has led her."

"Not so the infinite relations—below" (1040)

1983 SHURR, *Marriage*, p. 153
According to this poem "those who love on earth are doomed to eventual separation . . . but 'On High' this will not be so."

1985 JOHNSON, *Emily Dickinson*, pp. 147–48
The poem's "expression of faith is leavened by a characteristic bitterness toward the indifference of heaven."

"Not that he goes—we love him more" (1435)

1988 McHUGH, "Interpretive Insecurity," pp. 52–53
"The questions which spin out from their embedding in the poem's

single act of complex proposition ARE its spiritual charge, and they are questions that guide us away from answerability."

"Not to discover weakness is" (1054)

1982   MOSSBERG, *Emily Dickinson*, p. 209 n. 8
Here "impregnability comes about through a consciousness of the faith others have in your ability not to be vulnerable. Impregnability is not 'strength' but comes only by avoiding one's 'weakness,' through 'artifice.' "

"Not what we did shall be the test" (823)

1971   LEVIN, "Some Uses of the Grammar," pp. 21, 23, 24, 26
Considers how recoverable deletion operates in the poem.

1984   WOLOSKY, *Emily Dickinson*, p. 110
"Sacrifices are requisite, not only for their consequent reward, but because allegiance to God seems to preclude an allegiance to this world."

"Not with a club the heart is broken" (1304)

1981   ALEXANDER, "Reading Emily Dickinson," pp. 11–12, 15
"The gradual but determined restructuring of the line lengths is too subtle to prepare the reader for the final stanza's abrupt shift in tone; yet in retrospect, the whole feel of the poem can be sensed to have altered stanza by stanza."

1983   SHURR, *Marriage*, pp. 191–92
The poem reflects on "the marriage as an event with continuing effect on her life" and "analyzes the possible causes of her broken heart."

1988   PHILLIPS, *Emily Dickinson*, pp. 193–94
Questions interpreting the poem as a confession of the poet herself. It is "an examination of both a psychological phenomenon and a moral dilemma, hardly peculiar to an acutely sensitive poet."

"Now I knew I lost her" (1219)

1984   POLLAK, *Dickinson*, pp. 142–43
"Poems such as these in which her self-analysis is deflected by her analysis of someone else's neglect of her tend to be cluttered and under-developed. . . . these poems arouse our suspicion that Dickinson was an overdemanding friend . . . ."

"Obtaining but our own extent" (1543)

1986 ROBINSON, J., *Emily Dickinson,* pp. 76–77
The poem suggests "that we get in life or the hereafter only what we earn—a most un-Calvinist idea, and an acerbic one . . . ."

"Of all the souls that stand create" (664)

1978 ABAD, *Formal Approach,* pp. 136–39
Contrasts with "The soul selects her own society" to illustrate different qualities of lyric poems.

1979 BUDICK, "When the Soul Selects," pp. 352, 358–59
". . . concealed within the fragmented, hyphen-perforated form of the poem . . . runs a seething undercurrent of attack in which Dickinson charges her election-fixated preferences with wreaking havoc on the cosmos and herself."

KHAN, "Conception of Love," pp. 21–22
This poem offers Dickinson's "philosophical conception of death as a transitional moment viewed from the post-mortal perspective."
Reprinted: Khan, *Emily Dickinson's Poetry,* pp. 93–94

1982 MARCUS, *Emily Dickinson,* pp. 56–57
"The notion of separating the before and the after, and the description of life as a process of shifting sands, suggest the greater reality and stability of the afterlife."

1983 MILLER, C., "How 'Low Feet' Stagger," pp. 139–40, 154 n. 13
"Dickinson's truncated participial adjective 'create' in [this poem] . . . suggests both infinite potential and incompleteness."

1984 LEONARD, D. N., "Dickinson's Religion," pp. 342–43
The poem "implicitly identifies the 'one' that the persona has chosen as her own soul." It shows "Dickinson renouncing the world in favor of herself and her self-reliant pursuit of spiritual transcendence."

1987 CULJAK, "Dickinson and Kierkegaard," pp. 153–54
"Death is not to be feared in that it occasions the fulfillment of self. . . . The self which exists has merged fully with the self which is becoming at the moment of death, the threshold of immortality."

POHL, "Poet and a Scientist," p. 6
Poem gives strong support to identification of Major Edward Hunt as the inspiration for Dickinson's love poetry.

"Of all the sounds despatched abroad" (321)

1983 SHURR, *Marriage*, p. 22
The poem seems to develop "a comparison between the way the wind moves across the landscape and the way the hand of a lover moves across a woman's body."

"Of bronze and blaze" (290)

1977 AGRAWAL, *Emily Dickinson*, p. 104
The poem "clearly illustrates the lack of any communication between the divine and the human."

1979 HAGENBÜCHLE, "Sign and Process," p. 148
". . . it remains ambiguous whether the 'Competeless Show' refers to the overwhelming wonders of nature, or the permanence of her own work, or both. At any rate, it is the unbridgeable difference between the two realms which affects the poet."
Reprinted: *Dickinson Studies*, pp. 77–78

KELLER, K., *Only Kangaroo*, pp. 23, 228
"In her concept of womanhood at this early point in her work as poet, she feels she achieves what a man may not: instead of struggle and activity, an amazing abundance."

1982 MARCUS, *Emily Dickinson*, pp. 30–31
General consideration as one of Dickinson's "more descriptive philosophical poems of nature." "Unlike 'These are the days,' this poem shows Emily Dickinson alienated from the natural processes that symbolize immortality."

SALSKA, *Poetry of the Central Consciousness*, pp. 92, 175, 181–82
"Presumably less autonomous as well as subject to 'alarms,' the poet's art resists time more effectively than the supreme but brief spectacle of the northern lights."
Revised and reprinted: Salska, *Walt Whitman and Emily Dickinson*, pp. 80, 176, 183

1984 POLLAK, *Dickinson*, pp. 246–47
"Mortality, Dickinson suggests, is more typically an experience of inadequacy, anxious proximity to alarm, concern with reputation, with physical needs, and with the ultimate terror of irreversible anonymity. The poem momentarily reverses this terror . . . ."

1985 JOHNSON, *Emily Dickinson*, pp. 40–42, 197 n. 40
This poem "may serve as the paradigm for Dickinson's awareness of natural process in contrast to her own mortality."

1986 BLOOM, H., *American Women Poets*, pp. 3–5
The poem "overtly is 'about' the northern lights, but actually is mediated by Emerson's essay,'The Poet'. . . ." Considers poem's ironies.

1987 BLASING, *American Poetry*, p. 236 n. 9
The poem illustrates "how grammatical deviance undermines statement."

STONUM, "Dickinson Against the Sublime," pp. 32–35
The poem "begins with a generally orthodox episode of the romantic sublime and then curiously, even somewhat awkwardly, transforms the usual significance of that episode by extending it into an imagined futurity."

1988 WOLFF, *Emily Dickinson*, pp. 432–34
"The reason we do not experience Him as the Great Destroyer is that we do not experience Him in any conclusive way at all. The only thing we can know is the display, which may or may not portend a Presence behind it . . . ."

1989 HOCKERSMITH, "'Into Degreeless Noon,'" pp. 288–89, 294 nn. 17–18
"In this poem, Dickinson portrays a speaker confronted with a manifestation of the vastness of the universe. . . . [She] uses this episode to portray the process of reflection which concludes that, although men are mortal, they may achieve a limited immortality through their ability to create."

LEONARD, D. N., "Certain Slants," pp. 126, 128, 129, 130–31, 132
"The speaker recognizes that nature is simply the better poem, God, the superior artist." Relates to other poems in fascicle 13 and its "running meditation on the relation between nature and the artist."

"Of Brussels it was not" (602)

1984 RUDDICK, "'Synaesthesia,'" p. 65
The poet's use of "mellow" is too ambiguous for it to qualify as an example of "literary synaesthesia."

"Of consciousness her awful mate" (894)

1985 JOHNSON, *Emily Dickinson,* pp. 66–67
"The perceptual quest . . . involves the debilitating self-consciousness of a triple scrutiny, and the poem describes . . . a Chinese-box theory of perception."

1986 ROBINSON J., *Emily Dickinson,* pp. 56–58, 107
The poem "is without substance beyond the reference of its own drama: here, an ineffectual wish to be free set against overwhelming opposition. There is judgement, but it is an expression of power, not ethics."

1988 UNO, "Optical Instruments," pp. 240–43
"In this poem we can see Emily Dickinson's ambivalent attitude toward science and technology, and toward religion, just as 'Consciousness' and 'Soul' are 'Mate' although both of them are 'awful' to each other. Science and technology and religion are fused here without any contradiction."

1989 KNAPP, *Emily Dickinson,* pp. 117–18
In this poem "Dickinson tries to center her vision, to force open the doors that separate the known from the unknown, and thereby experience that sacred space 'Behind the Eyes of God—' that inner lens or mirror leading to the soul."

"Of course I prayed" (376)

1983 SHURR, *Marriage,* pp. 82, 104, 142–43
The poem relates to Wadsworth and Dickinson's marriage to him. It "represents a relationship that began in counselling, for religious motives, and which proceeded with typically clerical advice long after it had changed to something far more humanly intense and personal."

TEICHERT, "Divine Adversary," pp. 22–23
Examines poem's image of God and the implications of "the question of divine indifference."

1985 SALSKA, *Walt Whitman and Emily Dickinson,* p. 152
"The cause of rebellion, the factual content of the experience, is not even clearly specified because it is irrelevant. Essentially the poem is organized by the contradictory pulls of emotional response to the predicament and the apprehension of its futility."

1987   CULJAK, "Dickinson and Kierkegaard," pp. 147–48
Here the poet "suggests that non-existence might be preferable to existence without purpose. God's indifference robs man of purpose, and the poet's immediate response is anguish."

LEDER and ABBOTT, *Language of Exclusion,* p. 160
"This poem, like many Dickinson poems, paints the picture of a bleak, deistic universe that uncaringly spins its way."

MOREY, "Dickinson-Kant II," pp. 12, 13
This is "a peevish, egotistic poem . . . highly lyric in its wish not to have been born. It is not a suicide plaint directly, but more of a Job's lament, not wanting to be an apprentice of life."

1989   KNAPP, *Emily Dickinson,* pp. 128, 133
"Hiding her sorrow in expertly used puns and plays, the narrator wonders whether prayer is a form of play, a game, a joke; whether one is being 'smart' or smarts after the disappointment following the ritual."

"Of death I try to think like this" (1558)

1978   RUDAT, "Dickinson and Immortality," pp. 85–87
This poem "is at the same time informed by similarities and dissimilarities to allusive contexts both in Virgil and Milton."

1983   PESCHEL and PESCHEL, "Am I in Heaven," pp. 477–78
". . . a poem in which she conquers her fear of death by thinking about death in terms of what she understands and loves: life."

"Of glory not a beam is left" (1647)

1989   HAGENBÜCHLE, "Visualization and Vision," p. 65
"The graphic sign of the asterisk is both an evocation of absence and a metonym for the written text of the dead poets who are remembered by their work only; by contrast, the stars point at the realm of (romantic) ideals which living writers pursue."

"Of God we ask one favor" (1601)

1981   TRAVIS, "Dickinson's 'Of God,'" pp. 31–32
". . . taking the conventional idea of *felix culpa* as a point of reference, she uses the ideas of 'magic' and 'Happiness' on earth to question the rationale of sin and fall, the source of punishment, and the belief in redemption only after death, by God's grace."

1984 WOLOSKY, *Emily Dickinson,* pp. 117–18

"The critique presented here is nevertheless presented as appeal. . . . As an assault on divine distance, it is an effort to bridge that distance and to reach God, if only to admonish him."

1987 MOREY, "Dickinson-Kant II," pp. 12, 13–14

"She is questioning the Calvinist doctrine of original sin. . . . The tone is quiet, studied, even, but the unorthodoxy of her position would seem blasphemous to a Puritan."

"Of life to own" (1294)

1983 SHURR, *Marriage,* pp. 131, 157

"This remarkably compressed poem . . . can only be taken as another late reflection on, an intensely brief scenario from, her state of sexual deprivation after the anomalous marriage."

"Of nearness to her sundered things" (607)

1983 ROSENTHAL and GALL, *Modern Poetic Sequence,* pp. 69–70, 71

Discusses relationship between this, the second poem in fascicle 16, and the first, "Before I got my eye put out."

"Of paradise' existence" (1411)

1981 KIMPEL, *Dickinson as Philosopher,* pp. 280–81

"The philosophical intelligence which is expressed in this poem . . . is an awareness that any particular status of life beyond the earth is an inference. And, furthermore, it is not an inference based upon any evidence provided by a knowledge of a reality transcendent of the earth . . . ."

1983 JUHASZ, *Undiscovered Continent,* pp. 144–45

This poem "seems to be a gloss, and much more successful revision, of 'To know just how He suffered—'. . . Again the issue is not only the existence but the location of eternity, and the means of approach is, again, emphatically, knowing."

1985 KAJINO, "Moment of Death," p. 37

In this poem "we witness the poet defining death as the messenger who implies the existence of God or heaven," the messenger who bisects "our being: one half in this world and the other in heaven."

"Of so divine a loss" (1179)

1981 STEINER, "Image Patterns," p. 65
Relates to other Dickinson poems concerning "the woman in her dealings with Power."

"Of their peculiar light" (1362)

1978 HORIUCHI, *Possible Zen Traits,* p. 357
"This quatrain suggests the idea of priming a pump—a ray is kept for later use to clarify the sight being sought."

"Of this is day composed" (1675)

1984 WOLOSKY, *Emily Dickinson,* pp. 17–18
"Morning and noon . . . betray and delude, so that even their positive beauties are subverted and finally negated. . . . In the end, glory has not only been displaced by but is shown to have never been anything but a penury without remedy."
Reprinted: Wolosky, "Syntax of Contention," p. 174

1987 BARKER, *Lunacy of Light,* p. 59
Discussion of Dickinson's use of sun imagery. Here "the light of day is a seductive but abandoning figure . . . ."

"Of tribulation these are they" (325)

1983 SHURR, *Marriage,* pp. 61, 70, 144
Relates to other "martyr" poems. This poem "is about 'we' who suffered Anguish and Tribulation but not Surrender or Defeat, and who now are clothed in white like the martyrs in Revelations." Speculates on biographical significance.

1989 GARBOWSKY, *House without the Door,* pp. 81–82
The poem "encapsulates Dickinson's pattern of flight and the meaning of home. The protection the poet felt within her home is typical of agoraphobes . . . ."

OLIVER, *Apocalypse of Green,* pp. 130–32
"The poem presents a conjunction of earthly and spiritual desires. . . . [It] insists on the need for 'tribulation' and determination not to 'surrender' or acknowledge 'defeat' if worldly success or spiritual salvation is to be attained."

"Oh future! thou secreted peace" (1631)

1989 OLIVER, *Apocalypse of Green,* pp. 122, 200
Considers along with other Dickinson poems concerning "grace."
"This seems to be Dickinson's last word about grace and that last word
is a question."

"Oh shadow on the grass" (1187)

1989 OLIVER, *Apocalypse of Green,* p. 106
"While waiting for some sign that she has been elected, Dickinson
seems to believe someone else may instead be chosen. The tone of this
poem is pessimistic; the probability is slim, and certainty is not possible."

"Oh sumptuous moment" (1125)

1985 JOHNSON, *Emily Dickinson,* pp. 94, 212 n. 4
The poem expresses "a joy both sobered and rarefied by the fact
of loss. . . . Characteristically, Dickinson focuses not upon the gloating
momentary satisfaction but upon the increased value of future starvation."

"On a columnar self" (789)

1984 SEWALL, "In Search," p. 527
Comments on geological detail in Dickinson's poems, here "columnar" and "granitic."

1985 JUHASZ, "Tea and Revolution," pp. 146, 148–49
"The intellectual battle being waged between the self's solitary beliefs . . . and forces external to it is given embodiment in forms whose
tangibleness emphasizes opposing strengths."

1986 NEW, "Difficult Writing," pp. 10–11, 25 n. 8
The poem "questions the movement toward easy certainties, the
overhasty constitution of false oppositional centers. In this poem Dickinson casts an ironic eye on the 'columnar,' or situated, self."

ROBINSON, J., *Emily Dickinson,* pp. 55, 56
"It is one of those places where her verse becomes compensa-
tory. . . . Someone genuinely self-reliant would not have been so insecure
in it as to write verse defending it."

1987 BLASING, *American Poetry,* pp. 235–36 n. 5
Suggests an ironic reading of the poem. ". . . the 'Columnar Self,' then, is the self in print, rectified by the male power of the signifier that it has erected."

LEDER and ABBOTT, *Language of Exclusion,* pp. 50–51
This poem is "her culminating expression of self-confidence and self-reliance as an intellectual female. The poem freshly employs the language of architecture as a metaphor for self-development to create an image of the self in construction."

1989 JUHASZ, "Reading Dickinson Doubly," pp. 219, 220–21
"The point of the poem is that the self relies upon itself, not God, so that whether He is considered an aspect of self, or as the only thing in the universe that isn't comprised by the self, He becomes secondary to an understanding of where power resides."
Revised and reprinted: Juhasz, "Reading Doubly," pp. 87–88

"On my volcano grows the grass" (1677)

1984 KELLER, L., and MILLER, "Rewards of Indirection," p. 552
The poem "expresses the sense of strength Dickinson derives from opposing the surrounding world."

1986 ROBINSON, J., *Emily Dickinson,* p. 152
Links this poem to others employing the volcano image.

1986 FINCH, "Patriarchal Meter," pp. 170, 171
Considers "semantic-metrical connections." "The poem makes an unusually clear statement of the sense of confinement and frustration and the threatening tension that accompany the renunciatory poetics of Dickinson's hymn stanza."

1989 KNAPP, *Emily Dickinson,* pp. 163–65
"The 'volcano' in Dickinson's poem is a *kratophany* (a manifestation of force). Charged with dynamism and equated with spiritual illumination, eruption leads to a breakthrough of an idea: its transformation from a latent power in the unconscious to its concretization in the consciously written word."

"On such a night, or such a night" (146)

1988 WOLFF, *Emily Dickinson,* p. 180
"Transcendent pain demands some stronger reaction than pity. The

strategy of [this poem] addresses precisely this demand as it makes the effort to move beyond mere pity."

"On this wondrous sea" (4)

1977 AGRAWAL, *Emily Dickinson,* pp. 69, 119
"The inner self steers the course of life making an inward journey into the mysterious psyche whose surface, like [the] sea's, is tranquil, but beneath which is turbulence—the chaotic condition of the sub-conscious and the unconscious."

MONTEIRO, G., "Pilot-God Trope," pp. 42, 46–47
This "doublet poem" may be read as "a rather orthodox religious poem" or "a 'Christianized' love poem."

1979 PATTERSON, *Dickinson's Imagery,* p. 198
Relates to other references to the West in Dickinson's poetry.

1985 ANANTHARAMAN, *Sunset in a Cup,* pp. 90–91
The poem is "a brief dialogue between the 'thee' of the poem and the 'pilot' on the subject of 'eternity'. The first stanza expresses the doubt of the persona as to which land is she being sailed."

"Once more, my now bewildered dove" (48)

1979 ESTES, "Search for Location," pp. 208, 217 n. 4
This early poem "expresses great hope that the poet will discover her location if she keeps searching. The memory of Noah who sent out a dove from the ark several times before learning that the flood waters had receded is the basis of optimism."

"One blessing had I than the rest" (756)

1987 TAYLOR, C., "Kierkegaard," pp. 572–73
"This 'Blessing' has been only an intimation of paradise, of perfect sizes and unlimited dreams. Recognizing its own limited perspective, the speaking voice acknowledges that even its own negative opposition is empty speculation."

1980 JOHNSON, "'Pearl of Great Price,'" pp. 211–13
The poem provides "a synthesis of all the major concerns which recur throughout her work: perception; her preoccupation with measurement . . . and size; the 'value' of the individual, striving quester; the pos-

sibility of a paradise within; . . . a justification of the ratios of earthly loss and artistic gain."

Revised and reprinted: Johnson, *Emily Dickinson*, pp. 9, 136–39, 211 n. 27

1983 JUHASZ, *Undiscovered Continent*, pp. 63–65, 78, 80, 82, 86, 92, 130
    "In its process the poem reveals how the equivalent perfection of despair—its ultimate and overwhelming totality, its dreadful 'contentment'—must be fought with precisely those weapons that despair is so adept at destroying: the ability to gauge."

1984 WOLOSKY, *Emily Dickinson*, pp. 10–11, 13, 14, 15
    "The paralysis of fragmented parts becomes indistinguishable from the immutable oneness of eternity. The poem is thus itself posing the problem of containment, of its contours and its valence."
    Reprinted: Wolosky, "Syntax of Contention," pp. 168–69, 170, 172

1985 EBERWEIN, *Dickinson*, p. 184
    The poet thought she had "crossed circumference . . . and the experience released her from her sense of limitation until the glorious awakening was withdrawn to leave her with a tragic sense of deprivation and betrayal. She has been granted a glimpse beyond circumference but has been denied access to the promised joy."

1989 OLIVER, *Apocalypse of Green*, pp. 175, 176–77, 233, 234
    This poem and "Which is best? Heaven" compare "the relative merits of an earthly Heaven and a spiritual one, and in both the persona opts for the earthly." Here Dickinson "describes a life so rich, so full, that there is no need for either judgment or Heaven."

"One crown that no one seeks" (1735)

1985 EBERWEIN, *Dickinson*, p. 250
    The poet here examines "the paradox of voluntary agony, pointing out that the pain other men avoided was actively pursued by Christ . . . ." Consideration of crucifixion imagery in Dickinson's poetry.

1987 OBERHAUS, " 'Tender Pioneer,' " pp. 347, 349–50, 352
    "The hieroglyph and meditational focus of [this] emblem poem is the Crown of Thorns Jesus wore when presented to Pontius Pilate." Relates to other Dickinson poems on the life of Christ.

"One crucifixion is recorded only" (553)

1986 ROBINSON, J., *Emily Dickinson*, pp. 130–31
    "There are—in a vein of thought which is decidedly Emersonian—

as many Calvaries as there are people, although an observer might be conscious only of the public Calvary, the famous one."

1987 OBERHAUS, "'Tender Pioneer,'" pp. 351–54, 358
Stanza-by-stanza analysis. Secular interpretations of this poem are called into question. "Dickinson's internalization of biblical texts is . . . that of the great poets of the Bible and that of the epitome of Christian poets, George Herbert."

1988 WOLFF, *Emily Dickinson,* pp. 456–58
". . . when the notion of the Divinity loses its hold upon our imagination . . . Christ becomes noteworthy not because He was divine, but because He was human; the meaning of Calvary is defined not by transcendent values, but by earthly ones."

1989 DIEHL, "Murderous Poetics," pp. 339–40
In this poem "the speaker universalizes Christ's suffering only to defuse the full impact of her closing lines, which identify her specifically as the imminent Christ."

"One day is there of the series" (814)

1987 BLASING, *American Poetry,* pp. 173, 180
Comments on effect of poem's alliteration.

"One dignity delays for all" (98)

1980 LAIR, "Fracture of Grammar," pp. 161–62
". . . the meaning of the entire poem may hinge upon the syntactic interpretation of the single word 'pomp.'"

1984 OLPIN, "Hyperbole: Part II," p. 24
"The poem ironically places strong emphasis on the element of human choice in making a 'claim' for that inevitable phenomenon, death. The irony is further compounded by the fact that the dead person whose honor it is to be the principal person in the parade will not be able to experience it."

"One joy of so much anguish" (1420)

1981 KIMPEL, *Dickinson as Philosopher,* pp. 191–93
The poet's reaction is "not of pity for herself, and not of envy for the living creatures outside of her window. It is rather the awareness that loving what is on the outside of her room, she is immobilized by her own nature to move out to enjoy it and to take part in it."

"One life of so much consequence"

1985   EBERWEIN, *Dickinson*, pp. 178–79, 270
"Joy, as threatening to the self-imprisoned consciousness as despair, provides intimations of possibilities outside the self, and the final lines suggest comfort beyond the painful mortal circumference even though the circuit world desperately protects itself against penetration by infinity."

"One life of so much consequence" (270)

1980   JOHNSON, " 'Pearl of Great Price,' " pp. 206, 214 nn. 8–9
The poem's pearl has been mistakenly "taken to be a figure for a romantic lover, but Dickinson is surely talking about herself and her own solemn new existence."
Revised and reprinted: Johnson, *Emily Dickinson*, pp. 128–29, 208–09 nn. 13–14

1982   TOEGEL, *Emily Dickinson*, pp. 59–60
The poem "touches on the poet's total commitment to a life of poetry and a stoic acceptance of the suffering and hardship that such a commitment incurs. . . . If we follow the flow of the italicized words, we perceive clearly the poet's intent."

1983   SHURR, *Marriage*, pp. 27–28
Relates to other "poems of risk and wager" in the fascicles. This poem contains "explicit links between this sense of risk and the day of her unique marriage."

1987   COOK, C., "Psychic Development," p. 130
"Long before Carl Jung wrote about archetypes, Dickinson used the sea to represent an unknown part of herself that contained the pearl, the gem of her inner self. She has seen her pearl in the sea of the unconscious, and she will take it though that means forfeiting the life she knows."

SEWALL, "Emily Dickinson," pp. 70–71, 72
"Which is the vehicle and which the tenor? Is she using religious metaphors to describe a romantic love? or romantic imagery to describe her longing for religious fulfillment? Or do both converge on her literary ambition?"

"One need not be a chamber to be haunted" (670)

1979   GILBERT and GUBAR, *Madwoman*, pp. 403, 622, 624–25, 627
The poem "comments upon the real significance of the gothic

genre, especially for women: its usefulness in providing metaphors for those turbulent psychological states into which the divided selves of the nineteenth century so often fell."

JUHASZ, "'Undiscovered Continent,'" pp. 87, 88–89, 93
Consideration of Dickinson poems in which "the enclosure and confinement experienced in the place of the mind is established with an architectural vocabulary."
Revised and reprinted: Juhasz, *Undiscovered Continent,* pp. 14, 16–17, 23, 73

1980 GREEN, "Spatial Drama," pp. 198–99, 200 n. 13
"This spatial imagery is continued in the dramatic inscape of [this poem], where the poet suggests that body/soul is analogous to a house in its possession of corners and corridors where specters and horrors, bred by the brain, may lurk."

1981 SCIARRA, "Woman Looking Inward," pp. 36, 37, 39–40
The poem deals with "the search for self" and expresses the poet's "intimidation when confronted with her own intellection."

1982 SALSKA, *Poetry of the Central Consciousness,* pp. 64–65
"Even though the conflict remains unresolved, the self's helplessness in confrontation with itself is made sufficiently clear."
Revised and reprinted: Salska, *Walt Whitman and Emily Dickinson,* p. 54

VAN DYNE, "Double Monologues," pp. 465, 468
The poem shows us "Dickinson's speaker standing watchfully by her subjective self in order to examine the dimensions and co-habitants of her chamber of consciousness."

1986 MOREY, "Dickinson-Kant: The First Critique," pp. 60, 62–63
"The duality of the individual is dramatized much as in a Freudian confrontation of the parts of the personality or psyche." Reviews critical interpretations.

1988 WOLFF, *Emily Dickinson,* pp. 463–64
"'Because I could not stop for Death—' makes a useful contrast to this poem."

1989 GARBOWSKY, *House without the Door,* pp. 130–32, 139
". . . if the poem is seen as the culmination of a series of poems in which the self and the soul—the 'Me and Myself'—are pitted against each other, then it accurately presents the fear of fear within the panic victim."

"One of the ones that Midas touched" (1466)

1984   TSELENTIS-APOSTOLIDIS, "I will be Socrates," pp. 16–17
    Questions poet's choice of the Jason myth to compare to the oriole and suggests that she may have confused the myth of the Golden Fleece with that of the Golden Apples.

1988   WEISSMAN, " 'Transport's Working Classes,' " pp. 417–18
    "Dickinson's oriole gathers more forbidden qualities to itself than any of her other animals. . . . [She] jams together a whole array of un-christian glories to honor this thieving bird, who specializes in robbing a farmer's best fruit."

    WOLFF, *Emily Dickinson*, pp. 529–31
    Examines ways in which the legends of Midas and of the prodigal son function in this poem that "focuses not upon her faith, but upon her art."

"One sister have I in our house" (14)

1981   MORRIS, A., "Two Sisters," p. 325
    This poem "sets the terms, predicts the details, and appropriates the participants" of the clash between Vinnie and Sue.

1984   POLLAK, *Dickinson*, pp. 138–40, 141, 143
    This poem and "You love me, you are sure" were "addressed to Susan Gilbert Dickinson and reflect the quest of a childlike persona for a surrogate mother."

"One thing of it we borrow" (1464)

1983   SHURR, *Marriage*, p. 155
    "She asks the power to forget while fiercely retaining the right to remember. The beloved is surely a lively presence in the poem, spoken as it is immediately to him."

"One year ago jots what" (296)

1979   PATTERSON, *Dickinson's Imagery*, pp. 25–26, 33, 152, 203
    This poem, "rich in oral symbolism, . . . hints at the lack of some final consummation."

1983   SHURR, *Marriage*, pp. 25–26, 40–41, 63–65
    The poem "celebrates the first anniversary of Dickinson's anom-alous marriage, with specific autobiographical details."

1985 EBERWEIN, *Dickinson*, p. 25

"Clearly the speaker of this and similar poems responds apprecia-tively to the enhanced self-image bestowed by her lover, by the sense of infinite possibility he conveys to her, even though the greatness arises from pain."

1988 WOLFF, *Emily Dickinson*, pp. 372–75, 376, 414

". . . the strategy of the entire poem is predicted [*sic*] upon the assumption that to be able to *name* a thing fully and adequately demon-strates mastery over it."

"Only a shrine, but mine" (918)

1980 PORTERFIELD, *Feminine Spirituality*, pp. 137–38

"The images in this stanza are the religious realities important to Elizabeth Seton. Emily Dickinson regards herself as a nun."

"Only God detect the sorrow" (626)

1986 OBERHAUS, " 'Engine against th' Almightie,' " pp. 155, 157

"This meditation manifests Dickinson's acceptance of the cen-tral Christian tenet of the Trinity, though in less solemn tones than else-where . . . ."

"Opinion is a flitting thing" (1455)

1987 BARKER, *Lunacy of Light*, pp. 63–64

"Since the sun seems as fickle and short-lived as public opinion, Dickinson would rather possess only 'Truth.' " Discussion of Dickinson's use of sun imagery.

"Our journey had advanced" (615)

1979 CAMERON, *Lyric Time*, pp. 109–12, 124, 133, 260, 267 n. 15

"The point at which the multiple conceptions of boundary intersect and the fact of the intersection is of significance, for the poem concludes by obliterating the very distinctions it has been at such pains to estab-lish."

Reprinted: Cameron, *"Et in Arcadia,"* pp. 56–58, 67, 74

1983 LEONARD, D. N., "Dickinson's 'Our journey,' " pp. 29–31

"Dickinson's carefully controlled ambiguity" in this poem "con-veys profound doubts about the nature of the noumenal world beyond the phenomenal one. The poem involves the ultimate questions and recognizes their unanswerableness."

1985 EBERWEIN, *Dickinson*, p. 202
The poem presents "the penultimate episode in a quest narrative. . . . God, the omnipresent defender of the mysterious community beyond circumference, seems to offer welcome."

JOHNSON, *Emily Dickinson*, pp. 183–85
In this poem "the poet offers an especially complex vision of the relationship between death and perception."

KAJINO, "Moment of Death," pp. 37–39, 40
In this poem "we feel that at the same time she sees herself as a mortal being who is 'reluctant' to go through 'The Forest of the Dead,' she transcends the limits of mortal consciousness and witnesses God at every gate in her advance to the world of immortality."

1988 WOLFF, *Emily Dickinson*, pp. 336–38
". . . as soon as the reader attempts to formulate a coherent image of the event that is being described, the obstinate paradox of virtually every significant mapping element in the verse frustrates the most persistent effort."

1989 OLIVER, *Apocalypse of Green*, pp. 87–88, 230–31
"Through the battle-field imagery Dickinson portrays death as a necessary transition. The persona has no choice, but at the same time, has nothing to lose since God is at every Gate. The poem can even be considered a gloss on her more famous poem, 'Because I could not Stop for Death'. . . ."

"Our little kinsmen after rain" (885)

1986 ROBINSON, J., *Emily Dickinson*, p. 71
Suggests that the poem derives from "A bird came down the walk" and shows how Dickinson "could move with wonderful flexibility in a number of ways from what might seem to be a single experience."

"Our little secrets slink away" (1326)

1982 MOSSBERG, *Emily Dickinson*, p. 169
"Her exultance in her courage is . . . ironically undercut by her fear of naming her undertaking, and contributes to the reader's under-

standing of her anxiety in her craft. Perhaps the reader is meant to share or shoulder the responsibility for her lyric nervousness."

"Our lives are Swiss" (80)

1985   JOHNSON, *Emily Dickinson*, pp. 146–47
"Like all of Dickinson's best early work, this poem states her religious dilemma with honesty and precision yet retains a note of youthful zest . . . , a sense of awe before the magnitude of the quest lying ahead."

1986   ARNDT, "Limits of Language," pp. 20–21
Supports the contention that "the significance and excellence of Dickinson's poetry lies exactly in its conscious and purposeful effort to be anti-logical, non-developmental and non-rationally associative."

1987   MARTIN, J. E., "Religious Spirit," p. 500
"A compressed allegory, the poem makes use of three symbols, the Swiss, the alps and Italy."

"Our own possessions, though our own" (1208)

1979   ESTES, "Search for Location," p. 216
"When mapping locations is impossible, absolute possession is the only way to maintain order. She must grasp what is precious so that it will not disappear."

"Ourselves we do inter with sweet derision" (1144)

1986   ROBINSON, J., *Emily Dickinson*, p. 79
"Such a religion which had not the confidence to take love beyond the grave must surely basically doubt itself, for all its fervent declaration."

"Ourselves were wed one summer, dear" (631)

1978   FADERMAN, "Homoerotic Poetry," pp. 21, 23–24
"While the poem is apparently about losing a beloved, she seems to have gone not to her death but rather to a man and a life of domesticity. In any event, it is clear from the penultimate line that both the lover and the beloved of this poem are women."

1980   CUNNINGHAM, *Dickinson*, pp. 42–44, 55
Paraphrase. The poem could not be addressed to Sue (Susan Gilbert Dickinson) because it is addressed to someone who died young.

1981 PORTER, *Dickinson,* pp. 205–06
The poem is a "companion piece to 'I think I was enchanted,' and associates the wedding figure with Browning."

1983 MORRIS, A., " 'The Love of Thee,' " pp. 110, 111
This poem and "Like eyes that looked on wastes" explore "the idea of a royal marriage between queens."

1984 POLLAK, *Dickinson,* pp. 100, 137, 141–42, 144, 155
"Together, [Dickinson] and Sue were 'Queens' or powerful women and Sue's marriage is compared . . . to a coronation. Dickinson, however, was dethroned by it."

1985 EBERWEIN, *Dickinson,* pp. 104–05, 174
The poem's frustrated speaker "blames her hardship—her abrupt transition from queen to shivering drudge—on the other woman, who had acted out the presumably normative wifely role and thereby enticed her into it. A bitter poem, it expresses Dickinson's resistance to the implications of bridal."

1987 LEDER and ABBOTT, *Language of Exclusion,* p. 141
The poem "does not resolve whether these two were 'wed' to each other or to other people at the same time. . . . This is not the only time Emily Dickinson plays with changes in gender roles."

"Out of sight? What of that" (703)

1979 PATTERSON, *Dickinson's Imagery,* pp. 125, 129
"Although not precisely an invitation to suicide, the poem seems to urge the other person . . . to risk flight into the next world for the blue that is unavailable in this." Considers symbolic significance of poem's blue and amber.

1989 OLIVER, *Apocalypse of Green,* pp. 178, 179
"It is far better, she insists, to assume the existence and merits of heaven and try to attain it than to debate its existence."

"Over and over, like a tune" (367)

1986 JONES, " 'Royal Seal,' " pp. 36–37
"Neither the rite itself nor its relation to future status are the center of this poem . . . ; the grandeur of the music and the march aid in the recollection of an earthly experience. But by using the ritual of baptism, Dickinson is able to convey the rare and majestic qualities inherent in the memory."

"Over the fence" (251)

1981 STEINER, "Image Patterns," p. 69

"Knowing her ability of climbing, the girl asserts herself but ends up being subjected to the established definitions of masculinity and femininity, as summed up in the contrastive images of 'climbing fence' vs. 'staining apron.'"

1982 MOSSBERG, *Emily Dickinson*, pp. 117–19, 122, 131, 150

Here Dickinson "presents her relationship with God, and the moral dilemma she experiences as a woman poet in her society, as a daughter-father conflict. Although the backdrop of the poem is light, the issues the poem presents are serious and represent Dickinson's deepest concerns."

Revised and reprinted: Mossberg, "Nursery Rhymes," pp. 52–53

1983 SHURR, *Marriage*, pp. 31, 72, 171–72

Relates to other poems in the fascicles that indicate "the speaker and her lover have found a paradise that is forbidden."

1987 BARKER, *Lunacy of Light*, pp. 45, 46

Here "'strawberries' could be words, poems themselves. Of significance in this poem is that Dickinson wants to pick her own berries—but she is blocked from doing so by two obstructions . . . ."

MILLER, C., *Emily Dickinson*, pp. 169, 170

"That God, rather than a nearer father, would scold suggests that these berries represent forbidden fruit of any variety. The poem specifies, however, that it is not the fruit but her climbing 'Over the fence' . . . that is forbidden."

1988 REED, "Masculine Identity," p. 283

"The powerful male figure in the poem deprives the helpless female figure of her food or the possibility of having her strawberries." Relates to other images of oral deprivation in Dickinson's poetry.

"Pain expands the time" (967)

1980 JUHASZ, "'To make a prairie,'" p. 22

"What makes time different in the brain is the experience of pain. This poem focuses upon pain's propensity to heighten sensation. In pain one's sense of time is 'expanded'. . . ."

Revised and reprinted: Juhasz, *Undiscovered Continent*, pp. 46–47

1984 WOLOSKY, *Emily Dickinson*, pp. 83–84

"By its calendar time itself is measured. The eternity that should redeem is instead engulfed by it. Its moment encompasses entire ages. It

thus stands only in relation to itself and loses any tie to a possible redemptive term."
    Revised and reprinted: Wolosky, "Dickinson's War Poetry," p. 37

1988   FURUKAWA, " 'Finite Infinity,' " pp. 22–23
    "The poem describes the infinite capacity of the soul for pain."

1989   KNAPP, *Emily Dickinson*, pp. 176–78
    "In Dickinson's private metaphoric code, pain is viewed both per-
sonally . . . and impersonally. . . . Resorting to mathematical structure
and to the thinking process that gave her the stability for which she
yearned, the poem is structured in visual permutations and progressions,
increasing in gravity and concluding in loss."

"Pain has an element of blank" (650)

1979   CAMERON, *Lyric Time*, pp. 10, 30, 161–62, 167, 168, 169, 171, 177,
186, 202
    " 'Blank—' is the renunciation of temporal category, the lapse of
memory that makes the present the be-all and end-all, the defunct imagination that cannot be required to think beyond what is."

1982   MARCUS, *Emily Dickinson*, pp. 70, 94
    "Just as the sufferer's life has become pain, so time has become
pain. Its present is an infinity which remains exactly like the past."

1988   WOLFF, *Emily Dickinson*, pp. 470–71, 472
    " . . . the effect of this kind of pain upon time is a wry irony. . . .
Now . . . time seems not an enemy to individual coherence, but a friend—
some fixed system within which individual experience can be ordered."

"Papa above" (61)

1978   BURKE, "Religion of Poetry," pp. 17, 18–19, 20, 25 n. 6
    "While appearing (and perhaps attempting) to pray, she is already
crying out against an unjust God."

1979   GILBERT and GUBAR, *Madwoman*, pp. 189, 598–99, 631
    "Her ironic hyperbole suggests . . . her lucid awareness of the lit-
erary and theological paradigms she might find for her relationship with
her father, and finally it suggests her consciousness of the extent to which
she herself desired to destroy or subvert that relationship."

1984 OLPIN, "Hyperbole: Part II," p. 7

"It would be easy to say that the whole perspective of the poem is one of reduction, but it is more complex than this. There is rather a clash of the big with the small and the powerful with the weak."

ST. ARMAND, *Dickinson and Her Culture*, pp. 165–66, 167

"The picture of a snug and secure celestial mouse, nibbling away at eternity in the wainscot of heaven, could hardly be called a pious commentary on the orthodox idea of paradise."

WALLACE, *God Be with the Clown*, pp. 82–83, 84

"The comedy here serves two primary functions: it enables Dickinson to affirm conventional truths about God, immortality, and the suffering self without sentimentality or sententiousness; it also enables her to bring God down to a manageable size."

1986 MUNK, "Recycling Language," pp. 237–38

"Dickinson had no sympathy for rats . . . , so that any 'Mansion' reserved for one is equivocal, at best. And if this 'Mansion' is ludicrous, what of the whole structure of belief that contains it?"

OBERHAUS, " 'Engine against th' Almightie,' " pp. 163–64, 171 n. 27

Relates to other "prayer" poems of Dickinson and examines implications of mouse/rat image.

1987 BARKER, *Lunacy of Light*, pp. 96, 174, 202 n. 14

"This poem expresses how very rebellious Dickinson felt herself to be; . . . she couched her meaning in such a childlike metaphor that few readers would suspect the power behind the rodent's teeth."

"Paradise is of the option" (1069)

1985 SIMONS, "Willed Paradise," pp. 175–82

Word-by-word analysis of poem's implications, associations, and possible meanings, employing a "psychoanalytic interpretive scheme."

"Partake as doth the bee" (994)

1983 MARCELLINO, " 'Partake as doth the Bee,' " pp. 66–67

Comments on ways in which Dickinson's classical knowledge informs the poem. "Essentially what Dickinson said in the poem was that one must be abstemious in picking roses in Amherst, a small town compared to Paestum . . . ."

"Perception of an object costs" (1071)

1979 GONNAUD, "Nature, Apocalypse," pp. 136–37
"With the 'Object Absolute' lying for ever beyond the reach of consciousness, its ultimate reality cannot be predicated, so that beauty depends entirely upon the arrangements of perception."

HAGENBÜCHLE, "Sign and Process," pp. 147–48
"Not only is perception here understood in terms of loss and gain, but loss . . . even seems to presuppose the gain. . . ." Compares Dickinson's view of perception with Emerson's.
Reprinted: *Dickinson Studies*, pp. 76–77

1980 DUNCAN, "Joining Together," pp. 118–19
"The Perfectness that Perception upbraids . . . is not the Object Absolute, but the very process of rendering Object into Idea. Perception upbraids itself because the idea it renders is as far from grasp, finally, as the original object . . . ."

JUHASZ, " 'To make a prairie,' " pp. 23–24
". . . when the mind perceives an object, the object cannot be the object as it was without the perception, determined in itself and not by anything outside itself. . . . But what is gained in the process by means of the loss of the object absolute (the price paid) is the meaning of the object . . . ."
Revised and reprinted: Juhasz, *Undiscovered Continent,* pp. 40, 47–48, 50, 181–82 n. 13

REISS, "Dickinson's Self-Reliance," p. 28
"Here perception actually is everything, all there is to gain, because we cannot possess the 'Object Absolute.' . . . We 'upbraid' the completeness of the Object Absolute because our perception of it is incomplete."

1981 CAMPBELL, "Poetry as Epitaph," pp. 662–63, 665
"Perception, in its essence, is both a result *of* loss and a reply *to* loss. That very act which creates the object . . . also fractures the object from the self."

ORSINI, "Romantic Use of Science," p. 61
"Through leaps of intuition and imagination, man creates a 'fair' world, but one that may be no truer, in any absolute sense, and no more realizable than the objective phenomenal world that eludes his grasp."

1985 CARTON, *Rhetoric*, pp. 125–26
"Perception's value for Dickinson lies in its process and, specifi-

cally, in the momentary 'transitional surface' that accommodates its simultaneous presentation of the fairness, and confession of the farness, of her ultimate object."

"Perhaps I asked too large" (352)

1986 JUHASZ, "Writing Doubly," pp. 5–6, 7
"The doubleness present throughout this poem is an expression . . . of the ontological situation of women in patriarchal culture."

McNEIL, *Emily Dickinson*, pp. 15–16
The poem "shows cosmic confidence, poetic command and personal doubt, while having nothing to say about fame or reputation. It also frankly uses imagery drawn from Dickinson's daily life as a woman, with no sense that this shouldn't mix with 'firmaments'."

"Peril as a possession" (1678)

1981 JUHASZ, " 'Peril as a possession,' " pp. 29–31, 34
"Bearing pain is the means of possessing it; the fear that comes from the possession of peril is not terror but awe, a heightened appreciation that brings with it vision or insight."
Revised and reprinted: Juhasz, *Undiscovered Continent*, pp. 54–55, 58, 78, 82, 83, 92, 94

"Pink, small, and punctual" (1332)

1983 DU PRIEST, "ED's 'Pink,' " p. 20
The poem's "images, associations, and etymological seeds" suggest the poem is about "the flower of the bosom, the female nipple ready for nursing."

"Praise it, 'tis dead" (1384)

1981 KIMPEL, *Dickinson as Philosopher*, pp. 109–11
Examines poem for its contribution to "an understanding of [Dickinson's] reflecting about human life and its moral obligations."

PORTER, *Dickinson*, pp. 191–92
Comments on poem's style and diction, with reference to worksheet.

"Prayer is the little implement" (437)

1978 BURKE, "Religion of Poetry," pp. 18, 20–21
"If there is no awe, no communication, if prayer is merely a means of flinging desperate petitions at an unhearing God, it is indeed a doubtful device, an 'apparatus.'"

1980 FRY, "Writing New Englandy," p. 27
The poem's success "depends upon defeating expectations" and here they "are based upon a general religious practice about which the poet entertains most serious doubts."

1982 MOSSBERG, *Emily Dickinson*, p. 128
"She satirizes the secular use of prayer. . . . She debases the relationship between God and humanity into a mere transaction, a matter of mechanics. Underlying the satire is bitterness toward The Father for denying people his presence."

1983 WALKER, N., "Humor as Identity," p. 63
"Wit, here as elsewhere, provides the detachment from convention which allows her an identity separate from that which religious commitment would demand."

1984 WOLOSKY, *Emily Dickinson*, p. 121
"Whether in supplicating contention or in contending supplication, she still gropes toward the realms of Presence and does so as a linguistic act."

1986 BYERS, "Possible Background," pp. 35, 36, 38 n. 4
Suggests possible source in James Montgomery's hymn, "Pray'r is the Soul's Sincere Desire."

OBERHAUS, "'Engine against th' Almightie,'" pp. 155–56, 167, 168
Relates to George Herbert's definition of prayer and considers other critical interpretations of the poem.

1987 OBERHAUS, "Herbert and Emily Dickinson," pp. 346, 360
Notes ways in which this poem resembles Herbert's "Prayer."

"Presentiment is that long shadow on the lawn" (764)

1978 ABAD, *Formal Approach*, pp. 15, 23, 37, 39–40, 41n, 66n, 98, 103, 134, 180, 399, 418
Examines as a poem of "personal definition" with particular attention to the poem's "long shadow on the lawn."

1980 JUHASZ, "'To make a prairie,'" pp. 14–15, 17, 25
The poet "equates her feeling with an act in nature, one that, we understand as we read on into the poem, is governed by natural laws. Such rhetorical devices turn an individual perception into a truism."
Revised and reprinted: Juhasz, *Undiscovered Continent*, pp. 30, 31–32, 51

1982 MARCUS, *Emily Dickinson*, p. 35
"As do most of Dickinson's philosophical nature poems, this one shows the poet confronting mystery and fright with a combination of detachment and involvement."

1986 ROBINSON, J., *Emily Dickinson*, pp. 172–73
"Definitions usually subtract words from the contexts where they operate (and accrete meaning) and make them transportable. This poem shows how hers work in the opposite way."

1988 WOLFF, *Emily Dickinson*, pp. 476–77
"What dominates this poem is not the internal conception, 'Presentiment,' but the extended description of the natural world has been invoked as a kind of definition."

"Proud of my broken heart, since thou didst break it" (1736)

1983 SHURR, *Marriage*, pp. 190–91
"The lines are a protest of love and separation, but of companionship in suffering, exactly fitting the diction of other marriage poems."

"Publication is the auction" (709)

1982 MARCUS, *Emily Dickinson*, pp. 39–40
General consideration as one of Dickinson's poems on "Poetry, Art, and Imagination."

1983 HOPE, "*Saintly Veil*," pp. 291–92
"Overtones of traditional meanings of the snow give resonance to Emily Dickinson's brief, intense, personal definition of her stance towards her own poetry, its silence and its secrecy."

SHURR, *Marriage*, pp. 43–44, 114–15, 143
Here Dickinson "mounts her objections to a correspondent who has suggested publication, for money, of her poetry. Her climactic argument would appeal strongly to a clergyman, would perhaps not even be understood by anyone else."

1984 BENFEY, *Problem of Others*, pp. 35–36
"The private realm is conceived of . . . as bodiless, though it may receive 'Corporeal illustration.' The 'Garret' suggests both poverty and the head, where the mind is located. To retain one's purity is to protect one's privacy. And that means not publishing."

EBERWEIN, "Doing Without," p. 218
"To read this poem only as an ironic attempt at disguising her authorial pain is to miss the genteel Yankee pride that spits out the key word 'Auction.' "

POLLAK, *Dickinson*, pp. 229–31
"A categorical distinction between masculinity and femininity informs the text, but Dickinson finds it necessary to delete the specifically female component from her justification of economic deprivation as the rationale for a literary career."

WOLOSKY, *Emily Dickinson*, pp. 167–68
"The language of contract . . . asserts here that thought and its expression are committed to heaven. Publication would betray the compact and debase what is in its essence an inward communion."

1985 COOK, A., *Thresholds*, p. 181
"Natural beauty, emblematic purity, unreal blanketing, cold, and here a pricelessness in two senses are signified by the snow, as all these attributes are at one or another time invested by the poet in death."

DICKENSON, *Emily Dickinson*, pp. 107–09
The poem "reflects the tension she must have felt between her own ambition and society's disapproval—with more than a hint of whistling in the dark and posing . . . ."

1986 McNEIL, *Emily Dickinson*, pp. 37–38, 56, 68, 111
By using the "image of a slave auction, Dickinson indicates that these sellers enslave their own minds." Discusses complex "snow" image.

ROBINSON, J., *Emily Dickinson*, pp. 60–61, 109
"In writing as she did she evidently saw publication as a matter of reputation, that is as a personal thing rather than a way of building something communal or sharing."

1987 LEDER and ABBOTT, *Language of Exclusion*, pp. 12–13
Illustrates "how, by way of extended metaphor and ironic toning, Dickinson minimizes the value of writing for publication."

1989 DOBSON, *Strategies of Reticence,* pp. 53–54

"The poem suggests that in extreme cases publication is justified by poverty and religious or moral content also sanctions publication but that the public sharing of the '*Human*' spirit, or . . . personal expression, is disgraceful."

NEKOLA, "'By Birth a Bachelor,'" p. 152

"Dickinson's famous dismissal of publication as an 'Auction' . . . also voices the sentiment of contemporary ideology, which presented fame as a false prize for women, one that would take them away from their true throne in the home and leave them wandering, homeless."

OLIVER, *Apocalypse of Green,* pp. 119–20

"Certainly the last stanza affirms that Dickinson has no price, either in this life or in the next. If God's grace is not freely given, then she will accept it on her own terms, or not at all."

WILSON, *Figures of Speech,* pp. 272–73, 275

"It is difficult to imagine a more uncompromising rejection of the practices of the literary marketplace. But there are oddities in the poem, oddities that may cut against the grain of its explicit argument."

"Pursuing you in your transitions" (1602)

1981 PORTER, *Dickinson,* p. 40

Notes "strained compaction" of lines sent to convalescing Helen Hunt Jackson. The poet is simply saying that "pursuing Helen in all her travels and occupations is like pursuing a mote in a sunbeam and that she is really capturable only in fantasy."

1982 SALSKA, *Poetry of the Central Consciousness,* pp. 95, 96

"The paradoxical plight of the mind yearning for comprehensiveness and certainty, but equipped with tools glaringly inadequate to the ambitions, is the theme of [this poem]."

Revised and reprinted: Salska, *Walt Whitman and Emily Dickinson,* p. 83

"Put up my lute" (261)

1979 PATTERSON, *Dickinson's Imagery,* pp. 155, 221 n. 40

"Clearly the strain to which Memnon vibrates is love's music, and the 'Sunrise' to which he yields . . . is love's sunrise or dawn." Discussion of Dickinson's use of African symbolism.

1981 DIEHL, "Dickinson and Bloom," pp. 437–38
". . . the predicament of the poem revolves around how the 'I,' who must depend upon an unwilling, indeed, formidable adversary, can extract from him the Word that will force him to respond—thus, in the very production of the miraculous sound, robbing him of his independence, his free will, and his power."

DIEHL, *Romantic Imagination,* pp. 66–67, 69 n. 2
"The words 'surrendered' and 'vanquished' strengthen the aura of aggressive intimacy between the Singer and Memnon, the lover and her beloved adversary, the poet and her silent muse."

1984 TSELENTIS-APOSTOLIDIS, "I will be Socrates," pp. 19–20
The poem expresses the poet's "frustration in not being able to move those people whom she wishes to move by her art. The reference is to a colossal statue on the banks of the Nile . . . ."

1988 PHILLIPS, *Emily Dickinson,* pp. 121–22
Notes literary source in poems of Robert Browning.

"Quite empty, quite at rest" (1606)

1981 KIMPEL, *Dickinson as Philosopher,* pp. 196–97
"Thinking of nature as a living and loving being, she relates herself to what she regards as capable of expressing a love that she herself is capable of extending."

"Rather arid delight" (1679)

1988 WEISSMAN, "'Transport's Working Classes,'" p. 421
"This is a sane, humorous, sad, realistic view of sex and the single woman."

"Read, sweet, how others strove" (260)

1983 SHURR, *Marriage,* pp. 70, 144
This is one of several poems that "suggest that she and her addressee model their behavior on the Christian martyrs." The addressee is probably Charles Wadsworth.

"Rearrange a 'wife's' affection" (1737)

1981 KHAN, "Poetry of Ecstasy," pp. 29–31
Here "the paradox of ecstasy of despair is presented through a

metaphorical analogue of attainment of wifehood. . . . The speaker goes on to describe the pleasure-pain paradox implicit in troth."
Revised and reprinted: Khan, *Emily Dickinson's Poetry*, pp. 56–57

STEINER, "Image Patterns," pp. 68, 69
"The woman's protest against conventional notions of power and powerlessness is articulated in [this poem], where terms like 'dislocate,' 'Amputate,' and 'bearded' stand for the masculine vocabulary . . . ."

1982 MOSSBERG, *Emily Dickinson*, pp. 4, 6, 24, 173–74, 176, 178–79
The poem, "which fuses the themes of sexual conflict and secrecy," explores the reason "Dickinson has to keep her avocation a secret until her death."

1983 GILBERT, "Wayward Nun," pp. 33–34
". . . without presuming to speculate about the 'facts' Dickinson may or may not be describing through this secularized crucifixion imagery, it is possible to see that her fictionalizing of those 'facts' tells us something crucial about the transformative energy her white dress represents."

SHURR, *Marriage*, pp. 15–17, 32, 60, 174–75
"The poem is quite frank about Dickinson's 'secret,' and it may be a secret which the family wanted kept for their own sake as well as hers." Considers as a "marriage" poem that may refer to an aborted child.

1984 POLLAK, *Dickinson*, pp. 169–72
"Because the speaker is unable to project herself imaginatively into a redeemed future scene, the poem's mode is neither sentimental nor domestic, but agonistic. Here, Dickinson has married the reality of sexual rage, which she unconsciously associates with the destruction of her womanhood."

1985 EBERWEIN, *Dickinson*, pp. 106–08, 282 n. 15
Suggests the poem be read as "a dramatic monologue addressed by a secretly pledged 'wife' to her skeptical 'husband' who may even be trying to escape from their tie by questioning her continued love."

1986 SMITH, S. B., "'Radical Dualism,'" pp. 39–40
"Here Dickinson poses as both male and female, reechoing Margaret Fuller's call for less stereotyped roles for men and women and consequently for a new, radical dualism."

1987 JEROME, "Type of the Modern," pp. 75–78
"One can see in this poem both a public self that is polite, restrained, and formal, and a scarlet secret self of intense emotion, daring

imagination and bold unconventionality. . . . In part the poem is a protest against society's requirement of hypocrisy and repression."

LEDER and ABBOTT, *Language of Exclusion,* pp. 136, 140
"Its theme and many of the images make it a compendium of Emily Dickinson's concerns about marriage. . . . In this poem . . . love in this life is only possible through Christlike or heroic suffering on the part of the woman."

1989   RICHWELL, "Poetic Immortality," pp. 13–14
The poem "is a good example of the way Dickinson's aesthetic of renunciation affects her metaphorical equation between fame and love. . . . The wifely persona and the theme of poetic immortality go hand in hand."

" 'Red Sea' indeed! Talk not to me" (1642)

1984   MARTIN, W., *American Triptych,* pp. 138–39
"Again, while undermining hierarchical religion and male mastery, Emily Dickinson associates diversity and vitality with the female earth and constricting domination with the male God and his heaven." Contrasts with Isaac Watts's "God of the Seas, thy thundering Voice."

1985   ST. ARMAND, "Dickinson's 'Red Sea,'" pp. 17–20
"Rather than a feminist manifesto," the poem is "a dramatic monologue, spoken . . . by the God who is the romantic poet, the true transforming power above and beyond all meretricious questions of gender."

"Rehearsal to ourselves" (379)

1979   CAMERON, *Lyric Time,* p. 144
"Clean-cut as absence, memory is murder because of its perpetual killing-off in the mind of presence. Memory defines its space . . . and simultaneously fills it with its own representation."

1981   ALEXANDER, "Reading Emily Dickinson," pp. 5–6, 15
"Pleasure and pain must be taken as the sources of the poem rather than its central concern. . . . The re-enactment of the lost lone pleasure is what the poem describes so chillingly: rehearsal as recreation."

1982   MOSSBERG, *Emily Dickinson,* pp. 192–93
"Dickinson could be talking about the fact that she has to feel wounded or to wound herself in order to write. She will not stop using

the word, which causes pain, because the anguish is necessary to her art."

1983   JUHASZ, *Undiscovered Continent,* pp. 121–23, 124–25
"The act of the imagination is here considered as less real . . . than the original experience—it is pretending or rehearsal only—but *only* is enough to bring the dead to life. Even if, in fidelity to the drama which it rehearses, the death, too, must be continually reenacted."

1985   CARTON, *Rhetoric,* p. 44
" 'Rehearsal,' here, is not a prelude but a vicious mimicry of fulfillment that can only dramatize its absence. . . . its bliss lies in the perverse destruction of its object, a murder that—since the object is a complete and original selfhood—constitutes suicide."

1987   MILLER, C., *Emily Dickinson,* p. 67
Notes "instance of syntactic doubling—here unusually complex because 'Commemorate' changes grammatical class (from uninflected verb to adjective) as well as function (from predicate to modifier of subject)."

1989   DIEHL, "Murderous Poetics," p. 326
"It is the self who is killed through this murder. What is won, nevertheless, is the figurative reshaping of the situation so that she becomes agent rather than victim, even if the end be the same."

" 'Remember me' implored the thief" (1180)

1983   SHURR, *Marriage,* p. 184
"Unless it is her child, the epithet 'my Guest' does not seem to describe any of the deaths in Dickinson's recent experience."

1986   BRUMM, "Religion and the Poet," p. 26
Here Dickinson's "legal terms aid us in understanding a complicated religious doctrine."

"Remembrance has a rear and front" (1182)

1983   JUHASZ, *Undiscovered Continent,* pp. 15, 19
"Memory is the house, the inhabitant is 'ourselves.' Again, a fiction of container and contained is established only to be denied by the conclusion of the poem. The 'Fathoms' that pursue us are our own memory, after all: self is haunted by self."

"Remorse is memory awake" (744)

1978 CAMERON, "Naming as History," pp. 234, 236
In this poem "the definition exists for the purpose of dismissing the situation with which it purports to deal."
Reprinted: Cameron, *Lyric time*, pp. 35–36, 38; Ferlazzo, *Critical Essays*, pp. 197–98, 199

1983 JUHASZ, *Undiscovered Continent*, p. 123
"The understanding that virtuous behavior (feeling remorse), God's institution, brings about an equivalence of hell only underlines . . . how complex is Dickinson's assessment of Christian stringencies."

1984 WOLOSKY, *Emily Dickinson*, pp. 77–78
"Remorse, rather than leading to a cure, itself becomes the disease. The divine power to heal and redeem suffering becomes instead the source of illness and of pain. The process of introspection is reversed."

1986 MOREY, "Dickinson-Kant: The First Critique," pp. 50, 51, 56
This is "a sublime, fearful definition poem, blasphemous in its final stanza. It is a negative poem, attacking the attitude and accusing God for its duration."

1989 ROGERS, K., "Introducing Dickinson," p. 54
Suggestions for teaching the poem to college students.

"Removed from accident of loss" (424)

1980 JOHNSON, " 'Pearl of Great Price,' " pp. 206–07
Examines the basic symbolic elements (the sea, the pearl, the Malay native) and the speaker in this poem and "The Malay took the pearl."
Revised and reprinted: Johnson, *Emily Dickinson*, pp. 130–31

"Renunciation is a piercing virtue" (745)

1977 AGRAWAL, *Emily Dickinson*, pp. 138–39, 147
"She gives a big rebuff to those who preach to renounce the terrestrial world and to look towards the spiritual world."

1978 CAMERON, "Naming as History," pp. 237–39, 248
"The relationship between renunciation and loss remains tentative throughout the poem. . . . Definition here . . . is a way of teaching the will to desire what an external force has deemed necessary."
Reprinted: Cameron, *Lyric Time*, pp. 40–41, 52, 153; reprinted in part: Ferlazzo, *Critical Essays*, pp. 201–02

1979 Nathan, "Soul at White Heat," pp. 51–52
Relates to Augustine's *Confessions*.

1981 Alexander, "Reading Emily Dickinson," pp. 13–14, 15
This poem "makes its connection with the hymn meter . . . by the number of stresses in logically linked word strings." The poet "has renounced the 'old' or familiar form while shaping the poem. . . . The poem is thus, at least in one sense, a comment on its own experiment."

Porter, *Dickinson*, pp. 45–46
Paraphrase is used to illustrate the poem's "radical deletion and transposition that obscure clauses, confuse subjects and objects, and generally knot the syntax chain."

1982 Burbick, "Irony of Self-Reference," pp. 91–92
"Renunciation, which can be seen as a necessary requirement of transcendence, is instead self-serving; it is a virtue that acts as a self-justification."

Guthrie, "Dickinson's Illness," p. 20
Relates to the poet's eye problems. "Because God will reward her with a much better pair of eyes after her death, 'Covered Vision,' or a life of voluntarily curtailed perception, must be endured not so much for the sake of recovering her health, but as a test of her will."

Johnson, "Emily Dickinson," pp. 7–9
"The poem argues for a distrust of perception . . . only when perception becomes a limited (and hubristic) 'Covered Vision,' one which has no awareness of its pre-eminent 'larger function.' To lose perspective is to lose everything."
Revised and reprinted: Johnson, *Emily Dickinson*, pp. 52–53, 90–91, 199–200 nn. 13–14

Kantak, "Unemersonian Aspects," p. 39
Notes effect of contrasting Saxon and Latinate elements.

Marcus, *Emily Dickinson*, pp. 66–67
Relates to other Dickinson poems on "Suffering and Growth." The poem indicates that the poet "has only partial faith in the piercing virtue of renunciation."

Mossberg, *Emily Dickinson*, pp. 184, 189
"In order to achieve mortal fame, Dickinson must choose against herself: renounce her feminine identity and become a neuter, lifeless 'it.' But the 'larger function' of self-denial will make her life on earth as a woman appear 'small.'"

1983 JUHASZ, *Undiscovered Continent*, pp. 129–31, 184–85 n. 26
"With the full power of Puritan expression behind her, but turned to her own purposes, Dickinson is talking about giving up certain experiences as they happen in the literal world . . . that they might happen, but differently, in the world of the mind."

SANAZARO, "Renunciation," pp. 19–20
Considers the poem as "a significant, formal declaration of Dickinson's own liberation from male approval and an objective representation of the struggle to reason herself away from the cluttering world of external 'realities' such as husband, home, and family."

1986 BURBICK, "Economics of Desire," pp. 370–71
"Dickinson sees clearly that the social demand of 'renunciation,' especially as it is interiorized by women, actually requires physical and mental wounding."

JUHASZ, "Renunciation Transformed," pp. 253–55, 259, 261
Explores the nature and implications of Dickinson's "renunciation." "Renunciation transformed is Dickinson the poet using imagination and language to create that larger function—in her mind and on the page."

1987 COOK, C., "Psychic Development," pp. 124–25
"In this poem, renunciation is positive; it is a *virtue,* but it hurts—it pierces the body and the heart that has to give up something it wants. . . . She renounces her role in society in order to be worthy of her own creative talents; she must choose between her social life and her creative life."

1989 RICHWELL, "Poetic Immortality," pp. 10–12
The poem "not only offers valuable insights into Dickinson's love life but also makes a powerful statement about her attitude toward publication and fame."

"Reportless subjects to the quick" (1048)

1978 HORIUCHI, *Possible Zen Traits*, p. 353
Notes "a faint oriental Zen-like atmosphere."

1985 PHILIP, "Valley News," p. 72
"The suggestion can fairly be made that Dickinson's explorations of the psyche here produce a speculative approach to language that equally looks forward to modern theory. This poem approaches a metalanguage . . . ."

"Rests at night" (714)

1983 SHURR, *Marriage,* p. 103
"This nightly vigil with her poetry sets her apart from the rest of men, who rise with nature and the Sun, and sleep when they sleep."

1987 BARKER, *Lunacy of Light,* pp. 77–78
"Dickinson's use of the phrase 'go on,' . . . implies . . . that whatever activities these noontime people pursue may be rather trivial, just as some people's chatter goes on."

"Revolution is the pod" (1082)

1982 MARCUS, *Emily Dickinson,* pp. 77–78
Here Dickinson "writes in a more genial and less harsh manner about suffering as a stimulus to growth. . . . The function of revolution, then, like suffering, is to test and revive whatever may have become dead without our knowing it."

1984 ANDERSON, C., "Deep Dyed Politics," pp. 3–7
A close analysis of the poem's "imagery and key words demonstrates that it is . . . a vigorous assessment of the nature of political systems."

"Robbed by death, but that was easy" (971)

1983 SHURR, *Marriage,* pp. 28, 122
The poem is "Dickinson's last statement of her relationship to 'the Brave Beloved' in the fascicles. . . . Putting off the fulfillment of her marriage until after death is 'Staking our entire Possession/ On a Hair's result'—so balanced are the possibilities for and against such eventual fulfillment."

"Safe despair it is that raves" (1243)

1981 KIMPEL, *Dickinson as Philosopher,* p. 13
"In this poem she expresses an acute understanding of what can take place when strong emotions are directed through an outlet productive of satisfaction rather than being repressed."

"Safe in their alabaster chambers" (216)

1972   RAO, *Essential Emily Dickinson,* pp. 117–18
General introduction to the poem aimed at "postgraduate students of literature in Indian Universities."

1979   KELLER, K., *Only Kangaroo,* pp. 190–93, 198–99
". . . in Sue's presence Emily Dickinson would stoop to writing what Sue could read, even if insensitively, but when out from under her sometimes domineering eye she could rise to a taller, tougher stature—and to far better verse. The Sue versions, after all, got discarded."

1981   ALEXANDER, "Reading Emily Dickinson," pp. 9–10, 12, 14
Compares 1859 and 1862 versions. "The important change shows itself in the understanding the poem displays."

ORSINI,"Romantic Use of Science," pp. 64, 65
". . . the materialist's denial in the second stanza sounds no more decisive than the idealist's affirmation in the first. Dickinson holds both views in perfect balance . . . ."

1982   MARCUS, *Emily Dickinson,* pp. 84–85
Relates to other Dickinson poems on death and immortality.

1985   ANANTHARAMAN, *Sunset in a Cup,* pp. 57–65
"The poem will get a unique sense of proportion if the nature images used there are discerned and understood properly." Examines form and structural components.

EBERWEIN, *Dickinson,* pp. 44, 129, 130, 131–33, 154, 196, 212, 218, 281 nn. 3–5
Discusses as "an example of Susan Dickinson's editorial advice."

1986   McNEIL, *Emily Dickinson,* pp. 51, 122–25, 135, 167
Considers implications of poem's images, particularly "dots—on a Disc of Snow." "Although—perhaps *because*— [this poem] is one of the most uncompromising poems about death in our language, it displays a certain cold joy."

ROBINSON, J., *Emily Dickinson,* pp. 53–55, 61, 81, 142
"There is something amiss that members of 'the Resurrection' have not been raised up. But the poem is written less to mock them, shut up in their solid beliefs, than to disconcert by suggesting that reality is immune to any belief."

1987   BAWER, "Audacity," p. 11
The poem "strikingly captures the antithesis between the passivity of death and the vibrancy with which life charges on through the centuries."

1988   WOLFF, *Emily Dickinson*, pp. 187, 245, 316–21, 587 n. 15
"The unifying insight of the poem is the falsity of Christ's promises and of the natural symbols that are said to portend them." Compares and analyzes variant versions.

1989   HOCKERSMITH, " 'Into Degreeless Noon,' " pp. 287–88
The poem "implies that, in their 'Alabaster Chambers,' the 'meek' have already 'inherited' the legacy that Christianity promises them; they 'inherit the earth' of the grave."

KNAPP, *Emily Dickinson*, pp. 50, 95–97
"Dickinson's message is sacrilegious." In this poem she "scornfully alters and mockingly rejects the meaning of Jesus's beatific message offering mortals eternal recompense." Line-by-line examination of images.

MILLER, C., "Approaches," p. 226
"In this poem, Dickinson clearly compares the world of the dead in stanza one with that of the living in stanza two, but she leaves the reader to determine the point of the contrast."

"Said Death to Passion" (1033)

1982   LEE, " 'This World is not Conclusion,' " p. 230
Relates to other Dickinson poems on death. "The conceit of a 'Debate' and our habit of making Death some distant point of arrival suggests the view of a poet long versed in issues of human illusion and mortality."

"Sang from the heart, sire" (1059)

1979   DIGGORY, "Armored Women," pp. 141–42
"The love or reverence revealed in this poem may be painful because it is not reciprocated, but there is also pain involved in the act of revelation itself. The poem is remarkable not only for its revelation but also for its devices of concealment."

1981   DIEHL, *Romantic Imagination*, pp. 155–58
Examines the nature of the poem's "sire" and considers "imagistic connections between Shelley and Dickinson."

1983   SHURR, *Marriage,* pp. 93, 144, 182
The poem "describes her suffering and twice memorializes the 'Death' which has caused it, but which is, paradoxically, her only sign of 'Wealth.' This is the poem which identifies the beloved addressee as a clergyman . . . ."

"Satisfaction is the agent" (1036)

1978   TILMA-DEKKERS, "Immortality," pp. 168–69
"Sufficient supply ('Satisfaction') would be indicative of a larger supply, with which to satisfy our needs would be 'Satiety'. It would, however, still be finite. Just as 'Satisfaction' is contrasted with 'Want', so is 'Satiety' contrasted with 'Infinity.' "

1980   HOMANS, *Women Writers,* pp. 181–83, 185
The poem "opposes opposition only by way of a rhetorical strategy based on oppositions. . . . On one level the poem states that satisfaction and satiety are opposites, affectively, at the same time reminding us that they are the same, by reminding us of their common root."
Reprinted: Homans, "Emily Dickinson," pp. 425–26, 427; reprinted in part: Homans, "Dickinson and Poetic Identity," p. 143

1983   JUHASZ, *Undiscovered Continent,* pp. 91–92, 93, 95, 100, 101, 120, 121
The poem "shows how close to delight is active pain, how close to despair is inactive pleasure. All depends upon the ratio or proportion between the emotions being measured. Yet the poem also suggests that there is a place between delight framed by distance and delight possessed . . . ."

"Savior! I've no one else to tell" (217)

1978   TAYLOR, C., "Kierkegaard," pp. 571–72
"The 'imperial Heart' presumably has a realm, but the speaker is unable to solve the riddle of that realm's location, and the italics emphasize her surprise as she leaps from thoughts of her own limited strength to doubts of God's capacity."

1980   LaBELLE, "Dickinson's 'Savior!' " pp. 34–35
Difficulty in interpretation may be "caused by the poem's participation in two very different but traditional conventions—that of the religious poem addressed to God in the familiar terms most identified with George Herbert, and that of the Petrarchan love poem in which the lover is presented as a ruler over the heart of the speaker."

1981   KIMPEL, *Dickinson as Philosopher*, pp. 240–41
"The meaning of 'Savior,' as this term is used in this poem, . . . is as elementary as the faith itself which she affirms in turning beyond herself to a reality she trusts for saving her from despondency."

1983   SHURR, *Marriage*, pp. 67, 175
"It may be that the poem laments the loss of the husband after the anomalous marriage ceremony, but Dickinson's diction and imagery build a metaphor out of the subject of pregnancy and childbearing. And the death of the newborn is implied in the metaphor, if it is a metaphor, since the newborn is now with God . . . ."

1985   EBERWEIN, *Dickinson*, pp. 257–58
"To read the poem as it stands is to think of the speaker as resolving a conflict between human and divine loves by committing herself and her lover to Christ. Yet a prior variant gives quite a different impression."

" 'Secrets' is a daily word" (1385)

1981   KIMPEL, *Dickinson as Philosopher*, pp. 93–95
"The very seriousness . . . with which she regards the moral obligation imposed by a 'secret' indicates her moral demands, not only upon herself, but also her expectations of what others should demand of themselves."

"Severer service of myself" (786)

1983   SHURR, *Marriage*, pp. 39, 41, 116, 119
"The poem comes late among the fascicles and explicitly ties her sorrow to loss of the beloved . . . her suffering is caused by loneliness, the loss of the beloved to whom she wrote so many love poems."

1984   POLLAK, *Dickinson*, pp. 199–202, 203
"The severe service this speaker has taken it upon herself to perform is the work of drugging consciousness by subjugating herself to a disciplined regimen designed to extinguish her memory of loss."

1989   OLIVER, *Apocalypse of Green*, pp. 55–56, 77
". . . treats death as a termination of the life process rather than as a transition between two forms of life. The poem is a rather pessimistic depiction of the struggles of the living to fill their lives with meaningful activity after the death of loved ones."

"Sexton! my master's sleeping here" (96)

1983 SHURR, *Marriage,* pp. 55, 93
Examines biographical implications.

1984 PORTER, "Dickinson's Readers," p. 114
Takes issue with Shurr's interpretation in which he "finds evidence that Wadsworth counseled Dickinson in a borrowed clergyman's study. But surely, in good graveyard fashion, the Master's chamber from which in spring 'the snow creeps slowly' is not a pastor's study but a grave."

"Shall I take thee, the poet said" (1126)

1979 HAGENBÜCHLE, "Sign and Process," p. 151
"Whatever way we read these stanzas, the moment of wording appears to coincide with the moment of epiphany. The search for the word, the meaning, and the vision become one."
Reprinted: *Dickinson Studies,* p. 85

1984 WOLOSKY, *Emily Dickinson,* pp. 152–53
In this poem "devoted to poetics, the exact role of the secular and the sacred word is stated through a masterful syntactic obfuscation."

1985 CARTON, *Rhetoric,* pp. 89–90, 124
"The poet's judiciously chosen nominee is not elected here; nomination fails. But the act or enterprise of nomination creates an occasion for the vision that it cannot articulate and perhaps sustains a prospect that it cannot fulfill."

SMITH, B. J., "'Vicinity to Laws,'" pp. 45–47
Examines linguistic and cognitive levels on which the poem's legal language operates.

1986 MUNK, "Recycling Language," pp. 245–46
"In terms of biblical typology, just as Christ, the *Logos* or Word, filled the Messianic vision of the Old Testament, so, in a moment of poetic grace, the 'Word' fills Dickinson's poetic 'Vision.'"
Revised and reprinted: Munk, "Musicians Wrestle," p. 6

1987 SEWALL, "Emily Dickinson," pp. 83, 85
This poem "confronts the problem of the very source of the word itself—how the poet comes by it. Is it conscious thought-process? By inspiration? . . . The poem depicts a little drama of the poetic process."

"Shame is the shawl of pink" (1412)

1979 DIGGORY, "Armored Women," pp. 138–39
"The one quality of this poem that is not a feminine cliché is its refusal to concede helplessness, despite the affectation of a 'helpless Nature.' . . . Dickinson redefines traditional images of feminine vulnerability and endows them with all the strength of armor."

"She dealt her pretty words like blades" (479)

1982 MARCUS, *Emily Dickinson,* pp. 63–64, 66, 68
Relates to other Dickinson poems on society. "The pretty and glittering words suggest the pleasure which a clever woman takes in her speech while being at least partly aware of how much her words hurt those whom she is addressing."

"She laid her docile crescent down" (1396)

1981 DIEHL, *Romantic Imagination,* pp. 63–64
"The power of the stone depends directly on the consciousness of others. . . . Death itself . . . becomes the bond between object and person which lends the relic meaning."

MONTEIRO and ST. ARMAND, "Experienced Emblem," pp. 197–204, 266
The poem can best be understood in the context of the popular and contemporary emblem tradition with which Dickinson was familiar.

"She lay as if at play" (369)

1984 OLPIN, "Hyperbole: Part II," p. 26
Finds similarity between this poem's theme and that of John Crowe Ransom's "Bells for John Whiteside's Daughter."

1988 WOLFF, *Emily Dickinson,* p. 277
In the second stanza "the sexual innuendo becomes patent. And in the last stanza . . . sexuality becomes violent: prying these eyelids open so that they *must* regard the new day of Heaven is but ravishment displaced."

"She rose to his requirement, dropt" (732)

1979 GILBERT and GUBAR, *Madwoman,* pp. 588–91, 634
"The irony of the woman/wife's situation as it is described here is

"She rose to his requirement, dropt"

that in 'rising' to the rigorous 'Requirement' of a husband she has . . .
been cast out of the holy, Wordsworthian sea of imagination where she
had dwelt as a girl."

1980 JOHNSON, "'Pearl of Great Price,'" pp. 209–10, 215 n. 15
 "The poem is clearly Dickinson's meditation to herself about the
choices in her life: she imagines the compromise a conventional existence
would try to force upon her, and further imagines how she might fulfill
her duties both to a husband and to her own gifts."
 Revised and reprinted: Johnson, *Emily Dickinson,* pp. 133–35, 210 n.
22

1982 MARCUS, *Emily Dickinson,* pp. 60–61
 "Very probably an attempt to look objectively at the rewards and
losses of those real-life marriages in which Dickinson did not share, this
poem may also contain parallels to her own condition as imagined wife
and as poet."

 THOTA, *Emily Dickinson,* pp. 113–14
 "The real problem is posed in the last stanza. 'It lay unmentioned,'
and the idea is developed within the circumference of the experience of
love as the pearl develops in the sea. The pearl is there, but concealed."

1983 JUHASZ, *Undiscovered Continent,* pp. 114–16, 117, 118
 "Even as, through its manipulation of analogical implications, [the
poem] exposes the traditional goal, and life, of most women as destructive, reductive, so it undercuts, as well, the traditional meanings allotted
to the transition that must occur between childhood and adulthood."

 WALKER, N., "Humor as Identity," pp. 65, 66
 "The speaker in this poem is a detached commentator, an observer
of the transformation of a woman's ostensible self from subject to object."

1984 POLLAK, *Dickinson,* pp. 161–63
 "Having discovered the unmentionable—that in rising to *his* requirements, she has scanted her own—Dickinson's typic woman liberates
herself from the power of social convention by reappropriating the powers
of imperfection, of introspection, and of silence."

1985 EBERWEIN, *Dickinson,* pp. 105–06, 174
 "What did it mean for a wife to rise to her husband's requirement . . . ? To judge from the imagery of this poem and its elegiac tone,
it meant loss: of girlhood, play, possibility, and wonder."

1986 DOBSON, "'Invisible Lady,'" pp. 51, 54 n. 14
 "Here being 'Woman' and 'Wife' is once again equated, and de-

fined . . . as 'honorable Work.' In order to attain this identity, however, the woman described in this poem must sink her own potential."
Reprinted: Dobson, *Strategies of Reticence,* pp. 74, 146 n. 11

1987   Cook, C., "Psychic Development," p. 125
"The woman is caught in a social trap; in order to be honorable, she is to marry, but if she marries, she has to forget her development—a plaything—and concentrate on being a wife."

LEDER and ABBOTT, *Language of Exclusion,* pp. 137–38
"Whether this is God Himself or Husband Himself, the images of irritants—even 'Pearl' building from an irritant and 'Weed' as the fruition of this union—are not the answer we expect. The reality of this imagined, supernatural, or actual marriage is unmentioned and unmentionable."

MILLER, C., "Dickinson's Language," p. 82
The poem's masculine pronoun probably "refers to the woman herself, conferring masculine status on her to mark the oceanic depth, breadth, and wealth of the life she does not reveal."

ROGERS, K., "Introducing Dickinson," p. 55
Suggestions for teaching the poem to college students, with emphasis on "the speaker's evaluation of marriage."

WALKER, N., "Voice, Tone," pp. 109–11
Suggests contrasting with "A wife at daybreak I shall be" for teaching purposes. "From a cultural standpoint, these poems reveal Dickinson's understanding of the myth and the reality of marriage for women in the nineteenth century . . . ."

"She sights a bird, she chuckles" (507)

1981   PORTER, *Dickinson,* pp. 71, 72
"The poem begins with a precise description . . . and ends in an allegory of denial, bliss fled." This is "no real cat at all, but rather the figure of man himself put in the way of disappearing hope."

1983   ALLEN, M., *Animals,* p. 38
"The traditionally female cat . . . comes as the only female authority in Dickinson's poetry, where in the few cases in which animals are female, they are generally associated with clothing, frivolity, or meekness."

1989   ROGERS, K., "Introducing Dickinson," p. 53
Suggestions for teaching the poem to urban college students.

"She staked her feathers, gained an arc" (798)

1986   NEW, "Difficult Writing," pp. 8–10, 11
"Dickinson is toying here with a whole system of religious deference, and yet if the tone is too blithe, we should note that the possible consequences of an embrace of circumference are quite grave."

STONUM, "Calculated Sublime," pp. 118–19, 121
"This may be the most impressively optimistic poem Dickinson ever wrote. . . . The bird's triumph is precisely what Dickinson everywhere testifies to desiring for herself and nowhere claims to have achieved so definitively."

"She sweeps with many-colored brooms" (219)

1980   PORTERFIELD, *Feminine Spirituality,* pp. 3–4, 5
"If this poem about nature works by its association with feminine cycles and sweepings, it is rendered all the more humanly profound by its spiritual associations."

1982   DOWNEY, *Child's Emily Dickinson,* pp. 64, 66
In this poem "Emily tells us about a fairy who rides through the sky with colored brooms on Halloween. . . . When the fairy's brooms fade into stars, Emily leaves because it is time to go to bed and get rested for the beautiful day that follows."

1985   BUDICK, *Emily Dickinson,* pp. 8–9, 12, 26, 194
In this poem there is "something slightly chilling about the wispy clutter of images that sweeps across the landscape, a haunting intimation of perplexing discontinuities that may well end, the poet suggests, in dissolution."

1989   LEONARD, D. N., "Certain Slants," pp. 126–27, 128, 130
"While it is possible to dismiss the poem as a clever lyric whose tone inexplicably varies at the end, one is rewarded by . . . considering the poem within its fascicle setting."

"She went as quiet as the dew" (149)

1979   PATTERSON, *Dickinson's Imagery,* p. 96
"Perhaps the poet thinks herself less skillful than the astronomer because he finds a new 'star' and she can only lose one."

"Shells from the coast mistaking" (693)

1980   JOHNSON, " 'Pearl of Great Price,' " p. 208
Relates to other Dickinson poems employing the pearl image. Here the poet "separates pearl and speaker in order to illustrate that they are inseparable, a single entity."
Reprinted: Johnson, *Emily Dickinson*, p. 132

" 'Sic transit gloria mundi' " (3)

1983   MARCELLINO, "Pronounce Latin," pp. 11–12
Knowledge of how Dickinson probably pronounced Latin sheds light on poem's rhyme scheme.

1984   WHITMAN, "Rhyme Scheme," p. 50
Comments on poem's rhyme scheme.

1987   BLASING, *American Poetry*, p. 185
Examines stanza 8. "Both gravities—the Newtonian and Biblical falls, 'fact' and 'myth'—are joined *and* separated in the word 'gravitation.' "

"Size circumscribes—it has no room" (641)

1979   ESTES, "Search for Location," p. 212
"Size sets its own limit and does not measure its proportions against such insignificant things as flies, or even such important ones as calumnies. Thus 'size' connotes expansive amplitude. By viewing the vast expanse of circumference, the poet can learn that she, too, possesses expansiveness."

1983   SHURR, *Marriage*, p. 96
"The poem attempts to describe the 'size' which her present status has conferred, . . . beyond even the reach of lying rumors. . . . She seems to be claiming exemption from ordinary norms of behavior on the basis of the lovers' unique personal experience, in the last two lines."

1985   EBERWEIN, *Dickinson*, p. 162
In this "satirical poem on growth," the poet hints at "the advantages she derived from the very narrowness of her circuit. . . . If 'Size circumscribes,' perhaps minuteness liberates to some extent."

"So from the mould" (66)

1983 KHAN, "Dickinson's Phenomenology of Evolution," pp. 60, 65
"Dickinson's poetic imagination is spell-bound at the metamorphosis implicit in the instinctive evolution in nature." This poem "expresses her wonder at this aspect of phenomena."
Revised and reprinted: Khan, *Emily Dickinson's Poetry*, pp. 103, 109

1987 BARKER, *Lunacy of Light*, p. 121
"Although certainly these images of life springing anew from the 'mould,' or from death, are Christian in character, and although certainly Dickinson was influenced by biblical metaphor, this imagery also reflects her own particular poetic strategy."

"So give me back to death" (1632)

1983 SHURR, *Marriage*, p. 167
"The poem looks back over a long stretch, acknowledges a recent important change, and anticipates an event soon to occur. . . . The long stretch is her frequently affirmed attitude toward death, that it holds nothing for her to fear as long as it offers final union with the beloved."

1984 MARTIN, W., *American Triptych*, p. 111
"This lyrical and flowing poem expresses Emily Dickinson's intense sorrow [at Judge Lord's death] and deepening awareness of her own mortality. There is no attempt to diminish the intensity of the pain with false promises of reunion in an afterlife."

"So has a daisy vanished" (28)

1985 BUDICK, *Emily Dickinson*, pp. 51–53
Dickinson is here "suggesting that sacramental symbolism may not tell us anything more than we already know. And it may actually distract us with doubts that might otherwise not have arisen."

"So I pull my stockings off" (1201)

1986 DOBSON, " 'Invisible Lady,' " pp. 46, 54 n. 7
"Compromise of one's own will is shown to be a swindle here. . . . She here equates good behavior and bad behavior; neither is a guarantee of fair treatment by God. One might as well be bad."
Reprinted: Dobson, *Strategies of Reticence*, pp. 66, 145 n. 4

1988   WOLFF, *Emily Dickinson,* pp. 186–87, 215
"Does such a God deserve obedience? Will He honor it if He receives it? The child in the poem concludes that the record speaks against God, and so this child chooses Disobedience *for its own sake:* 'Wading in the Water.'"

1989   OLIVER, *Apocalypse of Green,* pp. 140–41
"The lightness of tone and the absence of recrimination make the poem appear less critical of God's ways than of man's understanding of God's ways."

"So large my will" (1024)

1988   STOCKS, *Modern Consciousness,* pp. 100–01
"This poem, from its viewpoint in old tradition, makes its own gentle appraisal of the validity or the scope of the existentialist will. The poem reads like a putting to rest of the restless existentialist impulse in her deeper vision of the real."

"So much of heaven has gone from earth" (1228)

1983   RIPLEY, "Dickinson's 'So much of heaven,'" pp. 27–30
"The language of lawyer and trial does not fit a problem of 'simple' belief. Dickinson uses this conflict to justify not her faith, but her unorthodox means of retaining it: mystery, ambiguity, and ultimately, self-denial."

"So much summer" (651)

1981   PORTER, *Dickinson,* pp. 88, 103–04
The poem illustrates "how much pressure the hymn mold put on Dickinson's syntax. . . . The poem is nothing so much as a cubist dispersal of natural arrangement to conform to an arbitrary form."

"So the eyes accost and sunder" (752)

1981   PORTER, *Dickinson,* p. 108
Comments on poem's syntax and "lack of organization."

"Soil of flint, if steady tilled" (681)

1979   PATTERSON, *Dickinson's Imagery,* pp. 149, 195
Considers poem's use of African imagery.

"Some keep the Sabbath going to church" (324)

1972   RAO, *Essential Emily Dickinson,* pp. 133–34
General introduction to the poem aimed at "postgraduate students of literature in Indian Universities." "The poem reflects Emily's rebellious attitude towards the Puritanic Practice [*sic*] of going to church."

1978   BURKE, "Religion of Poetry," pp. 18, 19, 22
The poem shows the poet's growing propensity to rely on her own capacity for spiritual realization rather than on some prescribed formula."

1981   STEINER, "Image Patterns," p. 67
"The religious imagery . . . is counterbalanced by nature imagery . . . , the message being that service can take a variety of shapes, not only the one dictated by society."

1983   SHURR, *Marriage,* pp. 35, 69, 142
Suggests the poem is addressed to a clergyman, specifically Wadsworth. Here, "if we are correct in concluding that all the fascicle poems are addressed to the beloved, she alludes archly to him as among those who 'keep the Sabbath, in Surplice'—a garb that serves to distinguish the clergy from the laity."

1986   MUNK, "Recycling Language," pp. 239–40, 250 n. 33
"The elevated tone of a religious sermon is undercut by bird songs . . . and by puns; both serve to undo the decorum of orthodoxy."

1987   MARTIN, J. E., "Religious Spirit," pp. 504–05
In this poem "Dickinson contrasts traditional religious practice with that characteristic of a religion of nature, unique and subjective."

1988   REYNOLDS, *Beneath the American Renaissance,* p. 36
"This poem may be regarded as a clever adaptation of the antebellum religious style: not only does it shift worship from the church to nature and sing praise to short sermons, but it actually converts God into an entertaining preacher obviously trained in the new sermon style."

1989   GARBOWSKY, *House without the Door,* p. 80
". . . when we place this poem within the context of Dickinson's life, its pantheistic suggestions fade to reveal Dickinson's fear of crowds and public gatherings."

"Some one prepared this mighty show" (1644)

1984   BENFEY, *Problem of Others,* pp. 43–44
"The poem expresses a version of the 'argument from design': the

most convincing proof of God's existence is that the universe bears evidence of design beyond man's capacity." Examination of what "tickets" signify in Dickinson's poetry.

"Some rainbow coming from the fair" (64)

1988   WOLFF, *Emily Dickinson*, p. 434
"When God refuses to acknowledge our prayers, it is a matter of His will; a reaction of anger is appropriate, and residual hope for some recognition can be sustained. Here, however, unresponsiveness is a matter of intrinsic incapacity, and both anger and hope seem absurd in the face of this inanimate impassivity."

"Some say goodnight at night" (1739)

1984   ANDERSON, D., "Presence and Place," pp. 214–16
Dickinson "leaps immediately from the sense of departure in 'parting' not to the anticipatory joy of returning but to a full and stable 'presence'—a presence as direct as simple experience is in comparison with the mediated experience of words . . . ."

"Some things that fly there be" (89)

1978   HECHT, "Riddles," p. 16
The poem seems to imitate "some of the formal principles of the riddles in the book of Proverbs."
Reprinted: Hecht, *Obbligati*, pp. 106–07

1983   BENVENUTO, "Words within Words," pp. 50–51
Examining definitions and etymology of poem's "riddle," as they appear in the dictionary Dickinson used, may shed light on poem's meaning.

1988   WOLFF, *Emily Dickinson*, pp. 288–89
"Is the 'Riddle' the all-too-real dead body, waiting to be magically resurrected from decay into that new life? . . . Is the 'Riddle' the promise of Redemption? How 'still,' how persistently and enduringly, it 'lies' and deludes us!"

"Some too fragile for winter winds" (141)

1986   HUGHES, G., "Subverting the Cult," p. 24
". . . what seems at first to be yet another poem in which Dickinson boldly affronts the God of her fathers is so suggestively polarized

between life-endangering males and death-offering, or death-accepting females that additional orthodoxies are plainly being called into question as well."

"Some we see no more, tenements of wonder" (1221)

1984　WoLOSKY, *Emily Dickinson,* p. 43
Death "poses a problem that cannot be resolved with any certainty—a problem, Dickinson suggests, equally arising from the 'Dust' of the grave in general . . . and from the 'Drums' of war in particular."

"Some work for immortality" (406)

1981　PERRINE, "Dickinson's 'Some—Work,' " pp. 32–33
Confusion in interpretation is caused by its second stanza; the "theme of this poem should be compared with that of . . . 'Essential Oils—are wrung.' " Paraphrase.

1984　POLLAK, *Dickinson,* pp. 247–48
Here "Dickinson initially views her poetic identity as a function of her relationship to her employer, 'Immortality.' . . . Eventually, 'Immortality' rectifies temporal injustice. Untransformed by Dickinson's language, the idea is a cliché: easy come, easy go."

1988　McHUGH, "Interpretive Insecurity," pp. 51–52
"There is hardly a syntactical unit here which cannot be variously connected with the elements surrounding it. . . ." Examines the poet's virtuosity, which permits "the greatest possible number of competing readings."

1989　OLIVER, *Apocalypse of Green,* p. 215
"In this poem, though immortality is of a higher order to her, she is unable to explain the reasons for her preference in other than time-bound language."

"Some wretched creature savior take" (1111)

1984　WoLOSKY, *Emily Dickinson,* p. 109
"Dickinson rejects the savior's salvation and turns the mercy of clerical discourse against its own purposes. She seeks distance from the source of love rather than union with it. What emerges is a sharp divergence between the earthly and heavenly stances."

Somewhat to hope for (1041)

1983   JUHASZ, *Undiscovered Continent,* p. 63
"Parallel construction links *hope* and *suffer,* implying that the awareness of a future tense makes any present endurable, because it must by definition give way at some point to something else, i.e., the future. The opposite is also implied . . . ."

"Somewhere upon the general earth" (1231)

1978   KHAN, "Romantic Tradition," pp. 59–60
"The poem deals with the possibility of a knowledge of immortality which would enable the lovers to meet in the post-mortal life."
Revised and reprinted: Khan, *Emily Dickinson's Poetry,* pp. 71–72

1980   CUNNINGHAM, *Dickinson,* pp. 44–46
Comments on implications of the poem's diction, particularly in the first stanza.

1985   EBERWEIN, *Dickinson,* p. 185
"Having experienced brief release from her confining circuit, she delights in God's expansiveness as represented to her by nature and concludes the poem with a prayer . . . ."

"Soto! Explore thyself" (832)

1984   POLLAK, *Dickinson,* p. 20
In writing these lines the poet "did not mean that the process of observation is influenced by one's social context. Rather, she meant that the process of observation is culture-free."

1989   McCLURE, "Expanding the Canon," pp. 76, 77
Here Dickinson "uses the frontier as a metaphor . . . for exploration of the 'undiscovered continent' of the mind."

"Soul, wilt thou toss again" (139)

1984   LEONARD, D. N., "Dickinson's Religion," pp. 339–40
This poem "presents the struggle within the individual soul between good and evil, angels and demons. But while Dickinson seems to negate the power of personal will to decide the soul's ultimate disposition, she describes the exercise of choice at a subtle and paradoxical level."

1989   OLIVER, *Apocalypse of Green,* pp. 106–07
"Although the poem concedes the improbability of winning, the human soul is not completely at the mercy of an arbitrary deity's choice in that the soul has some control, albeit a limited one, over the final outcome."

"South winds jostle them" (86)

1981   CAMPBELL, "Poetry as Epitaph," pp. 662–63
"The poem, on one level, is an exploration of the nature of language as sign and of sign as an epitaphic gesture which claims to make present and, at the same time, enunciates absence."

"Speech is a prank of parliament" (688)

1984   WALLACE, *God Be with the Clown,* p. 102
"The poem starts with a joke that would seem more appropriate to a satire of Parliament than to a serious poem about grief beyond words. . . . All three lines are entertaining diversions from the real center of the poem—the unspeakable grief that stops the heart cold."

"Speech is one symptom of affection" (1681)

1984   WOLOSKY, *Emily Dickinson,* pp. 164–65
"Dickinson here parallels faith in things invisible and spiritual to words inaudible and 'within.' . . . In elevating the inward word, Dickinson's position approaches Augustine's."

1986   MCNEIL, *Emily Dickinson,* pp. 93–94
In this "highly condensed poem, Dickinson admits that speech can play a role, though a limited one, in the special circumstance of love." The poem also suggests that "the most perfect communication does not actually get 'heard' by anyone, even a lover."

"Split the lark and you'll find the music" (861)

1979   GONNAUD, "Nature, Apocalypse," p. 135
"Emily Dickinson sides against the presumption and foolishness of man more than she defends a mystic view of Nature." Notes Emersonian qualities.

1981   ORSINI, "Romantic Use of Science," pp. 58–59, 60, 61, 63, 65
In this poem "Dickinson implies that it is not the scientific method,

however incomplete, that is unsound, merely its application. The poet-scientist had simply gone too far."

1983   ALLEN, M., *Animals,* p. 51
The poem "not only conveys the energy involved in producing music, but it makes the song so nearly inseparable from the lark as to suggest the force unifying the atom, the cohesion that exists only with the most concise."

SHURR, *Marriage,* pp. 36, 151, 181
"The poem is not about poetic theory but about her love for her husband." Suggests it may refer to a "painful abortion" the poet may have suffered.

1984   BENFEY, *Problem of Others,* pp. 64, 72, 91, 93–94
"Saved suggests salvation, and the sacrificial tendency of the poem is unmistakable. Sacrifice and fidelity are tied, here, as they are in the crucifixion. Thomas's doubt and his demand for proof are as faithless and murderous as the demands of the crucifiers."

1986   McNEIL, *Emily Dickinson,* pp. 1, 95–96, 104, 135, 164
"The lark quite literally embodies the truth that music floods out of those who are born singers. The lark-song and the blood-flow are one, a 'passion' unto death."

1987   MOREY, "Dickinson-Kant II," pp. 23, 24
"Tho fidelity is the main idea presented, the tone is one of longing."

1988   WOLFF, *Emily Dickinson,* pp. 362–63
"God thinks it necessary to kill each and every one of us before He can determine whether we do, in fact, possess the requisite faith. Here He proceeds in a manner that seems a mockery of Christian custom."

"Spring comes on the world" (1042)

1983   JUHASZ, *Undiscovered Continent,* pp. 104–05
Relates poem's bee and blossom analogy to that in "Come slowly, Eden."

"Spurn the temerity" (1432)

1981   KIMPEL, *Dickinson as Philosopher,* p. 221
"She may give some evidence in this poem of having changed her attitude toward her own earlier disparagement of the teachings of the church . . . ."

PORTER, *Dickinson*, p. 44
Although its brevity "obliges the reader to supply much of the connective tissue," the poem's sense is roughly: "Let us not rush to the promised judgment, for the trials of doubt are happiness compared to the final wager of annihilation."

"Still own thee, still thou art" (1633)

1981   DIEHL, *Romantic Imagination*, pp. 168–69
"The poem wants answers and is willing . . . to wrestle with the dying, for response. . . . the intensity of inquiry stems not from a life of despair but from an increasingly complete hegemony of consciousness that is deprived only of what it most craves to make it complete."
Reprinted: Bloom, H., *American Poetry*, p. 454; Bloom, H., *Emily Dickinson*, p. 150

"Struck was I, nor yet by lightning" (925)

1984   POLLAK, *Dickinson*, pp. 186–88
"In telling the story of her unnatural devotion to a lover who persistently slays her, Dickinson attempts to reconcile her fear of male dominance with her passion for its power."

"Success is counted sweetest" (67)

1972   RAO, *Essential Emily Dickinson*, pp. 13–14, 52, 73–74, 80, 108–09
General introduction to the poem aimed at "postgraduate students of literature in Indian Universities."

1978   ABAD, *Formal Approach*, pp. 132–33, 134–35, 153, 369
". . . we can argue fairly reasonably that [this poem] is *either* didactic, since it merely defines an idea of success, or mimetic, since it simulates someone's meditation as she reacts to an event."

1980   HOMANS, *Women Writers*, pp. 176–77, 178, 180, 181, 189
The poem is "surely a bitter parody . . . of orthodox thinking" in which the poet "finds an equivalence of valuelessness" rather than "a balance of price and purchase."
Reprinted: Homans, "Emily Dickinson," pp. 421–23, 424, 425, 430; reprinted in part: Homans, "Dickinson and Poetic Identity," pp. 139–40, 141, 142, 143

1982 MARCUS, *Emily Dickinson*, pp. 11, 76–77
This poem "about compensation . . . proceeds by inductive logic to show how painful situations create knowledge and experience not otherwise available."

TOEGEL, *Emily Dickinson*, pp. 65–66
"The victors have only their victory which they may not be able to savor fully, not having had the education of defeat."

1983 GIBSON, "Poetry of Hypothesis," pp. 229–30
Suggests that when Thomas Niles, the poem's first publisher, "emended the last line, substituting 'agonizing' for 'agonized,'" he made it a better and "more Dickinsonian" poem.

1984 WALLACE, *God Be with the Clown*, p. 97
"The familiar poem embraces a comic paradox as a sure defense against loss. . . . Failure and success, frustration and satisfaction, defeat and victory are comically inverted."

WOLOSKY, *Emily Dickinson*, pp. 84–85
"Dickinson seems to be asserting that even need has value. Experience of the worst, she suggests, heightens the experience of the good."
Revised and reprinted: Wolosky, "Dickinson's War Poetry," pp. 37–39.

1985 DICKENSON, *Emily Dickinson*, pp. 44, 105–06, 118, 123
Examines editorial changes made by Thomas Niles. "The changes are petty, but petty-minded: they lessen the poem's originality without improving on its perfectly clear meaning and sound grammar."

1986 BAKKER, "Emily Dickinson's Secret," p. 344
"The justification of defeat seems to lie in a greater awareness of the value of victory, a value negated by the emphasis on the existential agony of the man dying in defeat."
Reprinted: Bunt et al., *One Hundred Years*, p. 242

MOREY, "Dickinson-Kant: The First Critique," pp. 51, 56
"The perceptions of the defeated person are graphic with the distinct celebration of music and flags being bundled into a concept of living success as opposed to a permanent defeat of territory and death."

1987 LEDER and ABBOTT, *Language of Exclusion*, pp. 26, 108, 112, 114
"The poem's assumptions betray Dickinson's socialization as a woman to ennoble self-sacrifice." Links with other poems that have Civil War as background.

1988 CORN, "Dickinson's Losses," pp. 18–19
    Examines "the facets of success being explored" in this poem. Suggests that the "kind of 'success' suggested is the triumph of achieving religious faith."

    REED, "Masculine Identity," p. 280
    In this poem "we see the fear of oral deprivation defended by reaction formation."

1989 DOWNEY, "Mathematical Concepts," pp. 23–24, 30
    Exemplifies Dickinson's use of "indirect variation."

"Summer begins to have the look" (1682)

1985 JOHNSON, *Emily Dickinson*, pp. 109–10
    "The structure of this poem illustrates with special clarity the pattern of Dickinson's thought when she is attempting to draw inferences about immortality from natural phenomena." Discusses along with other Dickinson poems about the passing of summer.

1987 HESFORD, "Creative Fall," pp. 85–86
    Relates to other "fall" poems and other poems in which Dickinson "draws on the Judeo-Christian tradition of reading and interpreting nature as a book, a second scripture, replete with meaning."

"Summer has two beginnings" (1422)

1989 OLIVER, *Apocalypse of Green*, pp. 75, 230
    "The full flowering in June is dependent upon the vegetative death in October. Both seasons are temporary, recurrent, and dependent on one another. The poet cannot be certain that human death is analogous to the 'deciduous' plan of nature."

"Summer we all have seen" (1386)

1981 PORTER, *Dickinson*, pp. 95–96, 97
    Examines worksheets of this poem to illustrate poetic techniques and methods. Considers significance of specific word choices.

1983 SHURR, *Marriage*, pp. 186–86
    Examines biographical significance. Suggests that "'Embryo' is not a metaphor for anything within the world of this poem; it is rather the very subject of the poem itself."

1989 OLIVER, *Apocalypse of Green,* pp. 74–75, 86, 230
"Whether the knowledge attained only through death be the secret of everlasting life or a more sinister 'doom,' it must finally be accepted through faith, and the poem makes clear that only a few can truly believe."

"Sunset at night is natural" (415)

1984 WALLACE, *God Be with the Clown,* pp. 100–01
". . . if an unpredicted eclipse or death occurs, it must be a mistake; God's watch must be wrong. The final unexpected joke is a shock, both protecting against and expressing the anguish in the poem."

1987 MILLER, C., *Emily Dickinson,* pp. 103–04
An aspect of "the speaker's relation to her subject and her audience" is revealed by the poem's "pattern of assertion and contrast."

"Sunset that screens reveals" (1609)

1978 FRANKLIN, "Three Additional," pp. 110–11
Description of manuscript, a working draft of this poem.

1979 NATHAN, "Slanted Truth," p. 39
Compares with "Delight's despair at setting" concerning Dickinson's views on the elusiveness of truth. "One must work at seeing the truth, which is many-layered; fraud, on the other hand, is 'glaring and dazzling,' all surface and no depth."

1987 BARKER, *Lunacy of Light,* p. 108
". . . the paradoxical act described in this poem is one of uncovering—or recovering—the truth by *allowing* it cover—or privacy, or respect. In addition sunset here feeds the imagination . . . ."

"Superfluous were the sun" (999)

1988 STOCKS, *Modern Consciousness,* p. 76
Comments on the poet's use of "the deeper grammatical layers of the language . . . for an introspective exploring mode of expression, . . . developing what is germinal and as yet undetermined in her consciousness into the spoken word . . . ."

"Superiority to fate" (1081)

1984 LEONARD, D. N., "Dickinson's Religion," pp. 340–41
"The poem is faithful, even in its equivocation, to Emerson's concept of self-reliance. . . . The paradox itself intrigues her: fate, necessity, and chance are present and inescapable, yet the soul can achieve its own will by constant striving."

1986 ROBINSON, J., *Emily Dickinson,* p. 22
". . . she challenges the idea of having objectives and seeking to reach them, of judging life by targets which are or are not attained. Such purposefulness . . . makes someone vulnerable to circumstance, whereas her hope . . . is that someone who manages in different terms may be liberated."

1989 ROGERS, K., "Introducing Dickinson," pp. 54–55
Suggestions for teaching the poem to college students, with emphasis on vocabulary.

"Suspense is hostiler than death" (705)

1987 MILLER, C., *Emily Dickinson,* p. 104
"The disjunctive effect of the repeated *But*s and the dashes of line 5 reflect the speaker's surprise at encountering anew the 'Suspense' she thought had died."

1989 GARBOWSKY, *House without the Door,* pp. 118–19
The poem includes "a possible reference to the threat of panic attack."

OLIVER, *Apocalypse of Green,* pp. 81–82
"Unlike death, the suspense regarding death does not die. . . . The real treachery of the suspense is that its promises of immortality may be deceptive, leading only to oblivion."

"Sweet mountains, ye tell me no lie" (722)

1981 DIEHL, "Dickinson and Bloom," pp. 430–32, 441 n. 26
"Dickinson adopts, in this poem, the authority of Christ to identify a faith of her own, one associated with the alternative power of women, a discipleship based on female identity."

1982 BARNSTONE, "Women and the Garden," pp. 162–63
"Unlike the God the Father of Genesis the 'Sweet Mountains' do not 'lie' about her existence by squeezing her into the role of the silent,

subservient wife. Nor do they condemn her for her failure or her doubting nature . . . ."

1983   DIEHL, " 'Ransom,' " pp. 167–68
"The poem asks for the belief of the mountains in the 'I' who usurps Christ's role but adopts a diametrically opposite position, beneath the hill as Christ was at its summit. This 'wayward nun' is, moreover, at once savior and worshipper."
Reprinted: Bloom, H., *American Women Poets,* pp. 33–34

1987   BARKER, *Lunacy of Light,* pp. 110–11
"Dickinson's evening is a time when masculine deity is finally and blessedly silent so that she, as a rebellious nun herself, can commune with her own maternal deities."

"Sweet, safe houses" (457)

1984   OLPIN, "Hyperbole: Part II," pp. 22–24
"The poem is an ironic attack upon faith in the pomp and comfort of the grave and upon the funeral rite that supposedly gives dignity and subtracts from the horror of death."

"Take all away" (1365)

1981   KIMPEL, *Dickinson as Philosopher,* p. 287
The poet here is "affirming that after all images of a hereafter are dismissed, the one affirmation which is worthy of respect is the unembellished declaration that there is an immortality."

1983   JUHASZ, *Undiscovered Continent,* pp. 167–68
This epigram "both attacks and condones death, turning on its two definitions of 'all': the one conventional, the other radical."

1984   MARTIN, W., *American Triptych,* p. 123
"In many respects this selflessness is an intensification of the conditioned egolessness of traditional womanhood. By carrying the Victorian dictate of feminine receptivity to its extreme, Dickinson discovered what mystics call the joy of cosmic fusion, or being one with the universe."

"Take your heaven further on" (388)

1977   BENNETT, "Language of Love," p. 15
". . . the imagery which the poet uses here and her stance with the poem . . . was developed largely within the context of a love passion that

was not only unrequited but, by its very nature, forbidden and hence of necessity bound to be extraordinarily painful."

"Taking up the fair ideal" (428)

1978 CARTON, "Dickinson and the Divine," p. 251
"Whenever we take our ideal, Dickinson suggests, whenever we clearly view the object of our quest, we perceive it to be flawed. Its flaw, however, reflects our own limitation or failure."
Reprinted: Carton, *Rhetoric*, pp. 131–32

1985 BUDICK, *Emily Dickinson*, pp. 116–17
"To dismiss idealism too lightly is, in Dickinson's view, an error. But to fixate on the ideal, to live entirely within and for the immaterial realm of an ideal universe, is a problem of equal magnitude . . . ."

1989 OLIVER, *Apocalypse of Green*, pp. 185–86
"If we remain steadfast to our ideal, if we have faith, the imperfections in the ideal or our imperfect understanding of the ideal will be remedied."

"Tell all the truth but tell it slant" (1129)

1978 HECHT, "Riddles," pp. 18–20
Considers poem's "religious significance."
Reprinted: Hecht, *Obbligati*, pp. 109–10

1981 ANDERSON, V., "Disappearance of God," pp. 15–16
"The poet takes on herself the responsibility to endure on her own a direct, painful exposure to the truth so that others might be spared such an ordeal. Again the poet is serving a function often attributed to Christ."

1982 MARCUS, *Emily Dickinson*, pp. 44–45
General consideration as one of Dickinson's poems on "Poetry, Art, and Imagination."

1984 WALLACE, *God Be with the Clown*, pp. 78–79
Contrasts Dickinson's use of comic persona with Whitman's. "Paradoxically, Whitman's hyperbolic self-aggrandizement becomes a kind of modesty, while Dickinson's hyperbolic self-deprecation becomes a kind of hubris."

1985 LAWSON, "Slant on Immortality," pp. 24, 25–26, 27, 29
"Dickinson's 'Truth,' . . . is the 'superb surprise' of her God of

the center and, as the poem shows, He is also the 'omitted center' of the poem, because it is not possible for mortal eyes to behold Him or speak of Him directly."

1986 MILLER, C., "'A letter is a joy,'" p. 35
"By the logic of this poem, indirection or 'slant' in language protects the hearer, and the speaker's or poet's role becomes implicitly maternal. The thoughtful user of language protects her reader/children from frightening truth by talking around it . . . ."
Revised and reprinted: Miller, C., *Emily Dickinson,* pp. 16, 184

1988 MOREY, "Dickinson-Kant III," p. 21
Here "the word *truth* can be seen to cover all knowledge, relationships, progress, in fact all the Kantian categories which constitute the filtering *mens*."

UNO, "Optical Instruments," pp. 237–38
"Here, expression and sight are fused. . . . the two different processes, reasoning and sensation, are combined to describe the poet's principle of dualism, of 'observing' (seeing and/or expressing) things 'slantly.'"

1989 DOBSON, *Strategies of Reticence,* pp. 103–04
This poem "seems to posit an aesthetic based on gradual revelation of abstract truth; . . . the revelations of this poem are associated with the 'Delight' and 'superb surprise' of all poetry that deals with great and difficult truths."

"Tell as a marksman were forgotten" (1152)

1988 PHILLIPS, *Emily Dickinson,* pp. 173–75
"The restraint with which the poet voices consternation about what a gesture of freedom might have cost had Tell not been a man of self-control, skill, and Christian faith is less eloquent than the rhetoric of protest against God's treatment of Moses" in "It always felt to me a wrong."

"That after horror, that 'twas us" (286)

1979 CAMERON, *Lyric Time,* pp. 106–08, 110, 112
"The attempt to glimpse death's visage while escaping its grip, . . . to straddle the line between ignorance and knowledge, is an abortive one

in [this poem], and Dickinson acknowledges that fact. One cannot have knowledge and be protected from its consequences at the same time."
Reprinted: Cameron, *Et in Arcadia*," pp. 53–55, 57, 58

1982   BUCKINGHAM, "'That after Horror,'" pp. 34–35
Takes issue with Cameron's 1979 interpretation, which "runs counter to its central and unifying conviction that human consciousness may not penetrate the boundary at life's farthest edge."

1983   SHURR, *Marriage*, pp. 31, 61
". . . it may be that the poem reflects on a sudden and serious illness that ended happily, but there are two people involved and much in the poem suggests rather a moral danger luckily overcome." Relates to a meeting between Dickinson and Wadsworth.

1984   OLPIN, "Hyperbole: Part II," pp. 19–20
"The human grin and the mechanical man here personified as death fulfill another central criterion for the comic according to Bergson . . . ."

1986   LOVING, *Emily Dickinson*, pp. 8–9
". . . the fear described is that the present negates our true identity in the irrecoverable past and that we will pass nameless and without a 'Moment's Bell' into oblivion."

ROBINSON, J., *Emily Dickinson*, pp. 121, 123–24, 128
"There is a politics of memory. Memory may be a victory celebration. Here, however, it is a defeat. With the instant speed of the imagination, the past may become the present."

1987   MILLER, C., *Emily Dickinson*, pp. 142–43
"Dickinson's own rhythms, loose rhymes, and abbreviated (therefore often cryptic) metaphors of description sound less unusual when placed besides Watts's hymns than when compared with the work of her contemporaries."

1988   WOLFF, *Emily Dickinson*, pp. 264–68, 269, 270, 445, 446, 497
The poem "records the final moments of Christ's hold over our collective imagination, the twilight of the Christian era when strong, confident faith is disjointedly falling apart."

1989   OLIVER, *Apocalypse of Green*, pp. 142–43, 147, 153
"The split-second salvation by Christ from the jaws of Death has something of the macabre in it. The very thought of the possibility of losing to death or annihilation 'by a Hair' is too horrible to contemplate . . . ."

"That I did always love" (549)

1981 KIMPEL, *Dickinson as Philosopher*, pp. 257–58
"This poem includes at least two assertions which might be regarded as propositions in a philosophy about the nature of love, when such a philosophy is not encumbered by emotive or unconventional uses of language."

1989 OLIVER, *Apocalypse of Green*, pp. 220–21
"In the second stanza she adds the term *immortality* as the predicate of her major premise and of her conclusion: Life has immortality; Love is Life; therefore, Love has immortality. It is life that is the larger class and thus provides the immortality which love as a member of the class is entitled to."

"That it will never come again" (1741)

1978 CARTER, "Dickinson and Mysticism," p. 87
The poem suggests "that it may be the *lack* of permanence in nature, the insecurity upon which the material universe is founded, that stimulates man's rage for order and his thirst for the Divine."

1986 ROBINSON, J., *Emily Dickinson*, pp. 145, 147
"Her emotional and poetic practice is to love the thrill of the imminent and to linger in a departure because in such moments, related to the firm or solid state but not confined to it, she seemed to have the most secure real, least prone to doubt."

1989 OLIVER, *Apocalypse of Green*, pp. 59–60, 64, 229
The poem contains one of Dickinson's most explicit statements of the "idea that the intrusion of death compels, or should compel, the living to greater concern for the quality of this life."

"That odd old man is dead a year" (1130)

1981 KIMPEL, *Dickinson as Philosopher*, pp. 49–50
"A discouragement is expressed in this poem which is accentuated to the extreme of despondency. It contrasts the vitality with which a human being begins life, with a hope of achieving what justifies it, and then progressively comes to a sense of defeat, as if the promise for life had been deceptive."

"That she forgot me was the least" (1683)

1978 FADERMAN, "Homoerotic Poetry," p. 24
"It is the other woman alone who is to blame. The speaker acknowledges that she had nothing to offer her beloved except faithfulness; but the unchanging devotion of the speaker, who poses here as the woman's anonymous lover, became an embarrassment to the beloved."

"That short potential stir" (1307)

1980 CLEARY, "Classical Education," pp. 128–29
The poem, "most Horatian, in language, form, and theme," suggests that Dickinson was influenced by the Greek and Roman classics "in more than a merely formal way."

"The admirations and contempts of time" (906)

1978 HUGHES, J., " 'Time's Sublimest Target,' " pp. 32–35
The poem's "literal meaning . . . could confirm traditional Christian answers, but the echoes of the words and the confusion over pronoun reference confirm the fact that this poem lacks the definitiveness that only death can provide."

TILMA-DEKKERS, "Immortality," pp. 174–75
". . . the 'Open Tomb' affords us 'Compound Vision': the convex and concave vision make up the total vision of Reality."

1981 DIEHL, *Romantic Imagination*, p. 148
"Whatever the specific genesis of the poem . . . here Dickinson takes as her subject the change in perspective, the shift in point of view, that follows death. The vision is 'compound,' life's opposite providing a new light by which to view the finite as the soul stares, Janus-like, back and forward through time."

PORTER, Dickinson, pp. 13, 119, 192–93
Examines elements that precipitate the poem's "swift movement from description into style, from rhetorical persuasion into language dance, and from conventional sentiment into wit."

1984 MARTIN, W,. *American Triptych*, pp. 142–43
"This 'Compound Vision' composed of what is and is not there, presence and absence, past and future, 'Convex' and 'Concave,' enables us to distinguish and appreciate the texture of the moment that is thrown into relief by the reality of death."

WOLOSKY, *Emily Dickinson,* pp. 19–20

"Not just end, but end as synecdochic wholeness provides the retrospective stance that makes forward motion possible and that determines its axiology. And only such final totality allows time's 'Contempts' to be borne."

Reprinted: Wolosky, "Syntax of Contention," pp. 175–76

1985   COOK, A., *Thresholds,* pp. 184–85

"Death provides, abidingly, the assessment for life through a 'Compound Vision' that takes the power of Wordsworthian retrospection, so to speak, and transposes it from the present's look at the past to an absolute future's look after death at a simultaneous present."

JOHNSON, J., *Emily Dickinson,* pp. 3–4, 173–74

This is *"the* poem of Dickinson's 'bardic' stance, presenting her transcendence over death in its character as an existential terror, an insuperable threat. . . . [It] focuses upon death as the doorway, *within* consciousness to a perception so glorified that it seems synonymous with transcendent poetic vision."

1986   MOREY, "Dickinson-Kant: The First Critique," p. 66

"The Dying is looking back on an ecstasy, after a state of being, or moment of consciousness-raising, something important enough to be considered a watershed in one's life.

1988   UNO, "Optical Instruments," pp. 235–36, 237, 242

Examines poem's scientific references. "The term 'Compound' must have derived from a reflecting telescope, in which a 'Convex' lens and a 'Concave' mirror are used."

"The angle of a landscape" (375)

1981   KIMPEL, *Dickinson as Philosopher,* pp. 162–64

"What is significant in this poem is her orientation to a reality other than herself."

1983   SHURR, *Marriage,* p. 93

"The poem inventories the things she can see through her window" from her bed. The poem's "Steeple" refers to Wadsworth.

1984   ST. ARMAND, *Dickinson and Her Culture,* pp. 223–24

"Her duty remains to record the exact details and to infer the spiritual significance of the canvas, almost oriental in its simplicity, that is set before her. Her task is prospective rather than retrospective, and she

341

studies the patterns and features of the landscape as the physiognomist would survey a visage . . . ."

1985   JOHNSON, *Emily Dickinson,* pp. 115–16, 117, 207 n. 12
Here "the poet transforms a daily event in her life . . . into a meditation upon what is permanent in her world, what is transient, and their relative values."

1987   MILLER, C., *Emily Dickinson,* pp. 92–93
The poem's hypotaxis illustrates "the differences between Shelleyan and Dickinsonian complexity."

1988   WOLFF, *Emily Dickinson,* pp. 286–88, 312, 436, 460, 498
". . . the speaker of this verse is surely a poet by Emerson's definition, someone who can 'see' the comprehensive plan of nature. Yet this landscape is little more than a Design of desolation."

1989   KNAPP, *Emily Dickinson,* pp. 103–04
In this poem "Dickinson ridicules Emerson's notions concerning the benevolence of nature, which she sees rather as a ravishing and spoliating force that works in keeping with the dictates of God, the Supreme Designer."

"The auctioneer of parting" (1612)

1979   CAMERON, *Lyric Time,* pp. 148–49
In this poem "meaning yields to the more dominant sense of space left in its midst, as if space were a clearing, a doing away with the detail that life and its interpretation require."

"The bat is dun with wrinkled wings" (1575)

1983   ALLEN, M., *Animals,* p. 42
". . . there is no sign of gloom about him. His 'quaintly halved' wings reflect the artistry of precision in one who is considered abhorrent not because he is destructive but because he is different."

1988   WEISSMAN, " 'Transport's Working Classes,' " p. 419
"By saying that nature's creatures are also God's, Dickinson has brought God back to her poetic fold; by calling God adroit and eccentric she has brought him down from his forbidding heights and made him a fellow and a friend."

"The battle fought between the soul" (594)

1984 WOLOSKY, *Emily Dickinson,* pp. xvii–xviii
"In presenting this image of inner strife . . . Dickinson does so in terms provided by the world outside her. The poem was written in 1862: the very period when Antietam and Bull Run had begun to reveal fully the horrors of the Civil War."
Reprinted: Wolosky, "Voice of War," pp. 20–21

"The beggar lad dies early" (717)

1981 MONTEIRO and ST. ARMAND, "Experienced Emblem," pp. 214–17, 266
Examines as an "instance of Dickinson's almost piecemeal translation of an emblematic motif into poetry."

1989 DOBSON, *Strategies of Reticence,* pp. 3, 92
The poem "suggests no action and displays no real anger. It simply relates a situation and promises the conventional recompense in heaven."

"The Bible is an antique volume" (1545)

1978 YODER, *Emerson,* pp. 192–93
"Orpheus as founder of the ancient theology and revealer of sacred truth risks the oblivion of other 'faded Men.'"

1982 BARNSTONE, "Women and the Garden," pp. 154–55, 156
The poem contains clues to "the biblical Eden Dickinson rejects and the alternative gardens she creates."

MARCUS, *Emily Dickinson,* p. 91
"The poem may be a complaint against a Puritan interpretation of the Bible and against Puritan skepticism about secular literature. On the other hand, it may merely be a playful expression of a fanciful and joking mood."

1984 MARTIN, W., *American Triptych,* pp. 137, 138
"Not only does Dickinson relegate theology to the province of men and boys, but she criticizes the punitive orientation of the Judeo-Christian heritage with a reference to the myth of Orpheus whose music charmed the rulers of the underworld."

TSELENTIS-APOSTOLIDIS, "I will be Socrates," pp. 11, 18–19
"The fundamentally amoral, poetic and magical quality of Orpheus—deeply religious nevertheless—is what she prefers over the prosaic and unimaginative Puritan preaching. . . . The one religion sings, the other speaks."

1985 EBERWEIN, *Dickinson*, p. 79
"The poem calls for a freshening tone in Bible stories at the expense of moralizing; it prefers captivation of the reader to condemnation."

1986 BUELL, *New England Literary Culture*, p. 66
"Its gnomic method echoes in another key the dryness that it chides. The poem looks through the window of Calvinism at Orpheus playing in the distance."

ROBINSON, J., *Emily Dickinson*, pp. 42, 43, 81
"With the levity which characterizes such protests," the poet objects to "the mystification and dishonesties and picture-book simplification of the Bible, objects most to its resting on the coercions of external authority rather than intrinsic interest . . . ."

1988 ST. ARMAND, "'Your Prodigal,'" pp. 368–69, 371
Family correspondence sheds light on the poem's evolution.

"The bird did prance, the bee did play" (1107)

1981 PORTER, *Dickinson*, pp. 108–09
"It seems that Dickinson brought the poem to a close without the mold of a clear idea of what the poem was to say in its totality. It ends short of completion, the result of writing cut loose from discipline and the challenge and check of a design."

"The bird her punctual music brings" 1585)

1979 NATHAN, "Soul at White Heat," p. 44
Relates elements of poem to traditional modes of meditation.

"The bird must sing to earn the crumb" (880)

1977 AGRAWAL, *Emily Dickinson*, p. 118
"'The Bird' serves as a powerful symbol of the inner self in [this poem]. . . . The inner self must be alive to the demands of time made

upon life and must sing to the tune of life's music. Only then it may get its sustenance from life."

1981   PORTER, *Dickinson*, p. 186
The issue here is "not merely Milton's questioning of artistic purpose in a randomly destructive world; it is the question 'Who am I?' a plaintive seeking for a purpose to hold the extraordinary power and to make a target for the words."

"The birds begun at four o'clock" (783)

1979   CAMERON, *Lyric Time*, pp. 177–78
Examines ambiguities in poem's grammar.

1980   HARTMAN, *Criticism in the Wilderness*, pp. 122–26, 127, 128, 129, 130
Considers along with "At half past three a single bird." "Read in sequence, their quest for purity appears in a revealing and frightening way."

1984   ANDERSON, D., "Presence and Place," pp. 211–13
"What distinguishes the miraculous dawn is not any special sanctity but common availability—its closeness."

1986   STONUM, "Calculated Sublime," pp. 119–20, 121, 126
". . . her response begins with the confusion and the sense of being overwhelmed that normally inaugurate the sublime." But she goes on to acknowledge "that the singing is beyond her power to appropriate. The poem refuses the sublime . . . ."

"The blackberry wears a thorn in his side" (554)

1977   AGRAWAL, *Emily Dickinson*, p. 117
The poem's blackberry "symbolizes a man conscious of the anguish of his existence, who, without grudging it, goes on proffering his love and affection to all who frequent him."

1979   BARNES, "Telling It Slant," pp. 230–31
Relates Dickinson's use of the proverb, "The nightingale sings with a thorn in its breast," to a comment in a letter from Susan Dickinson.

PATTERSON, *Dickinson's Imagery*, pp. 15–16, 21, 107
Considers as one of several "boy poems written about 1862 [which] deal with the pain of lost love."

1986   Doreski, " 'Exchange of Territory,' " pp. 59–60
"Dickinson's real subject here is the felicity of vegetable imagery and the limits of personification."

"The blunder is in estimate" (1684)

1983   Juhasz, *Undiscovered Continent,* pp. 146–47
"Dickinson's criticism of our clichés for talking about eternity both proposes another set of terms, based on another perception of distances involved, and calls attention to the analogical function, too frequently forgotten, of all these words."

1984   Martin, W., *American Triptych,* p. 143
"For Dickinson, eternity is the unfolding present, not a destination or location."

"The bobolink is gone" (1591)

1966   Benjamin, *Province of Poetry,* p. 117
Study questions.

1983   Shurr, *Marriage,* pp. 169–70
Relates to aspects of Wadsworth's life. The poem is a "celebration of the personality of the recently dead husband as it was revealed in one of the major incidents of his career."

"The bone that has no marrow" (1274)

1981   Kimpel, *Dickinson as Philosopher,* pp. 149–50
Dickinson is "clearly aware of a problem with which philosophers have wrestled throughout the centuries [which is] . . . how it is possible that a human being who is what he is, can also become something other than what he is."

1984   Olpin, "Hyperbole: Part II," pp. 29–30
Relates poem's comic techniques to those employed by Dickinson in other "death poems."

"The brain is wider than the sky" (632)

1972   Rao, *Essential Emily Dickinson,* pp. 16–17, 146–47
General introduction to the poem aimed at "postgraduate students of literature in Indian Universities."

1979 JUHASZ, "Undiscovered Continent," pp. 95–96

"This poem attests to the mind's supremacy over everything in the external world, to its easy equivalence with God. Its actuality, as substantial as sea or sky, is revealed through a vocabulary of measurement, capacity and color."

Revised and reprinted: Juhasz, *Undiscovered Continent*, pp. 26–27, 177

PATTERSON, *Dickinson's Imagery*, p. 125

This poem "assigns the color blue to the brain, not in the commonplace sense of melancholy but rather in the sense of the infinity . . . that is symbolically associated with the blueness of sky and sea. . . . The poet is saying . . . that her brain has the quality of the infinite."

1980 HOMANS, *Women Writers*, pp. 193–94

"It is impossible to find here an order of valuation, and the poem teaches us not to wish to impose one."

Reprinted: Homans, "Emily Dickinson," p. 433

1982 MARCUS, *Emily Dickinson*, pp. 79–80

Relates to other Dickinson poems on "Suffering and Growth." Dickinson "seems to be asserting that imagination or spirit can encompass, or perhaps give, the sky all of its meaning."

VAN DYNE, "Double Monologues," pp. 465–67, 468, 473

The poem shows us "Dickinson's speaker standing watchfully by her subjective self in order to examine the dimensions and co-habitants of her chamber of consciousness."

1986 MOREY, "Dickinson-Kant: The First Critique," pp. 58–59

"The experience must come first; the understanding and recounting it involve linguistics which can only be an imperfect itemized accounting."

ROBINSON, J., *Emily Dickinson*, pp. 64–65

It is the "superiority of thought to matter which informs [this poem] with its conceit that sky and sea are smaller than the intelligence which grasps sky and sea as ideas."

1988 WOLFF, *Emily Dickinson*, pp. 462–63

"At first, this sweeping assertion of the 'Brain's' capacities may appear an ultimate confirmation of the primacy and authority of self, and in one sense it is. Yet the self that has been thus empowered is paradoxically limited, for every significant other self has been obliterated through absorption."

"The brain within its groove" (556)

1983 JUHASZ, *Undiscovered Continent,* pp. 20–21
"Natural acts serve as comparisons for mental events in these poems of geographical vocabulary, but what happens in the mind is always more significant, more interesting, and different."

1989 GARBOWSKY, *House without the Door,* p. 120
The poem "dramatically reveals the sense of mental disorder and disintegration experienced by victims of panic attack."

"The bustle in a house" (1078)

1972 RAO, *Essential Emily Dickinson,* pp. 154–55
General introduction to the poem aimed at "postgraduate students of literature in Indian Universities."

1982 MARCUS, *Emily Dickinson,* pp. 87–88
Relates to other Dickinson poems on death and immortality. "Few of Emily Dickinson's poems illustrate so concisely her mixing of the commonplace and the elevated, and her deft sense of everyday psychology."

1988 WOLFF, *Emily Dickinson,* pp. 484–85
"Taken as a whole, the poem addresses not so much a phenomenon of dying as a process of living: it venerates the incalculable value of quotidian domestic activities . . . ."

"The butterfly obtains" (1685)

1988 STOCKS, *Modern Consciousness,* p. 42
"The focus here is clearly on the social relationship. The free spirit, symbolised by the butterfly, is subjected to society's utilitarian appraisal, and found wanting."

"The butterfly's assumption gown" (1244)

1982 MARTIN, J. M., "Nature and Art," pp. 26–28
Compares and contrasts with "The butterfly's Numidian gown." Nature functions in both as a metaphor for art. The poems illustrate how Dickinson "was unable to separate nature from her day-to-day descriptions of it."

WESTBROOK, *New England Town,* pp. 195–96
"In the second stanza Dickinson is saying that the butterfly, fully

equipped for its assumption, seems to have found Amherst no less preferable than heaven."

"The butterfly's Numidian gown" (1387)

1982 MARTIN, J. M., "Nature and Art," pp. 26–28
Compares and contrasts with "The butterfly's assumption gown." Nature functions in both as a metaphor for art. The poems illustrate how Dickinson "was unable to separate nature from her day-to-day descriptions of it."

1987 BARKER, *Lunacy of Light*, p. 68
Here the poet "uses a butterfly to represent a female figure struggling with its most 'profound Responsibility.'"

"The chemical conviction" (954)

1981 PORTER, *Dickinson*, p. 175
This "marvel of compression" is "distorted in language by the hymn's procrustean bed."

1985 DICKINSON, *Emily Dickinson*, p. 95
"It takes a scientific metaphor, the law of the conservation of matter, to convince Dickinson of the resurrection of the body. . . . But Dickinson's language betrays her doubts."

"The child's faith is new" (637)

1985 EBERWEIN, *Dickinson*, p. 183
This poem, which "generalizes on the loss of innocence to experience and on that loss's result in cynicism about God's promises," is related to other poems in its fascicle; taken together they supply "evidence for the poet's having crossed circumference with God's help."

"The color of a queen is this" (776)

1981 RUDDICK, "'Color of a Queen,'" pp. 90, 91, 93
In this poem "the poet identifies three main groups of associations evoked in her mind by purple."

"The color of the grave is green" (411)

1983 ROSENTHAL and GALL, *Modern Poetic Sequence*, pp. 48, 54, 57–58, 65
"She is not talking of a physical grave at all; her concern is with

the 'Duplicate' grave within the human psyche." Considers as part of the sequence in fascicle 15.

"The daisy follows soft the sun" (106)

1978 CUDDY, "Latin Imprint," pp. 79–80
    The opening lines illustrate "Dickinson's purposeful reliance on both Latin and English rules, depending on her need."

1979 GILBERT and GUBAR, *Madwoman,* pp. 600–01, 602
    The poem "seems to be both an intensely felt address to the patriarchal sun as Father/Master/Lover and a careful elaboration of a courtly conceit."

1980 HOMANS, *Women Writers,* pp. 203–04
    "The poem parodies the faulty relations between the sexes that obtain when the conventional attributes are assigned, such as the equation of weakness with femininity and of power with masculinity."
    Reprinted: Homans, "Emily Dickinson," pp. 440–41

1983 HOMANS, "'Oh, Vision,'" pp. 118–19
    ". . . at the level of the theme of romantic love the daisy reverses the two figures' apparent relation of authority and humility, while at the level of rhetorical structure the metaphor that underlies both the poem's and the relationship's structure is exposed as illusion."

    MORRIS, A., "'The Love of Thee,'" pp. 104–05
    Relates poem to "the major iconographic pattern of the Master material: the relation between the Daisy and the Sun." It "reminds us that the daisy . . . is named for its tropism, its involuntary orientation to the sun."

1985 HOMANS, "Syllables of Velvet," pp. 576–80, 592 n. 13
    Although this poem "has many of the features of the lyric of romantic desire, it subverts that plot in several ways." Relates to Wordsworth's "Lucy" poems.

"The dandelion's pallid tube" (1519)

1979 DE EULIS, "Whitman's 'The First Dandelion,'" pp. 29–32
    Compares and contrasts with Whitman's "The First Dandelion." Examining the different ways in which the two poets responded to the occasions that brought the poems into being sheds light on "their respec-

tive attitudes towards the function of natural object as 'natural artifact' in verse."

1989   OLIVER, *Apocalypse of Green*, p. 76
"Somewhat different from the cyclical regeneration seen in nature of death and rebirth is the implication of a change of form as well, as the dandelion changes form without an interval of death."

"The day came slow till five o'clock" (304)

1972   RAO, *Essential Emily Dickinson*, pp. 128–29
General introduction to the poem aimed at "postgraduate students of literature in Indian Universities."

1980   PORTERFIELD, *Feminine Spirituality*, pp. 147–48
"The ambush that ends the picnic, and the Musket that hurries the Lady, are images that depict the encounter of day and night as a battle of the sexes."

"The day that I was crowned" (356)

1976   SHANDS, "Malinowski's Mirror," p. 315
Here Dickinson pursues the theme of transformation. "In this poem she uses the theme of the common element, that element that occurs in common form in coal and in its transcendent form in diamonds."

1979   KELLER, K., *Only Kangaroo*, p. 290
"The terms . . . have been wrenched from their institutional contexts, not allowed their conventional connotations, and made to serve something entirely different, the heretical assertion of autonomous being . . . ."

1986   JONES, " 'Royal Seal,' " p. 40
The poem employs a terminology and reflects "a ritualism reminiscent of a New England baptism."

"The day undressed herself" (716)

1978   MILLER, R., "Transitional Object," pp. 451–52
"Here she is striving to present with particularity and concrete clarity the way in which that large phenomenon of the sun setting manifests itself to the small yet observant human eye."

1979 PATTERSON, *Dickinson's Imagery,* pp. 41, 121, 192
    "The viewpoint throughout is subtly, quite unconsciously, but passionately voyeuristic, and it is the strength of the poem . . . ."

"The days that we can spare" (1184)

1982 THOTA, *Emily Dickinson,* pp. 21, 22
    In lines 5–6 "Dickinson poses a fundamental question about the concept of reality, whether aesthetic or theological. . . . Each individual through his own experience and knowledge must try to arrive at his own concept of reality, which can at best be tentative and relative."

1984 WOLOSKY, *Emily Dickinson,* p. 20
    "Time's arithmetic, an impressive figure for prosody, here entails the totality that governs linguistic and empirical pattern. On it, Dickinson's ability to compute, comprehend, and evaluate duration depends. Without it, duration scatters, leaving the poet stranded."
    Reprinted: Wolosky, "Syntax of Contention," pp. 176–77

"The devil had he fidelity" (1479)

1981 KIMPEL, *Dickinson as Philosopher,* pp. 212–13
    Dickinson's "acquaintance with Milton's *Paradise Lost* is most likely indicated in [this poem], which reaffirms Milton's view that the Devil or Satan was a rebellious archangel, whose intelligence in every way equalled God's."

1989 OLIVER, *Apocalypse of Green,* pp. 172, 234
    "If the Devil were but more faithful and less treacherous, his ability would render him an asset; in fact, he could achieve divinity. . . . Perhaps Emily Dickinson's views of Satan owe something to *Paradise Lost,* just as Milton's epic had influenced the theology of many of her contemporaries."

"The difference between despair" (305)

1980 JUHASZ, " 'To make a prairie,' " pp. 16–17
    This poem "demonstrates the complexity that analogy and parallelism often achieve."
    Revised and reprinted: Juhasz, " 'Peril as a Possession,' " pp. 32–34; Juhasz, *Undiscovered Continent,* pp. 36–38, 57, 62, 63, 78, 80, 130

"The ditch is dear to the drunken man" (1645)

1982 OLPIN, "Hyperbole: Part One," p. 22
Often described as "a satire of the village drunk," the poem is perhaps "more a satire of the village's standards and the 'Honor leagues away.'"

1989 OLIVER, *Apocalypse of Green,* pp. 84, 129
"The poem carries to a striking extreme the extension of the parallel of Christ's sacrifice not only to human . . . but to inanimate life. The ditch assumes Christ's role as advocate for this fallen man with oblivion imminent and honor out of reach."

"The drop that wrestles in the sea" (284)

1982 MADIGAN, "Mermaids," pp. 45–46
Relates to sea imagery in Dickinson's poetry. "Here we see the poet treating the problem of self-identity and self-loss."

1983 SHURR, *Marriage,* pp. 30, 70–71, 137
". . . an erotic poem in which the speaker would merge herself totally with the beloved, forgetting that 'Ocean' is already married to 'Amphitrite.'"

1984 TSELENTIS-APOSTOLIDIS, "I will be Socrates," pp. 19, 20
"What is of great interest in [this poem] is Emily's constant fascination with the sea; the sea as image of the intense experience of life, the sea as the emblem of the unknown as was used in the Homeric epic of Odysseus' voyage."

1986 JUHASZ, "Renunciation Transformed," pp. 256–57, 259
"In the terms of the poem itself and not beyond it, the poet pleading 'Me?' is acknowledging her defeat, her loss of psychic locality. The literalness of her final question gives away her final abasement, for she has relinquished her true power, that of language. She has indeed lost herself in a sea of love."

JUHASZ, "Writing Doubly," pp. 7, 9–10
". . . the poem incarnates contradictory albeit simultaneous interpretations of the same situation, as the speaker finds herself seeking to win the love of a powerful man both on his terms and on her own."

1987 MONTEFIORE, *Feminism and Poetry,* pp. 169–70
"This gnomic fable of the Drop, aroused by love to wrestle for her own identity, is structured on a contradiction. . . . Nothing but the will to

be herself makes her exist as 'Me', and yet the identity by which she escapes annihilation by the smiling oceans is her selfless love."

1988   WOLFF, *Emily Dickinson,* pp. 271–72, 334, 579 n. 7
"The 'I' and 'Thee' are mortal woman and possessive God; the 'Drop' is a Christian who has already won faith, and the 'Sea' is the primordial power of the Divinity."

"The earth has many keys" (1775)

1980   DUNCAN, "Joining Together," p. 128
Discussion of the line "Beauty is nature's fact."

"The face I carry with me last" (336)

1983   SHURR, *Marriage,* pp. 8, 35, 78, 142
This is "another marriage poem in which the crown she receives in marriage is greater than any which Gabriel ever received." The poem is apparently addressed to a clergyman, probably Wadsworth.

"The farthest thunder that I heard" (1581)

1983   SHURR, *Marriage,* pp. 133, 168–69
Relates to the "narrative program so fully developed in the fascicles. And whoever the beloved might be supposed to be, it must also be significant that the poem was brought to completion just after the death of Wadsworth."

1988   STOCKS, *Modern Consciousness,* pp. 60–62
"She is contrasting in the poem the 'oxygen' of ordinary everyday life with the 'electricity' of the visionary light."

1989   FALK, "Kinds of Difficulty," pp. 151–54
Discussion of the poem's difficulties of syntax, logic, and its use of "the indeterminate symbol."

FALK and PACKER, "Workshop Discussion," pp. 159–74
Transcript of a workshop discussion of the poem.

PACKER, "Poem 1581," pp. 155–58
Examines the poem's intricacies as "ambiguously represented" in its "central trope: the relationship between lightning and thunder."

"The fascinating chill that music leaves" (1480)

1981 KIMPEL, *Dickinson as Philosopher,* pp. 214–15
"In this poem she contrasts the effect of music in her life with what the Puritans maintained about the effect of music upon Christians."

1988 WOLFF, *Emily Dickinson,* p. 480
"Ironically, under these circumstances, the song itself becomes a kind of wounding . . . it cannot lead to the Divinity that resides behind the material world. . . . Art has become foreshortened because nature is neutral and indifferent."

"The feet of people walking home" (7)

1981 PORTER, *Dickinson,* pp. 43–44
Notes how the meaning of "Larceny—legacy—" depends on "the reader's obliging pause to recover, in his mind and not in the poem itself, the absent sense." The two words "carry the freight of at least eight or nine words that must be supplied silently."

1984 TSELENTIS-APOSTOLIDIS, "I will be Socrates," p. 8
The poem clarifies Dickinson's "attitude towards the classics."

1985 ANANTHARAMAN, *Sunset in a Cup,* p. 111
In this poem "Dickinson shows a traditional undoubting approach to Christianity and to the immortality it offers. 'Home' in this poem stands for 'heaven'. . . ."

JOHNSON, *Emily Dickinson,* pp. 144–46
This early poem is "distinct from her mature work . . . in its overt expression of a death wish . . . and it indicates that Dickinson's stance of 'confident despair' has not yet been achieved. Rather the poem's expression of 'faith' seems to mask or forestall a despair that cannot be qualified."

"The fingers of the light" (1000)

1982 THOTA, *Emily Dickinson,* p. 87
Compares with John Donne's "The Sunne Rising."

"The first day that I was a life" (902)

1983 SHURR, *Marriage,* pp. 11, 115–16
"The third stanza may well be the most important editorial statement in all the fascicles. It stands as a reflective moment . . . on the cen-

tral experience from which the fascicle impulse developed: her love, her anomalous marriage, and the poetic uses she found for it."

"The first day's night had come" (410)

1979   GILBERT and GUBAR, *Madwoman*, pp. 625–26
". . . the psychic rending described in this poem is mirrored in a style heavily interrupted by ambiguous punctuation marks, each seeming to represent a chasm of breath between one phrase and the next."

1980   TAYLOR, M., "Shaman Motifs," p. 5
Relates poem to elements of the"shaman experience."

1982   MOSSBERG, *Emily Dickinson*, pp. 21, 26–27, 29
This "drama of identity conflict, narrated by the artist persona," shows that "she is able to function as an artist despite, or perhaps because of, the dysfunction of her brain, her mind, and even her soul."

1983   ROSENTHAL and GALL, *Modern Poetic Sequence*, pp. 48, 49, 53–54, 55–57, 58, 60
The poem "presents a protagonist—a sensibility, rather—unspecified as to sex or other external characteristics, staving off madness and chaotic self-disintegration in the wake of some unnamed catastrophe." The poem, which shows affinities to the poetry of Yeats, is related to fascicle 15.

SHURR, *Marriage*, pp. 11, 42, 80–81, 178
Dickinson's relationship with Wadsworth is reflected in this poem.

1984   WALLACE, *God Be with the Clown*, pp. 103–04, 135
Discusses as a companion piece to "A day! Help! Help! Another day."

1985   BUDICK, *Emily Dickinson*, pp. 175, 176
"Without consciousness . . . there is no link between the phenomenal and the transcendent."

EBERWEIN, *Dickinson*, p. 124
"Those knowledgeable in gothic fiction may notice a normative aspect even to Dickinson's attempts to express and experience madness by playing the madwoman role. It was, after all, one of the conventional female parts . . . ."

1986   ROBINSON, J., *Emily Dickinson*, pp. 128–29
Here Dickinson faced "the possibility that her identity was in doubt. . . . However, against the tenor of the poem's closing question,

the mere allocation of a social name is a victory and the mere act of placement in a secure memory is also a victory."

1989 GARBOWSKY, *House without the Door,* pp. 18, 90, 91–94, 101, 107, 109–10, 117, 122
"What she is describing here are two major effects of panic attack: the first is the fear of recurrence and the second is the fear of personality disintegration. . . . all the symptoms of agoraphobia are present."

RINGLER-HENDERSON, "Poem 315," pp. 68–69
Relates to "He fumbles at your soul." The poems share "a pervasive sense of fear, a relentless inescapable pain which when it finally arrives in all its power blocks the consciousness and 'stills' the brain."

"The first we knew of him was death" (1006)

1989 OLIVER, *Apocalypse of Green,* p. 123
"Dickinson may be saying that Lincoln's death (seen as a sacrifice for his country) brought him on the human level a renown similar to the spiritual 'renown' that Christ's death procured for him."

"The flake the wind exasperate" (1361)

1981 PORTER, *Dickinson,* p. 66
Illustrates the poet's use of hidden metaphors. "All that applies to the snowflake in this minute morality play is in human terms . . . and therefore the career of the snowflake has something to illustrate about a deceased person whose life was troubled."

"The flower must not blame the bee" (206)

1979 PATTERSON, *Dickinson's Imagery,* pp. 35, 163
"Since the rose-lady herself is 'from Vevay,' and since the bee, who is writing the poem, assuredly would not beg to be rejected, the most plausible explanation is that the mischievous bee is now installed as footman and proposes to exclude all later arrivals."

"The frost of death was on the pane" (1136)

1984 OLPIN, "Hyperbole: Part II," pp. 27–28
"Tho the comic here is certainly muted in the desperate attempt to hold back death's onslaught, the techniques used are those of other comic poems; and the techniques themselves give an absurd and grotesque dimension to death."

"The frost was never seen" (1202)

1981 DIEHL, *Romantic Imagination,* pp. 10, 51–54
Contrasts with Coleridge's "Frost at Midnight," possibly the "parent text" of this poem. Comparison of the two poems suggests "a pattern that emerges generally in Dickinson's relation to the Romantic poets."

1984 BENFEY, *Problem of Others,* pp. 110–13
"The poem does not deny us access to nature. It denies that analysis and search and vigilance . . . will bring us nearer to nature." Examines Diehl's 1981 reading of the poem.

1985 JOHNSON, *Emily Dickinson,* pp. 112–13
Although Dickinson "will not assume that the 'secret ministry' of frost is a sign of harmonious reciprocity between man and nature, neither will she make it the sign of a cruel natural extinction. In her poem she evokes the mystery without explaining it . . . ."

"The gentian has a parched corolla" (1424)

1981 KIMPEL, *Dickinson as Philosopher,* pp. 177–78
"The gentian's unfailing addition to the beauty of autumn suggests how much would be added to human life if people were to be as faithful as these flowers are in the fulfillment of their ministry to human beings."

"The gentian weaves her fringes" (18)

1982 ETTER, "Dickinson's 'The Gentian,'" pp. 34–36
"All through this poem, Dickinson takes a common subject, clothes it in common, or at least familiar, images—uncommonly envisioned."

1983 SHURR, *Marriage,* pp. 52, 53, 54
Relates the poem to Dickinson's illness and her relationship with Wadsworth.

1985 BUDICK, *Emily Dickinson,* p. 65
The poem "is whimsical in a way that purposefully precludes our taking its promises as gospel."

1987 HESFORD, "Creative Fall," pp. 82–83
"Despite protestations to the contrary, the speaker's language . . . turns Sister Summer's funeral into an artful parade, culminating in a gaily blasphemous, mock-trinitarian blessing that seems a witty dance upon the departed's grave."

LEDER and ABBOTT, *Language of Exclusion,* pp. 159–60
"When nature and spirit are imaged as female and joined in 'sisterhood,' as in [this poem], Dickinson's 'supposed person' expresses faith in the redemptive power of the spiritual realm. However, when a patriarchal God is imaged as the arbiter, the delicate balance between nature and spirit is upset."

"The grass so little has to do" (333)

1983 WALKER, N., "Humor as Identity," pp. 59–60
The poem illustrates Dickinson's attitude toward and relationship with nature.

1988 MOREY, "Dickinson-Kant III," pp. 15, 16
". . . it is primarily a children's poem. The dark, tragic side of life is bypassed or sidestepped with rosy glasses, like Dr. Pangloss."

PHILLIPS, *Emily Dickinson,* pp. 92–93, 96, 98, 234 n. 38
"The poem, celebrating the majestic leisure of nature, expresses a feeling common to overworked people, but a primary source of the amusing reverie of a 'brood' mother is the poet's imagining an easier life when it was necessary, as it often was for her, to assume responsibilities in the Dickinson household."

"The hallowing of pain" (772)

1983 JUHASZ, *Undiscovered Continent,* pp. 59-60, 83, 96
"This is a poem about ultimates: what they offer and what they cost. Its subject is not just pain but its worship, a way to arrive at ultimate pain."

1986 ROBINSON, J., *Emily Dickinson,* p. 101
"There is 'a corporeal cost'. You have to abandon confidence in the contents of life for what the very fact of life itself might admit you to if only you could understand it."

1988 WOLOSKY, "Rhetoric or Not," pp. 225-26
Contrasts with Watts's hymn "When I survey the wondrous cross."

"The heart asks pleasure first" (536)

1982 MARCUS, *Emily Dickinson,* pp. 70–71
Relates to other Dickinson poems about "Suffering and Growth."

This poem "takes a passive stance towards suffering, but it also criticizes a world that makes people suffer."

1984   WOLOSKY, *Emily Dickinson,* pp. 99–100
". . . the religious configurations that constitute the poem's model are not entirely dismissed. Religious forms are treated seriously, if only to be defeated. And the poem, in its form, remains an appeal to the divinity it concomitantly scorns. Religion here is not renounced; it is bitterly confronted."

1987   MILLER, C., *Emily Dickinson,* pp. 137–38
The poem's "sequence . . . implies that no heart continues to ask for pleasure and that every heart will eventually have received enough pain to desire its own death."

1988   MOREY, "Dickinson-Kant III," p. 43
Considers along with other Dickinson poems concerning "the negative, disfunctional [*sic*] pain which the poet had not learned how to handle."

"The heart has narrow banks" (928)

1979   JUHASZ, "Undiscovered Continent," pp. 91–92, 93
Consideration of Dickinson poems in which a "geographical vocabulary" is used to "depict her experience of the mind's sudden expansion in times of crisis."
Revised and reprinted: Juhasz, *Undiscovered Continent,* pp. 21–22, 24

1981   MURPHY, "Wind Like a Bugle," p. 27
The wind is a symbol for one of Dickinson's "strongest fears, the possibility that she may ultimately be unable to maintain the precarious balance of her psyche."

"The heart is the capital of the mind" (1354)

1978   BURKE, "Religion of Poetry," p. 23
"Thru geographic imagery, Dickinson makes of a small, individual life an entire continent and implies that each individual bears within himself vast resources upon which he may call at will."

1980   BURBICK, "Revenge of the Nerves," p. 104
"Written in an historical period that was so concerned with nationhood, this poem is an ironic contrast to the political atmosphere of the time."

1982   THOTA, *Emily Dickinson*, pp. 138–39
   "Dickinson forces the reader to perceive the impersonal metaphors in the personal context of an individual's artistic process and the role of the mind and the heart, of the intellect and the emotion."

   TOEGEL, *Emily Dickinson*, pp. 32–33
   "The endless expansion of a 'capital,' a 'state,' or even a 'continent,' can be surpassed by the 'ecstatic Nation' of the Self . . . her mind's space is totally her own, completely private and knows no boundaries."

1983   JUHASZ, *Undiscovered Continent*, pp. 24–25, 73
   "By thus boldly graphing with a geographical vocabulary the contours of a world, by populating it with a complete society that is one self, Dickinson describes the richness of the mental life."

1987   COOK, C., "Psychic Development," p. 124
   The poem "shows that Emily Dickinson understood the different elements of her psyche, knew the importance of each of the elements, and recognized the fact that only when the two elements worked together was a person truly whole."

1989   McCLURE, "Expanding the Canon," pp. 77–78, 82
   In this poem "Dickinson's language is political; she treats the issue of power, the struggle for unity within herself, her own frontier."

"The heaven vests for each" (694)

1984   WOLOSKY, *Emily Dickinson*, pp. 132–33
   The poem is "a double text working at cross-purposes with itself. It at once declares the 'Clemency' of heavenly response to be common and then hastens to add that the fears this clemency will be withheld are only 'almost' silenced."

"The Himmaleh was known to stoop" (481)

1983   MILLER, C., "How 'Low Feet' Stagger," pp. 137–38, 153 n. 10
   The poem illustrates how Dickinson's use of "an unexpected pronoun" is used to undercut "expected hierarchical and gender relationships."

"The hollows round his eager eyes" (955)

1983   UNO, "Expression by Negation," p. 3
   "One can read this poem as Dickinson's declaration about her own use of expression in poetry. The blank around her words is a space where

one should read attentively." Here "negative expressions . . . are used skillfully to enhance the unobtrusive pain which is endured and unhelped."

1988   PHILLIPS, *Emily Dickinson,* pp. 183–84, 185, 235 n. 19
In this poem "the ironic point is that the man suffers in silence, which other people recognize but are helpless and unable to understand because he endures the pain in silence."

"The inundation of the spring" (1425)

1979   JUHASZ, "Undiscovered Continent," pp. 92, 93
Consideration of Dickinson poems in which a "geographical vocabulary" is used to "depict her experience of the mind's sudden expansion in times of crisis."
Revised and reprinted: Juhasz, *Undiscovered Continent,* pp. 22, 23, 24

"The lamp burns sure within" (233)

1979   PATTERSON, *Dickinson's Imagery,* p. 129
This poem's lamp " 'burns golden' even when its oil is gone, signifying the continuance of her love after the other's love has been withdrawn."

"The largest fire ever known" (1114)

1986   ROBINSON, J., *Emily Dickinson,* pp. 169–70
"The artful lie of art, confessing incompetence while demonstrating genius, shows in the poem as a properly self-effacing human manner. Where else could we be but in a world of seeming?"

"The last night that she lived" (1100)

1972   RAO, *Essential Emily Dickinson,* pp. 32–33, 155-56
General introduction to the poem aimed at "postgraduate students of literature in Indian Universities."

1978   ABAD, *Formal Approach,* pp. 157, 158, 160–63, 164, 194, 204, 205, 207, 229 n. 19, 285, 290, 392, 393, 409
Compares with T. S. Eliot's "Aunt Helen." Considers poems' formal aspects as "different species or forms of the so-called 'lyric poem.' "

1982   FAULKNER, "Emily Dickinson," pp. 811–12
"The strange linking of 'awful' with 'leisure,' the disruption of syntax at the line break, and the notion that the best belief can do is regulate leisure, all suggest in two lines the confusion and disruption for those who remain alive."

MARCUS, *Emily Dickinson*, pp. 85–86, 87, 88
"Conflict between doubt and faith looms large in [this poem]."

1984   ALLARD, "Regulation of Belief," pp. 34–36, 37
Examines effect of poem's dashes and relates to other Dickinson poems on the moment of death.

1985   COTTLE, *Language of Literature*, pp. 105–06
Discussion of the poem's grammar and diction.

EBERWEIN, *Dickinson*, pp. 204–06, 285 n. 2
"Within the circuit world of matter and time and intellectual awareness, the speaker and her fellow attendants feel a jealousy *for* the dying woman. . . . But it seems likely that the speaker also feels a jealousy *of* the departed one."

JOHNSON, *Emily Dickinson*, pp. 170–72, 173, 215 n. 15
Unlike other deathbed studies by Dickinson, the focus here is "not upon the experience of death, but rather upon the effect of death upon the living. As one might expect, Dickinson's attitude is complex . . . ."

1986   HUGHES, G., "Subverting the Cult," p. 23
"For all its precision, the poem manages a hushed reticence because its concreteness is selective."

STAMBOVSKY, "Witnessing Spirit," pp. 87–93
Detailed examination of this "brilliantly searching study of the consciousness of witnessing a death."

1989   KNAPP, *Emily Dickinson*, pp. 99–100
"Viewing the corpse in a kind of rite of passage from life to death is analogized in the poem's verbal patternings; language itself grows more and more deformed, progressively becomes lost, as if dwindling into nothing before the reader's very eyes."

"The leaves like women interchange" (987)

1983   WALKER, N., "Humor as Identity," p. 64
Examines ironies implicit in the poem's likening of women to leaves.

"The lightning is a yellow fork" (1173)

1989 KNAPP, *Emily Dickinson,* pp. 11, 180–83
Line-by-line examination of poem's language and images. In her displacing "connections between objects and words," Dickinson shares techniques with the Dadaists, Surrealists, and Symbolists.

"The lilac is an ancient shrub" (1241)

1978 TILMA-DEKKERS, "Immortality," pp. 166–67
The poem expresses the "impossibility of man ever finding his attempts at acquiring certainty of heaven rewarded."

1984 ST. ARMAND, *Dickinson and Her Culture,* pp. 288–90
"The crucifixion that is implicit in the romantic typology of sunset is here subsumed by Dickinson's study of the overwhelming, passional color of the scene. To analyze this phenomenon, in fact, would itself be a kind of crucifixion of her subject by the devoted artist . . . ."

1985 JOHNSON, *Emily Dickinson,* pp. 68–69
Here the poet "is communicating to the spiritually blind through a natural metaphor which they can understand, and she makes no effort to hide her condescension."

"The loneliness one dare not sound" (777)

1978 MANN, "Poet as Namer," p. 482
". . . the definition moves forward according to a process of progressive discrimination, a narrowing and clarifying of meaning until the reader understands precisely what this 'Loneliness' is to the poet."

1980 GREEN, "Spatial Drama," pp. 197–98
The poet writes of "a desolating loneliness in which the self fears even to examine the limits of the profundity of its sense of nihilism."

1981 KIMPEL, *Dickinson as Philosopher,* pp. 55–57
"A moral philosophy which regards honesty as the first condition for character could . . . cite this poem for pin-pointing the difficulty of a moral control of oneself. It is taking oneself under such stern scrutiny that one forbids himself to soft-pedal or 'skirt' an inventory of himself."

1983 GIBSON, "Poetry of Hypothesis," p. 225
Notes effect of "grammatical ambiguities" in last stanza, particularly in final line.

1986   REGUEIRO ELAM, "Haunting of the Self," pp. 93–96, 97, 98
   "The poem organizes itself around tropes of measurement—sounding, plumbing, surveying—and its impulse is to avoid measuring the self for fear that it may reveal itself to be boundless. Yet the process of writing the poem is, paradoxically, such a measurement."

"The lonesome for they know not what" (262)

1985   EBERWEIN, *Dickinson,* pp. 66, 172–73
   Examines the "strikingly circumferential imagery" employed here in dealing with "Dickinson's sense of herself as a stranger, . . . a Wordsworthian infant."

1989   LEONARD, D. N., "Certain Slants," pp. 126, 127–28
   "Read in the context of the fascicle's other sunset poems . . . the poem is about the living who yearn for the fulfillment of immortality" rather than "postmortem longing for a return to mortal existence."

"The longest day that God appoints" (1769)

1979   BARNES, "Telling It Slant," p. 229
   Examines the poet's use of the proverb; "far from offering solace, the poem borders on the bitterly cynical."

"The love a life can show below" (673)

1979   KHAN, "Conception of Love," pp. 19–20
   The poem "reads like an untampered document of Neoplatonic writing."
   Revised and reprinted: Khan, *Emily Dickinson's Poetry,* pp. 89–90

1985   BUDICK, *Emily Dickinson,* pp. 89–91
   The speaker's "full relish of the divine moment" is being hampered by "a suspicion that an emotionally unreliable universe, or at least an inconstant one, may not be innocently loving. It may be downright sardonic."

   JOHNSON, *Emily Dickinson,* p. 67
   "This poem, straining beyond the visible to something ineffable that is perceived by the poet's spirit, stresses that the 'diviner thing' is inconstant. . . . The extraordinary final stanza conveys a poignant fascination with that inconstancy as well as the poet's frustration in her attempt to capture it in language . . . ."

1987 MILLER, C., *Emily Dickinson,* pp. 85–86, 151
"As the noun 'love' is defined by cumulative verbs and a final object, love itself is defined only through its cumulative, somehow paradoxical, acts and effect."

"The luxury to apprehend" (815)

1988 LOUIS, "Sacrament of Starvation," pp. 357–58, 359
"The syntax affirms satisfaction in the middle of desolation, since the two main clauses balance one another logically: *the luxury makes an epicure of me; the luxury bestows a sumptuousness.* This self-referential power creates and satisfies the epicure's desire for a delicate 'Sumptuousness.'"

"The Malay took the pearl" (452)

1980 JOHNSON, "'Pearl of Great Price,'" pp. 206–07, 214–15 n. 10
Examines the basic symbolic elements (the sea, the pearl, the Malay native) and the speaker in this poem and "Removed from accident of loss."
Revised and reprinted: Johnson, *Emily Dickinson,* pp. 129–30, 209 n. 16

1982 MADIGAN, "Mermaids," pp. 50–52
"It is significant that the poet . . . identifies herself with the civilized man . . . and that her search for Eternity, an essentially non-rational pursuit, will always be thwarted by rational thoughts that lead to timidity, doubt and repression."

1984 POLLAK, *Dickinson,* pp. 155–56
"Dickinson satirizes the primitivism of male dominance, fears the sea-change of homosexual conquest, and laments an unlived life."

1985 EBERWEIN, *Dickinson,* p. 102
"The earl, delayed in his effort by excessive forethought and doubts of his worthiness, loses the treasure to a Malay diver who springs into instant action and retrieves the treasure without ever suspecting its value."

1986 BENNETT, *Loaded Gun,* pp. 52–53
Compares with other poems concerning her love for Susan Dickinson: "Your riches taught me poverty" and "I never told the buried gold."

"The manner of its death" (468)

1979 PATTERSON, *Dickinson's Imagery,* p. 162
". . . the court of 'St. James' figures as the symbol of artificiality and social pretense as opposed to ugly, unfashionable truths of suffering and death."

"The martyr poets did not tell" (544)

1981 CAMPBELL, "Poetry as Epitaph," pp. 666–67
"Because the work is a representation of the artist, it stands in place of him; he is dead to us as a living being. What *is* important is some understanding of exactly what the 'Pang' found in art is."

1982 SALSKA, *Poetry of the Central Consciousness,* pp. 100, 102
"Art is treated as order—aesthetic, psychological and moral. . . . By rejecting more immediate reliefs and by dedication to their art, 'the poets' and 'painters' turn ordinary human suffering into purposeful 'martyrdom.'"
Revised and reprinted: Salska, *Walt Whitman and Emily Dickinson,* pp. 87–88, 90

1984 POLLAK, *Dickinson,* pp. 248–49
"The poem's conclusion is apparently imperfectly motivated: a stoical sublimation of grief into language is rapidly reformulated as a perpetual vow of silence. Dickinson's vulnerability to criticism probably explains this vow."

"The mind lives on the heart" (1355)

1982 THOTA, *Emily Dickinson,* p. 139
". . . the intellect itself has no content of its own to express or to reveal. It only works on the emotional experiences. This conception of intellect approximates to Bergson's."

1987 OATES, "Soul at the White Heat," pp. 813–14
Dickinson is "well aware of the dangers of self-consumption. . . . The relationship between the conscious ego (mind) and the unconscious self or soul (heart) has never been more succinctly or forcefully argued."
Reprinted: Oates, *(Woman) Writer,* pp. 174–75

1988 WOLFF, *Emily Dickinson,* pp. 464–65
The poem acknowledges that "feeding upon nothing but self devolves into a kind of abhorrent spiritual cannibalism."

1989   Guthrie, "Near Rhymes," pp. 71–72
Suggestions for teaching the poem, with emphasis on effect of poem's near rhymes.

Knapp, *Emily Dickinson,* pp. 160–62
Here "the puritanical mask of modesty and emotional temperance has been removed in favor of aggressivity and cannibalism. . . . The energy stored in the word has nowhere been expressed with more savagery and voraciousness than in [this poem]."

"The missing all prevented me" (985)

1979   Cameron, *Lyric Time,* pp. 170–71
"The distinctive feature of [this poem] is its impersonality, the largesse with which departure characterizes not only psychological reality but also physical and natural fact."

1980   McClave, "Missing All," p. 4
"The real subject of the poem is the continuing sense and definitive act of *missing:* clearly this is what sets the terms of her existence, so that the mind has some choice in the drama of happenstance."

1981   Kimpel, *Dickinson as Philosopher,* pp. 29–30
"The thought in this poem . . . may not be too unlike the thought which is expressed by Jesus: 'For my yoke is easy, and my burden is light.'"

1982   Marcus, *Emily Dickinson,* pp. 43–44
General consideration as one of Dickinson's poems on "Poetry, Art, and Imagination."

1987   Gelpi, "Emily Dickinson's Word," pp. 43–44
"Consciousness of 'I am' shatters the unconscious participation in the cosmos, and the almost-memory of an absolute totality of 'All' makes subsequent experience seem the clash of contradictory contingencies."

"The mob within the heart" (1745)

1985   Juhasz, "Tea and Revolution," p. 149
This poem, which is "especially concerned with the relationship between the mind and the external world . . . [,] shows how some rebellions can best be achieved when no one in authority knows they are taking place."

"The months have ends, the years a knot" (423)

1983 BUDICK, "Temporal Consciousness," p. 228
"Only because time implies 'ends' are we assured that the 'Skein' of human 'Misery' will not stretch endlessly on."
Revised and reprinted: Budick, *Emily Dickinson*, p. 202

1988 STOCKS, *Modern Consciousness*, pp. 50–51
"Death and time (calendar time, in this instance) are fused together in this poem. Man, 'the noisy Plaything' who, though grown weary, cannot put himself away, is put away by nature's gift to life of built-in obsolescence, measured by the calendar."

1989 GARBOWSKY, *House without the Door*, p. 89
"We see Dickinson trying to control her fate, as she arranged and stitched her work together, ordering her life. It is precisely this lack of control that is at the heart of the poem . . . ."

"The moon is distant from the sea" (429)

1982 MADIGAN, "Mermaids," pp. 46–47
Although the poem is "virtually unintelligible," it "does have a kind of negative interest as an indication that the sea becomes a meaningful image to the poet only when it suggests what lies beyond the realm of ordinary experience."

1983 MILLER, C., "How 'Low Feet' Stagger," pp. 135–36
The poem illustrates how Dickinson "restructures role associations . . . through an unconventional use of pronouns."

SHURR, *Marriage*, pp. 19, 76–77
The beloved's "absence is lamented in her . . . figure of the Moon and its magnetic relationship to the Sea. They are far apart, yet the moon continues to attract."

1987 MOREY, "Dickinson-Kant II," p. 5
". . . valuable to a critic in showing Dickinson's heliotropic ambition to be perfect in her response to God's will."

"The moon upon her fluent route" (1528)

1983 KNIGHTS, "Defining the Self," pp. 369–70
In this poem "not only does the mind find objective forms for deep-seated attitudes, but the contemplation of those forms has played a nec-

essary part in the discovery of what is in the mind: subject and object form an indissoluble whole."

1984   WOLOSKY, *Emily Dickinson,* pp. 28–29, 30
The poem "peers into the vision of aimlessness and disorder which Nietzsche made his theme. Its language is consequent to that vision in its fragmentation, its disruption of sequence, and, not least, its linguistic imagery."
Reprinted: Wolosky, "Syntax of Contention," pp. 183–85

"The morning after woe" (364)

1983   SHURR, *Marriage,* p. 48
"The 'musical key' of human suffering, which nature cannot provide, is once again the Calvary situation into which her marriage has put her."

"The morns are meeker than they were" (12)

1980   HOMANS, *Women Writers,* p. 198
"Rather than humanizing nature, the speaker risks her life in naturalizing herself: for her to put on a trinket is, in the context of nature's language of gayer scarf and scarlet gown, to prepare for death."
Reprinted: Homans, "Emily Dickinson," pp. 436–37

1987   MARTIN, J. E., "Religious Spirit," p. 499
The poem "mirrors Dickinson's sense of the concrete, uniqueness of vision and expression, and human involvement with nature."

"The most pathetic thing I do" (1290)

1983   SHURR, *Marriage,* pp. 156, 191
The poem is linked to the poet's relationship with Wadsworth and the "sense of their mutual exile."

"The most triumphant bird I ever knew or met" (1265)

1986   STONUM, "Calculated Sublime," p. 128 n. 13
Here "the bird's resumption of daily life is a loss of dominion and a return to the transitive estate. Dickinson's transitive here means primarily in transit from birth to death, but the poem as a whole insists . . . on the absence of goals or objects at the moment of dominion."

1989   WOLFF, *Emily Dickinson*, pp. 526–27
". . . although the '*Bird*' may be 'triumphant,' the poem that proclaims its victory is curiously flat: it captures no rich, sonorous sensuosity, and it conveys no significant message. . . . the residual import of the poem is a sense of felt loss, a falling away."

"The mountains stood in haze" (1278)

1985   JOHNSON, *Emily Dickinson*, p. 68
"The first two stanzas exemplify Dickinson's remarkable descriptive powers, but the final stanza does not really follow from them; rather the poet makes an imaginative leap toward the abstract 'Act of evening' and the poet's closeness with the 'Invisible.'"

1987   BARKER, *Lunacy of Light*, p. 111
"We see the twilight 'speaking' the 'spire' as if this light that is no longer male-dominated now acts upon the tongue of the spire, causing it to speak a new language in a new, different light—one in fact composed of both light and dark."

"The murmur of a bee" (155)

1982   MOSSBERG, *Emily Dickinson*, pp. 169, 170, 171
The poem "reflects her decision in her own life to be a martyred, unknown, dutiful daughter by day, a woman of 'degree' in her night poetry. The mystery in the poem refers to the status she gains at Sunrise, which inaugurates a new day of martyrdom and concludes a night of momentum toward 'Possibility.'"

"The murmuring of bees has ceased" (1115)

1985   RASHID, "Voice of Endings," pp. 24, 28–29, 34 n. 9
Examines in the context of Dickinson's other uses of the cricket image.

1986   BUELL, *New England Literary Culture*, pp. 291–92
"Of the various ways in which this haunting poem could be read, one would be as a stylization of the experience of late autumnal emptiness . . . , an emptiness 'prophetic' of death and the End Times, but charged also with expectation, as the speaker anticipates some cosmic payoff . . . ."

"The mushroom is the elf of plants"

ROBINSON, J., *Emily Dickinson,* p. 146
". . . the bees have gone but their murmuring is in the mind as both a memory of the past and an expectation for next year, and so it is for 'separating Friends', for thought about them . . . ."

1987 HESFORD, "Creative Fall," p. 85
Dickinson gives "a rather heretical twist" to the "Judeo-Christian tradition of reading and interpreting nature as a book": the book's author is "not a supernatural Father God, but Mother Nature herself."

1988 WOLFF, *Emily Dickinson,* pp. 307, 311–12, 368
"Summer's last reprieve is construed as its 'Book' of 'Revelations,' yet this is a paradoxically negative indictment. . . . nature here has no grandeur, only loss . . . ."

"The mushroom is the elf of plants" (1298)

1982 OLPIN, "Hyperbole: Part One," pp. 18–19
"Here is an illusive figure that is described in the hyperbolic manner of the frontier hero, but its nature also suggests the ironic comedy common in Dickinson that seeks to find a meaning available only fleetingly or not there at all."

1986 ROBINSON, J., *Emily Dickinson,* p. 147
"The mushroom is an overnight traveller, so abrupt an arrival that it seems to be making alibis for itself by being in two places at once—here but gone, gone but here, like a bubble."

"The name of it is 'Autumn'" (656)

1987 HESFORD, "Creative Fall," pp. 83–84
"A gigantic body shedding its blood (the language perhaps owes something to both the conclusion of Emerson's 'The Poet' and to Civil War hymns), the real presence, the sacramental incarnation, of autumn is as terrifying as it is beautiful."

1989 DIEHL, "Terrains of Difference," pp. 87–90
"Dickinson's poem, despite certain overt similarities to Shelley's ["Ode to the West Wind"], nevertheless redefines the relationship between the self and the external, re-mapping the terrain of difference as it dissolves the Shelleyan distinction between the imagination and nature."

DIEHL and PACKER, "Workshop Discussion," pp. 95–113
Transcript of a workshop discussion of the poem.

PACKER, "Poem 656," pp. 91–94

The poem "toys not with our comprehension, but with our powers of literary discrimination. It teasingly invites us to consider it in execrable taste." Its "inspired tastelessness . . . is Dickinson's own brand of dead-pan humor . . . ."

"The nearest dream recedes unrealized" (319)

1981 MONTEIRO and ST. ARMAND, "Experienced Emblem," pp. 208–10

Relates to emblematic books of Holmes and Barber; here Dickinson transposes their emblem on *Vanitas*.

1984 BENFEY, *Problem of Others*, pp. 69–71

"Fulfillment, to the extent that we pursue it, chase it, is denied us. But by the ambiguity of the final two lines, Dickinson suggests that our relation to what is nearest us, to what is home to us, need not be one of pursuit. It may be one of acceptance."

1985 EBERWEIN, *Dickinson*, pp. 59, 64, 130

"The boy, frustrated at the escape of the playful bee he had thought so catchable, gapes like grown men and women . . . when they turn to God above for the 'steadfast Honey' of permanent sweetness that nature hints at but cannot provide and that God may not supply . . . ."

1986 MOREY, "Dickinson-Kant: The First Critique," pp. 49, 50, 51, 56

"The poem is framed by two lines of didacticism at either end with an extended metaphor inbetween [*sic*]. . . . This is Dickinson's comment on an immature attitude to life."

1989 RASHID, "Role of Dickinson's Biography," pp. 139–40

Suggests classroom approaches to the poem. ". . . in-class specu-lation about Dickinson's own possible 'nearest dreams' can enhance un-derstanding of the poem . . . ."

"The one who could repeat the summer day" (307)

1980 MACHOR, "Feminine Rhetoric," pp. 144–45

In this poem "diaphoric synthesis is achieved among the three stanzas by repetition of a presiding image: constancy."

1986 DORESKI, " 'Exchange of Territory,' " pp. 60, 61–62, 64

The poem is "a masterpiece because it accomplishes so much on a scale so appropriate to its terms and intentions." Relates to poetic se-quence of fascicle 27.

"The only ghost I ever saw" (274)

1983 SHURR, *Marriage,* pp. 62, 69, 142
"If one begins explication of the poem from its last words, the subject of the poem becomes clear; the only momentous Day recorded in Dickinson's poetry so far . . . was the day of her anomalous marriage."

"The outer from the inner" (451)

1984 MARTIN, W., *American Triptych,* pp. 128–29
"Whereas the ritualized awareness of roles makes possible the smooth functioning of society, it does so at the expense of more complex perceptions. It is dangerous to eliminate the protective mask or to relinquish ego boundaries in a social system that is based on predatory individualism."

WILT, "Playing House," p. 154
Considers as one of the "scores of highly charged lyrics" in which "the poet confronts the house she is before, or within, or has become."

"The pile of years is not so high" (1507)

1983 SHURR, *Marriage,* pp. 160–61
"The first two lines set up a time scheme which corresponds to the known visits of Wadsworth . . . ."

"The poets light but lamps" (883)

1978 MILLER, R., "Transitional Object," pp. 454–55
"Embedded in this metaphor is the interesting notion that true, the poem must have vital light, and true again, each age must have the proper lens to perceive, to concentrate, to disseminate that light. In a word: good poets need good readers."

1979 ESTES, "Search for Location," pp. 210–11
Reviews various critical interpretations of the poem's "Circumference."

1981 ANDERSON, V., "Disappearance of God," p. 16
"The sense of mission is implied: the poets seek nothing for themselves in this endeavor; they give up their lights so that others might have light to see their way illuminated."

1982 KNOX, " 'The poets light,' " p. 31
Examines poem's central metaphor, which is "so dense that it has misled various attempts at critical analysis."

1986 MCNEIL, *Emily Dickinson*, pp. 100–01
"Each different age is a lens disseminating, spreading and multiplying the 'circumference' of the poet, who is now a sunlike source of light. The angle at which the poet is seen will shift as culture changes, but the poet's illumination remains."

"The popular heart is a cannon first" (1226)

1982 MARCUS, *Emily Dickinson*, pp. 64–65
Relates to other Dickinson poems on society. This one may be "chiefly about the drilling of militia soldiers."

1988 REYNOLDS, *Beneath the American Renaissance*, pp. 428–29
"The popular culture she perceives is one that has been torn both from the future . . . and from historical memory. . . . It is fluid and ever-changing with the throes of the tumultuous present."

"The products of my farm are these" (1025)

1981 KIMPEL, *Dickinson as Philosopher*, p. 15
"The imagery in this poem conveys [the poet's] respect for the sensitivities of people who may take time to consider what she offers them. In offering her poetry as an addition to a 'neighbor's bin' she is aware that they are familiar with other poetry."

1988 WOLFF, *Emily Dickinson*, p. 209
The poem's "voice" might "belong to that husband-man of Emerson's essay, but with this proviso—the definition of his achievement must follow the priorities Dickinson has set for her 'Wife' speaker."

"The props assist the house" (1142)

1981 DIEHL, *Romantic Imagination*, p. 84
"By describing the process of 'making a life' in terms of carpenter and wood, Dickinson momentarily defines a conscious boundary to protect her from a threatening self-consciousness. She finds safety in the asexual, mechanical language of craft."

1984   WILT, "Playing House," p. 162
   This "brilliant process-poem" is one of many in which "the poet confronts the house she is before, or within, or has become."

"The province of the saved" (539)

1981   ANDERSON, V., "Disappearance of God," pp. 13–14
   "The lines reveal a poet who saw her role as salvific; the parallel between Dickinson and Christ is strong indeed at this point. . . . Her poetry becomes a kind of ministry."

1985   PHILIP, "Valley News," pp. 68–69
   "We should not under-estimate the extent to which the poem speaks from a position of dignity and purpose beyond the confines of a limiting theology. The 'Saved' that the speaker has joined are clearly no longer those who profess a traditional faith."

1987   MILLER, C., *Emily Dickinson*, pp. 94–96, 151
   "Dickinson proposes in this poem that one wholly, not just grammatically, identify a condition with its verbal root: the saved are those who save; the qualified those who qualify (both as transitive and intransitive verb). There is no passive or static possibility for salvation or meaning."

1989   OLIVER, *Apocalypse of Green*, pp. 83–84, 95 n. 47
   "Since the dead do not come back . . . , one cannot know with certainty about dissolution, defeat, or death, unless the *He* who has endured dissolution be Christ."

"The rainbow never tells me" (97)

1980   CLEARY, "Classical Education," pp. 125–26
   The poem shows that Dickinson's "knowledge of Roman history was not superficial."

1986   ROBINSON, J. *Emily Dickinson*, p. 89
   The poet is "constantly wary of 'terms' but also of beliefs inasmuch as beliefs represent rationalizations of the mysteries of life. . . . It is the life-stuff which enables philosophy to have any meaning."

"The rat is the concisest tenant" (1356)

1981   PORTER, *Dickinson*, pp. 71–72
   An example of the poet's turning a homely image "before our eyes into something else."

1982 THOTA, *Emily Dickinson*, pp. 140–41
This poem and "Grief is a mouse" are "examples of the perfection of Dickinson's technique of the fusion of emotion and thought."

1984 WILT, "Playing House," pp. 166–67
Considers as one of the "scores of highly charged lyrics" in which "the poet confronts the house she is before, or within, or has become."

1987 BARKER, *Lunacy of Light*, pp. 96–97
"In identifying with a rat or mouse, Dickinson states emphatically that she too will not participate in the world of the sun, dominated by men of noon and their rents, legal obligations, 'Decrees,' or normal, rational, logical 'wit.'"

"The reticent volcano keeps" (1748)

1987 BARKER, *Lunacy of Light*, p. 120
"Perhaps nowhere else is her enormous ambition so clearly outlined; she will keep to herself her 'never slumbering plan,' never revealing her ambitious 'projects.'"

"The riddle we can guess" (1222)

1978 TILMA-DEKKERS, "Immortality," p. 168
"The little poem reflects the attitude Emily Dickinson chose toward the unobtainable object of desire."

"The road to paradise is plain" (1491)

1983 JUHASZ, *Undiscovered Continent*, pp. 133, 148–49
The poem's "final, summarizing analogy, 'Mines have no Wings,' stands in the poem as corrective figure to the traditional images for paradise. It may be concrete, but its source is supposition, and its facts are ones found in the imagination."

"The road was lit with moon and star" (1450)

1988 WOLFF, *Emily Dickinson*, pp. 485–86
The poem affirms that "nature itself has inherent aesthetic configurations, mysteries, or secrets that cry out for poetic representation."

"The robin is a Gabriel" (1483)

1981 GUTHRIE, "Modest Poet's Tactics," p. 236
"Only by exercising supreme care in selecting his audience and by

maintaining a prosaic façade can the robin-artist continue to enjoy the benefits of privacy. But privacy is not the artist's chief goal; rather, it is the freedom to practice those skills which give him his covert, high status among the members of this circle."

1988 WEISSMAN, "'Transport's Working Classes,'" pp. 419–20
     "Even the most daring theological thought is not so immediately threatening to a reader's social comfort as this reminder that God's love and nature's joy also include the working classes."

"The robin is the one" (828)

1980 LAIR, "Fracture of Grammar," p. 163
     Comments on effect of substituting plural for singular verb form.

"The robin's my criterion for tune" (285)

1982 SOULE, "Robin," pp. 67–69, 81 n. 8
     In this poem Dickinson "focuses on the robin as a symbol of her poetic vision as she defines the realm of her poetry." Notes links to Emerson and Shakespeare.

1986 ROBINSON, J., *Emily Dickinson*, pp. 34–35
     In this poem where the poet acknowledges "that she sees 'New Englandly' she means simply that she is accustomed to robins, buttercups, autumn nuts and snow rather than cuckoos and daisies . . . ."

"The savior must have been" (1487)

1981 ANDERSON, V., "Disappearance of God," pp. 7–8
     "With a childlike willingness (docility), Christ performs his appointed tasks. . . . He is not distant, austere, and indifferent like God. Christ is a 'gentle' man who involves himself in the life of other men, even on 'so cold a Day.'"

1987 OBERHAUS, "'Tender Pioneer,'" pp. 345, 346–47, 358
     "By conflating Jesus' birth, life, and Crucifixion, Dickinson stresses that in choosing birth He chose human life, suffering, and death. . . ." Relates to other Dickinson poems about Christ.

"The sea said 'Come' to the brook" (1210)

1986 HUGHES, J. M., "Inner and Outer Seas," p. 205
"Perhaps Dickinson has written a nautical version of the Fall of Man after eating from the Tree of Knowledge."

"The service without hope" (779)

1987 MILLER, C., *Emily Dickinson,* pp. 60, 83–84, 196 n. 51
"By focusing unusual semantic as well as structural attention on its function words," the poem illuminates Dickinson's use of them.

"The show is not the show" (1206)

1982 MARCUS, *Emily Dickinson,* pp. 64–65
Relates to other Dickinson poems on society. "Attendance at a public entertainment brings out the showiness or pretense of those who attend more than it reveals anything spectacular in the event."

1987 MILLER, C., *Emily Dickinson,* pp. 66–67
Here as in other Dickinson poems, "ungrammatical and grammatical uses of language are equally intentional and manipulated with equal precision and skill."

"The sky is low, the clouds are mean" (1075)

1984 MARTIN, W., *American Triptych,* pp. 145–46
"Although Dickinson appeared to affect a childlike innocence, she rejected the pastoral convention of linking rural innocence with an unblemished heart."

"The smouldering embers blush" (1132)

1981 DIEHL, *Romantic Imagination,* pp. 153–55
The poem was "possibly written as a response to the mythic Prometheus, and perhaps with Shelley's *Prometheus Unbound* in mind."

"The snow that never drifts" (1133)

1983 BICKMAN, "'Snow that never drifts,'" pp. 139, 140–45
Reviews critical history and combines "the perspectives of Emerson with some key modern notions of the relation of language to perception and emotion." The poem may be viewed as "a meditation on the nature of analogy-making itself, a meta-statement about metaphor."

"The soul has bandaged moments" (512)

1979 CAMERON, *Lyric Time*, pp. 7–8
"Although the poem presents an ostensible contrast between 'Dungeoned' moments and 'moments of Escape—,' it does so partially in order to uncover the underlying dialectic of time and its annihilation . . . ."
Reprinted: Mullane and Wilson, *Nineteenth-Century*, p. 76

1980 GREEN, "Spatial Drama," pp. 196–97
The poem's drama "is conducted within the dark confines of the self."

TAYLOR, M., "Shaman Motifs," pp. 4–5
Relates poem to elements of the "shaman experience." "The first two stanzas suggest an invasion by a figure that appears analogous to Jung's shadow."

1984 MARTIN, W., *American Triptych*, p. 120
"Here Emily Dickinson uses the traditional distinction between female powerlessness and male aggression to structure her poem. Interestingly, by externalizing terror, she gains psychological and artistic control over the turmoil and despair that threatens to engulf her."

1985 EBERWEIN, *Dickinson*, pp. 125, 178
". . . the tone of these stanzas on manic release overpowers even the reader's judgment to the point that one regrets the psychological bomb's forced return to captivity and horror."

1986 BURBICK, "Economics of Desire," pp. 374–75
"The ability of the speaker's 'Soul' to flip between images of lover and goblin is unnerving. To depict desire as always vulnerable to control by death equates desire with threat."

ROBINSON, J., *Emily Dickinson*, pp. 121, 124–25
"If we seek the reassurance of paraphrase we could say that Emily Dickinson had been so miserable that she had wanted to die, but this crudely reductive account would falsify the verse. Death would not be a termination, it would be a release and a fulfilment, the reaching of the 'Rose'."

1988 PEECK-O'TOOLE, "Lyric and Gender," pp. 327–29
". . . the impetus behind the poem . . . is to delineate the stages by which the soul obtains its freedom—and loses it again." Examines the nature of the poem's "Goblin."

WOLFF, *Emily Dickinson*, pp. 359–61
". . . it is God's power to injure that this poem addresses, a power that can act quite literally as a prison."

YAEGER, *Honey-Mad Women*, pp. 240–41
In this poem "Dickinson constructs a sober vision of female creativity in which manic self-construction is followed by depression. . . . While Dickinson's verse flows with a sense of pleasure and empowerment, she is skeptical about emancipation."

1989 GARBOWSKY, *House without the Door*, pp. 18, 112, 113–15, 116, 129
"The poem focuses on the fluctuating course of panic attack, its suddenness, its diminishment, and then its reappearance. It is a chronicle, too, of the alternate states of fear, release from fear, and the return of fear . . . ."

GUERRA, "Dickinson's 'The Soul,'" pp. 30–32
The poem is clarified and enriched by interpreting its "Bomb" as "the stroke upon a bell"; this alternative definition appears in Dickinson's dictionary.

"The soul selects her own society" (303)

1972 RAO, *Essential Emily Dickinson*, pp. 127–28
General introduction to the poem aimed at "postgraduate students of literature in Indian Universities."

1977 REICHERT, *Making Sense*, pp. 10–12, 36
Aspects of the poem are used to demonstrate application of critical tools of synonymy, analogy, and paraphrase.

1978 ABAD, *Formal Approach*, pp. 135–39, 153, 181–82, 300 n. 38, 397
Contrasts with "Of all the souls that stand create" to illustrate different qualities of lyric poems. In this poem "we respond chiefly to the idea, but the idea *as someone's thought,* whereas in [the other poem] we respond chiefly to *someone's own reaction to a dramatic situation* . . . ."

HECHT, "Riddles," pp. 17–18
The poem's power "derives from a suppressed riddle, an unstated but implied parallel. As the soul is to its society (absolute, arbitrary, ruthless) so is God in His election and salvation of souls."
Reprinted: Hecht, *Obbligati*, pp. 108–09

1979   BUDICK, "When the Soul Selects," pp. 352, 353–56, 358, 360, 363
The poem "borrows linguistic trappings from Puritan theology and applies them to the phenomenon of Transcendentalism. . . . It demonstrates graphically as well as thematically how a kind of perception dependent upon symbols and types eventuates in a dangerous, corrupting distortion of cosmic reality."
Revised and reprinted: Budick, *Emily Dickinson*, pp. 138–43, 145

JUHASZ, "Undiscovered Continent," pp. 87–88, 94–95
Consideration of Dickinson poems in which "the enclosure and confinement experienced in the place of the mind is established with an architectural vocabulary."
Revised and reprinted: Juhasz, *Undiscovered Continent*, pp. 15–16, 25, 26, 73, 158

KELLER, K., *Only Kangaroo*, pp. 27–28, 157
". . . the poem is a woman enlivened *in* language by virtue of her self-sufficient, self-reliant, conscientious religious security."

WESTBROOK, *Free Will and Determinism*, p. 60
"It is an interesting poem in that it states both the soul's freedom to select its destiny (as Calvinists insisted it must do) and the finality of its act . . . , which carries a connotation of momentousness and irrevocability suggestive of the doctrine of the perseverance of saints."

1980   DUNCAN, "Joining Together," pp. 124–25
"Selecting entails rejecting; turning to requires turning from; being unmoved is a symptom of death as well as divinity; in shutting others out, the soul closes itself in, its self-containment exquisitely complete: it becomes its own tomb, a heart of stone."

MACHOR, "Feminine Rhetoric," p. 145
"Dickinson's polarization of meaning creates a tension among the stanzas, counterpointing them to one another in order to present the plurisignificance of the imagery."

PORTERFIELD, *Feminine Spirituality*, pp. 140–41
"This poem celebrates the fullness of solitude and suggests the sheer strength required for self-confidence."

1981   MONTEIRO, G., "Dickinson's Select Society," pp. 41–43
Finds echoes in the poem "not merely of Emerson's ideas taken in abstraction, but of Emerson's subjects couched in the Sage's very language."

1982 MARCUS, *Emily Dickinson,* pp. 57, 58–59, 60, 62, 64

"The chosen one is the beloved whose spirit she lives with or has perhaps taken into herself by the power of imagination. The soul has almost denied everything else in life to lock itself into its strange relationship with the chosen 'one.'"

MORSE, "History in the Text," pp. 331–32, 341–42

Budick's 1979 historical reading "disregards only one important fact about the text: that it is a poem." Notes "what appears to be something like a historical connection" between poem and passage by Emerson.

1983 DAICHES, *God and the Poets,* pp. 160–61

This poem "is in its way a model of what a poem is: It selects from the flux of experience its own society, its own unit of meaning and pattern of images which tell the truth about that unit, and then stops."

HOLLOWAY, "Death and the Emperor," pp. 69–70, 71

The poem's image of the Emperor's chariot is "derived from Elizabeth Barrett Browning's *Aurora Leigh* and, through it, from Dante Alighieri's *Purgatorio X.*"

1984 LEONARD, D. N., "Dickinson's Religion," pp. 342–43

"For Dickinson the soul in the select company of itself is in fellowship with God, whether God is understood as simply an aspect of the self or as a being wholly other. In any case, to admit another human being into this transcendent unity of self would be utterly destructive."

LUSCHER, "Emersonian Context," pp. 111–16

"Using Emerson as a framework and as a subject, [Dickinson's poem] defines and defends the act of poetic creation—her calling—as a selective concentration that measures, in relative solitude, particular moments in her Soul's conversation with her own society."

MARTIN, W., *American Triptych,* p. 86

"When read in the context of her religious struggle and fierce resolution to remain committed to this life instead of the next, the imperial—and imperious—metaphor of the queenly soul to describe her own consciousness takes on greater resonance."

WOLOSKY, *Emily Dickinson,* pp. 128–30

"Dickinson's is the terrible irony of a Puritan or Emersonian retreat into the soul in search of the divine, only to find herself trapped there. . . . The desired experience of inward infinity gives way to claustrophobia."

1985 COTTLE, *Language of Literature,* p. 102
A note on poem's grammar.

1986 BYERS, "Possible Background," p. 35
Suggests a possible source for this poem in *Hamlet.*

LOVING, *Emily Dickinson,* pp. 42, 48, 61, 80, 112
"The poem is unique for its pattern of regression. . . . The movement in the poem from mind ('Soul') through person (Elizabeth) to matter (the oyster) illustrates Dickinson's response to the human condition."

ROBINSON, J., *Emily Dickinson,* p. 55
"There seems to be more merit in rejecting the many than in rejoicing over 'the Society' selected, and to indicate that merit by declaring that it spurns even Emperors when it closes the valves of its attention is to betray a preoccupation with rank."

1987 FINCH, "Patriarchal Meter," pp. 172–73
Considers "semantic-metrical connections." The poem "retreats from its initial iambic pentameter line, a movement that metrically parallels the poem's verbal description of self-reliance and frugality."

SEWALL, "Emily Dickinson," pp. 72–73, 75
In this poem Dickinson "presents with stunning power the essence of an experience—'what it feels like' to make a final, ultimate commitment to a way of life that involves perhaps painful renunciation of many of the fine things of this world . . . ."

1988 REED, "Masculine Identity," pp. 281–82
Relates to "larger overall pattern in Dickinson's poetry that includes the themes of deprivation and separation or, in psychoanalytical terms, an interruption or denial of nourishment and nurture to be defended against by gaining exclusive control of the source of nourishment here expressed in the poet's desire for separateness."

WOLFF, *Emily Dickinson,* pp. 198–200, 505
"A speaker may reject both the world and God; nonetheless, they are of value in the poem because they provide a context for the speaker's act."

1989 GARBOWSKY, *House without the Door,* pp. 134, 135, 150
"By implication, the soul is keenly discriminating. . . . Impervious and imperial in her disregard of 'an Emperor,' she makes her choice, which is forever fixed and inscrutable."

ROBINSON, DOUGLAS, "Two Dickinson Readings," pp. 26–29, 34, 35 n. 4
In this poem "Dickinson's apocalyptic imagination is as it were deadlocked, split in an agon between an Emersonian expansion and a Poeian constriction that seems irresolvable."

"The soul should always stand ajar" (1055)

1980 HOPES, "Uses of Metaphor," pp. 17–18
"The energies of the poem, visitor and host, are represented in metaphor by both persona and symbol, active and static imagery."

1986 ANDERSON, P., "Bride of the White Election," p. 7
The poem is Dickinson's gloss on Song of Solomon 5:2–6.

1988 WOLFF, *Emily Dickinson,* p. 505
". . . the attitude of the verse invokes not some land of ancient Biblical splendor, but the township of Amherst in the year of our Lord 1865."

"The soul that hath a guest" (674)

1976 SHANDS, "Malinowski's Mirror," p. 323
Here Dickinson "presents an 'apologia' for solipsism, saying defiantly that she can supply her own needs for companionship and love. . . . The figure of speech correlated with megalomania and solipsism is hyperbole, and in this poem we see the systematic expansion of terms to some kind of ultimate."

1985 JUHASZ, "Tea and Revolution," pp. 147, 149
"This witty poem is at once a rationale for solitude and a reinterpretation, or transformation, of its meaning."

"The soul unto itself" (683)

1980 HOMANS, *Women Writers,* pp. 210, 211
"The terms 'friend' and 'Spy' represent the poet's efforts to render comprehensible this division between the soul and itself. The poet falls back on the oppositional structure of language, as a self-defense . . . ."
Reprinted: Homans, "Emily Dickinson," pp. 445, 446

1981   KIMPEL, *Dickinson as Philosopher,* pp. 87–89
The poet here affirms "that moral willing is unconditioned, and therefore, is dependent upon nothing external to the individual himself who exercises this initiative. . . . She is impressed with the mode of willing itself which constitutes the moral independence of human beings who so act."

1982   BURBICK, "Irony of Self-Reference," pp. 90–91
Examination of pronominal language; compares with "Me from myself to banish."

1986   MOREY, "Dickinson-Kant: The First Critique," pp. 60, 64
"If one accepts the levels of one's shadow, it is seen as an imperial friend; if one rejects or fights the primordial functions, they are seen as a Spy or Enemy."

1987   COOK, C., "Psychic Development," pp. 131–32
"If the 'Soul' that Dickinson talks about in this poem is her inner, masculine self and the 'itself' is her outer, feminine self, it is easy to see that this poem ends in a warning to the Soul that she will not lose control of her consciousness while seeking the unconscious."

CULJAK, "Dickinson and Kierkegaard," p. 153
"The poet suggests the necessity for a relationship between the dialectic aspects of the self, but also posits a disrelationship."

"The soul's distinct connection" (974)

1978   CAMERON, "Naming as History," pp. 244–45
The speaker's "incomprehension is a direct result of the lapsed connection between experience and its history or context. . . . The subject here lurks in the connections between the words, elusive and perceived indirectly."
Reprinted: Cameron, *Lyric Time,* pp. 47–48, 175–76, 180

TILMA-DEKKERS, "Immortality," pp. 171–73
"The tremendous power of the event is suggested in the word 'Calamity': the danger has turned from threat to actuality, and the poet is completely at its mercy."

1981   DIEHL, *Romantic Imagination,* p. 128
"Moments of danger or calamity shock us into an awareness of our connection with 'immortality,' here a trope for death. . . . This sudden vision, however, reveals danger, and Dickinson realizes the need to pro-

tect the self against the blinding effect of these flashes, instructive yet potentially damaging."

JUHASZ, "'Peril as a Possession,'" pp. 34–35
"The poem's two stanzas are analogous, and the un-'exploded' parallelism of their components indicates the nature of the relationship between soul and immortality."
Revised and reprinted: Juhasz, *Undiscovered Continent,* pp. 57–58, 83

1985   JOHNSON, *Emily Dickinson,* p. 70
"It is crucial to notice here the linking of 'danger' to the lightning flash of numinous perception: the soul has not yet ascended into its own spiritual landscape because that landscape is still essentially unknown, foreign."

1987   MARTIN, J. E., "Religious Spirit," pp. 500–01
"Immortality in this poem is not viewed primarily as a state of life in the future, but as an actual condition of the person here and now."

1988   UNO, "Optical Instruments," pp. 229–30
Here Dickinson "fuses two metaphors: lightning and photo-taking in order to show a kind of revelation."

"The soul's superior instants" (306)

1979   BUDICK, "When the Soul Selects," pp. 352, 359
"Despite the apparently ecstatic quality of the poem's summary revelation, the poem is filled with doubts, self-criticisms, and self-conscious sarcasms."

WESTBROOK, *Free Will and Determinism,* p. 58
"Some of her poems [such as this one] deal unmistakably with conversion or the sequels of it, leaving no other interpretation reasonably possible."

1983   JUHASZ, *Undiscovered Continent,* pp. 159–60, 161
"Here, as in others of her poems attesting to the power of the solitary soul, Dickinson makes herself god-like. This posture . . . is essential to our understanding of Dickinson's actual position."

SHURR, *Marriage,* pp. 99, 103, 133
"The two major themes of this phase—the beloved's presence-through-absence, and Dickinson's achievement of identity as a professional poet—converge" in this poem.

1985 BUDICK, *Emily Dickinson,* pp. 145–46
"Here Dickinson identifies strongly with the soul's lofty and singular position, and yet she also betrays a suspicion that the soul that has 'ascended' beyond the plane of the ordinary and the 'Mortal' to have revealed to it the knowledge of eternity and immortality is vulnerable and somewhat painfully isolated."

JOHNSON, *Emily Dickinson,* pp. 74, 202 n. 21
"The speaker and her perception of spiritual reality meet on equal terms, like independent monarchs; graciously the soul 'abolishes' what is mortal, and eternity 'discloses' its rarefied substance. The relation is thus reciprocal, cordial, the two identities clearly focused and discrete."

1986 MOREY, "Dickinson-Kant: The First Critique," p. 65
The poem "zooms in on the particular moments when one is aware of an altered state of being, whether Zen enlightenment, a mystical moment of contact, or another spiritual insight."

1989 OLIVER, *Apocalypse of Green,* pp. 108–09, 219
Notes disagreement on interpretation among critics. The poem "does place emphasis on what Dickinson considers the autocratic and unjust process of election."

"The spider as an artist" (1275)

1981 DIEHL, *Romantic Imagination,* p. 93
"Unappreciated and therefore totally independent, the spider is Dickinson's image of the working poet—one who despite the most persistent efforts of the caretakers of convention keeps forming poems out of the solitary self."

"The spider holds a silver ball" (605)

1979 GILBERT and GUBAR, *Madwoman,* pp. 633–35, 697 n. 69
". . . the fact that the spider's yarn is of pearl suggests in Dickinson's symbol-system both the paradoxical secrecy of his triumph and the female nature of his trade."

1984 MARTIN, W., *American Triptych,* pp. 132–34
Contrasts with Whitman's "A noiseless patient spider," illustrating the "essential differences between patriarchal and gynecocentric modes of perception."

OLPIN, "Hyperbole: Part II," p. 29
This poem "recounting the end of a spider, is a parody of the notion that the grand plans and works of men are ever subject to being arbitrarily cut off."

RAFFEL, *How To Read a Poem*, pp. 71–72
Examines the poem's metaphorical comparison, "the linkage between Dickinson's own life and career and these metaphorically brilliant and neglected human weavers."

ST. ARMAND, *Dickinson and Her Culture*, pp. 33–34, 323 n. 30
"This artistic spider is playful and much too self-indulgent for Puritan economy to tolerate, an aesthete who juggles words for his own amusement and who must pay the penalty of seeing both himself and his art swept into the abyss of time."

1985 JOHNSON, *Emily Dickinson*, pp. 44–45
"The poem implies . . . that artistic endeavor is valuable for its own sake . . . and that momentary triumphs of personal vision, even if they do not ensure immortality, are better than no triumphs at all."

"The spirit is the conscious ear" (733)

1989 LOEFFELHOLZ, "Dickinson Identified," pp. 170–71, 175–76
Suggests "possible posthumanist readings in both women's studies and English undergraduate classrooms."

"The spirit lasts, but in what mode" (1576)

1982 MOSSBERG, *Emily Dickinson*, pp. 28–29
"The poem is a metaphysical discussion of the relationship between the body's speaking apparatus and informing consciousness. . . . a trauma of identity and alienation that the pronominal disorder and syntactic structure reflect."

THOTA, *Emily Dickinson*, p. 143
Dickinson's "sharply focussed artistic consciousness . . . can be directly perceived in her poems about her technique. She considers the integral link between content and form in [this poem]."

1984 BENFEY, *Problem of Others*, pp. 43, 97–98, 101
The poem discovers "that to imagine the afterlife of the spirit requires one to imagine the life of the spirit, here, 'below.'"

Wolosky, *Emily Dickinson*, pp. 168–69
"Each aspect—spiritual and corporeal—seems necessary rather than inimical to the other. . . . Both are necessary to nature and to utterance . . . ."

1985   Eberwein, *Dickinson*, pp. 230–31
"Forced to pose questions from within the circuit that are unanswerable here, she instinctively directs her speculation outside. . . . The circumferential gate to circuit rumor withstands the energetic thrust of her prognosticating curiosity."

Swenson, "Big My Secret," pp. 30–31
Suggests that the poem's "Either" might be a typo for "Ether," or possibly both words were meant.

1988   Stocks, *Modern Consciousness*, pp. 21–22
"Between the Metaphysicals and her poem lie the Cartesian body-mind dualism and the other dissociations of the age. It is against this background, the wrenching apart of old unities, that her poem should be measured."

Weissman, " 'Transport's Working Classes,' " pp. 422–23
"Logic and experience combine in [this poem] to lead the reader through a series of statements that keep suggesting Dickinson's joyful faith in the immortality of the flesh."

"The stars are old that stood for me" (1249)

1978   Faderman, "Homoerotic Poetry," p. 24
"The speaker had believed that her worship of the other woman would only evoke 'Her infinite disdain,' but the beloved has been vanquished by pity, and thus has not gotten off scot free in the battle of their relationship . . . ."

1989   Diehl, "Murderous Poetics," p. 340
"Disdained by all around her, she vanquishes the adversary by her very defeat and thus slays victory."

"The stimulus beyond the grave" (1001)

1981   Porter, *Dickinson*, p. 92
This "does not mean the mystical banality it implies, but rather 'The stimulus (of the thought that I will see his countenance) beyond the grave' supports the bereaved like brandy."

"The sun and fog contested" (1190)

1982   MARTIN, J. M., "Nature and Art," p. 28
"This poem recalls the condescending attitude of the poet, for here we see another 'rule' of nature in that clarity overrules obscurity. The poet, by abstraction, clarifies nature by writing the poem and in Dickinson everyday weather becomes a universality."

1987   BARKER, *Lunacy of Light,* pp. 70–71
"At first glance another charming 'nature poem,' [this] may be, rather, one of Dickinson's most succinct criticisms of patriarchy."

"The sun is one, and on the tare" (1372)

1982   MARCELLINO, "Dickinson's 'The Sun Is One,'" pp. 29–30
"The poem states quite clearly . . . that since there is only one sun, it naturally shines as punctually both on the tare . . . as well as on the 'conscientious Flower' . . . and holds them both in equally high esteem or repute."

"The sun just touched the morning" (232)

1979   BAYM, "God, Father, and Lover," pp. 202–03
"One cannot miss the traditional religious imagery used here, as well as the Puritan concept of the self's unworthiness unless and only because graced by the arbitrary King, whom one must adore whether or not one is sanctified by him."

GILBERT and GUBAR, *Madwoman,* pp. 601–02
This poem "seems almost like a darkened revision of 'The Daisy follows soft the Sun.'"

1987   BARKER *Lunacy of Light,* pp. 59–60
"Certainly the poem may be about love's loss, but it can also be read as a poem about writing."

"The sun kept setting, setting still" (692)

1989   GARBOWSKY, *House without the Door,* pp. 115–16
The poem "recapitulates the classic physiological symptoms of panic attack."

"The sun kept stooping, stooping low" (152)

1987 BARKER, *Lunacy of Light*, pp. 109–10
"In larger terms, the sun as representative of the masculine principle is, in effect, relinquishing his domination to the feminine. And as these female hills therefore assume larger proportions, . . . the poet begins to feel a corresponding 'martial' energy."

LEDER and ABBOTT, *Language of Exclusion*, pp. 113–14
"There is a menacing quality to this highly metaphoric poem at odds with the subject matter. The stain upon the window and the armies' slow advance, especially when read in 1860, have dimensions it is hard to avoid."

"The sun went down—no man looked on" (1079)

1979 NATHAN, "Soul at White Heat," p. 48
Poem's elements are related to those of Augustinian meditation.

1984 MARTIN, W., *American Triptych*, pp. 123–24
"Struggling with complex problems such as the artificial distinction between subject and object that characterizes patriarchal modes of perception, Dickinson remained focused on the actual and immediate rather than on the transcendent dimension of her experience."

1987 COOK, C., "Psychic Development," p. 128
"She watched the sunset alone, and then in the darkness that followed she made contact with that nameless bird, her unconscious masculine traits, which stayed with her and viewed the crowning of the new day and of the creative forces in her."

"The sunrise runs for both" (710)

1979 PATTERSON, *Dickinson's Imagery*, pp. 126, 133, 183, 202–03
Relates to significance of East and West in Dickinson's poetry. Suggests the poem may have been written while Susan Dickinson was away.

1983 SHURR, *Marriage*, pp. 104–05
Suggests that the poem refers to the distance between the poet and Wadsworth.

1988 WOLFF, *Emily Dickinson*, p. 292
"What can we make of these echoing elements—daylight and au-

rora borealis, or Janus-faced dawn and dusk? 'Both lie—': the final line's brief, punning dismissal."

"The sunset stopped on cottages" (950)

1987   BARKER, *Lunacy of Light,* p. 62
Considers significance of sun in Dickinson's poetry. Here "it becomes unreliable to the point of impotence."

"The sweetest heresy received" (387)

1983   SHURR, *Marriage,* pp. 35, 104
Several of the love poems suggest the lover should be identified as a clergyman. Here "Dickinson explains her notion of marriage as its own religion, counter perhaps to his more orthodox views . . . ."

"The symptom of the gale" (1327)

1982   THOTA, *Emily Dickinson,* pp. 87–88
Compares with "Donne's verse-letter 'To Mr. Christopher Brooke,' about 'The Storme.'"

"The test of love is death" (573)

1987   OBERHAUS, "'Tender Pioneer,'" pp. 345, 347–49, 358
The speaker in this meditation "reflects upon the Cross that proved God's love, asserts that she attempts to imitate His love, confesses her imitation is imperfect, and finally asks for salvation not because she has earned it but because Christ promised and won it."

"The things that never can come back are several" (1515)

1985   EBERWEIN, *Dickinson,* pp. 66–67
The poem "offers comfort beyond that suggested in its introductory lines and opens a typological reading of the quest that suggests the illusory quality of loss rather than of gain. This vestige of Puritan language hints at Christian consolation."

1988   WOLFF, *Emily Dickinson,* pp. 513–14
The poem's usage "removes the notion of 'typic' from its usual *historical* and *mythic* context and applies it to ordinary, *quotidian existence,* claiming that each life, here and now, has its own privileged moments of insight—even, perhaps, of foreknowledge . . . ."

"The things we thought that we should do"

"The things we thought that we should do" (1293)

1981 KIMPEL, *Dickinson as Philosopher,* pp. 115–16
"Emily Dickinson is aware that there is no morally responsible acting without thinking. In other words, thinking about what should be done is the minimum condition for conduct."

"The thrill came slowly like a boon" (1495)

1988 WOLFF, *Emily Dickinson,* pp. 514–15
"Although these annihilating forces suffuse the verse, 'desolation' is specified as the 'only' missing element: the speaker's integrity is left intact, and the experience of conversion (or perhaps even of death itself) is rendered as no more than a change of 'Dress.'"

"The tint I cannot take is best" (627)

1987 CARTON, "Dickinson and the Divine," pp. 243, 245, 247
Examines relation of this poem to "Before I got my eye put out." Here "the speaker rejoices in the perpetual failure of her senses (particularly of her vision) to satisfy her."
Revised and reprinted: Carton, *Rhetoric,* pp. 5, 47, 50–51, 55, 60, 270 n.5

1982 MARCUS, *Emily Dickinson,* p. 43
General consideration as one of Dickinson's poems on "Poetry, Art, and Imagination." "Here, the emphasis is on the impossibility of art's capturing the essence of precious experience, especially of nature and of spiritual triumphs."

1984 ST. ARMAND, *Dickinson and Her Culture,* pp. 271–72
Considers "aspects of nineteenth-century landscape painting" observable in the poem, where they are "cast into Dickinson's particular local terms and metaphors."

1985 BLOOM, H., *Emily Dickinson,* pp. 5–7
"What precedents are there for such a poem, a work of unnaming, a profound and shockingly original cognitive act of negation? . . . It is, rugged and complete, a poetics, and a manifesto of Self-Reliance."
Reprinted: Bloom, H., *American Poetry,* pp. 26–28; Mullane and Wilson, *Nineteenth-Century,* pp. 83–84

1986 BLOOM, H., *American Women Poets,* pp. 5–6
Dickinson, "shrewdly exploiting her identity as woman poet, chooses another way to see, a way that unnames without defiance or

struggle. The best tint is what she cannot take, too remote for showing, impalpable, too exquisite to tell, secret, graspless."

"The treason of an accent" (1358)

1981   KIMPEL, *Dickinson as Philosopher*, pp. 97–98
"What obviously is common to both . . . versions is the term 'treason'. Such 'treason' or infidelity, however, has consequences which differ, according to the two versions."

"The trees like tassels hit and swung" (606)

1986   McNEIL, *Emily Dickinson*, p. 122
"The delicious half-satisfaction of nature's complex life seems to be experienced from inside and outside at once, so that what is happening in nature is perfectly matched to the random wandering of our senses and thoughts."

"The veins of other flowers" (811)

1980   HOMANS, *Woman Writers*, pp. 192, 193
The poem "appears to value nature's visual language over human language . . . in fact it is only through the poem's juxtaposition that the scarlet flowers have any relation to the others. Nature's language is at once superior to and dependent on a human viewpoint."
Reprinted: Homans, "Emily Dickinson," pp. 432, 433

1982   MILLER, C., "Terms and Golden Words," pp. 48–49, 50, 52
"In this poem, human language and, consequently, human creation are implicitly reductive: our grandest thoughts are released into the world only through our combination of syllables—incomplete, closed units of meaning and structure."

1985   BUDICK, *Emily Dickinson*, pp. 129–30, 164
The poet here suggests the "grim possibility that art not only cannot say it all, but that in trying to say it all, in attempting to 'conjugate' 'Terms,' art distorts and perhaps even destroys."

1986   ROBINSON, J., *Emily Dickinson*, p. 91
"This imposition of language on experience is clear enough to see as long as we are dealing with something external such as flowers. It becomes more intricate to follow when the experience on which abstract language is being imposed is itself abstract."

"The voice that stands for floods to me" (1189)

1984 BENFEY, *Problem of Others,* pp. 19–20
Considers "difficulties of interpretation" in this poem whose theme is "'meanness' and its relation to meaning."

"The way I read a letter's this" (636)

1979 CROSTHWAITE, "Way to Read a Letter," pp. 159–65
The poem "contains striking parallels to a passage . . . from *Villette,* by Charlotte Brontë."

1984 BENFEY, *Problem of Others,* pp. 48–50, 55
This is "Dickinson's major text on privacy and reading." Relates poem to "I dwell in possibility."

1986 LOVING, *Emily Dickinson,* pp. 85–86
"The poem is not about the receipt of a lover's missive but about the isolation necessary for the most serious kind of introspection. . . . The poem is about the delicate balance between society and the self, between all animal life . . . and the ego that strives to transcend animal or human limitations."

"The way to know the bobolink" (1279)

1988 WEISSMAN, "'Transport's Working Classes,'" p. 416
The poem's bobolink "violates social, political, and religious rules with his beauty and joy. . . . Reading this poem, we are forced to imagine a world without the restrictions that demand words like sedition, heresy, and apostasy."

"The whole of it came not at once" (762)

1981 KIMPEL, *Dickinson as Philosopher,* pp. 42–43, 53–54
"In this particular poem, Emily Dickinson is not merely referring to a particular disappointment in her life. She is rather affirming a generalization about suffering entailed in living."

1983 SHURR, *Marriage,* p. 181
"If Dickinson suffered a painful abortion which left her sick and bedridden for a whole summer, then two poems record vividly remem-

bered details." This is one; the other, "Split the lark and you'll find the music."

1988 WOLOSKY, "Rhetoric or Not," pp. 227–28
"This poem seems remote from the hymnal; yet, the hymnal frame gives to it, as to so many Dickinson poems, an extra resonance and force. Even original figures are often rooted in traditional ones."

"The wind begun to knead the grass" (824)

1982 MARCUS, *Emily Dickinson*, pp. 24–25
General consideration as one of the poet's nature poems. "It seems to please the speaker to see nature as both alien and familiar, wild and domestic."

OLPIN, "Hyperbole: Part One," pp. 17–18
Contrasts tone of different versions of the poem.

1983 BUDICK, "Dangers of the Living Word," pp. 210–11, 213, 216, 217, 220, 223 nn. 8–9
The poem "effects upon itself a version of disintegration and dissolution so complete that metaphorically, syntactically, and narratively it shatters into the jumbled multiplicity of the elements which it describes. Poetic cohesion, like cosmic cohesion, becomes almost totally unhinged."
Revised and reprinted: Budick, *Emily Dickinson*, pp. 14–16, 18, 104

1986 McNEIL, *Emily Dickinson*, pp. 117–19
Both versions of the poem "offer a complex display of gender in relation to perspective and possession of the place from which the poem comes."

MOREY, "Dickinson-Kant: The First Critique," pp. 46–47
Although this and "There came a wind like a bugle" are "companion poems, on the same subject, there is a difference in the syntax, ellipsis, and amount of abstraction . . . ."

"The wind didn't come from the orchard today" (316)

1982 OLPIN, "Hyperbole: Part One," p. 15
The poem "relies on sound manipulation and rime to create a comic and playful picture of the wind in an orchard."

"The wind drew off" (1694)

1981 DIEHL, *Romantic Imagination,* pp. 158–59
Considers "possible links" between this poem and Shelley's "Lines written among the Euganean Hills."

MARCELLINO, "'Beware an Austrian,'" pp. 53–54
Dickinson's probable knowledge of the Latin word *auster* (meaning "south wind") illuminates poem's final line.

1983 GALINSKY, "Northern and Southern," p. 159 n. 80
The poem's structure supports an interpretation of "Austrian" as "south wind," from the Latin word *auster.*

"The wind tapped like a tired man" (436)

1985 COOK, A., *Thresholds,* p. 189
"Even this poem, occupied entirely with the wind, cannot be divorced from hints of theology, given Dickinson's sense of humming as joining in the heavenly chorus, and given her revising the term for this particular bird into a generalized activity."

1987 BODIE, "Dickinson's 'The wind tapped,'" pp. 25–26
Suggests possible implications of poem's image of tunes blown in glass, which may refer to a glass harmonica.

"The winters are so short" (403)

1986 ROBINSON, J., *Emily Dickinson,* pp. 78–79
Here the poet says, "in a farmhouse-conversation way which binds country wisdom to biblical, that the restrictions of winter are scarcely worth observing; it is scarcely worth, that is, orienting life to the possibility of the worst."

1988 WOLFF, *Emily Dickinson,* pp. 284–85, 353
"No argument can counter the implacable power of the Divinity; no comfort can assuage the pain of His victims. Thus the poem ends abruptly, with a dismissal rather than a conclusion."

"The world stands solemner to me" (493)

1983 SHURR, *Marriage,* pp. 15, 152, 183–84
The poem "looks back upon the day of marriage and reflects on the experience in a calm and ordered way. . . . [It] ends with a direct

address identifying the husband as a clergyman and asking him for his advice on how to forget him."

1984 POLLAK, *Dickinson,* pp. 163–65
    "Idolizing a masculine erotic other, Dickinson imagines herself as the recipient of comparable adoration. Suggesting that marriage represents an antiprogressive state, Dickinson acknowledges the appeal of stasis."

1987 LEDER and ABBOTT, *Language of Exclusion,* pp. 137, 138
    "The poem perfectly delineates the Victorian marriage with the woman's soul burdened, clasped, and bound." Relates to other Dickinson poems on marriage.

"The worthlessness of earthly things" (1373)

1984 WOLOSKY, *Emily Dickinson,* p. 113
    "Zion she finds limitlessly in the natural world, precluding any longing for a heavenly Jerusalem. It provides its own arguments against the pulpit wisdom that would devalue it. For the evidence that would support nature's lack speaks instead in its favor."

"The zeroes taught us phosphorus" (689)

1979 PATTERSON, *Dickinson's Imagery,* pp. 16, 98, 117, 134, 188
    The poem "makes a detailed contrast between loveless North and erotic South . . . ."

1980 HOMANS, *Women Writers,* pp. 179–81, 186
    The poem "invites both ironic and non-ironic readings, and having established that the simple reversal of meaning is central to orthodox rhetoric, the poet allows orthodoxy's own principles to undermine themselves."
    Reprinted: Homans, "Emily Dickinson," pp. 423–24, 425, 428; reprinted in part: Homans, "Dickinson and Poetic Identity," pp. 141–42, 143

1984 MARTIN, W., *American Triptych,* p. 160
    "In this poem, Dickinson reasons syllogistically that just as cold gives meaning to heat, so death intensifies life's vitality."

1987 BLASING, *American Poetry,* pp. 186–87, 189
    " 'Zero,' then, is neither presence, since it signifies nothing, nor absence, since it is both a number and a word; rather, it proposes a system of delineating and designating presence and absence."

"Their height in heaven comforts not"

WILLIAMS, S., " 'Omitted Centers,' " pp. 28–30, 34, 35
Compares with "Water is taught by thirst" in order to demonstrate Dickinson's "development of the metonymic character of her work."

"Their height in heaven comforts not" (696)

1983 JUHASZ, *Undiscovered Continent,* pp. 137–40
The central argument of this poem, in which Dickinson directly confronts "the Christian myth of heaven," is "for personal experience against public doctrine, so that 'supposition' here means promises that masquerade as truth with nothing actually to support them."

1984 WOLOSKY, *Emily Dickinson,* pp. 104–05
"Heavenly glory is 'nought' to the poet, not because it may not exist, but because in its height it cannot be applied to earthly existence and makes no difference to it."

1988 WOLFF, *Emily Dickinson,* pp. 325–26, 330, 337, 587 n. 19
"This is a particularly American interpretation of the panoramic, unknown afterlife. . . . the incoherence, even danger of an unseeable, unexplored Paradise is rendered here by the substitution of abstract nouns . . . for the concrete nouns that would complete such locutions if they referred to that earthly frontier, the burgeoning American West."

1989 McCLURE, "Expanding the Canon," pp. 68, 74, 76–77, 82, 83
"Dickinson's use of frontier imagery illustrates how she adapted cultural mythology to express a personal vision."

OLIVER, *Apocalypse of Green,* pp. 199–200, 235
In this poem Dickinson "blames on her finitude her inability to fathom the nature of the afterlife."

"There are two Mays" (1618)

1981 KIMPEL, *Dickinson as Philosopher,* pp.114–15
The poet's "keen understanding of the nature of moral willing is expressed in this poem by contrasting the meanings of three words."

"There are two ripenings—one of sight" (332)

1979 PATTERSON, *Dickinson's Imagery,* pp. 25–26, 103, 184, 211 n. 38, 224 n. 11
Suggests possible source of poem's "teeth of Frosts" in John Ruskin's *Stones of Venice.*

1985 JOHNSON, *Emily Dickinson*, pp. 187–88

The poem is "a tiny, symbolic expression of Dickinson's theory of perception, envisioning death not as a hostile threat but as the crucial state in a natural, inevitable process."

"There came a day at summer's full" (322)

1972 RAO, *Essential Emily Dickinson*, pp. 131–33

General introduction to the poem aimed at "postgraduate students of literature in Indian Universities." ". . . at a deeper level, the poem is on the corrosive effects of time upon love or friendship."

1979 NATHAN, "Soul at White Heat," p. 46

Elements of the poem are related to those of Augustinian meditation.

1980 CUNNINGHAM, *Dickinson*, pp. 34–36

It is not renunciation that the poem presents; "rather it is anticipation, and anticipation with confidence."

DUNCAN, "Joining Together," p. 123

In the meeting narrated in this poem, "pleasure and pain, bliss and woe become indistinguishable. . . . In the figure of the Passion, . . . she not only identifies bliss and woe, she also fuses, empirically speaking, the secular and the sacred."

1981 KIMPEL, *Dickinson as Philosopher*, pp. 293–94

The poem "affirms a Christian faith about the continuity of consciousness, and as such, what she believes about the conscious retention in memory of all whom she loves. But what is not specifically Christian is her generalizing of the meaning of Calvary."

McGREGOR, "Standing with the Prophets," pp. 22–24, 25

"The poem shows a Puritan's sophisticated understanding of biblical typology and eschatology; it is saturated with scriptural allusion and moves intentionally within the framework of biblical eschatological thought and language."

STEINER, "Image Patterns," p. 66

Here "the 'Bond' between the lovers is one of suffering, a mutual 'Calvary' on earth which is part of the 'sacramental' union."

1982 MARCUS, *Emily Dickinson*, pp. 54–55, 57, 58, 59

"In this poem, the element of conflict and suffering is held in balance with, or made subservient to, the triumphs of love."

1983   BUDICK, "Symbolizing Eternity," pp. 1–12
"In its entirety the poem reconstructs our sense of what immortality is by making available to us a new kind of dynamic symbol of cosmic structure."
Revised and reprinted: Budick, *Emily Dickinson,* pp. 212–23, 227–28

GILBERT, "Wayward Nun," p. 27
"Defining herself and her lover as 'Sealed churches' and their erotic communion as a sacrament, she converts the Christianity she had begun to reject as a seventeen-year-old Mount Holyoke student into a complex theology of secular love."

HARRIS, N., "Naked and Veiled," pp. 23, 25–27, 29, 33
Contrasts with Plath's "A Birthday Present." Both poems "concern painful moments of imminent separation in love relationships."

KHAN, "Agony of the Final Inch," p. 30
"The paradox of human situation [*sic*] is that the climactic moment of union is precipitated into separation of antipodal nature. This tantalizing pain has its precedent only in the crucifixion of Golgotha or Calvary."
Revised and reprinted: Khan, *Emily Dickinson's Poetry,* pp. 34–35

SHURR, *Marriage,* pp. 11, 12–14, 17, 23, 28, 33, 36, 38–39, 48, 57, 60, 67, 73, 75, 80, 83, 89, 96, 98, 130, 132–33, 186, 191
This is "the single most rich and startling description of Dickinson's marriage experience." It celebrates the day "when the lovers exchanged marriage vows and crucifixes, parted definitively, though with the anticipation of reunion in heaven, and accepted the road to Calvary in this life as justification for their anomalous relationship."

1985   EBERWEIN, *Dickinson,* pp. 24–25, 113–14, 118, 124, 176, 251
"The darkening tone of this initially jubilant poem reflects the general pattern of romance within Dickinson's work. . . . The crucifix in this poem, however, witnesses to the hope of resurrection. Although a role model for suffering, Christ was also an example of triumphant martyrdom."

LOVING, "'Hansom Man,'" pp. 96–97
Both theme and structure of this "literary manifesto about language at the limits of civility" are similar to those of "Because I could not stop for death."

1986   BENNETT, *Loaded Gun,* pp. 62, 66, 84–86, 87
As a "love poem" it draws "its depth and power from experiences that predated her relationship" with the "Master." It appears to be about

the same experience as two poems ("Like eyes that looked on wastes" and "Ourselves were wed one summer, dear") about Susan Dickinson.

HURLEY, "Waiting for the Other Shoe," pp. 132–33
Discussion of the nature and effect of poem's rhymes.

JONES, " 'Royal Seal,' " pp. 35, 41–42, 50 n. 18
"Except for the ritualistic sign of the cross not practiced in Congregational churches, these lovers express their devotion through a sacramentalism that is markedly Puritan in its spirituality."

LOVING, *Emily Dickinson,* pp. 39–41, 90
"The poem is really about language at the limits of civility. . . . Both the theme and structure are remarkably similar to those of 'Because I Could Not Stop for Death.' "

1987 EBERWEIN, "Sacramental Tradition," pp. 67, 69
Examines the poem "within the specific context of Calvinist sacramental theology as understood by the nineteenth-century Congregational community within which Dickinson received her Christian formation."

MOREY, "Dickinson-Kant II," pp. 25, 27–28
Considers the "control" displayed here. The poem "may be justly considered too pat for sincerity . . . ."

1988 LOUIS, "Sacrament of Starvation," pp. 353–54
Here Dickinson "draws on Revelation to describe a non-Christian sacrament of love between individuals."

WOLFF, *Emily Dickinson,* pp. 412–13, 414
The poem's "lovers have disrupted the mythic order in having experienced the Redemption before the Crucifixion. . . . Ironically, theirs is a too-perfect union for sublunary creatures; only Heaven can contain them, and they must earn that Paradise 'through Calvaries of Love.' "

1989 OLIVER, *Apocalypse of Green,* pp. 123–26, 128, 129, 161 n. 44, 232
"The poem can easily be interpreted as operating on two levels, the natural and the supra-natural, which, however, are not mutually exclusive or related in any consequent way, but are integrally combined."

"There came a wind like a bugle" (1593)

1972 RAO, *Essential Emily Dickinson,* pp. 160–61
General introduction to the poem aimed at "postgraduate students of literature in Indian Universities."

"There comes an hour when begging stops"

1986 DERRICK, "Emily Dickinson," pp. 31–32, 34, 35–37
"Operating, as Heidegger postulates that all authentic language must, within the very nexus of change, [the poem] rescues permanence out of loss and thus allows us to understand them both, in their most fundamental character."

MOREY, "Dickinson-Kant: The First Critique," pp. 46–47
Considers along with "The wind begun to knead the grass." Although these are "companion poems, on the same subject, there is a difference in the syntax, ellipsis, and amount of abstraction . . . ."

"There comes an hour when begging stops" (1751)

1985 SMITH, B. J., "'Vicinity to Laws,'" pp. 43–44
Examines poem's legal vocabulary. "The law is kinder than total freedom; it implies concern."

1986 OBERHAUS, "'Engine against th' Almightie,'" pp. 156, 158, 159
"This disappointed but resigned speaker finds God's prohibitions kinder than His deferred response. . . . Despite the supplicant's 'begging' and 'long' pleading, God seems deaf to her prayer, as does Herbert's God in 'Deniall'. . . ."

"There is a finished feeling" (856)

1980 LAIR, "Fracture of Grammar," p. 160
Examines poem's syntactic ambiguity.

1985 JOHNSON, *Emily Dickinson*, p. 173
Death's presence "serves to validate the poet's identity, since death enables us to see 'Preciser what we are.' An inchoate sense of life's meaning is therefore accompanied by a greater exactness of perception."

1989 OLIVER, *Apocalypse of Green*, p. 59
"Though the first stanza seems to indicate a persona from beyond the grave, the second seems to apply more to the living. . . . Implicit rather than stated in the poem is the message that death forcefully reiterates of the transitory and irrecoverable nature of this temporal life . . . ."

"There is a June when corn is cut" (930)

1981 PORTER, *Dickinson*, pp. 174–75, 248
"The poem measures out difference in an attempt to understand. It is a poem of unsophisticated speculation but of language precision that creates high wit."

1984 WOLOSKY, *Emily Dickinson*, pp. 113–15
"The decision does go to earth, not to heaven. But the syntactic skirmish registers some contrary impulse."

1986 BENNETT, *Loaded Gun*, pp. 93–94, 277 n. 21
Analysis making "a sharp distinction between the two 'Summers' of the first two stanzas and the two 'Seasons' of the last two stanzas. The two summers are 1) the 'real' summer, 2) marriage. The two seasons are 1) marriage . . . , 2) the poet's frosty 'North.'"

1988 MORRIS, T., "Development," pp. 38–39, 40
This poem, "welded together out of a tremendous tension of style and symbol, is a rejection of the whole mystery of immortality in favor of a confidence trick by Nature that seems honest in comparison."

"There is a languor of the life" (396)

1989 GARBOWSKY, "House without the Door," pp. 122, 123–24
"Although the poem appears to concern death, it may reasonably be surmised that it refers to depersonalization."

"There is a morn by men unseen" (24)

1982 BARNSTONE, "Women and the Garden," pp. 163–64, 165
"The motivation for creating a single-sexed Eden is the same for both Marvell and Dickinson: freedom. . . . For Emily Dickinson . . . men represent lack of freedom precisely because of the constraints placed on women through the fear of sin."

1983 DIEHL, "'Ransom,'" pp. 159–60
"Puns and associative images create a complex web of meaning that reinforces the overall vision of the poem as a counter-revelation, another way for the poet to be, as opposed to the commonly received notion of poetic vocation and the daylight world of masculine orthodoxy."
Reprinted: Bloom, H., *American Women Poets,* pp. 26–27

SHURR, *Marriage,* pp. 28, 52
The poem "presents a detailed imaginary picture of heaven and expresses the desire to be there; nowhere in the poem is there anything but confidence in the reality of this heaven and a serene hope that she will eventually take up residence there."

1984 CHERRY, "Sexuality and Tension" p. 15
Here Dickinson resolves "the conflict produced by sexuality" by denying its existence. "The speaker is safe while amongst women and can even reach spirituality thru this chaste sensuality."

"There is a pain so utter" (599)

1979 CAMERON, *Lyric Time,* pp. 158–59, 160, 170
"Pain is the space where words would be, the hole torn out of language. [In this poem], in its self-consuming totality, it is amnesia."

1983 JUHASZ, *Undiscovered Continent,* pp. 44-46, 73, 78, 81
"Time's activities within the mind, in particular those of memory, are documented here, as one state in a process for coping is described. Language embodies time by rendering its actions with a concrete vocabulary of spatial dimension."

1984 POLLAK, *Dickinson,* pp. 209–10
"Extreme pain, Dickinson believes, destroys the memory of its occasion. . . . The soul cannot bear too much reality and commands a variety of amnesiac responses which blank out pain, all of which prefigure that ultimate amnesiac, death."

1988 WOLFF, *Emily Dickinson,* p. 468
". . . this unstructured and continuous state of pain is coextensive with life. And the starkest contrast between this poem and some study of imminent death is that here, no eye/I struggles against extinction: it cannot, for 'pain . . . swallows substance up—.'"

1989 GARBOWSKY, *House without the Door,* pp. 122, 123, 139
"This description of the trancelike effect of depersonalization brought on by the panic attack accurately describes its release function and the protective purpose it serves. By cutting the victim's feelings off, depersonalization prevents him or her from a more serious breakdown."

"There is a solitude of space" (1695)

1980 GREEN, "Spatial Drama," p. 195
Examines phrase "polar privacy."

1984 LEONARD, D. N., "Dickinson's Religion," pp. 334–36
The poem "implies that the price for the marvelous power of self-awareness is extreme loneliness and an accompanying sense of paradox at the root of one's identity."

1986 MOREY, "Dickinson-Kant: The First Critique," pp. 60, 64–65
Links with "This consciousness that is aware." Both poems "concern consciousness opening up to the unconscious" and "posit the fourth state after death."

1987   CULJAK, "Dickinson and Kierkegaard," p. 154
"The synthesis of self is here resolved; the 'polar' separation inherent in man ends with the moment of death. The 'sickness unto death' is finally cured."

1989   KNAPP, *Emily Dickinson,* pp. 178–79
"Unlike in some other Dickinsonian poems, 'polar privacy' or the experience of the space/time continuum (that fourth dimension) is here viewed as a positive force."

"There is a word" (8)

1978   HUGHES, J., " 'Time's Sublimest Target,' " pp. 29–31
This early poem "posits the riddle of time-death-eternity which Dickinson was so fearfully yet fearlessly to analyze. . . . Dickinson seems to withdraw from the specific instance of what may be eternity's fatality and consider the nature of existence in general."

1982   MILLER, C., "Terms and Golden Words," pp. 53–54, 55, 61 nn. 7–8
"As in other poems, the piercing word . . . is associated with Christ and here, implicitly, with the forces of death and salvation. . . . The poem's word most importantly resembles Christ . . . in its unification of the universal or ahistorical with the historical."

"There is a zone whose even years" (1056)

1978   TILMA-DEKKERS, "Immortality," pp. 178–79, 180
Examines with other Dickinson poems for her view of "consciousness."

1986   REGUEIRO ELAM, "Haunting of the Self," pp. 84–85, 88–89, 92, 99 n. 2
"The consciousness that is noon must also, necessarily, be the consciousness that 'constructs' that noon, the consciousness that cannot conceive of otherness or of an outside that opposes itself to consciousness' interiority."

1989   HOCKERSMITH, " 'Into Degreeless Noon,' " pp. 282–83
In this poem Dickinson "directly juxtaposes her concept of a timebound immortal consciousness and an eternal oblivion. . . . 'Noon' usually symbolizes timelessness or stasis in Dickinson's poetry. In this poem, Dickinson applies the symbol to two different concepts of timelessness."

MILLER, C., "Dickinson's Language," p. 80
Comments on effect of poem's uninflected verbs.

"There is an arid pleasure" (782)

1988 WEISSMAN, "'Transport's Working Classes,'" pp. 410–11, 421
"What *is* the arid pleasure? Both the long poetic tradition that associates flowers with women's genitals and Dickinson's own other poems about male bees and female flowers suggest that the answer is that the arid pleasure is masturbation, and joy is making love."

"There is another loneliness" (1116)

1986 ROBINSON, J., *Emily Dickinson,* pp. 55–56, 106
". . . the quality of a thinking mind showing its alertness by overturning stale assumption, comes to a stop in simple assertion. The assertion is of privilege and is made unchallengeable by refusing to declare the grounds on which its 'richer' is based."

"There is another sky" (2)

1977 AGRAWAL, *Emily Dickinson,* pp. 57–58
"The universe of self, full of diverse experiences, has everything different from the familiar manifest material world. It is ever bright . . . ."

1980 HOMANS, *Women Writers,* pp. 194–95
Relates to letter poet wrote to Austin Dickinson. "The 'brighter garden' is called into being in response to an inadequacy in real nature, so that as well as functioning as a metaphor for the writer's love, those lovely images compete with real nature on the literal level."
Reprinted: Homans, "Emily Dickinson," pp. 434–35

1981 CUDDY, "Expression and Sublimation," p. 30
The poem "is interesting for the unconsciously sexual connotation toward her brother and adumbrates the later sexual feelings represented by (or more likely sublimated in) the bee."

1984 ANDERSON, D., "Presence and Place," pp. 206–09, 211, 213, 214, 217, 219
"Compared to Bradstreet's more straightforward piety, Dickinson's poem is, in some sense, worldly, but Dickinson has divided experience just as decisively as did Bradstreet or Watts into the mutable and the immutable, the inessential and the deeply significant. . . . her landscape of promise is *here,* as close as a bee is when we can hear the hum."

1987 BARKER, *Lunacy of Light,* pp. 104–05, 201 n. 9
"Dickinson's imaginative garden . . . is a garden that grows by her own lights, a garden of art, of poetry." Relates poem to letter poet wrote to Austin containing it.

"There is no frigate like a book" (1263)

1972 RAO, *Essential Emily Dickinson,* pp. 158–59
General introduction to the poem aimed at "postgraduate students of literature in Indian Universities."

"There's a certain slant of light" (258)

1972 RAO, *Essential Emily Dickinson,* pp. 22–23, 121–22
General introduction to the poem aimed at "postgraduate students of literature in Indian Universities."

1977 AGRAWAL, *Emily Dickinson,* pp. 89–90, 121
"How overwhelmingly is the inner self afflicted by the despairing moments of painful experiences of life is portrayed in [this poem]."

1979 CAMERON, *Lyric Time,* pp. 5, 17, 100–03, 127, 130, 131, 179, 180, 199, 203
The poem is "about correlatives, about how interior transformations that are both invisible and immune to alteration from the outside world are at the same time generated by that world."
Reprinted: Cameron, *"Et in Arcadia,"* pp. 48–50, 51, 69–70, 72, 73

1980 KNIGHTS, "Poetry," p. 239
Comments on poem's diction and its use of silence. "The poem . . . is neither depressed nor self-pitying: it is too austere for that; and because the poet's strength matches the implacability she faces, the 'affliction' can properly be called 'imperial.'"

REISS, "Dickinson's Self-Reliance," p. 29
"Here 'Air' serves as a synecdoche for nature and as the nineteenth century metaphor for heaven. Death and the mood inspired by death are consequences of life, are a result of our own breath of life."

1981 DIEHL, *Romantic Imagination,* pp. 54–55
"Light, the element that bathes Wordsworth's landscapes, casts its shadow on this poem."

1982 MARCUS, *Emily Dickinson,* pp. 31–32, 33, 35
Here "the elevating and the destructive qualities of nature balance

one another." General consideration as one of Dickinson's "philosophical poems of nature."

NIGRO, "Imp of the Perverse," p. 7
Dickinson "uses the language of religion to evoke psychic dread. . . . her conclusion linking the passing of that light to the distance on the look of death, like symbolist imagery, is linguistically indefinite but emotionally precise in its intensification of estrangement."

1984   KAZIN, "Wrecked, Solitary, Here," pp. 165, 174–75
The poem "is in fact an exploration of 'Hurt,' the impact from afar, the shudder of awe in itself. . . . The *us* struck by 'Heavenly Hurt' has been all alone, but this poem of meticulous consciousness shows the 'distance' indeed *between* us and death."

POLLAK, *Dickinson*, pp. 218–21
"Dickinson expresses a passionate desire to reconstitute a natural universe predicated on a stabilizing relationship between the self and God. The poem describes the frustration of that desire, as nature reminds her of herself."

RUDDICK, "'Synaesthesia,'" pp. 69–70
Examination of synaesthetic elements in Dickinson's poetry. This poem's first two stanzas are cited as the poet's "best-known use of complex synaesthesia."

ST. ARMAND, *Dickinson and Her Culture,* pp. 161, 239–40
"The oppressive light of this poem acts as both penetrating spear and murderous blunt instrument; consequently, Dickinson suffers internal scourging, crucifixion, and death, with no immediate hope of resurrection."

1985   RENAUX, "Seasons of Light," pp. 28–29, 48–51
Employs A. J. Zokovskij's "theory of amplification" to analyze the poem; "it is through amplification that we can trace how form and content interact to convey meaning."

1986   ANDERSON, CHARLES, "Modernism," pp. 41–43
In this poem Dickinson "is much closer to T. S. Eliot's *Four Quartets,* written more than 75 years later, than to Emerson's little book entitled *Nature,* published just 25 years before."

HOLDEN, "Landscape Poems," pp. 161–63, 164–65, 167, 171, 172, 173, 174, 176
Examines as a "paradigm of how the achieved poem of landscape"

confronts the difficulty of creating action "in a setting which would seem to be inherently static and without people."

MARSTON, "Metaphorical Language," pp. 113, 114
"This poem suggests that the threat posed by death is for Dickinson an ultimate form of the threat posed by nature. Both nature and death impinge upon consciousness, and loss of mind's supremacy over nature, including the biological self, is what Dickinson fears most."

REGUEIRO ELAM, "Haunting of the Self," pp. 87–88
"The 'passing' of light and poem is . . . double-edged, for 'passage' bespeaks both presence and disappearance, and what the poem witnesses is the 'mark' of its own difference, of its own passage through itself. It traverses its own otherness, and 'seals' itself in the space of its own impossibility."

ROBINSON, J., *Emily Dickinson*, pp. 142–43
". . . it is the *strangeness* of the light in [this poem] which threatens; it is not permanent enough to become familiar, so it threatens as much by going as by coming . . . ."

1987   DAHL, "Dickinson's 'There's a certain slant,'" pp. 37–38
Suggests "a further possible connotative value" for the poem's "'Air'"; it is "also the air of 'the prince of the power of the air' (Eph. 2.2), the devil . . . ."

SEWALL, "Emily Dickinson," pp. 79–81
". . . in this awareness we live more intensely, closer to the divine in our nature. It takes the shock of such awareness—'the look of Death'—to wake us up."

1988   PHILLIPS, *Emily Dickinson*, pp. 153–54
"The imagery of the poem—an annunciation of reality, the solitude of human existence, that all the tropes and icons of earth sustain—is sacramental, but it denies there is any ultimate meaning which earthly eyes and ears can perceive beyond the final word, Death."

1989   GREENWALD, "Dickinson among the Realists," pp. 165–66, 167–68
Suggests classroom approaches.

KNAPP, *Emily Dickinson*, pp. 130–32
"The grimness of Dickinson's vision was instrumental in polarizing her thoughts, increasing her libido, and endowing her with the energy to face her dilemma consciously—through her art—as in [this poem]." Line-by-line examination of poem's images.

LEONARD, D. N. "Certain Slants," pp. 128, 129–30
In this poem "Dickinson's surreal personification, juxtapositions of the concrete and abstract, 'pictureless' imagery, and bold and multiple metaphorical suggestion prove her a literary pioneer no less original than Whitman or Hopkins."

MILLER, C., "Approaches," pp. 223–24, 227–28
The poem's "'internal difference' in 'Meaning' provides a kind of paradigm for what Dickinson intentionally creates: she describes the perimeters of her subject by creating a space of difference or uncertainty inside the closed circle of things we think we understand. She makes us question the adequacy of Meanings."

SHULLENBERGER, "My Class had stood," pp. 99–102
Suggestions for teaching the poem. "The poem offers a solemn yet steady gaze into the haunted house of nature and a precisely calibrated diagnosis of epiphany as pain and of the profound readjustment of the consciousness stunned into being by it."

"There's been a death in the opposite house" (389)

1981 STEINER, "Image Patterns," p. 69
"The outlook on death is so innocent and the imagery so narrowly provincial that it seems most appropriate to relate the pseudo-male mask in this case to Dickinson herself and memories of Amherst deaths."

1982 LEE, "'This World is not Conclusion,'" pp. 224–26
Relates to other Dickinson poems on death. Here "the occasion has been rendered almost parodically from the outside, a comment more upon life than upon its conclusion."

1986 DORESKI, "'Exchange of Territory,'" pp. 57–58, 59, 63
This poem "maps the eventual progress of the sequence [of fascicle 27] by suggesting how a poem can encompass a variety of ways of knowing. In its inclusiveness it forms a catalogue . . . of available perceptions."

MCNEIL, *Emily Dickinson,* pp. 127–28
"The first person speaker is an 'other', not a persona in the sense of a mask of the self so much as an effort to make a mask which will look as if it is hiding the features of someone else."

1988 PARKER, *Unbeliever,* pp. 106–10, 158 n. 30
"Given the pattern of defenses throughout Dickinson's poem, the conversion of emotions into objects, and the castigating satire of the

townspeople who act out the same defenses . . . the choice to speak in a male voice calls for more than ordinary scrutiny."

"There's something quieter than sleep" (45)

1979 BARNES, "Telling It Slant," p. 240
The poem's final stanza "suggests that this poem . . . is metaproverbial as well as metapoetic—that there are personal as well as esthetic motives behind one's 'proneness to periphrasis.'"

"These are the days when birds come back" (130)

1972 RAO, *Essential Emily Dickinson,* pp. 111–13
General introduction to the poem aimed at "postgraduate students of literature in Indian Universities."

1978 DOWNEY, "Antithesis," p. 13
Examines poem's use of the antithesis of "opposite motions."

1979 BUDICK, "Assignable Portion," pp. 1, 2–6, 7, 9, 10, 11, 13, 14–15 nn. 5–6
In this poem Dickinson "treats what she conceives of as the 'fraud' of symbolizing perception" which "can 'cheat' the perceiver into seeing the naturalistic universe as a symbol of Christian resurrection and which thereby distracts the individual from true faith."
Revised and reprinted: Budick, *Emily Dickinson,* pp. 54–60, 61, 65, 66, 67, 168, 171, 173, 187, 191–93, 214, 216

1981 FORD, T., "Indian Summer," pp. 542–50
Examines this poem and Robert Penn Warren's story "Blackberry Winter." In both works the "sudden reversals of nature's seasons become strikingly appropriate metaphors for the deeply disturbing and peculiarly human awareness . . . that those things which we had always regarded as absolute, timeless, changeless, permanently reliable are, in fact, subject to change."

1982 MARCUS, *Emily Dickinson,* pp. 28–29, 30, 31
General consideration as one of "Dickinson's more descriptive philosophical poems of nature."

SALSKA, *Poetry of the Central Consciousness,* pp. 37–38, 58
"What begins as a description of Indian summer is resolved into a dialogue between the sceptical intellect supported by the evidence of the senses and the longing heart which wants to suppress the rational faculty,

to become like a child for the reward of security and religious ecstasy which the union with nature can offer."

Revised and reprinted: Salska, *Walt Whitman and Emily Dickinson,* pp. 24–25, 48–49

1984   HATTENHAUER, "Feminism," p. 56

"Dickinson, unlike the birds in nature, cannot join Eden and innocence. However, neither can she fall into the experience of marriage and motherhood without being forced into the innocence of mind expected of Victorian women."

RUDDICK, " 'Synaesthesia,' " p. 67

Examines poem's final image, "blue and gold mistake," and finds it is not synaesthetic.

1986   MUNK, "Recycling Language," p. 236

". . . subtly transforms the language of orthodoxy." Poet attempts "to redeem religious rhetoric by associating it with early religious rites."

1987   EBERWEIN, "Sacramental Tradition," pp. 67, 74–76

The poem "applies eucharistic language to the natural world as though attempting to find compensation there for her alienation from the church."

1988   MORRIS, T., "Development," pp. 36–37, 38, 39, 40

Examines as part of a cluster of Dickinson poems on Indian summer to illustrate her stylistic development. This poem "does not confront the problem of faith. It poses outside the problem, and we can either appreciate or reject that pose, but not engage it in an argument."

TRIPP, *Mysterious Kingdom,* pp. 96–98, 101–06

"Its deep resonance resounds far beyond one seasonal cycle and thus reaches to the mystery and pathos of the cyclic manifestation of eternal beauty in transient forms. The poem is a subtle investigation of the reality and utility of this world's maya."

WOLFF, *Emily Dickinson,* pp. 307–09

"The poem's poignant beauty demonstrates how ardently we *want* to believe in the reciprocity that Wordsworth had postulated between mankind and nature, and how cruelly nature allows us to deceive ourselves into precisely such expectations."

"These are the nights that beetles love" (1128)

1983   ALLEN, M., *Animals,* pp. 41–42

"To show the explosive reaction resulting from the minute source is not a device for mock heroic humor alone. . . . The beetle that terror-izes the child and draws merriment from men is for her the source of both responses and more."

1984   St. Armand, *Dickinson and Her Culture*, p. 248
"The thunderstorm becomes a lesson in Victorian self-improve-ment . . . and ironically stimulates the imagination." Since "she cannot practice her usual strategy of physiognomy in the dark . . . she turns to the classification of those beetles who love such nights."

1985   Porter, "Searching for the Capital," p. 121
Notes that St. Armand (1984) misreads this poem "about June bugs" as a poem about a thunderstorm.

1988   Phillips, *Emily Dickinson*, pp. 157–58, 169
"The high burlesque does not mock the great Puritan poet's epic, *Paradise Lost* itself, but a lowly pest and the idea of its educative power; the comic effect results from the disparity between the trivial theme, the thunderous beetle, and the lofty style."

"These are the signs to nature's inns" (1077)

1981   Kimpel, *Dickinson as Philosopher*, pp. 216–17
"This poem affirms her view of the place of Nature in her life, which in every respect parallels what a religious faith would attribute to a divine reality, such as God. . . . This also is an important expression of her ambivalent attitude in considering her philosophy of religion . . . ."

"These fevered days—to take them to the forest" (1441)

1981   Kimpel, *Dickinson as Philosopher*, p. 175
Dickinson "understood that water purifies a distraught person even when it is not an element in a religious rite, and it is this spiritual role of water to which she refers in this poem."

"These held their wick above the west" (1390)

1985   Johnson, *Emily Dickinson*, p. 113
"Anything in nature so transient and inexplicable must be ac-knowledged, even when its ability to elude perception create[s] anxiety and disorientation, and effectually breaks any perceiver's 'mathematics' or pattern-making."

415

"These tested our horizon" (886)

1979 ESTES, "Search for Location," pp. 214–15
"Past experiences offer no insight to what waits beyond the horizon. The poet here locates herself in terms of what has happened, what she remembers seeing at a certain 'Latitude,' and not in terms of an external goal that is 'sure—for the Distance' which lies before her."

"They called me to the window, for" (628)

1986 LOVING, *Emily Dickinson*, pp. 57–58
The poem "provides a few clues to her psychic dilemma. . . . Dickinson's persona in this poem longs for the baptismal or life-giving experience."

"They dropped like flakes" (409)

1984 WOLOSKY, *Emily Dickinson*, pp. 37, 38, 45
Here "Dickinson compares the violence of battle . . . to the usual processes of nature. . . . The comparison of battle to snow and wind, far from making the death of soldiers seem more natural, makes nature seem sudden and frightening."
Reprinted in part: Wolosky, "Dickinson's War Poetry," pp. 25–26

1985 COOK, A., *Thresholds*, p. 183
" 'God can summon every face / On his Repealless—List' . . . this well expresses the balance in her doctrine between the Calvinist election ('List') and the ecumenical spirit ('every'), the latter emphasized by the inclusiveness, as well as the exclusiveness, of 'Repealless.' "

" 'They have not chosen me,' he said" (85)

1981 ANDERSON, V., "Disappearance of God," p. 11
"The poem shows a close identity between the speaker and Christ. Their circumstances in this life are markedly similar: each is a victim of rejection, and each is alienated, solitary, 'Broken hearted' because of this rejection."

1983 SHURR, *Marriage*, pp. 56, 191
". . . the 'dishonor' the Sovereign has suffered is unexplained, surely another clue that we as general readers intrude upon a private correspondence not intended for our eyes."

1985   EBERWEIN, *Dickinson*, pp. 13–14, 80, 249
This is "another poem about choices [which] serves as the obverse to 'For every Bird a Nest—.' . . . The speaker of the poem . . . identifies with Jesus in his capacity as rejected lover. She shares in his dishonor. Does she anticipate sharing in his eventual triumph?"

"They leave us with the infinite" (350)

1978   TAYLOR, C., "Kierkegaard," pp. 279–80
"The 'if true' does not change the speaker's certainty to doubt; rather, it shows that she has accepted the possible as a defining characteristic of the relationship between the self and God, and can imaginatively incorporate into faith the arguments of reason . . . ."

"They might not need me, yet they might" (1391)

1981   KIMPEL, *Dickinson as Philosopher*, pp. 105–06
"This expression of her concern for others . . . expresses a way of thinking and of living which indicate her awareness of a type of obligation which the needs of others imposed upon her."

"They put us far apart" (474)

1979   PATTERSON, *Dickinson's Imagery*, pp. 42, 97, 175, 202
The poem, which "describes love's martyrdom," is "so ingeniously worded as to avoid sexual identity."

1988   WOLFF, *Emily Dickinson*, pp. 414–16
". . . there is no real-world component to this love at all. Its nature is defined entirely by the transcendent, and ironically, its 'triumph' cannot be felt by the reader as anything more than a sleight of hand with words."

"They say that 'Time assuages'" (686)

1985   COTTLE, *Language of Literature*, p. 101
A note on the use of the subjunctive.

"They shut me up in prose" (613)

1980   PORTERFIELD, *Feminine Spirituality*, pp. 143–44, 182
"The poem implies that conventional household discipline could circumscribe human experience and reduce it to a prosaic formula. Domestic space could function like a prison."

1982   MOSSBERG, *Emily Dickinson,* pp. 3–4, 6, 17, 107–09, 135, 171, 206
n. 5
"Dickinson draws an analogy between the consequences of trying
to express herself as a little girl in her own father's house and trying to
express her voice in poetry when she is an adult in a world still governed
by a patriarchy telling its women how to behave. In both cases 'they' try
to make her 'shut up.' "

1983   MILLER, C., "How 'Low Feet' Stagger," pp. 140–41, 147, 151
Illustrates effect of poet's use of adjectives as adverbs. Here, in
"They might as wise," it "provides a flavor that is both more essential
and less restrictive than 'wisely' would have."

WALKER, N., "Humor as Identity," pp. 57–58
"The bird 'laughs' at his would-be captors: claiming the same freedom from the varieties of 'Prose' to which she is subject, Dickinson
laughs at both the conventions of language and the images of herself mirrored in the assumptions of those around her."

1986   McNEIL, *Emily Dickinson,* pp. 125–27, 164, 177, 191 n. 4
The poem "is both an account of childhood and of the denial of
adulthood. . . . Dickinson's bird-speaker, not consistently mythologized,
connects freedom with mature song and does not allow that one can exist
without the other."

POLLAK, "Second Act," pp. 163–64
The poem "illustrates the tension between the romantic myth of
childhood freedom and the reality of the Dickinsonian persona's powerlessness."

1988   PHILLIPS, *Emily Dickinson,* pp. 9–10
Suggests that the poem's persona may not be Dickinson and offers
possible sources for the poem in the poet's reading.

"They talk as slow as legends grow" (1697)

1986   McNEIL, *Emily Dickinson,* pp. 63, 85–86
" 'Predestined' and 'portentous' link the empty predictability of
gossip with sacred speech, the implication being that there, too, we all
know what the conclusion is going to be."

1989   OLIVER, *Apocalypse of Green,* pp. 102, 104, 111
"Just as the human author in the poem already knows the plot to
be developed and refrains from revealing it, so also by implication does
God, the author of man's destiny, keep this destiny 'Portentously
untold.' "

"They won't frown always, some sweet day" (874)

1986   DOBSON, " 'Invisible Lady,' " pp. 45, 48
"The poem goes beyond being 'shut up in prose' to embody the essential expressive dilemma of the woman writer—to be silent is to win approval, but to be a silent writer is a deadly contradiction in terms."
Reprinted: Dobson, *Strategies of Reticence*, pp. 63, 68–69

"This chasm, sweet, upon my life" (858)

1979   GILBERT and GUBAR, *Madwoman*, pp. 628–31, 632, 639
The poem "sardonically parodies the saccharine love poetry that ladies were expected to write. . . . The chasm in being that Dickinson perceives turns out . . . to be her own life, and specifically the female body in which she is helplessly (but turbulently) embedded."

1982   MOSSBERG, *Emily Dickinson*, p. 29
"To repair herself . . . would mean 'Death' to 'Him,' a masculine component within her that needs psychic wounds. Because of 'him' she must endure a life of mental pain and divided consciousness."

1986   GILBERT, "American Sexual Poetics," pp. 150–51
Discussion of Dickinson's "rejection of genre," as seen in this poem, in which "Dickinson's speaker enacts precisely the catastrophe . . . that Whitman wards off through contemplation."

"This consciousness that is aware" (822)

1981   DIEHL, *Romantic Imagination*, pp. 134–35
"Ambivalence exists within the possible meanings of the single hound . . . ."

1982   BURBICK, "Irony of Self-Reference," pp. 92–93
Examines pronominal language.

MARCUS, *Emily Dickinson*, p. 78
Although the poem deals with death, "it is at least equally concerned with discovery of personal identity through the suffering that accompanies dying. . . . Neither boastful nor fearful, this poem accepts the necessity of painful testing."

MOSSBERG, *Emily Dickinson*, p. 25
"The extent to which consciousness is traumatized is stressed by the depersonalized references to the self. Consciousness is presented here in emphatically neuter terms: 'It' or 'itself' dominate the poem not only by repetition but by the syntax."

SALSKA, *Poetry of the Central Consciousness,* pp. 68, 97–98, 187
"The 'properties' of consciousness and its 'adequacy' must do as the basis of whatever certain knowledge is accessible to man."
Revised and reprinted: Salska, *Walt Whitman and Emily Dickinson,* pp. 57–58, 85–86, 193

1983   BUDICK, "Temporal Consciousness," pp. 229–30
"In attempting to traverse the 'interval' between this world and the next, consciousness does not succeed in bringing the soul to heaven. Rather it manages to impose on heaven all of the corrupt materialistic conditions of earth."
Revised and reprinted: Budick, *Emily Dickinson,* pp. 144, 176, 203–04

JUHASZ, *Undiscovered Continent,* pp. 161–63
In this poem "death is the object of the great adventure, but the adventure itself is the act of knowing, the business of consciousness."

1984   MARTIN, W., *American Triptych,* pp. 117–18
"In Dickinson's poetic scenario, the prepared heart is modulated into intense existential awareness." Here "consciousness replaces Christ and self-awareness supersedes salvation."

1985   EBERWEIN, *Dickinson,* pp. 82–83, 208
The poem "demonstrates the continuity of Puritan personality traits and a Puritan myth structure in the struggle for immortality."

JOHNSON, *Emily Dickinson,* p. 180
"The poem begins with a statement about 'Consciousness' and ends with one about 'identity'; the poem's major claim is that they are synonymous."

1986   MOREY, "Dickinson-Kant: The First Critique," pp. 60, 64–65
Links with "There is a solitude of space." Both poems "concern consciousness opening up to the unconscious" and "posit the fourth state after death."

REGUEIRO ELAM, "Haunting of the Self," pp. 96–98, 99 n. 7
"The soul at the end of the poem is condemned to be adventure most unto itself, which is to say that it must be subject and object of its experiences, sealed in by its own will to adequacy. The consciousness that is aware of nature and death must ultimately be aware of itself, and this means to be hounded by itself—to see . . . its own abyss."

1987   CULJAK, "Dickinson and Kierkegaard," p. 149–50
"Her characterization of the individual self . . . comes very close

to the Kierkegaardian dialectic. . . . She asserts the necessity of individual isolation and recognizes the process which constitutes selfhood."

1988 STOCKS, *Modern Consciousness*, p. 56

The poem's "four short stanzas are dense with the properties of an existentialist attitude . . . the awareness of death as an abiding presence and a crucial event, the hunt for personal identity in a world that reduces personal identities to 'mortal numeral' or swamps them in superficial social relationships."

WOLFF, *Emily Dickinson*, pp. 466–67

". . . the principal actor is also the principal victim, 'Consciousness.' Death is an ultimate of anguish . . . because it is the moment of supreme seclusion."

1989 HOCKERSMITH, " 'Into Degreeless Noon,' " p. 281

". . . it is her own consciousness that 'hounds' . . . the speaker. She is being tormented by her continual awareness of her own existence in time."

"This dust and its feature" (936)

1988 WOLFF, *Emily Dickinson*, p. 335

Expresses the poet's fear that "the 'self' would be entirely engrossed into some larger, amorphous entity, God or the cloud of saved souls."

"This is a blossom of the brain" (945)

1977 AGRAWAL, *Emily Dickinson*, p. 129

In this poem Dickinson tells us "how the inner self, the soul, is involved in the creation of poetry."

1982 MARCUS, *Emily Dickinson*, pp. 41–42, 43

This poem "may be taken as a deliberate extravaganza or a serious assertion of Emily Dickinson's feelings about art as a religion and her participation in it."

1984 MARTIN, W., *American Triptych*, p. 159

Links with other instances of flower imagery in Dickinson's poems that illuminate "her evolution from passive, dependent femininity to autonomous womanhood."

"This is my letter to the world"

1989 MUNK, "Musicians Wrestle," pp. 12–13
"The poem, as 'Flower of the Soul,' is 'fathered,' as it were, by 'Spirit' in a manner analogous to the conception of Christ, an analogy that ED systains [*sic*] thruout."

"This is my letter to the world" (441)

1982 MARCUS, *Emily Dickinson*, pp. 36–37, 38
General consideration as one of Dickinson's poems on "Poetry, Art, and Imagination."

1983 SHURR, *Marriage*, pp. 45, 101
Considers implications of the poem regarding the audience for whom Dickinson wrote her fascicle poems.

1986 MILLER, C., "'A letter is a joy,'" pp. 31, 34
"The poet's artlessness is patently a pose here. . . . Nonetheless, the metaphor of poet as letter writer aptly characterizes Dickinson's art."
Reprinted: Miller, C., *Emily Dickinson*, pp. 8–9, 15, 179

ROBINSON, J., *Emily Dickinson*, pp. 106–07
"By making her seem national martyr and national monument it entirely falsifies what she was actually doing—irrespective of whether or not she ever posted the so-called letter."

1987 LEDER and ABBOTT, *Language of Exclusion*, pp. 3–5
"The fact that Dickinson placed #441 in a fascicle with [two other Civil War poems] clearly moves us to consider #441 as a Civil War poem, though its treatment is more oblique than the other two."

1988 OAKES, "Welcome and Beware," pp. 188–89, 192, 195
Considers the nature of the poem's speaker and the role assigned to the reader.

1989 RICHWELL, "Poetic Immortality," pp. 25–26
In this poem nature "serves the typical inspirational role the lover fills in Shakespeare's sonnets."

"This me, that walks and works, must die" (1588)

1985 EBERWEIN, *Dickinson*, p. 231
Relates poem's "circumferential imagery" to other poems from 1883. "The poem expresses confidence in the heavenly 'Tracts of Sheen'

into which the child has advanced but frustration at the closing of the door to insight."

1986 LOVING, *Emily Dickinson*, pp. 108, 113
"The poem resembles Frost's 'Fire and Ice' in its negative capability."

"This quiet dust was gentlemen and ladies" (813)

1982 MARCUS, *Emily Dickinson*, p. 65
Relates to other Dickinson poems on society. This poem "attributes a certain superficiality or pointlessness to the cycle of nature."

"This was a Poet—It is that" (448)

1981 ANDERSON, V., "Disappearance of God," p. 15
This is "one of the key poems expressing [Dickinson's] conception of the poet. . . . The poet is an almost godlike observer of the human scene; it is the poet's Christlike suffering that seems to have brought her to such a position."

1982 MARCUS, *Emily Dickinson*, pp. 40–41
General consideration as one of Dickinson's poems on "Poetry, Art, and Imagination."

1984 EBERWEIN, "Doing Without," pp. 207–08
"Rather than producing a new substance, the poet distills the essence from ordinary reality, squeezing eternity out of the temporal. . . . The lasting essence of organic matter must be forced into usefulness by pressure at once destructive and liberating."
Revised and reprinted: Eberwein, *Dickinson*, p. 138

1985 BUDICK, *Emily Dickinson*, pp. 112, 121–23, 127–29, 168
The poem is "the vehicle for a brilliantly sensitive statement about how language, so magnificent and powerful in its triumphs, can, if not managed properly, complete the process of reductive fragmentation that idealist thought initiates."

CARTON, *Rhetoric*, pp. 28–30, 124
"Dickinson's most straightforward tribute to the poet . . . betrays, upon examination, an uneasiness with its own claims and an ambivalent relation between its speaker and the poet figure."

1987 MILLER, C., *Emily Dickinson*, pp. 28–29, 45–46, 59, 73, 76–78, 86, 118–22, 127, 128, 195 n. 36

Examines poetic techniques employed, including repetition, disjunction, and nonrecoverable deletion. "The ambivalence between admiration and ironic disdain finds expression in [the poem's] uneven syntax."

1988 WOLFF, *Emily Dickinson*, pp. 216, 532, 583–84 n. 35

"'Amazing Grace,' is significant in several ways to this poem."

1989 RICHMOND, "Teaching ED," pp. 38–39

Dickinson here "offers both a theory of artistic evolution and that theory executed in the poem divulging it."

WILSON, *Figures of Speech*, pp. 233–34, 236

The poem seems to be an "unproblematic celebration of the transcendent worth of the makers of verse." It could, however, "perfectly well have been an obituary poem for one of her favorite poets, and not a summary of her own program for her work."

"This world is not conclusion" (501)

1981 KIMPEL, *Dickinson as Philosopher*, pp. 228–31, 277

"This poem in every respect is . . . a parallel of St. Augustine's *Confessions*. . . . Basic to this poem is a confident affirmation that there is an order of reality which is other than the world, and is transcendent of it in the sense that it is 'beyond' it."

ORSINI, "Romantic Use of Science," pp. 63–64

"Obviously this poem never proves the narrator's initial thesis, but it does at least spare her religious beliefs, since the evidences of the senses, of science, appear no more conclusive than her lofty spiritual yearnings."

PORTER, *Dickinson*, pp. 106–07

This poem illustrates "the absence of a controlling design."

1982 MARCUS, *Emily Dickinson*, pp. 81–82, 96

The poem "shows a tension between childlike struggles for faith and the too easy faith of conventional believers, and Emily Dickinson's anger, therefore, is directed against her own puzzlement and the double-dealing of religious leaders."

1983   BENVENUTO, "Words within Words," pp. 49–50, 53, 55 n. 7
Suggests instances where examining definitions and etymologies of key words in the poem, as they appear in the dictionary Dickinson used, may shed light on poem's meaning.

1984   BENFEY, *Problem of Others*, pp. 14, 16
This poem "could almost be a gloss" on a passage from Emerson's "Montaigne; or, The Skeptic."

1985   EBERWEIN, *Dickinson*, pp. 227–28
"The hope of immortality finds insufficient supports in human wisdom. Science, philosophy, and theology all prove inadequate to the task with dogmatic pulpit pronouncements the most ludicrously insufficient."

1986   BUELL, *New England Literary Culture*, pp. 133–34
"She is just as aware of the precariousness of doctrinal structures as Emerson, but she feels the problems and possibilities of her position more keenly because she sees these structures both as all-important and as bankrupt."

1988   WOLFF, *Emily Dickinson*, pp. 269–70, 440
Observes "the systematic way [the poem] examines the leakage and finally the loss of faith."

"Those cattle smaller than a bee" (1388)

1983   ALLEN, M., *Animals*, pp. 45–46
"Dickinson's featuring of the disdained and the small not only refreshes the stale subject of nature but revolutionizes a system that places all value in the grandiose. Thus the fly's offense is for her a charmed moment."

1984   WALLACE, *God Be with the Clown*, pp. 25–26
"Dickinson's shocked offense over the flies is comic—they've affronted her by being impolite—and the dimension of her shock and offense is comically exaggerated by the incongruity between the two halves of her metaphor, the relative sizes of cattle and fly."

1988   PHILLIPS, *Emily Dickinson*, pp. 158–59
"Describing 'the Fly,' Dickinson combines the perspective and language of Swift's Gulliver in the land of Brobdingnag with that of a woman who sometimes 'hayed a little for the horse' . . . in the barn and often 'minded' the flies in a fastidious household."

"Those dying then" (1551)

1978 TAYLOR, C., "Kierkegaard," pp. 573–74, 580
"Here, reason self-consciously affirms the need for belief in the act of viewing belief from the perspective of one who has abdicated it."

1979 ESTES, "Search for Location," pp. 216–17
"In the darkness which hides location, life must remain small and closed-in for fear of confronting the unknown."

1982 MARCUS, *Emily Dickinson,* p. 83
This poem, which "takes a pragmatic attitude towards the usefulness of faith, . . . is effective because it dramatizes, largely through its metaphors of amputation and illumination, the strength that comes with convictions, and contrasts it with an insipid lack of dignity."

1984 OLPIN, "Hyperbole: Part II," p. 10
"The meaning of faith is given a special and peculiar emphasis in [this poem] . . . that seems to indicate that a game of hide-and-seek without a rival player is at least better than no game at all."

WALLACE, *God Be with the Clown,* p. 90
"Comedy enables Dickinson to ridicule and affirm religious ideas simultaneously."

1986 LOVING, *Emily Dickinson,* p. 93
"The qualification [of the final two lines] is not an argument for Emersonian self-reliance but one for the *ignis fatuus* of the brooding self, that flickering illusive flame at the end of the tunnel that insists that whatever the character of the soul its destiny is achieved in the present."

1987 BLASING, *American Poetry,* p. 181
"The violent juxtaposition of the metaphoric 'hand' with a surgical term like 'amputated' reduces the metaphoric to the literal and thus disarticulates the whole anthropomorphic myth of God, for a reduction of the metaphoric to the literal is in effect a loss of faith."

"Those not live yet" (1454)

1978 TILMA-DEKKERS, "Immortality," pp. 177–78
". . . our consciousness in its full sense, the awareness of our total existence, though partial in our mortal state, is nevertheless complete in immortality: our existence does, like the disk, not have a beginning and an end . . . ."

1982 MARCUS, *Emily Dickinson,* pp. 89, 90
Relates to other Dickinson poems on death and immortality. This poem "may be Emily Dickinson's strongest single affirmation of immortality."

1983 JUHASZ, *Undiscovered Continent,* pp. 164–67, 185–86 n. 17
The poem articulates the "profound association between consciousness in its complex manifestations , death, and eternity, as elements that must define one another."

1985 EBERWEIN, *Dickinson,* pp. 161, 233, 234
"Rather than terminating one life or separating two, death functions here as the drawbridge above the stream that links two shores on one road, and as a hyphen combining apparently disparate ideas in one concept. Time connects with immortality; it is neither subsumed by it nor eliminated."

1987 COOK, C., "Psychic Development," pp. 133–34
"Death does not stop the conscious mind; it connects it—as a hyphen connects two parts of a word—with the unconscious, the sea. The connection of these two parts of the mind creates the perfect whole that Jung refers to as the total personality . . . ."

"Tho' I get home how late—how late" (207)

1985 ANANTHARAMAN, *Sunset in a Cup,* pp. 111, 112
"The locale is the consciousness of the poet. The persona is imagining how 'transporting the moment' will be . . . when she will reach 'home.'" Considers the idea of "home" in Dickinson's poetry.

"Tho' my destiny be fustian" (163)

1984 BOGUS, "Not So Disparate," p. 44
Relates to Elizabeth Barrett Browning's "Where's Agnes?"

1989 WILSON, *Figures of Speech,* pp. 229–31
The poem is "a greeting-card exercise" and should not be "deciphered" in terms of Dickinson's life.

"Though the great waters sleep" (1599)

1982 MADIGAN, "Mermaids," p. 56
"God did not give man physical existence ('this Abode') in order

to eliminate the Infinite. The 'great Waters' are still there to be explored. The minds of many may be unconscious of the vastness, but for those who are more adventurous the 'Deep' will always prove a temptation."

"Three times we parted, breath and I" (598)

1985 JOHNSON, *Emily Dickinson,* p. 158
Here "the process of death is dramatized within the context of Dickinson's typological sea, here representing the threat of extinction, the disorienting chaos of experience, and finally the eternal 'mystic mooring'. . . ."

1989 DIEHL, "Murderous Poetics," pp. 335–36
In this poem, which "takes a drowning as its ostensible subject, the struggle between death and breath assumes dialectical intimacy."

"Three weeks passed since I had seen her" (1061)

1985 JOHNSON, *Emily Dickinson,* p. 214 n. 6
This "poem stressing perception expresses a fear that it is the living, not the dead, who are 'out of sight,' suggesting that the perceiving consciousness is totally isolated from knowledge."

"Through the dark sod, as education" (392)

1979 GILBERT and GUBAR, *Madwoman,* pp. 645–46
". . . we have to suspect that the festival she is secretly imagining . . . is a female Easter, an apocalyptic day of resurrection on which women would rise from the grave of gender in which Victorian society had buried them alive . . . ."

JOHNSON, *Emily Dickinson,* pp. 177–78, 179
"This wholly joyous vision of quest emphasizes the quester's identity, the purity and exalted spiritual status represented by her 'whiteness.'" Examines the poem's "many familiar symbolic elements."

"Through the strait pass of suffering" (792)

1978 CAMERON, "'Loaded Gun,'" pp. 433–34
"Holding to one's course, and the evenness of rhythm therein im-

plied, might be defined as the inability to feel, the pulse that refuses to quicken, or so Dickinson suggests in [this poem]."

Reprinted: Cameron, *Lyric Time*, p. 84; Bloom, H., *Emily Dickinson*, pp. 122–23

1983 MILLER, C. "How 'Low Feet' Stagger," pp. 140, 141
Examines effect of using adjective as adverb in phrase "Martyrs—even—trod."

SHURR, *Marriage*, pp. 33, 116, 140, 144
The poem "seems as cold and rigorous in its diction as the doctrine it espouses."

1986 MILLER, C., " 'A letter is a joy,' " pp. 33–34
The multiple copies Dickinson made of this poem suggest "that the poet's primary intent in writing the poem was not . . . to point towards any single occasion. . . . The poem expresses a truth Dickinson values and finds useful."
Reprinted: Miller, C., *Emily Dickinson*, pp. 13–14

"Tie the strings to my life, my Lord" (279)

1983 SHURR, *Marriage*, p. 40
The poem "imagines both the lovers in a carriage, riding willingly together toward Judgment. The poem really mirrors not a death wish but another . . . version of their acknowledged oneness, their certain union in heaven, and their secure feelings toward Judgment because of their sacrifice."

1984 BOGUS, "Not So Disparate," p. 41
Suggests source in Elizabeth Barrett Browning's *Aurora Leigh*.

1989 GARBOWSKY, *House without the Door*, pp. 105, 108, 110
The poem may be about "a death to a way of life, rather than an actual death. In agoraphobia, the last stages of withdrawal are complete when the patient is 'housebound, immobilized and restricted to a point where there are few new stimuli to which conditioning may occur.' "

OLIVER, *Apocalypse of Green*, pp. 149–50
"The fact that the sentiments expressed seem somewhat too firmly accepting, too lacking in the doubt and reluctance found in many other Dickinson poems on the subject makes one wonder . . . if she might be trying to convince herself of belief rather than expressing firmly held convictions."

"Till death is narrow loving" (907)

1981   DIEHL, *Romantic Imagination,* pp. 141–43
   "As she echoes Shelley's attack on monogamy which begins 'Narrow / the heart that loves,' Dickinson seems to be responding to her precursor's aim throughout the poem. Death itself becomes the crucial and determining factor in the capacity to love, not the poet's death, but the death of the one she loves."

1983   SHURR, *Marriage,* p. 121
   "Dickinson proposes her own marriage as requiring a greater love than the standard marriage, with its promise of love until death."

1985   DICKENSON, *Emily Dickinson,* pp. 91–92
   "Redemption through the active imitation of Christ . . . is one component of Dickinson's religious belief. It is beautifully embodied in this difficult poem which combines the themes of religion and reclusion."

1989   DIEHL, "Murderous Poetics," pp. 333–34
   "The issue here is both poetic and personal entitlement. . . . it is the complex association of personal identity, allegiance, and poetic integrity that this poem addresses."

"Time feels so vast that were it not" (802)

1979   ESTES, "Search for Location," pp. 211–12
   "By her use of the term 'circumference' . . . Dickinson emphasizes the great difficulty of defining one's location and of discovering order in the surrounding world. Here she posits a bold method to overcome the fearful limitlessness of a circumferential world by establishing herself at its center."

1984   WOLOSKY, *Emily Dickinson,* pp. 130–31
   "Circumference here . . . is situated at the outermost boundary of time and the innermost boundary of eternity. The two are in some sense continuous, although the continuity is as between spheres which remain separate."

1985   EBERWEIN, *Dickinson,* pp. 18, 19, 162, 269, 270
   The poem "presents most directly the advantage of the diminished circle with the awareness it necessarily fosters of amplitude beyond. . . . Credit for preventing circumference from engrossing her finity goes to God, who opens perspectives on infinity to her even within her circuit."

JOHNSON, *Emily Dickinson*, pp. 90–91

". . . because she has learned to estimate, to employ her own system in exploring the vast range of human experience, she finds that the temporal dimension is itself so magnificently complex that it could 'engross' all her time and talents, her very being."

1986 NEW, "Difficult Writing," pp. 17–18

"What Dickinson probes is precisely the idol-making power of the mind, its tendency to formally fix, or compass, time within the parameters of its own limitations."

" 'Tis little I could care for pearls" (466)

1980 JOHNSON, " 'Pearl of Great Price,' " pp. 208–09, 215 n. 12

The poem's subject is not death but "ecstatic life in poetry." The speaker's "joy is such that she hyperbolically claims to care no longer for pearls, her sense that she has mastered human experience ('the ample sea') bringing her to a position of absolute wealth and power."

Revised and reprinted: Johnson, *Emily Dickinson*, pp. 132–33, 209–10 n. 19

1985 SALSKA, *Walt Whitman and Emily Dickinson*, p. 156

"The images employed to illustrate the rule do not lead to its gradual inference; . . . the poem leaves the reader with the impression of the speaker groping for some final clinching image or formula and failing to find it."

" 'Tis not that dying hurts us so" (335)

1981 STEINER, "Image Patterns," p. 67

"The voice pronouncing 'We are the birds that stay' sounds resigned here but it carries the potential of protest . . . ."

1984 STAUB, "Dickinson Diagnosis," pp. 43–44

"In accordance with the consolation literature of her day, Dickinson softens the terrors of dying and death. . . . Dickinson's analogy of the bird's flight 'home' aligns comfortably with the sentimental notion of a slow journey towards salvation."

" 'Tis one by one the Father counts" (545)

1985 JOHNSON, *Emily Dickinson*, pp. 92–93, 204 n. 16

In this poem Dickinson "envisions human beings as 'cypherers' groping through darkness toward certain answers, and God as a kind of benign, fair-minded schoolmaster."

1986 STONUM, "Calculated Sublime," pp. 124–25
"The poem insists upon the difference between mathematical skill and the patriarch who teaches it, that is, between the rules of mathematics and of the father."

1988 STOCKS, *Modern Consciousness*, pp. 82–83
"Although God uses the methods of the prevailing socio-economic order—of the counting, statistical Benthamite society—He nevertheless leaves some open spaces, cypherless tracts amidst the counting, . . . for the imagination to enter."

" 'Tis opposites entice" (355)

1980 HOMANS, *Women Writers*, pp. 180–81
The poem "considers the satanic deception . . . that whatever the believer lacks must be the good. Opposites may entice but it is because they are constructed to do so; the valuation conferred by lack is a distortion."
Reprinted: Homans, "Emily Dickinson," pp. 424–25; Homans, "Dickinson and Poetic Identity," pp. 142–43

1982 DITTA, "Jewel and Amethyst," pp. 30, 31–37
The poem "is at once a statement about poetic method and a demonstration of it. But more than this, as a statement the poem advances a philosophical doctrine in which method in its broadest sense becomes identical with meaning, and acquires both metaphysical and esthetic value."

1983 SHURR, *Marriage*, pp. 88, 104
The final quatrain suggests that Wadsworth's "first love would be assumed to be God; that she would move in to substitute for God as the object of his love; and that their separation increases his love."

" 'Tis seasons since the dimpled war" (1529)

1983 HOMANS, " 'Oh, Vision,' " pp. 123–24
"In addition to the characteristic common to this kind of poem of a violent stalemate leading to stasis, this poem shares with 'Like Eyes that looked on Wastes—' an insufficiency of terms, owing to, or causing, the identity between the protagonists."

" 'Tis so appalling, it exhilarates" (281)

1978   TAYLOR, C., "Kierkegaard," pp. 577–78
"Fully conscious of the terrible consequences of faith, she nevertheless delights in its absurd paradox and uses reason to explicate the welcome horror."

1979   CAMERON, *Lyric Time*, pp. 15, 98–100, 103, 131
"Since the task of Dickinson's poem is to distinguish between process and conclusion, intimation and knowledge, the dread of terror and its safe arrival, it rests its case on the implicit assertion that you cannot top or bottom a superlative. The content of the superlative thus matters very little . . . ."
Reprinted: Cameron, "*Et in Arcadia*," pp. 47–48, 51, 73

1982   SALSKA, *Poetry of the Central Consciousness*, pp. 63–64
"Terror's ghastly freedom comes not so much from its 'objective' strength as from the fact that the speaker's intellectual initiative stops: the mind can seize no fact 'to grapple' with and is overcome."
Revised and reprinted: Salska, *Walt Whitman and Emily Dickinson*, pp. 53–54

1985   BUDICK, *Emily Dickinson*, pp. 158, 159
The poem's narrator discovers that "mental solipsism is no antidote for the dangers and tensions of mortality."

JOHNSON, *Emily Dickinson*, pp. 154–55, 214 n. 19
"The speaker is one whose consciousness has fully accepted the reality of death, and the poem describes both her appalled reaction and the more permanent reaction of exhilaration. . . . No longer immured within a dream-state, she discovers the liberating effect of death upon her imagination."

1987   LEONARD, D., " 'Chastisement of Beauty,' " pp. 250–51
"Prayer, suspense, torment, dying, a ghost, and 'Wo' [*sic*]—none of these things is the true subject of the poem; they are metaphors for sublime emotions evoked by the contemplation of death."
Reprinted: *University of Dayton Review*, pp. 41–42

1988   WOLFF, *Emily Dickinson*, pp. 223–24
"This progression of actions whereby we are encouraged to 'look' at things that cannot be seen compels a reader to understand that for Dickinson, eyesight or vision . . . is that power by which individuals impose order on human experience and thereby assert authority over it."

1989   GARBOWSKY, *House without the Door,* pp. 107–08, 111
"... the ordeal is recorded in the present tense, presumably because it is an ongoing experience with still more to come." Relates to characteristics of agoraphobia.

" 'Tis so much joy! 'Tis so much joy" (172)

1982   MOSSBERG, *Emily Dickinson,* pp. 167–69
In this poem "Dickinson poses the dangers of abandoning the security of conventional behavior for a higher goal, yet the nature of her bold venture remains paradoxically unnamed. Dickinson will risk all, but she cannot tell what for."

1988   WOLFF, *Emily Dickinson,* pp. 334–35
"Ironically, the ultimate danger is not that Heaven might *fail* to exist, but that it might *prove* to exist."

1989   OLIVER, *Apocalypse of Green,* pp. 188–89
"Failure will bring nothing stronger than defeat; nothing worse than that which has been anticipated can happen. On the other hand, winning would yield 'Heaven,' which . . . might be almost too overpowering."

" 'Tis sunrise, little maid. Hast thou" (908)

1979   GILBERT and GUBAR, *Madwoman,* pp. 623, 628, 629
"Here the poet . . . speaks not as the vulnerable victim she usually pretends to be but, ironically, as the murderous madwoman whom she ordinarily fears. Her tone is sepulchrally 'kind,' as if to parody the sinister and patronizing benevolence with which Victorian little maids were addressed by well-intentioned relatives and clergymen."

1987   BARKER, *Lunacy of Light,* p. 88
"Although perhaps a parody of the graveyard verse that filled gift books and magazines of the mid-nineteenth century, [this poem] may also suggest Dickinson's painful awareness that her culture provided no actual place for little maidens with big minds, thereby actually encouraging them, in a sense, to die."

" 'Tis true they shut me in the cold" (538)

1982   MOSSBERG, *Emily Dickinson,* p. 153
"The daughter goes so far as to assume, first, that God will punish her parents for their treatment of her . . . and, second, that it is through

her intervention—like that of the Son himself—that they will be forgiven."

1986   OBERHAUS, " 'Engine against th' Almightie,' " p. 164
"The prayer follows the three-fold Ignatian meditation form favored by the seventeenth-century poets, the first stanza comprising the composition of place with the speaker evoking a kind of crucifixion, the second, an appeal to the understanding, and the third, an affective appeal to the will."

1989   OLIVER, *Apocalypse of Green*, pp. 151–52, 175
"This simple enough poem explains that the differences between life and death are too great for the living to comprehend their unintentional harm, and since she has forgiven them, she hopes God will also forgive. If not, she respectfully declines His forgiveness of her." Notes biblical echoes.

"Title divine is mine" (1072)

1976   SHANDS, "Malinowski's Mirror," pp. 325–26
"The intricate play in the figures of speech in this poem may be especially noteworthy in relation to others having the same kind of implication. . . . In her imagination, Miss Dickinson equates the status of being a bride with that of being bridalled . . . ."

1987   CAMERON, " 'Loaded Gun,' " pp. 434–35
"Between the nothing that is the self and the nothing to which the self gets reduced when it capitulates to another, we see our options clearly. . . . Yet options exist because we must take them. We cannot, as Sartre points out, not choose. This recognition is the moment the poem records."
Revised and reprinted: Cameron, *Lyric Time*, pp. 85–87; Bloom, H., *Emily Dickinson*, pp. 124–26

1980   PORTERFIELD, *Feminine Spirituality*, pp. 136–37
"The royal life she celebrates offered her the consummation of her imagination but required the bridle of religious discipline and the shroud of living out the experience of her own death."

1981   KHAN, "Poetry of Ecstasy," pp. 26–28
"The theme of the poem seems to be a situation of Tantalus—a paradoxical ecstasy of despair—the despairing distance separating the ideal or desire from its fulfillment."
Revised and reprinted: Khan, *Emily Dickinson's Poetry*, pp. 52–54

PORTER, *Dickinson,* pp. 167, 195, 206–08, 283

"It is a model of evasion, of language crafted to carry emotion without verifiable reference. . . . Wifehood, in fact, is diminished in each comparison and by the tone of condescension. Confused, the poem claims total knowledge but in its core has no knowledge at all, only hysteria." Relates to other "wife and bride poems" of Dickinson.

1982   MARCUS, *Emily Dickinson,* pp. 9, 60, 62

This poem "deals primarily with the fantasy of a spiritual marriage to a man from whom the speaker is physically separated. . . . she seems quite aware that . . . the whole thing is a bitter delusion." Relates to other Dickinson poems on marriage.

MOSSBERG, *Emily Dickinson,* pp. 186–87

"Divinity, wife, royalty she is not; but her steadfast devotion to her muse confers on her 'Acute Degree'—a status won by pain. It is in contrasting her life to other women that Dickinson is most wistfully, savagely witty."

1983   GILBERT, "Wayward Nun," p. 29

In this "poem that is both searingly sincere and a triumph of irony, Dickinson describes the way she herself has been transformed through the sufferings of love into a paradoxical being, an *Empress* of *Calvary,* a Queen of Pain. . . . Surely this poem's central image is almost the apotheosis of anguish converted into energy . . . ."

JUHASZ, *Undiscovered Continent,* pp. 110–14, 117

"This is what the poem is about: her sense of marriage, union, love. Her sense of victory. Her feeling. . . . this sense of herself as both undiminished by love and as experiencing a love that will not end . . . is created by figurative language and stands in direct contrast to her knowledge of loves and marriages in the everyday world."

SHURR, *Marriage,* pp. 26, 133, 138–39

"The poem is a definition of the particular kind of marriage Dickinson experienced, and several of the themes she established elsewhere regarding that day come together here . . . ." Relates to other "wife" and "bride" poems.

1984   CHERRY, "Sexuality and Tension," pp. 16–17

". . . both alternatives give the woman someone else's name. She is unable to appropriate language for her own purposes."

KELLER, L., and MILLER, "Rewards of Indirection," pp. 545–46

The poem illustrates the way in which Dickinson's "riddle-like descriptions and her reliance on nondeclarative rhetorical patterns resemble the protective strategies some twentieth-century linguists consider typical of women's speech."

MARDER, *Exiles at Home*, p. 118
"There is little evidence that Wadsworth, a stable family man, ever encouraged her, yet she imagines herself suffering the same fate as other women leading conjugal lives."

MARTIN, W., *American Triptych*, pp. 103–04
"This is a love poem, but it is also an announcement of her power—her capacity to experience intense emotions and to survive their annihilating potential. . . . She is not ruled by a master—she reigns over herself."

POLLAK, *Dickinson*, pp. 88–89, 158, 165, 174–77
"One of its themes is that to be both married and unmarried sunders body and spirit, and that the speaker's words are designed to reunite them."

1985 CARTON, *Rhetoric*, pp. 85–87, 88, 89, 99, 123
The poem "demonstrates the way in which the sign, freighted with natural and material associations, blocks or crushes the ideal that it seeks to contact and redeem."

1986 BENNETT, *Loaded Gun*, pp. 73–74, 77–78, 80, 81, 82, 91
Read "within the context of other poems Dickinson wrote on the marriage theme prior to 1862 . . . it is clear that Dickinson meant 'Title divine' to be about her mature identity as woman . . . ."

DOBSON, " 'Invisible Lady,' " pp. 49, 52–53, 54 n. 14
"This poem appears, on one level at least, to reflect Dickinson's decision to 'marry' her art and achieve the divine identity of poet."
Reprinted: Dobson, *Strategies of Reticence*, pp. 71, 75–76, 146 n. 11

JONES, " 'Royal Seal,' " pp. 41, 45–46
"Although the poem ends tentatively, . . . the bold assertion of the opening line continues dominant, declaring that a suffering akin to that of Christ has bestowed upon her a 'divine' rank."

MCNEIL, *Emily Dickinson*, pp. 24, 55, 87–88
The poem "deals with speech as it is influenced by gender."

1987 COOPER, M., "Androgynous Temper," pp. 143–44, 145
"This poem is a good example of self-imaging in the realm of traditional womanhood."

1987 SMITH, M., "'To Fill a Gap,'" pp. 15–18
"Considering the kind of copies Dickinson sent to each of them, [this poem] is more likely to be about Dickinson's love for Sue than for Bowles."

1988 BEPPU, "'O, rare for Emily,'" pp. 182–85, 186
Compares variant versions. The variations are "significant" when considering the poem's relationship to Shakespeare's *Antony and Cleopatra*.

WOLFF, *Emily Dickinson*, pp. 200, 396–97
"Ironically, this poem does not employ the Voice of the 'Wife'; instead . . . it trades upon the attitudes and tonalities of the saint, who is willing to renounce the rewards of this world."

"To be alive is power" (677)

1981 KIMPEL, *Dickinson as Philosopher*, pp. 83–84
"This poem not only ventures the comparison of one aspect of human nature with the nature of God, . . . it also ventures to credit a human being with a capacity to will which is not contingent upon God's grace."

1984 LEONARD, D. N., "Dickinson's Religion," pp. 341–42
In this poem Dickinson "stresses the paradoxical essence of the choosing being: God-like, yet finite, that person actually creates himself or herself. This is Dickinson at her most triumphant."

MARTIN, W. *American Triptych*, pp. 136–37
"This poem contains the kernel of Dickinson's cosmology: life as an end in itself is inherently powerful, while life dedicated to control can create the illusion of omnipotence but ultimately exposes the limitations of human will."

"To be forgot by thee" (1560)

1983 SHURR, *Marriage*, p. 166
"The intention behind the poem seems to be to hold firmly in place the reasons for the beloved never to forget her, even though they now stand on different sides of the experience of death."

"To die takes just a little while" (255)

1987   BARKER, *Lunacy of Light*, p. 63
Relates to other poems in which Dickinson denigrates the sun's capabilities.

"To die without the dying" (1017)

1981   LEONARD, J., "Poems of Definition," pp. 20–21
Here "the omission of the defined term helps to strip away its religiously connotative effect and allows the paradox to be examined in its essential form, as a material phenomenon rather than a religious dogma."

1986   ANDERSON, P., "Bride of the White Election," pp. 6–7
"The essential paradox of Christianity is summed up tersely in the first two lines, while the poet's reaction in the last two shows a growing understanding of what Christian maturity means—death to self."

ROBINSON, J., *Emily Dickinson*, pp. 100–01
Here the poet "is at her most extreme, saying that we need to ignore all the contingencies which make our experience—of which the physical fact of dying is one—as if there were a kind of pure life form on which mere body-life obtruded."

"To fight aloud is very brave" (126)

1972   RAO, *Essential Emily Dickinson*, pp. 74, 110–11
General introduction to the poem aimed at "postgraduate students of literature in Indian Universities." Paraphrase.

1979   DAHL, "Dickinson on Tennyson," pp. 94–99
"Not to read 'To fight aloud' against the background of 'The Charge of the Light Brigade' is to miss much of its meaning and subtle art."

1984   WOLOSKY, *Emily Dickinson*, pp. 55–56
"Dickinson sees her inward strife as like the strife of objective battlefields. Her imagination makes her own world in the image of the world of war."

"To fill a gap" (546)

1980   McCLAVE, "Missing All," pp. 3–4
"'Air' is a particularly apt metaphor for the dilemma that the poet suggests because it remains outside any matter of causality, being literally and figuratively unaccountable."

1983   SHURR, *Marriage,* p. 85
"By the exact contours of the gap in her life she is always conscious of precisely what is missing. The absence of the beloved is the only form of his conscious presence in her life."

1986   McNEIL, *Emily Dickinson,* pp. 169, 179
"The poem vehemently rejects sublimation. Desire requires its original object, that which incited it; desire is not transferable."

1987   BLASING, *American Poetry,* pp. 177–78
". . . if we regard the poem as establishing the distinction between gaps or abysses and the things capable of filling them . . . we will see that the very idea of a gap is generated by the poem itself. Such a poem invites readings but rules out any authoritative reading."

"To hang our head ostensibly" (105)

1983   MILLER, C., "How 'Low Feet' Stagger," p. 143
Although here "we cannot tell the sex of either the 'You' or of the plural I, the poem . . . concentrates collective power in an otherwise weak or subordinate singular and contrasts that figure with some person (or, 'You' plural, persons) of authority."

1989   GALPERIN, "Posthumanist Approach," p. 114
Examines the "feminist trajectory in Dickinson" through teaching a specific sequence of poems, including this one.

"To hear an oriole sing" (526)

1972   RAO, *Essential Emily Dickinson,* pp. 19, 142–44
General introduction to the poem aimed at "postgraduate students of literature in Indian Universities."

1980   DUNCAN, "Joining Together," pp. 117–18
"Epistemologically . . . Dickinson is a practicing idealist, and she knows it, as this well-known poem says stanza after stanza."

1981 KIMPEL, *Dickinson as Philosopher,* pp. 64–66
The poem "states a view which rejects realistic theories of knowledge that maintain properties of realities external to experience are the principal determinant of experience."

1984 BENFEY, *Problem of Others,* pp. 20–23, 90, 94
The poet's subject here is "whether what we hear will be *singing,* whether we have ears to hear. It may be a common thing if we are equal to it . . . ; otherwise only the gods will hear it."

1988 OAKES, "Welcome and Beware," pp. 186–88, 189
Examines "the disparity between speaker and reader" that Dickinson emphasizes in this poem.

1989 GUTHRIE, "Near Rhymes," p. 75
Considers effect of poem's use of near rhyme.

TRIPP, "Test for Transcendentalism," p. 5
Compares Dickinson's and Thoreau's views of birds and their singing, both "unquestionably transcendental." "Although each may investigate an idea differently, a common pattern of insight remains, as here in the necessary subjectivity of spiritual rapport."

"To her derided home" (1586)

1986 McNEIL, *Emily Dickinson,* pp. 9, 131–32
"Jesus offers joy, but to whom? Dickinson's answer is one of the most condensed in her poetry, perhaps because she is making herself consider the possibility of never having joy and knowledge together."

"To his simplicity" (1352)

1981 KIMPEL, *Dickinson as Philosopher,* pp. 107–09
"This poem interprets moral duty as unconditioned, just as Kant interprets it. It is unconditioned in the sense that no consideration other than fulfilling requirements imposed by one's duty is morally worthy of approval."

"To interrupt his yellow plan" (591)

1986 ROBINSON, J., *Emily Dickinson,* p. 76
Compares with "It's easy to invent a life." "There is the same self-

absorption with dignity and regulation, yet all the while in this implacable scheme there are human beings, tiny, explosively alive."

"To know just how he suffered would be dear" (622)

1983   JUHASZ, *Undiscovered Continent,* pp. 141–43, 145
"At every point the quest for information is foiled: what remains is speculation. Thus speculation itself persists as the best form of knowledge for this situation: at any rate, the only one we have."

1985   EBERWEIN, *Dickinson,* p. 206
"The question in this case is not one of election. . . . Her concern is much more for the emotional implications of leave-taking from the circuit world. She wants to know the strength of its appeal, evidently hoping for continuing evidence of human love right to the point of death."

"To learn the transport by the pain" (167)

1979   O'HARA, " 'Designated Light,' " pp. 190–92
"This poem is an interpretation of the sublime experience in the Romantic tradition."

1981   DIEHL, *Romantic Imagination,* pp. 101–02
"Dickinson proclaims that anguish is fundamental to the sublime, patient 'laureates'—the poets of the dead. Their sanctified voices pass, inaudible, beyond the poets of earth . . . ."

STEINER, "Image Patterns," p. 68
". . . centers on the contrastive images of transport . . . and pain. . . . The assertive voice derives its power from its change of perspective, from viewing pain as agony to viewing it as triumph."

1989   PARSONS, "Refined Ingenuities," pp. 14–15
"The concluding stanza swiftly reverses the direction of the poem and warns us away from a serene assenting to this strange theological economy of suffering and music."

"To lose one's faith, surpass" (377)

1985   SALSKA, *Walt Whitman and Emily Dickinson,* pp. 152–53
"Faith imaged as 'Estate,' belief as a title deed, and its loss as the condition of 'Beggary' remain legal abstractions which fail to capture the immediate quality of experience, the personal sense of loss."

"To lose thee, sweeter than to gain" (1754)

1989 FULTON, "Moment of Brocade," pp. 26–27
"The sandy ocean floor is Other to the ocean's dominant One. Its position, like woman's, is that of 'sterile perquisite' or unfruitful privilege. Yet without such a hidden pedestal the sea's visible aspect could not exist."

"To make a prairie it takes a clover and one bee" (1755)

1980 JUHASZ, "'To make a prairie,'" pp. 24–25
"The mind's idea of a given object creates it, makes it, insofar as, through the act of perception, mind provides object with meaning. And, since the mind can also think of an object that is unperceived, in that sense it creates the object before perception."
Revised and reprinted: Juhasz, *Undiscovered Continent*, pp. 49–50, 51

1981 PADDOCK, "Metaphor as Reason," pp. 70–71
The poem "constitutes a relatively precise statement of Dickinson's poetic methods, wherein silences replace statements."

1985 BUDICK, *Emily Dickinson*, pp. 178–80, 181–82
"The philosophical system that informs the symbolic logic of [this poem] . . . is perhaps most usefully thought of as material-idealism, the coexistence of reality's constituent phases in total equality of status and in absolute separateness."

"To make one's toilette after death" (485)

1983 SHURR, *Marriage*, pp. 17–18, 87, 190
"The 'death' of the beloved, in the first stanza, would be 'easier' to bear than the moral and religious imperatives, the 'Decalogues,' that have separated them from physical contact, from the eyes which can no longer fondle her bodice."

"To make routine a stimulus" (1196)

1985 JOHNSON, *Emily Dickinson*, p. 169
"The daily routine of existential life . . . can be transformed into a continual 'stimulus' when viewed within the context of death; only within the tormented human consciousness does the perceiver have the power to grow, to 'repair.'"

"To mend each tattered faith" (1442)

1987 LEDER and ABBOTT, *Language of Exclusion,* p. 161
". . . she is able to achieve faith in the moral correctness of her controversial career when the agent of redemption is conceived as female, in this case a simple seamstress."

"To my quick ears the leaves conferred" (891)

1984 BENFEY, *Problem of Others,* pp. 62, 100
"To animate leaves and the walls of caves is . . . to turn the world of things into a world of spies. . . . What the speaker longs for is not privacy taken as secrecy so much as invisibility."

1985 JOHNSON, *Emily Dickinson,* p. 40
"In this poem the speaker attempts to escape some outer, hostile perception—an extreme example of poetic perception externalized through placing the speaker (with maximum discomfort) into the natural landscape."

"To my small hearth his fire came" (638)

1983 JUHASZ, *Undiscovered Continent,* pp. 108–09, 118, 119
The poem shows, "by calling attention to the artifice of its own imagery, how the experience of delight, initiated by love explicitly sexual, creates its own timeless brand of time."

1985 EBERWEIN, *Dickinson,* p. 183
Relates to other poems in the fascicle, which together supply "evidence for the poet's having crossed circumference with God's help."

"To one denied to drink" (490)

1980 MURPHY, "Definition by Antithesis," p. 23
This poem, which illustrates development in Dickinson's use of "definition by antithesis," is "a bitter and scornful rejection of the Calvinist God and his mode of dealing with the human race."

1987 MILLER, C., *Emily Dickinson,* pp. 55–56
"Why, she pointedly wonders, beyond sadistic enjoyment of another's misery, give her knowledge of a heaven, or perfection, or joy she could otherwise merely abstractly 'surmise'? In all these questions, the primary power of the speaker lies in the freedom to ask them."

"To own the art within the soul" (855)

1983 DIEHL, "'Ransom,'" pp. 172–73
"Dickinson's possessive pronoun converts the terms of her deprivation into a potential resource whose hidden reserves will never fail because they lie buried deep within."
Reprinted: Bloom, H., *American Women Poets*, pp. 37–38

"To pile like thunder to its close" (1247)

1981 DIEHL, *Romantic Imagination*, pp. 78–79, 126–27
". . . having equated love and poetry with God, she asserts that they require the same complete sacrifice. As one cannot see God and live, one cannot experience the equal power of love or poetry and expect to survive."

1983 HOMANS, "'Oh, Vision,'" p. 125
"The poem leaves us with the paradoxical definition of poetry as post-linguistic . . . and of love as post-experiential. The moment at which language becomes poetry is precisely the moment when we cease to be able to understand it . . . ."

1986 JUHASZ, "Writing Doubly," pp. 8, 13–14
"Central to the poem's vision, and structure, is the attempt to sustain a both/and ontology. . . . even as the poem's definition of poetry turns out to be a definition of love as well . . . so the poem continues on to explain how this very coevality is the essence of the sacred."

1987 MILLER, C., *Emily Dickinson*, pp. 52–53, 69–70, 71, 85, 86–87, 97, 98, 99–100, 101, 126–30
"Dickinson articulates what is almost an Emersonian view of the human relation to God in this poem: through the most profound human actions (writing poetry, loving) one unites with the divine Oversoul, and the poet reaches farthest toward the upper range of human power."

1988 WOLFF, *Emily Dickinson*, pp. 475–76
"Elsewhere in Dickinson's poetry this process of life which leads inevitably and inexorably toward death is viewed pejoratively as *God's* experiment; in this poem, however, it seems to be *our* experiment. . . . As the pod inheres in the flower, so death inheres in life."

1989 MILLER, C., "Approaches," p. 226
Considers way in which nonrecoverable deletion creates ambiguity in poem's penultimate line.

"To put this world down, like a bundle"

MILLER, C., "Dickinson's Language," pp. 80–81
Comments on questions raised by poem's uninflected verbs.

RICHWELL, "Poetic Immortality," pp. 4, 6, 29–30
"Because she uses the conventional vocabulary of womanly fulfilment as a kind of private symbolism in which to imagine recognition as a writer, Dickinson's affirmations of womanhood and her statements about poetic immortality are one and the same."

"To put this world down, like a bundle" (527)

1989   LOUIS, "Dickinson's 'To put this world down,'" pp. 32–33
"Dickinson is the poet of forced renunciation. One particularly brilliant analysis of renunciation as a compromised Christian ideal appears in [this poem]."

"To tell the beauty would decrease" (1700)

1983   MATTHEWS, "Importance of Silence," p. 16
"Tho the poet's intellectual faculties struggle for the word to denote, to state explicitly that something, they fail. Still, the recompense for this failure is the rapture of *feeling* rather than *explaining* the spell. Poetry, then, tries not to explain, but to recreate that spell."

1984   WOLOSKY, *Emily Dickinson,* pp. 166–67
"As in Augustine, the outward word signifies an inward experience. And the inward experience is in greater proximity with, and partakes in, the world of silent truth . . . ."

1987   BLASING, *American Poetry,* p. 177
"'It' in line 4 means both the sea and the word *sea:* as the word *sea* is to the actual, 'syllable-less' sea, the sea itself is to an invisible, eternal sea."

"To the stanch dust" (1402)

1983   SHURR, *Marriage,* pp. 186–87
"The poem describes a secret burial. The 'We' of the love poems are the agents of the affair. . . . The baby has become a harmonious part of nature; its secret will be kept."

"To try to speak and miss the way" (1617)

1982 MOSSBERG, *Emily Dickinson,* p. 27
"At fifty-four years old, Dickinson is still describing the problem of trying to express herself (as a man); she feels unable to because her soul is a 'Mutineer' who refuses to be subjugated. The compromise that the self makes is that it then tries, instead of 'speaking,' to conceal its problems."

"To venerate the simple days" (57)

1978 FRANKLIN, "Three Additional," pp. 114–15
Describes manuscript that contains second stanza in Dickinson's handwriting.

" 'Tomorrow'—whose location" (1367)

1981 KIMPEL, *Dickinson as Philosopher,* pp. 113–14
"She is convinced that a mark of moral maturity is an intelligence to acknowledge that there is no dodge or shirking of responsibilities."

"Tried always and condemned by thee" (1559)

1983 SHURR, *Marriage,* pp. 165–66
". . . what possible human situation could fit the allegorical scene? . . . It is possible that here the 'thee' is the divine judge, and the 'reprieve' she asks for is excuse from his condemnation of her adulterous wishes."

"Triumph may be of several kinds" (455)

1980 LAIR, "Fracture of Grammar," pp. 163–64
"The subjunctive undercuts the ringing assurance of the Calvinistic sermons Miss Dickinson had heard and reveals the poet's timorousness in the face of so awesome a metaphysical spectrum as is evoked by talk of death, or truth, of temptation, and of final judgment. The grammar conveys the hesitation."

1982 MOSSBERG, *Emily Dickinson,* p. 183
"Dickinson associates the 'Rack' with the pain that renunciation brings. At the same time, of course, she is making herself a martyr in the same way that Christ does, and in her poetry she intimates that she, too,

will be acquitted, precisely for her refusal to accept the 'temptation' of a normal life."

1983 SHURR, *Marriage,* pp. 31, 99–100
The poem describes, "in ascending order, different kinds of 'Triumph'; [it] concludes with a 'Severer Triumph' which one experiences only with an inner sense of moral righteousness."

1989 OLIVER, *Apocalypse of Green,* pp. 66, 93 n. 14
The poem's final two lines "qualify significantly the power of death and affirm the human ability to overcome death by introducing the theme of Faith and Judgment."

"Trust in the unexpected" (555)

1985 SMITH, B. J., "'Vicinity to Laws,'" p. 50
Examines way in which poem's legal language works.

"Trusty as the stars" (1369)

1988 STOCKS, *Modern Consciousness,* pp. 83–84, 117
"Even if the celestial mechanics are all of heaven we know, at least their mathematical certainties are the source and guarantee of the life-sustaining certainties and stabilities of nature."

"'Twas a long parting, but the time" (625)

1983 HOMANS, "'Oh, Vision,'" p. 128
"Death is not a simple confirmation of dualism, a separation of the limitless spirit from the limiting flesh." The poem argues "against the notion of an antithesis between body and soul. The pure gaze . . . images a language where signifier and signified are becoming one."

SHURR, *Marriage,* pp. 98–99, 133
"Dickinson here triumphantly declares that [she and her beloved] can have their love and a successful Judgment before God as well."

1988 WOLFF, *Emily Dickinson,* pp. 379–80
". . . what ought by tradition to be the Judgment Day becomes instead a festive marriage ceremony . . . and the relationship between the woman and man not only takes precedence over the Lord's activities, but also imposes structure upon eternity."

" 'Twas fighting for his life he was" (1188)

1984 WOLOSKY, *Emily Dickinson,* p. 40
"The subject of this poem is clearly an internal experience, of which battle remains figurative. But the sense of inner crisis and, not least, of violence seems not only expressed through, but modeled on, exterior combat."

" 'Twas here my summer paused" (1756)

1981 PORTER, *Dickinson,* pp. 200–01, 229, 245
"Bride here means to know despair fully, to marry fate, and thereafter to be inseparable from it. It is to marry loss and absence. The poem's crushing weight of desolation is carried in only thirty-five words." Relates to other Dickinson poems employing wife and bride images.

" 'Twas just this time last year I died" (445)

1981 STEINER, "Image Patterns," p. 70
". . . the girl is presented as dead and remembering her death which coincided with harvest time, i.e., was embedded into nature. Thus, nature imagery constitutes a substantial part of the poem's imagery, together with images taken from the customs of the seasons and the family circle."

1983 SHURR, *Marriage,* p. 26
"The expression of the first line may seem odd for a marriage poem, but in a very real sense . . . the marriage was a death to earthly enjoyment, with the only hope of fulfillment in heaven."

1988 PHILLIPS, *Emily Dickinson,* pp. 87–89, 91, 92
Suggests elements in the poet's life that may have contributed to the poem.

1989 GARBOWSKY, *House without the Door,* pp. 108–09, 110
Relates to other poems in fascicles 15 and 16 that "reflect the physiological and psychological experience of the agoraphobic as she lives through the state of panic and beyond."

" 'Twas like a maelstrom with a notch" (414)

1978 MANN, "Dream," pp. 23–24
Here as in other Dickinson poems the dream "metaphorically bridges the gap between the world outside and the poet's consciousness,

and the images follow one another as equivalents of mental processes having a logic all their own."

1979 CAMERON, *Lyric Time,* pp. 93–95, 98, 100, 110, 130
"The entire poem . . . casts its subject into doubt. The fact of death and the psychic anguish that anticipates it are really no longer separate. In effectively annihilating the boundary between the two, Dickinson forces us to transcend a line that we know, in reality, it is impossible to transcend."
Reprinted: Cameron, *"Et in Arcadia,"* pp. 43–44, 47, 48, 57, 72

1980 TAYLOR, M., "Shaman Motifs," pp. 5–6
Relates poem to elements of the "shaman experience." "Having suffered herself, like the shaman, the narrator speaks for all those enduring the same passage."

1981 GARBOWSKY, "Maternal Muse," pp. 14–17
Relates to a story by Harriet Prescott published in the *Atlantic Monthly* in 1860. "The poem strongly resembles Miss Prescott's story in imagery and vocabulary as well as in content and structure, suggesting a causal relationship between the two."

1982 MARCUS, *Emily Dickinson,* pp. 74–75
"This poem probably treats the same kind of alienation, lovelessness, and self-accusation found in 'After great pain' and 'I felt a Funeral.' "

1983 JUHASZ, *Undiscovered Continent,* pp. 70–73, 74, 75, 77, 78
"Three analogues move rapidly from a felt correspondence between this mental state and nature to dramatic situations, 'fictions,' where metaphors more closely delineate the space of the mind. . . . Language may itself be an agent in the vanquishing of pain, although the insight and control that it produces need not necessarily diminish the pain."

ROSENTHAL and GALL, *Modern Poetic Sequence,* pp. 48, 54, 58–61, 67
Considers as part of the sequence in fascicle 15. ". . . the murderous, forced renunciation suggested in the two previous poems is weighed against the crushing guilt of letting go and yielding to desire."

SHURR, *Marriage,* pp. 81, 82
Relates to other poems in the fascicle. In this poem a meeting between Dickinson and her beloved is connected "with her madness, or at least with her extreme distress, and clearly reflects the role of the beloved in it."

1985   BUDICK, *Emily Dickinson,* pp. 153–55, 157
"The dream and the reality, the maelstrom and death, become in-
terpenetrating currents in the vast ever-churning, ever-narrowing funnel
of symbols that the poem describes."

1986   ROBINSON, J., *Emily Dickinson,* pp. 125–27
". . . she seems to have thought of a notch in the same connection
as a mark on the whites of spinning wheels where they have passed
through floods. . . . The poem has a number of such exact markers which
scrupulously calibrate only how near or how far we are from the disaster
which . . . is always replaced by a new version of approaching calamity."

1987   CULJAK, "Dickinson and Kierkegaard," p. 148
Here Dickinson "explores the pain caused by the lack of purpose
for existence by alluding to the quintessential existential character,
Job . . . ."

1988   OAKES, "Welcome and Beware," pp. 199–201
"The poem resists an interpretation which gives it an extractable
meaning because from a metonymic perspective, it doesn't 'develop,' it
only includes, signaling pure context; and its principle of 'coherence' is
the intimate, troubling speaker-audience connection."

WOLFF, *Emily Dickinson,* pp. 354–59, 377, 472, 479
". . . the function of this narrative is to demonstrate that the
speaker can at least hold an integral self together until the inevitable end
and that she can wrest meaning from her own travails and convey that
meaning to others."

**1989   GARBOWSKY, *House without the Door,* pp. 68, 94–101, 106, 107,108,
109, 110, 111, 112, 114, 116, 118, 123, 129**
"The mental, emotional, and physical states described here are
identical with panic attack—the 'hallmark of the agoraphobic syndrome.'"

KNAPP, *Emily Dickinson,* pp. 77–80
"Contention and tension, even all-out was is the narrator's only
weapon against the brutality of emotional, intellectual, and spiritual domination. To allow the 'Maelstrom,' a manifestation of universal energy, to
crush the individual, is to accept defeat and allow annihilation."

OLIVER, *Apocalypse of Green,* pp. 143–44, 147
"The implicit choice offered to her is not between death and life,
since death ultimately claims all, but rather between an oblivion following
death or some form of rescue by God's judgment."

" 'Twas love, not me" (394)

1982 MOSSBERG, *Emily Dickinson,* pp. 132–33, 205 n. 1
"Not only does she suggest that God is a trifle forgetful about such matters as the crucifixion, and perhaps even a bit blind or senile . . . but she provides a logic for God's mistake that hinges on her own Christ-like goodness."

1983 SHURR, *Marriage,* pp. 32, 112
The poem argues that if "God is Love" then "He should be punished—not she, for her love is only participatory in His." In this poem "her 'Love' and her 'Guilt' are so inextricably intermeshed that she cannot tell them apart."

" 'Twas such a little, little boat" (107)

1985 JOHNSON, *Emily Dickinson,* pp. 18–19
"The poem does not warn against being 'lost'—for this is an ineluctable fact of existence—but against the failure to mature, to grow out of a childish sense of safety, of unquestioning faith in a benevolent universe."

1989 KNAPP, *Emily Dickinson,* pp. 68–70, 73
"The very fact that the 'craft' is drawn into chaotic waters, where it loses its orientation, offers the narrator the possibility of bringing order to disorder and to grapple with life's options." Examines poem's development of the boat metaphor.

" 'Twas the old road through pain" (344)

1979 CAMERON, *Lyric Time,* p. 110
Contrasts with "Our journey had advanced" and notes "significant differences between the two narrations."
Reprinted: Cameron, "*Et in Arcadia,*" pp. 56–57

" 'Twas warm, at first, like us" (519)

1978 CAMERON, "Naming as History," pp. 239–40, 244, 246
"In the space created by the words, at the center of which lies recognition (as in the space created by the lowering of the corpse, at the center of which lies grief), definition is by default."
Reprinted: Cameron, *Lyric Time,* pp. 42–43, 47, 49, 202; reprinted in part: Ferlazzo, *Critical Essays,* p. 203

1981 PORTER, *Dickinson,* pp. 193–94, 222
"Aside from the devouring egotism of her style the subject corpse is itself never depicted beyond the pronoun 'it.' Death is instead an array of language analogues . . . ."

1985 JOHNSON, *Emily Dickinson,* p. 164
"Clearly this insentient body creates a reaction of terror in the speaker, and the controlled poetry serves to heighten its effects. . . . The body is 'like Adamant' both in its inert weightiness and in what the speaker imagines to be an adamant refusal to communicate with the living."

1988 WOLFF, *Emily Dickinson,* pp. 315–16
"Nothing has been learned. Or perhaps the only thing that can be learned is the process itself. Life: begun in warmth, concluded with a short, cold drop into the grave."

"Two butterflies went out at noon" (533)

1979 MONTEIRO, G., "In Question" pp. 219–25
Supports theory that the 1862 poem and the 1878 penciled worksheet draft are two separate poems and suggests that the source for the latter poem might have been Rabelais.

1985 CUDDY, "Shelley's Glorious Titan," p. 34
The poem might be a "eulogy inspired by Shelley's death." It "speaks of an incident that might well relate to the drowning of Shelley and Edward Williams."

EBERWEIN, *Dickinson,* pp. 144–45
Examines revised version of poem to illustrate poet's technique.

1986 DAHLEN, "Powers of Horror," pp. 9–10
This is "not a poem about two butterflies; it is a poem about disappearance."

1988 MONTEIRO, G., *Robert Frost,* pp. 13–14, 18
Cites as an antecedent for Frost's "My Butterfly."

"Two lengths has every day" (1295)

1983 BUDICK, "Temporal Consciousness," p. 237–38
"'Eternity' can be reached in one of two ways. . . . In either case, . . . [it] will occur 'At Fundamental Signals/ From Fundamental

Laws.' It will be a product of the laws of the universe, and of the laws of consciousness . . . ."

Revised and reprinted: Budick, *Emily Dickinson*, p. 227

1984 Martin, W., *American Triptych*, p. 142

"Just as time measured in hours, minutes, and seconds constricts awareness, so the traditional notion of an afterlife as a specific time and place following death impoverishes our experience of the present."

1985 Johnson, *Emily Dickinson*, pp. 174–75

". . . the process of epistemological quest, the poem implies, takes place within life, and eternity is only an enhancement or a continuation of these personally earned rewards."

1988 Furukawa, " 'Finite Infinity,' " p. 23

Eternity "is in a state of both movement and stillness at once. This is because the extreme ecstacy [*sic*] of both 'Hope' and 'Horror' transcends human comprehension, and goes beyond to eternity."

"Two swimmers wrestled on the spar" (201)

1980 Nower, "Soul, Take Thy Risk, Part 1," p. 7

"Here the ocean symbolizes the risk of spiritual 'wrestling,' the land symbolizes security, an end to uncertainty, spiritual peace, or even Christianity."

1981 Diehl, *Romantic Imagination*, pp. 178–79

"The poem explodes the event, opening it to its own narrative emphases—wrestling, human responsibility, the concentration on the eyes in death."

Reprinted: Bloom, H., *American Poetry*, p. 460; Bloom, H., *Emily Dickinson*, pp. 156–57

1984 Martin, W., *American Triptych*, pp. 99–100

This poem "expresses the conflict she was experiencing between two aspects of herself—the romantic and the creative. . . . Signaling a resolution to Dickinson's struggle between autonomy and dependence, this poem affirms her creative identity."

1985 Anantharaman, *Sunset in a Cup*, pp. 103–07

Contrasts with "A little east of Jordan." Here the poet "has used this Biblical myth to project her own emotions—a fear of her own destiny as a nonbeliever."

1988   WOLFF, *Emily Dickinson,* pp. 139, 140, 145, 192, 203, 247, 271, 579
n. 7
"The elements of separation and the threat to coherent identity
that Dickinson's eye/face language so often conveys are indeed central to
this poem."

"Two were immortal twice" (800)

1986   NEW, "Difficult Writing" pp. 22–23
"What is this reversed 'Divinity' but God in the convex mirror . . .
of human perception? Eternity, only accessible through Time, must reverse itself in order to disclose itself. This reversal, this disclosure based
on multiplication and so on falsification, is the inevitable process of human vision."

"Unable are the loved to die" (809)

1981   KIMPEL, *Dickinson as Philosopher,* pp. 250, 259–60
The poem's terminology is "hellenic rather than essentially Christian. Yet it is not entirely without a Christian character . . . ."

1982   BARNSTONE, "Women and the Garden," p. 161
"The peace of God's Eden comes only before of after life, whereas
the harmony of love's Eden, to which Dickinson aspires, comes upon
tearing down the walls that imprison the lovers' minds. Love, then, is
'Deity,'. . . ."

1985   COOK, A., *Thresholds,* p. 187
"This astonishing psychological perception, whereby an oceanic
feeling is created by the lovers, takes the principle of life and transposes
it into what governs the afterlife: 'Vitality' into 'Divinity.' "

"Uncertain lease develops lustre" (857)

1985   JOHNSON, *Emily Dickinson,* p. 117
Here the poet "employs the familiar imagery of earthly values to
indicate the worth of transient experience. . . . It is time's 'Uncertain
lease' that gives the lustre to what prizes the poet does achieve, the tran-
sience and formlessness of experience actually intensifying poetic gains."

"Under the light, yet under" (949)

1988 PHILLIPS, *Emily Dickinson,* pp. 154–55
"The rhythms of children's games . . . may seem inappropriate to the imagery of the grave . . . , but they are subtly allusive in underscoring the relationship between the ebullience of the young together in play and the futile wish for the skill to hurl a discus to the dead light-years away."

UNO, "Optical Instruments," pp. 233–35
"In this poem Dickinson tries to express the distance between the living and the dead, by contrasting the astronomical view with that of the nearby familiar images of 'the Grass and the Dirt.'" Considers significance of poem's scientific references.

"Undue significance a starving man attaches" (439)

1982 MOSSBERG, *Emily Dickinson,* pp. 140–41
"The phrase 'And therefore—Good—' gives away Dickinson's attitude about fulfillment and her true need or desire to be fed. Her rather perverse aesthetics prefer the unattainable. . . . Given this aesthetic, we can judge that her 'hunger' is perpetuated, if not contrived."

"Unfulfilled to observation" (972)

1983 SHURR, *Marriage,* pp. 117–18
"The Sun that illuminated her life, the Bliss of her marriage, has suffered 'a Revolution/ In Locality'—but waits for her still, permanently, in some other horizon."

1985 JOHNSON, *Emily Dickinson,* p. 148
"Although heaven exists in this poem and is merely 'Unfulfilled to Observation,' the poem nevertheless contains an implicit rebelliousness and anger at being shut out."

"Unit, like death, for whom" (408)

1979 CAMERON, *Lyric Time,* pp. 15, 43
". . . the simile in the first line remains perplexing because it presents an identic connection as if it were an analogic one."

1983 SHURR, *Marriage,* pp. 29, 177–78
"It is curious that *two* are buried here, and that they are identified

as mother and child. . . . The last two lines intensify the moral and emotional atmosphere in which the mysterious burial takes place."

1984   BENFEY, *Problem of Others,* pp. 42–43, 44
   The poem's "tickets" imply "that death is a spectacle, for which
one acquires seats. They also suggest . . . that death is a journey, for
which one acquires berths."

"Unto like story trouble has enticed me" (295)

1984   WOLOSKY, *Emily Dickinson,* pp. 142–43
   The poem is "fully typological, presenting both personal and historical experience as intersecting in the eternity of Christ's sacrifice."

1985   EBERWEIN, *Dickinson,* pp. 74–75
   "Like other poems she grouped with this one in fascicle 12 . . .
this celebrates the power of imagination liberated through art to overcome
impotence and loneliness."

1988   STOCKS, *Modern Consciousness,* pp. 57–58, 114
   "Written in or about 1861, it reaches across the century to ally
itself . . . with the radical tendencies of some varieties of post-Second
World War existentialism."

1989   RICHWELL, "Poetic Immortality," pp. 19–20
   "The ultimate act of martyred heroism that Dickinson admires in
this poem is crucifixion. It is a potent symbol for acute personal suffering
and for the victory over death that poetry represents for her."

" 'Unto me?' I do not know you" (964)

1984   WALLACE, *God Be with the Clown,* pp. 83–84
   "The entire poem is a parodic extension of Jesus's biblical injunc-
tion, 'Suffer the little children to come unto me.' Initially, *this* child isn't
about to go off with a stranger. By the end of the poem one suspects she's
ready to hop in the car."

1986   HUGHES, G., "Subverting the Cult," p. 25
   "In the context of the cult of domesticity and of the consolation
mentality which used its codes to connect this life with the next, the civil-
ities of the opening exchange . . . introduce dynamics of powerlessness
and exploitation and this makes Jesus' intentions seem less than honorable."

1987   OBERHAUS, "Herbert and Emily Dickinson," pp. 354–57, 361
Dickinson's poem so closely resembles George Herbert's "Dialogue" in "theme, form, development, and poetic strategies that it might even be a response to the earlier poem."

"Unworthy of her breast" (1414)

1978   HORIUCHI, *Possible Zen Traits*, pp. 357–58
"Here the sin element, the sense of guilt that Puritans were never quite free of might be the point in question: that scathing test, her exacting light is what conscientious souls must pass under."

"Victory comes late" (690)

1979   PATTERSON, *Dickinson's Imagery*, pp. 33, 129–30
"The subject is love, and the 'Eagle's Golden Breakfast' that '*dazzles*' her is suggestively erotic on the oral level so common in her work. If Bowles, who was pretty well informed, had been urging her to take her women friends less seriously, this is her answer."

1981   STEINER, "Image Patterns," p. 64
"When in [this poem] the dominant images are hunger, starvation, and coldness, this is meant to demonstrate that God's goodness is a myth and that His provisions hardly suffice to feed the smallest of birds . . . ."

1982   MOSSBERG, *Emily Dickinson*, pp. 39, 115–16, 127, 137
". . . what is interesting in this poem about God's neglect is that God is given the maternal role of nurturing. But God fails as a mother because he has her father's traits: he is stingy, careless, neglectful, powerful, and sadistic."

1984   OLPIN, "Hyperbole: Part II," p. 4
"The basic irony perhaps is that this penny-saving Deity should still hold as much cause for awe as he does."

WOLOSKY, *Emily Dickinson*, pp. 61–62, 63
The poem "moves from a concern with military to a concern with theological victory, and the latter subsumes the former. . . . the whole structure of divine/human interchange is the poem's subject." Here "specific historical sorrow becomes general metaphysical accusation."

1986   MONTEIRO, K., "Dickinson's 'Victory,'" pp. 30–32
More than "an expression of unrequited earthly love," the poem

shows Dickinson's "vision of the tragedy of war and of the revivalist religion, which she found unsatisfying."

"Volcanoes be in Sicily" (1705)

1988 WOLFF, *Emily Dickinson,* p. 185
"The vision is that of a child—old enough to go to school, but young enough still to say aloud the truth that adults push from consciousness, that violence is not found exclusively 'someplace else.'"

"Warm in her hand these accents lie" (1313)

1984 WOLOSKY, *Emily Dickinson,* p. 158
"Dickinson does not finally resolve the dissociation between her words and the power that truly saves by establishing language as a separate sphere. The disjunction of earth from heaven, of language from the Word, constitutes for Dickinson the problem, not the solution."

" 'Was not' was all the statement" (1342)

1984 WOLOSKY, *Emily Dickinson,* p. 139
". . . in the guise of commentary [on Genesis 5:24] that would illuminate the text, she appropriates its words to show how dark and sudden they remain."

"Water is taught by thirst" (135)

1980 HOMANS, *Women Writers,* pp. 178–79, 181
"The speaker who believes in the instructional value of relativity can do so only through deafness to the poem's tonal contrast, but we can criticize the poem's ethic of relativity only by relying on such a principle in reading the poem's language."
Reprinted: Homans, "Dickinson and Poetic Identity," pp. 141, 142, 143; Homans, "Emily Dickinson," pp. 423, 424, 425

MURPHY, "Definition by Antithesis," pp. 21–22
"The poem is a discursive, analytic treatment of the idea of definition by antithesis . . . ."

1987 WILLIAMS, S., " 'Omitted Centers,' " pp. 28–29, 35
Compares with "The zeroes taught us phosphorus" in order to demonstrate Dickinson's "development of the metonymic character of her work."

"We, bee and I, live by the quaffing" (230)

1981 STEINER, "Image Patterns," p. 70
". . . together with the images of 'Clover' and 'Thyme,' nectar constitutes a cluster of sexually-charged imagery."

1982 OLPIN, "Hyperbole: Part One," p. 21
Notes qualities of frontier humor in the poem.

1986 BORUCH, "Dickinson Descending," pp. 874–75
"Dickinson's mockery of such questions—'Do we "get drunk"?'—and her attempt here to recover a delicious drunken state by jokes and camaraderie may have been . . . her answer to the rigid moral vicissitudes raking America midcentury."

1987 DI GIUSEPPE, "Maiden and the Muse," p. 53
Examines poem's "bee" metaphor.

1988 REYNOLDS, *Beneath the American Renaissance,* pp. 424–25
"With characteristic playfulness, Dickinson strips the dark-temperance mode of terror and of feminist implications by using the drunkard's wife as a metaphor in an apolitical poem that celebrates a summer day."

"We can but follow to the sun" (920)

1988 WOLFF, *Emily Dickinson,* p. 481
"This poem focuses not upon the legend that has been lost, but upon the flat, residual fact: despite the poet's deft success in using nature to *define* elements of the self, human beings and nature have no more than an accidental relationship."

"We do not know the time we lose" (1106)

1984 WOLOSKY, *Emily Dickinson,* pp. 100–01
The poet here "expresses and defines . . . her genuine need of faith. . . . The life of a friend is as exposed and as fragile as is mere chance. All that appears solid and substantive ultimately becomes specter and sand."

"We do not play on graves" (467)

1984 LLOYD, "Adult Voice," pp. 25, 27–30
Two suggested readings of the poem, "taken together, . . . show how Dickinson, thru her manipulation of childish and adult perception of

death, generates an impressive number of possible responses to that reality."

OLPIN, "Hyperbole: Part II," p. 25
"The real reason [not to play on graves] is that the mourners will disrupt and 'crush our pretty play'; the faces of mourners and a sharp human reminder of death are more apt to ruin play than the grave's physical dimensions."

"We don't cry, Tim and I" (196)

1981   KIMPEL, *Dickinson as Philosopher,* pp. 138–44, 145
The poem is "a record of what anyone might do in moments of questioning the wisdom of what he has done."

1986   POLLAK, "Second Act," p. 168 n. 11
Takes issue with Gelpi's 1975 explication.

1988   HARRIS, S., "'Cloth of Dreams,'" pp. 5–6, 16 n. 9
"Dreams are at first mocked in this poem as being equivalent to that mythic place traditional religion has made of heaven. But that momentary dream . . . reveals a reality too frightening in its clarity . . . ."

WOLFF, *Emily Dickinson,* pp. 179, 238
"Alas, the Tiny Tim of this poem does not touch a reader's heart, and the cloying supplications of the child-speaker sink into such plaintiveness that the verse hovers at the edge of inadvertent caricature."

"We dream—it is good we are dreaming" (531)

1978   MANN, "Dream," p. 23
"The poet discovers that her dream of death is a concrete reality, and discovers, in the process, that the use of dreams to investigate certain elements of her inner experience can lead to significant knowledge."

1981   DIEHL, *Romantic Imagination,* pp. 79–81
"Her 'play,' a ritual of blood, becomes bearable only in this condition of oneiric semi-consciousness. Ironically, just because it is a mythic drama, the stakes are total, the injuries internal."

1985   BUDICK, *Emily Dickinson,* pp. 150–53, 155, 157
The poem suggests "that a Transcendentalist solution to the bewildering finality of death may be no solution at all."

JOHNSON, *Emily Dickinson,* pp. 150–52, 212–13 n. 13
"The rhetoric of this poem is powerful, but it would seem to rep-

461

resent an impasse for the poet's quest: it implies, finally, that perception must be selective, that to face the tragic possibility is to enter a state of death-in-life and to lapse into silence."

1987 MILLER, C., *Emily Dickinson,* pp. 80–81
Examines the poem's "primary structuring device," which is the "ambiguous movement between nonspecific pronouns and definite pronouns used without antecedent."

"We grow accustomed to the dark" (419)

1979 ESTES, "Search for Location," pp. 213–14
"Complete accuracy in making the journey is impossible. Yet, 'Life steps almost straight.' We must accept such imperfections when the eye sees only the darkness of midnight."

JUHASZ, "Undiscovered Continent," pp. 92–93
Here "an event in the external world is contrasted, by means of the same vocabulary, with an event in the mind; their similarities underline their differences—in significance, in complexity."
Revised and reprinted: Juhasz, *Undiscovered Continent,* pp. 22–24

1988 WOLFF, *Emily Dickinson,* pp. 452–53, 455
This poem, in which God is present "only obliquely or by default," suggests that "the poet has a new kind of mission. She must investigate the meaning of God's demise."

WOLOSKY, "Rhetoric or Not," pp. 221–23
"As tropes common to the hymnal emerge in Dickinson's overtly secular poem, the way in which they are manipulated indirectly signals a theological intention."

1989 GARBOWSKY, *House without the Door,* pp. 101–02, 103, 109, 118, 149–50
The poem "suggests an adjustment to an abnormal situation. Perhaps the speaker . . . is depicting a period of respite between the violence of panic attacks . . . ."

"We knew not that we were to live" (1462)

1986 LOVING, *Emily Dickinson,* p. 106
"The tense shift between the first two lines . . . startles us into the awareness that we are still perilously alive in the present, after allowing

in the first line the objective distance possible only in our focus upon the unchangeable past."

"We learn in the retreating" (1083)

1984   WOLOSKY, *Emily Dickinson,* pp. 86–87
"Retreat, rather than defeat, is Dickinson's martial, negative trope here. And the poem ostensibly argues, at least at the outset, that retreat has heuristic value."

"We learned the whole of love" (568)

1978   HECHT, "Riddles," pp. 22–24
"It is not only that, in the terms of this poem, divine love unfits us for worldly love; it is the further paradox that a perfect understanding of love (which is ignorance) makes love inexpressible, an ineffable mystery, a *riddle*."
Reprinted: Hecht, *Obbligati,* pp. 114–17

1983   SHURR, *Marriage,* pp. 105–06
"The lover here is by no means a divine lover . . . yet the situation is described for one who would appreciate its being cast in religious terms." The poem seems to reflect the poet's relationship with Charles Wadsworth.

"We like March" (1213)

1979   PATTERSON, *Dickinson's Imagery,* pp. 126, 178
Suggests the "British Sky" reference may relate to the fact that Kate Turner was in England in 1872 and 1873.

"We met as sparks, diverging flints" (958)

1981   DIEHL, *Romantic Imagination,* p. 149
The poet describes "the approach of life in terms of a fusion of fire, an intermingling of sparks reminiscent of Shelley's smouldering images. . . . Unlike Shelley's vision of merging meteors, Dickinson sees the meeting as transitory, although it defines a new 'angle of vision.'"

KIMPEL, *Dickinson as Philosopher,* pp. 16–17
"She is concerned that the light which she treasures for illuminating her life may also enlighten the life of others. In this concern . . . she

"We miss her, not because we see"

expresses an obvious similarity of concern to Plato as he considers the
responsibilities of an enlightened person . . . ."

"We miss her, not because we see" (993)

1981   PORTER, *Dickinson,* pp. 47–48
"It is not possible to dismiss the poem as simply a variation on a
Sunday school slogan . . . for Dickinson by her garbled language has
turned it so strange, to the point of unintelligibility, that a deeper significance is suggested."

1985   JOHNSON, *Emily Dickinson,* p. 159
The poem, "perhaps the most unambiguously hopeful she ever
wrote . . . is remarkable for its lack of bitterness, since the secret of immortality, after all, is still 'foreclosed.' "

"We outgrow love like other things" (887)

1987   MOREY, "Dickinson-Kant II," pp. 25, 28
Relates to other Dickinson poems showing "adjustment or at least
control" as a response to loss.

"We play at paste" (320)

1980   CRONENWETT, " 'We Play at Paste,' " pp. 28–32
History of ownership of the manuscript, which travelled "some
7000 miles in almost 70 years only to reside in a manuscript collection two
blocks from its origin."

1982   MARCUS, *Emily Dickinson,* pp. 44, 46, 96
The poem "can be viewed as a comment on spiritual or personal
growth, but it is probably chiefly concerned with the growth of a poet's
craftsmanship."

1986   ANDERSON, P., "Bride of the White Election," pp. 8–9
The poem, often misinterpreted because early scholarship is ig-
nored, presents Dickinson's "view of mortal and immortal life. The
'paste' and 'sands' of this life prepare us for the 'Pearl' and 'gem' of
eternal life."

MCNEIL, *Emily Dickinson,* pp. 25–27, 28, 137
Dickinson uses the poem's simple words "in a manner which parallels the poem's act of process."

1988   MAZUREK, "'I Have No Monarch,'" p. 130

"The movement from paste to pearl, sand to gem, is typical of Dickinson's discovery of wonder in the everyday, of significance in the apparently lowly. The form of the poem is irregular; the condensation . . . modern."

WOLFF, *Emily Dickinson*, p. 459

"Hovering behind this verse is a traditional religious notion. God's Kingdom was described as the 'Pearl of Great Price' for which all of life's limited pleasures ought to be traded; 'Paste' might be taken as generic for this world, and 'Pearl' for Heaven."

"We pray to heaven" (489)

1981   FAST "'The One Thing Needful,'" pp. 159–60

"The poem describes efforts like those of both the orthodox and the consolation writers to define and contain the mysteries of both death and eternity. The speaker rejects the imposition of limiting terms to heaven, proposing a more appropriate, *because more elusive* (and *less* familiar) vocabulary."

KIMPEL, *Dickinson as Philosopher*, p. 286

"This obviously is a disparagement of a flippant discourse about an aspect of human life which she believes is entitled only to the most august and sober of treatment."

1982   JOHNSON, "Emily Dickinson," pp. 13–14

This poem "indicates that heaven is not 'a place,' and in a tone which makes it an appropriate reply to the speaker of 'I never saw a moor.'"

Revised and reprinted: Johnson, *Emily Dickinson*, pp. 58–59

1983   JUHASZ, *Undiscovered Continent*, pp. 133, 145–46

"Heaven, at once center and circumference, becomes the fitting location for 'Omnipresence,' which is the soul's condition. A location that is more conceptual than it is physical, thus defined here with abstract rather than concrete words."

1988   WOLFF, *Emily Dickinson*, pp. 326–27

"Presumably, to be in Heaven is to be with God. And yet here is the paradox: God is *everywhere*, 'Omnipresence.' Where is He *not?* Where is He *more?*"

"We see comparatively" (534)

1979 PATTERSON, *Dickinson's Imagery,* pp. 51, 105, 167
In the poem "she at first appears to be talking philosophically, even generally, about changing attitudes resulting from the growth of experience, but the emotionalism, indeed, the hot anger, of the two final stanzas leaves little doubt that she is writing out of a bitter personal disappointment." Relates to other "angle" poems.

1984 WOLOSKY, *Emily Dickinson,* p. 65
"We know the 'towering high' in opposition to the low. Without such opposition, distinctions, and therefore definitions, could not be drawn. The issue seems epistemological. Contrast is essential to understanding. For Dickinson, however, there are inevitable theological implications to the epistemological problem."
Revised and reprinted: Wolosky, "Dickinson's War Poetry," pp. 38–39

"We send the wave to find the wave" (1604)

1979 BARNES, "Telling It Slant," pp. 234–35
The "choice of construction, both syntactically and propositionally, conforms to and thereby reflects [Dickinson's] own demonstrated predilection for the proverbial mode."

1987 MILLER, C., *Emily Dickinson,* p. 148
"Although this poem may be read as an elaboration of a truism— that one must give to receive, or that some losses cannot be prevented— it also ironically suggests that distinguishing present and absent sea . . . is 'vain.' The 'wise distinction' persists in failing to recognize the absurdity of damming what is not there and cannot be kept anyway."

"We should not mind so small a flower" (81)

1981 KIMPEL, *Dickinson as Philosopher,* p. 178
"What is possibly the most significant aspect of this poem is the terminology of religion to interpret the effect of a flower upon the Poet . . . ."

1984 RUDDICK, " 'Synaesthesia,' " pp. 75, 76
Comments on intersensory imagery in poem's "So silver steal a hundred flutes."

"We shun because we prize her face" (1429)

1985 JOHNSON, *Emily Dickinson*, pp. 88, 203 n. 9

"The lines are perhaps a rationalization of the poet's neurosis; certainly they express an amazingly selfish outlook on human relationships, since the beloved is valuable only as a 'prize' of the poet's imagination . . . ."

"We shun it ere it comes" (1580)

1978 DIEHL, " 'Come Slowly,' " p. 576

"Although Dickinson does not say here that she is explicitly describing her response to the advent of the muse, she has outlined what for her becomes a typical drama, whether the 'it' refers to a season, a lover, or poetic inspiration."

Reprinted: Diehl, *Romantic Imagination*, p. 19

"We talked as girls do" (586)

1984 POLLAK, *Dickinson*, pp. 146–47

"The 'Grave' is a social and psychological reality that was never comprehended by the women themselves. It symbolizes both the death of their relationship and the destruction of their community from within."

"We talked with each other about each other" (1473)

1981 KIMPEL, *Dickinson as Philosopher*, pp. 145–46

The poem may be "her reflecting upon two different aspects of her life, each having a mode of a nature different from the other."

1983 SHURR, *Marriage*, pp. 161–62

Use of the word "reprieve" links this poem to "It came his turn to beg." Suggests that the meeting recorded here was with Wadsworth.

"We thirst at first—'tis nature's act" (726)

1985 EBERWEIN, *Dickinson*, pp. 58, 144, 232

This poem "articulates her sense of herself as temporarily estranged from the fulfillment out of which she has come and to which she is destined."

"Went up a year this evening" (93)

1980 GREEN, " 'You've seen Balloons,' " p. 12

". . . uses the symbol of a balloon ascent implicitly to reenact the death process of spiritual ascension. The poem is full of a beautifully calm confidence in the existence of a Paradise to which our spirits rise."

"Were nature mortal lady" (1762)

1982 THOTA, *Emily Dickinson*, p. 79

"What makes this a metaphysical poem is the conceited reference to nature as any other mortal 'society-lady,' who is always busy changing places for the sake of a suitable climate."

"Wert thou but ill, that I might show thee" (961)

1980 DIEHL, "American Self," pp. 6–7

"The intimate yet deeply ambivalent aspects of this relational vision extend to all confrontations between Dickinson and the other— whether he be lover, consciousness, the unacknowledged energies of creativity, or death itself."

"What care the dead for chanticleer" (592)

1979 PATTERSON, *Dickinson's Imagery*, pp. 189–90, 203, 224 n. 16

The poem "reads at first like a generalized account of physical death. . . . It becomes clear that the poem is a bitter reproach . . . ."

1981 PORTER, *Dickinson*, pp. 41–42

Suggests a "syntactical restoration" of the final two stanzas of this contorted poem.

1985 JOHNSON, *Emily Dickinson*, pp. 161–62

This poem and "A long, long sleep, a famous sleep" contain ironic characterizations of the dead and their "independent, enviable status" and "a new and luxurious life of 'idleness.' "

1989 HOCKERSMITH, " 'Into Degreeless Noon,' " pp. 285–87

Illustrates Dickinson's use of "structure and tone" to contrast "her vision of death with that of Christianity,"

"What I see not, I better see" (939)

1978 CROSTHWAITE, "Dickinson's 'What I see not,' " pp. 10–12
A comparison of this poem with Shakespeare's sonnet 43 "indicates a relationship which is striking both for the affinities present and for the singularity with which Emily Dickinson pursued the shared idea."

1985 JOHNSON, *Emily Dickinson,* pp. 61, 72, 201 n. 19
"The object of the poem's 'Faith' and the identity of 'Thee' in line 10 remain mysterious, but whether the poem describes human or spiritual longing, this perceptual 'Best Moment' is surely intuitive and fleeting."

1989 RICHWELL, "Poetic Immortality," p. 28
Although "Dickinson's words are the same as Shakespeare's . . . her sense is entirely different. . . . the brief death of sleep that Shakespeare writes about becomes in Dickinson the eternal sleep of death."

"What if I say I shall not wait" (277)

1982 MOSSBERG, *Emily Dickinson,* pp. 111–12, 119
"What is most important about these examples of the little girl or daughter triumphing over a punitive society which seeks to quell her voice—Dickinson's self-image as a poet—is how the little girl . . . functions as both a metaphor for repression . . . , and a representation of her own experience and identity as a little girl."

1983 SHURR, *Marriage,* pp. 40, 84
"It takes a rather unimaginative seriousness to read this poem, so full of wit and hyperbole, as a suicidal threat. It is a lover's mock protest, rather, addressed to her beloved 'thee.' "

1984 POLLAK, *Dickinson,* pp. 188–89
The poem "derives its power from Dickinson's shocking swerve away from the expected associations of freedom with life and of imprisonment with death."

1989 GARBOWSKY, *House without the Door,* p. 8
The poem addresses suicide. "It is not the force that she recalls which holds her, but 'Dungeons,' the feeling of being trapped or locked in. After this act of defiance and the achievement of freedom, all else pales in importance . . . ."

"What inn is this" (115)

1985   BUDICK, *Emily Dickinson*, pp. 52, 53
Here the poet "presents her sacramentalism as a series of questions that simultaneously describes and probes conventional sacramental relationships."

"What is 'Paradise'" (215)

1982   BARNSTONE, "Women and the Garden," pp. 157–58
" 'Eden' and 'Paradise' are equated, both being the location of immortality where 'farmers' 'hoe' innocently in the garden. Who the 'farmers' are is who she is not . . . ."

WESTBROOK, *New England Town*, pp. 196–97
"Doubtless Dickinson would wish the last four questions answered affirmatively, reassuring her that Paradise is not very different from Amherst. But in one respect she hopes it will be different—that there she will not be isolated as 'unconverted'. . . ."

1983   SHURR, *Marriage*, pp. 69, 144
It is probably Wadsworth's sermonizing to which the poet is responding in this poem.

1984   WALLACE, *God Be with the Clown*, pp. 81–82, 84
"She asks humorously innocent questions, pretending to see the figurative in terms of the literal, the spiritual in terms of the physical, and the exalted in terms of the common."

1985   CARTON, *Rhetoric*, pp. 87–88, 123
If the poem "somewhat domesticates the mysterious, it also mystifies the oppressively commonplace."

"What mystery pervades a well" (1400)

1977   AGRAWAL, *Emily Dickinson*, pp. 114–15
"Referring to the Christian doctrine of nature that the divine spirit pervades it . . . Dickinson says that the adherents of this doctrine have neither been able to learn nature nor to explain how the Holy Ghost 'haunts' nature."

1980   HOMANS, *Women Writers*, pp. 189–90
"Those who get near to nature know her less by comprehending

her resistance to our inquiries, but they also know her less because to get near to nature is to die, and to know everything less."
Reprinted: Homans, "Emily Dickinson," pp. 430–31

REISS, "Dickinson's Self-Reliance," pp. 28–29
". . . there is no cause to pity those who do not understand the spirit of nature, because that spirit is almost completely unknowable. For most who cite nature, nature reflects their own image. Those who can penetrate nature's reflection see the abyss."

1982 MARCUS, *Emily Dickinson*, pp. 27–28
"Although it is more expository than most of Dickinson's philosophical nature poems, it still maintains a balance between abstraction, metaphor, and scene."

1984 BENFEY, *Problem of Others*, pp. 6, 66–67, 77–78
This is "a poem about 'relatedness,' and about a willingness to forgo certainty and knowledge, and accept intimacy and 'nearness.'"

1987 MARTIN, J. E., "Religious Spirit," pp. 502–04
"Here Dickinson most brilliantly captures in symbol and imagery the problem of immanence and transcendence at the heart of being."

1988 MOREY, "Dickinson-Kant III," p. 44
The poem "discusses the premonition of negative emotions or stages of pain which are within us, but usually untapped in childhood."

STOCKS, *Modern Consciousness*, pp. 70–72
"The picture of the grass and the poet at the well's edge, the grass unafraid, the poet with her burden of consciousness, expresses a recovered unity with nature at a high level of human awareness and understanding, the poet fulfilling her role as nature's consciousness and tongue."

WOLFF, *Emily Dickinson*, pp. 486–87
". . . the poem's penultimate stanza firmly dismisses both a Trinitarian reading of nature and Emersonian transcendentalism. If nature's 'mystery' is to be revealed, some new process of aesthetic investigation must be invented."

"What soft, cherubic creatures" (401)

1980 LAWES, "'Dimity Convictions,'" pp. 127–28
Examines attributes of dimity that make its use particularly apt in this poem.

1982   MARCUS, *Emily Dickinson,* pp. 62–63, 65, 66, 68
Relates to other Dickinson poems on society. Comments on poem's diction, attitudes, and allusions.

1983   WALKER, N., "Humor as Identity," pp. 64–65
"The severity with which Dickinson treats the 'gentlewoman' image testifies to both its pervasiveness and her personal rejection of it."

1984   WALLACE, *God Be with the Clown,* pp. 32–33
Here "Dickinson turns her satiric rod against the kind of artificially elevated woman she could not be. Chastizing mere social respectability and shallow thinking, Dickinson ridicules her culture's 'soft, cherubic creatures' for being satisfied with a half-life."

1987   LEDER and ABBOTT, *Language of Exclusion,* pp. 136, 140, 155
"It is Dickinson's unease with the accepted women's way of dealing with passion and desire that may have led her to write [this poem]. Clearly she saw at least some other women as refusing to welcome any but the most ladylike religious, as well as earthly, experience."

1988   WOLFF, *Emily Dickinson,* p. 279
"Yes, the porcelain females are laughable; however, it is the God Whose 'Redemption' can occur only if He 'assaults' us and 'violates' us Who is the real target of the poem's outraged contempt."

1989   OBERHAUS, "Dickinson as Comic Poet," pp. 120–21, 122
The poem's speaker "not only rejects haughty gentlewomen in the here and now; she also concludes, alluding to Scripture, that because of their arrogant self-righteousness they will be rejected in the hereafter . . . ." Examines the poem's "comic strategies."

"What twigs we held by" (1086)

1981   KIMPEL, *Dickinson as Philosopher,* pp. 51–52
"The type of suffering expressed in this poem . . . arises . . . from reflecting on her own persisting inclination to trust what she repeatedly learned did not justify her trust."

1985   JOHNSON, *Emily Dickinson,* p. 186
"The poem is not an easy wish-fulfillment . . . for it takes into account the struggle of the quester's uphill journey and simply posits a happy ending. . . . This ecstatic conclusion to her journey not only involves everlasting light, but also a perceptual confrontation—seeing God—which inspires in Dickinson a characteristic awe."

1988 UNO, "Optical Instruments," pp. 231–33, 234, 235
Examines poem's scientific references, particularly "Discs" and "a Saturn's Bar."

"What we see we know somewhat" (1195)

1983 JUHASZ, *Undiscovered Continent,* pp. 136, 137–38, 140–41
The poem "discusses the conflict between empiricism and supposition, but this time supposition's daring, even criminal, procedure is the subject." Links with "Their height in heaven comforts not."

"What would I give to see his face" (247)

1985 BUDICK, *Emily Dickinson,* pp. 73–75
"The poem delights in the comedy of the situation, and yet the sense of loss and the accompanying criticism of God are serious."

1988 WOLFF, *Emily Dickinson,* pp. 273–74, 333, 587 n. 8
"Who is this courting God? A ruthless Shylock demanding his pound of flesh, without exception and without compassion. His contract is *literally 'Extatic,'* for its terms demand that the soul be wrenched from the body."

"Whatever it is, she has tried it" (1204)

1988 WOLFF, *Emily Dickinson,* pp. 496–97
"The woman's life has been curtailed; one more 'subject' of God's royal power 'is finished.' Yet the 'subject' of some long disagreement may be ended as well."

"When bells stop ringing, church begins" (633)

1985 COOK, A., *Figural Choice,* p. 33
"The dizzying series here, based on an imaginal process, has the air of providing entries for some theological lexicon of the true spiritual function of the things of the world."

EBERWEIN, *Dickinson,* pp. 151–52
Use of "cog" and "circumference" in other Dickinson poems clarifies this poem's meaning.

"When diamonds are a legend" (397)

1979 PATTERSON, *Dickinson's Imagery,* pp. 84, 145
Relates "symbols associated with South America" and "diamond" image to uses in other Dickinson poems.

"When Etna basks and purrs" (1146)

1977 COPPAY, "Internal Analysis," pp. 19, 20, 30–36
Finds the "sense of compression [is] produced by internal semantic relationships, rather than external syntactic gaps. My results thus negate Levin's [1971] account of compression and support Riffaterre's hypothesis of textual self-sufficiency."

1979 PATTERSON, *Dickinson's Imagery,* pp. 81, 136–37, 142, 174, 223 n. 79
"Although the poem has no manifest personal application, it would be a mistake not to suspect one." Relates poem's use of "Garnet," "Naples," and "Etna" to uses in other Dickinson poems.

1981 DIEHL, *Romantic Imagination,* pp. 176–77
"Whereas Emerson and Dickinson are both drawn to the vision of an imminent power that smoulders undetected, Dickinson 'personalizes' this vision."
Reprinted: Bloom, H., *American Poetry,* pp. 458–59; Bloom, H., *Emily Dickinson,* p. 155

1986 ROBINSON, J., *Emily Dickinson,* p. 151
"The volcano image gives her the drama of greater power revealing itself to shake the lives of the previously complacent with revelations of the real. It is a drama which depends on deceptive appearance, so in [this poem] it is when the volcano is quiet that the city is apprehensive . . . ."

"When I count the seeds" (40)

1985 BUDICK, *Emily Dickinson,* pp. 53–54
"Counting and cunning may be helpful. They are antecedents of earthly renunciation. But without belief and faith they are veritably useless."

1989 OLIVER, *Apocalypse of Green,* pp. 71–72
"The poem is cast almost in the form of a logical argument: the persona recognizes through her senses the regenerative process of nature;

by analogy she compares human death to this process, but finds that only faith will allow her to consider the comparison trustworthy."

RICHWELL, "Poetic Immortality," p. 27
This is very likely Dickinson's adaptation of Shakespeare's sonnet 12. "With her preference for eternity over the present, Dickinson turns the sense of Shakespeare's sonnet on its head."

"When I have seen the sun emerge" (888)

1987   BARKER, *Lunacy of Light*, p. 71
The poem's final lines contain an image that "suggests a sense of entrapment in a world that does not allow her an instrument with which to create her own sounds, music, or ideas."

"When I hoped I feared" (1181)

1987   HESFORD, "Creative Fall," p. 89
"Because she has suffered the deep knowledge the serpent affords, she can construct her own charm against his charm, can depose doom by dooming herself to a life without the fearful hope offered by serpent-haunted conventional religion, to a daring self-constituting life."

"When I hoped, I recollect" (768)

1983   SHURR, *Marriage*, pp. 11, 106–07
The poem is "an attempt to schematize the conflicting emotions caused by the marriage experience."

"When I was small, a woman died" (596)

1987   LEDER and ABBOTT, *Language of Exclusion*, pp. 111–12
"The explicit meaning of the poem is a tribute to a brave soldier and his mother's pride which extends beyond the grave, but the poem actually focuses on the woman rather than the warrior. . . . the poet *and* the mother participate in war and Christlike sacrifice."

"When Katie walks, this simple pair accompany her side" (222)

1984   BOGUS, "Not So Disparate," p. 43
Suggests inspiration in Elizabeth Barrett Browning's "My Kate."

"When we stand on the tops of things" (242)

1986   Robinson, J., *Emily Dickinson*, pp. 43–44
"The poem is thoroughly Puritan in its division of people on other than earned merit and in its expectation of light which is only hinted at now. Yet it does not issue in ideas of duty and guilt but in security."

"Where bells no more affright the morn" (112)

1986   Singley, "Reaching Lonely Heights," p. 78
Notes ways in which poem echoes Sarah Orne Jewett's story "A White Heron."

1987   Leder and Abbott, *Language of Exclusion*, pp. 144, 145
"The poem appears in a cluster which are speculations on immortality. . . . She is clearly interested in portraying a changed landscape in which she has no control and in which the images of the new technology stand for death."

"Where ships of purple gently toss" (265)

1982   Thota, *Emily Dickinson*, p. 84
Contrasts Dickinson's "response to diffodils" [*sic*] with that of Wordsworth. "Dickinson does not portray nature as it is; but discusses her as she viewed and felt at the moment of experiencing the scene."

"Where thou art, that is home" (725)

1978   Hecht, "Riddles," p. 8
"The carefully balanced rhetorical and syntactical structure of this poem is far nearer Herbert's practice than Emily Dickinson's."
Reprinted: Hecht, *Obbligati*, p. 98

1982   Mossberg, *Emily Dickinson*, pp. 129–30
"Dickinson's speaker does not care what happens to her, whether it is incarceration or crucifixion, or in what form God's notice is given (whether it is esteemed status or 'Shame'). Her strategy is to transform her deprivation into her sign of election."

1983   Shurr, *Marriage*, pp. 39, 78, 120
Considers as an "assessment" of the poet's love relationship. "The spices and rowing recall the erotic Eden poems."

"Whether my bark went down at sea" (52)

1985   Johnson, *Emily Dickinson,* pp. 14–16, 34
"The combination of process and stasis in the poem illustrates the dynamic relationship between two separate quests: the active, poetic quest imaged by the bark and its possible fates, and the perceptual quest imaged by the bodiless 'eye.'"

"Which is best? Heaven" (1012)

1979   Barnes, "Telling It Slant," p. 230
Finds the poem's use of the proverb less effective than similar treatment in an earlier letter.

1985   Dickenson, *Emily Dickinson,* pp. 92–93
"Dickinson is rarely willing to give everything, and cannot help doubting. But her scepticism here extends even to her own choice of this world over the next. She knows she may change her mind later, but she recognizes that by then it will be too late for redemption."

Kajino, "Moment of Death," pp. 35–36, 39–40, 44
"It may be said that at the end of the poem, the poet imagines herself at the moment of death when she is forced to leave this world and has only the possibility of the 'Heaven to come' to face."

"While it is alive" (491)

1983   Shurr, *Marriage,* pp. 178–79, 184
Suggests that the poem's "it," the unborn child, might have been the poet's own.

1984   Benfey, *Problem of Others,* p. 97
"While the body is alive, body and spirit seem so intimate that 'Division' is unthinkable . . . ."

1985   Anantharaman, *Sunset in a Cup,* pp. 81–82
"In this poem the persona's consciousness becomes like an ancient archaeological sight [*sic*] with layers upon layers of an 'sceptical awareness' of non-separation . . . ."

"Who goes to dine must take his feast" (1223)

1981   Kimpel, *Dickinson as Philosopher,* pp. 63–64
"Failure to cultivate sensitivity to what might enhance the quality of life is a moral failure. It is of such moral failure that this poem speaks."

"Who has not found the heaven below"

1984   BENFEY, *Problem of Others,* pp. 18–19
      In this poem about "our relation to the world" the poet's stress lies on "preparing our vision, making ourselves worthy of the world, fit lovers of it."

"Who has not found the heaven below" (1544)

1984   BENFEY, *Problem of Others,* pp. 68–69
      The poem's thrust "is not so much to deny the distinction between heaven and earth as it is to deny a comfortable assurance that we need only wait, and the unknown will make itself known."

      MARTIN, W., *American Triptych,* pp. 139–40
      Contrasts with a verse by Isaac Watts. "Dickinson rebelled against Watts's metrics, just as she resisted Calvinist theology. Sometimes she satirized his strict scansion, which she found too confining . . . ."

"Who never wanted maddest joy" (1430)

1978   BURKE, "Religion of Poetry," p. 23
      "Self-denial becomes positive, for in denying the desired element we are, paradoxically, experiencing and enjoying it psychologically. The paradoxical compensation inherent in self-denial, then, becomes evident."

1979   POLLAK, "Thirst and Starvation," pp. 33, 38, 40–41, 42
      In this poem Dickinson establishes "a psychological law . . . which in effect posits an absolute cleavage between reality and imagination." Examines the "concept of the Banquet of Abstemiousness."
      Revised and reprinted: Pollak, *Dickinson,* pp. 126–27

1983   JUHASZ, *Undiscovered Continent,* pp. 96–97
      "Insanity is equivalent to drunkenness, both producing loss of control. On the other hand, wanting, reaching, desiring are themselves exciting and without harmful side-effects: 'Desire's perfect Goal—.' "

1988   WOLFF, *Emily Dickinson,* pp. 210, 213, 215
      "By rendering relinquishment *itself* as a sensual delight," the poem's "Banquet of Abstemiousness" "seems to border on the perverse."

"Who occupies this house" (892)

1979   DIGGORY, "Armored Women," pp. 143–44
      Contrasts with Frost's "Stopping by Woods." "In both poems the

ultimate object of contemplation is death, for Frost's refusal of the woods is a refusal to sleep, and the 'house' which Dickinson approaches proves to be a grave. What distinguishes the poems is the different position from which each poet observes the object."

1981 KILLINGSWORTH, "Dickinson's 'Who occupies,'" pp. 33–35
The poem's theme is the "inadequacy of metaphorical thinking as a means of dealing with the mystery of death."

1982 MOSSBERG, *Emily Dickinson*, p. 122
Here "Heaven is a paradigm of alienation for the little girl. . . . we see Dickinson's ambivalence to her identity as a girl emerge as the primary reason for her homelessness on earth and in heaven."

"Who were 'the Father and the Son'" (1258)

1979 PATTERSON, *Dickinson's Imagery*, p. 20
". . . the child, hitherto protected by the infant sense of immortality, is now introduced to the idea of its own death as the consequence of original sin."

1982 BARNSTONE, "Women and the Garden," pp. 156–57
"The process of growth forces the faithful to 'alter' belief for the sake of truth. Heaven becomes embarrassing, for the requirement for achieving immortality is to 'shun' the voice of consciousness."

MOSSBERG, *Emily Dickinson*, p. 125
"She thinks that if God Himself had told her when she wanted to know, and presumably had answered her prayer instead of leaving her in an ignorance of dread, 'We better Friends had been, perhaps.' As it is, she is convinced that it is too late for any rapprochement."

1985 EBERWEIN, *Dickinson*, pp. 240–41
Although Dickinson blames "distorted religious formation in childhood for adult defenses against the Deity . . . the poem expresses a residual trust."

1989 DIEHL, "Murderous Poetics," p. 338
"No longer 'fortified' by childhood innocence, her only retaliation becomes a tortured self-reliance. This is not, however, the Emersonian brand . . . ."

"Whoever disenchants" (1451)

1981 KIMPEL, *Dickinson as Philosopher*, p. 96
"This poem compresses into four lines some of the sternest aspects

of morally serious reflecting. . . . Her terminology '*whoever* disenchants' affirms a universal moral obligation which she believes cannot be justifiably broken under any circumstance."

"Whole gulfs of red, and fleets of red" (658)

1984   WOLOSKY, *Emily Dickinson,* p. 38
"This is a traumatized view of sunset. War here serves as the model in terms of which Dickinson perceives the day's decline and which renders that decline terrible and fearful."
Reprinted: Wolosky, "Dickinson's War Poetry," pp. 26–27

1985   BUDICK, *Emily Dickinson,* pp. 11, 12, 194
In this poem "Dickinson's choice of imagery and analogy, as well as her poetic form, serve to remind us that the blood that courses bounteously through the veins and arteries of the living universe, the color that defines shape and season and gives them meaning, may be the same blood, the same color, that spills out upon the landscape and stains it in death."

"Whose are the little beds, I asked" (142)

1988   HARRIS, S., " 'Cloth of Dreams,' " p. 12
Relates to other instances in Dickinson's "dream letters and poems" where the theme is "sexual awakening."

" 'Why do I love' you, sir" (480)

1981   PORTER, *Dickinson,* pp. 48–50
Paraphrase. "What the poem says . . . is intelligible only if we are willing to unpack the syntax, lay the lines out, and then recompose the poem." Examines the "obscurities in this Browningesque poem."

"Why do they shut me out of heaven" (248)

1982   MOSSBERG, *Emily Dickinson,* pp. 110–11, 123, 170
". . . her dilemma is whether to be 'still' and 'timid' and get into heaven with Prose, or to write real poetry and suffer the alienation of the outcast, ostracized and exiled for disobedient boldness as a woman and as a poet."
Revised and reprinted: Mossberg, "Nursery Rhymes," pp. 49–50, 51–52

1986   McNEIL, *Emily Dickinson*, p. 43
The poet expresses simultaneously "the pathos of the excluded and the commanding irony of one who knows herself superior."

1987   MILLER, C., *Emily Dickinson*, pp. 54–55, 169–70, 172, 173
Notes ironic use of "could" in this poem, which, like "Over the fence," compares "the child/speaker's role with God's."

1989   OLIVER, *Apocalypse of Green*, pp. 139–40, 141
Considers critical interpretations of the poem. "These interpretations do not preclude, and in fact seem to complement a reading of the poem as an ironic comment on the arbitrary nature of judgment, at least as explained by orthodox religion."

"Why make it doubt, it hurts it so" (462)

1979   GILBERT and GUBAR, *Madwoman*, pp. 603, 607
The poem "attests to the fearful power with which the dreaded and adored man of noon has rended Dickinson's mind, shattering logic, syntax, and order. . . . 'They,' 'it,' 'Itself,' and 'me' continually shift meanings here . . . ."

1983   GILBERT, "Wayward Nun," pp. 26, 40
The poem is "obviously tormented and almost certainly autobiographical. . . . Gasping and elliptical, it seems like a speech spun out of delirium; reading it, we become witnesses to a crisis in love's fever, watchers by the sickbed of romance."

1985   SALSKA, *Walt Whitman and Emily Dickinson*, p. 154
"The use of the 'it' pronoun blurs the meaning of the poem . . . ."

1986   McNEIL, *Emily Dickinson*, pp. 44–46
Examines poem's tone of "masochistic longing." "Dickinson hints that the Master for whom her creature would die like a faithful dog may not actually be a person but an idea, a 'Vision', which the creature itself may have invented."

1988   TRIPP, *Mysterious Kingdom*, p. 122
Comments on poem's diction and syntax.

"Wild nights—wild nights" (249)

1977   MONTEIRO, G., "Pilot-God Trope," pp. 42, 46, 47–48
The poem is structured by the "Pilot-God trope"; it may be read as "a rather orthodox religious poem" or "a 'Christianized' love poem."

481

1978 FADERMAN, "Homoerotic Poetry," pp. 20, 26 n. 5
"When understood as a love lyric in which the principals, both being women, have no pre-defined roles or set sexual functions the poem no longer contains the puzzling role-reversal that has so often been observed."

1979 ESTES, "Search for Location," pp. 208–09, 212
"Because of its sexual suggestiveness, many critics discuss [this poem] as a love poem. However, it also applies to Dickinson's intense search for a permanent location in a world of flux."

1980 NOWER, "Soul, Take Thy Risk, Part 1," p. 7
Speculates on the nature of the poem's "Thee."

1981 DIEHL, *Romantic Imagination,* p. 159
The poem "bears more than an external relation" to Shelley's "Good-night," "also a poem about remaining together, staying close or voyaging from the beloved."

MONTEIRO and ST. ARMAND, "Experienced Emblem," pp. 223–28, 266
"What has not been recognized is that the poem . . . is actually a doublet in that it can be read both as a secular love lyric employing religious imagery and as a devotional piece drawing on traditional tropes."

STEINER, "Image Patterns," p. 66
"The longing of the boat for 'mooring' in the sea is not only that for being submerged by the other, but also indicates that mixing with another Power is a means of escape."

1982 MADIGAN, "Mermaids," pp. 47–48, 49
The poem seems "to speak of a desire to avoid the pitfalls of conventionality and to live as intensely as possible even though catastrophe may result."

MARCUS, *Emily Dickinson,* pp. 57–58
Relates to other Dickinson love poems. "The suggestions of masculinity in this poem's speaker may reveal in Dickinson an urge to be active in creating a situation that she usually anticipates more passively."

SALSKA, *Poetry of the Central Consciousness,* p. 67
"By giving up the guidance of the mind . . . the speaker has deprived herself of the possibility of at least struggling to influence her position; and the situation fills her with apprehension. Leaving oneself open to the play of uncontrolled emotions results in passiveness, in numbness, an attitude both tempting and destructive."

Revised and reprinted: Salska, *Walt Whitman and Emily Dickinson,* pp. 56–57, 98 n. 32

1983 KHAN, *Emily Dickinson's Poetry,* pp. 13–14
"The analogues for the 'luxury' of the 'Wild Nights' are drawn from two sources: biblical mythology and nature."

SHURR, *Marriage,* pp. 17, 18, 19, 67, 86
". . . Dickinson here introduces her frequently used theme of 'Eden' as the paradise of sexual security and enjoyment. Once again, those who would see this as a divine poem have much to contend with . . . ."

1984 CHERRY, "Sexuality and Tension," p. 18
"Loss is what energizes this poem and creates its movement. Sexuality, tho acknowledged, is beyond the power of the speaker."

SALSKA, "Emily Dickinson's Lover," p. 136
What makes the poem "disquieting is the way in which it gives us the essence of passion without its personal context." The lover's "elemental presence serves to analyse the contradictory impulses within the self."
Revised and reprinted: Salska, *Walt Whitman and Emily Dickinson,* pp. 137, 138, 142

1986 McNEIL, *Emily Dickinson,* p. 15
The poem's final image "is one of choosing to be contained by the lover. Mooring tonight is a way of remaining eternally in the oceanic paradise of Eros."

1987 MONTEFIORE, *Feminism and Poetry,* pp. 168–69
"This passionate poem articulates desire for a person whose presence promises dangerous, reckless excess at the same time as complete protection from disturbance—interpretations which logically contradict each other."

1988 REED, "Masculine Identity," pp. 283–84
In this poem we see "a major defense structure in the overall poetry, and that is to assume the masculine identity, to become the phallic force and thereby effectively prevent the intrusion of the male or the father into the oral situation, into the situation of security and separateness."

REYNOLDS, *Beneath the American Renaissance,* pp. 434–35
Dickinson's "treatment of the daring theme of woman's sexual fantasy in this . . . poem bears comparison with erotic themes as they

appeared in popular sensational writings. . . . Unlike popular erotic literature, the poem portrays neither a consummated seduction nor the heartless deception that it involves."

WOLFF, *Emily Dickinson,* pp. 382, 383–84, 416
". . . the word 'luxury' points explicitly to the lovers' pleasure: according to Dickinson's dictionary, it means 'voluptuousness in the gratification of appetite . . . lust.'"

1989 GILBERT and GUBAR, *No Man's Land,* vol. 2, p. 112
The sea of Kate Chopin's *Awakening* "has much in common with the mystically voluptuous ocean" of Dickinson's poem.

"Will there really be a 'Morning'" (101)

1984 WALLACE, *God Be with the Clown,* p. 85
"Dickinson's satiric exposure of the supposed experts whose 'knowledge' can't begin to answer her simple questions is so innocently framed here that one could easily miss the sly smirk underlying the humorous pose."

1988 WOLFF, *Emily Dickinson,* p. 289
"Perhaps this New England 'Pilgrim' seeks only directions to the place of eternal 'Morning'; more probably, however, she seeks some explanation for the 'lies' that have claimed each day's 'Morning' as an *evidence* that God will rescue us from the grave."

"Witchcraft has not a pedigree" (1708)

1986 ROBINSON, J., *Emily Dickinson,* pp. 95–96
Links with "Estranged from beauty none can be." "Beneath the images of the two poems we have a recurrence—two separate maps of the same place: of what precedes our birth and exceeds our death."

"Witchcraft was hung in history" (1583)

1986 ROBINSON, J., *Emily Dickinson,* pp. 14–15, 24
". . . the opposition in the poem is not really between now and then; it is between then and always. It is not that we now know better, having learned from experience. It is that the past provides clear evidence of the way that human history is superfluous and in contrast there is another sort of history which is real."

"With pinions of disdain" (1431)

1987   MILLER, C., *Emily Dickinson*, p. 175
Links to speakers in other Dickinson poems whose "responses to the confining world" are characterized by disdain.

"Within my garden rides a bird" (500)

1981   THOMAS, "Emerson's Influence," pp. 38–40
This poem and "A route of evanescence" illustrate "growth in the poet's attitude toward nature and herself, as well as the influence of Emerson's theories of nature."

1984   WALLACE, *God Be with the Clown*, pp. 90–93
This poem "uses the mode of light verse to explore the serious theme of human unknowing."

1986   MOREY, "Dickinson-Kant: The First Critique," pp. 35–36, 37–38, 43
Examines along with "A bird came down the walk" in order to explore a Dickinson–Kant relationship.

"Within that little hive" (1607)

1978   MANN, "Dream," pp. 20, 26 n. 2
"Whatever the focus of intense, connotative significance upon the word 'Honey,' reality and dream are conceived as opposing orders whose juxtaposition or interpenetration has some importance for the poet."

"Without a smile, without a throe" (1330)

1987   BLASING, *American Poetry*, p. 186
Examines Dickinson's "jumbling of letters and graphemes" in this poem.

"Without this there is nought" (655)

1984   WOLOSKY, *Emily Dickinson*, pp. 161–62
"The ultimate ramifications of this irreconcilable positing of time and eternity against each other are, for Dickinson as poet, its consequences in the world of discourse. Torn between the two, Dickinson is finally torn with regard to the speech act itself."

"You cannot put a fire out" (530)

1987 BARKER, *Lunacy of Light,* pp. 116–17
"The poet knows that even though cultural and familial pressures may suppress her, her own 'fire'—or creative drive—cannot be extinguished . . . ."

"You cannot take itself" (1351)

1981 KIMPEL, *Dickinson as Philosopher,* pp. 125–28
Considers philosophical implications of Dickinson's "tautological assertion that whatever the self is, cannot be taken from what it is."

1988 WOLFF, *Emily Dickinson,* p. 465
"The ruthless strength of the opponent justifies and limits the extremity of the speaker's attitude. However, when the Divinity's power vanishes, this exclusive concern of self for self begins to take on the tonalities of an emotional aberration."

"You constituted time" (765)

1983 SHURR, *Marriage,* pp. 7, 112
". . . Dickinson argues that her beloved was to her a 'Revelation' of Eternity; since Eternity is the revelation of God, she has had to 'adjust' herself to this new idolatry, The poem is argued quite abstractly; but a concrete presentation of the same subject is offered in [poem] 649."

1986 NEW, "Difficult Writing" pp. 19–21, 22, 23
"In a paradoxical, contradictory syntax that confounds binary opposition, the poet affirms God's absoluteness and her own relativity while at the same time acknowledging the reduction, or idolatry, or her terms even as she posits them."

"You know that portrait in the moon" (504)

1985 BRASHEAR, "Dramatic Monologues," pp. 70–71
Discussion of Dickinson's development of the monologue form. Here "she stages a moonlight meeting between a woman and her lover."

"You left me, sire, two legacies" (644)

1984 WOLOSKY, *Emily Dickinson,* p. 134
". . . the poem goes beyond complaint to reproach. But the reproach remains dialogical."

1988   STOCKS, *Modern Consciousness,* p. 27
The "Sire" to whom the poem is addressed "is, surely, man him-self, *Homo sapiens*—more specifically, in the terms of our tradition, the fallen Adam. Both the love and the pain, in the Christian scheme, are written on the Cross, plain for all to read; yet they are the twin legacies of the fall."

1989   DIEHL, "Murderous Poetics," pp. 331–32
"The vastly self-contradictory poems that attest to Dickinson's abasement before the male other and her wish to sacrifice all for him derive their source from *his* dual legacy to her."

"You love me, you are sure" (156)

1984   POLLAK, *Dickinson,* pp. 138–39, 140, 141
This poem and "One sister have I in our house" were "addressed to Susan Gilbert Dickinson and reflect the quest of a childlike persona for a surrogate mother."

"You love the Lord you cannot see" (487)

1983   SHURR, *Marriage,* pp. 101–02, 143
Suggests the poem "describes the life of a clergyman with literal exactness" and probably refers to Wadsworth.

"You said that I 'was great' one day" (738)

1981   GUTHRIE, "Modest Poet's Tactics," pp. 232–33
"By using a persona, Dickinson may be attempting to cast the re-sponsibility for finding an appropriate place for herself in society . . . into a friend's hands, thus freeing herself from the task."

1983   SHURR, *Marriage,* pp. 7, 11, 54, 96–97
"The poem is directly addressed to the absent 'Thee,' and it is one of the few poems in which one of their conversations is actually recalled and cited."

1988   PHILLIPS, *Emily Dickinson,* pp. 107–08, 115
The poem "has origins in Jane Eyre's story of her devotion to Rochester and the efforts she made to cheer, to tease, and to 'suit' him."

"You see I cannot see—your lifetime" (253)

1982   Ditta, "Jewel and Amethyst," pp. 35–36
"That the I-you in the poem refers to the Poet–Persona distinction being discussed seems clear . . . ."

1983   Shurr, *Marriage,* p. 74
"In the first stanza Dickinson assumes that her lover's longing and loneliness are equal to hers. The exercise is a painful one . . . ."

"You taught me waiting with myself" (740)

1983   Shurr, *Marriage,* pp. 7, 119–20, 143–44
"Addressing her clergyman lover . . . she sums up the enduring residue of their relationship. . . . There is, in the last lines, serene conviction of their certain union after death."

"You'll know her by her foot" (634)

1981   Guthrie, "Modest Poet's Tactics," pp. 234–35
In its present form, it "represents a departure from what was probably Dickinson's original purpose in writing this poem, that is, to assert her qualifications as a poet despite an initially awkward or prolonged apprenticeship."

1988   Dickie, "Discontinuous Lyric Self," pp. 541–44, 550–51
"Offering instruction on how to know a bird, Dickinson provides too an inquiry into self-representation. . . . To know by the foot is not a simple knowledge nor is it a different way of knowing something that exists outside the poem; it is rather a form of knowing by excesses only available in brief and metrical form."

"You'll know it as you know 'tis noon" (420)

1982   Miller, C., "Terms and Golden Words," pp. 49–50, 51, 53, 59
"The speaker's advice to the reader at the end of the poem suggests that the poet's intention in differentiating 'terms' from 'intuition' is more didactic than comparative."

"Your riches taught me poverty" (299)

1980   Cunningham, *Dickinson,* pp. 16–19
The poem's "pearl" is "plausibly the experience of conversion."

1985   DIEHL, "At Home With Loss," p. 177
Relates this "grim version of Emersonian compensation" to the poet's inability to "resolve the conflict between ravishing other and receptive self" and to the lack of "continuity between the patriarchal power and the female experiential self."

1986   BENNETT, *Loaded Gun,* pp. 53–55, 90
". . . the only poem in which Dickinson ever felt totally free to express in direct and undisguised form the love she felt for this extraordinary and very much underrated woman [i.e., Susan Gilbert Dickinson]."

"You're right—'the way is narrow'" (234)

1983   SHURR, *Marriage,* pp. 69, 144
Here Dickinson quotes from (probably) Wadsworth, whose "sermonizing had suggested a financial analogy for salvation." She follows the reasoning of his sermon "but abandons it as inadequate at the end."

1985   CARTON, *Rhetoric,* pp. 88–89, 123
"To risk destitution is to court an ineffable plenitude, as Dickinson does in [this poem], when she exposes some of her central metaphors as contemporary theological clichés, divorcing herself from the poem's culturally overdetermined claims by casting them as the quoted assertions of a phantom interlocutor."

1989   OLIVER, *Apocalypse of Green,* pp. 145, 168
". . . this Biblical paraphrase is complicated by the inclusion of terms from business and commerce and by the emphasis that Dickinson gives to some of the words in the poem. . . . Nevertheless, there is no ironic intent in her insistence that the 'good men' must earn their 'dividends.' "

"You've seen balloons set, haven't you" (700)

1980   ARMITAGE, "Crackerbox Humor," p. 12
"This poem, along with several others that feature a gallery of village and national types and local events, is an excellent example of Dickinson's crackerbox humor."

GREEN, " 'You've seen Balloons,' " pp. 11–18
This is "a symbolic re-enactment of her wavering, opposing convictions about a number of important issues. These include death and immortality, belief and doubt, success and failure and the poet's twin ac-

tions of perception and creation. . . . it is about the precariousness of belief and achievement."

1984   CHERRY, "Sexuality and Tension," pp. 19–20
   "The tension in the poem is probably produced more by the conflict between the female balloon and the decidedly male clerks, than by the balloon's encounter with death. For, at least, death acknowledges her as a worthy combatant . . . ."

1987   MILLER, C., *Emily Dickinson*, p. 66
   "Making both verbs plural in this poem doubly emphasizes the contrast between the tragic but 'imperial' singularity of the poet/balloon and the plural anonymity of the members of the crowd."

1988   WOLFF, *Emily Dickinson*, pp. 439–40
   "No simple story, . . . this verse records a colossal decline as Christ, the overreacher, the poet, and the possibility for some transcendent meaning in our everyday world all subside together. . . . Dickinson mingles other mythic traditions with [the poem's Christian implications]."

Bibliography

Abad, Gémino H. *A Formal Approach to Lyric Poetry*. Quezon City, Philippines: U of the Philippines P, 1978.

Agrawal, Abha. *Emily Dickinson: Search for Self*. New Delhi: Young Asia, 1977.

Alexander, Bonnie L. "Reading Emily Dickinson." *Massachusetts Studies in English* 7.4-8. 1 (1981): 1–17.

Allard, Joseph. "Emily Dickinson: The Regulation of Belief." *Modern American Poetry*. Ed. R. W. (Herbie) Butterfield. London: Vision; Totowa, NJ: Barnes & Noble, 1984. 22–40.

Allen, Gay Wilson. *American Prosody*. New York: American Book, 1935.

Allen, Mary. *Animals in American Literature*. Urbana: U of Illinois P, 1983.

Anantharaman, Priyamvada Tripathi. *The Sunset in a Cup: Emily Dickinson and Mythopoeic Imagination*. New Delhi: Cosmo, 1985.

Anderson, Celia Catlett. "Deep Dyed Politics in ED's 'Revolution is the Pod.'" *Dickinson Studies,* no. 49 (June 1984): 3–8.

Anderson, Charles. "The Modernism of Emily Dickinson." *Emily Dickinson: Letter to the World*. Ed. Katharine Zadravec. Washington, DC: Folger Shakespeare Library, 1986.

BIBLIOGRAPHY

Anderson, Douglas. "Presence and Place in Emily Dickinson's Poetry." *New England Quarterly* 57.2 (June 1984): 205–24.

Anderson, Peggy. "Dickinson's 'Son of None.'" *The Explicator* 41.1 (Fall 1982): 32–33.

———. "The Bride of the White Election: A New Look at Biblical Influence on Emily Dickinson." *Nineteenth-Century Women Writers of the English-Speaking World*. Ed. Rhoda B. Nathan. Contributions in Women's Studies, No. 69. New York: Greenwood, 1986.

Anderson, Vincent P. "Emily Dickinson and the Disappearance of God." *Christian Scholar's Review* 11.1 (1981): 3–17.

Arensberg, Mary, ed. *The American Sublime*. Albany: State U of New York P, 1986.

Armitage, Shelley. "Emily Dickinson's Crackerbox Humor." *Thalia: Studies in Literary Humor* 3.1 (Spring–Summer 1980): 11–15.

Arndt, Murray D. "Emily Dickinson and the Limits of Language." *Dickinson Studies,* no. 57 (1st Half 1986): 19–27.

Attebery, Brian. "Dickinson, Emerson and the Abstract Concrete." *Dickinson Studies,* no. 35 (1st Half 1979): 17–22.

Bachinger, Katrina. "Dickinson's 'I heard a fly buzz.'" *The Explicator* 43.3 (Spring 1985): 12–15.

Baddeley, Laura Seager, and Nadean Bishop. "Perpetual Noon: The Mystic Experience in the Poetry of Emily Dickinson." *Studia Mystica* 7.1 (Spring 1984): 6–22.

Bakker, J. "Emily Dickinson's Secret." *Dutch Quarterly Review of Anglo-American Letters* 16.4 (1986): 341–50. Rpt. in Bunt, G. H. V., E. S. Kooper, J. L. Mackenzie, and D. R. M. Wilkinson, eds. *One Hundred Years of English Studies in Dutch Universities*. Seventeen papers read at the Centenary Conference, Groningen, 15–16 January 1986. Amsterdam: Rodopi, 1987. (*Costerus,* n.s. 64)

Barker, Wendy. *Lunacy of Light: Emily Dickinson and the Experience of Metaphor.* Carbondale: Southern Illinois UP, 1987.

Barnes, Daniel R. "Telling It Slant: Emily Dickinson and the Proverb." *Genre* 12.2 (Summer 1979): 219–41.

Barnstone, Aliki. "Women and the Garden: Andrew Marvell, Emilia Lanier, and Emily Dickinson." *Women and Literature* 2 (1982): 147–67.

———. "Houses within Houses: Emily Dickinson and Mary Wilkins Freeman's 'A New England Nun.'" *Centennial Review* 28.2 (Spring 1984): 129–45.

Bawer, Bruce. "The Audacity of Emily Dickinson." *New Criterion* 5.5 (Jan. 1987): 7–16.

Baym, Nina. "God, Father, and Lover in Emily Dickinson's Poetry." *Pu-*

ritan Influences in American Literature. Ed. Emory Elliott. Illinois Studies in Language and Literature 65. Urbana: U of Illinois P, 1979. 193–209.

Beauchamp, William. "Riffaterre's *Semiotics of Poetry* with an Illustration in the Poetry of Emily Dickinson." *Centrum: Working Papers of the Minnesota Center for Advanced Studies in Language, Style, and Literary Theory,* n.s. 1.1 (Spring 1981): 36–47.

Benfey, Christopher E. G. *Emily Dickinson and the Problem of Others.* Amherst: U of Massachusetts P, 1984.

Benjamin, Edwin B. *The Province of Poetry.* New York: American Book, 1966.

Bennett, Paula. "The Language of Love: Emily Dickinson's Homoerotic Poetry." *Gai Saber* 1.1 (Spring 1977): 13–17.

———. "ED and the Value of Isolation." *Dickinson Studies,* no. 36 (2d Half 1979): 40–49.

———. *My Life a Loaded Gun: Female Creativity and Feminist Poetics.* Boston: Beacon, 1986.

Benvenuto, Richard. "Words within Words: Dickinson's Use of the Dictionary." *ESQ: A Journal of the American Renaissance* 29 (1st Quarter 1983): 46–55.

Beppu, Keiko. " 'O, rare for Emily!'—Dickinson and *Antony and Cleopatra.*" *After a Hundred Years: Essays on Emily Dickinson.* Ed. Emily Dickinson Society of Japan. Kyoto, Japan: Apollon-sha, 1988. 175–89.

Berg, Temma F., ed. *Engendering the Word: Feminist Essays in Psychosexual Poetics.* Urbana: U of Illinois P, 1989.

Bickman, Martin. " 'The snow that never drifts': Dickinson's Slant of Language." *College Literature* 10.2 (Spring 1983): 139–46.

Bishop, Nadean. "Queen of Calvary: Spirituality in Emily Dickinson." *University of Dayton Review* 19.1 (Winter 1987–88): 49–60.

Blasing, Mutlu Konuk. *American Poetry: The Rhetoric of Its Forms.* New Haven: Yale UP, 1987.

Bloom, Clive. *The "Occult" Experience and the New Criticism: Daemonism, Sexuality and the Hidden in Literature.* Sussex, Eng.: Harvester, 1986; Totowa, NJ: Barnes & Noble, 1987.

Bloom, Harold, ed. *Emily Dickinson.* Modern Critical Views. New York: Chelsea, 1985.

———. *American Women Poets.* Critical Cosmos Series. New York: Chelsea, 1986.

———. *American Poetry to 1914.* Critical Cosmos Series. New York: Chelsea, 1987.

Bodie, Edward H., Jr. "Dickinson's 'The wind tapped like a tired man.'" *The Explicator* 46.1 (Fall 1987): 25–26.

Bogus, S. Diane. "Not So Disparate: An Investigation of the Influence of E.B.B. on the Work of ED." *Dickinson Studies*, no. 49 (June 1984): 38–46.

Bonheim, Helmut. "Narrative Technique in Emily Dickinson's 'My life had stood a loaded gun.'" *Journal of Narrative Technique* 18.3 (Fall 1988): 258–68.

Boruch, Marianne. "Dickinson Descending." *Georgia Review* 40.4 (Winter 1986): 863–77.

Brashear, Lucy. "'Awake ye muses nine': Emily Dickinson's Prototype Poem." *South Atlantic Bulletin* 45.4 (Nov. 1980): 90–99.

———. "Emily Dickinson's Dramatic Monologues." *American Transcendental Quarterly*, no. 56 (Mar. 1985): 65–76.

Brumm, Anna-Marie. "Religion and the Poet: ED and Annette von Droste-Huelshoff." *Dickinson Studies*, no. 59 (2d Half 1986): 21–34.

Buckingham, Willis J. "Dickinson's 'That after Horror—that 'twas *us*.'" *The Explicator* 40.4 (Summer 1982): 34–35.

Budick, E. Miller. "'I had not minded—Walls—': The Method and Meaning of Emily Dickinson's Symbolism." *Concerning Poetry* 9.2 (Fall 1976): 5–12.

———. "The Assignable Portion: ED on the Dilemma of Symbolic Perception." *Dickinson Studies*, no. 36 (2d Half 1979): 1–15.

———. "When the Soul Selects: Emily Dickinson's Attack on New England Symbolism." *American Literature* 51.3 (Nov. 1979): 349–63.

———. "Symbolizing Eternity: A Reading of Emily Dickinson's 'There came a day at summer's full.'" *Concerning Poetry* 16.1 (Spring 1983): 1–12.

———. "Temporal Consciousness and the Perception of Eternity in Emily Dickinson." *Essays in Literature* 10.2 (Fall 1983): 227–39.

———. "The Dangers of the Living Word: Aspects of Dickinson's Epistemology, Cosmology, and Symbolism." *ESQ: A Journal of the American Renaissance* 29 (4th Quarter 1983): 208–24.

———. *Emily Dickinson and the Life of Language: A Study in Symbolic Poetics.* Baton Rouge: Louisiana State UP, 1985.

Buell, Lawrence. "Literature and Scripture in New England Between the Revolution and the Civil War." *Notre Dame English Journal: A Journal of Religion in Literature* 15.2 (Spring 1983): 1–28.

———. *New England Literary Culture: From Revolution Through Renaissance.* Cambridge: Cambridge UP, 1986.

Bunt, G. H. V., E. S. Kooper, J. L. Mackenzie, and D. R. M. Wilkinson, eds. *One Hundred Years of English Studies in Dutch Universities.* Seventeen papers read at the Centenary Conference, Groningen, 15–16 January 1986. Amsterdam: Rodopi, 1987. (*Costerus,* n.s. 64)

Burbick, Joan. "Emily Dickinson and the Revenge of the Nerves." *Women's Studies* 7.1–2 (1980): 95–109.

———. "The Irony of Self-Reference: Emily Dickinson's Pronominal Language." *Essays in Literature* 9.1 (Spring 1982): 83–95.

———. "Emily Dickinson and the Economics of Desire." *American Literature* 58.3 (Oct. 1986): 361–78.

Burke, Sally. "A Religion of Poetry: The Prayer Poems of Emily Dickinson." *Emily Dickinson Bulletin,* no. 33 (1st Half 1978): 17–25.

Byers, John R., Jr. "The Possible Background of Three Dickinson Poems." *Dickinson Studies,* no. 57 (1st Half 1986): 35–38.

Bzowski, Frances. "A Continuation of the Tradition of the Irony of Death." *Dickinson Studies,* no. 54 (Bonus 1984): 33–42.

Cadman, Deborah. "Dickinson's 'I taste a liquor never brewed.'" *The Explicator* 47.2 (Winter 1989): 30–32.

Cameron, Sharon. "Naming as History: Dickinson's Poems of Definition." *Critical Inquiry* 5.2 (Winter 1978): 223–51.

———. "'A Loaded Gun': Dickinson and the Dialectic of Rage." *PMLA* 93.3 (May 1978): 423–37.

———. *Lyric Time: Dickinson and the Limits of Genre.* Baltimore: Johns Hopkins UP, 1979.

———. "*Et in Arcadia Ego:* Representation, Death, and the Problem of Boundary in Emily Dickinson." *American Women Poets.* Ed. Harold Bloom. New York: Chelsea, 1986.

Campbell, Karen Mills. "Poetry as Epitaph." *Journal of Popular Culture* 14.4 (Spring 1981): 657–68.

Carruth, Hayden. "Emily Dickinson's Unexpectedness." *Ironwood,* no. 28 (1986): 51–57.

Carter, Steve. "Emily Dickinson and Mysticism." *ESQ: A Journal of the American Renaissance* 24 (2d Quarter 1978): 83–95.

Carton, Evan. "Dickinson and the Divine: The Terror of Integration, the Terror of Detachment." *ESQ: A Journal of the American Renaissance* 24 (4th Quarter 1978): 242–52.

———. "'The True Romance': Philosophy's Copernican Revolution and American Literary Dialectics." *Philosophical Approaches to Literature: New Essays on Nineteenth- and Twentieth-Century Texts.* Ed. William E. Cain. Lewisburg, PA: Bucknell UP; London: Assoc. UP, 1984. 91–116.

―――. *The Rhetoric of American Romance: Dialectic and Identity in Emerson, Dickinson, Poe, and Hawthorne.* Baltimore: Johns Hopkins UP, 1985.

Cherry, Amy L. "'A Prison gets to be a friend': Sexuality and Tension in the Poems of ED." *Dickinson Studies,* no. 49 (June 1984): 9–21.

Cleary, Vincent J. "Emily Dickinson's Classical Education." *English Language Notes* 18.2 (Dec. 1980): 119–29.

Cody, John. "Dickinson's 'I taste a liquor never brewed.'" *The Explicator* 36.3 (Spring 1978): 7–8.

―――. "Dickinson's 'I can wade grief.'" *The Explicator* 37.1 (Fall 1978): 15–16.

―――. "Emily: Hazards, Billowbees and Rewards." *Midwest Quarterly* 22.3 (Spring 1981): 201–17.

Cook, Albert. *Figural Choice in Poetry and Art.* Hanover, NH: UP of New England, 1985.

―――. *Thresholds: Studies in the Romantic Experience.* Madison: U of Wisconsin P, 1985.

Cook, Carol L. "The Psychic Development of a Woman Writer." *University of Dayton Review* 19.1 (Winter 1987–88): 121–35.

Cooper, Michele F. "Emily Dickinson: The Androgynous Temper." *University of Dayton Review* 19.1 (Winter 1987–88): 137–45.

Cooper, Philip. "The Central Image of 'Because I could not stop for death.'" *Studies in English and American Literature.* Ed. John L. Cutler and Lawrence S. Thompson. Troy, NY: Whitston, 1978. 295–96. (*American Notes and Queries.* Supplement, Vol. 1)

Coppay, Frank L. "The Internal Analysis of Compression in Poetry." *Style* 11.1 (Winter 1977): 19–38.

Corn, Alfred. "Dickinson's Losses Regained." *Threepenny Review* 11.2, issue no. 34 (Summer 1988): 18–19.

Cottle, Basil. *The Language of Literature.* New York: St. Martin's, 1985.

Crabbe, John K. "A Thing without Feathers (J.510)." *Dickinson Studies,* no. 34 (2d Half 1978): 3–6.

Cronenwett, Philip. "'We Play at Paste': A Footnote on an Emily Dickinson Manuscript." *Resources for American Literary Study* 10.1 (Spring 1980): 28–32.

Crosthwaite, Jane. "The Way to Read a Letter: Emily Dickinson's Variation on a Theme by Charlotte Brontë." *American Transcendental Quarterly,* no. 42 (Spring 1979): 159–65.

―――. "Emily Dickinson's Ride with Death." *Massachusetts Studies in English* 7.4-8.1 (1981): 18–27.

Crosthwaite, Jane F. "Dickinson's 'What I see not, I better see.'" *The Explicator* 36.3 (Spring 1978): 10–12.

Cuddy, Lois A. "The Latin Imprint on Emily Dickinson's Poetry: Theory and Practice." *American Literature* 50.1 (Mar. 1978): 74–84.

———. "Expression and Sublimation: More on the Bee in ED's Poetry." *Dickinson Studies,* no. 39 (1st Half 1981): 27–35.

———. "Shelley's Glorious Titan: Reflections on ED's Self-image and Achievement." *Dickinson Studies,* no. 55 (1st Half 1985): 32–40.

Culjak, Toni Ann. "Dickinson and Kierkegaard: Arrival at Despair." *American Transcendental Quarterly* 1.2 (June 1987): 145–55.

Cunningham, J. V. *Dickinson: Lyric and Legend.* Los Angeles: Sylvester & Orphanos, 1980.

Dahl, Curtis. "'To Fight Aloud' and 'The Charge of the Light Brigade': Dickinson on Tennyson." *New England Quarterly* 52.1 (Mar. 1979): 94–99.

———. "Dickinson's 'There's a certain slant of light.'" *The Explicator* 45.3 (Spring 1987): 37–38.

Dahlen, Beverly. "A Reading: Emily Dickinson: Powers of Horror." *Ironwood* 28 (1986): 9–37.

Daiches, David. *God and the Poets: The Gifford Lectures, 1983.* Oxford: Clarendon, 1984.

Dalke, Anne French. "'Devil's Wine': A Re-Examination of Emily Dickinson's #214." *American Notes and Queries* 23.5-6 (Jan.–Feb. 1985): 78–80.

D'Avanzo, Mario L. "A Source in Wyatt." *Dickinson Studies* 42 (June 1982): 40–43.

Davis, Sophia M. "'Heavenly Father'—take to thee (An explication of poem J1461)." *Emily Dickinson Bulletin* 33 (1st Half 1978): 40–44.

De Eulis, Marilyn Davis. "Whitman's 'The First Dandelion' and Emily Dickinson's 'The dandelion's pallid tube.'" *Walt Whitman Review* 25.1 (Mar. 1979): 29–32.

Derrick, Paul Scott. "Emily Dickinson, Martin Heidegger, and the Poetry of Dread." *Western Humanities Review* 40.1 (Spring 1986):27–38.

Dickenson, Donna. *Emily Dickinson.* Berg Women's Series. Leamington Spa, Eng.: Berg, 1985.

Dickie, Margaret. "Dickinson's Discontinuous Lyric Self." *American Literature* 60.4 (Dec. 1988): 537–53.

Diehl, Joanne Feit. "'Come Slowly—Eden': An Exploration of Women Poets and Their Muse." *Signs: Journal of Women in Culture and Society* 3.3 (Spring 1978): 572–87.

BIBLIOGRAPHY

———. "Dickinson and the American Self." *ESQ: A Journal of the American Renaissance* 26 (1st Quarter 1980): 1–9.

———. "Dickinson and Bloom: An Antithetical Reading of Romanticism." *Texas Studies in Literature and Language* 23.3 (Fall 1981): 418–41.

———. *Dickinson and the Romantic Imagination*. Princeton: Princeton UP, 1981.

———. "'Ransom in a Voice': Language as Defense in Dickinson's Poetry." *Feminist Critics Read Emily Dickinson*. Ed. Suzanne Juhasz. Bloomington: Indiana UP, 1983. 156–75. Rpt. in Bloom, *American Women Poets*, pp. 23–39.

———. "At Home With Loss: Elizabeth Bishop and the American Sublime." *Elizabeth Bishop*. Ed. Harold Bloom. Modern Critical Views. New York: Chelsea, 1985. 175–88.

———. "Emerson, Dickinson, and the Abyss." *Emily Dickinson*. Ed. Harold Bloom. New York: Chelsea, 1985. 145–59. Rpt. in Bloom, *American Poetry*, pp. 449–62.

———. "In the Twilight of the Gods: Women Poets and the American Sublime." *The American Sublime*. Ed. Mary Arensberg. Albany: State U of New York P, 1986. 173–214.

———. "Murderous Poetics: Dickinson, the Father, and the Text." *Daughters and Fathers*. Ed. Lynda E. Boose and Betty S. Flowers. Baltimore: Johns Hopkins UP, 1989. 326–43.

———. "Poem 656. Terrains of Difference: Reading Shelley and Dickinson on Autumn." *Women's Studies* 16.1-2 (1989): 87–90.

———. "Poem 1651. Loving Language: The Poetics of Authority in 'A Word made Flesh.'" *Women's Studies* 16.1-2 (1989): 177–80.

Diehl, Joanne Feit, and Barbara Packer. "Poem 656: Workshop Discussion." *Women's Studies* 16.1-2 (1989): 95–113.

Diehl, Joanne Feit, Cristanne Miller, and Maurya Simon. "Poem 1651: Workshop Discussion." *Women's Studies* 16.1-2 (1989): 189–206.

Diggory, Terence. "Armored Women, Naked Men: Dickinson, Whitman, and Their Successors." *Shakespeare's Sisters: Feminist Essays on Women Poets*. Ed. Suzanne Juhasz. Bloomington: Indiana UP, 1979. 135–50.

Di Giuseppe, Rita. "The Maiden and the Muse: Dickinson's Tropes of Poetic Creation." *Quaderni di Lingue e Letterature* 12 (1987): 39–56.

Ditsky, John. "The Two Emilies and a Feathered Hope: Shared Imagery in Dickinson and Brontë." *Kyushu Amerika Bungaku* [Kyushu American Literature] 19 (1978): 28–31.

Ditta, Joseph M. "The Jewel and the Amethyst: Poet and Persona in Emily Dickinson." *Dickinson Studies* 42 (June 1982): 30–37.

Dobson, Joanne "'The Invisible Lady': Emily Dickinson and Conventions of the Female Self." *Legacy: A Journal of Nineteenth-Century American Women Writers* 3.1 (Spring 1986): 41–55.

———. *Dickinson and the Strategies of Reticence: The Woman Writer in Nineteenth-Century America.* Bloomington: Indiana UP, 1989.

———. "Poem 754: The Unreadable Poem." *Women's Studies* 16.1-2 (1989): 117–20.

Dobson, Joanne, Lillian Faderman, and Ellin Ringler-Henderson. "Poem 754: Workshop Discussion." *Women's Studies* 16.1-2 (1989): 133–48.

Dobson, Joanne A. "'Oh, Susie, it is dangerous': Emily Dickinson and the Archetype." *Feminist Critics Read Emily Dickinson.* Ed. Suzanne Juhasz. Bloomington: Indiana UP, 1983. 80–97.

Donohoe, Eileen M. "Undeveloped Freight in Dickinson's 'I read my sentence—steadily—.'" *Concerning Poetry* 15.2 (Fall 1982): 43–48.

Donohue, Gail. "Lyric Voice: 'I cannot live with You—.'" *Dickinson Studies,* no. 46 (Bonus 1983): 3–8.

Doreski, William. "'An Exchange of Territory': Dickinson's Fascicle 27." *ESQ: A Journal of the American Renaissance* 32 (1st Quarter 1986): 55–67.

Downey, Charlotte. "How the Mathematical Concepts Portrayed in the Language Patterns of Walt Whitman's and ED's Poems relate to Meaning." *Dickinson Studies,* no. 72 (2d Half 1989): 17–32.

Downey, Charlotte, R.S.M. *A Child's Emily Dickinson.* Providence, RI: n.p., 1982.

———. "ED's Appeal for a Child Audience." *Dickinson Studies,* no. 55 (1st Half 1985): 21–31.

Downey, Sister Charlotte, R.S.M. "Antithesis: How ED uses Style to Express Inner Conflict." *Emily Dickinson Bulletin,* no. 33 (1st Half 1978): 8–16.

Duncan, Jeffrey L. "Joining Together/Putting Asunder: An Essay on Emily Dickinson's Poetry." *Missouri Review* 4.2 (Winter 1980–81): 111–29.

Du Priest, Travis. "ED's 'Pink—small—and punctual.'" *Dickinson Studies,* no. 46 (Bonus 1983): 20.

Durnell, Hazel B. *Japanese Cultural Influences on American Poetry and Drama.* Tokyo: Hokuseido P, 1983.

Eberwein, Jane Donahue. "Dickinson's Nobody and Ulysses' Noman: 'Then there's a pair of us?'" *Dickinson Studies,* no. 46 (Bonus 1983): 9–14.

———. "Dickinson's 'I had some things that I called mine.'" *The Explicator* 42.3 (Spring 1984): 31–33.

———. "Doing Without: Dickinson as Yankee Woman Poet." *Critical Essays on Emily Dickinson*. Ed. Paul J. Ferlazzo. Boston: G. K. Hall, 1984. 205–23.

———. *Dickinson: Strategies of Limitation*. Amherst: U of Massachusetts P, 1985.

———. "Emily Dickinson and the Calvinist Sacramental Tradition." *ESQ: A Journal of the American Renaissance* 33 (2d Quarter 1987): 67–81.

Eddins, Dwight. "Emily Dickinson and Nietzsche: The Rites of Dionysus." *ESQ: A Journal of the American Renaissance* 27 (2d Quarter 1981): 96–107.

Eitner, Walter H. "ED: Another Daphne?" *Emily Dickinson Bulletin*, no. 33 (1st Half 1978): 35–39.

Elfenbein, Anna Shannon. "Unsexing Language: Pronominal Protest in Emily Dickinson's 'Lay this Laurel.'" *Engendering the Word: Feminist Essays in Psychosexual Poetics*. Ed. Temma F. Berg. Urbana: U of Illinois P, 1989. 208–23.

Emily Dickinson Society of Japan. *After a Hundred Years: Essays on Emily Dickinson*. Kyoto, Japan: Apollon-sha, 1988.

Erkkila, Betsy. "Emily Dickinson on Her Own Terms." *Wilson Quarterly* 9.2 (Spring 1985): 98–109.

Estes, David C. "'Out upon circumference': Emily Dickinson's Search for Location." *Essays in Literature* 6.2 (Fall 1979): 207–18.

———. "Granny Weatherall's Dying Moment: Katherine Anne Porter's Allusions to Emily Dickinson." *Studies in Short Fiction* 22.4 (Fall 1985): 437–42.

Etter, Kathryn. "Dickinson's 'The gentian weaves her fringes.'" *The Explicator* 40.3 (Spring 1982): 34–36.

Faderman, Lillian. "Emily Dickinson's Homoerotic Poetry." *Higginson Journal*, no. 18 (1st Half 1978): 19–27.

———. "Poem 754: Ambivalent Heterosexuality in 'My Life had stood—a Loaded Gun.'" *Women's Studies* 16.1-2 (1989): 121–25.

Falk, Marcia. "Poem 271." *Women's Studies* 16.1-2 (1989): 23–27.

———. "Poem 1581: Kinds of Difficulty in 'The farthest Thunder that I heard.'" *Women's Studies* 16.1-2 (1989): 151–54.

Falk, Marcia, Barbara Mossberg, and Maurya Simon. "Poem 271: Workshop Discussion." *Women's Studies* 16.1-2 (1989): 39–52.

Falk, Marcia, and Barbara Packer. "Poem 1581: Workshop Discussion." *Women's Studies* 16.1-2 (1989): 159–74.

Fast, Robin Riley. " 'The One Thing Needful': Dickinson's Dilemma of Home and Heaven." *ESQ: A Journal of the American Renaissance* 27 (3d Quarter 1981): 157–69.

———. "Poem 315." *Women's Studies* 16.1-2 (1989); 55–59.

Fast, Robin Riley, and Christine Mack Gordon, eds. *Approaches to Teaching Dickinson's Poetry.* Approaches to Teaching World Literature 26. New York: Modern Language Assn. of America, 1989.

Fast, Robin Riley, Suzanne Juhasz, and Ellen Ringler-Henderson. "Poem 315: Workshop Discussion." *Women's Studies* 16.1-2 (1989): 73–84.

Faulkner, Howard. "Emily Dickinson." *Critical Survey of Poetry: English Language Series.* Ed. Frank N. Magill. "Authors," vol. 2. Englewood Cliffs, NJ: Salem, 1982. 802–13.

Felstiner, John. "Translating Celan/Celan Translating." *Acts: A Journal of New Writing,* no. 8-9 (1988): 108–18.

Ferlazzo, Paul J., ed. *Critical Essays on Emily Dickinson.* Critical Essays on American Literature. Boston: G. K. Hall, 1984.

Finch, A. R. C. "Dickinson and Patriarchal Meter: A Theory of Metrical Codes." *PMLA* 102.2 (Mar. 1987): 166–76.

Fitzgerald, Nora M. "Dickinson's 'I took my power in my hand.' " *The Explicator* 43.2 (Winter 1985): 20–21.

Flatto, Eli, Ph.D. "Emily Dickinson's 'My Life Closed Twice': The Archetypal Import of Its Imagistic Number Two." *American Imago* 45.2 (Summer 1988): 225–27.

Fleissner, Robert F. " 'Frost . . . at . . . Play': A Frost-Dickinson Affinity Affirmed." *Research Studies* 46.1 (Mar. 1978): 28–39.

———. "Dickinson's 'Moor.' " *Dickinson Studies,* no. 34 (2d Half 1978): 7–12.

———. "Beauty-Truth RE-Echoed: The Keats-Dickinson 'Marriage' Annulled." *Higginson Journal,* no. 38 (1st Half 1984): 19–21.

Fletcher, John. "Poetry, Gender and Primal Fantasy." *Formations of Fantasy.* Ed. Victor Burgin, James Donald, and Cora Kaplan. London: Methuen, 1986. 109–41.

Fontana, Ernest. "Dickinson's 'Go not too near a house of Rose' (Poem 1434) and Keats' *Ode on Melancholy.*" *Dickinson Studies,* no. 68 (2d Half 1988): 26–29.

Ford, Boris, ed. *New Pelican Guide to English Literature.* Vol. 9: *American Literature.* Harmondsworth, Middlesex, Eng.: Pelican, 1988.

Ford, Thomas W. "Indian Summer and Blackberry Winter: Emily Dickinson and Robert Penn Warren." *Southern Review* 17.3 (July 1981): 542–50.

BIBLIOGRAPHY

Frank, Bernhard. "Dickinson's 'I saw no way—the heavens were stitched." *The Explicator* 48.1 (Fall 1989): 28–29.

Franklin, R. W. "The Manuscripts and Transcripts of 'Further in Summer than the Birds.'" *Papers of the Bibliographical Society of America* 72 (1978): 552–60.

———. "Three Additional Dickinson Manuscripts." *American Literature* 50.1 (Mar. 1978): 109–16.

———. "The Houghton Library Dickinson Manuscript 157." *Harvard Library Bulletin* 28.3 (July 1980): 245–57.

Freedman, William. "Dickinson's 'I like to see it lap the miles.'" *The Explicator* 40.3 (Spring 1982): 30–32.

Fry, August J. "*Writing New Englandy* [*sic*]: A Study of Diction and Technique in the Poetry of Emily Dickinson." *From Cooper to Philip Roth: Essays on American Literature*. Presented to J. G. Riewald on the occasion of his seventieth birthday. Ed. J. Bakker and D. R. M. Wilkinson. Amsterdam: Rodopi, 1980. 21–31. (*Costerus*, n.s. 26)

Fulton, Alice. "Her Moment of Brocade: The Reconstruction of Emily Dickinson." *Parnassus: Poetry in Review* 15.1 (Spring 1989): 9–44.

Furukawa, Takao. "Emily Dickinson's 'Finite Infinity' As a Double Vision." *After a Hundred Years: Essays on Emily Dickinson*. Ed. Emily Dickinson Society of Japan. Kyoto: Japan: Apollon-sha, 1988. 15–31.

Galinsky, Hans. "Northern and Southern Aspects of Nineteenth Century American-German Interrelations: Dickinson and Lanier." *American-German Literary Interrelations in the Nineteenth Century*. Ed. Christoph Wecker. American Studies—A Monograph Series 55. Munich: Wilhelm Fink Verlag, 1983. 124–65.

Galperin, William. "Assignment for an Introductory Literary Studies Class." Fast and Gordon (1989), *Approaches*. 178–79.

———. "A Posthumanist Approach to Teaching Dickinson." Fast and Gordon (1989), *Approaches*. 113–17.

Galperin, William H. "Emily Dickinson's Marriage Hearse." *Denver Quarterly* 18.4 (Winter 1984): 62–73.

Garbowsky, Maryanne M. "A Maternal Muse for Emily Dickinson." *Dickinson Studies*, no. 41 (Dec. 1981): 12–17.

———. *The House without the Door: A Study of Emily Dickinson and the Illness of Agoraphobia*. Rutherford, NJ: Fairleigh Dickinson UP; London: Assoc. UP, 1989.

Gelpi, Albert. "Emily Dickinson's Word: Presence as Absence, Absence as Presence." *American Poetry* 4.2 (Winter 1987): 41–50.

Gibbons, Reginald. "Poetry and Self-Making." *Triquarterly*, no. 75 (Spring–Summer 1989): 98–118.

Gibson, Andrew. "Emily Dickinson and the Poetry of Hypothesis." *Essays in Criticism* 33.3 (July 1983): 220–37.

Gilbert, Sandra M. "The Wayward Nun beneath the Hill: Emily Dickinson and the Mysteries of Womanhood." *Feminist Critics Read Emily Dickinson.* Ed. Suzanne Juhasz. Bloomington: Indiana UP, 1983. 22–44.

———. "The American Sexual Poetics of Walt Whitman and Emily Dickinson." *Reconstructing American Literary History.* Ed. Sacvan Bercovitch. Harvard English Studies 13. Cambridge: Harvard UP, 1986. 123–54.

———. " 'Now in a moment I know what I am for': Rituals of Initiation in Whitman and Dickinson." *Mickle Street Review,* no. 11 (1989): 46–55.

Gilbert, Sandra M., and Susan Gubar. *The Madwoman in the Attic: The Woman Writer and the Nineteenth-Century Literary Imagination.* New Haven: Yale UP, 1979.

———. "Tradition and the Female Talent." *Literary History: Theory and Practice.* Ed. Herbert L. Sussman. Proceedings of the Northeastern University Center for Literary Studies 2. Boston: Northeastern UP, 1984. 1–27. Rpt. in *The Poetics of Gender.* Ed. Nancy K. Miller. New York: Columbia UP, 1986. 183–207.

———. *No Man's Land: The Place of the Woman Writer in the Twentieth Century.* Vol. 1: *The War of the Words.* Vol. 2: *Sexchanges.* New Haven: Yale UP, 1988–89.

———, eds. *Shakespeare's Sisters: Feminist Essays on Women Poets.* Bloomington: Indiana UP, 1979.

Gilmore, Leigh. "The Gaze of the Other Woman: Beholding and Begetting in Dickinson, Moore, and Rich." *Engendering the Word: Feminist Essays in Psychosexual Poetics.* Ed. Temma F. Berg. Urbana: U of Illinois P, 1989. 81–102.

Gohdes, Clarence L. "Emily Dickinson's Blue Fly." *New England Quarterly* 51.3 (Sept. 1978): 423–31.

Gonnaud, Maurice. "Nature, Apocalypse or Experiment: Emerson's Double Lineage in American Poetry." *Vistas of a Continent: Concepts of Nature in America.* Ed. Teut Andreas Riese. Anglistische Forschungen 136. Heidelberg, Ger.: Carl Winter Universitätsverlag, 1979. 123–41.

Green, David. " 'You've seen Balloons set—Haven't You?' (J.700)." *Dickinson Studies,* no. 37 (1st Half 1980): 11–18.

Green, David L. "Emily Dickinson: The Spatial Drama of Centering." *Essays in Literature* 7.2 (Fall 1980): 191–200.

BIBLIOGRAPHY

Greenwald, Elissa. "Dickinson among the Realists." Fast and Gordon, *Approaches*. 164–69.

Gross, Seymour, and Frank Rashid. "Emily Dickinson and the Erotic." *Dickinson Studies*, no. 37 (1st Half 1908): 25–28.

Guerra, Jonnie G. "Dickinson's 'A bird came down the walk.'" *The Explicator* 47.2 (Winter 1989): 29–30.

———. "Dickinson's 'The soul has bandaged moments.'" *The Explicator* 48.1 (Fall 1989): 30–32.

Gunn, Giles. *The Interpretation of Otherness: Literature, Religion, and the American Imagination*. New York: Oxford UP, 1979.

Guthrie, James. "'Before I got my eye put out': Dickinson's Illness and its Effects on Her Poetry." *Dickinson Studies*, no. 42 (June 1982): 16–21.

———. "Near Rhymes and Reason: Style and Personality in Dickinson's Poetry." Fast and Gordon, *Approaches*. 70–77.

Guthrie, James R. "The Modest Poet's Tactics of Concealment and Surprise: Bird Symbolism in Dickinson's Poetry." *ESQ: A Journal of the American Renaissance* 27 (4th Quarter 1981): 230–37.

Hafley, James. "Emily Dickinson's Green Experiment." *The Single Hound* 1.1 (1989): 18–20.

Hagenbüchle, Roland. "Sign and Process: The Concept of Language in Emerson and Dickinson." *ESQ: A Journal of the American Renaissance* 25 (3d Quarter 1979): 137–55. Rpt. in *Dickinson Studies*, no. 58 (Bonus 1986): 59–88.

———. "The Concept of Ambiguity in Linguistics and Literary Criticism." *Modes of Interpretation: Essays Presented to Ernst Leisi on the Occasion of his sixty-fifth Birthday*. Ed. Richard J. Watts and Urs Weidmann. Tübingen, Ger.: Gunter Narr Verlag, 1984. 213–21.

———. "Emily Dickinson's Aesthetics of Process." *Poetry and Epistemology: Turning Points in the History of Poetic Knowledge*. Papers from the International Poetry Symposium Eichstätt, 1983. Ed. Roland Hagenbüchle and Laura Skandera. Eichstätter Beiträge 20; Abteilung Sprache und Literatur 6. Regensburg, Ger.: Verlag Friedrich Pustet, 1986. 135–47.

———. "Visualization and Vision in Emily Dickinson's Poetry." *Poetry and the Fine Arts*. Papers from the Poetry Sessions of the European Association for American Studies Biennial Conference, Rome, 1984. Ed. Roland Hagenbüchle and Jaqueline S. Ollier. Eichstätter Beiträge 24; Abteilung Sprache und Literatur 8. Regensburg, Ger.: Verlag Friedrich Pustet, 1989. 61–71.

Hagenbüchle, Roland, and Joseph T. Swann. "Dickinson and the Dialectic of Rage." *PMLA* 94.1 (Jan. 1979): 144–45.

Harris, Natalie. "The Naked and the Veiled: Sylvia Plath and Emily Dickinson in Counterpoint." *Dickinson Studies,* no. 45 (June 1983): 23–34.

Harris, Sharon M. "The 'Cloth of Dreams': Dream Imagery in Dickinson's Poetry and Prose." *Dickinson Studies,* no. 68 (2d Half 1988): 3–16.

Hartman, Geoffrey H. *Criticism in the Wilderness: The Study of Literature Today.* New Haven: Yale UP, 1980.

Hattenhauer, Darryl. "Feminism in Dickinson's Bird Imagery." *Dickinson Studies,* no. 52 (2d Half 1984): 54–57.

Hecht, Anthony, ed. *Obbligati: Essays in Criticism.* New York: Atheneum, 1986.

———. "The Riddles of Emily Dickinson." *New England Review* 1.1 (Autumn 1978): 1–24. Rpt. in Hecht, Anthony. *Obbligati: Essays in Criticism.* New York: Atheneum, 1986. 85–117.

Helms, Alan. "The Sense of Punctuation." *Yale Review* 69.2 (Dec. 1979): 177–96.

Herndon, Jerry A. "A Note on Emily Dickinson and Job." *Christianity and Literature* 30.3 (Spring 1981): 45–52.

Hesford, Walter. "'In snow thou comest': ED's Faithful Riddle." *Dickinson Studies,* no. 46 (Bonus 1983): 15–19.

———. "The Creative Fall of Bradstreet and Dickinson." *Essays in Literature* 14.1 (Spring 1987): 81–91.

Hockersmith, Thomas E. "'Into Degreeless Noon': Time, Consciousness, and Oblivion in Emily Dickinson." *American Transcendental Quarterly* 3.3 (Sept. 1989): 277–95.

Holden, Jonathan. "Landscape Poems." *Denver Quarterly* 20.4-21.1 (Spring-Summer 1986): 159–76.

Holland, Jeanne. "Emily Dickinson, the Master, and the Loaded Gun: The Violence of Re-figuration." *ESQ: A Journal of the American Renaissance* 33 (3d Quarter 1987): 137–45.

Holloway, Julia Bolton. "Death and the Emperor in Dante, Browning, Dickinson and Stevens." *Studies in Medievalism* 2.3 (Summer 1983): 67–72.

Homans, Margaret. *Women Writers and Poetic Identity: Dorothy Wordsworth, Emily Brontë, and Emily Dickinson.* Princeton; Princeton UP, 1980.

———. "'Oh, Vision of Language!': Dickinson's Poems of Love and Death." *Feminist Critics Read Emily Dickinson.* Ed. Suzanne Juhasz. Bloomington: Indiana UP, 1983. 114–33.

———. "Emily Dickinson and Poetic Identity." *Emily Dickinson.* Ed. Harold Bloom. New York: Chelsea, 1985. 129–44.

BIBLIOGRAPHY

———. "Syllables of Velvet: Dickinson, Rossetti, and the Rhetorics of Sexuality." *Feminist Studies* 11.3 (Fall 1985): 569–93.

———. "Emily Dickinson." *American Poetry to 1914*. Ed. Harold Bloom. New York: Chelsea, 1987. 411–48.

Hook, Andrew. *American Literature in Context, III: 1865–1900*. London: Methuen, 1983.

Hope, Quentin M. "*The Saintly Veil of Maiden White:* Snow and Divinity." *Arcadia* 18 (1983): 282–93.

Hopes, David B. "The Uses of Metaphor in Emily Dickinson's Poetry." *Dickinson Studies,* no. 38 (2d Half 1980): 12–20.

Horiuchi, Amy. *Possible Zen Traits in Emily Dickinson's Perception*. Kawagoe, Japan: Toyo University, 1978.

Howe, Susan. *My Emily Dickinson*. Berkeley: North Atlantic, 1985.

Hughes, Daniel. "Emily Dickinson as the Queen of Sheba and the Approach to Solomon Master." *University of Dayton Review* 19.1 (Winter 1987–88): 19–30.

Hughes, Gertrude Reif. "Subverting the Cult of Domesticity: Emily Dickinson's Critique of Women's Work." *Legacy: A Journal of Nineteenth-Century American Women Writers* 3.1 (Spring 1986): 17–28.

Hughes, James M. "Dickinson as 'Time's Sublimest Target.'" *Dickinson Studies,* no. 34 (2d Half 1978): 27–37.

———. "Inner and Outer Seas in Dickinson, Dana, Cooper, and Roberts." *Literature and Lore of the Sea*. Ed. Patricia Ann Carlson. Amsterdam: Rodopi, 1986. 202–11. (*Costerus*, n.s. 52)

———. "'I bring my rose.' ED's Gift of Power." *Dickinson Studies,* no. 63 (2d Half 1987): 33–42.

Hughes, James M., and Carlos Cortinez. "Where Do You Stand with God, Ms. Dickinson, Senor Borges?" *Borges the Poet*. Ed. Carlos Cortinez. Fayetteville: U of Arkansas P, 1986. 232–42.

Hurley, Andrew. "Waiting for the Other Shoe: Some Observations on Rhyme." *Auctor Ludens: Essays on Play in Literature*. Ed. Gerald Guinness and Andrew Hurley. *Cultura Ludens: Imitation and Play in Western Culture* 2. Philadelphia: Benjamins, 1986. 127–36.

Hymel, Cynthia Drew. "Singing Off Charnal Steps: Passivity in Dickinson's First Person Accounts of Death." *Dickinson Studies,* no. 41 (Dec. 1981): 3–11.

Iwata, Michiko. "Something from Nothing in Emily Dickinson's Poetry." *After a Hundred Years: Essays on Emily Dickinson*. Ed. Emily Dickinson Society of Japan. Kyoto, Japan: Apollon-sha, 1988. 133–41.

Jerome, Judson. "Type of the Modern." *University of Dayton Review* 19.1 (Winter 1987–88): 69–78.

Johnson, Greg. "'Broken Mathematics': Emily Dickinson's Concept of Ratio." *Concerning Poetry* 13.1 (Spring 1980): 21–26.

―――. "'A Pearl of Great Price': The Identity of Emily Dickinson." *ESQ: A Journal of the American Renaissance* 26 (4th Quarter 1980): 202–15.

―――. "Emily Dickinson: Perception and the Poet's Quest." *Renascence: Essays on Value in Literature* 35.1 (Autumn 1982): 2–15.

―――. *Emily Dickinson: Perception and the Poet's Quest.* University: U of Alabama P, 1985.

Jones, Rowena Revis. "'A Royal Seal': Emily Dickinson's Rite of Baptism." *Religion and Literature* 18.3 (Fall 1986): 29–51.

Juhasz, Suzanne. "'But most, like Chaos': Emily Dickinson Measures Pain." *American Transcendental Quarterly* 43.1 (Summer 1979): 225–41.

―――. "The 'Undiscovered Continent': Emily Dickinson and the Space of the Mind." *Missouri Review* 3.1 (Fall 1979): 86–97.

―――. "'To make a prairie': Language and Form in Emily Dickinson's Poems about Mental Experience." *Ball State University Forum* 21.2 (Spring 1980): 12–25.

―――. "'Peril as a possession': Emily Dickinson and Crisis." *Massachusetts Studies in English* 7.4-8.1 (1981): 28–39.

―――. *The Undiscovered Continent: Emily Dickinson and the Space of the Mind.* Bloomington: Indiana UP, 1983.

―――. "Tea and Revolution: Emily Dickinson Populates the Mind." *Essays in Literature* 12.1 (Spring 1985): 145–50.

―――. "Renunciation Transformed, the Dickinson Heritage: Emily Dickinson and Margaret Atwood." *Women's Studies* 12.3 (1986): 251–70.

―――. "Writing Doubly: Emily Dickinson and Female Experience." *Legacy: A Journal of Nineteenth-Century American Women Writers,* 3.1 (Spring 1986): 5–15.

―――. "Poem 315." *Women's Studies* 16.1-2 (1989): 61–66.

―――. "Reading Dickinson Doubly." *Women's Studies* 16.1-2 (1989): 217–21.

―――. "Reading Doubly: Dickinson, Gender, and Multiple Meaning." Fast and Gordon (1989), *Approaches.* 85–94.

―――, ed. *Feminist Critics Read Emily Dickinson.* Bloomington: Indiana UP, 1983.

Kajino, Midori. "The Moment of Death in Emily Dickinson's Poetry." *Studies in American Literature* (American Literature Society of Japan) 22 (1985): 35–47.

Kammer, Jeanne. "The Art of Silence and the Forms of Women's Poetry." *Shakespeare's Sisters: Feminist Essays on Women Poets*. Ed. Suzanne Juhasz. Bloomington: Indiana UP, 1979. 153–64.

Kantak, V. Y. "On the Unemersonian Aspects of Thoreau and Emily Dickinson." *Indian Journal of American Studies* 12.1 (Jan. 1982): 33–44.

Kaplan, Cora. "The Indefinite Disclosed: Christina Rossetti and Emily Dickinson." *Women Writing and Writing About Women*. Ed. Mary Jacobus. London: Croom Helm; New York: Barnes & Noble, 1979. 61–79.

———. *Sea Changes: Essays on Culture and Feminism*. London: Verso, 1986.

Kazin, Alfred. "Wrecked, Solitary, Here: Dickinson's Room of Her Own." *An American Procession*. New York: Knopf, 1984. 161–80.

Keller, Karl. "Alephs, Zahirs, and the Triumph of Ambiguity: Typology in Nineteenth-Century American Literature." *Literary Uses of Typology from the Late Middle Ages to the Present*. Ed. Earl Miner. Princeton: Princeton UP, 1977. 274–314.

———. *The Only Kangaroo Among the Beauty: Emily Dickinson and America*. Baltimore: Johns Hopkins UP, 1979.

Keller, Lynn, and Cristanne Miller. "Emily Dickinson, Elizabeth Bishop, and the Rewards of Indirection." *New England Quarterly* 57.4 (Dec. 1984): 533–53.

Khan, M. M. "'King' Symbolism in Dickinson's Early Poetry." *Panjab University Research Bulletin (Arts)* 7.2 (1976): 13–18.

———. "Romantic Tradition and the Compound Vision of Love in Emily Dickinson's Poems." *Panjab University Research Bulletin (Arts)* 9.1-2 (Apr.–Oct. 1978): 53–69.

———. "Conception of Love and Immortality in Dickinson's Poetry." *Dickinson Studies*, no. 36 (2d Half 1979): 16–25.

———. "The Poetry of Ecstasy—Dickinson and Keats." *Panjab University Research Bulletin (Arts)* 12.1-2 (Apr.–Oct. 1981): 15–36.

———. "Dickinson's Phenomenology of Evolution and Imperfection and the Butterfly Symbolism." *Panjab University Research Bulletin (Arts)* 14.1 (Apr. 1983): 55–70.

———. "The Agony of the Final Inch: Treatment of Pain in Dickinson's Poems." *Dickinson Studies*, no. 47 (Dec. 1983): 22–33.

Khan, Mohammad Mansoor. *Emily Dickinson's Poetry: Thematic Design and Texture*. Series in English Language and Literature (SELL) 8. New Delhi: Bahri Publications, 1983.

Kier, Kathleen E. "Only Another Suspension of Disbelief: Emily Dickinson's 'I've heard an organ talk, sometimes—.'" *Massachusetts Studies in English* 7.4-8.1 (1981): 40–48.

Killingsworth, Myrth Jimmie. "Dickinson's 'Who occupies this house?'" *The Explicator* 40.1 (Fall 1981): 33–35.

Kimpel, Ben. *Emily Dickinson as Philosopher*. Studies in Women and Religion 6. New York: Mellen, 1981.

Kjaer, Niels. "Emily Dickinson, Job's Sister." *Dickinson Studies,* no. 65 (1st Half 1988): 19–24.

Knapp, Bettina L. *Emily Dickinson*. New York: Continuum, Frederick Ungar, 1989.

Knights, L. C. "Poetry and 'things hard for thought.'" *Times Literary Supplement,* 29 Feb. 1980: 239–41.

———. "Defining the Self: Poems of Emily Dickinson." *Sewanee Review* 91.3 (July–Sep. 1983): 357–87.

Knox, Heléne. "Metaphor and Metonymy in Emily Dickinson's Figurative Thinking." *Massachusetts Studies in English* 7.4-8.1 (1981): 49–56.

———. "Dickinson's 'The poets light but lamps.'" *The Explicator* 41.1 (Fall 1982): 31.

LaBelle, Jenijoy. "Dickinson's 'Savior! I've no one else to tell.'" *The Explicator* 38.4 (Summer 1980): 34–35.

Lair, Robert L. "Emily Dickinson's Fracture of Grammar: Syntactic Ambiguity in Her Poems." *The Analysis of Literary Texts: Current Trends in Methodology*. Third and Fourth York College Colloquia. Ed. Randolph D. Pope. Ypsilanti, MI: Bilingual/Editorial Bilingüe, 1980. 158–64.

Lakoff, George, and Mark Turner. *More than Cool Reason: A Field Guide to Poetic Metaphor*. Chicago: U of Chicago P, 1989.

Landow, George P. "Moses Striking the Rock: Typological Symbolism in Victorian Poetry." *Literary Uses of Typology from the Late Middle Ages to the Present*. Ed. Earl Miner. Princeton: Princeton UP, 1977. 315–44.

Larsen, Jeanne. "Text and Matrix: Dickinson, H. D., and Woman's Voice." *Engendering the Word: Feminist Essays in Psychosexual Poetics*. Ed. Temma F. Berg. Urbana: U Illinois P, 1989. 244–61.

Lawes, Rochie Whittington. "Emily Dickinson and 'Dimity Convictions.'" *University of Mississippi Studies in English,* n.s. 1 (1980): 127–28.

Lawson, Elizabeth. "ED: a slant on immortality." *Dickinson Studies,* no. 56 (2d Half 1985): 24–37.

Leder, Sharon, with Andrea Abbott. *The Language of Exclusion: The Poetry of Emily Dickinson and Christina Rossetti.* Contributions in Women's Studies, no. 83. New York: Greenwood, 1987.

Lee, A. Robert. "'This World is not Conclusion': Emily Dickinson and the Landscape of Death." *Anglo-American Studies* 2 (1982): 217–32.

Leonard, Douglas. "'Chastisement of Beauty': A Mode of the Religious Sublime in Dickinson's Poetry." *American Transcendental Quarterly* 1.3 (Sept. 1987): 247–56. Rpt. in *University of Dayton Review* 19.1 (Winter 1987–88): 39–47.

Leonard, Douglas Novich. "Dickinson's 'Our journey had advanced.'" *The Explicator* 41.4 (Summer 1983): 29–31.

———. "Emily Dickinson's Religion: An 'Ablative Estate.'" *Christian Scholar's Review* 13.4 (1984): 333–48.

———. "Pictureless Trope: a Dickinson Experiment." *Dickinson Studies,* no. 57 (1st Half 1986): 28–34.

———. "Certain Slants of Light: Exploring the Art of Dickinson's Fascicle 13." Fast and Gordon (1989), *Approaches.* 124–33.

Leonard, Garry M. "The Necessary Strategy of Renunciation: The Triumph of Emily Dickinson and the Fall of Sylvia Plath." *University of Dayton Review* 19.1 (Winter 1987–88): 79–90.

Leonard, James S. "Dickinson's Poems of Definition." *Dickinson Studies,* no. 41 (Dec. 1981): 18–25.

Levin, Samuel R. "Some Uses of the Grammar in Poetic Analysis." *Problèmes de l'Analyse Textuelle/Problems of Textual Analysis.* Ed. Pierre R. Léon, Henri Mitterand, Peter Nesselroth, and Pierre Robert. Montréal: Didier, 1971. 19–31.

Lewis, Kevin. "A Theologian on the Courtly Lover Death in Three Poems by Emily Dickinson, Anne Sexton, and Sylvia Plath." *Lamar Journal of the Humanities* 8.1 (Spring 1982): 13–21.

Lindenberger, Herbert. "Walt Whitman and Emily Dickinson." *Erkennen und Deuten: Essays zur Literatur und Literaturtheorie—Edgar Lohner in Memoriam.* Ed. Martha Woodmansee and Walter F. W. Lohnes. Berlin: Erich Schmidt Verlag, 1983. 213–27.

Lloyd, David. "The Adult Voice in Dickinson's Child Poems." *Dickinson Studies,* no. 49 (June 1984): 22–31.

Loeffelholz, Mary. "Dickinson Identified: Newer Criticism and Feminist Classrooms." Fast and Gordon (1989), *Approaches.* 170–77.

Louis, M. K. "Emily Dickinson's Sacrament of Starvation." *Nineteenth Century Literature* 43.3 (Dec. 1988): 346–60.

———. "Dickinson's 'To put this world down, like a bundle.'" *The Explicator* 47.2 (Winter 1989): 32–33.

Loving, Jerome. "Emily Dickinson's Workshop." *Review* 5 (1983): 195–201.

———. "Dickinson's 'Hansom Man.'" *Le Sud et Autres Points Cardinaux.* Paris: Presses de l'Université de Paris-Sorbonne, [1985]. (Actes du Colloque de 1984, Centre de Recherches en Littérature et Civilisation Nord-Américaines. Civilisations, no. 12)

———. *Emily Dickinson: The Poet on the Second Story.* Cambridge, Cambridge UP, 1986.

Luckett, Perry D. "Dickinson's 'My life closed twice.'" *The Explicator* 40.3 (Spring 1982): 32–34.

Luscher, Robert M. "An Emersonian Context of Dickinson's 'The Soul selects her own Society.'" *ESQ: A Journal of the American Renaissance* 30 (2d Quarter 1984): 111–16.

McClave, Heather. "Emily Dickinson: The Missing All." *Southern Humanities Review* 14.1 (Winter 1980): 1–12.

McClure, Charlotte S. "Expanding the Canon of American Renaissance Frontier Writers: Emily Dickinson's 'Glimmering Frontier.'" *The Frontier Experience and the American Dream: Essays on American Literature.* Ed. David Mogen, Mark Busby, and Paul Bryant. College Station: Texas A & M UP, 1989. 67–86.

McGann, Jerome J. "The Text, the Poem, and the Problem of Historical Method." *New Literary History* 12.2 (Winter 1981): 269–88.

McGregor, Elisabeth. "Standing with the Prophets and Martyrs: ED's Scriptural Self-Defense." *Dickinson Studies,* no. 39 (1st Half 1981): 18–26.

Machor, James L. "Emily Dickinson and the Feminine Rhetoric." *Arizona Quarterly* 36.2 (Summer 1980): 131–46.

McHugh, Heather. "Interpretive Insecurity And Poetic Truth: Dickinson's Equivocation." *American Poetry Review* 17.2 (Mar.–Apr. 1988): 49–54.

McNeil, Helen. *Emily Dickinson.* New York: Pantheon; London: Virago, 1986.

Madigan, Francis V., Jr. "Mermaids in the Basement: Emily Dickinson's Sea Imagery." *Greyfriar: Siena Studies in Literature* 23 (1982): 39–56.

Mann, John S. "Dream in Emily Dickinson's Poetry." *Dickinson Studies,* no. 34 (2d Half 1978): 19–26.

———. "Emily Dickinson, Emerson, and the Poet as Namer." *New England Quarterly* 51.4 (Dec. 1978): 467–88.

BIBLIOGRAPHY

Marcellino, Ralph. "Emily Dickinson's 'Beware an Austrian.'" *Classical Bulletin* 57.4 (Feb. 1981): 53–54.

———. "Dickinson's 'The Sun Is One.'" *The Explicator* 40.3 (Spring 1982): 29–30.

———. "How did Emily Dickinson Pronounce Latin?" *Classical Bulletin* 59.1 (Jan. 1983): 11–12.

———. "Dickinson's 'Partake as doth the Bee.'" *Classical Bulletin* 59.4 (Oct. 1983): 66–67.

Marcus, Mordecai. *Emily Dickinson: Selected Poems.* Lincoln, NE: Cliffs Notes, 1982.

———. "Dickinson and Frost: Walking Out One's Grief." *Dickinson Studies,* no. 63 (2d Half 1987): 16–29.

Marder, Daniel. *Exiles at Home: A Story of Literature in Nineteenth Century America.* Lanham, MD: UP of America, 1984.

Marhafer, David J. "Reading a Poem by Dickinson: A Psychological Approach." *English Journal* 77.1 (Jan. 1988): 59–63.

Marston, Jane. "Metaphorical Language and Terminal Illness: Reflections upon Images of Death." *Literature and Medicine* 5 (1986): 109–21.

Martin, John E. "The Religious Spirit in the Poetry of Emily Dickinson and Theodore Roethke." *Religion and Philosophy in the United States of America.* Proceedings of the German-American Conference at Paderborn. 29 July–1 Aug. 1986. Vol. 2. Arbeiten zur Amerikanistik 1. Essen, Ger.: Varlag Die Blaue Eule, 1987. 497–518.

Martin, John M. "Nature and Art: Two Undiscussed Poems by ED." *Dickinson Studies,* no. 42 (June 1982): 26–29.

Martin, Wendy. *An American Triptych: Anne Bradstreet, Emily Dickinson, Adrienne Rich.* Chapel Hill: U of North Carolina P, 1984.

———. "Emily Dickinson." *Columbia Literary History of the United States.* Ed. Emory Elliott. New York: Columbia UP, 1988. 609–26.

Matthews, Pamela R. "Talking of Hallowed Things: The Importance of Silence in Emily Dickinson's Poetry." *Dickinson Studies,* no. 47 (Dec. 1983): 14–21.

Mazurek, Raymond A. "'I Have No Monarch in My Life': Feminism, Poetry, and Politics in Dickinson and Higginson." *Patrons and Protégées: Gender, Friendship, and Writing in Nineteenth-Century America.* Ed. Shirley Marchalonis. New Brunswick, NJ: Rutgers UP, 1988. 122–40.

Mermin, Dorothy. "The Damsel, the Knight, and the Victorian Woman Poet." *Critical Inquiry* 13.1 (Autumn 1986): 64–80.

Miller, Cris. "Terms and Golden Words: Alternatives of Control in Dickinson's Poetry." *ESQ: A Journal of the American Renaissance* 28 (1st Quarter 1982): 48–62.

Miller, Cristanne. "How 'Low Feet' Stagger: Disruptions of Language in Dickinson's Poetry." *Feminist Critics Read Emily Dickinson.* Ed. Suzanne Juhasz. Bloomington: Indiana UP, 1983. 134–55.

———. " 'A letter is a joy of earth': Dickinson's Communication with the World." *Legacy: A Journal of Nineteenth-Century American Women Writers* 3.1 (Spring 1986): 29–39.

———. *Emily Dickinson: A Poet's Grammar.* Cambridge: Harvard UP, 1987.

———. "Approaches to Reading Dickinson." *Women's Studies* 16.1-2 (1989): 223–28.

———. "Dickinson's Language: Interpreting Truth Told Slant." Fast and Gordon (1989), *Approaches.* 78–84.

———. "Poem 1651." *Women's Studies* 16.1-2 (1989): 181–84.

Miller, Martha LaFollette. "Parallels in Rosalia de Castro and Emily Dickinson." *The Comparatist: Journal of the Southern Comparative Literature Association* 5 (May 1981): 3–9.

Miller, Mary Cender. "Emily Dickinson's Oriental Heresies." *After a Hundred Years: Essays on Emily Dickinson.* Ed. Emily Dickinson Society of Japan. Kyoto, Japan: Apollon-sha, 1988. 143–58.

Miller, Ruth. "Poetry as a Transitional Object." *Between Reality and Fantasy: Transitional Objects and Phenomena.* Ed. Simon A. Grolnick and Leonard Barkin, in collaboration with Werner Muensterberger. New York: Aronson, 1978. 449–68.

Montefiore, Jan. *Feminism and Poetry: Language, Experience, Identity in Women's Writing.* London: Pandora, 1987.

Monteiro, George. "The Pilot-God Trope in Nineteenth-Century American Texts." *Modern Language Studies* 7.2 (Fall 1977): 42–51.

———. "*Love & Fame* or *What's a Heaven For:* Emily Dickinson's Teleology." *New England Quarterly* 51.1 (Mar. 1978): 105–13.

———. "Dickinson's 'For every bird a nest.'" *The Explicator* 37.1 (Fall 1978): 28–29.

———. "In Question: The Status of Emily Dickinson's 1878 'Worksheet' for 'Two butterflies went out at noon.'" *Essays in Literature* 6.2 (Fall 1979): 219–25.

———. "Dickinson's 'I reason, earth is short.'" *The Explicator* 38.4 (Summer 1980): 23–26.

———. "Dickinson's Select Society." *Dickinson Studies,* no. 39 (1st Half 1981): 41–43.

———. "Dickinson's 'I heard a fly buzz.'" *The Explicator* 43.1 (Fall 1984): 43–45.

———. "Manzanilla." *The Explicator* 43.3 (Spring 1985): 16–17.

———. "Dickinson's 'Abraham to kill him.'" *The Explicator* 45.2 (Winter 1987): 32–33.

———. "Dickinson's 'Because I could not stop for death.'" *The Explicator* 46.3 (Spring 1988): 20–21.

———. *Robert Frost and the New England Renaissance.* Lexington: UP of Kentucky, 1988.

———. "Emily Dickinson's 'Like Brooms of Steel' and Its Precursors." *Single Hound* 1.2 (1989): 19–23.

Monteiro, George, and Barton Levi St. Armand. "The Experienced Emblem: A Study of the Poetry of Emily Dickinson." *Prospects: The Annual of American Cultural Studies* 6 (1981): 187–280.

Monteiro, Katherine A. "Dickinson's 'Victory comes late.'" *The Explicator* 44.2 (Winter 1986): 30–32.

Morey, Frederick L. "Dickinson-Kant: The First Critique." *Dickinson Studies,* no. 60 (2d Half 1986): 1–70.

———. "Dickinson-Kant, Part II (covering the second critique, that of Practical Reason)." *Dickinson Studies,* no. 64 (2d Half 1987): 3–30.

———. "Dickinson-Kant, Part III: The Beautiful and the Sublime." *Dickinson Studies,* no. 67 (2d Half 1988): 3–60.

Morris, Adalaide. "'The Love of Thee—a Prism Be': Men and Women in the Love Poetry of Emily Dickinson." *Feminist Critics Read Emily Dickinson.* Ed. Suzanne Juhasz. Bloomington: Indiana UP, 1983. 98–113.

Morris, Adalaide K. "Two Sisters Have I: Emily Dickinson's Vinnie and Susan." *Massachusetts Review* 22.2 (Summer 1981): 323–32.

Morris, Timothy. "The Free-rhyming Poetry of Emerson and Dickinson." *Essays in Literature* 12.2 (Fall 1985): 225–40.

———. "The Development of Dickinson's Style." *American Literature* 60.1 (Mar. 1988): 26–41.

Morse, Jonathan. "History in the Text." *Texas Studies in Literature and Language* 24.4 (Winter 1982): 329–46.

Morton, Mary L. "How Language Works: Learning with Dickinson." Fast and Gordon, *Approaches.* 47–51.

Mossberg, Barbara. "Poem 271. Dressing for Success: Emily Dickinson's Accomplished 'A solemn thing—it was—I said.'" *Women's Studies* 16.1-2 (1989): 29–34.

―――. "Double Exposures: Emily Dickinson's and Gertrude Stein's Anti-autobiographies." *Women's Studies* 16.1-2 (1989): 239–50.

Mossberg, Barbara Antonina Clarke. *Emily Dickinson: When a Writer Is a Daughter.* Bloomington: Indiana UP, 1982.

―――. "Emily Dickinson's Nursery Rhymes." *Feminist Critics Read Emily Dickinson.* Ed. Suzanne Juhasz. Bloomington: Indiana UP, 1983. 45–66.

Mossberg, Barbara Clarke. "A Rose in Context: The Daughter Construct." *Historical Studies and Literary Criticism.* Ed. Jerome J. McGann. Madison: U of Wisconsin P, 1985. 199–225.

Mullane, Janet, and Robert Thomas Wilson, eds. *Nineteenth-Century Literature Criticism.* Vol. 21. Detroit: Gale Research, 1989.

Munk, Linda. "Recycling Language: Emily Dickinson's Religious Wordplay." *ESQ: A Journal of the American Renaissance* 32 (4th Quarter 1986): 232–52.

―――. "Musicians Wrestle Everywhere: ED, C. G. Jung & the Myth of Poetic Creation." *Dickinson Studies,* no. 72 (2d Half 1989): 3–16.

Murphy, Brenda. "ED's Use of Definition by Antithesis." *Dickinson Studies* 38 (2d Half 1980): 21–24.

―――. "Wind Like a Bugle: Toward an Understanding of Emily Dickinson's Poetic Language." *Dickinson Studies,* no. 41 (Dec. 1981): 26–37.

Nathan, Rhoda. "The Slanted Truth: Thoreau's and Dickinson's Roles." *Thoreau Journal Quarterly* 11.3/4 (July–Nov. 1979): 35–40.

―――. "The Soul at White Heat: Emily Dickinson & Augustinian Meditation." *Studia Mystica* 2.1 (Spring 1979): 39–54.

Nekola, Charlotte. "'By Birth a Bachelor': Dickinson and the Idea of Womanhood in the American Nineteenth Century." Fast and Gordon (1989), *Approaches.* 148–54.

New, Elisa. "Difficult Writing, Difficult God: Emily Dickinson's Poems beyond Circumference." *Religion and Literature* 18.3 (Fall 1986): 1–27.

Newman, Robert D. "Emily Dickinson's Influence on Roethke's 'In Evening Air.'" *Dickinson Studies,* no. 57 (1st Half 1986): 38–40.

Nigro, August. "Emily Dickinson: An Imp of the Perverse." *Proceedings of the Second Annual Conference of EAPSCU.* Hosted by Millersville State College, 23–25 Sept. 1982. Compiled by Malcolm Hayward. N.p.: English Assn. of the Pennsylvania State Colleges and University, [1983].

BIBLIOGRAPHY

Norris, Kathleen. "Let Emily Sing for You Because She Cannot Pray . . ." *Cross Currents: A Yearbook of Central European Culture* 36.2 (Summer 1986): 219–29.

Nower, Joyce. "Art And The Movement: Soul, Take Thy Risk—Reflections on the Poetry of Emily Dickenson [*sic*]." *The Longest Revolution* [Part 1] 4.4 (Apr.–May 1980), 7; [Part 2] 4.5 (June–July 1980): 7.

Oakes, Karen. "Welcome and Beware: The Reader and Emily Dickinson's Figurative Language." *ESQ: A Journal of the American Renaissance* 34 (3d Quarter 1988): 181–206.

Oates, Joyce Carol. "Soul at the White Heat: The Romance of Emily Dickinson's Poetry." *Critical Inquiry* 13.4 (Summer 1987): 806–24.

———. *(Woman) Writer: Occasions and Opportunities.* New York: Dutton, 1988.

Oberhaus, Dorothy Huff. "'Engine against th' Almightie': Emily Dickinson and Prayer." *ESQ: A Journal of the American Renaissance* 32 (3d Quarter 1986): 153–72.

———. "'Tender Pioneer': Emily Dickinson's Poems on the Life of Christ." *American Literature* 59.3 (Oct. 1987): 341–58.

———. "Herbert and Emily Dickinson: A Reading of Emily Dickinson." *Like Season'd Timber: New Essays on George Herbert.* Ed. Edmund Miller and Robert DiYanni. Seventeenth Century Texts and Studies 1. New York: Lang, 1987. 345–68.

———. "Dickinson's Poem 698." *The Explicator* 46.4 (Summer 1988): 21–25.

———. "Dickinson as Comic Poet." Fast and Gordon (1989), *Approaches.* 118–23.

O'Connell, Patrick F. "Emily Dickinson's Train: Iron Horse or 'Rough Beast?'" *American Literature* 52.3 (Nov. 1980): 469–74.

O'Hara, Daniel T. "'The Designated Light': Irony in Emily Dickinson ('Dare you see a soul *at the White Heat?*')" *Boundary 2* 7.3 (Spring 1979): 175–98.

O'Keefe, Martha L. "I Hide Myself Within My Flower." *After a Hundred Years: Essays on Emily Dickinson.* Ed. Emily Dickinson Society of Japan. Kyoto, Japan: Apollon-sha, 1988. 57–66.

Oliver, Virginia H. *Apocalypse of Green: A Study of Emily Dickinson's Eschatology.* American University Studies. Series 24: American Literature 4. New York: Lang, 1989.

Olpin, Larry. "Hyperbole and Abstraction (The Comedy of Emily Dickinson): Part One." *Dickinson Studies,* no. 44 (2d Half 1982): 3–22.

———. "In Defense of the Colonel." *Higginson Journal,* no. 42 (1st Half 1985): 3–14.

Olpin, Larry R. "Hyperbole and Abstraction (The Comedy of Emily Dickinson): Part II." *Dickinson Studies,* no. 50 (Bonus 1984): 1–37.

Orsini, Daniel J. "Emily Dickinson and the Romantic Use of Science." *Massachusetts Studies in English* 7.4-8.1 (1981): 57–69.

Ostriker, Alicia. "Being Nobody Together: Duplicity, Identity, and Women's Poetry." *Parnassus: Poetry in Review* 12.2-13.1 (Spring/Summer/Fall/Winter 1985): 201–22.

Ostriker, Alicia Suskin. *Stealing the Language: The Emergence of Women's Poetry in America.* Boston: Beacon, 1986.

Packer, Barbara. "Poem 656: Dickinson and the Contract of Taste." *Women's Studies* 16.1-2 (1989): 91–94.

———. "Poem 1581." *Women's Studies* 16.1-2 (1989): 155–58.

Paddock, Lisa. "Metaphor as Reason: Emily Dickinson's Approach to Nature." *Massachusetts Studies in English* 7.4-8.1 (1981): 70–79.

Parker, Robert Dale. *The Unbeliever: The Poetry of Elizabeth Bishop.* Urbana: U of Illinois P, 1988.

Parsons, Thornton H. "Emily Dickinson's Refined Ingenuities." *The Single Hound* 1.1 (1989): 12–17.

Patterson, Rebecca. *Emily Dickinson's Imagery.* Ed., with an introduction by Margaret H. Freeman. Amherst: U of Massachusetts P, 1979.

Pearce, Frank, "The Bards and the Bees." *Studies in English and American Literature.* Ed. John L. Cutler and Lawrence S. Thompson. Troy, NY: Whitston Publishing, 1978. 293–94. (*American Notes and Queries.* Supplement, Vol. 1)

Peeck-O'Toole, Maureen. "Lyric and Gender." *Dutch Quarterly Review of Anglo-American Letters* 18.4 (1988): 319–29.

Perkins, James A. "History of Explication of P 1052: 'I never saw a Moor—.'" *Dickinson Studies* 63 (2d Half 1987): pp. 30–32.

Perrine, Laurence. "Emily Dickinson's 'I know that He exists." *CEA Forum* 8.3 (Feb. 1978): 11–12.

———. "Dickinson's 'A house upon the height.'" *The Explicator* 36.3 (Spring 1978): 14–15.

———. "Dickinson's 'As by the dead we love to sit.'" *The Explicator* 36.3 (Spring 1978): 32–33.

———. "Structure and Pronominal Reference in 'It was not Death' (J.510)." *Dickinson Studies,* no. 38 (2d Half 1980): 34–36.

———."Dickinson's 'Some—work for immortality—.'" *The Explicator* 40.1 (Fall 1981): 32–33.

Peschel, Richard E., and Enid Rhodes Peschel. "'Am I in Heaven Now?': Case History, Literary Histories." *Soundings: An Interdisciplinary Journal* 66.4 (Winter 1983): 469–80.

Petry, Alice Hall. "Two Views of Nature in Emily Dickinson's 'In Winter in My Room.'" *Modern Language Studies* 9.2 (1979): 16–22.

———. "The Ophidian Image in Holmes and Dickinson." *American Literature* 54.4 (Dec. 1982): 598–601.

Philip, Jim. "Valley News: Emily Dickinson at Home and Beyond." *Nineteenth-Century American Poetry.* Ed. A. Robert Lee. London: Vision; Totowa, NJ: Barnes & Noble, 1985. 61–79.

Phillips, Elizabeth. *Emily Dickinson: Personae and Performance.* University Park: Pennsylvania State UP, 1988.

Pohl, Frederick J. "A Poet and a Scientist." *Dickinson Studies,* no. 63 (2d Half 1987): 3–14.

Pollak, Vivian R. "Thirst and Starvation in Emily Dickinson's Poetry." *American Literature* 51.1 (Mar. 1979): 33–49.

———. *Dickinson: The Anxiety of Gender.* Ithaca, NY: Cornell UP, 1984.

———. "The Second Act: Emily Dickinson's Orphaned Persona." *Nineteenth-Century Women Writers of the English-Speaking World.* Ed. Rhoda B. Nathan. Contributions in Women's Studies, no. 69. New York: Greenwood, 1986. 159–69.

Porter, David. "Emily Dickinson: The First Modern." *New Boston Review* 6 (Jan.–Feb. 1981): 17–19.

———. *Dickinson, The Modern Idiom.* Cambridge: Harvard UP, 1981.

———. "Dickinson's Readers." *New England Quarterly* 57.1 (Mar. 1984): 106–17.

———. "Searching for the Capital of the Mind." *The Kenyon Review* 7.4 (Fall 1985): 116–22.

Porterfield, Amanda. *Feminine Spirituality in America: From Sarah Edwards to Martha Graham.* Philadelphia: Temple UP, 1980.

Privratsky, Kenneth L. "Irony in Emily Dickinson's 'Because I could not stop for death.'" *Concerning Poetry* 11.2 (Fall 1978): 25–30.

Rachal, John. "Probing the Final Mystery in Dickinson's 'I heard a Fly buzz' and 'I've seen a Dying Eye.'" *Dickinson Studies,* no. 39 (1st Half 1981): 44–46.

Raffel, Burton. *How To Read a Poem.* New York: A Meridian Book-New American Library, 1984.

Raina, B. N. "Dickinson's 'Because I could not stop for death.'" *The Explicator* 43.3 (Spring 1985): 11–12.

Rao, J. Srihari, ed. *Essential Emily Dickinson*. Bara Bazar Bareilly (U.P.): Prakash Book Depot, 1972.

Rashid, Frank D. "Emily Dickinson's Voice of Endings." *ESQ: A Journal of the American Renaissance* 31 (1st Quarter 1985): 23–37.

———. "The Role of Dickinson's Biography in the Classroom." Fast and Gordon (1989), *Approaches*. 134–41.

Reed, Michael. "Masculine Identity and Oral Security in the Poems of Emily Dickinson." *Journal of Evolutionary Psychology* 9.3-4 (Aug. 1988): 278–86.

Regueiro Elam, Helen. "Dickinson and the Haunting of the Self." *The American Sublime*. Ed. Mary Arensberg. Albany: State U of New York P, 1986. 83–99.

Reichert, John. *Making Sense of Literature*. Chicago: U of Chicago P, 1977.

Reiss, John. "Emily Dickinson's Self-Reliance." *Dickinson Studies,* no. 38 (2d Half 1980): pp. 25–33.

Renaux, Sigrid. "The Seasons of Light." *Ilha do Desterro* 14.2 (1985): 27–52.

———. "Dickinson's 'A light exists in spring.'" *The Explicator* 46.4 (Summer 1988): 21.

Reynolds, David S. *Beneath the American Renaissance: The Subversive Imagination in the Age of Emerson and Melville*. New York: Knopf, 1988.

Richmond, Lee J. "Teaching ED and Metaphor: towards modern poetic practice." *Dickinson Studies,* no. 72 (2d Half 1989): 33–42.

Richwell, Adrian. "Poetic Immortality: Dickinson's 'Flood-subject' Reconsidered." *Dickinson Studies,* no. 69 (1st Half 1989): 1–31.

Ringler-Henderson, Ellin. "Poem 315." *Women's Studies* 16.1-2 (1989): 67–71.

———. "Poem 754." *Women's Studies* 16.1-2 (1989) 127–31.

Ripley, Richard J. "Dickinson's 'So much of heaven has gone from earth.'" *The Explicator* 42.1 (Fall 1983): 27–30.

Robinson, David. "Text and Meaning in ED's 'A Pit—but Heaven over it—' (J1712)." *Emily Dickinson Bulletin,* no. 33 (1st Half 1978): 45–52.

Robinson, Douglas. "Two Dickinson Readings." *Dickinson Studies,* no. 70 (Bonus 1989): 25–35.

Robinson, Fred Miller. "Strategies of Smallness: Wallace Stevens and Emily Dickinson." *Wallace Stevens Journal* 10.1 (Spring 1986): 27–35.

Robinson, John. *Emily Dickinson: Looking to Canaan.* Faber Student Guides. London: Faber, 1986.

Rogers, Katharine M. "Introducing Dickinson in a Basic Literature Course." Fast and Gordon (1989), *Approaches.* 52–55.

Rogers, William Elford. *The Three Genres and the Interpretation of Lyric.* Princeton: Princeton UP, 1983.

Rosenthal, M. L. "Volatile Matter: Humor in Our Poetry." *Massachusetts Review* 22.4 (Winter 1981): 807–17.

Rosenthal, M. L., and Sally M. Gall. *The Modern Poetic Sequence: The Genius of Modern Poetry.* New York: Oxford UP, 1983.

Rudat, Wolfgang E. H. "Dickinson and Immortality: Virgilian and Miltonic Allusions in 'Of death I try to think like this.'" *American Notes and Queries* 16.6 (Feb. 1978): 85–87.

Ruddick, Nicholas. "'The Color of a Queen, is this—': The Significance of Purple in Emily Dickinson's Poetry." *Massachusetts Studies in English* 7.4-8.1 (1981): 88–98.

———. "Dickinson's 'Banish air from air—.'" *The Explicator* 40.4 (Summer 1982): 31–33.

———. "'Synaesthesia' in Emily Dickinson's Poetry." *Poetics Today* 5.1 (1984): 59–78.

Sadowy, Chester P. "Dickinson's 'He touched me, so I live to know.'" *The Explicator* 37.1 (Fall 1978): 4–5.

St. Armand, Barton Levi. *Emily Dickinson and Her Culture: The Soul's Society.* Cambridge: Cambridge UP, 1984.

———. "Dickinson's 'Red Sea.'" *The Explicator* 43.3 (Spring 1985): 17–20.

———. "Veiled Ladies: Dickinson, Bettine, and Transcendental Mediumship." *Studies in the American Renaissance* (1987): 1–51.

———. "'Your Prodigal': Letters from Ned Dickinson, 1879–1885." *New England Quarterly* 61.3 (Sep. 1988): 358–80.

———. "Heavenly Rewards of Merit: Recontextualizing Emily Dickinson's 'Checks.'" *After a Hundred Years.* Emily Dickinson Society of Japan. Ed./Kyoto, Japan: Apollon-sha, 1988. 219–38.

St. Armand, Barton Levi, and George Monteiro. "Dickinson's '"Hope" is the thing with feathers.'" *The Explicator* 47.4 (Summer 1989): 34–37.

Salska, Agnieszka. *The Poetry of the Central Consciousness: Whitman and Dickinson.* Lodz, Pol.: Uniwersytet Łódzki, 1982. (*Acta Universitatis Lodziensis:* Folia Litteraria 7)

———. "Emily Dickinson's Lover." *Studies in English and American Literature: In Honour of Witold Ostrowski.* Warsaw: Państwowe Wydawnictwo Naukowe (Polish Scientific Publishers), 1984. 135–40.

———. *Walt Whitman and Emily Dickinson: Poetry of the Central Consciousness.* Philadelphia: U of Pennsylvania P, 1985.

Sanazaro, Leonard. "Renunciation and Emily Dickinson's Will to Create." *Higginson Journal,* no. 34 (June 1983): 19–20.

Sciarra, T. "A Woman Looking Inward." *Dickinson Studies,* no. 39 (1st Half 1981): 36–40.

Selley, April. "Emily Dickinson as Kinky Kangaroo." *Higginson Journal,* no. 28 (June 1981): 3–12.

Sewall, Richard B. "In Search of Emily Dickinson." *Michigan Quarterly Review* 23.4 (Fall 1984): 514–28.

———. "Emily Dickinson." *Voices and Visions: The Poet in America.* Ed. Helen Vendler. New York: Random, 1987. 51–89.

Shands, Harley C. "Malinowski's Mirror: Emily Dickinson as Narcissus." *Contemporary Psychoanalysis* 12.3 (July 1976): 300–34.

———. "The Goblin Bee: Anxiety in Relation to Poetry, Physics, and Semiotics." *American Journal of Semiotics* 4.3-4 (1986): 1–27.

Sharma, Radhe Shyam. "Emily Dickinson's 'I Heard a Fly Buzz—When I Died': A Reconsideration." *Indian Journal of American Studies* 8.1 (Jan. 1978): 50–54.

Shimazaki, Yoko. " 'Dare you see a Soul *at the White Heat?*': A Study of Emily Dickinson's Inner World." *After a Hundred Years: Essays on Emily Dickinson.* Ed. Emily Dickinson Society of Japan. Kyoto, Japan: Apollon-sha, 1988. 87–111.

Shullenberger, William. "My Class had stood—a Loaded Gun." Fast and Gordon (1989), *Approaches.* 95–104.

Shurr, William H. *The Marriage of Emily Dickinson: A Study of the Fascicles.* Lexington: UP of Kentucky, 1983.

Siegfried, Regina, A.S.C. " 'Faith is a fine invention' (J185): A Bridge Poem in Fascicle 12." *Higginson Journal,* no. 38 (1st Half 1984): 22–23.

Simon, Maurya. "Poem 1651." *Women's Studies* 16.1-2 (1989): 185–87.

———. "Poem 271." *Women's Studies* 16.1-2 (1989): 35–37.

Simons, Louise. "Emily Dickinson's Willed Paradise: In Defeat of Adam and Repeal." *American Imago* 42.2 (Summer 1985): 165–82.

Simpson, Jeffrey E. "The Dependent Self: ED and Friendship." *Dickinson Studies,* no. 45 (June 1983): 35–42.

Singley, Carol J. "Reaching Lonely Heights: Sarah Orne Jewett, Emily Dickinson, and Female Initiation." *Colby Library Quarterly* 22.1 (Mar. 1986): 75–82.

Smith, B. J. "ED: 'Vicinity to Laws.'" *Dickinson Studies,* no. 56 (2d Half 1985): 38–52.

Smith, Lorrie. "Some See God and Live: Dickinson's Later Mysticism." *American Transcendental Quarterly,* n.s. 1.4 (Dec. 1987): 302–09.

Smith, Martha Nell. "'To Fill a Gap.'" *San Jose Studies* 13.3 (Fall 1987): 3–25.

Smith, Susan B. "'Radical Dualism': Emily Dickinson and Margaret Fuller." *Higginson Journal,* no. 45 (Bonus 1986): 31–41.

Soule, George H., Jr. "Emily Dickinson and the Robin." *Essays in Literature* 9.1 (Spring 1982): 67–82.

Stambovsky, Phillip. "Emily Dickson's [*sic*] 'The last Night that She lived': Explorations of a Witnessing Spirit." *Concerning Poetry,* no. 19 (1986): 87–93.

Staub, Michael. "A Dickinson Diagnosis." *Dickinson Studies,* no. 54 (Bonus 1984): 43–46.

Steiner, Dorothea. "Emily Dickinson: Image Patterns and the Female Imagination." *Arbeiten aus Anglistik und Amerikanistik* 6.1 (1981): 57–71.

Stocker, Edgar P. "We Roam in Sovereign Woods." *Dickinson Studies,* no. 42 (June 1982): 43–50.

Stocks, Kenneth. *Emily Dickinson and the Modern Consciousness: A Poet of our Time.* New York: St. Martin's; Basingstoke, Hampshire, Eng.: Macmillan, 1988.

Stonum, Gary Lee. "Emily Dickinson's Calculated Sublime." *The American Sublime.* Ed. Mary Arensberg. Albany: State U of New York P, 1986. 101–29.

———. "Dickinson Against the Sublime." *University of Dayton Review* 19.1 (Winter 1987–88): 31–37.

Stout, Janis P. "Breaking Out: The Journey of the American Woman Poet." *North Dakota Quarterly* 56.1 (Winter 1988): 40–53.

Sudol, Ronald A. "Elegy and Immortality: Emily Dickinson's 'Lay this laurel on the One.'" *ESQ: A Journal of the American Renaissance* 26 (1st Quarter 1980): 10–15.

Swenson, May. "Big My Secret, But It's Bandaged." *Parnassus: Poetry in Review* 12.2-13.1 (Spring/Summer/Fall/Winter 1985): 16–44.

Tackes, George A. "Dickinson's 'He put the belt around my life.'" *The Explicator* 42.1 (Fall 1983): 26–27.

Taylor, Carole Anne. "Kierkegaard and the Ironic Voices of Emily Dickinson." *Journal of English and Germanic Philology* 77.4 (Oct. 1978): 569–81.

Taylor, Linda J. "Form, Process, and the Dialectic of Self-Construction: 'After Great Pain' and Three Modern Poems." *University of Dayton Review* 19.1 (Winter 1987–88): 91–101.

Taylor, Marcella. "Shaman Motifs in the Poetry of Emily Dickinson." *Dickinson Studies,* no. 38 (2d Half 1980): 5–11.

Teichert, Marilyn C. "The Divine Adversary: The Image of God in Three ED Poems." *Dickinson Studies,* no. 46 (Bonus 1983): 21–26.

Thomas, Jeanette M. "Emerson's Influence on Two of ED's Poems." *Dickinson Studies,* no. 41 (Dec. 1981): 38–42.

Thota, Anand Rao. *Emily Dickinson: The Metaphysical Tradition.* New Delhi: Arnold-Heinemann; Atlantic Highlands, NJ: Humanities, 1982.

Tilma-Dekkers, E. M. "Immortality in the Poetry of Emily Dickinson." *Dutch Quarterly Review of Anglo-American Letters* 8 (1978): 162–82.

Toegel, Edith. *Emily Dickinson and Annette von Droste-Hülshoff: Poets as Women.* Potomac, MD: Studia Humanitatis, 1982.

Travis, Mildred K. "Dickinson's 'Of God we ask one favor.'" *The Explicator* 40.1 (Fall 1981): 31–32.

Tripp, Raymond P., Jr. *The Mysterious Kingdom of Emily Dickinson's Poetry.* Denver: Society for New Language Study, 1988.

———. "A Phsyiological [*sic*] Test for Transcendentalism." *Thoreau Society Bulletin,* no. 187 (Spring 1989): 4–5.

———. "Spiritual Action in 'My Life had stood—a Loaded Gun—.'" *Papers on Language and Literature* 25.3 (Spring 1989): 282–303.

Tselentis-Apostolidis, Persephone. "And I Will Be Socrates: Greek Elements in the Poetry of Dickinson." *Dickinson Studies,* no. 52 (2d Half 1984): 3–21.

Tsuri, Nobuko. "The Wind After a Hundred Years." *After a Hundred Years: Essays on Emily Dickinson.* Ed. Emily Dickinson Society of Japan. Kyoto, Japan: Apollon-sha, 1988. 7–14.

Turco, Lewis Putnam. *Visions and Revisions of American Poetry.* Fayetteville: U of Arkansas P, 1986.

Uno, Hiroko. "Expression by Negation in ED's Poetry." *Dickinson Studies,* no. 47 (Dec. 1983): 3–13.

———. "Optical Instruments and 'Compound Vision' in Emily Dickinson's Poetry." *Studies in English Literature* (English Literary Society of Japan), 64.2 (Jan. 1988): 227–43.

BIBLIOGRAPHY

Van Dyne, Susan R. "Double Monologues: Voices In American Women's Poetry." *Massachusetts Review* 23.3 (Autumn 1982): 461–85.

Walker, Cheryl. *The Nightingale's Burden: Women Poets and American Culture before 1900*. Bloomington, Indiana UP, 1982.

———. "Locating a Feminist Critical Practice: Between the Kingdom and the Glory." *Women's Studies* 16.1-2 (1989): 9–19.

Walker, Julia M. "ED's Poetic of Private Liberation." *Dickinson Studies*, no. 45 (June 1983): 17–22.

Walker, Nancy. "Emily Dickinson and the Self: Humor as Identity." *Tulsa Studies in Women's Literature* 2 (1983): 57–68.

———. "Voice, Tone, and Persona in Dickinson's Love Poetry." Fast and Gordon (1989), *Approaches*. 105–12.

Wallace, Ronald. *God Be with the Clown: Humor in American Poetry*. Columbia: U of Missouri P, 1984.

Weissman, Judith. "'Transport's Working Classes': Sanity, Sex, and Solidarity in Dickinson's Late Poetry." *Midwest Quarterly* 29.4 (Summer 1988): 407–24.

Wells, Anna Mary. "ED Forgeries." *Dickinson Studies*, no. 35 (1st Half 1979): 12–16.

Westbrook, Perry D. *Free Will and Determinism in American Literature*. Rutherford, NJ: Fairleigh Dickinson UP; London: Assoc. UP, 1979.

———. *The New England Town in Fact and Fiction*. Rutherford NJ: Fairleigh Dickinson UP; London: Assoc. UP, 1982.

Whitman, A. Wilson. "Emily Dickinson's Rhyme Scheme." *Classical Bulletin* 60.3 (Summer 1984): 50.

Wienold, Götz. "Some Aspects of Meaning in Literature." *Dispositio: Revista Hispanica de Semiotica Literaria* 3.7-8 (1978): 127–35.

Williams, David R. "'This consciousness that is aware': Emily Dickinson in the Wilderness of the Mind." *Soundings: An Interdisciplinary Journal* 66.3 (Fall 1983): 360–81.

———. *Wilderness Lost: The Religious Origins of the American Mind*. Selinsgrove, PA: Susquehanna UP; London: Assoc. UP, 1987.

Williams, Sherri. "'omitted centers': Dickinson's Metonymic Strategy." *San Jose Studies* 13.3 (Fall 1987): 26–36.

Wilson, R. J. "Emily Dickinson and the Problem of Career." *Massachusetts Review* 20.3 (Autumn 1979): 451–61.

Wilson, R. Jackson. *Figures of Speech: American Writers and the Literary Marketplace, from Benjamin Franklin to Emily Dickinson*. New York: Knopf, 1989.

Wilt, Judith. "Emily Dickinson: Playing House." *Boundary 2* 12.2 (Winter 1984): 153–69.

Winther, Per. "On Editing Emily Dickinson." *American Studies in Scandinavia* 11 (1979): 25–40.

Wolff, Cynthia Griffin. "Dickinson's 'Much madness is divinest sense.'" *The Explicator* 36.4 (Summer 1978): 3–4.

———. *Emily Dickinson*. Radcliffe Biography Series. Reading, MA: Addison-Wesley, 1988.

———. "Emily Dickinson, Elizabeth Cady Stanton, and the Task of Discovering a Usable Past." *Massachusetts Review* 30.4 (Winter 1989): 629–44.

Wolosky, Shira. *Emily Dickinson: A Voice of War*. New Haven: Yale UP, 1984.

———. "Emily Dickinson's War Poetry: The Problem of Theodicy." *Massachusetts Review* 25.1 (Spring 1984): 22–41.

———. "A Syntax of Contention." In *Emily Dickinson*. Ed. Harold Bloom. New York: Chelsea, 1985. 161–85.

———. "Emily Dickinson: A Voice of War." *American Women Poets*. Ed. Harold Bloom. New York: Chelsea, 1986. 17–22.

———. "Rhetoric or Not: Hymnal Tropes in Emily Dickinson and Isaac Watts." *New England Quarterly* 61.2 (June 1988): 214–32.

Wortman, Marc. "The Place Translation Makes: Celan's Translation of Dickinson's 'Four Trees—upon a solitary Acre—.'" *Acts: A Journal of New Writing,* no. 8-9 (1988): 130–43.

Yaeger, Patricia. *Honey-Mad Women: Emancipatory Strategies in Women's Writing*. New York: Columbia UP, 1988.

Yoder, R. A. *Emerson and the Orphic Poet in America*. Berkeley: U of California P, 1978.